Politics, Parties, and Pressure Groups

By V. O. Key, Jr.

PROFESSOR OF GOVERNMENT
HARVARD UNIVERSITY

*Fourth
Edition*

Politics, Parties, and Pressure Groups

Thomas Y. Crowell Company

New York

FIRST EDITION

First Printing, January, 1942
Second Printing, February, 1943
Third Printing, September, 1944
Fourth Printing, May, 1945
Fifth Printing, July, 1946
Sixth Printing, December, 1946
Seventh Printing, February, 1947

SECOND EDITION

First Printing, September, 1947
Second Printing, May, 1948
Third Printing, October, 1948
Fourth Printing, January, 1950

THIRD EDITION

First Printing, August, 1952
Second Printing, October, 1952
Third Printing, November, 1953
Fourth Printing, August, 1955
Fifth Printing, September, 1956

FOURTH EDITION

First Printing, March, 1958
Second Printing, August, 1958

Library of Congress Catalog Card Number 58-6098

Manufactured in the United States of America
By Vail-Ballou Press, Inc., Binghamton, N.Y.

To

F. M. S. and W. C. H.

Preface

I<small>F HE</small> has a decent respect for the opinions of his professional colleagues, the author of a fourth edition of a textbook should be able to set out persuasive justifications for the new version. Let it be remarked, then, that this is not a routine revision in extent sufficient only to make obsolete the stocks of the earlier edition in the hands of the second-hand book dealers. Although its broad structure remains about the same, the work has been almost completely rewritten. A principal purpose of the revision has been to take into account the findings of recent research on American politics. Perhaps in no field of American political science in recent years has the research output been either so voluminous or so impressive as in the area of political parties and politics generally.

The author of a textbook, or so it seems to me, has an obligation to do more than simply to summarize and synthesize the findings of his colleagues who have industriously explored aspects of the field. He should also himself contribute something to the common store of knowledge. That obligation, it is hoped, has received at least a minimum fulfillment by the pieces of original inquiry reported at various points in the book. The revision has also provided an opportunity to set some sectors of the data of American politics into new interpretative frames, which may add new meaning to old data.

My chief obligation in this work is obviously to the authors of the many articles and monographs on which I have relied; that debt, I trust, has been invariably recognized in the footnotes. Chapters 16 and 20 rest principally on an extensive set of analyses made by Eliot Chace; for cheerful assistance on these and many other chores I am mightily obliged to her. To Norma Tilley I am also indebted for preliminary analyses, especially those that formed the basis for chapter 24. In accord with convention, I must add the assertion, not likely to be challenged, that I committed all the errors both of fact and of judgment that appear in these pages.

V. O. KEY, JR.

Cambridge, Massachusetts

Contents

Part Two: The Party System

Part Four: Party and the Electorate

Politics, Parties, and Pressure Groups

1 | The Nature of Politics

GOVERNMENT is a universal, if not always an admirable, feature of society. The most primitive tribes and the most industrialized nation states have their governing processes. Whatever the religion, the race, the color, or the stage of technological development of a people, they need some sort of governing apparatus. Threats from enemies outside require the management of men and resources for defense—and perhaps for assault. The maintenance of the domestic peace and tranquillity requires means for keeping order and for settling disputes among men. In short, without governmental authority to provide for the common defense and to maintain domestic order, human society could scarcely exist, even though utopians dream of that day of human perfection when government shall be forever dissolved.

Government, though universal, is also most diverse. The task of governing may be performed by the elders as an incident to their paternal and priestly functions; or it may be carried on by a clearly differentiated, specialized organization. The range of governmental functions may be narrow or broad. Government's main concern may be the resolution of squabbles between citizens; or its activities may extend from the education of children, through the care of the aged, to the management of the economy. The holders of authority may be few or many. Government may act at the caprice and whim of the rulers or it may operate in accordance with sharply defined sets of constitutional standards. It may exploit the many for the benefit of the few; or it may exploit the few for the benefit of the many.

However diverse the processes and forms of governance may appear to be, tribal chieftains, tyrants, ruling aristocracies, and chief executives of modern republics have something in common: they possess authority; they exercise power. Their success depends on their skill in the fulfillment of their roles as holders of power; the demands of those roles, to be sure, differ greatly from time to time, from situation to situation, from culture to culture.

Government must cultivate a cheerful and willing obedience. Yet its armory of ultimate sanctions includes powers over property, liberty, and life itself. The ubiquity of the relationship of governor and governed, of ruler and ruled, leads students of politics to single out power as the basic characteristic of that human behavior of professional interest to them. Who exercises power? For whose benefit? In what manner? To what ends? According to what principles, if any? By what right? Such questions occupy the philosophers of politics and even the precinct captains. With them prime ministers, presidents, and princes must also be concerned.

Politics As Power

These observations give an uncommonly broad connotation to the term politics. They equate politics with governance, with the process and practice of ruling. In everyday usage politics may be taken to cover only such matters as the battles of the Republicans and Democrats, low and unprincipled humbugging of the people, skillful negotiation, or all the incomprehensible things "they" do in Washington. For the moment, let the term apply more broadly to workings of governments generally, their impact on the governed, their manner of operation, the means by which governors attain and retain authority. So defined, politics encompasses the phenomena dealt with in courses of study ranging from police administration, to constitutional law, to international relations. Through all these and other aspects of the governing process runs the common thread of power.

What is power? If the essence of politics lies in power, precise definition of that term is in order. Often power is regarded as if it were a substance that could be poured into a keg, stored, and drawn upon as the need arises. A person has or does not have power. Wall Street has the power. The labor barons have the power. The inner ring of Democratic (or Republican) politicians has power. A clique of businessmen and military bureaucrats runs the country.

Such notions of power as a substance in a keg, something a person does or does not have, convey a truncated or partial conception of the reality of power. These usages describe only a single aspect of certain relationships among human beings. Politics as power consists fundamentally of relationships of superordination and subordination, of dominance and submission, of the governors and the governed. The study of politics is the study of these relationships. George E. G. Catlin, an English political theorist, defines "politics as a study of the act of control, or as the act of human or social control." [1] In a similar vein Harold D. Lasswell, an American political scientist, says, "The study of politics is the study of influence and the influential." [2] To comprehend politics one must look not only at the man who draws power from a keg, so to speak, but at the relation between him and those his actions may affect. In this relationship lies the essence of politics.

The sociologists in their concept of role, which is a bit recondite, come close to this view of politics as power. Within the political system many types of individuals possess influence or the right to command. Their positions come to be clothed with customary duties whose fulfillment evokes relatively predictable responses from those affected. No matter who fills the position, or a role in the language of sociology, about the same responses may be expected. Thus, pick at random a moderately intelligent individual with quick reflexes and good eyesight, drape him with a policeman's uniform, and put him to directing traffic. Matters will probably proceed as if our man were a duly sworn officer. By virtue of the role, that is, the actions expected of such an individual and the responses expected from all concerned, he might be said to possess power. Yet when he fills a role he occupies a position as an actor in a system of human relationships. The political order in a sense consists of a system of such patterned roles, from the players of which specified behaviors are expected by others. A president, no less than a policeman, fills a role. Or, it might be said, he possesses power by virtue of the office he holds.

If one views power as relational, he must hasten to reject some of the popular connotations of the term "power." The word carries by implication its own adjectives and may suggest unlimited authority. In fact, the

[1] *A Study of the Principles of Politics* (New York, 1930), pp. 68–69. Quoted by permission of The Macmillan Company, publishers.
[2] *Politics* (New York: Whittlesey House, 1936), p. 1.

power relationship may shade off from one of brute force to the most gentle persuasion. Nor should the term "power" be allowed to conjure up solely visions of commands coming from "above." The power relationship is reciprocal, and the subject may affect the ruler more profoundly than the ruler affects the subject. As Lasswell puts it, "Power is an interpersonal situation; those who hold power are empowered. They depend upon and continue only so long as there is a continuing stream of empowering responses." [3] Nor should description in terms of power be taken as a contention that all political activists are motivated solely, or even primarily, by a drive for power. Yet the leader of the most holy cause, if he is successful, is tied to many people by relationships of power. Obviously political power (in the keg sense of the word) is something more than an end in itself, although for many practitioners of politics the deference that accompanies the achievement of positions of leadership may be deeply satisfying.

Structures of power. Though political power in the relational sense ultimately distills down to the relations between individuals A and B, the isolated political act takes on a fuller meaning when regarded in the framework of the totality of political relations within the society. A working political system consists of a multiplicity of these individual relationships which, collectively, tend to be organized or shaped into characteristic forms.

Political speculators, from Aristotle on, have occupied themselves with the classification of states according to differentiations in their structures of political power. That is, they have sought to identify the types of patterns or systems of relationships of political power. Familiar is the overly simple classification of constitutions—or structures of political power in our terminology—into monarchies, aristocracies, democracies, which groups regimes according to the number of persons holding authority: one, few, many. An additional characteristic of power relationships enters into the classification when tyranny is differentiated from monarchy, oligarchy from aristocracy, mob rule from democracy. Authority may be exercised with justice and with restraint or arbitrarily and capriciously whether vested in one, few, or many.

Such categories do not necessarily picture the real world of governance, for each regime has its individual peculiarities. One dictatorship may be a tyranny in the ancient sense, another not, and a third differ from both. Instead of being separable into sharply differentiated classes political systems differ in degree, and one category gradually shades off into another. Moreover, the realities underlying formal institutional ar-

[3] *Power and Personality* (New York: Norton, 1948), p. 10.

rangements have a perverse way of changing while the façade remains unaltered. Nevertheless, mention of these varieties of power structures may serve to illustrate the idea that power relationships within all societies tend to be organized into systems of authority.

Democracy, Self-Government, and Power

An observer of politics aware of the many kinds of power structures that have existed through history, or even over the globe at a particular time, has no difficulty in picturing political phenomena in terms of power. He may arrive at a generalization of the sort stated by Gaetano Mosca, an Italian political theorist:

> In all societies—from societies that are very meagerly developed and have barely attained the dawnings of civilization, down to the most advanced and powerful societies—two classes of people appear—a class that rules and a class that is ruled. The first class, always the less numerous, performs all political functions, monopolizes power, and enjoys the advantages that power brings, whereas the second, the more numerous class, is directed and controlled by the first, in a manner that is now more or less legal, now more or less arbitrary and violent.[4]

The idea of a ruling class grates on democratic ears. The citizen of a democracy may assert that Mosca's generalization describes a system unknown to him. Indeed, the theory of democracy turns upside down the ancient relationships of authority and proposes that power rest in the people who govern themselves. The rulers become identical with the ruled. The conception of politics as a system of power relationships clashes with such doctrines as that of "popular self-government," the idea of the "general will," and the belief in government "of the people, by the people, and for the people."

Yet even the most casual observer of democratic processes finds difficulty in observing the transmutation of the general will into statute. He quickly sees that some people have much more of a voice in what government does than do others. He has no difficulty in discerning that not all democratic orders are cut from the same cloth. A democracy may have within it a touch of aristocracy; it may have a dash of tyranny; and on occasion it may even be powerless to act. Even so, the political regimes classified as democratic, despite their individual peculiarities, possess characteristics that differentiate them from tyrannies, from dictatorships, from aristocracies. Those characteristics relate to the pattern or organization of the power structure, to the manner of exercise of authority, and to the ends sought through government. The most appropriate analytical approach is to assume that certain patterns in the structure and dynamics

[4] *The Ruling Class* (New York: McGraw-Hill, 1939), p. 50.

of political power are more or less peculiar to democratic orders and to seek to identify those special characteristics rather than to assume that the power analysis is inapplicable to democratic systems.

Succession to authority in democracies. Democratic systems have evolved a characteristic solution of the problem of succession to posts of authority —a basic question that vexes all sorts of regimes. Hereditary monarchies left the matter to a biological lottery which, at times, worked well enough. Hereditary aristocracies had much the same solution. Quite as often one set of rulers replaced another by coup d'état or by revolution. Modern dictatorships confront no new problem when the ·dictator nears senility and the issue of succession demands attention. How to accomplish transfers of authority without serious disturbances in the life of the state has been a topic for political speculation through the ages. The democratic solution is to fill the principal posts of authority by elections. A working system of elections cannot, of course, be created by fiat. Successful utilization of elections to determine succession to authority seems to come only with a cultural habituation to such a technique, under circumstances of general agreement on a broad range of fundamental issues both substantive and procedural, and doubtless in association with other factors neither well understood nor easily defined. Nevertheless, a major accomplishment of the architects of democracies has been the contrivance of orderly modes of succession to places of authority.

The democratic formula goes beyond the question of succession in its ancient form. It not only provides a means for filling posts of authority when they become vacant; it assures that they will become vacant at frequent intervals without either the messiness of a beheading or the inconvenience of a revolution. The democratic technique for the determination of succession is thus combined with a method for the termination of the life of a government. An election poses the questions whether the ruling clique shall be continued in power and, if not, by whom shall it be succeeded. Democratic orders merge into a single ritual a substitute for older techniques of determining the heir to authority and a functional equivalent for the varieties of ways by which peoples rid themselves of unwanted rulers.

Consultation and consent in democracy. The exercise of authority in democratic orders is characterized by a deference to the ruled, which is associated with techniques for consultation with the people or their representatives and with means for the expression of popular consent to governmental action. The relations involved in consultation and in obtaining consent became by historical transformation also means for holding governments accountable for their past actions. In a way, democratic doctrine prescribes that the people ought to get what they want no matter how wrongheaded they may be. Those charged with governance may educate, persuade, or assume the risk of making decisions that either turn out to be unpopular or to yield precisely what the people wanted but were unaware of it until they had lived with it for a while. Deference to the wishes of the ruled does not mean deference to the will of each individual—which would amount to anarchy. Most commonly democratic doctrines accord authority to popular majorities, although the theorists often spin out limitations of one kind or another on the majority. Whatever the exact form, democratic ideas, in their insistence on the consent of the ruled, differ sharply from theories that legitimize authority by such doctrines as the divine right of kings. Democratic practice, however, may often differ only in degree from that of regimes resting on doctrines other than that of popular consent. Dictators, absolute monarchies, governing aristocracies must also take into account the moods of the multitude; withdrawal of popular favor, mutterings of discontent, sabotage, and underground conspiracies may have their consequences in modification of policy as well as in repressive measures.

A corollary of the doctrine of consent and of the practice of deference to the ruled is freedom for expression of dissent from the actions of authority, with the expectation that protests will be heard and, if not heeded, at least considered and not followed by reprisals. Monarchs, to be sure, heard petitions, but in democratic orders freedom of dissent is associated with the right to join with others in efforts to seek redress by ousting the government—through electoral means. The people may not really govern themselves, but they can stir up a deafening commotion if they dislike the way they are governed—all of which points to the somewhat relaxed nature of the power relations of democratic regimes.

Dispersion of points of authority in democratic orders. A closely related characteristic of democratic orders—or at least of the American democratic order—is a wide dispersion of power (in the sense of a substance in a keg). Acutal authority tends to be dispersed and exercised not solely by governmental officials but also by private individuals and groups within the society. Moreover the power structure tends to be segmented: authority over one question rests here and over another, there. All this contrasts with the model of a clear and rigid hierarchical pattern of power. On one matter the President's decision may govern; on another, the wishes of the heads of a half dozen industrial corporations will prevail; on a third, organized labor or agriculture will win the day; and on still another, a congressionally negotiated compromise completely satisfactory to none of the contenders may settle the matter. Even the journalists may cast the deciding vote on some issues. Thus the locus of power may shift from question to question and even from time to time on the same question. "Power in America," says David Riesman, "seems to me situational and mercurial; it resists attempts to locate it in the way a molecule, under the Heisenberg principle, resists attempts simultaneously to locate it and time its velocity." [5]

Dispersion of power inevitably brings with it competition among centers of power, a behavior certainly not limited to democratic orders; though perhaps in democratic orders that competition occurs under different ground rules, over a broader range of matters, and with different consequences than in nondemocratic regimes. In some eras the rivalry among dispersed centers of power and influence becomes so salient that the entire political process is interpreted as one of the reconciliation of their conflicts. John Dickinson observed:

The task of government, and hence of democracy as a form of government, is not to express an imaginary popular will, but to effect adjustments among the various special wills and purposes which at any given time are pressing for realization.

Almost the whole range of political problems are problems of what may be called adjustment—of devising ways and means to curb particular "wills" or "interests," and thus clear the track for the realization of other wills and interests in fuller measure. This is the task of governmental decisions ranging in importance from where to locate a new street or sewage-disposal plant to whether or not to go to war. Government, from this point of view, is primarily an arbitrator, and since practically every arbitration must result in giving to one side more of what it thinks it ought to have than the other side is willing to admit, every governmental act can be viewed as favoring in some degree some particular and partial "will," or special interest. It is therefore meaningless to criticize government, whether democratic or not, merely because it allows special interests to attain some measure of what they think themselves entitled to. The question is rather whether it allows the "right" side, or the "right" special interest, to win; and the "right" special interest means only the one whose will is most compatible with what we, as critics, conceive to be the right direction for the society's development to take.[6]

An incidental but significant aspect of the dispersion of power is the existence of a multiplicity of points of initiative for collective action, which may be either governmental or nongovernmental. Governmental initiative, moreover, may set off either governmental or nongovernmental action. Nongovernmental initiative, in turn, may spark governmental action or it may set in motion moves for the achievement of essentially public ends through nongovernmental organization.

[5] *The Lonely Crowd* (New Haven: Yale University Press, 1950), p. 252.
[6] "Democratic Realities and Democratic Dogma," *American Political Science Review,* 25 (1930), pp. 291–292.

A politics of limited objectives? Perhaps, too, a democratic politics must be a politics of limited objectives at least in the short run. That is, given the mode of managing succession to authority and the related characteristics of democratic orders, what are the limits of change that will be tolerated through electoral and representative procedures without the invocation of force in defense by those adversely affected? Casual observation suggests that democratic procedures operate on the expectation that changes in the short run will be comparatively narrow, that the "outs" will not be liquidated or deprived of their liberty, at least not without due process, and that all concerned will live to fight it out again in another campaign.[7] This point sometimes appears in the form of the contention that a democratic order can operate effectively only on the foundation of a widely shared consensus on fundamentals. That consensus defines the limits of political conflict, and those who advocate measures outside that range may expect to be treated roughly.

If the limitation of political conflict to tolerable bounds requires that democratic politics be a politics of limited objectives in the short run, it may also be, paradoxically, that a durable democratic order must rest on a presupposition of unlimited objectives over the long run. The mystique of democracy nourishes a belief that the wrongs of today, persistent though they may seem, will be corrected in some remote tomorrow. Perhaps any regime that struggles for stability must implant such expectations in the minds of its people. Yet democratic doctrine seems especially adapted to the encouragement of such a faith, for it contemplates an evolving system in which the dispossessed of today may hope to become the top dogs of tomorrow.

Other significant characteristics of democratic power systems could be set out but these suffice to suggest the bewildering skein of power relations within a modern democratic society as well as something of their nature. Government controls but is itself controlled. Private centers of power influence, even command, both private individuals and government. Dispersed centers of power interact with each other, all in a most complex and kaleidoscopic pattern.

Institutions of Democracy

Associated with these characteristics of a democratic system of authority are institutions congenial to the fulfillment of the requisites of such an

---

[7] It would be erroneous to conclude that those in office in the United States never jail political opponents. Some prosecutions look extraordinarily like attempts to take advantage of the technicalities of the law to discourage the opposition. They only illustrate the point that bills of rights have a broad significance for the workings of the political system quite apart from their bearing on the liberty of the citizen not a partisan activist.

order. Nondemocratic regimes have their executives, their courts, their councils, and even representative bodies of a sort. Democracies supplement that traditional apparatus of government with instrumentalities that link the governed more closely with the governors and facilitate the management of succession to authority, the reconciliation of the claims of competing points of authority, and the consultation of the governed. Such machinery alone is not the whole of a viable democratic order; considerable civic education and human adaptation must occur to permit the mechanism to operate. Even the institutions themselves are not designed and built overnight. They are the product of long evolution, of trial and error, of not a little blind groping—all tutored by purpose and aided by an occasional deliberate choice that turns out to be both rational and fortunate in its consequences.

No single type of institutional apparatus is requisite to a democratic order, although elements common at least in name appear in most systems that purport to be democratic: political parties, elective representative bodies, other popularly chosen officials, and electoral systems. Yet each of these institutions may differ from nation to nation. Moreover, they combine in each situation to produce a more or less unique whole, a system in which the function of each part is conditioned by its place in relation to the other elements of the individual order.

Political parties. Political parties constitute a basic element of democratic institutional apparatus. They perform an essential function in the management of succession to power, as well as in the process of obtaining popular consent to the course of public policy. They amass sufficient support to buttress the authority of governments; or, on the contrary, they attract or organize discontent and dissatisfaction sufficient to oust the government.

In more than a poetic sense political parties are lineal descendants of two sorts of groups that recur in the annals of governance: those that conspire to overthrow the government and those that rally around to defend and maintain the regime. The party system sublimates that ancient conflict into behaviors no more bellicose than the oratory of an election campaign. To regard the party of the outs of the moment as akin to the old-time rings of conspirators banded together to overthrow the government may seem far fetched, and their kinship may be more analogical than genealogical. Nevertheless, political parties in combination with other institutions and procedures (all in the context of appropriate behavior patterns acquired by both the citizenry and the leadership echelons) provide means for handling the problem of succession to authority more or less peacefully. Whether the party system constitutes the only way in which succession may be arranged presents another type of question. Democratic orders seem to have discovered no other technique for the purpose, although at some times and in some jurisdictions, especially in smaller units of government, party organizations are most rudimentary.

Representative bodies. The institutional paraphernalia of democratic orders commonly includes some sort of representative body or bodies, with at times other elective officials as well. Consultative councils representative of the interests within society antedated the rise of modern democracies, but their place in the governmental system came to be altered as they were linked to the electorate through the party system and elections. That linkage developed concurrently with the rise of democratic ideologies, which defined new roles for representatives: they became, at least according to some theories, agents and advocates of their constituents. Whatever norms guide the actions of representatives in a particular system, the apparatus of representation symbolizes the consultation of the governed and its actions tend to be regarded as equivalent to the command of the popular majority if it had the capacity and inclination to command. Of equal significance may be the role of representative bodies as conduits for the communication of popular discontent with the operations of government and as forums for the expression of dissent.

Electoral procedures. The practices and procedures of popular elections may be regarded as another democratic institution, which is intertwined, of course, with the system of parties and representation. Elections alone do not make an order democratic. Dictatorial regimes have their plebiscites, which reflect a fraudulent deference to the potency of the ideology of democracy. Characteristically the electoral practices of democracies are associated with party systems which propose to the electorate a choice, as well as with a general disposition to accept the verdict of the count of heads. The march of millions of people to the polls constitutes a dramatic symbolization of the ideas of democratic theory. On occasion, to be sure, the voters may act as puppets manipulated by small groups of willful men; or the electorate may be swayed by demagogues bent only on duping the people; or ballots may be a flimsy cover for a cohesive army of plunderers. Withal, over the long pull elections in a democracy mark great turning points in public policy, express mass approval of actions taken, set limits to the course of governmental policy, ratify the work of governments or cast them into oblivion or dishonor.

Nonparty associations and groups. In the give and take between government and governed, the formal apparatus of government may be supplemented by a system of private associations, which, in the United States, are called pressure groups. These associations may perform a representative function by communicating the wishes of their members to public authorities; or they may bring "pressure" to bear upon the government. The same groups may be consulted by government. They may even exercise forms of private authority which differ little from governmental authority. At times their influence on the actions of formal government may be so potent that they in fact control the exercise of public authority. In other instances they may perform creative functions in the contrivance of proposals for public policy. Pressure groups may be in alliance with a political party and they often seek to influence the outcome of elections.

Other linkages of government and citizenry. All these more or less formalized and organized features of the structure and nature of power relations are supplemented by other kinds of interaction between government and the governed. These cannot be neatly classified or characterized but in general they consist of communications between official and citizen which occur in a context of official concern about public attitudes. Governments infrequently undertake measures of great import without attempting to estimate the probable public reaction. That estimate may rest on intuition or on systematic appraisals of the public mind. The flow of mail from citizens to representatives and to executive and administrative offices constitutes another link between citizen and government. The ruminations and reports of the journalists are perused in official quarters and may touch sensitive spots and have their effects on public action. None of these types of interaction between government and governed is peculiar to democratic orders, yet for their maximum development conditions associated with democratic regimes (e. g., freedom of press, the right of petition, protection against official reprisal for expression of protest) must prevail to some degree.

Other Aspects of Power

Most of this book will be devoted to an analysis of the American version of these institutions and practices of democracy: political parties, pressure groups, elections, representation. The student should be warned, however, that these methods of developing more or less rational consent to the course of governmental action by no means cover all the complexities of the American—or any other—regime. Democratic institutional forms and procedures can operate only within an appropriate matrix of public attitudes and beliefs—a proposition amply demonstrated by many abortive attempts to transplant democratic institutions to unsuitable environments. Furthermore, the governing process as a whole from time to time employs techniques far removed from the democratic methods of consultation and give-and-take between government and governed. Democratic forms may serve as a screen for tyranny or for gang rule, at least within restricted areas and for short periods of time. Such techniques of governance, which have a way of becoming mixed with the conventional methods of democracy, deserve brief mention in this introductory conspectus of the nature of politics.

Custom. The means for the development and maintenance of the customs of a people form an essential element of the political system, although their function as such is not often explicitly recognized. Politically relevant customs include a considerably wider range of behavior than narrowly political conventions. Thus, by custom the members of the electoral college cast their votes for the candidates named by the national convention of their political party. By custom Senators may invoke the right of "senatorial courtesy" and cause the Senate to deny its consent to certain appointments by the President. Beyond such customs connected with the institutions of government are politically relevant attitudes shared by the mass of the people. Although such attitudes profoundly affect the actions of government, their identification presents no little difficulty. Important on the American scene are such attitudes as the disposition to compromise; the willingness to accept the outcome of elections; the insistence on "fair" procedures at least for those playing the game within the accepted limits; the tendency to frown on excessive and arbitrary authority; a comparatively weak sense of class identification together with a relatively strong sense of identification with the community as a whole; a moderate reverence for politicians. All such attitudes and the related customary behaviors may be regarded as equivalent to the political element of the anthropologist's concept of culture.[8]

A political order enlists for its maintenance and perpetuation all the mechanisms for the dissemination and inculcation of attitudes and beliefs and all the means for their transmission from generation to generation. The school, the church, the family, the press, radio and television, literature, patriotic ceremonials, and other institutions and practices mold the oncoming generation and re-enforce the faith of the old.[9] In modern

[8] Gabriel Almond has developed the concept of political culture in his "Comparative Political Systems," *Journal of Politics*, 18 (1956), pp. 391–409.

[9] The communications specialists approach the same phenomenon in somewhat different terms. Thus, Karl W. Deutsch observes: "The inner source of political power—the relatively coherent and stable structure of memories, habits, and values—depends on existing facilities for social communication, both from the past to the present and between contemporaries. Such communication requires facilities for storing, recalling, and recombining information, channels for its dissemination and inter-

societies the school system in particular functions as a formidable instrument of political power in its role as a transmitter of the goals, values,
and attitudes of the polity.[10] In the selection of values and attitudes to be
inculcated, it chooses those cherished by the dominant elements in the
political order. By and large the impact of widely accepted goals, mores,
and social values fixes the programs of American schools. When schools
diverge from this vaguely defined directive and collide with potent groups
in the political system, they feel a pressure to conform.

The ideal of equality of opportunity vests in the American educational
system another function of deep significance for the political order. In a
rigidly structured society vertical mobility is apt to be slight: the sons
and daughters of each social class "inherit" a status. The offspring of
favored classes enjoy special opportunity, including access to education,
and are apt to constitute most of the favored classes of the next generation. The sons and daughters of the less-favored classes, even though
potential geniuses, are likely to remain in the status to which they were
born. The philosophy of American education proclaims that each young
person shall have an educational opportunity to develop fully his abilities
—a doctrine that is part and parcel of democratic theory. Jefferson,
hence, was not out of character as a democratic theorist when he proposed
an educational system to skim off at various educational levels persons
of genius and provide further training for them at public expense. "The
object," he said, "is to bring into action that mass of talents which lies
buried in poverty in every country, for want of the means of development, and thus give activity to a mass of mind, which, in proportion to
our population, shall be the double or treble of what it is in most countries." [11] Such a doctrine, revolutionary in its day, provides a basis for an
educational system that serves as something of an escalator for the social
system. Even though upward mobility is in substantial degree an article
of faith rather than a fact, the faith has a political significance of no small
import.

Violence and force. Democratic standards exclude reliance on force and
violence in domestic politics. Indeed, a great accomplishment of democratic orders consists in their contrivance of substitutes for force. Yet
even in democratic orders violence and the threat of violence play a

action, and facilities for deriving further information, as well as new changes in
purposes and values, from these processes."—*Nationalism and Social Communication*
(New York: Technology Press and John Wiley, 1953), p. 49.

[10] The second edition of this book contains a chapter (No. 21) on "Education as
Politics." Consult that chapter and its bibliography.

[11] Quoted in *The Jeffersonian Cyclopedia*, J. P. Foley, ed. (New York: Funk and
Wagnalls, 1900), p. 275.

part.[12] In political conflict the use of violence is almost always an under-lying potentiality. If the stakes are not deemed fundamental, if deeply cherished values are not at issue, if the customs discourage resort to force, adjustments through pacific means may be acceptable to the contenders. Yet the circumstances under which only pacific means are used are tran-sient and may be easily upset. Furthermore, nonviolent methods for the settlement of political conflict sometimes work because of the threat of violence in the background.

Although the actual employment of violence in our society is frequent enough, the saber more often exerts its influence without being drawn. Regimes are always prepared to defend their positions with force if the need arises. Armies have their domestic potentialities as well as their foreign uses.[13] On the other hand, those groups that deem themselves insufferably oppressed may cease to be satisfied with debate and resort to arms. Social reform has at times been accelerated by the fear that "there might be a revolution," although modern military technology makes revolt an unfruitful endeavor. Tenuous is the line between conditions under which arbitration of differences by discussion brings acceptable results and the conditions under which violence flares up. However the line is drawn, the content of the category of issues soluble only by the sword constantly changes. Issues that at one time generate bloody internal dissension at another time are settled by means no more sanguinary than the ceremonial bellicosity of parliamentary conflict.

The American order has had its share of violence. One great sectional dispute, that over slavery, could be terminated only by war. Incidents of violence punctuate the long history of employer-employee relations, with aggressors on both sides. For many decades employer force, either in the hands of company militia or allied public police, contributed significantly to the maintenance of the status of the employing groups. Workers, when they could, met force with force.[14] Ultimately public authority com-manded other modes for the solution of employer-employee differences.

[12] The second edition of this book includes a chapter (No. 20) devoted to the political role of force. For suggestive brief treatments of the subject, see C. E. Merriam, *Prologue to Politics* (Chicago: University of Chicago Press, 1939); James Marshall, *Swords and Symbols* (New York: Oxford University Press, 1939). See also S. P. Huntington, *The Soldier and the State* (Cambridge: Harvard University Press, 1957).

[13] Thus, in 1934 at a time of widespread unrest, the Assistant Secretary of War, Harry H. Woodring, advocated a larger army to "cope with social and economic problems in an emergency" and to provide "secret insurance against chaos."—Quoted by Merle Curti, *Peace or War* (New York: Norton. 1936), p. 266. Earlier President Coolidge had pointed to the uses of the armed forces in "domestic tumults."

[14] See Robert Hunter, *Violence and the Labor Movement* (New York: Macmillan, 1914).

Similarly, violence and the threat of violence have fixed in no small measure the status of the Negro. Lynchings, the threat of lynchings, and threats of violence have formed a part of the bundle of sanctions, official and private, that maintain the dominance of white over black in the South.

Economic sanctions. Not infrequently the formal mechanisms of political power are supplemented by economic sanctions or persuasives, often pecuniary in form. The actions of government in arbitration among competing centers of power may merely formalize bargains driven with dollars behind the scenes. Or money may aid mightily in the organization of popular support. Bribery and bread and circuses have an ancient, if not honorable, political lineage. The essence of the economic sanction in the power relation consists in the use of things of material value to cement support or to control. The accord of public honor and the compulsions of public duty govern some men while more mundane considerations move others.[15]

No taxonomy of economic sanctions of political significance need be attempted here, but the moral opinion of the community divides economic sanctions into those regarded as corrupt and those treated as correct. In the first category belongs bribery. In some political conflicts the greased palm may cast the deciding vote. While enduring political systems are not built by bribery, it has in one form or another played a potent role in public decisions in many confused, disorderly, and rapidly changing social situations. By definition, bribery can occur only in those relations in which private individuals seek to influence the holders of formal authority. Yet at times bribery is difficult to distinguish from political extortion in which the holders of authority exact a price for their action or inaction.

In American localities from time to time impressive power structures —virtual dictatorships—have been constructed by corrupt techniques. The tolerance of prohibited lines of commerce—gambling, prostitution, and other trades catering to tastes beyond the law—is sometimes regarded as simply a result of bribery and nothing more. Yet these arrangements also may tie to the political leadership groups powerful in electioneering and fruitful as a source of funds for political warfare. In the total political context a bloc is built into a dominant political coalition. The informal award of valuable "licenses" to pursue illegal endeavors parallels in its effects the use of public jobs, purchases, contracts, and other material perquisites to gain the support of particular elements of the community.

[15] Chapter 23 of the first edition of this book is devoted to an analysis of pecuniary sanctions.

The line separating the corrupt from the correct is tenuous indeed. Material advantages and expectations of material advantage occupy no small place in the construction of political coalitions and in the maintenance of systems of power. From the normal actions of government some groups receive preference; others suffer disadvantage. The motives behind such actions may be both disputed and obscure. A work-relief program may be denounced as a calculated move by venal men to purchase the vote of the shiftless, or it may be praised as a bold humanitarian program to alleviate the hardships of those destitute through no fault of their own. And it may be a little of both. In any case, the forms of material benefit at the disposal of government multiply with the expansion of governmental functions: tariffs to industry, subsidies to farmers, privileges to licensed activities in a variety of forms, benefits to the aged and the incapacitated, privileges to the users of the public domain—to mention only a few. Policies on all these and other such matters affect the relations of power within the society.

These introductory pages outline a conception of politics to serve as a setting for the more detailed analyses that follow. The general drift of the argument has been that politics should be equated with governance in its broadest sense. So commodious a definition has its pedagogical disadvantages since American usage commonly attributes a narrower meaning to the term politics. Yet perhaps a better understanding of the institutions of American politics may be gained by examining them, and speculating about them, against a backdrop of such a general conception of the nature of the political process.

To equate politics with governance brings within our definition all types of governments. The analysis has identified the salient characteristics that differentiate democratic regimes from other sorts of power structures in order better to place democratic systems in the family of governments. These features include such matters as the democratic solution to the problem of succession to power; the assumption that government should operate on a foundation of popular consent; the expectation of extensive consultation between governors and governed; freedom of dissent and criticism; the dispersion of points of authority and centers of initiative within the system; and, in general, an extensive practice of give-and-take between governors and governed.

The democratic organization of authority includes certain institutions appropriate to the characteristics of democratic governance. The most conspicuous are political parties, pressure groups, election procedures, and representative bodies. Their workings do not account by any means for all politics in the sense of the totality of governance. A man from Mars studying the process of American governance would bring within his purview the workings of the civil courts in the adjudication of private rights, the application of the criminal laws, the operations of the administrative regulatory authorities, the functions of the great administrative departments, and a variety of other activities of government. In our focus on the institutions more or less peculiar to democracy—pressure groups, political parties, and related agencies—we should not be unmindful that we deal with only a segment of the governing process.

Part One | **PRESSURE GROUPS**

A PRINCIPAL instrumentality of democratic politics, as the introductory chapter pointed out, is the system of political parties. A foundation for consideration of the American party may be laid by an inspection of pressure groups. At bottom, group interests are the animating forces in the political process; an understanding of American politics requires a knowledge of the chief interests and of their stake in public policy. The exercise of the power of governance consists in large degree in the advancement of legitimate group objectives, in the reconciliation and mediation of conflicting group ambitions, and in the restraint of group tendencies judged to be socially destructive. Hence, an examination of pressure groups and of the interests from which they arise throws light on the materials that politicians must manage, on the problems with which they must cope.

The most common basis for group action is economic. As the authors of *The Federalist* long ago concluded:

the most common and durable source of faction has been the various and unequal distribution of property. Those who hold and those who are without property have ever formed distinct interests in society. Those who are creditors, and those who are debtors, fall under a like discrimination. A landed interest, a manufacturing interest, a mercantile interest, a moneyed interest, with many lesser interests grow up of necessity in civilised nations, and divide them into different classes, actuated by different sentiments and views.[1]

Economic motivation does not explain all. *The Federalist*, in an un-Marxian manner, pointed to other bases of group interest, such as "zeal for different opinions concerning religion, concerning government, and many other points, as well of speculation as of practice; an attachment of different leaders ambitiously contending for pre-eminence and power." And, when all else is lacking, "the most frivolous and fanciful

[1] *The Federalist*, No. X.

distinctions" are sufficient to excite the "most violent conflicts." Whatever the bases of group action may be, the study of politics must include an analysis of the objectives and composition of interest groups within a society.

A striking feature of American politics is the extent to which political parties are supplemented by private associations formed to influence public policy. These organizations, commonly called pressure groups, promote their interests by attempting to influence government rather than by nominating candidates and seeking responsibility for the management of government. The political interests of agriculture, for example, may be advanced through lobbying and propaganda activities of pressure groups, such as the American Farm Bureau Federation. Such groups, while they may call themselves nonpolitical, are engaged in politics; in the main theirs is a politics of policy. They are concerned with what government does either to help or to harm their membership. They do not attempt to assume, at least openly, the party's basic function of nominating candidates and seeking responsibility for the conduct of government, although the division of labor in the political system between parties and pressure groups is not always clear-cut. Pressure groups may campaign for party candidates and may even become, in fact if not in form, allied with one or the other of the parties. Yet by and large pressure groups, as they seek to influence the exercise of public power, play a distinctive role. They supplement the party system and the formal instruments of government by serving as spokesmen for the special interests within society.[2]

[2] For general surveys of pressure-group activity, see Pendleton Herring, *Group Representation before Congress* (Baltimore: Johns Hopkins Press, 1929); D. C. Blaisdell, *American Democracy Under Pressure* (New York: Ronald, 1957); K. G. Crawford, *The Pressure Boys* (New York: Messner, 1939); Stuart Chase, *Democracy Under Pressure* (New York: Twentieth Century Fund, 1945). For a theoretical analysis of group role, see David B. Truman, *The Governmental Process* (New York: Knopf, 1951), ch. 2.

2 | Agrarianism

THE STRUCTURE of political power may be pictured as a more or less unstable equilibrium among competing interests—in our times the accent has been on instability. Or, to change the figure and shift the focus of attention, the politician might be regarded as a person riding a bicycle on a tight rope and juggling an indeterminate number of irregular objects, each moving through an unpredictable orbit. Whether the figure precisely fits the phenomenon, the political equilibrium among social groups is from time to time disturbed. One class or group becomes discontented with the existing state of things and the processes of politics go into operation to create a new equilibrium. The politician finds himself in the middle—and belabored from all sides—as he seeks to contrive a formula to maintain peace among conflicting interests.

Examination of the role of agriculture in American politics will account for one major unit in our galaxy of political interests; it will also illustrate the manner in which maladjustments develop in the relations among great groups of the population. Disturbances that produce deprivation or a sense of injustice generate movements for redress which often find ultimate expression in the statute books. The reactions of American agriculture to the profound changes it has undergone constitute a striking indication of the political problems that flow from a drastic alteration in the position of a major sector of the economy.

Agriculture in American Life: Long-Term Trends

The gradual cumulation of the effects of secular changes dating approximately from the Civil War has profoundly altered the position of agriculture in American politics. The proportion of rural people in the total population has sharply declined—a change that has been accompanied by loss of political position to the cities. Furthermore, changes in the economy have subjected the farm population in special degree to the impact of economic fluctuations and created the practical necessity for novel types of public policy.

Rural rear-guard action. The adaptation of the political system to the marked decrease in the proportion of rural population remains yet to be completely accomplished. Although by 1950 the proportion of the population living on farms had declined to 16 per cent, the influence of agriculture remains far greater than might be expected from its numerical strength. Census after census has recorded the movement of people from farms and the growth of cities, yet rural dwellers have fought a stubborn rear-guard action to delay full political recognition of the fact that America, once predominantly agrarian, has become predominantly industrial.

In their endeavors to retain their position, farmers have been able to draw on a tradition that ascribes special moral values to farm people. Rural attitudes and rural people, so the belief has been, constitute the reality and the strength of America. Thomas Jefferson asserted that farmers were "the chosen people of God, if ever He had a chosen people"; cities were "essentially evil" and "ulcers on the body politic." These ideas did not die with Jefferson, and partly from the strength of such notions agriculture has enjoyed a strategic advantage in politics.

Although the free and independent rural yeomanry has long since lost its position of dominance, it retains a most respectable authority. Rural overrepresentation in legislative bodies contributes concretely to the maintenance of a powerful farm influence which manifests itself in legislation favorable to rural dwellers generally, as well as to farmers.

Market shrinkage and technological advance. The trends in the division of population between country and city bring a relocation of the centers of political influence. Yet other long-term changes in the position and nature of agriculture gradually created the economic circumstances productive of modern agrarian political problems. The net effect of one set of these changes was that there came to be too many acres in cultivation and too many people trying to make a living by farming. The export market for farm products declined after 1900 except for temporary war-time spurts in demand; it required the produce of 27,000,000 fewer acres to meet export requirements for the period 1935–1939 than for 1925–1929. Long-term dietary changes operated to the disadvantage of some classes of farmers and to the advantage of others. The decline in flour and potato consumption has been notable. Another market for farm products disappeared with the replacement of the horse and mule by truck and tractor. Between 1918 and 1953, about 70,000,000 acres formerly used to produce food for draft animals became available for other uses.

The effects of these market losses were partially offset by the increasing population, but meanwhile on the supply side farmers were becoming more efficient producers. Technological advances—mechanization, increased use of fertilizers, improved cultural practices, better insecticides, upbreeding of farm plants and animals—brought, at first gradual then startling, increases in productivity per farm worker. In 1820 one farm worker produced enough for himself and three other persons. By 1920, this figure had risen to nine and by 1945, to 14 other persons.[1] In the 1940's productivity grew extremely rapidly. In 1950, on the average, a single farm worker produced 50 per cent more than he had a scant 20 years earlier. In 1920 3.6 per cent of farms had tractors; in 1950, 46.9 per cent.

So long as population grew rapidly enough to offset market shrinkages and increases in productivity, farming was an expanding business even though it was becoming proportionately less important in the total economy. Yet since 1910 the farm-labor force has declined absolutely as well as relatively. From 1920 to 1955 the farm population dropped by about 10,000,000, almost one-third of the 1920 total. From 1950 to 1956 alone population living on farms declined by 11 per cent. In part, the downward adjustment of the agricultural labor force takes care of itself. Sons of farmers move to the city; farmers become filling-station operators. Yet these shifts occur slowly and the lag in the transfer of the excess population from the farms complicates the problem of coping with those farm problems that would exist even if there were not too many farmers.

Commercialization of agriculture. Another long-term alteration in the character of agriculture—more significant for the modern political ills of the farmer than the declining numerical importance of the farmer—has

[1] S. E. Johnson, "Technological Changes and the Future of Rural Life," *Journal of Farm Economics,* 32 (1950), pp. 225–239.

been the commercialization of agriculture. In the good old days, not so many decades ago, the farmer and his family subsisted in considerable degree on the produce of the farm. Moreover, the major factor in production was labor: the labor of the farmer and his family. To the extent that the farm productive unit was self-contained, it was insulated from the forces of the market.

Gradually farmers came to devote themselves more and more exclusively to the raising of crops to be sold in the market. The dependence of the farmer on the market made him subject to all the storms of the economic system generally. When the price of wheat fluctuated in Minneapolis, the farmer in North Dakota was affected. When the price of hogs dropped in Chicago, the impact struck in Iowa. A sag in the price of milk in New York City made itself quickly felt on the upstate dairy farms.

Commercialization of agriculture also subjected the farmer to the impact of market fluctuations on items he came to purchase for his own consumption and for use in production. Wage rates, the price of tractors, and the cost of gasoline are links that tie the commercialized farmer far more closely to the economy than was his predecessor who plowed with horses and mules and relied on himself and his family for human labor. In short, the farmer gradually became an entrepreneur who invests, hires, and manages rather than toils. The farm manager with his account books, his payrolls, and his capital equipment tends to replace the free and independent tiller of the soil who could afford to be radical and on occasion breathe fire. As a businessman, even an industrialized farmer, he comes to feel a common interest with the business community generally.

These fundamental alterations in the farmer's place in the economy occurred earlier in some areas than in others. They affected the producers of some commodities before they reached the producers of others. Yet the key to the understanding of farm politics in the United States in the first half of the twentieth century lies in the understanding of the peculiar position of agriculture in the economic system as a whole. The farmer came to be vulnerable to the stresses of the economic system generally, though he acquired in the process no weapons for economic self-defense. When overproduction and lower prices threaten, business groups may with some success act together to curtail production and safeguard themselves without the interposition of government. Millions of independent agricultural producers find such concerted action impossible; hence they enter politics to seek their "fair" share of the national income.

Cycles of Agrarian Discontent: The Nature of Political Movements

While the long-term changes in the relation of supply and demand for agricultural products have necessitated painful adjustments in farm plant and labor force, more significant in the stimulation of agitation about the farm question have been the special effects of economic fluctuations on agriculture. The commercialization of farming—and the decline in reliance on farm output for subsistence—linked the farmer to the economy and subjected him to the blows of the business cycle. Yet the consequences went a bit further: owing to the peculiar workings of the economic system, downswings of the business cycle strike the farmer far more severely than other sectors of the economy.

A factor of great significance in the setting off of political movements is an abrupt change for the worse in the status of one group relative to that of other groups in society. The economics of politics is by no means solely a matter of the poor against the rich; the rich and the poor may live together peaceably for decades, each accepting its status quietly. A rapid change for the worse, however, in the relative status of any group, rich or poor, is likely to precipitate political action. Depressions have been closely associated with intensification of farmers' political activity. Agrarian agitation, at times a bit boisterous and disturbing to the conservative elements of society, has not occurred at a uniform pitch but has had its dull periods and its shrill points correlated somewhat with variations in the fortunes of farmers. Although the entire story of agrarian discontent need not be recounted here, episodes can be used to illustrate the recurring pattern of economic maladjustments that generate popular movements to demand rectification of supposed injustices.

Economic adversity and the Granger movement. The Granger movement was an early example of the relations between economic deprivation and political unrest. The Grange reached its peak strength in the 1870's and served as a vehicle for the expression of agrarian discontent in the corn- and wheat-growing region embracing the upper Mississippi Valley from Ohio to the western rim of settlement in Kansas and Nebraska—a relatively newly developed area, devoted in special degree for the time, to the production of crops for market. In the late 'sixties and early 'seventies falling prices, caused mainly by the reduced demand following the Civil War, brought distress to western farmers. They blamed chiefly the railroads, the bankers, and monopolies for their plight. Of these misdoers, the railroads bore the brunt of Granger protest, and the movement bore fruit in early legislation to regulate railroad rates. The railroads, however, were not left with the entire blame: commission men and other middlemen were accused of taking an unduly large slice of the farmer's dollar; high rates of interest and the difficulties of meeting payments on heavy mortgages directed antagonism also toward the holders of mortgages.

Although it had been founded in 1867, the Grange, or the Patrons of Husbandry, had only a slow growth until the early 1870's when the pinch of economic adversity tightened. During 1873, the year of the panic, and 1874 the organization spread rapidly and at its peak had about three-quarters of a million members. Although the Grange extended into many states, the most highly organized region was the quadrilateral from Ohio to Dakota Territory, to Kansas, to Kentucky, to Ohio.

The Grange declared itself to be a nonpartisan organization. Instead of attempting to nominate and elect candidates under its own banner, it employed those methods now known as pressures. Both the state Granges and the National Grange adopted resolutions on proposed legislation; delegations were sent to present to legislatures the Grange's views; candidates for public office were asked to indicate their stand on measures of interest to farmers.

During 1875–1880 the Grange suffered a sharp decline in membership. Although the organization persists to this day, in the period 1880–1900 other farm organizations and movements succeeded it in the center of public attention. They rose and fell and left little in the way of lasting organizational apparatus.

Agricultural depression and farmer agitation, 1921–1952. Drops in prices and in economic activity strike farmers more harshly than they do other types of producers. In contrast, in boom times the prices of farm products rise to exceptionally high levels, to the temporary advantage of farmers. Industrial prices, that is, the prices that farmers must pay for commodities they consume and use in production, are relatively sticky while the prices for farm commodities are highly variable. A complex of factors accounts for this difference in price variability, but a major cause rests in the contrasting organization of the agricultural and nonagricultural sectors of the economy. Relatively small numbers of industrial producers operate in ways to minimize price fluctuations, a result that may come about even in the absence of collusion in price fixing. Participation in farm production, on the other hand, of millions of producers, along with other factors, creates circumstances that make the prices of farm products far more responsive to changes in supply-demand relationships.

The characteristic behavior of farm prices reflects itself in the graph in Figure 2.1, which shows the index of farm prices as a percentage of the index of prices paid by farmers since 1910. In effect, the figure shows the variations in the purchasing power of the prices of farm products. In World War I, farm prices raced upward far more rapidly than did the prices paid by farmers. In 1917 a bale of cotton would buy more fertilizer or more farm implements than it would have bought in 1914. After the shrinkage of war-induced demand, the curve drops quite rapidly, and in the sharp depression of 1921 farmers enjoyed a position of severe disadvantage in dealing with their suppliers. As the graph moves across the page, a substantial recovery may be noted in the mid-twenties, only to be followed by the deep trough of the Great Depression.

Economic deprivation suffices to generate political discontent. Yet the fact that economic distress affects the farmer more severely than it does the nonfarm producer contributes a special quality to agrarian political demands. When the curve in Figure 2.1 falls far below 100 per cent of parity, a demand arises to restore parity, to work toward a "fair" level of income for a sector of society subjected to unavoidable hazards by the

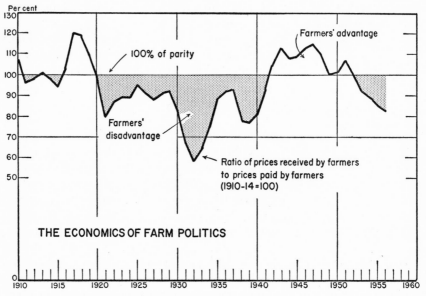

Figure 2.1. Ratio of Index of Prices Received by Farmers to Index of Prices Paid by Farmers (1910–1914 = 100), 1910–1956

workings of the economic system. Whether the idea of parity is defensible in terms of economics may be doubted, but its political appeal cannot be denied.

The precipitous decline in the economic position of agriculture after World War I, which may be seen in Figure 2.1, set the stage for the modern system of farm lobbying. The American Farm Bureau Federation became the principal means for the expression of farmer grievances in the 1920's. The Federation developed in close association with the county-agent system, which had been formed to disseminate among farmers the findings of agricultural research carried on by the land-grant colleges and the United States Department of Agriculture. The Smith-Hughes Act of 1914 had provided federal grants to state extension services, under the supervision of the land-grant colleges, which, in turn, made arrangements with county authorities to employ county agricultural agents.

Better to reach farmers with practical instruction in farming methods, local associations of farmers were formed, often by the county agents. The name "farm bureau" happened to be applied to an early association created as a unit of a chamber of commerce. On occasion the members of the bureau contributed to the salary of the county agent and almost invariably a close relation prevailed between the agent and the bureau. In due course, county farm bureaus federated into state farm bureau federations. In 1919 delegates from 31 states met in Chicago to create a national federation of these state farm organizations. The formation of small groups of farmers to facilitate the demonstration of new farming methods had set in motion forces that led to the formation of the American Farm Bureau Federation, an organization to become extremely effective in advancing the cause of the farmer.

The Federation set to work by establishing a legislative office in Washington and by defining its mission in blunt and straightforward terms: "First, to ascertain definitely, by referendum or otherwise, the farmers' attitude on pending legislation affecting agriculture; second, to thoroughly inform members of Congress concerning the farmers' legislative needs and requests; and, third, to report to the membership fully concerning the support or lack of support of individual congressmen." The Federation followed through and in 1921 and 1922 the agricultural bloc virtually wrested control of Congress from the party leaders. That bloc, a coalition of Senators and Representatives of both parties from agricultural districts, was formed "as a result of a series of helpful conferences at Farm Bureau legislative headquarters." [2] They agreed upon a program of measures and Congress passed bills to control grain exchanges, to regulate packers and stockyards, to increase appropriations for construction of rural highways, and to increase tariffs on farm products.[3]

Although the measures adopted by Congress under the spur of the farm bloc were helpful, the status of agriculture remained fundamentally unchanged in 1925 and 1926. The disadvantage of the farmer, in terms of the relationship between agricultural and industrial prices, continued to prevail. Agrarian spokesmen pointed to the tariff protection long enjoyed by industry and asserted that national policy compelled American farmers to produce food and fiber at ruinously low prices to facilitate the expansion of the export market for industrial products. The McNary-Haugen bill was brought forward as a means for reducing the gap between industrial and agricultural prices. The original bill was rejected by the House in June, 1924. Another version was defeated in 1926. Although backed

[2] O. M. Kile, *The Farm Bureau Movement* (New York: Macmillan, 1921), p. 188.
[3] See Arthur Capper, *The Agricultural Bloc* (New York: Harcourt, Brace, 1922).

with enthusiasm by the corn-belt states, the bill fell before the combined opposition of the Northeast and the South. In February, 1927, however, the bill, further modified, won congressional approval only to meet with executive veto. Again, in May, 1928, still another version of the bill was passed, and was again rejected by the President.[4]

The midwestern farm states carried their battle into the 1928 Republican convention and threatened rebellion against domination of the party by industry and finance. They failed to persuade the convention to commit itself to the McNary-Haugen plan, but Hoover, triumphant in 1928, came into office committed to "do something" about the farm problem. Congress, at a special session in 1929, created the Federal Farm Board with a mandate to "promote the effective merchandising of agricultural commodities in interstate and foreign commerce, so that the industry of agriculture will be placed on a basis of economic equality with other industries." Congress appropriated $500,000,000 for the board to buy and sell surpluses to stabilize prices, but the efforts of the Farm Board were doomed to fail. The board recognized "control of excessive production as absolutely essential" to improvement of the status of the farmer, yet all that it could do was to urge voluntary restraint to hold production to the limits necessary to maintain higher prices.

Though the Farm Bureau Federation did not openly endorse the Democratic presidential candidate in 1932, its president, Ed O'Neal, declared: "We must elect those who are true friends of agriculture, those who will pledge themselves to carry out our program." Roosevelt favored a large part of the Federation's program; farmers had no difficulty in identifying their "true friend." In 1933 Congress speedily enacted the Agricultural Adjustment Act, legislation agreed upon by farm leaders. The act declared "the present acute economic emergency" to be, in part, "the consequence of a severe and increasing disparity between the prices of agricultural and other commodities, which disparity has largely destroyed the purchasing power of farmers for industrial products." The policy of Congress was to "re-establish prices to farmers at a level that will give agricultural commodities a purchasing power with respect to articles that farmers buy, equivalent to the purchasing power of agricultural commodities" before World War I. The means of achieving this end was primarily control of production, which involved ultimately the determination by public authority of the amount of each of the major commodities

---

[4] See John D. Black, "The McNary-Haugen Movement," *American Economic Review*, 18 (1928), pp. 405–427; Theodore Saloutos and John D. Hicks, *Agricultural Discontent in the Middle West, 1900–1939* (Madison: University of Wisconsin Press, 1951); Gilbert C. Fite, *George N. Peek and the Fight for Farm Parity* (Norman: University of Oklahoma Press, 1954).

that should be produced by each farmer. The hope was thus to limit agricultural production and thereby to raise farm prices.

The passage of the Agricultural Adjustment Act of 1933 initiated a long series of governmental actions, with the object of achieving parity for the farmer. In one way or another most of the legislation sought to manage farm production by controlling production, by stimulating consumption, or by fixing prices. Production or acreage allotments were employed from time to time, sometimes in association with government purchase and storage programs at prices higher than would have been obtained on a free market. Among the measures to increase consumption, the school-lunch program was conspicuous although disposition through foreign aid also played a role. Some legislative acts dealt with a group of basic commodities while special legislative controls were established for tobacco, sugar, and dairy products.

During the 1930's experimentation with farm policy brought limited relief but it remained for the demands induced by World War II to lift the prices of farm products above parity. Stimulation, rather than limitation, of production became the order of the day and the administrative mechanisms built up in the 1930's were used to guide production into desired lines. The Korean War prolonged the demand for farm products, but its termination soon stimulated the concern of the American farmer about agricultural policy.

Eisenhower's farm slump. The proposition that farm prices and income serve as a crude index of the political temperature of the farmer finds further illustration in the intensification of the debate on farm policy in the years from 1952 to 1956. A tapering off in the demand for farm products, together with the surpluses built up by a combination of increased agricultural efficiency and the stimulation of price supports, caused a rapid decline in farm prices beginning in late 1952. The behavior of farm prices over this period appears in Figure 2.2, which presents in more detail and for a shorter period the price indices of farm and industrial products that underlie Figure 2.1. Note in Figure 2.2 that the prices received by farmers, in relation to the prices they paid, steadily deteriorated from 1952 and by 1956 had dropped markedly below the 1952 level. (The index of all farm prices averages out the gyrations in the prices of individual commodities, and Figure 2.2 includes also the index of prices for meat animals to suggest the variability in the prices of individual farm products.) Net agricultural income in 1955 was 27 per cent less than in 1951, a shift that did not sit well with farmers who saw other sectors of the economy enjoying a high level of prosperity.

The Eisenhower Administration initiated, under Secretary of Agricul-

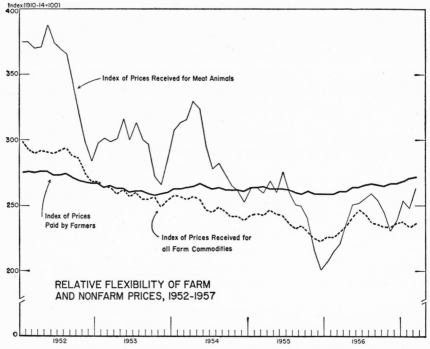

Figure 2.2. Indices of Prices Received by Farmers and of Prices Paid by Farmers (Monthly Data), 1952–1957

ture Ezra Taft Benson, a program looking toward the liquidation of agricultural surpluses and the reduction of the levels of farm price support, measures calculated to encourage a downward movement of agricultural output and a cityward movement of farm population.[5] As farm price declines continued, midwestern farmers in particular became more vocal in their unhappiness. In the 1954 congressional elections the Republican vote sagged most noticeably in farming areas most seriously affected by price declines. A Democratic Congress, with the aid of Republicans from the farm states, in 1956 adopted a high-support farm bill only to have it vetoed by the President. Yet the Administration, fearful of the potential repercussions in the farm regions, then adopted policies far more favorable to the farmer than it had evidently originally in-

[5] The drift of Administration policy had been predictable from the 1952 Republican platform which favored "a farm program aimed at full parity prices for all farm products in the market place." It expressed opposition to "restrictions on the American farmers' ability to produce" and proposed commodity loans at a level necessary "to maintain a balanced production."

tended.[6] Those policies did not suffice to prevent in 1956 a loss of several Republican House seats or a decline in Eisenhower's popular vote in farming districts west of the Mississippi.

From spontaneous movement to crystallized interest: Permanent mobilization. One of the morals of the preceding recital is that movements of political protest tend to develop when a sector of the population regards itself as unjustly treated or as the victim of circumstances. For fifty or sixty years after the Civil War, farmers' movements tended to sweep the country at times of economic crisis; movements developed more or less spontaneously in response to frustration and deprivation. Once the vicissitudes that gave birth to the agitation disappeared, the organization formed to carry the movement withered. When the pain left, the farmer quit squawking and went back to the plow.

The alternation of vitality and feebleness in farm organization has apparently been replaced by a permanent mobilization for political action; organizations of farmers maintain a constant alert. This development of farm organizations parallels the growth of collective endeavor in all sectors of American society. The character of modern public policy requires that farm organizations—like tariff lobbyists and public utility legislative representatives—give unremitting attention to the actions of government. Instead of a slumbering, rustic giant roused only by depression and adversity, farm organizations, well-organized and competently led, maintain an interest in public policy as keen and continuous as that of any business or labor group. In a sense public policy—by creating public bounty and by making the income of agriculture in part a matter of political decision—has given farmers a powerful incentive to join together in cohesive organization.

The broad objectives of farm organizations have been stated in terms of the achievement of a principle of fair treatment for a disadvantaged sector of the economy, but often their operations have had the odor of the old-style tariff lobby. Nevertheless, farmers, given the way the economic system operates, occupy a peculiarly vulnerable position. Their troubles have been magnified by the problems of adjusting the farm plant and labor force to the reduced scale dictated by the new agricultural technology. Even were that adjustment out of the way, the perverse re-

[6] For treatments of governmental policy toward agriculture, see D. C. Blaisdell, *Government and Agriculture* (New York: Farrar & Rinehart, 1940); Bela Gold, *Wartime Economic Planning in Agriculture* (New York: Columbia University Press, 1949); M. R. Benedict, *Farm Policies of the United States, 1790–1950* (New York: Twentieth Century Fund, 1953); Lowry Nelson, *American Farm Life* (Cambridge: Harvard University Press, 1954).

fusal of the economic system to solve everything automatically in accord with the rules of classical economics makes it most improbable that the farm problem will soon evaporate. Despite the forbidding administrative and economic problems involved in governmental interposition, farm spokesmen will probably for a long time continue to invoke the aid of government to maintain what they regard as an equitable status for agriculture.[7]

Cleavages within Agriculture: Farm Spokesmen

Platform drafters appeal to the farmers and political orators allude to the sterling virtues of their rural constituents, but only in a poetic sense can one speak of "the" farmer. The agricultural population constitutes no homogeneous block of voters with like political interests and aspirations. Conflicts in party loyalties and divergencies in economic interest divide agriculture into many segments, each with its own special concern about public policy. Although farmers may respond warmly to those candidates who succeed in building an image of themselves as genuine friends of the farmer, only on a most limited number of issues do farmers as a whole share a common interest.

Producers of different crops often have different problems. Tobacco farmers, dairymen, and citrus growers have little in common and each group pursues its own ends. One class of farmers may produce the raw materials for another and their political objectives may clash, as when dairymen and poultrymen of the Northeast protest against high support prices for feed grains. Often competition between different types of farmers spills over into the political arena, as in the fight between dairymen and growers of oil-bearing products over legislative discrimination against oleomargarine. The varying positions of commodities with respect to the world market bear on the political orientation of their producers. Thus, dairymen advocate protectionist measures to block cheese imports.

Farm producers differ widely in the scale of their operations, a factor that generates political differences within the agricultural population. Although no farm is really big as economic enterprises go, large-scale farms, which numbered 103,000 or 2.8 per cent of the 3.7 million commercial farms in 1950, accounted for slightly more than one-fourth of the value of farm products sold.[8] Large family-scale farms, 10.3 per cent

[7] See J. K. Galbraith, "Economic Preconceptions and the Farm Policy," *American Economic Review,* 44 (1954), pp. 40–52.

[8] In addition to the farms classified as commercial, in 1950 there were 1.7 million residential and part-time farms which accounted for only 2.5 per cent of the value of farm products sold. The figures are from R. L. Mighell, *American Agriculture, Its Structure and Place in the Economy* (New York: Wiley, 1955), p. 56.

of all commercial farms, were responsible for another one-fourth of the value of farm products. Thus, less than 15 per cent of the farms produced one-half of the marketed farm products. At the other end of the scale, smaller farms making up 43 per cent of all commercial farms accounted for only 10 per cent of the value of farm products sold. These lifeless figures conceal extremes of wealth and poverty not without political significance.[9]

Many of these differences among agricultural producers are reflected in the structure of farm organizations. A goodly number of associations formed along commodity lines advance the cause of their memberships. Illustrative are the American Cranberry Growers Association, the American Livestock Association, the American Sugar Cane League, the National Apple Institute, the National Beet Growers Federation, the American Pork Producers Association, the National Cooperative Milk Producers Federation, and the National Wool Growers Federation. Farm organizations shade over into associations in which food processors have a hand, and it is not uncommon for leaders of food-processing industries to adorn their ears with wisps of straw and attempt, with some success, to camouflage themselves as farmers to gain legislative advantage.

The great general farm organizations loom larger in the public eye than do the specialized farm groups. They also parallel broad ideological cleavages within the farm population. These organizations are the National Grange, the American Farm Bureau Federation, and the National Farmers' Union; each attempts to cover the nation although none is entirely successful. Each is equipped with the customary organizational apparatus—annual national meetings, designed to be representative of the membership, together with the necessary executive and administrative staffs—to determine the wishes of the membership and to direct pressure, at the appropriate times, upon Congress and other national governmental agencies.[10]

National Grange. In its early days the National Grange, with its belligerent radicalism, aroused anxieties in Wall Street but it has become a comparatively conservative farm organization. It pictures itself as "the oldest and largest farm organization in America and the only Farm Fraternity in the World." It is a "social, educational and economic force,

[9] See Department of Agriculture, *Development of Agriculture's Human Resources, A Report on Problems of Low-Income Farmers* (Washington, 1955).

[10] For a survey of farmers' organizations, see Wesley McCune, *The Farm Bloc* (Garden City: Doubleday, Doran, 1943). See also his *Who's Behind Our Farm Policy?* (New York: Praeger, 1956), a survey of business organizations interested in farm policy.

plus a neighborly and community building agency." It places emphasis, according to its literature, "on moral and spiritual idealism. It is a fraternity with a beautiful ritual." Founded as a fraternal order, the Grange retains its ritualistic forms. Its chief officer is the National Master while the supreme authority in ritualistic matters is the Assembly of Demeter, presided over by the High Priest of Demeter.

The Grange draws the bulk of its membership from the Northeast. It exists on a firm basis in the New England states, but the state granges with the largest membership are New York, Ohio, and Pennsylvania. A secondary area of Grange strength is the Pacific Northwest, where powerful state organizations exist in Washington and Oregon. With two-thirds of its membership in the Northeast, National Grange policies reflect the rural conservatism of these states and the interests of farmers advantageously situated in relation to rich domestic markets.

The Grange early manifested lukewarmness toward New Deal programs to control agricultural production, primarily, it may be supposed, because Grange members did not have so much to gain thereby as did southern and midwestern farmers whose views were represented by the Farm Bureau Federation. The resolutions and literature of the Grange long had a timbre not unlike Republican campaign speeches, but the Grange, like the Republican party, eventually altered its tone. As federal farm programs became firmly established, the Grange developed policy proposals of its own, proposals which varied with the circumstances and took into account the special problems of its membership.

In its 1956 program the Grange took a middle course between the advocates of high-support prices and those who proposed to abandon all farm programs and let the market control production and prices. It urged transitional measures looking toward the eventual removal of production controls. Yet even in its long-term program it recommended price supports when necessary to "achieve stabilized farm parity income and to meet emergency requirements for food or fiber." It sought to promote the welfare of middle-income farm families "which receive all or a major portion of their income from farm operations" and low-income farm families. The Grange recognized the right of "corporation-type" farmers to operate freely, but it maintained "that neither their needs nor the general welfare justifies the use of public funds to supplement or support their income."

At one time the Grange aligned itself firmly with protectionist manufacturers on foreign trade policy; it demanded repeal of the Reciprocal Trade Agreement Act. Eventually the Grange came around to a position of advocacy of reduction of barriers to international trade and of measures to regain foreign markets for American farm products. Trade unions find little favor with the Grange, which opposes "all efforts of labor unions to organize farmers or farm workers." [11] The Grange took some credit for blocking repeal of the Taft-Hartley Act and it has recommended enactment of "right-to-work" laws by the states. Although the Grange sees a place of usefulness for labor unions to "offset the power of organized or big industry and finance," its detailed views on labor policies can give little comfort to labor organizations.

American Farm Bureau Federation. The American Farm Bureau Federation, with a tinge of arrogance, asserts that it is the voice of the farmer. A powerful voice it is indeed but it speaks principally for the corn and cotton farmer. About one-half of its membership is in the Midwest and another one-third in the South. From the circumstances of its origin in local groups of farmers organized by the county agents, it developed and continues to maintain close relationships with the land-grant colleges and their state extension services. [12] In a sense the Federation speaks for a coalition of cotton, corn, and the agricultural services associated with the land-grant colleges. Its great legislative success in the 1930's resulted in part from the fact that it brought the South and the Midwest into alliance, a problem that had plagued the agrarian politicians of the 1920's. The maintenance of the coalition of cotton and corn requires the development of Federation programs acceptable to both regions, a task that at times creates serious internal stresses in the organization. The defeat of the 1957 corn bill in Congress showed that all was not well with the alliance of cotton and corn.

Although comparative measurements of political strength are hazardous, the Farm Bureau is certainly the most powerful of the three general farm organizations. Any legislative or administrative measure, concludes the historian of the Bureau, "that is opposed by the AFBF is not likely to get far. On most agricultural matters, except possibly some highly specialized cooperative or crop matter, it is not too much to say that unless AFBF actively supports it the chances of its success are slight." [13] To make known its views, the Federation employs able leaders and pays them well. It maintains a research staff to aid it in reaching its decisions; through its "department of information" it educates the general public as well as its own membership.

In presenting the views of the farmer to Congress, Federation officials

[11] The official historian of the Grange, its High Priest Emeritus, concludes that with erratic weather, insect pests, and other such problems the farmer has "all the headaches he can possibly bear" without adding that of organized labor.—C. M. Gardner, *The Grange—Friend of the Farmer* (Washington: The National Grange, 1949), p. 170.

[12] For a general survey, see E. deS. Brunner and E. Hsin Pao Yang, *Rural America and the Extension Service* (New York: Teachers College, 1949).

[13] O. M. Kile, *The Farm Bureau Federation through Three Decades* (Baltimore: The Waverly Press, 1948), p. 389.

are guided by resolutions voted by the annual convention, which is, of course, closely guided by the Federation officials. They employ the usual methods of testifying before congressional committees, interviewing Congressmen, and stirring up pressure on statesmen in their home districts. By enlisting the support of its affiliated state and county organizations, the Federation can, when the occasion demands, turn enormous pressure on Congress. Its Washington representatives watch the legislative process and guide the strategy of battle.[14]

The Federation promotes the cause of the more prosperous farming classes of its midwestern and southern constituency with great zeal and ability. The types of measures appropriate to that cause differ from time to time. The Federation had an influential hand in the formation of the early New Deal agricultural legislation and collaborated closely with the Department of Agriculture. In the early 1940's, however, it came into conflict with the Democratic Department of Agriculture. The bases of conflict were complex. One factor was simply rivalry for farm leadership, but more fundamental was a difference over the means to be employed to maintain farm income—and over what farmers' incomes were to be maintained. In 1946 Allan Kline, of Iowa, became president of the Federation, at which time it moved toward a policy of flexible price supports at a lower level, a doctrine that made a good deal of hard economic sense but which incidentally would hasten bankruptcy for the smaller, less-efficient farmer.[15] The Federation strongly, and successfully, opposed in 1949 the Brannan plan, a proposal by the Democratic Secretary of Agriculture, which placed emphasis on "parity income" rather than "parity price" and included features of benefit to consumers of agricultural products.

With the election of Eisenhower, the Federation again came to enjoy close relations with the Department of Agriculture. Its friends occupied high posts in the Department and the Administration's farm legislative recommendations generally followed lines congenial to it.[16] In turn, the

[14] In the 1942 debate on appropriations for the Farm Security Administration, Representative Hook asserted: "One of the most revolting things that has come to my attention since I have been a member of Congress was the fact that Edward O'Neal, head of the Farm Bureau Federation, sat in the gallery yesterday afternoon signaling and directing the efforts of those on the floor of the House to sabotage one of the finest Government agencies that this Government has had in the interest of the small farmer and the war program. I say this advisedly because I saw it with my own eyes, and I refer to many others, including my good friend Jed Johnson of Oklahoma, who observed the same tactics."—*Congressional Record* (daily ed.), March 13, 1942, p. 2502.

[15] See E. L. Butz, "The Politics of Agricultural Subsidies," *Proceedings,* Academy of Political Science, 35 (1952), pp. 54–68.

[16] See C. M. Hardin, "The Republican Department of Agriculture—A Political Interpretation," *Journal of Farm Economics,* 36 (1954), pp. 210–227. On Republican-

Federation supported Eisenhower in his 1956 dispute with the Democratic Congress over farm legislation. It by no means proposed that government abandon agriculture to the free market; rather it advocated flexible price supports which could be managed to adjust production downward and to avoid the accumulation of surpluses. In keeping with its large-farmer orientation it argued, in connection with the soil bank proposal, that "no limits be placed on the amount that the individual producer may earn or receive under the plan," in contrast with the Grange view that the larger farming enterprises should have to look out for themselves without government aid. Simultaneously, the Federation recognized the seriousness of the problem of "rural under-employment" leading to low living standards and urged that further "consideration and study" be given to the problem.

In its general position the Federation probably sided with the implacable economic trends that were to triumph in the long run. Whether public policy can, or should, long offset the technological developments making it difficult for small farmers to exist was debateable if not questionable. Yet in taking its position the Federation leadership ran counter to the short-run interests of many of its members, aroused charges that it misrepresented the farmers, and strained the unity of the organization. The southern wing of the Federation remained cool toward flexible supports and some southern state federations took public stands in opposition. Even in its midwestern strongholds, rival, and perhaps fly-by-night, farm organizations arose to present a contrary view.[17]

An early indication of the emerging big-farmer orientation of the Federation was its successful campaign to kill the Farm Security Ad-

ism among Farm Bureau members in Wisconsin, see L. D. Epstein, *The Wisconsin Farm Vote for Governor, 1948–1954* (Madison: University of Wisconsin, Bureau of Government, 1956).

[17] The role of the Farm Bureau hierarchy in the agricultural discontent of the middle 1950's suggests an animadversion on the function of organized groups in restraining as well as in representing their membership. The chances are that, at least under some conditions, an extensive, powerful, and politically sophisticated group leadership structure may restrain the more boisterous, reflex actions of the rank and file against adverse circumstances. In the absence of an operating group structure and hierarchy, leaders of the moment may rise and fan the flames of discontent of a disadvantaged class of persons. A long-established leadership, however, may take a more restrained position because of its estimate of what is feasible by way of remedial action and perhaps because of a tendency of well-organized hierarchies to become somewhat conservative. Mobs act differently from disciplined regiments. In a broad sense, the organizational apparatus of private groups may, under some times and circumstances, serve as an instrument to govern—to restrain—in quite as great a degree as it may be an instrument of agitation. All this is not, of course, to deny that other sorts of factors also bore in the particular situation on the actions of the Federation, not the least of which was the close communion between its midwestern hierarchy and the Republican leadership.

ministration, a unit of the Department of Agriculture born in early New Deal days to rehabilitate low-income farmers. It reached a class of farmers neglected by the principal programs of farm credit and production management. Moreover, it concerned itself with the wages and working conditions of farm workers, even migratory workers upon whom farm proprietors with heavy seasonal labor requirements were especially dependent. Early in 1942 the Federation launched a barrage against the Farm Security Administration, which was not invulnerable to charges of inefficiency. Its opposition was interpreted, however, as the action of an organization representative of large-scale farming, which did not want "any governmental agency to help restore tenants, sharecroppers, and farm laborers to ownership and operation of their own farms" to the detriment of the interests of its members.[18]

A feature of Federation policy has been its vigorous attempt to establish and maintain itself as the predominant, if not the sole, spokesman for the farmer. At least a color of truth pervades the cynical observation that the Federation fights for the Iowa corn grower, speaks for the Alabama cotton planter, but most of all it looks out for the American Farm Bureau Federation. Before the extensive development of agricultural administrative apparatus in the 1930's, the principal agencies dealing with farmers were the state extension services connected with the state land-grant colleges. Commonly the Federation and the state colleges were joined together in informal alliance to their mutual advantage. Administrative actions by the Federal Department of Agriculture that by-passed the state colleges aroused the opposition of the Federation, which saw farm programs moving into the hands of organizations less susceptible to its influence. It reacted with special vigor against direct federal consultative and service relations with groups of farmers, apparently on the basis of the doctrine that only it should speak for farmers.

The Federation has been most impatient with the Soil Conservation Service which deals directly with local soil conservation districts. It has urged that the Service's functions be devolved upon the state extension services, and in 1953 administrative actions by Secretary Benson were attacked by the National Association of Soil Conservation Districts as calculated to bring the soil conservation program within the orbit of the state extension services and the Farm Bureau. A system of county land-use planning committees by which the Department of Agriculture proposed to consult with farmers on the form and administration of agricultural programs met a quick death as the Federation moved in on the appropriations committee. Farm Bureau leaders, perhaps mindful of the

[18] Representative Dingell in *Congressional Record* (daily ed.), March 13, 1942, p. 2505.

Federation's origins in official stimulation, regarded these and other measures as designed to create new and competing organizations of farmers. We will, the President of the AFBF said, "crack down on any group that will do that." [19] At one stage the Federation even proposed that all the important farm programs be placed in control of state committees to be appointed "from nominations by the State director of extension after consulting with State-wide farm organizations." In a number of states, such a policy would have constituted virtual delegation of public authority to the Farm Bureau.[20]

On issues outside the agricultural sphere, the Federation often takes a stand parallel to that of the principal business groups. On labor questions it tends to throw its weight with business, and some state federations have spearheaded movements for legislation to restrict organized labor. It favors legislation to exempt that part of corporation income paid out as dividends from the corporation income tax. In 1956 it supported the elimination of national control of the field price of natural gas. On such matters peripheral to agriculture, Federation leaders at times come perilously close to converting their organization into a tool of business without much regard to the concern of farmers with the issues at stake. On the other hand, the Federation looks to business for support on farm issues and may feel obliged to reciprocate.

National Farmers' Union. The National Farmers' Union is differentiated from other farm organizations by its tradition, its ideology, its program, and the location of its membership. Founded in Texas in 1902 by men who had been active in the Farmers' Alliance, the Union carries on the tradition of old-fashioned, militant agrarian radicalism. Its membership centers in such Great Plains states as Oklahoma, Nebraska, and the Dakotas, and strong state affiliates exist in Wisconsin, Minnesota, Montana, and Colorado. The geography of its membership makes the politics of wheat an important item on its agenda, and the special uncertainties of

[19] The story of the influence of the Federation on the administrative structure of farm programs is long and involved. See Grant McConnell, *The Decline of Agrarian Democracy* (Berkeley: University of California Press, 1953) and C. M. Hardin, *The Politics of Agriculture* (Glencoe: Free Press, 1952).

[20] The abiding jurisdictional jealousies of the Farm Bureau Federation may be a specific manifestation of a general tendency of organized groups to seek to monopolize the right to organize and speak for particular constituencies. When governmental agencies, for example, set up advisory committees that represent unorganized as well as organized segments of particular industries, trade associations often utter hypocritical protests about dictatorial inclinations to ignore the recognized and established spokesmen of business. Illustrative of the same phenomenon is the ill-concealed antipathy of the American Legion toward other groups of veterans. Jurisdictional anxieties are by no means limited to labor unions.

farming on the western rim of arable land find reflection in its outlook.

The ideas of the co-operative movement occupy a prominent place in the Union's political creed and at times internal debate has been spirited on the issue of the relative emphasis to be given the development of co-operatives as against legislative means for the advancement of the cause of the farmer. The more extreme pronouncements of the Union contemplate the ultimate replacement of private enterprise by co-operatives as the "only means by which the potential abundance of this Nation may be made available to all its people and by which true democracy may be maintained and safe-guarded." In keeping with its doctrines, the Union has sponsored co-operative terminals, elevators, insurance enterprises, creameries, and agencies for the purchase of farm supplies and the sale of farm products.

The Union advocates measures to encourage and protect the owner-operated, family farm. It opposes the "factory farm" and commercialized agriculture. Its faith in farming as a "way of life" brings it into conflict with the Farm Bureau Federation, which tends to regard farming unsentimentally as a way to make money. On other matters also, it has opposed the Farm Bureau. In 1956, for example, it advocated high and rigid price supports while the Federation supported the Republican Administration's flexible price-support program.

A remnant of the drive toward farmer-labor collaboration of the Populist days remains in the program of the Union. It maintains friendly relations with labor organizations and participated actively in the movement for the adoption of the Employment Act of 1946. It does not begrudge labor's gains. It supported the Brannan plan, a widely discussed scheme proposed by President Truman's Secretary of Agriculture, which would have both maintained prices to farmer and given urban consumers farm commodities at prices fixed by the market. The Union acclaimed the plan as "an historic advance in agricultural policy-making because it grows out of and recognizes the great truth that each group in our society depends upon all the others and that governmental programs must serve fairly the needs of all groups." Farm Bureau leaders take a more jaundiced view of most such measures that might benefit urban consumers.[21]

Given its traditional strain of reformism—attachment to the family farm, opposition to monopoly, advocacy of co-operatives, friendliness to labor—the Farmers' Union in recent decades has been on the Democratic side of the fence. Republican politicians and leaders of competing farm

[21] On the Farmers' Union generally, see W. P. Tucker, "Populism Up-To-Date: The Story of the Farmers' Union," *Agricultural History*, 21 (1947), pp. 198–208, and "The Farmers' Union: The Social Thought of a Current Agrarian Movement," *Southwestern Social Science Quarterly*, 27 (1946), pp. 45–53.

organizations have not been above charging that the Union's native American radicalism amounted to un-Americanism.[22]

Farm workers. Organization of agriculture has been limited mainly to farm owners and managers. Agricultural labor and farm tenants have not found their political voice through organization. The IWW made an early attempt to organize farm labor. It claimed in the years 1916–1918 a membership of 18,000, chiefly casual workers in the corn and wheat belts, for its Agricultural Workers Organization. Within a few years the IWW practically disappeared. In the early 'thirties the Southern Farm Tenants Union came into existence, in part to resist the imposition of a disproportionate share of the adjustments involved in crop reduction upon tenants and sharecroppers. It also made attempts to obtain better pay for seasonal agricultural workers, but its strength was limited and its small membership was concentrated mainly in Arkansas. In 1946 the Union, now called the National Farm Labor Union, became an AFL affiliate and extended its activities to the organization of citrus workers in Florida and California. The heavy need for seasonal labor in agriculture creates a migratory labor force exceptionally subject to exploitation. Migratory workers, moreover, because they are migratory, lack the political capacity for self-protection enjoyed by relatively immobile groups of laborers.

In most instances in which farm workers have been organized effectively enough to attempt to strike, they have been suppressed with a ferocity that would make even the most reactionary industrialist blush with shame. In addition, farm organizations have generally sought, and often succeeded, in excluding farm labor from the benefits of labor legislation, such as unemployment insurance, workman's compensation, and wage and hour rules. "We vigorously support," resolved the Farm Bureau Federation in 1955, "the agricultural and seasonal exemptions of the Fair Labor Standards Act." At the same time the Bureau concluded that the provisions of the Social Security Act covering agricultural workers paid $100 or more in cash by one employer in one year were "impractical and burdensome for farmers who are employers of part-time workers, transients, or aliens admitted to the United States on a temporary basis." Amendments to make the legislation "workable" were recom-

---

[22] In 1950, in a published letter, the executive secretary of the Utah State Farm Bureau Federation, asserted that Democratic Representative W. K. Granger, a candidate for re-election, had exhibited an animosity toward all "farmers' organizations except the Communist-dominated Farmers Union." The Union and its adjunct, the Farmers Union Service Corporation, sued the Utah State Farm Bureau and won $25,000 in damages. Representative Granger had introduced a bill that would have compelled complete separation of the Farm Bureau and the State Agricultural Extension Services, a step strongly opposed by the Farm Bureau Federation.

mended. In some instances farm organizations have obtained exemptions in the application of labor legislation to such processes as canning, packing, and the operation of creameries, matters essentially industrial in nature.

Unity and division among farmers. This brief review of the major general farm organizations should make it clear that agriculture cannot be regarded as a unit either politically or economically. Distinctions of objective founded on economic interest are supplemented by contrasts in broad political ideology which find reflection in the programs of farm groups. Farm organizations only infrequently unite for legislative purposes. Under the impact of economic disaster they may work together or under special circumstances, they may join in coalition, as in the lobbying of the principal farm organizations, save the Farmers' Union, in World War II for special treatment under price-control policies. More typically, the major farm organizations urge upon Congress conflicting programs.

The Genesis and Course of Political Movements

The preceding discussion has served to indicate some of the political concerns and characteristics of agriculture, an important though declining element of the American political complex. The analysis has, moreover, been designed to go beyond the specific example and to point toward ideas of utility in the understanding of the political process generally.

Political systems may exist in a stable, even static, form over long periods. The holders of power are unchallenged; the allocation of rights, privileges, and benefits remains acceptable on all sides; every man knows his place and keeps it. In modern states so serene a political condition does not prevail for long. The equilibrium—the balance, the ordered course of affairs, the established pattern—is disturbed from time to time by some change that generates discontent. Such dislocations tend to set off movements in demand of a correction of the balance or for the creation of a new order. Discontent may find expression through a political movement, a more or less spontaneous rising of the people concerned, or it may be manifest in the intensified activities of existing organized groups. The farmers' movements, sketchily surveyed here, merely exemplify this more general pattern of maladjustment, agitation, and governmental action.

What is it that sets off political agitation, that brings demands for governmental action, that arouses groups, even stimulates the creation of new groups, to clamor for attention and for greater consideration in the decision-making processes of the community? In the example chosen, agriculture, particularly certain segments of it, had suffered severe economic deprivation. This change in circumstances generated discontent and led to demands for political remedies. It would be wrong to contend from this instance that all political movements are set in motion by a change in objective external conditions or by material deprivation. Yet some new element must be introduced into a situation to stimulate resort to political action. That new element may be an economic change, which dislocates pre-existing relationships; it may be a threat to a status already enjoyed; it may be mass frustration in any one of a variety of forms.

The frequency with which alterations in economic circumstances ignite political agitation gives rise to the theory that economic factors underlie all political activity. It seems clear, however, that other factors may be influential in setting into motion movements leading to a new political equilibrium. New scientific discoveries, for example, may direct attention to conditions hitherto unperceived, or may point to possibilities previously unknown, and be instrumental in stimulating political action. The discovery of immunization against certain diseases by vaccination and other methods, for example, laid the basis for political crusades for compulsory, universal vaccination. An idea, or ideal, may be a factor of great force in movements leading to the reshaping of public policy. How is one, for example, to explain the movements for the expansion of manhood suffrage? The woman suffrage movement? Or what single factor was at the bottom of the prohibition movement? Or why does a movement begin at any particular time rather than at an earlier time? A concrete condition may exist over long periods, and at some particular moment unrest flares up to redress a long-standing wrong. Simple explanations of the origins of political disequilibrium must be regarded with reserve.

The introduction of a new element creating demands for a readjustment in the social situation does not invariably lead to political agitation. In one situation discontent may lead to legislative action and in another it may work itself out in the nonpolitical sphere. In the 1920's certain leaders, such as President Coolidge, counseled the unhappy farmers to abide by the operation of beneficent economic laws. They meant that farmers producing at high cost should reduce their costs, produce something else on their lands, or seek a livelihood in industry; that agriculture should adjust itself to the changed situation by the inexorable process of bankruptcy for high-cost producers. The farmers refused to or could not take that course of action, and governmental remedies were sought. Harold Lasswell says: "Although political movements begin in unrest, all social unrest does not find expression in political movements. Under some conditions, a community which is visited by plague may pray; under other conditions, the community will demand the retirement of the health commissioner." [23] To use a less remote example: at one time when unemployment increased, a citizens' committee would solicit funds to maintain a soup line for those in distress; now pressure is brought on public authorities to increase the appropriation for unemployment relief. In one culture drought-stricken farmers may pray for rain; in another they may petition Congress to appropriate for the installation of irrigation works. Thus the content of the governmental sphere changes.

When conditions are ripe for the rise of a political movement, a leader may come on the scene with a remedy. It is essential that the functions of leadership, agitation, and education in political movements be perceived. Before there can be a political movement, the persons making up the movement must be conscious of a common cause, a common injury, a common goal. How is this consciousness created? Fundamentally by the sharing of experience; and leaders, agitators, propagandists furnish the channels for the communication of a consciousness of common interest. The agitator thus serves as a medium both for cementing together those with a common concern and for expressing that concern. The leader converts the mutterings at the crossroads, in the taverns, and wherever men gather, into a movement; that is, a joint effort by a considerable number of persons to influence the course of events. Often would-be leaders misjudge the timeliness of their actions, and there is no response to their offer to lead. In such instances the time is not at hand to convert the discontent of scattered individuals into a cohesive movement.

As a sense of common cause grows a remedy is evolved. For the agrarian unrest after World War I the McNary-Haugen bill served as a goal. As a rallying cry for his movement, Dr. Townsend evolved the "Townsend Plan"; Henry George, the "Single Tax"; William Jennings Bryan, free coinage of silver at sixteen to one. As movements become more complex many measures may be brought under the canopy of a single slogan: the "New Deal"; the "full-dinner pail"; the "return to normalcy." For effective agitation, the most complex measures must be reducible to simple slogans. The remedy around which a political movement is rallied need not be workable. In fact, the remedies advocated by messiahs often are, as the saying goes, "snares and delusions." Yet the expression of discontent is symptomatic of need for readjustment; even if the proposed therapy is futile the pressure may compel the government to devise a substitute treatment. For example, the Townsend Plan, which proposed two hundred dollars a month for every person over sixty, was

[23] "The Measurement of Public Opinion," *American Political Science Review,* 25 (1931), pp. 311–336.

claimed by all the experts to be unworkable, but the pressure of Dr. Townsend's movement helped bring about the enactment of the Social Security Act, with a different method of caring for the aged. At times movements operate to dissipate frustrations by the mere expression of discontent, or they are worn down by the resistances of existing institutional patterns. In some instances—notably American municipal reform movements—discontent is blotted out by the enactment of an ordinance that symbolizes success for the movement but has no perceptible effect on the course of events.

Not uncommonly an element of a movement is a diagnosis that blames all the misfortunes of the affected group on some convenient scapegoat: the railroads, the Jews, Wall Street, the capitalists, union bosses, municipal bosses.[24] These diagnoses have simple, dramatic qualities and, therefore, a high propaganda value. Yet they may be incorrect and may result in grave injustice, in uncontrollable outbursts of political discontent. Nonrational sorts of political disturbances characterized by a high concentration of attention to the devil in the situation may also be quite futile in alleviating the maladjustments that started all the commotion in the first place.

In the course of their growth, movements usually acquire an organizational apparatus and recruit a secretariat or a bureaucracy. Once the movement achieves its immediate objective, it may disappear, though its institutional machinery often gains virtual immortality. The movement may evolve into an organization that grasps new issues and new causes to keep itself alive. Most pressure groups, in fact, originate in an effort to cope with some immediate problem and then persist as an organization to deal with new matters of concern to the membership.[25]

The foregoing discussion of the natural history of political movements suggests that one of the principal tasks of those who govern is to identify and deal with maladjustments that give rise to social discontent and political movements. The skill and insight with which a politics of prevention is followed will determine whether those who govern will continue to govern. Social maladjustments tend to be neglected until they give rise to strong movements in demand of action; in rare instances all the techniques of social research are brought into play to observe, foresee, and plan thoroughly to meet rising problems. Those who govern may

[24] For a similar analysis, see E. C. Lindeman, *The Community* (New York: Association Press, 1921), ch. 9.

[25] For discussions of the nature of social movements, see R. M. MacIver, *Social Causation* (Boston: Ginn, 1942); Hadley Cantril, *The Psychology of Social Movements* (New York: Wiley, 1941); Rudolf Heberle, *Social Movements* (New York: Appleton-Century-Crofts, 1951).

choose to wear down by delay and obstruction rather than deny or suppress. More often they do not have the wit to see that corrective measures are in order; otherwise the personnel of governments would not change so frequently.

3 | Workers

INDUSTRIALIZATION has been at the root of most of the great domestic political issues in the United States since the War between the States. The rise of manufacturing and the development of associated financial, transport, and distributive organizations generated changes of profound political significance. The expansion of new economic interests brought struggles for a redistribution of political power; and with the erection of mighty structures of private industrial power came demands from disadvantaged groups for governmental redress of grievances. Agrarian protest movements that swept the country in the latter part of the nineteenth century failed to stay the hand of the new colossus of finance and industry. After the turn of the century, in the Progressive movement and in Woodrow Wilson's crusade for the "new freedom," the middle classes and the small entrepreneur fought only a delaying action against the same antagonist.

In the battle for power in the state the worker has proved to be, at least potentially, the strongest force loosed by the process of industrialization. The growth of industry in the United States thrust into numerical preponderance a working class sharply distinguished in status from the farmer and the small entrepreneur. In the main without property, this class found itself arrayed against those possessing title to this world's goods. With its resources limited to skills of mind and of muscle, it occupied a situation of great insecurity. Without cash reserves, its very food and shelter were dependent on the vagaries of business conditions that determined the regularity of the pay envelope. The only mode for defense and offense open to the industrial worker was collective action, since he was almost powerless as an individual.

The American industrial laboring class emerged in an ideological climate superficially hospitable to political action. Doctrines of political equality and of the right of self-government seemed to pave the way for the new toiling masses to grasp power and to mold the state to suit their wishes. Moreover, while American workers were increasing in number, socialist ideas were blossoming around the globe. Heady doctrines were being proclaimed: workers should unite and take what was justly theirs. Moreover, if they merged the ideas of socialism and democracy, they would not have to take what they wanted—all they had to do was to vote for it. He who would understand politics in the large may ponder well the status of labor: a numerically great force in a society adhering to the doctrine of the rule of numbers, yet without proportionate durable political power as a class.

Political Consequences of the Emergence of New Occupations

When in a liberal-democratic state substantial numbers of people begin to earn their living in a new way, it is fairly safe to predict that a redistribution of political power will occur. The emerging group seeks a share in political power mainly for the purpose of altering public policies which were designed to meet the needs of the old order. If the new group becomes a substantial proportion of the population, radical shifts in political power may take place and the framers of public policy may come to be preoccupied with an entirely new set of problems.

Occupational change and the political equilibrium. The occupational and status changes associated with industrialization in the United States since 1870 brought large segments of the population into the wage-earning class. As this group expanded, it demanded alterations in the political order; and as it grew in numbers, its demands were heard more respectfully. The census does not yield data to show well those changes in occupational status that are probably most significant politically. Yet the changes in the industrial classification of gainful workers, which are pictured in Figure 3.1, indicate well enough the timing and magnitude of the broad shifts in the occupational pattern in the United States.[1] By 1890 manufacturing and related pursuits employed as many persons as did agriculture, and after 1910 industrial workers rapidly increased in numbers as farm employment declined. Underlying the trends reflected in the curve in Figure 3.1 were many changes in ways of life, changes both obvious and subtle, that created new political needs and new factors in the process of politics.

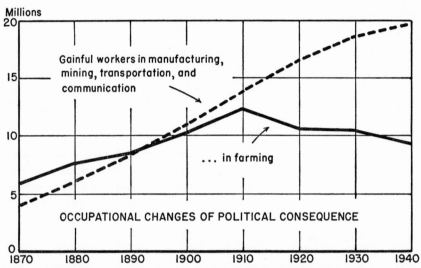

Figure 3.1. Trends in Numbers of Gainful Workers in Manufacturing, Mining, Transportation, and Communication and in Farming, 1870–1940

Frailty of class consciousness. Although industrialization created a large new class of wage earners, the conditions under which the industrial working class emerged were such that a relatively feeble class consciousness developed. The frailty of the sense of class membership and of class cause affects profoundly the role of labor in politics. To constitute a politically effective group, individuals must share common aspirations and antipathies. It may be contended that the interests of all wage earners are the same; but, until workers as individuals believe this to be true, there can be no crystallized consciousness of common cause, and, hence, no labor solidarity in action.

Radical differences in the sense of class attachment are associated with variations in skill among wage earners. Many workers do not regard

[1] The figure is based on data presented by Dewey Anderson and P. E. Davidson, *Occupational Trends in the United States* (Stanford: Stanford University Press, 1940).

themselves as members of a "working class"; they feel, rather, an attachment to the middle class. A striking cleavage in attitude prevails between factory workers and white-collar workers. Among manual workers like differences, though not so wide, prevail. Evidence on the general point has been reported by Richard Centers from the results of a poll of a national sample on the question: "If you were asked to use one of these four names for your social class which would you say you belonged in: the Middle Class, Lower Class, Working Class, or Upper Class?" [2] The results, which show striking differences between white-collar and manual workers, were as follows:

	Upper Class	Middle Class	Working Class	Lower Class
White-collar	2%	61%	34%	0.6%
Skilled manual	2	26	71	1
Semiskilled	1	14	83	1
Unskilled	—	18	75	7

Workers, thus, do not uniformly share a sense of class consciousness. To an extent varying among different subgroups of workers, they identify with the middle class. Other cleavages also cut through the wage-earning class. Economic competition among workers sometimes manifests itself in jurisdictional disputes among trade unions, which are often quite as bitter as conflicts between employees and employers. National, religious, and racial differences project themselves into the labor movement. Rivalries between workers of different national origins are not uncommon. Skill groups are sometimes divided among Jewish and Gentile unions; Catholics as a matter of religious principle oppose socialist tendencies within unions. In some industries and in some localities the Negro has presented a special problem in union organization, although since 1935 a gradual reduction in union discrimination against Negroes has occurred.

Incompleteness of labor organization. The frailty of class consciousness among American workers, and other factors as well, are reflected in the slow growth of labor organization and in the fact that many workers re-

[2] *The Psychology of Social Classes* (Princeton: Princeton University Press, 1949), p. 86. Other studies indicate that the form of Centers' question probably affected the distribution of responses, i. e., that with a different question form a smaller proportion of persons would have identified themselves with the "working class." See Neal Gross, "Social Class Identification in the Urban Community," *American Sociological Review*, 18 (1953), pp. 398–404. See also J. G. Manis and B. N. Meltzer, "Attitudes of Textile Workers to Class Structure," *American Journal of Sociology*, 60 (1954), pp. 30–35. Among persons who are in fact working class, those psychologically identified with that class are more frequently Democratic than are those who regard themselves as middle class. See Heinz Eulau, "Identification with Class and Political Perspective," *Journal of Politics*, 18 (1956), pp. 232–253.

main even yet unorganized. In 1956 union membership accounted for only about one-third of the total nonagricultural labor force, which included many categories of workers not readily susceptible to organization, such as household workers, farm workers, and professional and technical workers. Some industries are, of course, almost completely unionized, while in others extremely few workers belong to unions.

Factors peculiar to individual trades or industries have affected the rate of growth of unions. The union movement, for example, made headway among the skilled crafts long before it became established in the mass-production industries. Industries characterized by small operations were organized before those in which huge firms dominated. In addition, certain broad conditions have from time to time stimulated spurts of unionization generally. Of special interest from the political viewpoint has been the extraordinary growth of unionism at times of widespread unrest. Unions grew rapidly in the early 1880's when both farmers and workers were agitated about the operation of the social system. Similarly, in the 1930's the growth of unions occurred under circumstances of disenchantment with the workings of American institutions. The great sit-down strikes of the 1930's had about them at least a tinge of the revolutionary. Other periods of marked expansion of unions have occurred when sharp increases in the price level coincided with a scarcity of labor.[3] A rising cost of living gave incentive to organization and the scarcity of labor gave bargaining leverage to unions. Illustrative are the upward jumps in union membership during World War I and World War II, which appear in the graph in Figure 3.2.[4]

In this century unions have enjoyed their most marked growth in periods when the government looked benignly on the labor movement. At these times—World War I and the New Deal–World War II period —the Democratic party controlled the national government and encouraged unionization. The sharp rise in union strength in the New Deal era may not have been "caused" by government policy, but the toleration of this development by Democratic leadership contributed toward the broadly pro-Democratic orientation of organized labor.

Obstacles to the political assimilation of emerging groups. A newly emerging group faces a different problem as it seeks power in a society

[3] See John T. Dunlop, "The Development of Labor Organization: A Theoretical Framework" in R. A. Lester and Joseph Shister, *Insights into Labor Issues* (New York: Macmillan, 1948), pp. 163–193; Joseph Shister, "The Logic of Union Growth," *Journal of Political Economy*, 61 (1953), pp. 413–433.

[4] Figure 3.2 rests on data presented by Irving Bernstein, "The Growth of American Unions," *American Economic Review*, 44 (1954), pp. 301–318. On the extent of unionization and the rate of union growth within each state 1939 to 1953, see National Bureau of Economic Research, *Thirty-sixth Annual Report* (1956), pp. 45–48.

Figure 3.2. Growth in Union Membership in the United States, 1900–1955

than does a declining group that attempts to retain its influence. A new group meets the resistance of those already on the ground who share their power only grudgingly. A new group is likely to challenge the cherished values of the old order; an old group merely has to defend what is regarded as right, proper, and respectable. The older holders of power control the instruments of government and may use them to resist, to suppress, to weaken the newcomers, who may be regarded even as revolutionaries who would upset the ancient order.

In the long history of attempts to unify the American working classes, time and again labor suffered reverses as it collided with the reigning ideologies and interests. In his interpretation of the American labor movement Perlman places great emphasis on the strength of the institution of private property and the incompatibility of the objectives of organized labor with private property. Whether labor seeks its ends by political means or by bargaining, its objective is to restrict the control of the employer over his property.[5] The claims of labor have to a considerable degree been on matters that employers have been most reluctant to yield, and in this attitude employers have often been able to ally with themselves substantial proportions of the general public. For decades the demand for collective bargaining and for union recognition was met by private armies, sometimes supported by police and troops. When the National Labor Relations Act of 1935 guaranteed the right of collective bargaining, employers' resistance did not evaporate overnight. Sabotage of the law was widespread.

To carve out a place for itself in the politico-social order, a new group may have to fight for a reorientation of many of the values of the old order. Early unions were assailed as anarchist or socialist. Eventually they became accepted, only to have the cry of communism raised against them. Organized labor is still regarded with hostility by substantial segments of society and some of its practices find little acceptance among the public generally. Moreover, many labor leaders even yet live under a psychology of siege: they believe, not entirely without reason, that industrial leadership merely tolerates unions or that business would, given a fighting chance, attempt to crush unionism. Nevertheless, during the last half century organized labor established itself fairly securely as an element of the social system. Organized labor amounted to something less than an instrument for "all the toiling masses" but it came to exercise great influence on many public questions and to possess a veto, if not the affirmative power of decision, on others.

Is industrial labor past its peak? If there is validity in our general proposition that the emergence of new types of occupational groupings tends to bring alterations in the pattern of political power, it may be that occupational changes have been, and are, in the making which will have far-reaching political consequences. The proportion of factory workers in the total labor force has long since ceased increasing. Great growth has occurred in technical, clerical, administrative, and sales personnel. Among manual workers larger proportions are now skilled and semiskilled; and the census category of "skilled workers" conceals upgrading in the character of work performed and in the status of workers.

Crude measures of some of these trends, as well as projections to 1975, are shown in Figure 3.3. Such shifts in occupational characteristics and distribution occur slowly, yet as they cumulate over the decades they may have basic effects on the American polity. The growth in professional,

[5] *A Theory of the Labor Movement* (New York: Macmillan, 1928), ch. 5.

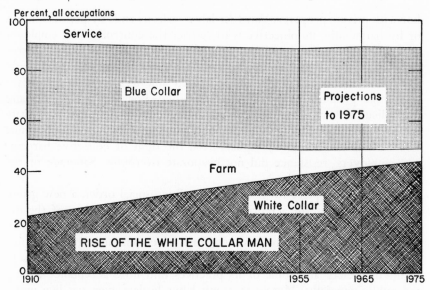

Per cent, all occupations

Figure 3.3. Distribution of Employment Among Major Occupational Groups with Projections to 1975 by the Bureau of Labor Statistics

administrative, and other white collar occupations augurs for a strengthening of middle-class Republicanism. The probable consequences of the rise in income, educational level, and status of skilled workers are not so clear. The result might well be an intensification of a labor-oriented political outlook among these groups rather than a conversion to a middle-class or business view.[6]

Government of Trade Unions

Persons interested in acting together to gain political influence, to improve their economic status, or to accomplish some other joint end do not rise spontaneously as one man and in unison shout their demands. A segment of society that seeks to improve or defend its status usually works through a relatively elaborate organization, which formulates and expresses its wishes. This machinery for collective action constitutes a group government strikingly similar to that of the state itself. An examination of the organization of American labor will throw light on its characteristics significant for political action and will also illustrate problems of organization and leadership common to all private groups. Moreover,

[6] See Arthur Kornhauser and others, *When Labor Votes* (New York: University Books, 1956); C. Wright Mills, *White Collar* (New York: Oxford University Press, 1951); N. N. Foote and P. K. Hatt, "Social Mobility and Economic Advancement," *American Economic Review*, 43 (1953), no. 2, pp. 364–378.

even a cursory inspection of the government of labor will suggest fundamental questions about the role of private organizations in the process of governance broadly defined.

In both their formal structure and their more subtle patterns of behavior the governments of private groups resemble the apparatus of the state. Private groups have their parliaments, their cabinets, their administrative agencies, and their courts. They have, too, their taxes, their crimes, their systems of group education, their procedures for purging dissentient elements. As they strive toward group consensus, private groups operate an internal politics not unfamiliar to the observer of the politics of the state. Although it might be supposed that the objectives of private associations, vis-à-vis the state or other groups, would be self evident, they seldom are. Generally conflicts of interest, of ideology, of aims exist and must be settled if the group is to go forth united to fight its battles.

AFL-CIO: A confederacy. When in 1955 the American Federation of Labor and the Congress of Industrial Organizations merged as the AFL-CIO, newspapers dilated on the powerful creation of the act of unity. The realities differed from the dispatches. The AFL-CIO, like its predecessor organizations, is a confederacy of national and international unions; and confederations are notoriously weak. The constituent units of the AFL-CIO, such as the Auto Workers, the Bricklayers, the Rubber Workers, and the Machinists, enjoy states' rights with a vengeance. Each "national and international union is entitled to have its autonomy, integrity and jurisdiction protected and preserved." Moreover, the AFL-CIO constitution recognizes that its affiliated national unions have the right of secession. In short, the common interests of national labor organizations—with the exception of a few independents, such as the Mine Workers and the railroad brotherhoods—suffice to cause them to associate together but not to establish a powerful central government over themselves.

The biennial convention of the AFL-CIO is its "supreme governing body" and might be compared with a parliament or, perhaps more accurately, a conference of ambassadors. Representation of the constituent national unions varies roughly with their membership. The convention hears reports from the AFL-CIO functionaries, elects officers, and adopts resolutions. The executive council functions somewhat as the cabinet of a parliamentary government. It consists of the president and the secretary-treasurer along with the 27 vice-presidents of the AFL-CIO. The vice-presidents are, in turn, usually presidents of their respective national labor organizations.

The president and the secretary-treasurer preside over the Washington headquarters of the AFL-CIO, but they, as the officers of a confederation of labor baronies, operate within a sphere restricted both constitutionally and practically. The AFL-CIO governmental superstructure was built in the tradition of union autonomy of the older AFL. Yet the AFL-CIO constitution also took a few hesitant steps toward a greater centralization of authority, which represented also a projection of trends in the older organizations.[7]

Indicative of constituent autonomy in the AFL was the consideration by its 1940 annual convention of the problem of cleansing some of its member unions of racketeers. The principle of "states' rights" limited the convention to a condemnation of racketeering union leaders and to a direction to the executive council to use its "influence" to bring about a house cleaning in the unions concerned. By 1953 AFL constitutional doctrine had moved a long distance and its convention took the "revolutionary" step, as some labor leaders termed it, of expelling the International Longshoremen's Association from the Federation. Expulsion does not in itself cure a malodorous situation and the AFL followed through, unsuccessfully as it turned out, with an attempt to form a new union of longshoremen. Such an exile from the labor movement may ultimately become a sanction with some effect against wrong-doing. At least, by 1956 the ILA, lonely in its exile, was petitioning for re-admission, although it failed to convince George Meany, AFL-CIO president, that it had cleansed its ranks of racketeers. Another illustration of the AFL doctrine of autonomy is provided by a debate in the 1944 convention on the question of discrimination against Negroes by some of the constituent unions. What could the Federation do about it? The answer was that each national and international union was "clothed with autonomous authority to formulate, shape, and administer its own affairs."

In principle, the CIO operated on the same confederate principle as the AFL. In its early days the CIO central headquarters exercised considerable power because many of its newly formed unions depended on subsidies from the parent body. As the new unions developed strength and sources of revenue, they became autonomous. Yet the CIO national leadership took strong action against several of its internationals which were dominated by Communist factions. These unions were expelled and the CIO financed organizing committees to recruit workers in the industries concerned into new unions with an untainted leadership.[8]

---

[7] On the amalgamation of the AFL and CIO, see A. J. Goldberg, *AFL-CIO, Labor United* (New York: McGraw-Hill, 1956).

[8] See Max M. Kampelman, *The Communist Party vs. the C.I.O.* (New York: Praeger, 1957).

These centralizing trends affected the new AFL-CIO constitution. Unions dominated by communists, fascists, or other totalitarians are ineligible for membership and the aim is to "protect the labor movement from any and all corrupt influences." A committee on ethical practices has the duty of assisting the executive council in keeping the organization free of communism and corruption; and a committee on civil rights has a similar duty to assist in bringing about as soon as possible conformity with the principle of nondiscrimination. Yet the ultimate power of the AFL-CIO over its constituent unions is expulsion, which could be followed by an organizing campaign to woo the unionists concerned away from their old leaders, at best a costly and difficult process. Fundamentally the rule of autonomy continues to prevail. The AFL-CIO can expel a union, but expulsion of a large union may hurt the AFL-CIO more than it does the expelled union.

Soon after the AFL-CIO was formed those labor leaders actively concerned about corruption in the constituent nationals began to breathe life into the new committee on ethical practices. An obvious target for the committee was the Teamsters' Dave Beck, who, early in 1956, responded to a reporter's inquiry whether the committee had considered having him on the carpet: "I don't know and I don't give a damn. We're an autonomous union and nobody's going to tell us how to run our affairs." [9] To cope, in the absence of constitutional power to discipline, with so large a union as the Teamsters was a formidable task for the AFL-CIO top command. The committee moved first against three smaller unions: the Laundry Workers, the Distillery Workers, and the Allied Industrial Workers. The executive council ordered them to clean house on pain of suspension from the AFL-CIO. Meanwhile a Senate committee had deflated Mr. Beck's influence by disclosure of irregularities in Teamster finances and in May, 1957, the AFL-CIO executive council removed him as a vice president and member of the Council. Yet in his post as president of the Teamsters he was beyond reach of the AFL-CIO. Under the impact of the senatorial investigation, the denunciations of his colleagues of the AFL-CIO, and protests from his own union, he decided not to run for re-election to that post.

As might be surmised from this description of its structure, no little effort must be devoted to the task of keeping the AFL-CIO from flying apart. Yet sufficient unity may be maintained at the top level of labor organization to perform certain essential functions. A primary function of the national organization is the formulation and advancement of the political objectives of labor before Congress, within the administrative agencies, and in campaigns. Beyond this the national machinery, within

[9] *Wall Street Journal*, February 14, 1956.

severely restricted limits, needs, as a matter of public relations if for no other reason, to police its constituent units in so far as it can. Finally, the top leadership can attempt to settle jurisdictional conflicts among individual unions.

Constituent units of AFL-CIO. The constituent units that enjoy "states' rights" within the AFL-CIO are about 140 national unions formed on either craft or industrial lines. The older form of labor organization, the craft union, predominated in the AFL. Well over half of the AFL nationals had less than 50,000 members each at the time of the merger. Its largest nationals were the United Brotherhood of Carpenters and Joiners of America, the International Brotherhood of Electrical Workers, the International Association of Machinists, and the International Brotherhood of Teamster, Chauffeurs, Warehousemen and Helpers of America. The CIO had been created by secession from the AFL by the United Mine Workers and other unions dedicated to the organization of workers along industrial rather than craft lines. By far the largest CIO nationals were the United Auto Workers and the United Steel Workers, each with over one million members.

Each of the nationals is in turn built upon a base of local unions, of which there are probably 60,000 to 70,000 in the country. The local may be formed on a plant basis in an industrial union or it may consist of the craftsmen, e. g., plasterers, within a locality. While the details differ from union to union, each national has a governing apparatus of its own. Ordinarily a national convention, consisting of representatives from the locals, is the top governing authority. The convention elects the national's president and he usually works with an executive committee or board. The presidents of the large nationals are in the public eye as the major labor leaders of the country and they commonly exert great influence in the councils of the labor movement as a whole.

While the relationships between the national headquarters of a union and its locals vary from union to union, the government of the typical national would probably be described by the political scientists as unitary. The national union superstructure historically developed to supplement and to make effective the operations of independently formed locals. The geographic mobility of goods had made futile the bargaining efforts of scattered independent locals, and the geographical mobility of labor likewise created problems for the local. The national union gradually emerged and acquired varying controls over locals in the admission and disciplining of members, the calling of strikes, compliance with contracts, wage policies, work rules, and the like. In some situations the national may take over the management of the local. In others, it may review actions by locals, such as disciplinary measures. Over the long run the authority of the nationals has grown both to prevent abuses and to permit effective bargaining over large areas.[10]

Democracy and oligarchy in labor organization. The governmental apparatus of labor as a whole resembles representative institutions generally. The formal line of mass control moves from the local to the national to the AFL-CIO in a pattern not unfamiliar to students of government. Yet in private, as in public, organizations the constitutional prescriptions do not necessarily coincide with actual institutional workings. In fact, the internal governments of unions range from the most tightly controlled oligarchy—perhaps an occasional tyranny—to a system closely approximating a competitive two-party system. Spectacular instances of corrupt and boss-controlled unions have attracted attention to the internal politics of unions.[11] Amidst assertions that all is dictatorship or that all is a sweet and reasonable democracy, there should be no mistake: the hierarchies of labor organizations, whether accountable or not accountable in specific situations, wield an authority over their members, as do all quasi-governmental institutions.

Before the merger the national conventions of the AFL-CIO commonly were smoothly managed by the controlling oligarchy of leaders. A statement at the 1936 AFL convention by the late Charles P. Howard, president of the International Typographical Union, could have been used to describe many AFL and CIO national conventions: "During the years I have been a delegate to conventions of the American Federation of Labor I have observed the strongest cohesion in a controlling group for the purpose of determining every question from election of officers to selection of the city in which the convention is to meet the following year." [12] Doubtless, if the AFL-CIO merger shakes down into a stable organization, its biennial convention, despite its formal role as the "supreme governing body" of AFL-CIO, will also come to operate decorously under the guidance of the official clique.

[10] The basic structure of organization, be it craft or industrial, is scarcely adaptable to the political needs of labor in state and local spheres. The state federations of labor developed to fill this gap. Local unions, whatever their national connection might be, could affiliate with their state federation of labor which performed primarily political and lobbying functions on state matters. The CIO organized structurally similar state industrial union councils. Both AFL and CIO had arrangements for similar coalitions or alliances within cities. The AFL-CIO merger plan called for these state and local co-ordinating bodies to be consolidated within two years.

[11] A recent bibliography contains 429 titles on trade-union government. See D. L. Tagliacozzo, "Trade-Union Government, Its Nature and Its Problems, A Bibliographical Review, 1945–55," *American Journal of Sociology*, 61 (1956), pp. 554–581.

[12] AFL, Annual Convention, 1936, *Proceedings*, p. 72.

That such a national convention should be under firm control should occasion no astonishment. The dominance of the official leadership may be observed in national gatherings representative of all sorts of private associations. The lack of conflict within the convention may result not only from the power of the leadership: it may come also from the compromise of differences in advance. Nevertheless, the stability of labor leadership assured by the bureaucratic pattern of succession at times produces an inflexible and unimaginative top echelon. The formation of the CIO arose in part from a breach between the old-guard oligarchy of the AFL and militant leaders who advocated a vigorous organizing campaign in the mass production industries. The processes of recruitment had not brought to the top leaders capable of contriving policies to command the support of the entire labor movement.

Within each national union, the oligarchy of professional union workers tends to manage politics. The existence in the International Typographical Union of two parties that regularly compete for control of the organization is exceptional. Even such an election as that of the United Steel Workers in 1957 when David J. McDonald drew only two-thirds of the votes in his bid for re-election is unusual. More generally the "organization slate" for national offices runs without opposition. Philip Taft reports that slightly more than 80 per cent of 764 officers chosen by seven unions over the period from 1910 to 1944 were unopposed in the voting. Uncontested elections are no necessary indication that a leadership is unresponsive to the sentiments of its followers; that fact may merely result from an assiduous cultivation of the membership. Yet ample citation may be made of instances in which union leadership has maintained its position by chicanery or violence. Some leaders have "dissolved parliament" for long periods—the officers of the Tobacco Workers called no convention from 1900 to 1939; the Granite Cutters held no convention between 1881 and 1912.

Union hierarchies represent the union member in negotiations with employers but, in turn, union hierarchies also govern the union member —within the range of union powers and subject to varying degrees of "popular" control by the member. The conduct of the collective business of the union requires a degree of discipline. To refuse to go out on a strike, to work for less than the agreed wage, to violate the union's working rules may defeat the common purpose. Further, discipline is required to enable the union leadership to fulfill its commitments to those employers with whom it makes agreements. In a sense union hierarchies have edged into the process of industrial administration and have a hand, through bargaining, in the formulation of policy on promotions, transfers, layoffs, fringe benefits, methods of production, and other such matters. In the application of these rules the union hierarchy may also make itself heard. If we regard the process of governing as the imposition of rules of behavior, unions in reality govern as well as agitate. And the caricature of a business agent dragging off the job workers reluctant to strike is matched by instances of business agents exhorting exasperated workers to restrain their tempers and stay on the job.

That union hierarchies exert an authority over the union member there can be no denying. For unions to perform the functions they do, that authority probably needs to exist. The control of its exercise is the problem. It may be doubted that a competitive internal politics necessarily assures rectitude, responsiveness, and fairness from a group hierarchy. At any rate, continuing political turmoil within unions may not be compatible with their effectiveness. Unions themselves have established internal appellate and supervisory procedures to monitor the actions of their locals. The AFL, the CIO, and the merged AFL-CIO gradually assumed a more admonitory attitude toward their errant affiliates, a tendency that gained encouragement from scattered irregularities in the management of the new large welfare funds. Yet the processes of constitutional evolution in private associations seem both as slow and as erratic as are those in the adaptation of governmental institutions generally.[13]

Political Ideology of Labor

The circumstances conditioning the formation of American labor organization contributed to the creation of the peculiar political ideology of the American labor movement. That ideology rejected the socialist formula for improvement of the worker's lot by nationalization of industry and followed a line of *laissez faire* fundamentally like that of American business. Yet over the past half century the ideology of labor, like that of most other sectors of society, has undergone modification.

[13] The literature on trade-union government is voluminous. The following items have been helpful in the above synthesis: Jack Barbash, *Labor Unions in Action* (New York: Harper, 1948); A. L. Gitlow, "Machine Politics in American Trade Unions," *Journal of Politics*, 14 (1952), pp. 370–386; Herbert Harris, *Labor's Civil War* (New York: Knopf, 1940); Will Herberg, "Bureaucracy and Democracy in Labor Unions," *Antioch Review*, 2 (1943), pp. 405–417; G. H. Hildebrand, "American Unionism, Social Stratification, and Power," *American Journal of Sociology*, 58 (1953), pp. 381–390; Joel Seidman, "Democracy in Labor Unions," *Journal of Political Economy*, 61 (1953), pp. 221–231; George Strauss, "Control by the Membership in Building Trades Unions," *American Journal of Sociology*, 61 (1956), pp. 527–535; Philip Taft, *The Structure and Government of Labor Unions* (Cambridge: Harvard University Press, 1954); Lloyd Ulman, *The Rise of the National Trade Union* (Cambridge: Harvard University Press, 1955).

Traditional doctrine of AFL. Over a long period the AFL insisted about as vociferously as business that the true doctrine was that of *laissez faire:* let the state leave labor alone; it would care for itself through organization, collective bargaining, and the strike. Government intervention was frowned upon, since it might deprive labor of its freedom to employ the economic weapons at its command. The Federation supplemented its strict *laissez faire* policy when employers made effective use of the state to combat labor unions. In 1906 it proclaimed "Labor's Bill of Grievances," which demanded, among other things, the exemption of labor unions from the antitrust laws and a cessation of the use of the injunction in labor disputes. Even here the Federation did not seek the positive aid of the state; it merely desired that it be freed from state coercion so that it might fight out its battle with employers on more even terms.

In other legislative demands the Federation sought only negative governmental assistance. Labor might ask that immigration be restricted, that Chinese be excluded, that convict labor not be used in competition with free men; but it wanted to be left free to determine the essential items of the labor contract—wages and hours—through bargaining with the employer. In situations in which collective bargaining was not a suitable method, the Federation asked for positive legislation for the benefit of certain classes of workers, such as government workers. It also urged legislation for the benefit of groups under some special handicaps such as women, children, and seamen. Labor thus placed great faith in collective bargaining; it sought legislation chiefly to deal with matters beyond the scope of bargaining.

A marked change in union political philosophy first appeared in the railroad brotherhoods, not affiliated with the AFL, and the railroad unions of the Federation. When the government undertook to regulate railroad rates and thereby to determine the income from which wages could be paid, it was inevitable that the railroad unions would need to exert their political strength to advance their cause. The strategic importance of railroads in the economy made railroad strikes matters which government could not consider as private disputes. The government had to take a hand in their prevention and settlement. Moreover, the strike was less effective in dealing with great railroad corporations than in negotiating with small employers. The hostility of the railroads after World War I made it difficult for labor even to maintain the right to organize without governmental assistance. Simple reliance on "economic power" was not enough for railroad employees. Their political strength and activity have been reflected in a long series of legislative acts, including the Railway Labor Act of 1926 which guaranteed to them the right to organize. Yet the railroad unions only modified rather than reversed the doctrine of *laissez faire*. They flirted with the idea of government ownership of the railroads but wound up with a government guarantee of the right to exist and to bargain.

Despite the railroad labor deviation, the AFL doctrine of *laissez faire* persisted beyond the day of its usefulness. Dogmas, philosophies, and ideas have a strength of their own. The comparative conservatism of the traditional AFL doctrine rested also on factors other than the strength of a tested doctrine of the past. The building trades, as Professor Taft has pointed out, long played a significant part in the formation of Federation policies. These unions, not faced by the necessity of coping with the power of giant concerns, "felt they had nothing to gain from government intervention in economic matters." [14] A deeper consideration may well be that during its history the American labor movement has had to resist attempts by single-taxers, anarchists, socialists, communists, and others to capture it. Sometimes results disastrous for labor came from such intrusions, and labor leaders adopted as protective coloration a fervent affirmation of the dominant ideologies of the society.

Modification of AFL doctrine. After 1930 the AFL modified its traditional position in some respects but retained a hard core of its ancient doctrine. The extraordinary persistence of the doctrine of *laissez faire* appeared vividly in the hesitance of the Federation to endorse the principle of unemployment insurance. The 1930 convention voted down a proposal to do so. In 1931 the executive council again recommended against unemployment insurance. The workers, the resolution stated, "are being asked by the promoters of compulsory unemployment insurance in the United States to yield up their birthright, to practically surrender in their struggle for liberty, by enactment of legislation deliberately calculated to give the employers increased control over the workers." In 1932 the Federation finally endorsed the principle of unemployment insurance.

While the AFL came to support other social welfare legislation also, it continued to assert a central interest in the maintenance of the widest practicable range of freedom to exert its economic powers through bargaining. Bargaining may raise wages, improve working conditions, and shorten hours, but workers are concerned about a great many other things. In time the AFL manifested a broader interest in the promotion by legislation of matters beyond the job focus. By 1939 William Green, president of the AFL could say: "We now seek benefit for the workers

[14] Philip Taft, "Labor's Changing Political Line," *Journal of Political Economy,* 45 (1937), pp. 637–638.

and all our fellow men by the use of either direct economic strength or legislation as the situation demands. Neither alone can suffice." [15]

Impact of the CIO on labor ideology. The older political ideology of the AFL flowed logically from the doctrine of job unionism. At bottom the older political objectives concentrated on the establishment of the right of unions to exist, to bargain, to strike, and to promote the interests of organized workers by economic weapons. Once this framework of rights was established, the task of the union was to improve the condition of its members by its own strength here and now and not to venture forth on quixotic political crusades for the working classes generally or for ends with no immediate bearing on wages and working conditions.

Upon this hallowed doctrine the CIO had a powerful impact, yet the collision left intact at least the heart of the traditional faith. The maintenance of the basic right to exist for the industrial unions of the CIO required a far more benevolent government attitude toward organized labor. Giant corporations could not so readily be coerced by the strike and threat of strike as could the smaller employers with whom AFL unions had characteristically dealt. In a sense the CIO was a creature of the New Deal. Both the circumstances of its birth and the necessities in the formation of industrial unions gave its leadership a sharp awareness of the uses of its political allies. Yet once it established the right to exist in the newly unionized industries, the CIO's fundamental doctrine came to resemble that of the AFL on the central importance of collective bargaining.

In its concern with legislation of general interest to workers, the CIO introduced an intensity and range of activity alien to the AFL. The younger CIO leadership, liberally sprinkled with intellectuals, attempted far more to improve the status of the working classes generally by legislation than did the old-time leadership of the AFL. The CIO came, in fact, to be interested in about every major government policy: budgets, foreign trade, the level of domestic investment, the rate of interest—all these and other matters affect the health of the economy and the CIO worried about all of them.

Over time the differences between the political doctrines of the AFL and CIO narrowed. The *laissez faire* doctrine of reliance on bargaining strength eroded as it came to be recognized that the right to bargain itself might depend on government protection. Beyond this, both unions moved toward the view that the proper functions of a union extended to the promotion of legislation for benefits beyond matters of wages and

[15] William Green, *Labor and Democracy* (Princeton: Princeton University Press, 1939), p. 67.

working conditions. Yet, on the fundamental question of the character of the economic system, the dominant labor ideology did not challenge the established order. Neither CIO nor AFL questioned, as Selig Perlman put it, "the basic management mandate independent of government or labor." That is, the owner remains the boss, no matter how much he may be hedged about by agreements through bargaining. "It is this," continues Perlman, "which marks off the American labor movement from most other national movements; it is a labor movement upholding capitalism, not only in practice, but in principle as well." [16]

Changing scope of labor lobbying. Through time the scope of labor's lobbying activities has changed as has the political ideology of labor. Throughout its history it has manifested the keenest interest in proposals to restrict the use of the power of the state against labor and to protect the right of organized labor to exist. In an earlier day legislation to outlaw "yellow dog" contracts and to limit the issuance of injunctions in labor controversies received enthusiastic support. Great efforts went into the lobbying campaigns for the National Labor Relations Act and subsequently against the Taft-Hartley Act. Although even yet legislative matters affecting the existence and mode of operation of labor organizations receive highest priority, lobbying effort now also goes to the support of measures to improve the status of the worker by legal action. This broadening of interest occurred in the 1930's, with the CIO taking the lead and the AFL moving, slowly and reluctantly, in the same direction.

Individual internationals have their particular legislative axes to grind on job-connected proposals. The Bricklayers have an abiding interest in housing programs. The Miners are lukewarm toward hydroelectric power developments and favor the conservation of oil and gas. The Watchmakers become more exercised about Swiss competition than do the railroad brotherhoods. The building trades support building codes that may promote both the public safety and employment for their members.

Any national convention of labor expresses views on a wide range of matters beyond the categories mentioned: foreign policy, civil rights, education, the postal system, the condition of colonial aborigines—no problem is beyond the purview of organized labor. Yet the adoption of a resolution does not necessarily set the legislative committee to working on the question in the lobbies of Congress. Energies in the promotion of legislation tend to be concentrated on those matters of most immediate concern. Old-time labor leaders mildly object to the expansion of the agenda of labor resolutions. The grand chief engineer of the Brotherhood

[16] "The Basic Philosophy of the American Labor Movement," *Annals of the Am. Acad. of Pol. and Soc. Sci.*, 274 (1951), pp. 57–63.

of Locomotive Engineers observes that the rail unions have escaped some types of criticism because they have not tried "to tell everybody how to run the country from State Department policy on down."

Political Tactics of Organized Labor

Labor adapts its political strategy and tactics to its political ideology, which gives first priority to the maintenance of the right of labor to organize and to play a role in the determination of working conditions through collective bargaining. The improvement of the lot of the toiling masses generally through direct governmental action occupies a distinctly secondary place on labor's agenda. Given its doctrinal position, labor's political objectives are comparatively narrow and its political tactics are tailored accordingly. In short, organized labor does not seek responsibility for running the country. It wants to maintain the right to exist—and to keep others from using the government to push it around. The major shifts in tactics and the chief upsurges in political activity of organized labor have been either responses to threats to its right to exist or efforts to remove legal limitations on its operations.

Rejection of a labor party. In the setting of the American two-party system and the American political tradition, the political strategy consonant with the limited political objectives of labor consists in working within the major parties and in lobbying for legislative action. Although a few old socialists dream of the day when trade unions will form a new political party, labor organizations themselves, with a few local exceptions, have stuck to their knitting and rejected the notion of a labor party. In the American Federation of Labor Samuel Gompers firmly established the doctrine that it was inexpedient for labor to attempt to form an independent political party to seek control of the government. In 1906 he pointed out that to advance through a labor party would require waiting "until labor elects a majority of the legislature and a governor and then a President of the United States, who shall appoint the justices of the Supreme Court. I am afraid we are going to wait a long time! Trade unionists don't propose to wait so long to secure material improvement in their conditions." [17]

Labor's nonpartisan doctrine. The principle that guides the AFL-CIO in its campaign efforts is the so-called nonpartisan doctrine. Under this principle not only does labor reject the idea of a labor party; it also rejects the alternative of affiliation with either major party and dedicates itself

[17] Samuel Gompers, *Labor and the Common Welfare* (New York, 1919), p. 128. Quoted by permission of E. P. Dutton & Co., Inc., copyright owner.

to rewarding its friends and punishing its enemies, whatever their party affiliation may be. The American Federation of Labor developed the nonpartisan doctrine under both the leadership of Samuel Gompers and the impact of experience. Gompers' favorite formulation of the policy was that labor should be partisan for principle and not for party. Partisanship for principle, of course, resolves itself into partisanship for candidates who concur with labor's principles and Gompers asserted ". . . we must make manifest that we have political power and that we intend to use it." The CIO adopted the same doctrinal position.

The nonpartisan doctrine fits the political facts of life in congressional and legislative campaigns. Labor has friends and enemies in both parties. The AFL-CIO Committee on Political Education can, on the basis of legislators' records, separate the sheep from the goats. Both its predecessor agencies, the CIO-PAC and the AFL-LLPE, prepared prior to each congressional campaign analyses of the voting records of Senators and Representatives on measures of interest to labor. These records form a part of the basis for endorsement by the union agencies responsible for political action. In 1948 the AFL Labor's League for Political Education opposed all Senators and Congressmen who had supported the Taft-Hartley Act no matter "how many favorable votes" they had cast on other issues. In 1944, under different circumstances, the CIO-PAC did not limit itself to the consideration of the record of the candidate on labor issues narrowly defined. It made the test of its endorsement the attitude of congressional candidates toward the New Deal generally.

In practice, the campaign efforts of organized labor are not uniformly distributed in support of all its friends or in opposition to all its enemies. Campaign resources are allocated according to the necessities of the moment. Intensive efforts may be made in support of outstanding friends who are faced by strong opposition. Thus, in 1954 labor exerted itself in the campaign for re-election of Senator Paul H. Douglas, of Illinois. Labor may concentrate resources behind a candidate who has a chance to defeat an unfriendly sitting legislator. In 1954 labor rallied behind Patrick V. McNamara in his Michigan senatorial race against Homer Ferguson, Republican. In some states or districts candidates are so firmly entrenched that support of friends is superfluous or opposition to enemies futile.

The application of the nonpartisan doctrine to presidential campaigns has been somewhat less straightforward than to legislative campaigns. The first endorsement of a presidential candidate by an AFL convention occurred in 1952 when Adlai Stevenson received the nod. Prior to that time the convention had been held after the presidential polling, and the labor view had been expressed by means less formal than convention endorsement. Samuel Gompers in association with other ranking labor leaders supported Bryan in 1908, Wilson in 1912 and 1916, Cox in 1920, and La Follette in 1924. The AFL avoided "official" endorsement of presidential candidates, although its president and other leaders might in their "personal" capacities endorse a candidate. In 1948, for example, most of the members of the AFL executive council, "in their private capacities," became members of the "AFL Committee for Truman." The CIO executive board in both 1948 and 1952 endorsed the Democratic presidential candidate. In 1956 the AFL-CIO general board endorsed Stevenson and Kefauver, although that move was opposed by a handful of labor leaders including Dave Beck, of the Teamsters, and Maurice Hutcheson, of the Carpenters.

While on occasion individual nationals and internationals have endorsed Republican presidential candidates, the leadership of organized labor as a whole has been on the Democratic side. A few Republican senatorial and congressional candidates win labor endorsements and some Democratic candidates, especially in the South, earn the disfavor of labor, but labor in recent decades has infrequently felt moved to exertion on behalf of Republican candidates. Yet organized labor continues to assert, and to some degree to maintain, an independence of party. "We must ever be vigilant," the director of the AFL-LLPE asserted, "to keep our local leagues completely independent and nonpartisan. We must not become the tail to any political party. . . . We must always be in a position to support candidates on the basis of their record, and not on the basis of personal favors and party prejudices." [18] Sidney Hillman of the CIO spoke the language of William Green of the AFL in 1944 when he said: "We will neither attempt to capture nor submit to capturing by either of the political parties." Given the alternatives offered to organized labor in recent decades, the nonpartisan policy makes of labor, as one of its leaders has remarked, "nonpartisan Democrats."

A few local deviations from the nonpartisan doctrine need to be noted. In some states and localities trade unions have played a role in the organization of labor parties. The principal surviving example, the Liberal party of New York, rests chiefly on the support of the Ladies Garment Workers. This party continues to exist probably in part because it does not operate like a conventional party. It usually nominates as its candidates persons who are also the nominees of a major party, ordinarily but not invariably the Democratic. The vote for the Democratic candidate "on the Liberal line" of the voting machine may provide the margin for victory. New York's election laws, by permitting nominations by more than one party, create the legal conditions necessary for the maintenance

[18] *Minutes of the National Committee of Labor's League for Political Education,* October 5, 1949, pp. 8–9.

of an unusual type of party. The marriage of convenience between labor and the Democratic party takes other forms in other places. In Michigan the Democratic party began to come out of the doldrums as labor organization grew and the Democratic organization was heavily infiltrated by labor leaders. In Minnesota trade-union leaders take their place in Democratic councils. The more common relation is one of informal collaboration as occasion requires and circumstances permit. Union officials are often recognized by a place on the national convention delegation. Around 200 unionists attended the 1952 Democratic convention as delegates or alternates.[19]

Episodes in labor political activity. The nonpartisan doctrine is a standing principle of organized labor, but the magnitude of the efforts devoted to campaigns vary considerably from time to time. These variations find partial explanation in the primacy in labor's program of the maintenance of the right to organize—of freedom to exist and to operate as trade unions. Bursts of political activity and serious reconsiderations of the political role of labor have tended to occur when organized labor has been threatened. At times its right to exist has been under attack; at other times its freedom to operate has been challenged.

The extensive use of injunctions against labor unions and the application of the Sherman Antitrust Act to labor organizations helped to spur the AFL to political activity after the proclamation of its 1906 Bill of Grievances. The AFL formed its Labor Representation Committee to campaign for the election of friendly Senators and Representatives. Although by modern measures, the campaign efforts were small in scale, the AFL conventions regularly heard reports of defeats and victories. The AFL claimed some credit for the 1910 Republican loss of the House of Representatives. Eventually in 1914 the Clayton Act prohibited the issuance of injunctions by federal courts in labor disputes "unless necessary to prevent irreparable injury to property or to property right . . . , for which injury there is no adequate remedy at law." Labor leaders hailed the act as the "Magna Carta of Labor," though they had not reckoned that the courts would interpret it to change the status of the injunction in labor disputes but little.

In the years after World War I organized labor fought a losing political battle. The postwar reaction brought a determined effort to weaken, if not to destroy, labor organization. In the roaring 'twenties the injunction and all the other weapons in the employer armory were brought into

[19] See Max M. Kampelman, "Labor in Politics" in Industrial Relations Research Association, *Interpreting the Labor Movement* (Madison: The Association, 1952), pp. 171–191.

play. The reaction went so far that in 1924 the AFL could find no reason to favor the presidential candidate of either major party and supported the independent candidacy of Robert M. La Follette. Evidently the unhappy experiences of the 1920's left the AFL leadership shell-shocked. The political activities of labor seemed weak until the CIO initiated its energetic political program.

The National Labor Relations Act of 1935 guaranteed to employees the right "to form, join, or assist labor organizations, to bargain collectively through representatives of their own choosing, and to engage in concerted activities, for the purpose of collective bargaining or other mutual aid or protection." This legislation, with its promise of the use of the power of the state in defense of the right of unions to exist, was to provide a rallying point for labor political activities. In 1936, the Democratic Administration, under powerful attack from those who wished to repeal the act, found an ally in Labor's Nonpartisan League, a subsidiary of the CIO. The new industrial unions in a sense owed their creation to a friendly government and they exerted themselves to keep it friendly.

In World War II labor lobbyists resisted, with varying success, legislative proposals to limit the operations of unions, all justified by their sponsors on the ground of the necessity of uninterrupted war production. In 1943, after the firmer legislative line toward labor stemming from the congressional elections of 1942 became apparent, the CIO formed its Political Action Committee, which campaigned zealously for the Democratic ticket in 1944.

AFL political activity meanwhile continued less conspicuously and less energetically, but the congressional elections of 1946 set in motion forces that led to a much more determined effort to mobilize the political strength of organized labor. Republican triumph in the congressional elections of that year was so complete that the "friends of labor" were unable to muster enough votes to block the passage of the Taft-Hartley Act over the veto of President Truman. That act modified the Labor Relations Act of 1935, to the disadvantage of unions. Among some of its supporters, it was regarded as the first step toward the "complete elimination of governmental labor relations agencies" and the correction of "other errors of government initiated during the 1930's," such as the Social Security Act and the Fair Labor Standards Act.[20]

The threat to organized labor in the Taft-Hartley Act, as well as the fear of a general postwar reaction, stimulated labor political action. In 1947 the AFL created a political subsidiary, Labor's League for Political Education, to propagandize the labor viewpoint and to support candi-

[20] Fred A. Hartley, Jr., *Our New National Labor Policy* (New York: Funk & Wagnalls, 1948).

dates friendly to labor. It became an important source of finance for candidates supported by the AFL and collaborated informally with the CIO-PAC with which it was ultimately to be merged as COPE—the Committee on Political Education—of the united AFL-CIO. The threat, real or supposed, to organized labor in the Taft-Hartley Act gave common cause to the AFL and CIO and doubtless contributed to their eventual amalgamation.

As the debate on the Taft-Hartley Act wore on, the political alignment of organized labor became clearer. Truman's victory in 1948 on a pledge to repeal the Taft-Hartley Act may have put an end to the hope in some quarters that labor might be put in its place. Yet Truman was unable to fulfill his campaign promise. Nor did Eisenhower fulfill his commitment to bring about modifications in the act. As his first term unfolded labor leaders became more and more certain that they could not do business with a Republican Administration. Republican leadership itself was divided on the line to take toward organized labor. As the 1956 campaign approached Senator Barry Goldwater maintained a running fire against the political activities, fair and unfair, of labor leaders. A contrary view was advanced by such Republicans as Governor Goodwin Knight, of California, who thought it unwise to try to win labor votes by appealing over the heads of the leaders of labor. He had been able to do business in California with the AFL by a promise to oppose and, if necessary, to veto "right to work" bills and other legislation restricting union activities.

Organization for political action. Labor organization, since it evolved to meet other needs, is not designed to perform campaign functions effectively. The confederate character of labor organization leaves autonomy to individual national and international unions, and almost invariably a few national presidents are conspicuous exceptions to the general Democratic orientation of labor leadership. In its 1952 resolution of endorsement of Stevenson the AFL convention emphasized "that the affiliated unions . . . and each and every one of their members are free to make their own individual political decisions without any compulsion on our part." Among national leaders those who exercise this autonomy most frequently seem to be usually associated with the buildings trades. For many years William Hutcheson, of the Carpenters, occupied a high place in Republican councils and in 1952 Richard J. Gray, president of the Building and Construction Trades Department of the AFL, supported Eisenhower. In the lower reaches of the labor hierarchy Republican deviation is more frequent, and Republican candidates can ordinarily round up a committee of union officials to endorse them although commonly its members will be less prominent in the labor movement than those aligned with the Democrats.

Apart from the confusion induced by division among its top leaders, union organization can only most awkwardly be used to mobilize workers as voters. The accidents of history that vetoed attempts to organize all workers—skilled and unskilled whatever their craft or industrial pursuit —of particular geographical areas into single unions assured for labor a low political organizational potential. Workers are grouped into unions formed along craft, shop, plant, or industry lines, a structure ideal for bargaining with employers. Such an organization cannot readily be focused on union members in precincts, districts, or other geographical areas for the purpose of agitation and stimulation of voting. To this administrative difficulty must be added the fact that different unions have different traditions of political action. Some are more militantly led than others. Some have a more direct concern with the outcome of a particular election than others. Even without such variations the co-ordination of the campaign efforts of different unions with members in a particular locality is a most taxing operation. When it is attempted, the most astonishing confusion and conflict are not uncommon. Nor did the unification of the top levels of labor in the AFL-CIO alter this problem of organizing at the precinct level. The mechanisms for the communication of the advice of top leaders to the rank and file are most imperfect.[21]

In its campaign tactics organized labor needs to be aware of the possibility that at times its endorsement may have a net negative effect. Labor support may attract some votes but it may also repel a greater number. Under these conditions labor has learned that it needs to work, if it works at all, quietly and without hullabaloo.

Effectiveness of mobilization of labor vote. What of the effectiveness of labor organizations in the political mobilization of their members? In presidential politics for several decades union members have leaned Democratic. The proportions of union members supporting the Democratic ticket has changed from time to time. From slightly over 80 per cent in 1936 it declined to around 60 per cent in 1952. These gross figures, of course, conceal other variations. On the average, members of

[21] In a study of a local steel union it was found that a substantial proportion of the membership did not know of the union's activities in local campaigns. A frequent response to the request for views on the PAC was a variation of "What's PAC?" or "Who's he?"—Joel Seidman and others, "Political Consciousness in a Local Union," *Public Opinion Quarterly*, 15 (1951–52), pp. 692–702. In May, 1952, 70 per cent of a national sample of union members told Elmo Roper's interviewers that they had never received any literature from the union about candidates nor had any one from the union called at their home to talk about candidates.

the CIO unions have voted Democratic in higher degree than have persons affiliated with AFL unions. The solidarity of the labor vote doubtless also varies widely from union to union and from place to place, although no estimates of these variations are available.

What labor organizations have had to do with the Democratic orientation of unionists presents another question. The influence of organization is not solely an influence of its leadership. Group pressures of all sorts commonly bring a person's political orientation into conformity with that of his associates. Union members, for example, usually vote Democratic in higher degree than do groups of otherwise similar but unorganized workers. That difference may be caused by factors other than organization, but it has been established that those individuals most active in unions—by attendance at meetings and by participation in other union activities—are more likely to be Democratic than are the less active members of the same union.[22] In other words, men who spend time around the union hall are apt to be indoctrinated with the politics of the activists in the union.

Whether a labor vote exists that can be delivered by labor leaders is in a way a nonsense question. The influence of labor leaders over their members probably differs enormously with time and circumstance and in each instance is so intermingled with other influences as to be beyond measurement. Given the traditional partisan attachments of workers, the labor leadership could not shift many votes from a popular Democratic president to a Republican candidate.[23] The factors making for labor voting solidarity—the exertions of labor leadership and other factors as well—may be of most effect when questions of concern to workers as workers are salient. In 1948, with memories of the Taft-Hartley Act fresh and with anxieties about a possible economic let down, labor leadership probably had far greater influence than it did in 1952 when nonlabor questions were to the fore. In other instances the contribution of labor organization to the outcome may consist more in getting voters to the polls than in influencing the direction of the vote. Probably the influence of labor leadership can be most marked in direct primaries that involve contestants relatively unknown to the electorate.

Union members, like the rest of us, manage to get along with a multiplicity of loyalties which assume changing priorities in the monitoring of our behavior. Membership in a union does not mean that a person

[22] Bernard Berelson and others, *Voting* (Chicago: University of Chicago Press, 1954), p. 49.

[23] In 1940 John L. Lewis endorsed Willkie. Irving Bernstein found no evidence that the action moved many workers into the Republican ranks. See "John L. Lewis and the Voting Behavior of the C. I. O.," *Public Opinion Quarterly*, 5 (1941), pp. 233–249.

is invariably governed in voting by his interest as a union member. More-over, labor leaders compete with others for the vote of union members. Substantial numbers of union members regard politics as outside the proper sphere of union activity and larger numbers prefer to be informed of candidates' views of concern to the union rather than to be told how to vote. Yet the influence of labor organization should not be dismissed as of no import because labor endorsed candidates do not invariably win. Organization doubtless re-enforces the loyalties of the hard core of labor votes. At times labor leaders manage to get to the polls a larger vote than would be cast without their efforts. And on occasion their exertions may account for victory.[24]

Private Bureaucracy and Political Inertia

The discussion of the specific problems of agriculture led to the con-sideration of a much broader question: the process by which deprivations and dislocations of many sorts and many origins set off movements in demand of redress, adjustment, or even overthrow of the old order. In this chapter a similar sequence prevails. Organized labor has occupied the center of the stage but its analysis points to a political phenomenon in which many sorts of organizations share: namely, the role of organized groups in the maintenance of stability or the status quo. This resistance to disruption of the ordered course of things is thus the antithesis of the general pattern of behavior touched on in the preceding chapter.

The stabilizing role of the private group may readily be perceived if it is recognized that private organizations and groups, as well as officials, govern. At least this is so, if to govern is to set norms of behavior—what may not be done, what may be done, and how it shall be done—and to penalize deviations from those standards. That groups perform these functions is a commonplace of social science. The informal group, though it may lack officers, constitution, or other badges of being, may evolve its

[24] The following titles are useful on union political action: Alfred Braunthal, "American Labor in Politics," *Social Research*, 12 (1945), pp. 1–21; Fay Caulkins, *The CIO and the Democratic Party* (Chicago: University of Chicago Press, 1952); Chamber of Commerce of the United States, *Labor In Politics* (Washington, 1950); George Gallup, "How Labor Votes," *Annals of the Am. Acad. of Pol. and Soc. Sci.*, 274 (1951), pp. 118–124; Morton Leeds "The AFL in the 1948 Elections," *Social Research*, 17 (1950), pp. 207–218; Avery Leiserson, "Organized Labor as a Pressure Group," *Annals*, 274 (1951), pp. 108–117; Arnold M. Rose, *Union Solidarity* (Minne-apolis: University of Minnesota Press, 1952); H. Rosen and R. A. H. Rosen, *The Union Member Speaks* (New York: Prentice-Hall, 1955); Joel Seidman, "Organized Labor in Political Campaigns," *Public Opinion Quarterly*, 3 (1939), pp. 536–654; Philip Taft, "Labor's Changing Political Line," *Journal of Political Economy*, 45 (1937), pp. 634–650.

own etiquette of action and its own set of values and may possess means for their enforcement—means ranging from a mere frown to ostracism.

As private groups become crystallized into formal organizations their function of governance becomes more visible. The constitutions, governing machinery, and codes of fair competition of trade associations bear many of the earmarks of the apparatus of the state, and in the nebulous areas around the fringes of the antitrust laws they exercise powers like those of the state.[25] Professional associations with their codes of ethics and their committees on professional conduct bear a close resemblance to the law-giver and the police court. Churches command the obedience of their communicants and hold over their heads the threat of everlasting punishment. Labor unions have their codes and their means for penalizing action unbecoming a union member. Corporations, a special sort of group, have their structures of authority over hundreds of thousands of workers; their power may extend to vast resources and its exercise may have wide ramifications within the economy.

Such functions of governance, it may be said, are "nonpolitical." Even so, they are certainly politically relevant. Moreover, the governing function of private groups shade over almost imperceptibly into realms undeniably political or governmental. Groups often strive to control the exercise of public power or to obtain delegations of public authority. Notable instances occur among professional and semiprofessional associations which often obtain, in form or in fact, the authority to set standards for entry to the profession and to fix rules for the conduct of its practitioners. This tendency has brought the suggestion that the medieval guild is, to a degree at least, re-asserting itself.[26] In effect, the action of the private association becomes sanctioned by state authority. Or an underworld syndicate may obtain, through arrangements with the police, the power to "license" slot machines and to see that those operators not meeting its requirements are raided. Private groups not only set norms of conduct; they perform "service" functions similar to those of the state. Labor unions have their own welfare or social security systems and cor-

[25] Consider the system of promulgation of uniform rates by associations of insurance companies prior to the case of the *South-Eastern Underwriters*. Adherence to privately fixed rates was induced by refusal to reinsure the risks of nonmember companies, severance of relations wtih agents writing insurance for nonmember companies, and exclusion from the privileges of membership, which were real, of those concerns not in compliance with the association's rules. See "The Regulation of Insurance Rates," *Columbia Law Review*, 47 (1947), pp. 1314–1332.

[26] See J. A. C. Grant, "The Guild Returns to America," *Journal of Politics*, 4 (1942), pp. 303–335, 458–477; Francis P. DeLancey, *The Licensing of Professions in West Virginia* (Chicago: Foundation Press, 1938).

porations tax their stockholders for the support of charities in favor with the corporate management.

Quite apart from the formal governmental structure, if our contention is correct, the social system is bound together by an intricate network of governing relationships developed in the life of private groups. The broad political significance of this system—if, indeed, it may be called a system—seems plain enough. The system—the established way of doing things—constitutes a powerful brake on political change. Those who agitate for a new order invariably encounter the resistance of the old order which exists, in considerable degree at least, in the revered values more or less firmly anchored in group life. These patterns of behavior, traditional modes of action, group norms, or social equilibria—the concept employed in their description may not matter—possess a powerful capacity for their own perpetuation and resist movements that would disturb them.

The role of the group in the creation and maintenance of norms—and the direct political significance of it all—may be made more explicit. Doctrines or norms of special durability seem to be those propagated and perpetuated by group processes. The AFL, as has been noted, became devoted to a *laissez faire* doctrine and the strength of its adherence to that doctrine provoked grave debate on whether to endorse unemployment insurance even when millions of workers were jobless. It seems clear that group leadership and group processes function both to create group norms and to induce conformity. Group program and group policy do not emerge in finished form from a womb of determinism. Thus, the long persistence of the strength of the high-tariff policy in the American business community came in part from processes that generated a "public opinion" within business groups and even induced many elements of business to acquiesce in policies clearly to their immediate disadvantage. Or, the leadership of the American Medical Association manufactured a policy on health insurance and made it extremely bad form for a physician to dissent from the official line. The group defines norms, establishes patterns of behavior, and tends to exert its powers for their maintenance, often beyond their usefulness. Political movements that would alter the prevailing relationships must overcome the resistance of orthodox doctrines embedded in the working habits of group life.[27]

[27] These are not, to be sure, the only factors that make the way of the innovator hard. Some time ago Machiavelli observed: "And it ought to be remembered that there is nothing more difficult to take in hand, more perilous to conduct, or more uncertain in its success, than to take the lead in the introduction of a new order of things. Because the innovator has for enemies all those who have done well under the old conditions, and lukewarm defenders in those who may do well under the new. This coolness arises partly from fear of the opponents, who have the laws on their

A significant element in the stabilizing and braking function of private associations may be their hierarchical leadership which tends to be renewed by co-option. The self-perpetuation of the collective leadership of private associations was illustrated by the persistence in power of the oligarchies of labor organizations, yet the patterns of succession to leadership in other private organizations are not conspicuously dissimilar. The nature of the renewal of the personnel of hierarchies probably contributes to the stability of group doctrine. When advancement depends on the decision of those already in the charmed circle, a premium is likely to be placed on conformity and orthodoxy. The "elder statesmen" with ideas of another day hold onto their power and make life difficult for the "young Turks." The prevailing attitudes tend to be perpetuated. Hierarchies have an immortality of sorts; one man may be replaced but the organization goes on forever. Thus in armies, navies, the hierarchies of labor organizations, civil services, universities, corporations, trade associations, and all sorts of private groups co-option to the top often helps perpetuate the group orthodoxy.[28] And the doctrines and views of the leadership, whose existence is required by the necessities of group life, may become removed from the sentiments of the rank and file. Internal conflict that results in a turnover in private group leadership may have significance for the politics of the state as a whole.[29]

---

side, and partly from the incredulity of men, who do not readily believe in new things until they have had a long experience in them."—*The Prince*, ch. 6.

[28] Over the long run the increased collectivization of human activity (whether under corporate, voluntary association, or government auspices) may create inflexibility in the social system in that larger and larger proportions of human decision fall within the purview of fewer and fewer hierarchies, each characterized by the inflexibilities induced by the gyroscopic effect of co-option. Offsetting tendencies occur, to be sure, in the conscious recognition of the need for external inspection and criticism, as in management surveys, and in attempts to institutionalize innovation, as in industrial research.

[29] For a case study of the internal politics of a union and for observations suggestive of the nature of the general problem of democracy in voluntary associations, see Seymour Lipset and others, *Union Democracy* (Glencoe: Free Press, 1956).

4 | Business

Businessmen are a heterogeneous lot. The president of a life insurance company seeks safety in investment. The wildcat operator bets his fortune that oil will flow from a hole in the ground. Both are businessmen. The corporate bureaucrat, managing a railroad organization encrusted with traditional practices, and the management expert, guiding an automobile manufacturing company animated by an innovative spirit, are both businessmen. The steel magnate who espouses the inflexible views typical of heavy industry and the clothing maker who has anxieties about the disposable income of consumers call themselves businessmen. The barber-shop proprietor, the manager of far-flung chain-store enterprises, the corner grocer, the broker, the banker, the gadget maker, the shoe manufacturer, the undertaker, the tulip-bulb importer—all these and many others are "businessmen."

The variety of interests suggested by this enumeration might mean that discussion of "the businessman" in the political process would be a bootless undertaking. Perhaps one might better treat particular classes or groups of businessmen, for their interests are diverse and sometimes in conflict. Easy generalizations that businessmen believe this or that conceal a more complex reality in which a gradation of opinion prevails among different groups. Conflicts among business groups are commonplace, yet a network of common interest pulls the business community together on major issues when its security is threatened. Party lines, sectional lines, religious lines rarely divide businessmen when their common interests are in peril. Within the business community powerful factors operate to bring conformity to the predominant views. Unanimity is rare, but a predominant business sentiment usually crystallizes and makes itself heard on major issues affecting the group as a whole.

With the decline in the importance of agriculture, the preponderance of American wealth came to be controlled by businessmen. The power of wealth in politics is an age-old phenomenon. The holders of wealth, whatever its form, have great stakes in the outcome of the political struggle; they also have the time to devote to political maneuver or the money to employ others to do so. The power wielded by business in American politics may puzzle the person of democratic predilections: a comparatively small minority exercises enormous power. Agriculture, a waning sector of the economy, occasionally fights a rear-guard action against business. Labor assaults the business citadel from time to time with varying degrees of success. Yet, withal, business retains a position of potent leadership in public affairs.

Rise of Industry and Trade: Dynamics of Political Disequilibrium

In a static society the process of politics—of governing—is likely to be dull and uneventful. Since a major function of politics is the mediation of relations among groups of people, so long as there is no material change in the size, character, or aspirations of the major interests in a society the political pot remains at a low temperature. When the nature of relations among groups changes significantly, adjustments in political arrangements occur. The old rules of the game no longer serve. Maladjustments generate demands for new laws and new policies appropriate to the new circumstances. Individual acts of government—legislation, administrative actions, judicial decisions—constitute episodes in the continuing quest for an equilibrium among interests in society.

Business: Generator of imbalance and readjustment. While the sources of disturbance of the old order are legion, business has been prolific in producing disruptions of established group relationships. Paradoxically businessmen belligerently proclaim their conservatism yet consistently act as dedicated radicals. It was they—not the orators of the soapbox—who set in motion the forces that overturned the hallowed ways of our tranquil past. When the spirit of innovation roams the land, politicians must busy themselves in the accommodation of the institutions and laws to the new order. In America the great innovator has been the business-man; the secondary consequences of his actions fatten the statute books and lengthen the administrative codes.

The obvious impact on the political order of technological innovation scarcely needs to be spelled out. The effects of each of many technological developments in communication, transportation, and manufacture eventually permeated the entire society and were followed, as the night the day, by the contrivance of regulatory standards, procedures, and instruments. The invention of the automobile produced the motor vehicle code and the traffic court. Apart from such consequences of technological change, two other major developments associated with business merit special attention. The rapid growth of business changed the relationships between business and other social groups and raised ultimately the question of who should rule. In addition to the growth of business, radical changes in the internal nature of business occurred. Changes in the scale of business operation, in the nature of business rivalry, and in the structure of power within business drastically disturbed pre-existing relations between business and employees, business and customers, business and investors, and among different categories of businessmen. And these disturbances stimulated demands for redress, as well as the ingenuity of statesmen in the search for solutions.

Expansion of business in the national economy. In a gross sense the roots of the remaking of the political order may be traced to the growth of the place of business in the national economy. The power of business has been not inconsiderable, of course, from the beginning. Charles A. Beard demonstrated that the forces of wealth—money, trade, personalty in various forms—were influential in the adoption of the Constitution.[1] Yet business did not attain its full flowering until after the Civil War. The southern planter aristocracy, built on a foundation of slave labor and the cotton gin, was to hold sway until put to rout by the alliance of north-eastern business and northwestern free agriculture in the Civil War, the outcome of which Miriam Beard calls "the victory of American business over plantocracy."[2]

After the Civil War the trend toward a more highly industrialized society continued unabated; and with it came, not without friction, a marked shift in the balance of political power. In 1870 slightly over one-half of the gainfully employed were engaged in agriculture, fishing, and

[1] *The Economic Interpretation of the Constitution* (New York: Macmillan, 1913).
[2] *A History of the Business Man* (New York: Macmillan, 1938), ch. 24.

forestry, and far fewer in manufacturing. The ratios gradually shifted and by 1950 only about one-eighth of the civilian labor force found employment in agriculture.

The rapid growth of business, in comparison with other sectors of the economy, produced political changes both large and small. Eventually it raised the question whether business, instead of agriculture, was to govern the country. That question, a common interpretation holds, was settled by the election of 1896 which marked the triumph of business over the last great attempt of agriculture to assert its vanished sovereignty. Once the location of decisive power became unequivocally clear, government dedicated itself to the execution of the agenda of business.[3]

Organizational innovation. Apart from the expansion of business, which alone sufficed to compel governmental preoccupation with the problems of business, American businessmen have proved to be great innovators in the organization of economic activity. They made it both feasible and profitable to conduct business enterprises of unprecedented hugeness. In the construction of giant concerns and in the contrivance of working relations among them, business acquired a degree of independence from the invisible hand of Adam Smith. Business acquired a degree of power, of control, over the market, which could no longer alone be relied upon to govern the relations of businessmen with each other and with other sectors of the economy.

As business groups gained a power not sensitively subject to control by competitive forces, the traditional relations among groups of people were rudely disturbed. Large plants, at times virtually monopolizing the demand side of particular labor markets, altered the relations of employers and workers. Firms or combinations of firms capable of driving an isolated competitor to the wall brought new relations among businessmen in individual lines. Associations of firms able to dominate the market for a raw material put suppliers at a disadvantage. Suppliers who organized the market to dominate many users upset other relations. From all these and other innovations in business organization sprang the political pyrotechnics that burst around "big business" for decades.

The organizational revolution in American industry began in a movement of corporate merger and consolidation around the 1880's. The

[3] The chances are that the extraordinary growth of the American economy has had other consequences of profound significance for the American polity. An expanding economy creates new pelf, new places of power, new outlets for ambition in contrast with a stagnant economy in which a limited number of places of prestige are refilled as the old retire. Had a marked proportion of the energies devoted to economic development been dedicated to political agitation, the United States would have had a most turbulent politics.

process of consolidation moved with special rapidity from 1897 to 1903 and from 1925 to 1929. The earlier period saw the emergence of such noted corporate names as United States Steel, International Silver, United Shoe Machinery, American Can, Eastman Kodak, International Nickel, and International Harvester. Often the formation of such concerns had been preceded by a bitter competitive struggle for supremacy which eventuated in a merger to establish "order" in an industry rent by price wars.

The degree to which the movement toward concentration of control within industry has proceeded is warmly disputed by the experts on these matters, and the measurement of the extent of concentration indeed represents no mean technical problem. According to one estimate, by 1933 the 200 largest nonfinancial corporations controlled "approximately 19 to 21 per cent of the national wealth." In 1950, according to an estimate by the Federal Trade Commission, the 200 largest manufacturing companies accounted for 40.3 per cent of the total value of product of all manufacturing industries.[4]

Although the sinfulness and virtuousness of big enterprise may be debated endlessly, there can be no doubt that the organizational revolution has brought a radically new business structure. Instead of the atomized economy of many firms revered by the classical economists, an "organizational economy" has come to prevail.[5] In this new economy the great corporation becomes in a sense something of a government in itself.[6] The giant concern gains power over its suppliers and its customers, not necessarily by the attainment of a monopoly position but at times by its size alone.[7] Groups of corporations may act in concert through habit and the dictates of a strategy of survival rather than by old-fashioned conspiracies in restraint of trade. In short, managerial inventiveness created an economic organization the nature of which is both complex and disputed by the specialists.[8] Yet the political consequences of the new business or-

[4] *Report of the Federal Trade Commission on Changes in Concentration in Manufacturing* (1954), p. 115.

[5] The phrase is Calvin B. Hoover's. See his "Institutional and Theoretical Implications of Economic Change," *American Economic Review,* 44 (1954), pp. 1–14.

[6] See Adolph Berle, Jr., *The 20th Century Capitalist Revolution* (New York: Harcourt, Brace, 1954). See also M. S. Baratz, "Corporate Giants and the Power Structure," *Western Political Quarterly,* 9 (1956), pp. 406–415.

[7] Corwin D. Edwards, "Conglomerate Bigness As a Source of Power," in National Bureau of Economic Research, *Business Concentration and Price Policy* (Princeton: Princeton University Press, 1955), pp. 331–352.

[8] The literature is voluminous. Samples include: Walter Adams (ed.), *The Structure of American Industry* (New York: Macmillan, rev. ed., 1954); A. D. H. Kaplan, *Big Enterprise in a Competitive System* (Washington: Brookings, 1954); D. E. Lilienthal, *Big Business: A New Era* (New York: Harper, 1953); T. K. Quinn, *Giant*

ganization are plain enough. The erection within the social system of new points of economic power drastically altered the relationships among many categories of persons and brought new and continuing political problems.

Business Regulation: Intergroup Mediation

The upthrust of new types of business and of new business organizations radically altered the relations between groups within the nation. The old legal principles no longer governed these relations to the satisfaction of all concerned. The political system was called upon to mediate among social groups to maintain both the peace and a rough equity in the relations of men. While there developed numerous new types of group relations with their associated problems, several patterns arose with special frequency. The growth of large enterprises created new frictions commonly described as between big business and the public; on closer inspection, they often turned out to be frictions between two sorts of businesses, as railroads and shippers. Persistent maladjustments arose in the relations of employers and workers, which set off a continuing debate over the principles that should guide those relations. Among different types of business conflicts developed that led to demands for governmental intervention by one or the other of the contending groups.

In the broad variety of governmental actions bearing on business—and the affairs of business pre-empt an impressive proportion of the pages of the legal codes—no discernible thread of doctrinal consistency exists, save perhaps that business seeks to maintain the maximum freedom of action. Business, not unlike labor, likes to be left alone except when it needs government help. In some instances the business objective requires insistence on an unmixed doctrine of *laissez faire*. In others business demands the strictest governmental regulation of business—often, but not always, the other fellow's business. In a third type of situation the cause may be best promoted by government subsidy or aid. Under other circumstances, business may welcome regulation that mitigates the hazards of competition. Despite the extraordinary diversity of their political actions, business spokesmen expound more or less uniformly a philosophy of *laissez faire:* free competition, free enterprise, and the "American way." But this is an orthodoxy of ritual rather than of practice. In their actions businessmen pragmatically advocate state intervention today and restraint of the state tomorrow, a deviation from consistency by no means without its justification. To catalog all the actions of government

---

Business: Threat to Democracy (New York: Exposition Press, 1953); Edward S. Mason, *Economic Concentration and the Monopoly Problem* (Cambridge: Harvard University Press, 1957).

that mix into business and all the projections of business into government would require an encyclopaedia. A few categories of public policy will illustrate the broad theme that business regulation involves in considerable degree the mediation of intergroup cleavages created by the rise of industrialism.

Resistance to labor legislation. For a half century or more a central concern of organized business has been legislative proposals calculated to improve the lot of labor. These proposals—originating in the main from organized labor—have been a prime factor in bringing business competitors together in organizations for common defense. It would not be unfair to say that most of the major types of labor legislation have been, at least in their earlier stages, opposed with vigor by most business organizations. And the political role of business in this field has been in the main to delay rather than to prevent action. Once it loses the battle, business gradually learns to live with the new order.[9]

In its opposition to public intervention in the relations between employer and worker, organized business had the tactical advantage of being the defender of the orthodox political and economic doctrines. Individual rights over property, individual freedom, and individual responsibility pervaded the laws. New laws violated the ancient truths, or so it was argued. A workman's compensation act, for example, would make an employer financially responsible for injuries suffered by a worker through his own obtuse carelessness around obviously dangerous machinery. A ten-hour law would deprive both workers and employers of their freedom to fix by contract a longer workday. Unions indulged in practices that would limit the liberties of both worker and employer.

The wall of business resistance was first breached in situations in which strong humanitarian appeals could be brought to bear. Legislation to compel the elimination of hazardous conditions in factories came early as did industrial accident compensation laws. Laws limiting the hours of work of children preceded acts to prohibit child labor. On these and other related topics states enacted considerable legislation, but it was not until the Great Depression that advocates of labor legislation made spectacular headway. The 1929 crash and its aftermath drove business for a time from its dominant position, and new legislation radically altering the relations of business and labor came into being. Of all this legislation, that guaranteeing to labor the right to organize and imposing on business an obligation to bargain most significantly altered the structure of the social system. After the revision of this legislation by the Taft-Hartley Act of 1947,

[9] See R. E. Lane, *The Regulation of Businessmen* (New Haven: Yale University Press, 1954).

organized business and organized labor maintained a stalemate, each capable of preventing the other from bringing about changes in the statute. Yet there should also be mentioned laws fixing maximum hours and minimum wages, establishing systems of unemployment insurance, and a variety of other measures, all made politically possible by the depression and constitutionally legitimate by the new reading of the Constitution by the Supreme Court in the shadow of crisis.

Policy on monopoly and competition. The development of giant business organizations in a setting of economic individualism has made salient in American politics issues of monopoly and competition. Often the advocates of the application of public restraints against big business have been smaller businesses injured by the competitive tactics of the giants. The task of politics has been to achieve some more or less just balance between such groups. The consuming public, although never well organized, may also be regarded, at least symbolically, as a party to the political disputes involving the place of business within the economy.

The orthodox general public policy on monopoly and competition is clear enough. The Sherman Antitrust Act of 1890 declared contracts, combinations, and conspiracies in restraint of trade among the states illegal. The Federal Trade Commission Act of 1914 made unfair methods of competition in interstate commerce unlawful. On the whole, business proclaims the soundness of the principles of free, competitive enterprise, yet at almost every session one business group or another implores Congress to grant exceptions to the general proscription of combination. These prayers have brought results in numerous instances, and the politics of administration of antitrust legislation also produces variations in the impact of the law.

One class of exemption from antitrust policy is sought fundamentally to legalize arrangements to minimize competition. A striking instance occurred in the congressional debates from 1948 to 1950 over the question of policy toward basing-point pricing. Actions by the Federal Trade Commission, upheld by the Supreme Court after long litigation, had brought collusion in pricing through the use of the basing-point system within the prohibitions of the Clayton Act. The application of this principle to the cement industry stirred uneasiness in other industries with basing-point systems. (When used for collusive price-fixing, the system involved the publication of prices at basing points, which were usually producing points, and an understanding among producers that the price at any consuming point would be the nearest basing-point price plus freight to that point. A contractor would have to pay exactly the same amount for a barrel of cement whether he bought it from the plant across the street or from one 200 miles away.) A great hue and cry followed from business groups using the system to the effect that the law was uncertain, that it had become illegal to compete through the absorption of freight, that the bureaucracy was persecuting business. In fact, the law was a bit too certain. Nothing in the decisions prohibited the absorption of freight, in the absence of collusion to fix prices, and if bureaucracy was persecuting business it was doing so in the fulfillment of its sworn duty. Although the proponents of the exemption bill pushed it through Congress, the President vetoed it.[10]

In their campaigns for congressional approval of deviations from the antitrust principle, business groups can often so befog the issue that the interests at stake cannot be identified in the confusion. In 1945, for example, Georgia's Governor Arnall initiated antitrust actions against certain railroads, with the charge that prevailing rate-fixing combinations discriminated against the South and the West. The Association of American Railroads initiated a campaign to win the court case by persuading Congress to exempt railroads from the antitrust laws if their rate-fixing agreements were approved by the Interstate Commerce Commission. The AAR urged the necessity of legalizing long-standing practices of conferring in the fixing of rates; the matter was too intricate and complex to be left to the free play of competition. Between New York and Chicago, for example, traffic could be moved over 884 routes comprised of various combinations of 55 railroads and six water lines. To assure fair rates, or so the argument ran, carriers had to have rate conferences. The agreed rate structures in existence tended to freeze the prevailing geographical distribution of trade and industry and prevented shippers from receiving the full advantage of the lower costs of the most economical routes. At least that was the contention of southern and western critics of the railroads. The AAR carried the day; it lined up in support of the bill other associations the mere listing of which required 15 pages of small type. Yet in all the debate and discussion great confusion prevailed over precisely what was at stake.

In another category are modifications of antitrust policy designed to limit the exercise by large enterprises of their competitive advantage over lesser businesses. Important in this type of legislation are acts designed to maintain established channels of distribution, that is, to protect wholesalers and retailers against new and stronger competitors. Illustrative is the Tydings-Miller Act of 1937, an act adopted at the behest of retailers, principally druggists, to exempt certain price-fixing arrangements from the prohibitions of the Sherman Act. Associations of druggists had long

[10] For an account of the basing-point controversy, see Earl Latham, *The Group Basis of Politics* (Ithaca: Cornell University Press, 1952).

sought to limit competition by department stores and other price-cutting outlets and had boycotted manufacturers whose products were available to retail price cutters. The druggists hit upon the idea of the state fair-trade law which permitted manufacturers to contract with retailers to fix retail prices on their products; that is, it was not only "unfair" but could be made illegal for the chain druggist or the department store to sell Pond's Cold Cream at a lesser price than the neighborhood drug store.

These state fair-trade laws were held illegal as applied to goods sold in interstate commerce, and the National Association of Retail Druggists took the lead in pressuring Congress to grant an exception to the antitrust laws, which it did by the Tydings-Miller Act. The druggists enlisted the support of the National Association of Retail Grocers, the American Book Sellers Association, the National Automobile Dealers Association, and the National Association of Manufacturers. Department stores, mail order concerns, and cut-rate retailers generally were unable to amass sufficient strength to defeat the druggists. Once the act had been passed the druggists advised manufacturers to fix a minimum markup of 50 per cent over cost; various associations attempted to coerce manufacturers to fix the prices to the satisfaction of retailers. The actual effects on prices were most marked in large cities where on many drugs and related products, such as cosmetics and baby foods, prices charged by chain and department stores rose while prices in independent stores declined. A secondary effect, which ultimately threatened to undermine the law, was the rise of discount houses, called to life by the opportunity to make easy profits under the umbrella of high fixed prices.[11]

Another instance of legislation concerned with competition in distribution is the Robinson-Patman Act, which arose from the competitive pressures placed on wholesaling by chain stores and other mass distributors who could bypass the traditional distributive channels. By dealing directly with the manufacturer the mass distributors not only diverted business from wholesalers; they also obtained price concessions that put their retail competitors at a disadvantage, a factor not unconnected with the independent retailer support for the bill. Counsel for the United States Wholesale Grocers' Association drafted the original bill, but the propaganda presented the measure, not as a wholesalers' measure, but as a boon to the small, independent retailer, an individual high in the affections of the American politician. The legislation as enacted recognized the justice of differentials in prices by manufacturers to different types of customers but also sought to prevent mass distributors from abuse of their power of bargaining with manufacturers. In effect, Congress estab-

[11] See *Report of the Federal Trade Commission on Retail Price Maintenance* (1945).

lished a broad principle to guide the Federal Trade Commission in the mediation of the conflict among manufacturers, wholesalers, retailers, mass distributors.[12]

All these are merely episodes in the continuing process of mediating between bigness and those groups affected or threatened by it. The conflicts arise on many fronts and in many forms. Nor is the problem solely, or even primarily, a legislative problem, for questions of competition and monopoly are fought out before the administrative tribunals and the courts in the general policy framework fixed by whatever Administration is in power.

Regulation by license. Another field of government regulation may be conveniently defined by its administrative technique. In several important areas of the economy enterprises operate under license, permit, or a certificate of public convenience and necessity granted by state or federal authority. Commonly specified conditions must be met to obtain and retain the right to do business. As the new technology developed some types of enterprise turned out to be, or at least to be thought to be, natural monopolies. The protection of consumers from monopoly power was sought by conditional licenses—for example, a municipal franchise to a gas company might fix rates and other conditions of service.

Although the technique of regulation itself is irrelevant here, special types of political behavior seem to be associated with regulation by license. Genetically the animus of this sort of legislation is to control monopoly, but it may also create monopoly or semimonopolistic rights. Business groups may become vocal defenders of some aspects of the regulation to which they are subjected; they favor the obstacles to new entrants to the field inherent in the regulatory process. Furthermore, those enterprises subject to a regulatory statute have a deep concern about the administrative regulations issued under it. In a sense, regulation tends to breed pressure groups. All those subject to a regulatory law share a concern about the substance of the law and the manner of its administration and they organize to articulate that common interest. Moreover, rivalry between different groups of businesses operating under different regulatory statutes often takes a political form in that each jealously watches the range of action permitted to the other.

The enterprises that operate under license issued in one form or another by federal, state or local governments are mainly public utilities. They include most types of transportation, railroads, buses, truck lines, air transport. Important energy sources are on the list: producers and dis-

[12] For an illuminating analysis of legislation on distribution, see Joseph C. Palamountain, Jr., *The Politics of Distribution* (Cambridge: Harvard University Press, 1955).

tributors of electric power, gas distributors, interstate gas transmission lines, hydroelectric generators operating under license from the Federal Power Commission. Financial institutions such as banks, insurance companies, savings and loan associations, and credit unions exist under state or federal charter. Communications concerns, telephone, radio, television, telegraph operate under public permit which carries with it both privileges and responsibilities. Systems of proration in the production of petroleum have a kinship to regulation by license. State control of horse racing and race-track gambling is usually exercised through licensing.

The patterns of business politics induced by the licensing technique differ somewhat with the type of industry concerned and with the stage of development of the industry and its regulation. In the early stage of the development of television, for example, individual promoters maneuvered for licenses, that is, for the grant of a privilege of considerable value since the technical circumstances are such that only a few TV stations can be located in a single locality. As individual rights become settled, the TV industry as a whole develops a common interest and a common front in dealings with the Federal Communications Commission and Congress on matters of policy affecting the industry.

For some industries a major advantage accrues through the restriction on entry to the business that is incidental to regulation. Usually at the initiation of regulation all firms in the business are granted certificates of public convenience and necessity; newcomers have to negotiate an administrative hurdle to go into business and often the hurdle is high. Highway transport, for example, long resisted the initiation of regulation, but important elements of the industry saw the possibility of eliminating "cutthroat" competition by a restriction of entry to the business and by the fixing of rates by public authority. The major airlines similarly grew under the protection against competition from new lines afforded by the regulatory procedure and they have defended their sheltered position with determination against fringe competitors such as the nonscheduled carriers. Established banks similarly use their influence to discourage the chartering of new competitors. In all these and other similar lines of business, regulation with the aim of advancing the public interest can readily be subverted to promote the interest of the regulated.[13]

Occasionally the conditions under which regulated enterprises are permitted to do business restrict them unduly in their competition with another group of businesses. The legal standards that limit intergroup rivalry become the subject of political dispute. Thus, New York's bank-

---

[13] See Walter Adams and Horace M. Gray, *Monopoly in America, Government as Promoter* (New York: Macmillan, 1955); Marver Bernstein, *Regulating Business by Independent Commission* (Princeton: Princeton University Press, 1955).

ing law has limited the number of branches that savings banks might establish—a restriction placing them at a disadvantage in competition with the commercial banks in the growing suburbs. In 1953 savings bankers sought legislative relief but the commercial bankers wielded a superior influence in the legislature. In 1954 the commercial bankers again manned the lobbies in defense of the status quo and in 1956 they were still blocking the legislative proposals of the savings bankers.

Truckers and railroads compete for traffic but they also compete politically over the terms of public regulation. Federal regulation of trucking was not unwelcome to the railroads, for it was supposed that with the fixing of the rates for truckers their competition for traffic would become less keen. A running battle seems to be maintained between the Association of American Railroads and the trucking associations over questions of regulation. In 1955 the Presidential Advisory Committee on Transportation Policy and Organization advocated legislative changes which the railroads regarded as advantageous. The truckers claimed that the adoption of the recommendations would serve only to tie the hands of motor and water transport and to permit the railroads to indulge in discriminatory rate making and unfair competition. At times the state capital is the arena for the railroad-trucker conflict and the issue may be the permissable length or weight of trucks or the level of truck taxation.

Subsidies and services. Business manifests an odd ideological ambivalence. Almost any session of a major business organization will at one point endorse a resolution denouncing government bounty and at some later stage it will express discontent with the services rendered to industry by government. It may even resolve that the national defense or some other worthy objective justifies a subsidy for this or that business endeavor. And there may indeed be such a justification.

Subsidies appear in a variety of forms. Direct subsidies, simple payments from the treasury, are relatively few. Subsidies to shipping remain a prime example. Subsidies to airlines were for a long time concealed in mail payments and in costs of airports and aids to air navigation. Programs for the stockpiling of defense materials, while not in form subsidies, tend to guarantee a market for producers of some imperishable commodities. Government insurance or guarantee, as of home mortgages, may be a subsidy and attract the strongest support of the industrial groups affected. Legislation for accelerated tax amortization has from time to time resulted in heavy subsidies—interest free loans—to those concerns fortunate enough to obtain certificates under the laws. The protective tariff, of course, amounts to a subsidy, at least under certain conditions.

A business group may naturally regard with a cold eye what it considers a subsidy for a competitor. The railroads, for example, manifest no ardor for river-and-harbor appropriations. The railroads, the coal operators, and the United Mine Workers, thus, staved off the St. Lawrence Seaway for many years. Electrical utilities decry, and perhaps exaggerate, the subsidy element in public hydroelectric power as "creeping socialism," but they can reconcile themselves to the acceptance of an almost free, perpetual supply of energy at the hands of a government that permits private development of falling water.

Taxation. A surface agreement prevails among business groups on tax policy. All of them believe that taxes are too high. That agreement dissolves instantly when the question arises of what changes ought to be made in tax policy. The Chamber of Commerce of the United States and the National Manufacturers Association have long advocated greater reliance on sales taxes and a lesser dependence on income taxes, a view probably widely held among business organizations though exceptions do exist. The National Retail Dry Goods Association has opposed sales taxes.

The extraordinary complexity of the tax system—with particular excises on particular commodities, with tariffs on individual items, with other types of taxes limited to specified types of business–operates to create a differentiated interest among many groups in tax legislation. Truckers (who often enlist the Teamsters' Union in their cause) pressure legislators to keep trucking taxes low (and to shift the burden of road costs to passenger automobiles). Movie theater owners seek reductions of the admissions tax. Distillers resist increases in the excises on spirits and brewers oppose beer taxes. As many groups as there are specific duties on products maneuver to obtain favorable action. Associations of insurance companies are stirred by threatened changes in the taxes on their business. Petroleum companies defend the depletion allowance. One special privilege generates pleas for similar treatment for others. The complexity of tax legislation often makes the significance of individual changes beyond the understanding of all save a few experts, a circumstance that permits special treatment without great danger of public outcry.[14]

Complex linkage of government and business. These examples provide only meager suggestion of the nature of the tangle of relationships that has developed between business and government.[15] These relationships,

---

[14] See W. L. Cary, "Pressure Groups and the Revenue Code: A Requiem in Honor of the Departing Uniformity of the Tax Laws," *Harvard Law Review*, 68 (1954–55), pp. 745–780.

[15] Relevant is all the information a student may have acquired in courses in government and business.

complex and chaotic though they may be, add up to a working system in which organized groups, private centers of power, play a basic role. At times their leaders may be animated by the most stubborn and immediate self-interest. And it is easy to belabor them for their doctrinal inconsistencies. Yet in an order that permits wide ranges of freedom of action the actors are certain to come often into conflict. When the collisions of free groups produce intolerable damage to the public, the state intervenes to fix the rules of the game.

Spokesmen of Business

The foregoing recital of cleavages of interest within the business community conveys some conception of the diversity of political and economic objectives among business groups. The intricacies of political and economic relations create an endless number of clusters of firms, each with its own common concern and common enemies. Business is crisscrossed by divisions that set this category of enterprises off against that. The roster of business organizations reflects this diversity of business as well as the joining propensities of the American businessman. National and interstate trade associations, which consist of businesses in a single line of activity, number more than two thousand. Several hundred other nonlocal business associations, such as state chambers of commerce, have a broader membership than trade associations, while at least three thousand local business groups, such as chambers of commerce, exist. The Chamber of Commerce of the United States attempts to speak for the nation's business as a whole.

Almost every line of industrial and commercial activity has its association. The enumeration of a few organizations will suggest their variety: the American Petroleum Institute, the National Coal Association, the Associated General Contractors of America, the National Canners Association, the Distilled Spirits Institute, the American Cotton Manufacturers Association, the National Lumber Manufacturers Association, the American Iron and Steel Institute, the American Newspaper Publishers Association, the National Fertilizer Association, the Automobile Manufacturers Association, the Pin Manufacturers Institute, the National Retail Dry Goods Association, the American Federation of Retail Kosher Butchers, and the American Bankers Association.

Obviously these and hundreds of other business associations differ widely in their size, resources, and objectives. Some of them have staffs and budgets of considerable size, whereas in others one man manages a stable of associations. Some organizations are short-lived; others have existed for over 75 years. Nearly every organization claims to represent its industry as a whole, yet in almost half of them nearly 50 per cent of the cost is borne by a handful of members. Most business associations center their objectives on the narrow interests of their industries. The National Terra Cotta Manufacturers Association concerns itself with a far narrower range of public policy than does the Chamber of Commerce of the United States.

Most of the organizations perform functions other than public education and political activity. They exist for the exchange of technical information. They conduct research. Some trade associations appear to have been formed mainly to limit competition in one way or another. Nearly all business associations represent the industry before legislative committees and other public authorities when public action is desired or when public action threatens to impinge unfavorably on members of the association.

Chamber of Commerce of the United States. The most conspicuous spokesman for business is the Chamber of Commerce of the United States. It is a federation of other business organizations—state and local chambers of commerce, trade associations, and societies of businessmen not organized for private purposes—over three thousand in all. Unlike trade associations which may only incidentally be concerned with public policy, the major function of the Chamber is to speak for American business on issues of public policy. It cannot, however, take a stand on all issues of concern to all types of business. Its policy declarations are on matters "national in character, timely in importance, and general in application to business and industry." Given the conflicts of interest on particular issues among the diverse membership of the Chamber, it can speak with forthrightness chiefly on those broad issues on which business as a whole, or at least two-thirds of those voting at the annual meeting of the Chamber, have a common interest and a common view. On some issues it often takes a vague position, not unlike many planks in party platforms; on others, it is silent. The Chamber cannot fight, say, the issues peculiar to the rolling pin manufacturers, but must attempt to limit itself to issues of general concern. The necessity of seeking a formula acceptable to all on general issues sometimes gives the Chamber's pronouncements a tone of statesmanship—that is, a consideration of the interests of the nation as a whole—in sharp contrast with the attitudes of organizations that promote the narrow interests of a homogeneous industrial group. By the same token the Chamber has its internal disputes about the issues on which it shall speak. Its constituent groups attempt to commit it to the defense of their special cause. Thus, in 1956 the chemical industry successfully maneuvered to postpone action on policy recommendations in support of United States participation in the Organization for Trade Cooperation.

Policy proposals of the Chamber are in most instances adopted by the annual meeting on the basis of committee recommendations. These proposals, which remain in effect for three years, are codified annually for the information of all concerned. The annual collection of Chamber pronouncements fills a booklet of 150–175 pages.[16] So comprehensive a statement cannot be readily summarized but random excerpts will indicate its tone. The Chamber regards itself as "wholeheartedly committed to private enterprise in preference to government enterprise." While the Chamber does not reject all government interference in the economy, it generally urges the reduction of the scope of government control and opposes the initiation of new controls. With fair consistency the Chamber pleads for states' rights. The "dual system" of banking, involving the preservation of state-chartered banks, the Chamber argues, should be retained. Congress should not encroach upon state authority to establish water rights in interstate streams. Forest control should not be made solely a federal responsibility. With respect to education federal "financing inevitably leads to federal control. To avoid the one, we must and do vigorously oppose the other."

On labor policy the Chamber subscribes "to the right of employees to organize and bargain collectively whenever such action is the result of their own free and uncoerced choice." It opposes the union shop and advocates prohibition of sympathetic strikes and the outlawing of mass picketing. It contends that monopolistic practices by labor organizations should be subjected to legal controls just as employers are restricted. It argues for responsibility of labor organizations for injuries to persons and property through breach of contract or other unlawful acts.

The Chamber recognizes the circumstances that make high taxes necessary and admonishes its members to restrict their own requests to the government for services. It proposes a constitutional limitation on the taxing power of Congress "after adequate public hearings upon its possible scope." It urges a gradual reduction of the corporation income tax and the eventual elimination of the tax upon capital gains. On the tariff the Chamber speaks somewhat ambiguously: "a constructive and realistic tariff policy which will encourage the maximum flow of international trade but which at the same time will afford reasonable protection for American producers against destructive or otherwise unfair competition from abroad."

Although the annual meetings of the Chamber serve as sounding boards for the views of business, its work is not limited to these sessions. It maintains a staff at its headquarters in Washington to conduct research to serve as a basis for the deliberations of its committees and to make

---

[16] See the current year's pamphlet, *Policy Declarations of the Chamber of Commerce of the United States* (Washington).

known the views of organized business to Congress and to administrative agencies. Its committees analyze issues as they arise.[17] Its publicity staff prepares news for release to the daily press and to specialized journals. Its official organ, *Nation's Business*, presents the Chamber's views to the membership and to the public. During congressional sessions its staff follows closely the work of Congress and keeps the membership informed on legislative developments.[18]

National Association of Manufacturers. One of the most articulate organs of business is the National Association of Manufacturers, formed in 1895 to promote the cause of trade and commerce by aiding in the passage of legislation and by other means.[19] Like the Chamber of Commerce, this association has a heterogeneous membership and must concentrate its efforts on those matters in which its membership has common cause. Yet since the NAM has a much narrower membership than the Chamber, it is a more zealous and hard-hitting organization. Probably the greatest source of cohesion for the Association is an antipathy to organized labor, though this has become less marked as the decades have gone by.

After 1932, when the question of the place of organized labor became more salient, the NAM exerted itself in a propaganda campaign to sell to the public the symbol of "free enterprise," a most important component of which was opposition to increased power of organized labor. The fact seemed to be that a relatively small number of employers financed and used the NAM as a vehicle to resist the rise of labor strength. For a time the views of the NAM were so extreme that it probably had only a negative influence on legislation; its endorsement of a bill might be a kiss of death. "Of 38 major legislative proposals enacted into law between the years 1933 and 1941, the NAM opposed all but 7." [20]

Important elements of the NAM eventually concluded that they could not win the country to its point of view, and gradually the professed policy on labor was altered. The Association shifted to the position that collective bargaining could be tolerated under certain regulations and limitations. Even that shift involved sharp dissension within the NAM;

[17] In any good library the student will find several shelves filled with the publications of the Chamber.

[18] For an analysis of the work of the Chamber, see H. L. Childs, *Labor and Capital in National Politics* (Columbus: Ohio State University Press, 1930). An analysis of Chamber policies and views in the 1920's has been made by J. W. Prothro, *The Dollar Decade* (Baton Rouge: Louisiana State University Press, 1954).

[19] On some of the earlier political activities of the Association, see H. H. Wilson, *Congress: Corruption and Compromise* (New York: Rinehart, 1951), ch. 2.

[20] A. S. Cleveland, "NAM: Spokesmen for Industry?" *Harvard Business Review*, 26 (1948), pp. 353-371.

in 1946 a minority of the NAM board, representative of large and power-ful industries, "favored outright repeal of the Wagner Act, the Wage and Hour Act, and the Norris-LaGuardia Act." [21] The NAM finally conceded that government might intervene in labor-management relations and then contended for limitations and procedures on the bargaining process. In the Taft-Hartley Act 1947 Congress adopted largely, but not completely, the lines of action urged by the NAM. In the succeeding years the NAM met labor's demands for relaxation of restrictions of the Taft-Hartley Act, with proposals of its own for tighter limitations on labor in the bargaining process.

NAM spokesmen usually take a gloomy view of the trend of events as they expound their gospel. In 1955 its president told the assembled NAM at its Congress of Industry that the United States was "well on the way to the achievement of a Communist state as blueprinted by Marx." This standard doctrine is spelled out in campaigns to sell the NAM viewpoint on specific matters. Thus, in 1954 the NAM pushed a campaign against the guaranteed annual wage which was being advocated by the United Auto Workers. In 1955 it distributed literature on its tax program in which is set out its criticisms of existing policy and its proposals for change. They included a reduction of the progression in the income tax, the adoption of a manufacturer's excise tax, and a reduction in the rate of tax on corporate income. In 1954, of the NAM budget of $5,500,000, slightly over $2,000,000 went for a public information program.

Other business-wide organizations. Though the Chamber of Commerce and the NAM are the most conspicuous spokesmen for business, other organizations articulate other shades of opinion within the business com-munity. One of the more important of these is the Committee for Eco-nomic Development, incorporated in 1942. The CED represented a sharp departure in its outlook from that of the NAM. It seems evident that a group of business leaders came to the conclusion that both big business and big government were here to stay, that the policy of obstruction which had characterized the more vocal organs of business was self-de-feating, and that business had a responsibility to propose rather than merely oppose. The CED undertakes to develop through "objective re-search and discussion" recommendations which will contribute to main-tenance of employment, increasing productivity and living standards, and greater economic stability. It attempts to bring about public understand-ing of its recommendations to these ends but leaves the lobbying to others.

[21] R. W. Gable, "NAM: Influential Lobby or Kiss of Death?" *Journal of Politics*, 15 (1953), pp. 253-273.

With the aid of a research advisory board composed of leading economists, the CED studies problems it regards as of national interest. On the basis of these studies, committees of business executives struggle with the issues of policy and formulate recommendations. The Committee's attempt to fuse the expertise of the economist with the outlook of businessmen has resulted in policy statements that contribute in a responsible way to the solution of broad economic issues. It may well be that the declining proportion of romanticism, that is, a belief that the clock could be turned back to 1925, in the policies of the older business organizations can be attributed to the precept of the CED.

From time to time promoters manage to enlist support in the business community for campaigns in fierce advocacy of extreme viewpoints. Old business organizations tend to develop decorous manners. Other, more or less one-man organizations, give vent to the accumulated frustrations, the deep anxieties, the sharp animosities, and the partisan inclinations of some businessmen. In the 1930's the Liberty League, a club of disillusioned millionaires, fought the New Deal with more zeal than effectiveness. In the 1940's the Committee for Constitutional Government carried the torch. Its stated function was "educating the public on principles of constitutional liberty and economic freedom." Few of the policies of the New Deal and Fair Deal seemed to coincide with these principles, and the Committee's educational campaigns had a habit of intensifying at times of presidential campaigns and of concentrating in districts and states represented by "liberals." The Committee operated in effect as an unacknowledged auxiliary of the Republican party. The magnitude of the Committee's work is suggested by the fact that in a period of about four years it mailed from eight to ten million pieces of literature under the frank of friendly Congressmen. It thereby saved itself over a quarter of a million dollars on postage costs.[22] Many of the backers of the Committee could be found in 1957 lined up in support of the Campaign for the 48 States, an organization that sought, among other things, to limit the federal power of taxation and thereby to make futile lobbying for "Socialist" causes such as aid to education.

Diversity and unity. Although different segments of business are often arrayed in opposition, these fissures within the business class do not prevent the maintenance of an impressive business solidarity on broad political questions. The differences between shipper and carrier, between

[22] A goodly number of the most extraordinary reactionary propaganda organizations have been able to feed on business contributions. At times it has seemed that surely there was no crackpot who had failed to find a group of businessmen willing to support his "educational program" or to sponsor him as a radio commentator.

manufacturer and distributor, and between businesses of different regions are fought out in continuing skirmishes, but on the larger issues these differences tend to be subordinated to a greater unity.

One factor in the maintenance of this broad class unity consists in the disciplinary power of business organizations. The tendency of groups to develop norms of conduct and to bring the membership into conformity finds no clearer exemplification than in the workings of business groups. Although nonpolitical in their aims, they impose a partisan orthodoxy on their members far more effectively than do trade unions. The regimentation of the trade association, the board of directors, the Rotary Club, the chamber of commerce, or the country club brings the deviant into line with the political mores of the group—or at least keeps the dissenter quiet. Only the most hardy soul would express Democratic views at a session of the NAM.

Moreover, the operation of business associations—and of the hierarchies of corporations—creates a network of relations that ties together the scattered business leadership of the country. It is almost as if the business leadership were in a continuous political caucus. Conventions, committee sessions, board meetings, and corporate staff conferences, with their interlocking and overlapping memberships, build a system of face-to-face relations knitting the business community together. The airplane and the corporate expense account bring literally thousands of businessmen into conference every day, and they in turn have their relations back home with the less mobile elements of the business community. Such a communications system permits quick dissemination over the country of the views of the bellwethers and results in an almost continuous mobilization of business for political action.

Quite apart from the conformity induced by the fear of the frowns of one's fellows, pecuniary relations within the business system may be employed to repress dissent. The concentration of business in the large corporate organization establishes a large number of dependency relations (deposits in banks, retainers for attorneys, orders for suppliers, advertisements for newspapers, and the like) which may be used to purchase acquiescence or to penalize deviation. Or let a vulnerable manufacturer espouse unbusinesslike views, and he may discover that he has become an undesirable credit risk and that his customers are seeking other sources of supply. The intricate network of relationships within business creates mechanism for punishment as well as reward. Yet so effective is the system of business indoctrination that the cruder sanctions rarely need to be applied.

Business and Public Opinion: Aggression and Restraint

The politics of business involves far more than lobbying for or against legislation and mixing into election campaigns. Businessmen are a small minority highly vulnerable to political attack. They labor under serious political handicaps. They lack the strength of numbers. Moreover, their position lacks the moral authority that inheres in the cause of the sturdy agrarian yeomanry or the horny-handed toiler of the factory and foundry. To protect the broad status of business and to advance its cause businessmen have to depend on something other than their votes. They have to use their wits—and their money—to generate a public opinion that acquiesces in the enjoyment by business of its status in the economic order.

The politics of business, thus, must encompass a range of activity outside the limits of that ordinarily denominated as political. One phase of this activity includes aggressive attempts to mold the attitudes of both the general public and special publics. To gain public favor business associations and corporations employ in large numbers public-relations experts, those masters of the verbal magic that transmutes private advantage into the public good. While propaganda to win friends for specific legislative proposals or to make enemies for schemes opposed by business is important, of more fundamental significance is the continuing propaganda calculated to shape public attitudes favorably toward the business system as a whole or toward particular types of business. The assiduous dedication of effort to the capture of public favor lays a foundation of good will on which business groups may build in their efforts to obtain particular legislation or to obstruct undesired governmental actions.

The necessity of courting public favor carries with it, however, another type of business political behavior—at least if we define political broadly enough. The possibility of molding public opinion to conform with business ideologies has its limits, and a concern with public attitudes may compel business groups to alter their policies so that they can be sold to the public. Self-restraint, induced by anticipations of environmental reaction, may change the policy of the business group, particularly those groups dominated by a few concerns. The pursuit of some business policies, it may come to be recognized, will result in disfavor and perhaps in the eventual adoption of regulatory legislation at the behest of injured groups. The threat or possibility of governmental action may alter business behavior into a pattern more readily defensible in the forum of public opinion.

Early disregard of public opinion. Intense and continuing business concern about public attitudes is a comparatively recent development. The new industrial giants emerged from a competitive order in which the individual businessman, beset by competitors on all sides, exercised little power over his fellow man. Under these conditions a man's business could be genuinely his own private affair. No pressure of expediency or social necessity suggested the relevance of the doctrine that private business was clothed with a public interest. The older business attitudes persisted into the changed situation created by the revolution in the organization of business. Early corporate leaders held to the old doctrines and cared little what the public thought of them or of their industries. Moreover, the men who built up the great corporate concerns were often ruthless. The erection of great enterprises required men sturdy enough to suppress competition and skillful enough to build combinations, men who in another day might have been the barons, chieftains, and war lords. Then, too, they were engagingly frank. Witness the testimony of Henry Havemeyer, sugar refiner, in the 'nineties:

Senator Allen. . . . If you fix the price at 4 cents for granulated throughout the United States the others obtain it, don't they? And in that way the price is controlled.

Mr. Havemeyer. We undertake to control the price of refined sugar in the United States. That must be distinctly understood.

Senator Allen. And the price of refined sugar in the United States is higher to the American people in consequence of the existence of the American Sugar Refining Company than it would be if the different companies in your organization were distinct and independent companies?

Mr. Havemeyer. For a short time it is.

Senator Allen. And what difference does it make for the consumers in this country in a year, in your judgment?

Mr. Havemeyer. It has been in three years past three-eighths of a cent more on every pound they ate, as against doing business at a loss.

Senator Allen. And that would be about how much in round numbers?

Mr. Havemeyer. It is a large sum in the aggregate.

Senator Allen. How many millions?

Mr. Havemeyer. I should say it was close to $25,000,000 in three years.

Senator Allen. And you intend to keep your hold upon the American people as long as you can?

Mr. Havemeyer. As long as the McKinley bill is there we will exact the profit.

Senator Allen. Is that the result of the McKinley bill?

Mr. Havemeyer. We should not have achieved it without the McKinley bill; but a great deal of the profit is due to these men in consequence of combining the different interests and the skill and labor attending it.[23]

[23] Senate Report No. 606, 53rd Congress, 2nd sess. (1894), pp. 337–338.

Mr. Havemeyer's candid views were not exceptional: they represented a widespread attitude among business leaders who took the position that the public be damned. In some formulations, they advocated almost a doctrine of divine right. Thus, an executive of the anthracite mining industry in 1902 asserted that the rights of the laboring man would be protected, not by labor agitators, "but by the Christian men to whom God in his infinite wisdom has given control of the property interests of the country. . . ."

Toward the cultivation of public favor. After 1900 the political difficulties of the expanding corporate enterprise multiplied. Prosecutions of the trusts, investigations of the practices of big business, and the public resentment of bigness brought a gradual recognition by private business that it was no longer really private; that public favor had to be cultivated; that a concern for the general good, whether genuine or not, had to be manifested. Ivy Lee, the first of the great public-relations counselors, opened shop in 1903. He and his imitators found clients aware of the new trend of events, and eventually every corporate executive had at hand an advisor on public relations.

The public utility executives were among the first to set about systematically educating public opinion. Their industry had an exceptional political sensitivity and operated under the necessity of attempting to mollify those sectors of the public whose discontent might quickly be converted into demands for tighter regulation. President Vail of the Bell System in 1913 expressed the new viewpoint:

All industrials, particularly utilities, are face to face with problems, the solution of which will largely determine the future of the business; they are, in the last resort, subject to a control and regulation far stronger than that exercised by commissions or by legislators, that influence and power that makes and unmakes legislator and judges; the influence and power of public desire and public selfishness, which if not regulated or controlled will lead to chaos and disaster. The only regulation or control for this is that common sense which, directed by education and observation, and rightfully administered and regulated, will conserve the interests of all.[24]

The American Telephone and Telegraph Company's devotion of careful attention to its public relations paid off handsomely in the long run. It became our largest nonfinancial corporation, a natural target for political attack, and virtually a national monopoly. Yet it weathered the New Deal without ill results; its store of public goodwill made it an

[24] N. E. Long, "Public Relations Policies of the Bell System," *Public Opinion Quarterly*, October, 1937, p. 18.

unlikely object for attack by crusaders.[25] Lest the marvels of public relations be overestimated, it ought to be remembered that good service contributed to the goodwill enjoyed by the Bell System.

The public-relations specialist did not come into his own until after World War I, during which governmental propaganda agencies impressively showed the power of propaganda over the people. With this demonstration before them, industrialists more generally undertook to create a favorable context of public attitudes and business associations planned and executed large-scale programs of public education. One of the greatest efforts was by the National Electric Light Association, a group that later dissolved when the magnitude of its propaganda program became generally known. The rationale of its program, and indeed of most organized efforts to mold public opinion, was stated in 1925 by B. J. Mullaney, a utility leader:

I am fairly familiar with legislative practice and procedure and have not many illusions in that quarter. Sometimes the political road has to be traveled. When a destructive bill is pending in a legislature it has to be dealt with in a way to get results. I am not debating that. But to depend, year after year, upon the usual political expedients for stopping hostile legislation is shortsightedness. . . . In the long run isn't it better to lay a groundwork with the people back home who have the votes, so that proposals of this character are not popular with them, rather than to depend upon stopping such proposals when they get up to the legislature or commission? [26]

Business associations and individual corporations pursue their own objectives in public relations, yet it appears that beginning in World War II business interests more and more utilized their public-relations resources for the dissemination of political ideology. Particular objectives, particular legislative proposals, and short-term campaigns for this or that objective became overshadowed by an almost overwhelming propaganda of doctrine. With their unfortunate experiences with the New Deal behind them, with no goods to sell, with high tax rates which made advertising relatively inexpensive, corporations began to advertise ideology on a large scale. The popular periodicals carried advertisements pointing to the merits of the "American way" and to the virtues of free enterprise as well as now and then to the iniquities of socialism. The exploits of business under free enterprise were praised and the great achievements of American business in production and technology were publicized. The

[25] See Richardson Wood, "The Corporation Goes into Politics," *Harvard Business Review*, 21 (1942–43), pp. 60–70.

[26] Federal Trade Commission, *Summary Report . . . on Efforts by Associations and Agencies of Electric and Gas Utilities to Influence Public Opinion*, Sen. Doc. No. 92, Pt. 71A, 70th Cong., 1st sess. (1934), p. 17.

services of this or that corporation to scores of communities and the bounty that flowed from the corporation to its suppliers over the country were chronicled.[27] In this advertising a common ideological theme dominated: a theme of free enterprise, of "the American way," of the essential goodness of business. It was made to appear not only impertinent but unpatriotic to suggest that American business might have its blemishes. Under the circumstances of the decade in which the ideological permeation of corporate advertising occurred, business propaganda, if it had any influence at all, could have redounded only to the benefit of the Republican party.

While the gross impression from the propaganda programs of business may have been one of salience of political philosophy, campaigns to mold public opinion on particular policies probably gained strength from the saturation of the media with advertising calculated to sell ideas rather than merchandise. Thus the National Association of Electric Companies and associated groups took up the burden of selling the cause of the private utilities after the utility industry reached its nadir in public favor with the passage of the Public Utility Holding Company Act of 1935, the initiation of the TVA, and the construction of government-owned generating plants. All these measures were predicated on the need for regulation of an industry that enjoyed a monopolistic position that could be, and was, abused. Over a period of 15 or 20 years the propaganda campaigns of the association implanted a new image of the utilities in the public mind. Eventually proposals to limit federal hydroelectric power, criticisms of the Rural Electrification Administration, or advocacy of a higher return to the utilities were regarded as respectable doctrine rather than as favoritism toward utility magnates.

Although no careful analyses have been made of the effects of business campaigns to mold public attitudes, the utility campaign may suggest some clues. Sustained campaigns over long periods of time, through the power of repetition and through the shortness of public memory may have a marked effect on public attitudes. Further, the importance of campaigns politically may rest primarily in the fact that they may create a climate of opinion in which the propagandizer's political friends can act in his behalf without putting themselves in an indefensible position. Thus, in 1935, say, proponents of government "partnership" with private

---

[27] F. X. Sutton and others, *The American Business Creed* (Cambridge: Harvard University Press, 1956); L. I. Pearlin and M. Rosenberg, "Propaganda Techniques in Institutional Advertising," *Public Opinion Quarterly*, 16 (1952), pp. 5–26; M. H. Bernstein, "Political Ideas of Selected American Business Journals," *Public Opinion Quarterly*, 17 (1953), pp. 258–267; J. H. Bunzel, "The General Ideology of American Small Business," *Political Science Quarterly*, 70 (1955), pp. 87–102.

utilities would have brought down on their heads outraged cries of a sellout. In the 1950's, after over a decade of propaganda and after other factors had also had their effects, public reaction to advocacy of the utility cause by politicians seemed to be far less hostile.

No simple measure can readily be devised of the effects on public attitudes of the heavy expenditures of business associations and corporations to shape the public view on political issues and ideologies. Obviously large sums are completely wasted. Yet the chances are that the cumulative impact over the years is imposing. The great political triumph of large-scale enterprise has been the manufacture of a public opinion favorably disposed toward, or at least tolerant of, gigantic corporations, in contrast with an earlier dominant sentiment savagely hostile to monopolies and trusts. That fact is of fundamental importance in the workings of the American political system.

Feedback from public opinion. The relations of business and public do not amount simply to a one-way transmission of propaganda in which business and its public-relations specialists mold an infinitely malleable public. Business attempts to manipulate public opinion; but business itself —especially big business—is, within limits, manipulated by a public opinion beyond its control. As industrial power grew and the conscious policy of managing public attitudes to retain that power came to be adopted, big businessmen underwent a curious metamorphosis. They came to act like politicians; or, as they termed it, they became industrial statesmen. Similarly, they became sensitive to public criticism and they planned their major policies and decisions with a sharp eye to the anticipated public reaction. And, like politicians, their decisions have come to be influenced by the anticipated public reaction. The doctrine that corporate office is a public trust was promulgated; and to it, at least at times, more than lip service was paid.

Mr. Eugene Holman, president of Standard Oil of New Jersey, put the matter in this way:

There is another powerful influence on the policies of large-scale operations. Companies today are very largely influenced—and necessarily so—by public opinion. I believe the controlling force of public opinion is not always realized by some of us in this country. But the fact is that no management today— especially no big company management—can successfully develop its policies and practices without a keen awareness at all times of the public interest.[28]

The skeptic who insists that Mr. Holman's observations amount to nothing more than pious window dressing errs. Businessmen adopted his

[28] Eugene Holman, *The Public Responsibilities of Big Companies* (Standard Oil of New Jersey, 1948), p. 4.

view as they learned the consequences of ignoring public reactions and as they saw the limits on the management of public opinion. The public-relations experts soon discovered that their artistry could not make a business managed by scoundrels smell sweet; a clean-up job had to be done before they could do their work. It is apparent that many types of business behavior are influenced by "public opinion." Even pricing decisions, in the short run at least, may be so influenced. In some lines large concerns manifest solicitude for their small competitors; they are at least insurance against antitrust prosecutions. And, on occasion, the monopolist prudently seeks out another firm to share the market for the same purpose. Policies on labor matters and on production practices likewise bear the imprint of public reaction. Beyond such matters of internal management, the efforts of individual concerns and of business associations to mold public attitudes on broad political questions quite often are affected by judgments of existing public attitudes and predilections. The occasional internal commotions leading to shifts in the leadership of business associations have at times been battles over policy toward a public that had shown itself unmoved by the older policies of the association.

It would be absurd, of course, to make too much of the sensitivity of business to public opinion. Moreover, "industrial statesmanship" seems to be most notable among those firms, monopolistic or semimonopolistic, that both need to cultivate public favor and can afford to do so. In a truly competitive industry of many small firms the industry has no mechanism by which it can act as a unit to remedy the "abuses" of the industry or to take positions in response to public criticism. Nevertheless, in some types of industry the hovering spook of "public opinion" may be on hand at the directors' meetings to cast the deciding vote.

Accountability of Centers of Private Power

The substance of the preceding chapter suggested general observations about the existence of private governments within the social system. There the contention was that the governing process, if adequately defined, includes the workings of many centers of group power not ordinarily regarded as political. These power nuclei guide human behavior on a variety of matters and at times apply sanctions which may be harsh indeed. Professional societies promulgate standards of conduct and on occasion penalize nonconformers by deprivation of the right to practice. Labor unions may determine whether a man can get a job, as well as the manner in which he shall work; they may also in some circumstances exert almost a power of life and death over employers. And all private associations, from the Farm Bureau Federation to the American Legion, affect the attitudes of their members on questions of public policy and, to varying degrees, restrain the expression of dissent.

The materials of this chapter identify additional centers of private power: business associations and giant corporations. At times business associations, especially when they restrain trade, exercise potent sanctions to hold the members in line, and they may also affect the community as a whole for good or ill. While in the field of political and legislative action it is the business association that is most visible, it is probably comparatively insignificant in its social power alongside the 100 to 150 giant corporations that dominate American business. Corporations are, of course, far more tightly knit institutional entities than, say, the American Farm Bureau Federation or the Chamber of Commerce of the United States. They differ from associations or pressure groups, but their achievements in the organization of human effort endow them with power in relation to persons within the organization, with respect to their suppliers, their distributors, their customers, the communities within which they operate, and to the workings of the economy generally. Not only do they exercise power; they perform in a sense a public function. They are run, to be sure, to make money. Yet so essential is the proper management of their affairs to the public welfare that they tend to be clothed with a public purpose. Their shortcomings cannot be left, as in the fabled economy of atomistic competition, to be cured by the beneficent workings of the bankruptcy statutes. The bankruptcy of General Motors, if so improbable an event could be imagined, would be a public disaster. Nor can it be assumed, as the classical economist would have us believe, that the great corporation is kept sterile of power by a subordination to the forces of the market. Although the workings of these structures erected by organizational genius are only dimly understood, it is clear enough that corporate decisions have effects far beyond the factory gate.[29]

These observations, which constitute the merest suggestion of the variety of types of private centers of power, provide a backdrop for comment about another broad question of politics, namely, the problem of accountability of private centers of power. The American political tradition abhors irresponsible power, be it in private or governmental hands. Our political processes provide procedures for enforcing an accountability of those who hold public authority; they also provide, willy-nilly, ways and means, often tortuous and nearly always sluggish and cumbersome, for bringing to a reckoning those who abuse private power.

[29] For a stimulating essay on the emerging political role of the modern corporation, see A. A. Berle, Jr., *The 20th Century Capitalist Revolution* (New York: Harcourt, Brace, 1954). See also David E. Lilienthal, *Big Business: A New Era* (New York: Harper, 1953).

The freedom to build up private power complexes—be they huge corporations, business associations, labor organizations or what not—has as its reciprocal accountability. Hierarchies of private authority are a great convenience in the management of the affairs of mankind but they can be tolerated only so long as there is an ultimate accountability. Autonomous, private exercise of authority over matters of general concern becomes a dispensable luxury unless the assigned social purpose is fulfilled, an adequate observance of "due process" occurs, and only a few toes are stepped on. In a way, the drive for freedom in the exercise of private power on grounds that this promotes the public weal concedes an ultimate accountability. Businessmen probably have not thought this one through, for their exuberant estimates of what business can do if unrestrained may well intensify the severity of the enforcement of accountability when business performance sags below promise.

Under many circumstances the holders of private power may operate only in accord with statutory standards, but the phenomenon that excites attention at the moment is the enforcement of accountability outside the formal governmental processes. That phenomenon, often inchoate in form, rarely patterned in recurring sequences, highly variable in its efficacy, and erratic in its incidence, cannot be described in simple terms. Yet the informal enforcement of responsibility of private centers of power may well be one of the fundamental differentiating characteristics of a free society. Lest the entire idea of such accountability be dismissed as an imaginary construct, it is proper to raise such questions as: Accountability to whom? Accountability for what? Accountability by what means?

Nominally the holders of authority in private governments are accountable to their respective groups: the corporate management to the stockholders, the labor union hierarchy to the members, the pressure group leadership to its dues-paying constituency. Yet nothing seems clearer than the proposition that the internal political processes of organizations tend to be inadequate even to protect the rights of members of the groups themselves much less to take into account the interests of the larger public in the operations of governing centers of private groups. Corporate stockholders can go to court to obtain redress against abuses of power by corporate officers, but probably more significant in the protection of their immediate interests are the operations of informal controls developed outside government in the reporting requirements of the stock exchanges, in the probings of the security analysts, and in the pressures from institutional investors—all of which thrust corporate management into a gold-fish bowl. From time to time arbitrary and corrupt union leaderships oppress and exploit union members, a state of affairs which is beyond prevention by internal political processes of the union.[30] External controls must come into play to restrain abuses internal to the group.

The processes by which private centers of power are held accountable to their own immediate constituency scarcely touch the broader question of accountability for group actions with effects beyond the boundaries of the organization itself. The mechanisms by which this responsibility to the "public" is enforced, short of explicit governmental intervention, are diverse in form and effectiveness. It has long been evident that in the narrowly political sphere the power of some groups may be neutralized or held in check by the opposing power of other groups. Professor Galbraith has noted the workings of the same "countervailing power," as he christens it, in the economic sphere. The public may be protected from monopolistic or quasi-monopolistic control over prices by the rise of competing centers of power with capacity to bargain in the market place. Chain stores, for example, have a power to cope with the manufacturer; their ultimate sanction is to develop their own source of supply. Labor organizations rise to combat, in the labor market as well as in politics, the power of large employers. All the relations of conflict between great groups outside the government may, of course, seep over into political conflict. The efficacy of countervailing power, as Professor Galbraith points out, differs in different sets of circumstances and at different times. Yet in some situations a system of checks operates totally outside the public government to restrain the powers of private government.[31]

The broad conception of countervailing power is that the giants pit their strength against each other and the public incidentally benefits from the resulting balance or stalemate. Another more nebulous but pervasive mode of enforcing accountability of the holders of private power is by the vague but nevertheless real force of public opinion. Those who make decisions of public import tend to take into account the squawks their actions may evoke. Adolph Berle, an exceptionally well-informed observer, concludes: "Hardly any present-day board of directors or corporation management would take the position that it could afford to dis-

---

[30] Perhaps a safe prediction would be that legislation in function not unlike that governing the rights of corporate stockholders will ultimately develop to protect the union member.

[31] See J. K. Galbraith, *American Capitalism* (Boston: Houghton Mifflin, 1952). Critics of the doctrine of countervailing power believe that the doctrine, if regarded too seriously, might lead to the erroneous conclusion that it is only necessary to stand back and let the inevitable processes of countervailing power operate to protect the general weal. See George W. Stocking, "Saving Free Enterprise from its Friends," *Southern Economic Journal*, 19 (1953), pp. 431–444; Walter Adams, "Competition, Monopoly and Countervailing Power," *Quarterly Journal of Economics*, 67 (1953), pp. 469–492.

regard public opinion—or would last very long if it did." [32] Moreover, corporation managements spend money to discover the state of public opinion. One such business-supported inquiry concluded that the public, though it appreciated the productive skills of big business, had a "distaste for big business's power or misuse of power over the worker, the competitor, the consumer or other societal institutions." [33]

What goes on in the minds of corporate directors as diverse factors struggle for primacy in decision is rarely a matter of public record. Though the weight of "public opinion" in the process can only be conjectured, it is doubtless not uniform. The impact of public opinion is far more visible, although not necessarily more effective, in the actions of business associations, labor organizations, and other such groups. The reflections that occur to the leaders of such groups are suggested by the remarks of the chief of the Brotherhood of Locomotive Engineers about the AFL-CIO merger which he viewed with disfavor: "If there is one thing this country will not tolerate it is dictation to it by any power which seriously threatens the sovereignty of the nation itself." The greater the power, he said, "the smaller the area of unrestricted activity. The United States Bank learned this to its sorrow in the Nineteenth Century. The railroads still are learning it." Similar estimates of the price of a hostile public opinion doubtless have moved national labor leaders to attempt to clean up malodorous situations in some unions. A common sort of visible deference to public opinion consists in the trimming of legislative demands toward forms that are less likely to be generally regarded as outrageous. Even such brass-riveted outfits as the NAM and the AMA eventually modify their positions in the light of public reaction.

The inner guides of norms and conscience may be of greater significance in steering the behavior of the controllers of centers of private power than are sanctions of "public opinion" or the fear of hostile counteraction from other groups. Leaders of private groups are, after all, of the culture and sharers in its broad values. "It seems to me almost axiomatic," says Crawford H. Greenewalt, president of du Pont, "that, over the long stretch of corporate life, no business can prosper unless it serves the public interest in all of its many facets." Nor does he view the growth of the size of business units with alarm "for the pressures of society will inevitably produce their own controls and stabilizers. These pressures for the preservation of a particular moral code are great indeed, particularly in the area that has been called 'obedience to the unenforceable'—

[32] *The 20th Century Capitalist Revolution*, p. 56.
[33] Burton R. Fisher and Stephen B. Withey, *Big Business as the People See It* (Ann Arbor: Survey Research Center, 1951), p. 20-22. For another set of similar findings, see Elmo Roper, "The Public Looks at Business," *Harvard Business Review*, 27 (1949), pp. 165–174.

the things we do, not because they are required, but because they are right. This strength is much more potent and compelling than the law." [34]

Leaders of great business enterprises have their own ideas of the public interest, just as the rest of us do, but the important point is that they have a notion of public interest. Moreover, a comparison of Mr. Greenewalt's comments with Mr. Havemeyer's, quoted earlier in the chapter, suggests the radical change that has occurred in the viewpoint of business leaders over the past half century. While the world cannot be governed by relying on everybody to follow his own rules of fair play, the existence of private aggregates of power within the realm is more likely to be tolerable when a disposition toward "obedience to the unenforceable" prevails.

More tangible than these factors in its influence on the holders of private power is the threat of state intervention which could deprive them of their authority or regulate the manner of its exercise. The policies of private power centers are not infrequently modified to ward off new legislation. On occasion, so great is the sensitivity to the threat of public action, that a speech on the Senate floor may have about the same effect as would the enactment of a statute. Modifications of private practice to avert state intervention are perhaps most noticeable in great corporations which have within themselves the power to act to that end. Looser types of organizations, such as trade associations, professional societies, and labor federations, are deficient in the capacity to bind their members to action in avoidance, although the threat of state intervention may induce efforts to do so.

The broad point of these few pages has been that, within limits, private centers of power have an accountability, beyond that to their immediate membership, for the exercise of their authority. A few illustrations of the nature and mode of enforcement of this accountability have been set out. The identification of this type of behavior, which clearly exists, should not be confused with an estimate of the frequency of its occurrence or with its importance in the entire process of governance. Often private power seems to know no restraints of its own. At some times these informal modes of accountability are more potent than at others. Nevertheless the operation of a society that permits the accumulation of great aggregates of power in private hands requires the existence of informal modes of control and of enforcement of accountability. When those informal methods of holding to account fail, government must move in and exercise its formal power of coercion.[35] The price of freedom of centers of private power is their own behavior in the general interest.

[34] In a speech before the Bureau of Advertising of the American Newspaper Publishers Association, April 26, 1956.

[35] See A. T. Mason, "Business Organized as Power: The New Imperium in Imperio," *American Political Science Review*, 44 (1950), pp. 323-342.

5 | Other Interest Groups

FROM THE discussion of organizations resting on economic foundations it might be deduced that a group theory of politics is essentially a
theory of economic determinism. Under that theory it might be reasoned:
A steel industry exists; therefore an American Iron and Steel Institute will
exist and it will have predictable views about public policy. If a steel
industry exists, the chances are good that something on the order of the
Institute will exist, but what its views will be is not so predictable. Group
views are not cleanly cast from the matrix of economic circumstance;
they are hammered out by internal group debate and conflict. Moreover,
to equate a group theory with a theory of economic interest is to ignore
the many groups whose endeavors have only the most tenuous economic
basis. The Anti-Defamation League, the Americans for Democratic Action, the National Catholic Welfare Conference, the League of Women
Voters, the Daughters of the American Revolution, the American Cor-
rectional Association, and the American Friends Service Committee can
all raise quite a commotion and, under propitious circumstances, influence
public policy.

Obviously all sorts of groups that affect public policy have fundamental similarities; one common denominator is that the members of each group possess shared attitudes. These attitudes may or may not be related to the economic interest of the members of the group. Even if they are, they do not seep naturally in a predetermined form from a given set of circumstances. They develop somewhat unpredictably in the processes of interaction—the give-and-take—among the members of the group. Thus, many years ago the American Medical Association took a benign attitude toward health insurance proposals. Then gradually it swung around to the most spirited opposition in response to the shifting balance of power in its own internal politics.

In his group theory Professor David B. Truman holds that shared attitudes, not property, income, or other material concern, constitute group "interests."[1] If one adopts this conception of interest, the Izaak Walton League is as much an interest group as is the Gray Iron Founders Society. The members of each group share attitudes which underly its offensive excursions and defensive maneuvers in relation to government and to other private groups. Under this theory of the nature of interest and the associated conception of group as a condition of interaction among persons with shared attitudes (or a common interest), an interest group need not possess the apparatus of formal organization to carry weight in the political process. Even though no group machinery exists, politicians will take into account and seek to exploit the common attitudes of the home owners, the suburbanites, the good people of eastern Oregon, or the fine citizens of downstate Illinois. More commonly, of course, organization does exist and an executive secretary and a board of directors see that group attitudes are translated into resolutions and communicated to the points of decision.

The conception of group interest as shared attitude also permits one to take into account certain other aspects of politics that escape us if the notion of group is limited to organized group. Among the population are many categories of people with like attitudes but these classes of persons are quiescent politically and do not technically constitute groups. Once interactions develop among these people—communications, discussions, reactions, responses—an operative, although not necessarily an organized, group comes into existence and affects the balance of strength among groups already in being. These groups, called to life by events that activate the latent attitudes of their members, Professor Truman calls "potential" groups. A new highway, say, is to be routed through a residential district. The citizenry concerned are activated; the potential group

[1] For a statement of the essentials of his theory of the nature of groups, see David B. Truman, *The Governmental Process* (New York: Knopf, 1951), ch. 2.

quickly becomes a reality and its executive committee builds a fire under the state highway commission. Or a bill that appears to be a big steal seems about to be passed by the legislature. Mass meetings are called, indignant editorials appear, delegations call on the governor; a quiescent or potential group, based on a shared attitude of hostility toward thievery, becomes a reality for the duration of the crisis and then may lapse back into mere potential.

The idea of interest group that has been set out has sufficient breadth to include all the organizations dealt with earlier. It also covers others that have less of an economic base. Thousands of groups make themselves heard in the affairs of local, state, and national government. To catalogue all pressure organizations would be a task of census-like proportions. Their variety may be suggested by brief mention of several classes of groups before moving into the analysis of those groups treated at some length in this chapter.

One category of groups consists of those concerned with the scope and nature of public activities or with the nature of public regulation. Although commonly a pressure group moves the government to act (or not to act), at times organized groups come into being after the government has acted. The beneficiaries of governing activities are likely to be alert and insistent in presenting their recommendations on appropriations and legislation. Examples are the National Rivers and Harbors Congress, the National Reclamation Association, the National Rehabilitation Association, the Mail Order Association of America, and the National Rural Electric Cooperative Association. Similarly, groups may be concerned chiefly with the character of particular regulatory or tax measures. Organizations of public employees at times wield a powerful influence. Consider the capacity of postal employees in dealing with Congress or the successes of associations of firemen and of policemen in gaining privileges quite difficult to defend on grounds of equity.

Women are banded together in diverse groups with a concern about public policy. The League of Women Voters has a long record of lobbying in support of governmental measures ordinarily in the general interest, and the American Association of University Women has been active on some issues. The General Federation of Women's Clubs has stood for such proposals as the elimination of roadside billboards. Women, as women, have few common political interests, and, hence, women's organizations often have difficulty in finding issues in which their members have a joint concern and in avoiding issues that generate schisms. Women's groups with a multiclass membership maintain unity on only the most innocuous matters. Women's groups with a class membership, however, can push for sharply defined objectives without threatening their unity. Witness the Daughters of the American Revolution and the Women's Trade Union League; both are militant organizations but each tends to be representative of a single class.

Another differentiation among groups may be noted. Some groups— most of those discussed in earlier chapters—are permanent organizations that act from time to time as public issues arise of concern to their members. Another sort consists of organizations created, *ad hoc*, to agitate for or against specific proposals; they are usually fairly short-lived. They often serve to mobilize or to co-ordinate the efforts of several permanent associations with a common concern about legislation. Illustrative are the National St. Lawrence Project Conference, the National Committee for Repeal of Wartime Excise Taxes, and the National Committee to Defeat the Mundt Bill.

Pressure organizations are also clustered about state and local governments. Each state capital has its own complement of representatives of organized groups within the state. Often the division of functions between national and state government is paralleled by a division of spheres within a federated national private organization. The American Medical Association takes care of matters in Washington, while the state medical societies handle problems of states legislation and politics. State manufacturers' associations, state labor federations, state chambers of commerce, and other organizations are further examples.

A few of this miscellany of groups may be profitably subjected to brief analysis. Their prominence on the national scene justifies attention to veterans' organizations, religious groups, associations concerned with foreign policy, and professional associations. Consideration of their operations will also permit allusion to some patterns of behavior that are characteristic of many other groups.

Veterans' Organizations

"The American idea of war," said Thomas B. Reed, Speaker of the House, in 1897, "is to take the farmer from his plow, and return him to his plow—with a pension!" [2] Every war has been followed by the establishment of a society of veterans to bring pressure for the creation of conduits from the Federal Treasury to the pockets of the veterans. Yet it may be a fair question whether the pension objective is the basic cohesive element in veterans' organizations. Deeply etched recollections of shared experiences that set the soldier apart from the civilian undoubtedly cement such groups together, though their preoccupation with bonuses, pensions, and like matters is their most conspicuous characteristic.

[2] Quoted by Nicholas Murray Butler, *Across the Busy Years* (New York: Scribners, 1939), Vol. 1, pp. 298–299.

Grand Army of the Republic. Of organizations of old soldiers, the greatest, until the American Legion, was the Grand Army of the Republic, which consisted of Union veterans of the Civil War. The GAR played a peculiar role in American politics. About three million persons served in the Union armies in the Civil War. Normally they would be expected to be adherents of the Union, later known as the Republican, party. The political affiliations of the GAR membership and its sectional concentration gave the pension issue an especial appeal to Republican politicians. Pension appropriations would in most instances reach Republican hands and, in turn, would cement the Civil War veteran more thoroughly to the Republican party. The loyalties of northwestern war veterans, assured by pension legislation as well as by the Republican homestead policy, must be given a place among the factors which for many years held together the divergent interests of eastern finance and western agriculture within the Republican party.[3]

In form the GAR followed a policy of nonpartisanship but its relations, clandestine and not so clandestine, with the Republican party were both intimate and numerous. The nonpolitical façade of the organization permitted it to attract those of Democratic inclination. Once they are in the ranks, an Indiana GAR leader observed, we must quicken within "them a lively sense that those who fought and saved this country by force of arms are the same men who now try to uphold it by peaceful means with the same sentiment." In all gatherings of the old soldiers, he concluded, "the Republican party is indirectly benefited." Republican politicians had a hand in the formation of the GAR and, in turn, GAR politicians became Republican politicians. On occasion, Republican party committees subsidized the good works of GAR leaders among the old soldiers. The alliance of the GAR with the GOP is said to have been of special significance in the election of 1888 when the pension issue was sharply drawn between the parties. Cleveland had aroused the animosity of the veterans by vetoing certain pension legislation; the Republicans nominated Harrison, an old soldier. In Indiana, where the pension issue received a strong play, Republican speakers went about "representing Cleveland as an inhuman monster and Benjamin Harrison as an angel of mercy carrying a purse hanging mouth downward." Whether the GAR vote decided the election, the Harrison Administration proceeded to give the soldiers what they wanted to the accompaniment of considerable maladministration in the pension office.[4]

[3] The Confederate veterans looked to their state governments for pensions and consequently southern Democrats viewed coolly proposals for federal pension legislation.

[4] For a discerning study of the GAR, see Mary R. Dearing, *Veterans in Politics*

American Legion. The success of the GAR in extracting money from the Federal Treasury has been greatly overshadowed in magnitude by the operations of the American Legion. Formed after World War I, the Legion soon achieved a membership of around one million, or about one-third of those eligible for membership. It gave promise of eventually disappearing with the death of its generation of veterans, but a new crop of veterans came with World War II. The Legion's vigorous campaign to recruit younger veterans enabled it to claim a membership of over 2.5 million in 1956.

The Legion is organized in local posts, which are grouped in state legions, all capped by the national organization led by the National Commander. Legion policies are formulated at annual conventions, colorful gatherings that became somewhat more sedate during the interwar years with the advancing age of World War I veterans. During the interim between conventions the National Commander and the executive committee, with the aid of a staff of over two hundred at national headquarters, carry out Legion policies. The Legion constitution provides:

> The American Legion shall be absolutely non-political and shall not be used for the dissemination of partisan principles nor for the promotion of the candidacy of any persons seeking public office or preferment. No candidate for or incumbent of a salaried elective public office shall hold any office in the American Legion or in any Department or Post thereof.

In the interpretation of this clause there is in practice no limitation on the Legion in the promotion of public policy. Like the Farm Bureau Federation or the National Association of Manufacturers, the Legion does not nominate or endorse candidates for public office; nevertheless, it reserves freedom of action in making its wishes known and in bringing its strength to bear on legislative bodies on questions of public policy. The nonpartisan policy serves the same function in the Legion that it does in other pressure groups: that is, it prevents division on questions of candidates for public office and at the same time permits the maintenance of unity on those issues on which Legion members possess a common interest.

Although the Legion has branched out and taken an interest in a wide range of public issues, one of its central concerns has been the hope for additional compensation, perhaps ultimately a general pension, from the Federal Treasury. In 1920 the Legion succeeded in persuading Congress to raise the monthly pensions for disabled veterans from $30 to $100 a

(Baton Rouge: Louisiana State University Press, 1952). See also D. L. McMurry, "The Political Significance of the Pension Question, 1885–1897," *Mississippi Valley Historical Review*, 9 (1922), pp. 19–36.

month. In 1924 came its first great success when it induced Congress to grant adjusted service compensation, or the "bonus," which was, in effect, a bonus to be paid with accrued interest in 1945. In 1931 the Legion was back again asking, successfully, that veterans be permitted to borrow on their bonus certificates. In 1936 legislation providing for immediate payment of the bonus was passed. In its bonus campaigns the Legion was able to drive bills through Congress over the vetoes of Presidents Coolidge, Hoover, and Roosevelt. In 1955, probably in an attempt to head off general pension legislation, the President appointed a commission, under the chairmanship of General Omar N. Bradley, to inquire into the matter and to make recommendations. The commission recommended a co-ordination of veteran benefits with the general system of old-age insurance, a proposal quickly followed by sharp and effective dissent from the spokesmen of the Legion.[5] In 1956 veterans almost won the virtual equivalent of a general service pension.

In the public mind the Legion is identified chiefly with the bonus and pensions, yet it has been interested in a wide range of legislation. At a recent session of Congress the Legion legislative committee pressed for action on 124 pieces of legislation. It ordinarily takes a nationalistic position on foreign policy questions and favors strong defense measures.[6] A matter of major interest has been the question of hospital facilities for veterans. This service was originally limited to veterans disabled in the course of military duty, but under Legion pressure eligibility for public hospital and medical care has been broadened toward public medical care for all who have served in the armed forces regardless of whether the need arises from service-connected causes.[7] Another important point in the Legion program has been veterans' preference in public employment, a demand that veterans be given preference with little regard to their ability in comparison with other applicants. Over one-half of all federal civilian employees are veterans.

A handful of Legion politicians controls its national policies and defines its legislative strategy. When necessary, though it rarely is, the Legion

[5] President's Commission on Veterans' Pensions, *Veterans' Benefits in the United States* (Washington, 1956).

[6] Roscoe Baker, *The American Legion and American Foreign Policy* (New York: Bookman Associates, 1954).

[7] About two thirds of Veterans' Administration hospital patients are nonservice-connected cases chiefly in the neuropsychiatric and tuberculous categories. The service-connected case load consists to an unknown degree of cases with a most improbable linkage of illness to military service. The connection is at times defined by statute rather than by medical science. In effect, social welfare legislation develops for veterans as a class under fictions of service-connection, a necessity that would not arise with more adequate social welfare programs for people generally.

leadership can squelch discussion and ram a resolution through its national convention along with the best of the high-handed. In 1955, for example, in the face of a recommendation to the contrary by a committee that had conducted a most thorough investigation, the Legion convention in thirty seconds adopted a resolution denouncing UNESCO. *Life* observed that the convention did not represent the Legionnaires over the country but "only the handful of kingmakers who run the national Legion as their private dictatorship." [8] The pronouncements of the national leadership certainly do not flow up from the local Legion posts, whose meetings are more apt to be dedicated to conviviality than to heavy thought about the global problems that agitate the national leadership. On the other hand, probably a selective process occurs in which those veterans attracted to activity in Legion posts are not unhappy with the line promulgated from Legion headquarters in Indianapolis. In any case a dissenting Legion post would probably soon be in trouble.[9]

The Legion is not exceptional in its control by a small oligarchy. In his general theory of groups, Professor Truman has christened the leadership cliques of private groups as the "active minority." [10] In all kinds of groups a comparatively small and energetic crowd grasps control of the group machinery and proceeds to manage it and to speak in the name of the group. In labor unions, in farm organizations, in churches, and in chambers of commerce leadership and management are concentrated in a few hands. It does not necessarily follow that the leadership is out of line with sentiment within the group or that the group processes are "undemocratic." Yet it is a fact of group life that leadership tends to fall into specialized, even professionalized, hands.

Within a comparatively narrow range of public policy the Legion exerts a formidable, if not invariably controlling, influence. How is this power of the Legion, a comparatively small group of activists, to be explained? Undoubtedly war veterans, especially those disabled in battle, have a special claim on their country. The general sentiment supporting that claim creates a favorable atmosphere for the pressure activities of the Legion.[11] Moreover, from a political standpoint, a matter of no small

---

[8] October 24, 1955.

[9] In 1946 the National Commander of the Legion opposed a veterans' emergency-housing bill; a New York Legion post held a rally to support the bill. Shortly afterwards the local post was suspended. See Justin Gray, "The Legion Under Control," *New Republic*, May 10, 1948.

[10] *The Governmental Process* (New York: Knopf, 1951), pp. 139–155.

[11] The Legion can direct a stream of telegrams and letters to Capitol Hill, but it remains problematic whether to vote against the Legion increases a Congressman's chance of defeat at the next election. In opposing a 1956 measure designed in reality to introduce a general service pension, Representative W. H. Ayres, of Ohio, a

importance is the fact that the Legion has no compact and determined counter-pressure group against which it has to work. If the AFL, for example, strikes out for legislation, its lobbyists will likely collide with those of the National Association of Manufacturers. The Legion, however, in its main endeavors encounters less determined opposition, although it has had brushes with the American Medical Association.[12] The big guns of big business do not go into action effectively against Legion forays on the Treasury, a circumstance that gives plausibility to the hypothesis that a tacit alliance prevails between business and Legion leadership. For business the quid pro quo is the generally conservative position of the Legion. On labor matters in particular, the Legion, not so much by its public pronouncements as by the activities of its members and local posts, has earned the reputation of being aligned with business.[13]

Other veterans' groups. Although the Legion has been the largest veterans' organization, other groups have maintained a separate existence. The Veterans of Foreign Wars, formed after the Spanish-American War, limits its membership to veterans who have had overseas service and thereby excludes the home-front soldier. The program of the VFW is a "bread-and-butter" program much like that of the Legion. One of its recent legislative programs, for example, included 91 items, a large proportion of which related to the enlargement or maintenance of veterans' perquisites. The Disabled American Veterans, a relatively small group, consists of persons with disability incurred in military service, a condition of affiliation that gives its legislative demands a special moral force.

After World War II the older veterans' organizations campaigned vigorously to enlist the new generation of ex-soldiers. In its past record the Legion had both an asset and a handicap in its membership campaigns. The Legion had consisted mainly of the more prosperous veterans of World War I. As a consequence its program on issues apart from narrow "bread-and-butter" questions had been conservative, if not reactionary.

---

veteran himself, opined: "You would be amazed at the pressure they can employ through various individuals, but I honestly do not believe that the commander of any post, whether it be the American Legion, DAV, AMVETS, or Veterans of Foreign Wars, controls any vote other than his own. Sometimes I think he has difficulty in telling his wife what to do." *Congressional Record* (daily ed.), June 26, 1956, p. 9960.

[12] The AMA has urged a narrowing of eligibility for Veterans' Administration hospital care. The Legion's response is that "only a selfish interest" gives rise to such a view.

[13] Justin Gray, *The Inside Story of the Legion* (New York: Boni & Gaer, 1948); Marcus Duffield, *King Legion* (New York: Cape and Smith, 1931); R. S. Jones, *A History of the American Legion* (Indianapolis: Bobbs-Merrill, 1946); Dixon Wecter, *When Johnny Comes Marching Home* (Boston: Houghton Mifflin, 1944).

It had shown little sympathy for labor unions. It had shouted for nationalistic measures and for national defense but had shown little awareness of the threat of fascism. This record stimulated those of contrary political inclinations to attempt to form new organizations to attract the veterans of World War II.

The two principal new groups formed were the American Veterans of World War II (known as Amvets) and the American Veterans Committee (commonly called the AVC). Both groups are small, but Amvets, a cautious middle-of-the-road organization, has attracted less public attention than the AVC. The small but lusty AVC has had the temerity to challenge the old and mighty Legion on issues of public policy. The Legion, for example, had high regard for the House Committee on Un-American Activities, whereas the AVC declared it to be an abomination. The AVC stands for "Citizens First, Veterans Second." An organization espousing so novel a doctrine could scarcely be 100 per cent American in the view of the older veterans' group. The new organizations made little headway in recruiting members against the competition of the entrenched groups, which did their utmost to discredit and to freeze out the upstart societies. Yet the existence of even small dissenting groups serves the useful purpose of reminding legislators that not all veterans agree with the top brass of the Legion.

Nonparty Groups and Foreign Policy

Interest groups, as was argued earlier, rest on the shared attitudes of their members which may or may not be associated with a common economic interest. In either case the basis of the group is the shared attitude and not the objective economic interest. People may have different attitudes about the same economic concern and those attitudes may change from time to time. An association, for example, comes into existence because its members share attitudes and not because, say, they all happen to be retail merchants. This differentiation between attitude and material interest as the basis of group may be regarded, from observation of pressure groups in domestic politics, as a semantic trick rather than as a perceptive insight. A look at the activities of pressure groups designed to influence American foreign policy, however, makes much more apparent the fact that shared attitudes are the building blocks of groups. Those attitudes may, to be sure, be about some objective economic concern but they may also rest on beliefs, aspirations, memories, prejudices, generosities, hatreds.

Groups with external interests. A feature of peculiar significance in the formation of American foreign policy is the role of groups of citizens who, in a sense, also belong to groups abroad that may be affected by American policy. The pursuit of national interest externally is at times profoundly conditioned by the necessities of maintaining political support at home. Support at home for policy abroad is always a necessity; the American circumstances merely complicate and enlarge the problem of contriving foreign policy that will not arouse domestic dissent.

Groups of particular national origin are often most sensitive about American policies affecting the homeland. These groups perhaps make themselves felt more effectively through the electoral process, a matter to be treated elsewhere, than by the activities of their pressure organizations. A Congressman from an Irish district can be counted upon to twist the lion's tail occasionally without prodding by the Ancient Order of Hibernians in America or by the American League for an Undivided Ireland.[14] The land abounds with Irish, German, Italian, Scandinavian, and Polish societies. Such groups do some lobbying, but the volatility of their electoral preferences assures a respectful consideration of their sentiments by politicians even without a reminder from the lobby.

Religious groups on occasion seek to bend foreign policy to the cause of their coreligionists abroad. In recent years the Zionist Organization of America and related groups have worked energetically to influence policy toward Israel and policy on the admission to the United States of displaced persons. On the other hand, the American Council for Judaism is anti-Zionist and challenges what it calls the Zionist claim to speak for all Jews. The Council claims to be neither pro-Israel nor pro-Arab but pro-American. On some issues Catholic groups have sought to mold foreign policy in the interest of the Church abroad. Thus, during the civil disorders in Mexico in Wilson's Administration, Catholic lay societies and some lesser clerics took a critical line toward the Administration's refusal to intervene in the insurrection to protect the Catholic interest.[15] Later Catholic groups concerned themselves about policies toward Franco's Spain. Protestant churches on occasion seek State Department intervention to obtain more favorable treatment for their missionaries in Catholic countries.

[14] Thomas R. Marshall recorded that as governor of Indiana he had cheerfully approved a bill to require that The Star Spangled Banner be sung in its entirety in the public schools. He later learned that the bill had been put through the legislature by the Clan na Gael; the Celts wished the anthem to be sung in full because one stanza gave the lion's tail "a vicious and nerve-racking twist."—*Recollections of Thomas R. Marshall* (Indianapolis: Bobbs-Merrill, 1925), pp. 126–127.

[15] J. M. Blum, *Joe Tumulty and the Wilson Era* (Boston: Houghton Mifflin, 1951), pp. 91–106. For an analysis of attitudes on foreign policy of a wide range of private groups, see Gabriel Almond, *The American People and Foreign Policy* (New York: Harcourt, Brace, 1950), ch. 8–9.

Nationalists and Internationalists. While most of the great interest groups —agrarian, labor, business—make some pronouncements on foreign policy, other groups give it a prominent place in their program, and still others exist solely to influence it. One broad class includes organizations whose programs have a strongly nationalistic tone such as the patriotic societies and the major veterans' associations. The American Legion, thus, has consistently supported the maintenance of a powerful military establishment as a foundation for American foreign policy. It supported universal military training, for example, from 1922 to 1940 when that cause had little popularity. While the Legion favored American adherence to the United Nations, it generally views international involvement with a cautious reserve and urges that the United States operate and negotiate from impregnable military strength. The Legion expresses a "vigorous opposition to the participation of the United States in any form of world government or federation." Among the patriotic societies the Daughters of the American Revolution is conspicuous in the bellicosity of its nationalism. Somewhat less formidable, but no less forthright, are the Sons of the American Revolution.[16]

Radically different in outlook are organizations with an internationalist orientation. The nationalist groups regard themselves as hard-headed judges of the iniquities of the world that dictate that foreign policy should be at heart the wielding of a big stick from a position of strength. The internationalist groups, on the other hand, have a greater faith that by negotiation, by organization, by striving in one way or another a degree of peace and order can be introduced into the world. When their efforts verge on utopianism, these groups attract their quota of crackpots, although it must be said that it requires a fine discrimination to differentiate between those in the crackpot fringe of internationalism and their opposite numbers among the isolationists.[17]

In the years between World Wars I and II, before the ascent of Soviet Russia to great power and before the atom bomb, the peace movement developed considerable momentum under the leadership of internationalist and pacifist organizations. Disarmament plans, the World Court, the outlawry of war, neutrality, imperialism, and the elimination of the profits of war were some of the questions debated. On all these matters the internationalist organizations conducted an influential propaganda and their efforts affected some lines of governmental policy. One of the largest

[16] For the background of these and other similar groups, see W. E. Davies, *Patriotism on Parade, The Story of Veterans' and Hereditary Organizations in America, 1783–1900* (Cambridge: Harvard University Press, 1955).

[17] These remarks make it relevant to observe that in the explanation of political behavior psychiatry is at times more useful than economics.

and most effective organizations was the National Council for the Prevention of War established in 1921 as a clearinghouse for 17 national organizations. The Women's International League for Peace and Freedom, a small organization but ably represented on the Hill, won major credit for the initiation of the Nye investigation of munitions, whose findings contributed to the adoption of the Neutrality Act of 1935 as well as to the wide dissemination of the conception of munitions makers as merchants of death.[18] The League of Nations Association, later reincarnated as the United Nations Association, advocated collaboration with the League of Nations before its demise.

These and other such organizations were paralleled by groups dedicated to the study of problems of international relations and to the dissemination of information. By and large, however, these groups contributed to the stream of agitation hopefully looking for some way toward a peace which was not to come.[19] In an odd way the internationalists and isolationists complemented each other. One could capitalize on the hatred of war to keep military strength weak; the other, by contending that noninvolvement in international affairs was both feasible and wise, made military readiness seem superfluous. The net result was American paralysis as the world moved toward war in the 'thirties.[20]

The battle of the committees, 1940–1941. The activities of pressure organizations in the formation of American policy in the period immediately preceding our involvement in World War II constitute a notable example of how the leadership of public opinion even on great issues may move from the political parties into the hands of nonparty groups. The making of foreign policy in a democratic state presents problems of special delicacy in that government, if it is to be popularly responsive, cannot diverge markedly from public sentiment. On the other hand, the public needs to be informed and presented with the alternatives if it is to form a judgment. Commonly these functions are regarded as duties of the party system. Yet at moments when great choices have to be made, the parties may be impotent. They may be neutralized by their own inner conflicts over the issues that confront the nation. Or initiative may be foreclosed

[18] See Dorothy Detzer, *Appointment on the Hill* (New York: Holt, 1948).

[19] For a review of the period 1918–1936, see Merle Curti, *Peace or War, The American Struggle, 1636–1936* (New York: Norton, 1936), ch. 9.

[20] The student of 1960 may not easily comprehend the beliefs prevalent in 1940 about the feasibility of isolation. A few weeks before Pearl Harbor, the *Chicago Tribune*, representative of a widespread and doubtless sincere opinion, said: "What vital interest of the U.S. can Japan threaten? She cannot attack us. That is a military impossibility. Even our base at Hawaii is beyond the effective striking power of her fleet."

to them for the reason that an exceptionally high degree of public agreement may be requisite for action on some questions.

The circumstances of the late 1930's conspired to transfer the burden of leadership and debate in the foreign policy field in considerable measure to two nonparty groups, the Committee to Defend America by Aiding the Allies and the America First Committee. The Committee to Defend America grew out of the Non-Partisan Committee for Peace through the Revision of the Neutrality Law. Under the legislation in force the hands of the government were virtually tied. To embargo the shipment of arms to China and Japan, for example, would have weakened China and done little damage to Japan, a result not believed at the time to be in accord with the national interest. In September, 1939 President Roosevelt asked Congress to repeal the legislation forbidding the sale of arms to warring nations and to permit cash-and-carry sales. To drum up support for this recommendation, persons associated with the League of Nations Association took the initiative in setting up the Non-Partisan Committee for Peace under the chairmanship of William Allen White. This committee of several hundred persons—Republicans, Democrats, businessmen, religious leaders—put in motion a propaganda campaign and members of the committee set to work on Republicans in Congress.

After the Nazi movement into Norway and Denmark, White and his associates took the lead in forming the Committee to Defend America by Aiding the Allies. As the crisis developed, local chapters of the committee sprang up over the country—300 by July 1, 1940, three months after the establishment of the national committee. As events marched the committee maintained close liaison with the Administration. Although it advocated no measure opposed by the Administration, it could hardly be called an instrument of the Administration. It pushed for speedy action; its leaders fretted about the inertia of the government. As legislative issues arose, it laid down a barrage of telegrams on Congress. It carried on an extensive propaganda to build up support for such measures as the transfer of destroyers to Britain. It sought to bring the 1940 platforms of both parties into line with its program.[21] Apparently the Administration moved more slowly than majority opinion. Events in Europe were more influential than the Committee's propaganda in shaping public opinion, though the Committee doubtless brought into sharp focus public sentiment in support of a series of concrete actions.

The America First Committee led the isolationist or noninterventionist cause. Formed in September, 1940, it became the spearhead for the diverse strains of opposition to involvement in the European war and was headed

[21] For an account of the work of the committee, see Walter Johnson, *The Battle Against Isolation* (Chicago: University of Chicago Press, 1944).

by General Robert E. Wood, chairman of the board of Sears Roebuck and Company. The national committee consisted of prominent persons from over the country but its strength appeared to center in Chicago. It ran a newspaper advertising campaign, sponsored radio broadcasts, and encouraged the establishment of local chapters to further its cause. America First took the line that Britain's war was not America's war. It opposed the passage of the Lend-Lease bill; the Chicago chapter obtained 628,000 names on petitions against this legislation. It proposed a national advisory referendum on the question of war. Although its leadership drew heavily from the ranks of conservative midwestern Republicans, the America First Committee was plagued by allies it did not seek. It excluded pacifists from its membership, but it had their support as well as that of Socialists. Nazis and Fascists, too, infiltrated the organization; mushrooming organizations are especially vulnerable to infiltration. The America First Committee defeated no major Administration foreign policy proposal in Congress but its mobilization of noninterventionist opinion affected the course of government action. Its efforts, Professor Cole concludes, "undoubtedly helped to discourage" the President "from moving further and faster to help Britain defeat Hitler." [22] Certainly the strident debate made governmental action in any direction difficult. The resolution of the issue came not from our internal political processes but from the attack on Pearl Harbor. Shortly afterward the America First Committee's final statement asserted: "Our principles were right. Had they been followed war could have been avoided." [23]

Whether the battle of the committees exudes any clear moral may be

[22] Wayne S. Cole, *America First* (Madison: University of Wisconsin Press, 1953), p. 198. An assortment of unsavory organizations also agitated against intervention. On their activities, see John Roy Carlson, *Under Cover* (New York: Dutton, 1943); Michael Sayers and A. E. Kahn, *The Plot Against the Peace* (New York: Dial Press, 1945).

[23] The two broad streams of sentiment represented by the competing prewar committees continue to flow in American politics. The broad internationalist position of the Committee to Defend America came to be the prevailing doctrine, but various pressure groups rose to urge particular viewpoints. United World Federalists in 1947-1951 attracted heavy support to its campaign for world government, which ebbed after the outbreak of the Korean incident. See Bernard Hennessy, "A Case Study of Intra-Pressure Group Conflicts: The United World Federalists," *Journal of Politics*, 16 (1954), pp. 76-95. While the nationalist position continued to have strong backing from veterans and patriotic organizations, it was also urged with virulence by many small organizations, which were often nothing more than business enterprises operated by individuals with a knack for exploiting the gullibility of mankind. A heavy strain of professional anti-Communism ran through these organizations as well as a somewhat lesser streak of anti-Semitism. For the beginnings of many of these groups, see D. S. Strong, *Organized Anti-Semitism in America* (Washington: American Council on Public Affairs, 1941).

doubted, but it does point to a special characteristic of the American party system as well as to the special problems of a foreign policy responsive to public opinion. Commentators on the American system often make the point that some types of great public questions are avoided by the parties and are settled, if they are settled at all, by the mobilization of sentiment by nonparty processes. When the parties fail the political system spawns other institutions to occupy the vacuum and to carry on the battle over the issue. Something on this order happened in the fight between the Committee to Defend America and the America First Committee. While perhaps a preponderance of Democratic national leaders leaned toward intervention and the weight of sentiment in the Republican leadership was isolationist, the parties as parties feared to take the initiative in what, either way, was a most perilous undertaking. In effect, the country found itself realigned under the leadership of the committees along a battle line different from that between the parties. The Committee to Defend America managed to form the more powerful following in this new alignment.[24]

Clergymen in the Lobby

Organized religion seeks, both through action by the church itself and by lay groups, to influence governmental action. The prominence of these groups on the political scene creates an obligation to mention them. Yet the fulfillment of that obligation even in the broadest terms is a most hazardous enterprise. The most innocent comment about religious groups can arouse the sharpest reaction. Critical comment easily becomes bigotry or even an irreverent challenge to the work of the Lord. All of which suggests that the currents of religion run so deeply in our politics that people prefer not to talk about the topic lest discussion set off debates over questions irreconcilable because they present, at least potentially, conflicts of divergent absolutes.

Religious organizations. Protestants, Roman Catholics, and Jews are represented by a variety of organizations that have at least an incidental concern about questions of public policy. These organizations differ radically in the scale of their activities, in their methods, and in the range of their objectives. Some maintain large staffs in Washington; others may dispatch a man to Washington occasionally. Some eschew lobbying and limit themselves to public education; others make the strongest representa-

---

[24] Another instance in which private associations obtained action by Congress on a matter difficult to handle by partisan initiative was the repeal of legislation excluding Chinese. See the analysis by F. W. Riggs, *Pressures on Congress* (New York: King's Crown Press, 1950).

tions to Congress. Some concentrate on a single issue; others express themselves on a broad range of questions.

Among Protestant agencies perhaps the most conspicuous is the National Council of the Churches of Christ in the U.S. of A., which was formed in 1950 by a merger of the Federal Council of the Churches of Christ in America and other organizations. The Federal Council had been formed in 1908 as a loose federation of Protestant denominations and had had as one of its broad objectives to "secure a larger combined influence for the churches of Christ in all matters affecting the moral and social condition of the people." The Board of Temperance of the Methodist Church maintains its headquarters across the street from the Capitol. Although it is noted chiefly for its earlier campaigns in support of prohibition, its interests range more widely in the promotion of "the public morals" chiefly by educational means.[25] The Women's Christian Temperance Union, founded in 1874, continues as an organization for agitation by Protestant women on the liquor question. The Friends are represented in Washington through the Friends Committee on National Legislation. The Congregational Christian Council for Social Action has a legislative committee with an executive secretary in Washington.

The National Catholic Welfare Conference, formed in 1919 by the bishops of the United States, has its headquarters in Washington. Most of its activities have no direct bearing on public policy, but its Social Action Department has a continuing interest in welfare legislation. The National Conference of Catholic Charities, established in 1910, gained respect from Congress in part because of its able representation by Monsignor John O'Grady. The National Catholic Rural Life Conference keeps in touch with legislation on rural matters and makes the Catholic view known to Congress.[26]

Churches and social welfare. In the terrain of legislation for social betterment, the major religious organizations, Protestant, Catholic, and Jewish, appear—at least to an eye untutored in the niceties of ecclesiastical differentiations—to push generally in the same direction. The clergymen seem to be men of good will disposed to advocate reforms, both by private action and by legislation, to improve the lot of mankind. The Social Action Department of the National Catholic Welfare Conference

---

[25] The Anti-Saloon League was, of course, far more important in the prohibition movement. On the techniques of this organization, see the pioneer study by Peter H. Odegard, *Pressure Politics, The Story of the Anti-Saloon League* (New York: Columbia University Press, 1928).

[26] A brief account of the organization and objectives of the principal Christian church lobbies is set out by L. E. Ebersole, *Church Lobbying in the Nation's Capital* (New York: Macmillan, 1951), chs. 2–4.

has favored such propositions as stable employment, the availability of employment "at not less than a family living income," limitations of hours of labor, collective bargaining "as a basic right of labor," legal minimum wage standards, security in old age, decent housing for all people, and other such matters.[27] Compulsory health insurance has had both Catholic and Protestant backing. On the Protestant side the Federal Council of Churches of Christ contended for the right of labor to organize long before it was popular to do so and has set out such goals as "the provision of decent housing and assured medical care, equal access to employment and other benefits of our society regardless of race and creed, the wider distribution of income and power." [28]

In the advocacy of these broad social goals Catholic organizations seem to proceed with considerably less dissension in their ranks than do the Protestants. This may not be entirely a matter of differing ecclesiastical organization. The much stronger representation of upper-income business elements in Protestant denominations accounts for some dissent from the social gospel program of the National Council of Churches of Christ. Small organizations claiming to represent affiliated local Protestant churches in opposition to the National Council come and go, and occasional spurts of lay criticism of the Council's policy positions occur.[29]

Friction among churches. While the churches push in the same general direction over wide ranges of public policy, on other questions they differ among themselves. Some of their less incendiary differences, but nevertheless differences posing vexing problems for politicians, are about questions of the law and moral policy. The prohibition movement and subsequent efforts to restrain the liquor industry by such methods as restriction on advertising have been primarily Protestant movements. Catholics, no less devoted to temperance, doubted that prohibition was an effective means to the end. On public policy towards lotteries and other forms of gambling, the Federal Council of Churches urges a strong stand against an evil that not only demoralizes character but visits its losses mainly "upon the poor." The Catholic position is one of condemnation

---

[27] See the statement of principles made in 1938 by Bishop Edwin V. O'Hara, chairman of the Social Action Department, quoted in full by Anson Phelps Stokes, *Church and State in the United States* (New York: Harper, 1950), vol. III, pp. 13–14. Canon Stokes' monumental work may be examined with profit by those with an interest in the politics of church-state relations. An annotated bibliography is included in Vol. III at pp. 769–836.

[28] *Ibid.*, p. 8, quoting a 1937 statement of the Council.

[29] See P. A. Carter, *The Decline and Revival of the Social Gospel: Social and Political Liberalism in American Protestant Churches, 1920–1940* (Ithaca: Cornell University Press, 1954).

of lotteries if carried to excess but under certain conditions a lottery is not to be condemned as immoral. In practice Catholic policy seems to vary from place to place; in some localities Catholic clergymen have raised a powerful voice against the legalization of lotteries and against other forms of gambling. In other localities the issue of legalization of bingo when conducted for the benefit of churches has divided Protestant and Catholic. Thus, in New York in 1955 the Protestant Council of the City of New York fought a proposal to permit bingo for the benefit of churches. The New York Board of Rabbis took a similar position and resolved that the raising of funds through bingo games would not be "in consonance with the high standards of morality and dignity which the synagogue sets for the general community."

On these questions of public morals religious issues may become quite warm, but far deeper cleavages develop on aspects of public policy that may concern a high-priority church policy or that may affect a church as an institution. Legislation bearing on the dissemination of information about birth control stirs up the sharpest controversy between Catholic and Protestant. Statutes and court actions on the weight to be given religious factors in adoptions excite acrimonious debate.[30] Even more heated differences have developed on questions of education, a matter of basic import for churches. The extent to which public school facilities may be used for religious instruction has aroused controversy. The proposal that public funds should be available to parochial as well as to public schools sets off debate between Protestant and Catholic.[31]

Issues of the place of groups within the state. When pushed to their ultimate such issues raise broad questions of the relationship of church and state. Some observers forecast that with the growth of Roman Catholicism in a nation historically predominantly Protestant great political ingenuity will be required to contrive formulas to fix satisfactorily to all the division

[30] See Leo Pfeffer, "Religion in the Upbringing of Children," *Boston University Law Review*, 35 (1955), pp. 333–393. For analyses of conflict and litigation in other fields, see Pfeffer's *Church, State, and Freedom* (Boston: Beacon Press, 1953).

[31] Illustrative of the temper of some of these discussions was the statement of Francis Cardinal Spellman to Mrs. Eleanor Roosevelt in 1949 in connection with a proposal for federal aid to education then pending. Mrs. Roosevelt's doubt about the Cardinal's views brought the rejoinder that she had acted from "misinformation, ignorance or prejudice" and pointed to hers as a "record of anti-Catholicism" and of "discrimination unworthy of an American mother." In the final episode of the exchange the Cardinal stated the Catholic position to be not one of advocacy of "general support of religious schools." It was not one of advocacy of Federal financing of school construction or the support of teachers but one of advocacy of the view that children in parochial schools should benefit from aids for such purposes as school transportation, nonreligious textbooks, health aids, and other such incidental expenses.

of functions between church and state. Profound anxieties and suspicions based on estimates of developments possible in the long run color the debate on lesser current problems and tend to put them beyond the realm of rational political solution.[32]

In some ways the question of the relation of church and state is, in form at least, essentially the same question that arises in defining the relation of other kinds of groups to the state. Issues develop about the range of freedom of private groups and the degree of authority they shall be permitted to exercise. The rub comes when ecclesiastical claims conflict with the claims of the state or when the clergy insists that the authority of the state be brought to its service by the conversion of church policy into the law of the land. Other groups, too, on occasion make claims that conflict with the claims of the state and they insist that the authority of the state be brought to their service. The clergy would be quick to assert that their claims rest on a different foundation from those of a trade union, a business association, or the American Medical Association.

In the normal course of politics such conflicting claims between private groups and the state are compromised case by case in the give-and-take of the governmental process. The critical moment comes when neither side is disposed to give; the authority of both is brought into play and some public officials may be placed in a most uncomfortable position. Thus, in 1956 *Catholic Action of the South*, official organ of the Archdiocese of New Orleans, indicated that excommunication would be incurred by those who worked for a pending legislative proposal to force segregation in private schools, a measure supported by several Catholic legislators.[33] Such conflicts of loyalty are commonplace, although other private groups may rest their claims to loyalty on something less authoritative than a canon of the church. A union functionary who happens to be a member of a legislature may be bound by ties of loyalty to his union. Or a businessman is subject to sanctions of trade groups with which he is associated. One of the conditions requisite to the maintenance of a viable pluralistic order—with wide ranges of freedom of action accorded to private groups—is the minimization of the number of questions not readily compromisable and the avoidance of circumstances that assure collision of determined forces in diametric opposition.

[32] For candid discussions of these questions by Catholic laymen, see *Catholicism in America, A Series of Articles from the Commonweal* (New York: Harcourt, Brace, 1954). See also such titles as Will Herberg, *Protestant-Catholic-Jew* (Garden City: Doubleday, 1955); John J. Kane, *Catholic-Protestant Conflict in America* (Chicago: Regnery, 1955); Ray Allen Billington, *The Protestant Crusade, 1800–1860* (New York: Macmillan, 1938); Hans Rommen, "Church and State," *Review of Politics*, 12 (1950), pp. 321–340.

[33] *New York Times*, February 25, 1956.

The Professions

Although it is commonly said that all public questions are matters of general concern, many legislative decisions and administrative acts have immediate effect upon only a few people. In such situations the affected group can often determine what public policy shall be; the lack of challenge to its recommendations may be interpreted as unanimous consent. Its position of informal authority may be enhanced if the matter appears to require judgments on questions on which members of the group are expert. Such considerations bear on the fact that within certain restricted spheres the professions are quite as powerful as the Farm Bureau or the American Federation of Labor. Yet when professional associations venture beyond these areas their influence may wane. When their demands run counter to those of other well-organized groups, the conflict may end in compromise or defeat.

Control of entry to professions. Of great concern to professional associations is the control of entrance to the professions. Since the licensure of trades and professions is within the jurisdiction of the states, the chief political activities on this matter have been by state associations, but the national professional associations have provided leadership. State medical societies and state bar associations have consistently fought for the establishment by law of higher qualifications for the right to practice these professions. In the continuous drive to raise the standards of admission, the medical societies and bar associations have been animated by mixed motives. The medical men have sought to drive out the incompetent and the quack in the name of the public interest. The lawyers have attempted to prevent the licensing of persons who would be unable competently to serve their clients. Further, both professions have been motivated by a desire to restrict competition.

One method of controlling entrance to a profession is by permitting its numbers to grow until professional fees are forced down by competition to the point at which economic considerations make entrance into the profession unattractive. Another is to raise the educational requirements and make more difficult the entrance examinations. Lawyers and doctors have adhered to the latter doctrine—a sort of "planned economy" for the professions. But it cannot be said that their attempts to ration the supply of lawyers and doctors have been based on any thoroughgoing analysis of public need for these services.

Encouraged by the success of the lawyers and doctors, other groups have requested the intervention of the state in the matter of licensure. These groups, with more or less plausibility, justify their demands with the claim that they occupy a position analogous to that of the professions. Plumbers, accountants, engineers, electrical contractors, barbers, cosmetologists, pharmacists, architects, chiropractors, dentists, osteopaths, movie-projector operators, optometrists, real-estate salesmen, insurance agents, morticians, nurses, naturopaths, and others have persuaded legislatures to create licensing boards. In trades connected with the building industry the power to license is notably abused; its control by the leaders of local unions, acting in combination with builders' associations, is often used to restrain competition.

Tendency towards a system of guilds. A characteristic of the politics of the professional associations is their tendency to seek the reality, if not invariably the form, of a guild system. That is, in form the state may control the profession, but in fact the profession itself generally succeeds in fixing the requirements for entrance to the profession and in establishing the standards of professional conduct. In practice, a sort of pluralism has arisen in which the profession controls itself in the name of the state.[34] When legislative action is needed, the well-established professional societies can usually bring about its passage. "Within its field," says McKean, "the New Jersey Medical Society is very influential. It can usually block such bills as it does not like, and it can secure passage of the measures it approves." [35] In the administration of licensing laws the organized profession usually has a strong voice. The governor will give heed to its recommendations in the appointment of members of the examining board. Not infrequently the statutes require the governor to appoint from the nominees of the professional society, and sometimes the law even delegates the power of appointment to the association. The trend toward the guild system has gone to the logical extreme in the establishment in some states of an "integrated" or "self-governing" bar to which all licensed lawyers must belong and which exercises, by delegation from the state, the power to admit to the profession and to discipline for unprofessional conduct. Some state licensing and regulatory authorities can act only with the consent of the regulated group. Regulations of the South Dakota state optometry board, for example, do not become effective until approved by the state association of optometrists.[36]

[34] See Francis P. DeLancey, *The Licensing of Professions in West Virginia* (Chicago: Foundation Press, 1938). On the delegation of authority to an association to police over-the-counter securities markets, see H. V. Cherington, "National Association of Securities Dealers," *Harvard Business Review*, 27 (1949), pp. 741–759.

[35] *Pressures on the Legislature of New Jersey* (New York: Columbia University Press, 1938), p. 71.

[36] For a survey of legislative and judicial tendencies, see J. A. C. Grant, "The Guild Returns to America," *Journal of Politics*, 4 (1942), pp. 303–336, 458–477. Also

The profession attempts to protect its sphere from encroachments by new and competing groups. Orthodox medical practitioners have resisted efforts of chiropractors, osteopaths, and "drugless" healers to establish themselves. The first line of resistance has been on the question of licensure. Chiropractors, for example, have usually had to obtain positive legislation to permit them to practice before they could follow their calling without violating the state medical-practice acts. The medical men have usually been able to do no more than delay the chiropractors in their effort to obtain legislation. Then the battle shifts to other fronts. The unorthodox healers seek to obtain the right to practice in publicly supported hospitals and to serve the beneficiaries of workmen's compensation laws. The orthodox medical men fight in the name of the protection of the public against quacks; the newer groups demand the protection of the individual's right to choose his own physician. Similarly bar associations resist the practice of law by laymen. The encroachments of banks and trust companies in the field of estates and trusts have been fought by the lawyers, but large areas formerly exclusively in the province of the lawyer have been lost.[37]

Most lobbying by professional associations does not make the front pages. It concerns mainly questions related to the arcane lore of a professional group whose spokesmen enjoy a deference arising from their supposed expertness. When the professional association ventures beyond the narrow realm in which it is virtually accorded the right to make law, its influence may be tempered by opposition from other interested groups. On a matter of legal ethics the American Bar Association may be subject to less challenge than when it endorses the Bricker Amendment, a proposal about which the judgment of the lawyers may be no better than that of almost anybody else.

External relations of professions: The AMA and health insurance. The professional societies and many other private groups as well exercise a relatively autonomous authority over a wide range of matters. The governance of mankind would not be so vexing a task if each private group could be self-governing; then politicians would not have so much to worry about. Unfortunately in the exercise of its own authority and influence the private group sooner or later affects adversely other groups or interests within society. These conflicts require the interposition of government lest chaos prevail.

---

the note, "The State Courts and Delegation of Authority to Private Groups," *Harvard Law Review*, 67 (1954), pp. 1398–1408.

[37] See M. L. Rutherford, *The Influence of the American Bar Association on Public Opinion and Legislation* (Philadelphia, 1937), pp. 93–99.

A striking illustration of these broad remarks may be found in the reactions of the American Medical Association to proposals for the establishment of systems of health insurance, systems which could have altered practices that had long been governed by the customs and codes of the profession. The AMA campaign against health insurance also incidentally exemplifies the capacity of an extremely small group—less than a quarter of a million persons—to exert a most impressive resistance to political change. The AMA consistently opposed suggestions for health insurance in the 1930's and early 1940's but its major drive against the idea occurred in the years 1948–1952. In May, 1948 President Truman proposed a system of compulsory health insurance, and in December, shortly after he won the election, the AMA assessed its members $25 each for a nationwide plan of "education." In the next three and one-half years the AMA spent over $4.5 million in "educating" the American people about the hazards of "socialized medicine." A public-relations firm managed the campaign which, on the whole, allied organized medicine with the Republican party.[38] To inform the people about the dangers of "this un-American excursion into State Socialism," the AMA found it convenient to schedule $1,100,000 worth of advertising in the weeks immediately preceding the 1950 congressional elections, a step not calculated to aid the Democratic ticket. Although the AMA officially remained aloof from election campaigns, its leaders and the leaders of state and local medical societies formed political action committees—healing arts committees and the like—which organized the doctors for intensive opposition to such Democrats as Senator Herbert Lehman of New York, Senator Claude Pepper of Florida, Senator Frank Graham of North Carolina, and Senator Elbert Thomas of Utah. In the presidential campaign of 1952 the firm managing the AMA propaganda campaign moved over to handle the work of the National Professional Committee for Eisenhower-Nixon, whose chairman had also been chairman of the committee in charge of the AMA educational program. The Republican platform had declared against compulsory health insurance.

While the activities of the AMA could be interpreted as nothing more than a concerted effort by a group of upper-income professionals driven by a fierce determination to retain that status, the chances are that the episode can also be explained by other characteristics of behavior. Through the medical argumentation there runs a consistent thread of anxiety that health insurance would alter the medical craftsman's control of the manner of his work—of his relations with other practitioners and with his patients. Bureaucratic controls might be substituted for indi-

[38] For an account of the campaign, see Stanley Kelley, Jr., *Professional Public Relations and Political Power* (Baltimore: Johns Hopkins Press, 1956), ch. 3.

vidualism in the fixing of terms and conditions of work. The mores, customs, and habits that develop around work—jobways, so to speak— acquire a tenacity and a sanctity, whether the job be that of surgeon, lathe operator, or pedagogue.

The AMA campaign also bears on the origins of group attitudes. With a little administrative and political ingenuity, doctors could have built compulsory health insurance into a system that would have made it un- necessary for them to worry about collecting bills or about the ability of a patient to pay, all without disturbing their ways of work. Yet medical men opposed the scheme with awesome vigor. The attitudes of groups are molded and not innate. The attitude of the medical profession had been shaped by long and persistent indoctrination by the central bureauc- racy of the AMA. The indoctrination of a high-status, high-income, liter- ate class of persons and their political management, oddly enough, seem to be far more feasible than is the mobilization of lesser peoples who are supposedly easy to manipulate. The profession's leaders over a period of years did a thorough job of educating the rank and file; such dissent as remained was drowned out by the sheer volume of official AMA propa- ganda.[39]

Group capacity in resistance of political change. The health insurance campaign strikingly illustrates what seems to be a general capacity of even small groups within society to resist successfully proposals for politi- cal change. Unless their position can be made to appear completely un- tenable morally or equitably, those defending the status quo enjoy great advantage, a circumstance that may cause no end of fretting but which doubtless contributes to the stability of a social order. The early social reformers usually did not foresee the power that could be brought to bear against their proposals by comparatively small numbers of interested upper-class persons. Through their infiltration of other organizations, through their individual capacity as opinion leaders, through their lever- age over the drug industries, and through other such connections, the medical men delayed, if they did not permanently kill, health insurance.[40]

[39] Charles A. Wolverton, chairman of a House committee, felt it expedient not to identify in the record the AMA member whose letter expressed support of legisla- tion mild enough to be sponsored by the Eisenhower Administration: "It is my im- pression that a fair number of physicians share these sentiments. I honestly believe the central organization [of the AMA] in Chicago has no idea what the average physician wants his patients to have."—House Committee on Interstate and Foreign Commerce, 83d Cong., 2d sess., *Health Inquiry*, Part 7 (1954), p. 2230.

[40] All the debate may have had some effect. Earlier medical societies opposed pri- vately operated group practice and insurance plans and backed up the opposition with punishment of offending doctors by expulsion and deprivation of privileges. As the

Professional solidarity and ideological cleavage. Professional societies, just as other groups, have their difficulties in maintaining unity in their battles against the outside world. Their internal cleavages on occasion have a characteristic which doubtless exists but not in such salient form as in other sorts of groups. Broad questions of opinion on questions essentially of political ideology may cut across a professional group. Such a difference formed the basis of a long dispute within the American Medical Association which preceded its all-out effort against health insurance. The professional attributes which the members had in common did not lead them automatically to a uniform view on the question of health insurance. In terms of broad political philosophy one crowd veered in one direction and another in the opposite.

These ideological cleavages, when pushed to their ultimate conclusion, lead to organizational fission. The long and intimate identification of the bar associations with conservative views and interests contributed to the formation of the National Lawyers Guild. Its constitution specified as eligible for membership

. . . all lawyers who regard adjustments to new conditions as more important than the veneration of precedent, who recognize the importance of safeguarding and extending the rights of workers and farmers upon whom the welfare of the entire nation depends, of maintaining our civil rights and liberties and our democratic institutions, and who look upon the law as a living and flexible instrument which must be adapted to the needs of the people.

The Guild was organized mainly by lawyers of New Deal inclinations. Even prior to its formation, a few local groups had split off from the established bar associations for reasons not unlike those that motivated its founders.

Common Elements in the Miscellany

Although this chapter has ranged over the most disparate sorts of pressure societies, it has served to bring to attention characteristics of behavior common to many groups. Those points, which are of utility in understanding groups generally, may be summarized here.

---

clamor for some sort of prepaid medical service rose in volume, the AMA and the state societies moved over to acceptance and sponsorship of voluntary medical insurance (under medical control) which they urge as an alternative to government insurance. State societies have obtained state legislation to control and restrict group practice and prepayment plans. See J. H. Means, *Doctors, People, and Government* (Boston: Little, Brown, 1953), ch. 9. Also Oliver Garceau, *The Political Life of the American Medical Association* (Cambridge: Harvard University Press, 1941) and the note, "The American Medical Association: Power, Purpose, and Politics in Organized Medicine," *Yale Law Journal*, 63 (1954), pp. 938–1022.

A leading theory of the nature of interest groups suggests that such groups rest on shared attitudes rather than on material "interest." Those attitudes may or may not be related to a material concern. So defined, both the American Peace Society and the National Association of Manufacturers fall within the conception of interest group. This idea of group is useful in interpreting the political role of groups, for it permits an avoidance of the side issue of determinism.

The policies and programs of groups—and the shared attitudes on which they are based—are shaped by the interactions within the group, the experiences of its members, the environmental circumstances affecting the group, and other factors. Interest group activity is not, thus, to be regarded as a simple reflex action. Rather group objectives take shape from the deliberations, the debates, the strivings, and all the internal processes leading to group action.

In the formation of the views of interest groups the controlling oligarchy, the "active minority," usually plays an influential, if not a determinative, role. The leadership may indoctrinate the membership or it may, in the absence of adequate ties to the membership, speak in the name of the group without much guidance from group sentiment. The character of these internal group relations becomes a matter of public concern as the organs of the group seek to influence the course of public policy.

As private groups gain authority over their members the point may be reached when the power of the group conflicts with that of the state or, to put it in another way, when the individual is torn by a conflict between his loyalty to the private group and his loyalty to the state. A multiplicity of loyalties is commonplace in a complex social order; the maintenance of the social order requires both a minimization in the conflicts of those loyalties and suitable methods for the resolution of unavoidable conflict.

6 | Role and Techniques of Pressure Groups

THE TREATMENT of individual pressure groups and the analysis of selected aspects of their behavior leaves untouched the question of their place in the political system as a whole. This matter may be approached by an examination of the methods employed by groups generally in their relations with government. The general theme will be argued that pressure groups collectively may be regarded as a functioning element of the political order.

Interest groups have existed since the founding of the Republic, yet the great proliferation of organized groups came in the twentieth century. The evolution of our complex array of private organizations has been a secondary consequence of changes in the social order that created political needs met only inadequately by the older political institutions and procedures. Chief among these changes were the diversities introduced by specialization in the production and distribution of goods and services. This multiplication of specialized segments of society threw upon government an enormous new burden. Specialization has as its corollary interdependence; interdependence has as its consequence friction. New cleavages produced new frictions and put to government new problems in the mediation of conflicts born of the new relations among interests within society. The growing work load alone strained the capacity of representative and administrative institutions designed for a simpler day, but the old institutions were also ill-adapted to many of the newer problems brought to the government for settlement. The new types of interests needed new mechanisms to formulate and state their needs—instruments better suited to the purpose than the older type of geographical representation of interests.

Increased specialization almost inevitably means increased governmental intervention to control the relations among groups. In turn, governmental intervention, or its threat, stimulates the formation of organized groups by those who begin to sense a shared interest. This chain reaction may be set in motion not so much by government itself as by the formation of one organization to press its claims, through the government, upon other groups which in turn organize in self-defense. Almost every proposed law represents the effort of one group to do something to another. When a law or proposed law impinges on a class of individuals, they are likely to be drawn together by their common interest in political offense or defense. Organization begets counterorganization.[1]

The upshot of these processes has been the erection of an impressive system of agencies for the influencing of public attitudes and for the representation of group interests before Congress and other governmental agencies. Perhaps around 500 organizations have a continuing interest in national policy and legislation. The major groups may not number over two or three score, but hundreds of others have an occasional interest in legislation. A complete picture of the system of group representation would also take into account the great corporations which often deal directly with Congressmen rather than through trade organizations. The views of individual corporations tend to be made known with less fanfare than are the demands of organized groups. Often single firms constitute substantial proportions of their industries and they have a stake in public policy warranting advocacy by the individual firm. A corporation such as Pan-American Airways, with its intimate dependence on public policy,

[1] For example, according to A. H. Kelly the "precipitating factor in the organization of a state manufacturers' association in Illinois came in 1893. The General Assembly, inspired by pressure from the State Federation of Labor, Jane Addams and Florence Kelly of Hull House, and various Chicago trade union groups, in June enacted a statute limiting the hours of labor for women to eight per day. The response was immediate." Leading industrialists "organized the Illinois Manufacturers' Association, for the specific purpose of destroying the law."—*A History of the Illinois Manufacturers' Association* (Chicago: University of Chicago Libraries, 1940), pp. 3–4.

could scarcely rely solely on an association of air transport companies to look out for its interests.[2]

As he speculates about the place and significance of pressure groups the student may well keep in mind a warning about the popular stereotypes of these organizations. The term "pressure" itself can be quite misleading, for much of the work of these groups does not involve turning the heat on Congress. Nor is the notion that groups invariably seek indefensible special privilege correct; their objectives spread over as wide a spectrum of good and evil as do the motives of mankind generally.[3] The view that pressure groups are pathological growths in the body politic is likewise more picturesque than accurate. It is a safer assumption that the group system developed to fill gaps in the political system.

Techniques in Group Offense and Defense

The organized group exists in an environment of other groups and other institutions. With some groups it has conflicts of interest; with others it shares objectives. Governmental institutions, legislative and administrative, constitute elements of its environment as does that vague entity the general public. The group must either adapt its objectives to the limits fixed by this environment or seek to mold the environment toward acceptance of its objectives. This process is not necessarily one of constant struggle. An equilibrium—or a fairly stable position with something of a gyroscopic quality—tends to develop in the relations between a group and its surroundings. Yet at times the relationship becomes one of flux, with bursts of effort either by a particular group or by elements in its environment to alter the position of a particular interest in society. The focus here rests on the techniques utilized by groups in this interaction with their environment. These methods have been touched on incidentally in earlier chapters, but they may be summarized here in an analysis that arranges them according to the targets toward which group strength is directed.

[2] A notion of the scale of lobbying activities can be had from the fact that under the Federal Regulation of Lobbying Act reports of expenditures total over $4,000,000 per year. That figure is, however, no precise measure, for the reports include sums spent for purposes that are scarcely lobbying and no reports are filed on large expenditures to influence public opinion on legislation. The *Congressional Quarterly* periodically publishes analyses of lobbyists' reports.

[3] An old law of American politics runs to the effect that when the Government of the United States becomes seized of property of great value some group of highly respectable citizens will try to steal it to promote free enterprise, to protect states' rights, or in the name of some other worthy cause. In this endeavor they are certain to have the devoted support of at least one United States Senator. With equal certainty groups will arise to promote the most utopian or idealistic schemes that men can contrive, but unswerving senatorial encouragement of these movements is not inevitable.

Manipulating public opinion. Cultivation of public opinion occupies an important place only in the programs of organizations able to finance the costly task of manipulating mass attitudes. Public-relations efforts are essentially of two sorts. An intensive, short-term campaign may be designed to whip up public opposition to or support of a particular legislative measure. To be differentiated from the whirlwind campaign is the long-term effort to manage basic public attitudes toward support of a broad point of view or to create a favorable sentiment toward a particular corporation or industry.

Although labor and farm organizations seek public favor, the peculiar position of business creates for it a special reliance on programs to influence basic public attitudes. The public utilities have perhaps been the most consistent large-scale operators in opinion management; they seek to implant in the public mind the notion that there is something essentially good about electric power produced by "investor-owned" utilities, an endeavor that costs them hundreds of thousands of dollars annually. The American Petroleum Institute tells of the accomplishments of the oil industry in advertisements scented with ideological overtones: ". . . this will continue only as long as we maintain our American system of private free enterprise—the greatest force for scientific and industrial development the world has ever known." Individual corporations, through their institutional advertising, help carry the burden of long-term opinion-molding.

The assumption of these campaigns is that the creation of favorable public attitudes generally will make for smoother sailing when particular questions of public policy arise for decision.[4] The technique is that of the so-called "new lobby." In their origins these public-relations programs were thought to be a way of avoiding the malodorous practices of the "old lobby," which relied mainly on direct contacts with legislators, sometimes on a pecuniary basis. Thus, in 1956 a spokesman for the Natural Gas and Oil Resources Committee explained why his committee had spent about $1,750,000 for the education of the public on natural gas but had done no legislative lobbying: ". . . if the consumer understood he couldn't get supplies in a free economy unless the producer had an incentive, the problem was two-thirds solved." His committee left the other one-third of the job to others.

Though public-relations campaigns may build a status for a group in

---

[4] The general theory leads to activities that may seem remote from public policy. Thus, a public-relations firm, under commission from a railroad group to help resist the political efforts of trucking associations, undertook to feed into network programs scripts portraying truck drivers as sinister characters and to assure wide distribution of news photographs of highway accidents involving trucks. Truck interests fought back with advertisements about the heroic and kindly deeds of truck drivers.

the public mind, a group's deeds may have more effect on the public's impression of the group. Its record may put it in the doghouse beyond easy reprieve by ransom paid to the public-relations specialist. Or its record may command for it a public deference. The general status of the group supposedly bears importantly on its political effectiveness. The group may be accepted, respected, feared, heeded, or it may be regarded as ridiculous, inconsequential, irresponsible, suspect, even contemptible. The spokesmen for one group may be heard with respect; those of another may even have little opportunity to state its case. The views of one group may carry great weight; those of another may be deemed unworthy of much consideration.

In contrast with long-term campaigns are efforts to mobilize popular views on a specific legislative proposal. These campaigns range in magnitude from a few newspaper advertisements to those that involve outlays of millions of dollars. Illustrative of the large-scale programs was the AMA campaign against health insurance. At its beginning congressional mail—in the offices of the hundred Representatives studied—was running $2\frac{1}{2}$ to 1 in favor of health insurance; nine months later it ran 4 to 1 against it.

Both in their long-term campaigns and in their efforts to obtain passage of particular legislation, private associations give attention to the communications media, which are, within constricted limits, independent centers of power in the political system. Organized interests "lobby" the press and TV-radio, just as they do the government, and in so doing use means running from artifice to economic pressure. Professor Casey finds that newspaper editors regard religious and nationalistic groups as the most importunate in their demands. People seem to be extraordinarily sensitive about their religion and their national origin; communications media must tread lightly on these subjects or suffer the consequences.[5] Some newspapers have even accepted clerical censorship of religious stories in order to stave off a boycott. With respect to economic and social policy, the fact that publishing is a business of considerable scale itself contributes to the differentials among groups in their access to the press. Some readily obtain newspaper support; others cannot hope even to state their case through the press.[6]

[5] R. D. Casey, "Pressure Groups and the Press" in N. C. Meier and H. W. Saunders, *The Polls and Public Opinion* (New York: Holt, 1949).

[6] It would be most useful to have a thoughtful examination of the role of the communications media in the American governmental process. A basic assumption of democratic theory is that full information on public affairs will be made available to the people whose preferences thus informed will prevail in the long run. The guarantee of the freedom of the press supposedly promotes the dissemination of political information. No extensive investigation is required to conclude that news-

Persuading legislators. Pressure groups are most conspicuous in their activities in support of and in opposition to legislative proposals. They have developed this work into a fine art; whether applied in Washington or in state capitals, their methods are much alike. An association's staff is ordinarily in immediate charge of its legislative activities. The larger associations maintain permanent offices in Washington; whereas the more common practice in the states is to assign men to the capital during the legislative sessions. These men—lobbyists, legislative counsel—have often served in Congress or in the state legislatures. If they lack that experience, they are usually well informed on legislative procedure and tactics. Their tenure is likely to be longer than that of most legislators; and in the course of their service they may gain the confidence and respect of the legislators.

The use of the term "pressure" conjures up a picture of a wicked lobbyist attempting to coerce a righteous legislator to deviate from his disposition to follow the public interest. By and large the relations between organized interests and legislators must be described in other terms, although on occasion the crudest pressures are invoked for indefensible purposes. Each group has its friends and allies in Congress, men whose constituency and party connections dispose them generally favorably toward the group. Not infrequently, these men are ahead of the pressure groups in the advocacy of a cause and may even enlist the support of pressure organizations on specific matters.[7] From the farming states come Senators and Representatives who will aid the American Farm Bureau Federation. The National Association of Manufacturers and the AFL-CIO have their legislative allies from the industrial states.[8]

---

papers do not fulfill this function in an impressive manner. The cynical explanation that newspaper publishing is only a branch of the oldest profession contains a grain, but only a grain, of truth. The dedication of the newspaper to the recording of the history of the past 24 hours limits it severely as a disseminator of meaningful political intelligence. This self-imposed limitation makes the press an ideal medium for the reporting of natural disasters, baseball results, murders, robberies, stockmarket quotations, rapes, election returns, and not much else. Yet whether they function merely as neutral channels of communication or as centers of political initiative, the communications media occupy a position of fundamental significance in the structure of the political system.

[7] Representatives, for example, try to persuade the National Rivers and Harbors Congress to include their local projects in the list which the Rivers and Harbors group recommends to Congress for adoption. See A. A. Maass, "Congress and Water Resources," *American Political Science Review*, 44 (1950), pp. 576–593.

[8] Such a situation is indicated by the remarks of Clarence Cannon, Chairman of the House Appropriations Committee. He took occasion to say a word of "appreciation" to Mr. Ed O'Neal of the Farm Bureau Federation and his staff for their "assistance" to him and other members of the House interested in farm legislation. "We could not possibly have secured the enactment of appropriations to take care of the parity-

A major point of contact between Congress and the interest group is the committee hearing. On legislative proposals of importance, the appropriate committee of Congress holds public hearings. Representatives of organized groups appear to present their case. At times their presentation may rest on substantial factual research and provide genuine help to the committee in estimating the effects of a proposal; the hearings, incidentally, give committee members an opportunity to push as deeply as they wish into the motivations and interests of the group. The committee members may indulge in a bit of heckling and push the group representatives hard for justifications of their position. More and more the professional secretaries of pressure groups depend on the officials of their organizations to appear before committees: the full-time lobbyist is merely a "hired man"; he brings in the president and vice-presidents of the organization and coaches them on the bill, and they appear before the committees.[9]

While committee hearings are designed primarily to enlighten the committee members, they may also be an element of a broader propaganda strategy to advance or defeat a measure. The purpose may not be so much to inform the committee as to gain publicity in the press. The management of hearings may, indeed, be designed to give one set of organizations opportunity to build an impressive case and to handicap the opposition by drastic limitations on its hearing time.[10]

payment checks or soil-conservation checks without the wise counsel and support of Mr. O'Neal and the actual votes he enlisted in our support."—Hearing before Subcommittee of House Appropriations Committee, 77th Congress, 2nd sess., on Agriculture Department Appropriation Bill, 1943, Pt. 2, p. 627.

[9] The legislative counsel of the National Retail Lumber Dealers Association concludes: "The primary function of the lobbyist is to inform his client on the technical aspects of legislation, evaluate its chances of passage or defeat, and advise his client when to express his advocacy of or opposition to legislation. The function of dealing with Congressmen and Senators rests squarely on the shoulders of those affected by the legislation."—House Select Committee on Lobbying, Hearings, Pt. 2, p. 482.

[10] See Bertram Gross, *The Legislative Struggle* (New York: McGraw-Hill, 1953), ch. 15. The hearings on the Employment Act of 1946 provide an instructive example of collaboration between congressional sponsors and interest groups in the conduct of hearings. See Stephen K. Bailey, *Congress Makes A Law* (New York: Columbia University Press, 1950). On occasion all is not what it might seem on the surface of a legislative hearing. For example, in 1955 a House committee held a hearing on plans for the Air Force Academy; the architects' preliminary sketches, more or less in the modern style, were of structures using large expanses of glass and quantities of metal after the fashion of Lever House of New York. Frank Lloyd Wright turned up before the committee to dissent from the designs and others criticized the departure from the use of traditional American building materials. Intimations crept in that the plans were a bit radical, even un-American. The Veterans of Foreign Wars took the design as an "insult to our American heritage and traditions." It turned out that the hands behind the scenes guiding the show were those of the Allied Masonry Council and its public relations experts, people interested in the

Given the controlling influence of the committee on many legislative questions, often an interest group contents itself with an appearance before the committee and perhaps with interviews with committee members to make certain that the group's views are understood. The lobbyist then philosophically hopes for the best possible outcome on the assumption that he has presented his case on a complicated question with which the committee members have to wrestle. Problems of tactics arise, however, when it seems expedient to acquaint as many legislators as possible with the views of the group.

Of the measures considered by a session of Congress relatively few involve extensive mobilization of pressure. Of the bills of interest to even a large lobbying organization, on only a few will there be any effort to stir up pressure on Congress. Some lobbyists regard the barrage of telegrams on Congress as "death bed" politics to be resorted to only under dire circumstances. Others regard such techniques as ineffective. Indicative of the strategy of a seasoned lobbyist is the remark of an AFL legislative representative that his organization appeals to the general membership to write to their Congressmen only "infrequently" and then only "in an acute situation." Yet on occasion the AFL summoned to Washington the members of its legislative committee of over a hundred to make personal calls on the lawmakers.[11]

When pressure organizations attempt to direct upon a legislator influence from his constituency, they have a choice of two broad sorts of pressure: the "rifle" type and the "shot-gun" type. The first consists in enlisting the support of a few persons thought to have great influence with an individual legislator. Obviously its utility differs with the type of bill and the circumstances of the individual legislator. Some legislators, given the character of their constituency and their policy commitments, are strongly resistant to persuasion on some types of bills, and efforts to pressure them are a waste of time.[12] Yet on other measures, the same member may have only doubt about what he should do, and a word from an influential constituent may sway his vote.[13]

---

use of brick, stone, and other good traditional American building materials. The council had had in its maneuvers the collaboration of the Hon. John E. Fogarty, Representative from Rhode Island and former president of a local of the Bricklayers union. The Air Force decided to use more brick. See George Orick, "Off They Went Into the Wild Blue," *The Reporter*, Sept. 22, 1955.

[11] W. C. Hushing in J. B. S. Hardman and M. F. Neufeld (eds.), *The House of Labor* (New York: Prentice-Hall, 1951), pp. 143–44.

[12] Thus, a lobbyist against a bill to eliminate federal control of natural gas prices had on his list of Senators one group he considered "there was no sense in approaching." They came "from the producing states" and he thought "it would be a waste of time" to see them.

[13] The superior access of constituents to legislators is suggested by a comment by Senator John L. McClellan, of Arkansas: "If anybody wants to talk to me about

To bring to bear upon a Senator or a Representative pressures from persons influential with him requires an elaborate intelligence service. Some associations designate "contact" men who are thought to be known favorably to their Representatives. The National Association of Retail Druggists developed such a system in its fight for fair-trade legislation. The journal of the association described the system:

One of the outstanding achievements of the association through its Washington Office was the organization of the congressional contact committees. Under this plan, in 1935 and 1936, there were organized in each congressional district committees of pharmacists who were known to be friends of or intimately acquainted with Senators and Congressmen. These committeemen were the "minute men" upon whom the association relied to act, quickly and decisively, whenever the association's legislative program needed special attention. . . .

This year the congressional contact committees were reorganized on a county basis, nearly every county in the entire United States being represented on the contact committee lists in the Washington Office. These organizations, kept alive and enthused by the regular messages from the Capital, proved their effectiveness time and again this spring. Now, these committees are busy among the pharmacists and other independent businessmen of their counties, keeping a steady barrage of letters and telegrams directed upon the White House, in an effort to convince the President that he should reconsider his action in delaying the passage of the Tydings-Miller bill.

Other associations have built up such systems of contact men, and still others attempt on a smaller scale to bring to their support men thought to be influential with individual Congressmen. Such tactics may elicit as much resentment as support, but the nudge from a large campaign contributor, a powerful supporter, the man who holds the mortgage, or some other such individual may be decisive.

The "shot-gun" type of pressure campaign encourages all and sundry to wire their Congressmen. Often this sort of effort is but an incident in a short-term campaign designed to build up public favor for or against a particular piece of legislation. The object may be to panic Congress into action by promoting the appearance of a universal and insistent public demand. The opposing strategy will be to delay action until the dust settles in order that considerations other than the volume of artificially induced clamor may govern. The pressure organization may, indeed, in some of these campaigns on particular pieces of legislation succeed in activating a latent public sentiment to the service of its cause.[14]

legislation, if they are from my State, they certainly get to see me if they will be patient. If they are from some group or organization of people out of my State, then it depends upon the mood I am in at the time."

[14] More often they demonstrate the utter lack of public morality that permeates

Letters and telegrams have some effect on some legislators on some bills, but a safe guess would be that most of these missives fall on fallow ground. Legislators speak with disdain of a flood of communications similar in phraseology and obviously stimulated by some interested party.[15] Even if a legislator is disposed to be guided by these instructions, he soon finds that advice is offered often in ignorance of the parliamentary situation, at an untimely moment, or without an understanding of the details of the bill. Legislators, however, speak with tears in their voices of the influence of the letter written in pencil on a low-grade paper without complete mastery of the rules of English composition.[16]

Pressure-group lobbyists may play a role in shepherding a bill through the legislative mill. The processes of legislation are intricate and the channels can become clogged at many points. Lobbyists may give a push at this point and that to keep their bill in motion and may serve both as gadflies and strategic advisers to their legislative friends.[17] If the purpose is to defeat a bill, their skill and attention may be even more effective. The procedure of legislatures gives great advantage to those who seek to prevent action. At many stages, from committee consideration to executive approval, a bill can be killed, and an alert legislative counsel may perhaps carry the day at one step if not at another.

Implicit in the importunities of a lobbyist may be the threat that his organization will at the next primary or election throw its strength against the legislator who does not vote right. Historically the most impressive example of this type of persuasion has been the Anti-Saloon League which had enough of a following to determine the results of many elections.

the public-relations profession. Consider the memorandum from the public-relations department of the National Association of Home Builders to local associations: "Remember, the more noise you make, the more attention you will get. Go at it hammer and tongs. Make public charges that you can back up. Accuse your housing authority of squandering funds, of being inefficient and failing to live up to promises. Deride failure to clear slums and to house the poor. If you put on a vigorous assault, your newspapers will pay attention and your Congressman will see it."

[15] For example, in 1949 the National Tax Equality Association, a group seeking to tax co-operatives, sent to its members a half dozen sample telegrams and urged that wires be sent to legislators. One Senator in four days received 44 telegrams reading: "Urge your support of excise tax reduction, replacing revenue loss by taxing the untaxed." Eleven of his constituents followed a second form, 17 a third, 38 a fourth, 14 a fifth, and 21 elected to use the sixth form.

[16] See L. A. Dexter, "What Do Congressmen Hear: The Mail," *Public Opinion Quarterly*, 20 (1956), pp. 16–27; Frank Bonilla, "When Is Petition 'Pressure'?" *Public Opinion Quarterly*, 20 (1956), pp. 39–48.

[17] At times this relation looks a little raw. In 1952, Senator Spessard L. Holland, of Florida, obtained a suspension of the Senate rules to permit the chief lobbyist for the bill to transfer the off-shore oil lands to the states the privilege of sitting on the Senate floor to advise him during the debate.

Most groups that have a numerically large membership analyze the voting records of legislators and inform the membership of the candidates' stands on issues of concern to them. Such operations may affect some votes, but it is doubtful that most legislators need have much fear of such activity. The number of voters who know both the name of their Congressman and how he voted on any measure are quite small, and, of those, the candidate may gain as much by his vote on one measure as he loses on another. Moreover, often the admonitions of a pressure group only re-enforce other pressures on a legislator. A Representative from a working-class district may have his back stiffened by a word from the AFL-CIO but he need not fear a candidate backed say, by the state manufacturers' association. On the other hand, a Representative from a suburban Republican district who consistently supports labor measures has no right to be astonished if he faces primary opposition financed by those interests against whose wishes he has voted. In any case, it is not so much the rank-and-file legislator who receives the attention of pressure groups in campaigns as it is the conspicuous advocate or opponent of measures. The legislator who spearheads a movement that touches some interest in the pocketbook should give close attention to his political fences.

Any catalogue of methods of dealing with legislators would be incomplete without mention of the methods of corruption. That such techniques are employed is undeniable; the extent to their use is another matter. The prevailing supposition is that their use has declined over the past half century and that they survive chiefly in sporadic applications in state legislatures.[18] Instances of bribery—and near-bribery—seem to be associated with the maneuvers of relatively small groups interested in legislation that involves the grant or denial of privileges of great, immediate, monetary value. In such general category could be placed revelations during the 1930's and 1940's of the activities of small-loan companies, public utilities, race-track promoters, highway transport groups, gambling syndi-

---

[18] There is a lurid folklore of the old-fashioned lobby and its techniques. How accurate the stories were, or remain, is a matter of conjecture. One of the approaches "was to furnish sumptuous free meals without number, and great quantities of assorted intoxicating liquors to legislators." Another was to "let the persons to be influenced actually win large sums of money" in poker games. Still another was "to debase them morally by procuring for their entertainment lascivious women who were on the payroll of the lobbyist and who were willing to run the whole gamut, so to speak, of immorality." The author of the quoted remarks, Eugene D. O'Sullivan, former Representative from Nebraska, understood that the "practice of having legislators and others embraced in the toils of the harlots is still in vogue at the seat of many State governments but has been practically abandoned in Washington, D.C." —See *Congressional Record* (daily ed.), June 29, 1950, p. A5076.

cates, and the like.[19] Pecuniary ties between lobbyist and legislator may take forms other than an outright bribe. Thus, in the skirmishes over the 1956 natural gas bill an attorney for the Superior Oil Company spread about gifts of $2,500 which were later described as contributions to senatorial campaign funds made with no understanding about any Senator's vote on the bill. Human credulity has its limits, but the distinction between a campaign contribution and a bribe cannot always be made with certainty.[20]

What estimate is to be made of the significance of pressure-group representations in the determination of a legislator's votes? The unsatisfactory answer is that it "all depends." It depends in part on the strength of other factors bearing on legislative behavior and those factors vary from bill to bill, from time to time, and from legislator to legislator. The strength of party leadership may at times offset group pressures; the insistent but inarticulate demands of constituency may outweigh group representations. Another variable is the nature of the group itself. One group may be able to guide some legislators along the desired direction and another may be completely powerless. Still another variable may be the type of bill. All these factors and others are mixed in proportions that vary from legislator to legislator as well as from roll call to roll call. Such complexities warn against the easy generalization that Congressmen are invariably pushed around by lobbyists.

Relations with administrators. Pressure groups are at their most spectacular in their support of and opposition to legislation, but equally important are their continuous relationships with the administrative agencies of government. A group may be instrumental in obtaining the passage of legislation; it may follow through with pressure, aid, and encouragement to the agency charged with responsibility for enforcing the act. Legislation may be applied vigorously or otherwise, and the choice may not be unrelated to the concern of various groups about the matter.

[19] One by-product of these events was a Michigan statute attempting to reach a concealed form of bribery by prohibiting payment to legislators for services "in excess of the reasonable value of such service if the same was performed by a person not a member of the legislature," when the payer would benefit by the passage or defeat of a bill.—*Acts,* 1945, p. 208. This sort of relation occurs in reverse form when private interests try to sandbag a legislator by withdrawing their patronage from his business.

[20] If the data could be turned up, the conclusion probably would be that money is used (in any of a variety of ways) far more frequently to sustain friends than to convert opponents. Thus, the Nixon fund, brought to light in the 1952 presidential campaign, could scarcely be regarded as a means for influencing Senator Nixon. It only gave aid to a Senator committed to lines of policy congenial to the subscribers to the fund.

With the growing complexity of government, legislative bodies have had to delegate authority to administrative agencies to make rules and regulations. Administrators become legislators, and pressure groups inevitably direct their activities to the point at which authority to make decisions is lodged. Where power rests, there influence will be brought to bear.

Within the federal administration, procedures have evolved that regularize the role of private associations in the rule-making process. The Federal Administrative Procedure Act of 1946 requires most federal agencies to give public notice of proposed rules, to permit interested persons to present arguments, and to receive petitions for the issuance, amendment, or repeal of a rule. Pressure-group staffs keep track of such notices and when their organizations are affected prepare statements of the group position on the proposal. Such practices, to a degree at least, put the rule-making process into a gold-fish bowl and recognize a right of all concerned to be informed of proposed action and to be given an opportunity to make their views known.

In contrast, when rules are issued without such procedures a premium exists on access to administrators through the back door and the administrator may act without being confronted by the claims of all those to be affected. In 1955, a congressional investigation brought to light the easy access to the Department of Interior enjoyed by western utilities. Changes in regulations, to the advantage of the utilities, were issued in substantially the form recommended by the lobbyist whose advice had been requested by the Under Secretary of Interior. The action fell outside the terms of the Administrative Procedure Act, and the reversal of a policy of the Truman Administration was accomplished quietly and without fanfare.[21] Advocates of regularized procedures, in effect, assume that if the opponents of an action have an opportunity to stir up a commotion, the decision will be different. Thus, the American Public Power Association, after it saw that private utilities had an inside track to the Interior Department, urged Congress in 1956 to extend the Administrative Procedure Act to decisions on the marketing of electricity.

Pressure groups on occasion mount a propaganda campaign against administrative agencies, a campaign calculated to discredit the agency in the public eye and to direct pressure upon it to influence its decision. This may even extend to attempts to influence a quasi-judicial agency which is obligated to act somewhat as a court. In 1952 the Federal Trade Commission initiated a proceeding that involved a disputed interpretation

[21] See House Committee on Government Operations, 84th Cong., 1st sess., Hearings Before a Subcommittee (on Changes in Power Line Regulations), 1955 (Washington: Government Printing Office, 1956).

of fair-trade legislation. The Bureau of Education on Fair Trade, a lobbying outfit, proclaimed the action to be an effort to obstruct the will of Congress and urged all concerned to "Tell your Congressmen and Senators about this Threat Now." The bureau declined an invitation to appear before the commission as amicus curiae to present its views; it sought rather to affect the legal decision by pressure on the commission to drop the proceedings.[22]

A well-worn channel by which private groups attempt to influence administrative agencies about both general rules and decisions in individual matters is through Representatives and Senators. Congressmen, so the reasoning goes, control appropriations and legislation, and their word may approach intimidation in its effect on administrators. Legislative intervention may also jog a timid administrator to fulfill a plain duty or to moderate arbitrary practices. The administrative-legislative-lobby triangle at times includes group influence calculated to emasculate legislation by influencing Congress to make inadequate appropriations. Contrariwise, those groups desirous of adequate programs may re-enforce the requests of administrators for appropriations.

Appointments to administrative posts are by no means a matter of indifference to the association whose members are affected by the agencies in question. Organized labor is deeply interested in who is Secretary of Labor; organized business hopes that the Secretary of Commerce is a man acceptable to it. Other groups with specialized interests may cherish the wish that a friendly bureau chief will be appointed. Private groups seldom have publicly proclaimed "candidates" for these appointments; by less formal means they make their wishes known to appointing authorities. Often, groups with conflicting interests have an interest in the same appointment; their differences may be aired in the process of senatorial confirmation, if the equities are grossly violated by the designation of a person likely not to be impartial.

The notion should not prevail that the administrator and the organizations of those affected by his agency engage in endless strife. Apparently in the course of time a customary balance develops in their relations. The

[22] Federal Trade Commissioner Stephen J. Spingarn attracted considerable attention by his vigorous reaction to the propaganda of the fair-trade group and to other similar moves by a sector of the petroleum industry. In a press conference in December, 1952, he said: "What I am objecting to is a situation where people refuse to present their case on the merits, although they have a forum available to them, but instead hire high-powered public-relations counsel and go out into the propaganda market, not just of the United States, but of the whole world, to attack their own government in the most vicious and intemperate fashion, to say that it is corrupt and riddled with subversives, because they object to antitrust proceedings which have been brought against them, or to factual statements made in a fact-finding report."

administrator of a new piece of legislation may be in fairly steady conflict with the regulated groups until the administration shakes down, the bugs are ironed out of the legislation, and those subject to the law become reconciled to it. The resulting equilibrium may well draw the fangs of the legislation, but it may also reflect a condition of willingness to live and let live. The happy state of affairs reflected in a pattern of peaceful co-existence may be disturbed by changes in the political situation. The election of 1952, for example, gave many groups hope that they might alter the administrative environment and stimulated them to propaganda and lobbying efforts against administrative relations to which they had adjusted with reluctance.

Pressure groups and the courts. The role of the American courts in the determination of public policy brings them within the range of agencies with which, under some circumstances, pressure organizations must concern themselves. The records of presidential appointees to the Supreme Court undergo a searching scrutiny by pressure organizations, which are quick to oppose the confirmation of individuals thought to be biased against group interests. Given the customs of judicial action it is not good form to attempt to pressure judges. Yet interest groups often play an active role in the initiation of litigation to test the constitutionality of legislation; the existence of an organization incidentally permits a sharing of the costs of such cases. Outside the realm of constitutional questions, in some areas of public policy the reality of law is fixed not so much by the initiative of public authority as by the vigor of private litigation to establish and maintain rights. The role of the National Association for the Advancement of Colored People in supporting litigation to maintain Negro rights presents perhaps the most conspicuous instance of group activity over a long period to mold the law in its effects on a group of citizens.[23]

Intergroup lobbying. Officials are not the sole recipients of the attentions of lobbyists. Lobbyists also lobby each other.[24] Any proponent of action, or inaction, must take into account private as well as public centers of power able to obstruct or to help the cause. With potential friends and

[23] For an excellent account of the role of the NAACP in the steps leading to the Supreme Court ruling that injunctions may not be issued to enforce restrictive covenants, see Clement E. Vose, "NAACP Strategy in the Covenant Cases," *Western Reserve Law Review*, Winter, 1955.

[24] In 1954, as the National Institute of Municipal Law Officers met in San Francisco, each member was contacted by telephone by a spokesman for the natural gas industry in his home city. The attempt was to induce the NIMLO to adopt a resolution favorable to the relaxation of federal regulation of gas prices.

potential foes, a group's relations naturally differ. In many instances a group's objectives will run diametrically counter to those of some other group or constellation of groups. Such groups can only fight it out to a stalemate or to a compromise imposed by public authority. At times, however, opposition may be foreseen and coped with in advance. Modifications of a legislative proposal may remove its sting for groups with only a tangential interest in it or a concern about some incidental feature.

Group spokesmen lobby among potential friends for support. They often attempt to obtain endorsements from other groups with a secondary interest in a proposal. For example, in 1951 the marine committee of the Veterans of Foreign Wars adopted a resolution criticizing the State Department for directing its personnel to fly rather than travel by sea and thereby be bound by a statute requiring them to travel by American flag vessels. It turned out that a member of the VFW marine committee was also the vice-president of a shippers' association. All of which suggests parenthetical mention of the general practice of interests sharply affected by public policy of "boring from within" all opinion-forming groups to which they can obtain access. Intergroup lobbying sometimes verges on coercion.[25] Some associations regard it as sound strategy not to prejudice their main cause by involving themselves in side issues.[26]

Intergroup lobbying may be not a matter of winning reluctant allies but of bringing together groups with similar interests in a piece of legislation. The promotion of important legislative proposals often involves the formation of a committee to lead the efforts of a large number of groups with a common concern. Dr. Riggs points to the importance of such "catalytic groups," as he labels them, which exist either on an *ad hoc* or permanent basis. His study of the Citizens Committee to Repeal Chinese Exclusion indicates that this committee pulled together the efforts of a large number of organizations and that most of the witnesses who appeared before the congressional committee in support of repeal did so at the request of the Citizens Committee, which itself went unmentioned in

[25] The executive of a chain store group in reporting on the enlistment of support of the head of a co-operative creamery organization in opposition to a chain tax said: "It appears that considerable 'persuasion' may be necessary in order to induce Mr. Brandt to 'go to bat' for the chain stores in Minnesota, although it seems to be obvious that chains are among the very best customers of farmer cooperatives in that state."—Quoted by J. C. Palamountain, Jr., *The Politics of Distribution* (Cambridge: Harvard University Press, 1955), p. 172.

[26] The executive vice-president of the National Association of Real Estate Boards wrote in 1949: "I went to the offices of the American Medical Association and talked to them about our working together. There was nothing doing. They felt very decidedly that they could fight against socialized medicine most effectively and they did not want to mix up their issue with public housing and the like."—House Select Committee on Lobbying, Hearings, Pt. 2, p. 49.

the committee hearings.[27] Similarly, the "real estate lobby" was co-ordinated by the National Home Foundation. Weekly luncheons of 18 representatives of groups interested in building, construction materials, and real estate served as a means for exchanging views and for agreeing on those matters on which agreement was possible. In opposition, about 40 groups favoring public housing co-ordinated their efforts through the Housing Legislation Information Service.

Interest Groups and the Governing Process

The student may inquire what all these activities of organized groups have to do with politics. Campaigns and elections, it may be repeated, are not the totality of politics. Our conception of the political process is broad enough to cover all sorts of efforts to guide, influence, or affect governmental action. The striving for power, for status, for privilege is never-ending and not restricted to campaigns and elections. Administrators take action every day. Legislators make laws. Organized groups incessantly seek to influence these decisions which are, in a sense, the pay off of the process of politics in which elections are but episodes, albeit significant episodes. The decisions taken between elections constitute the basic stuff of politics, the pelf and glory for which men and groups battle. And the stakes of between-elections politics are great. A conservative estimate, say, of the costs imposed on consumers by the public policies borne of the efforts of the sugar lobby would be $100,000,000 annually.

A working conception of the political *process* must take into account the interactions among groups, interests, and governmental institutions that produce such decisions. Moreover, a working conception of the political *system* must make a place for organized interest groups: they not only seek to exert influence; they are a part of the political system—elements quite as integral to the system as are political parties.

Representative function of private groups. Obviously, organized groups, for good or ill, perform a function of representation in the political system. The characterization of the lobby as the "third house" puts the point vividly if somewhat exuberantly. The explanation of the development of this system of spokesmen for specialized segments of society probably rests in part on the shortcomings of geographical representation in a highly differentiated society. Legislators could speak authoritatively for the more or less homogeneous interests of their districts in a less complex society. The relative simplicity of legislative questions permitted

[27] F. W. Riggs, *Pressures on Congress, A Study of the Repeal of Chinese Exclusion* (New York: King's Crown Press, 1950).

easy accommodation of geographical representation to such necessity as existed for functional representation. The growth of the number of specialized interests in society and the increasing complexity of legislative questions created tasks beyond ready performance by spokesmen for geographical areas. No legislator could regularly be relied upon to look out for interests that spread across many districts. Organized groups supplement the system of geographical representation.

Representation does not consist solely in serving as a conduit for sentiments already in existence among the members of a group. Antecedent to the expression of group views is a process of creation of those views. Associations—or their committees—engage in the most extensive study and discussion in reaching decisions on their program for legislation. By this process differences within the group are ironed out and the association can approach the public and the government with a united front. The reconciliation of differences within interest groups facilitates the work of legislatures and of Congress by reducing the number of conflicts with which they have to deal, as well as by giving the government an authoritative statement of the group position. Government is then left with the task of ironing out conflicts between opposing groups.

The hammering out within private groups of consensus on public policy often produces legislative proposals that both reflect the views of the group and take into account the angularities of the situation with which legislation deals. Legislators, to be sure, could work out the details of policy proposals. On major issues, they may do so but countless lesser legislative schemes evolve within the groups to be concerned, greatly to the relief of legislators and often by no means to the detriment of the public interest.[28] In fact, the most efficacious statutes may well be those enacted at the behest of private groups which advocate measures to protect the group as a whole from the actions of its unethical fringe.

Representation includes more than advocacy; it extends to the maintenance of close watch on the legislative process to spot threats to the interest of the constituency represented. The staffs of pressure groups perform this intelligence function, an operation that requires skill, for often hidden away in bills are clauses with the most untoward effects, at times not intended by anybody concerned.[29] An alert lobbyist may pre-

[28] Illustrative of the legislative attitude is the observation of a publication of the National Lumber Manufacturers' Association that public officials prefer to have "the view of an industry, rather than to listen *ad infinitum* to the variant views of countless individuals."—Quoted by Donald Blaisdell, *Economic Power and Political Pressures* (Monograph No. 26, Temporary National Economic Committee, 1941), p. 3.

[29] Thus, a well-meaning soul, doubtless prompted by the shipping associations, proposes that 50 per cent of certain exports, encouraged by government policy, be transported in American vessels. The Florida Citrus Mutual hastens to call the

vent foolish or uninformed action. Whatever the portent of a bill may be, the group staff sounds the alarm to arouse the membership. One sometimes suspects that the staffs thrive on attempts to panic the members by horrendous accounts of what is in prospect in the way of public regulation. The group bureaucracy prospers as it succeeds in arousing fears, but individuals are likely to be much less well informed on what the legislative trend holds in store for them than are their lobbyists.[30]

To say that pressure groups perform a representative function is not to assert that public officials should not be wary of them. Most groups do not include nearly all persons of the class they purport to represent. The National Association of Manufacturers includes only a small proportion of the manufacturers of the nation. Probably two-thirds of the farmers are not affiliated with any farm organization. Members of pressure groups tend to be the more aggressive, often the more prosperous, or the larger units of the potential membership. Thus, the larger farmers affiliate with farm groups in a higher degree than do others. This greater frequency of affiliation from the upper brackets appears to be common to nearly all organized groups.[31]

Resolutions, programs, and platforms may reflect the views of the leaders and bureaucracy of the association rather than those of even a limited membership. At times, the controlling oligarchy may, of course, express sentiments widely held within the membership. On other occasions, the leadership of nonparty groups may be unfaithful to their trust or may misrepresent the views of the association. Still other situations may by no means be what they seem. An organization with an impressive letterhead and name purports to speak for thousands or hundreds of thousands of people when it consists of nothing more than an energetic promoter financed by some interest not eager to make its identity known. Or perfectly respectable organizations may be used as fronts. A recurring situation is illustrated by the remark of an official of the Association of American Railroads about a bill sponsored in the New Jersey Legislature

---

attention of the Florida Senators to the fact that under a similar requirement earlier it had been impossible to persuade any American line to divert refrigerated tonnage to Florida ports to transport fruit.—*Congressional Record* (daily ed.), July 3, 1956, p. 10590.

[30] Closely akin to legislative intelligence is the function performed by many groups of keeping their members posted on laws and regulations affecting them. Large corporations may keep track of these things themselves but trade associations perform this service for smaller concerns. The process at times shades over into the explanation of the factors underlying public policies which aids to a degree in obtaining acceptance and consent.

[31] For a case study and citations to the literature on the point, see J. C. Scott, Jr., "Membership and Participation in Voluntary Associations," *American Sociological Review*, 22 (1957), pp. 315-326.

by the Chamber of Commerce of the State of New Jersey: "Mr. Russell thinks it inadvisable to let it be known . . . that this bill was prepared by railroad counsel or is in any sense sponsored by any committee of the Association." Or false-front organizations may be established for short-term tactical advantage.

These observations make it plain that groups differ in their performance of the representative function. The spokesmen of some groups may be relied upon to present a case that has been preceded by extensive group deliberation. Others speak only for a small but active minority within the group. Some lobbyists gain reputations as men who will provide legislators with trustworthy information and advice; others follow hit-and-run tactics.

Legislation as intergroup negotiation. Another dimension of the role of organized groups in the political process may be seen in the phenomenon of legislation by negotiation. An act of a legislature may be in reality only the ratification of an agreement negotiated by the representatives of those private groups with an interest in a particular question. The legislative body, far from being pressured into conversion of private understandings into the law of the land, may act with an alacrity that comes from the pleasure of avoiding the agony of deciding a dispute between groups.

An illustration of this pattern, drawn from the work of the Vermont legislature, has been recorded in detail by Oliver Garceau and Corinne Silverman.[32] In 1951 the Associated Industries of Vermont found itself faced by a CIO-sponsored proposal to bring silicosis under the Workman's Compensation Act. The Associated Industries, on the other hand, wished to tighten the eligibility requirements for unemployment benefits, while the CIO favored an increase in both the duration and the level of benefits. In the negotiations the CIO, bargaining from a relatively weak position, agreed not to push its bills for more liberal unemployment benefits; the AIV agreed to drop its plea for tightened qualifications for benefits. The AIV conceded an occupational disease bill to deal with the silicosis question in a manner far less unacceptable to it than was the CIO proposal. All these negotiations took place in a situation that limited the demands each group could make. Enactment by the legislature came automatically when sponsors of the legislation announced that both industry and labor thought the bill should pass. The operation involved no buttonholing or pressuring of legislators, only a few of whom knew of the negotiations leading to the agreement.

[32] "A Pressure Group and the Pressured: A Case Report," *American Political Science Review*, 48 (1954), pp. 672–691.

In Illinois the process of legislation by negotiation has at times been formalized, according to studies by Gilbert Y. Steiner. Early in the century agreements between Illinois miners and operators "stipulated that neither party should introduce bills affecting the industry without previously consulting with the other." Under these arrangements the terms of a good many legislative proposals were fixed by collective bargaining. Labor might yield a point here and the operators concede a point there. An "agreed" bill would then be supported before the legislature by both the union and the operators, a set of circumstances likely to produce legislative results. Negotiation apparently became feasible in part because either group could block within the legislature proposals by the other.[33]

These examples of lawmaking by negotiation among private groups followed by formal legislative ratification raises the question of how frequently this pattern occurs. Does a large proportion of legislation find its way to the statute books by this means? The answer is that nobody knows, but probably a great many acts are preceded by varying degrees of negotiation and agreement among private groups. Often, predictable opposition from other groups moves the interest sponsoring legislation to yield a point in advance with or without negotiation. The pattern shades over into one in which members of the legislative committee mediate among affected groups and bring them to agreement.[34] Legislators, rather than undertake the onerous task of negotiating a compromise or the painful responsibility of deciding between conflict interests, may even postpone action until the groups concerned narrow their differences.[35] Administrative agencies at times take the lead in the negotiation of agreement among groups interested in legislation.

[33] For Professor Steiner's insightful analysis, see his *Legislation by Collective Bargaining* (Urbana: University of Illinois, 1951).

[34] The following interchange between Representatives illustrates the point:

"Mr. Gavin. I am tremendously interested in the bill also and I wanted to state that the bill as amended has been approved by the Izaak Walton League, the Outdoor Writers Association, the National Parks Association, the Wilderness Society, and the Wildlife Management Association.

"Mr. Bonner. The gentleman is correct; and I wish to advise him and the other Members of the House that we, and the committee, have had a difficult time working this bill out so that it would receive unanimous support of both the commercial fishing interests and the sportsmen of the Nation, which the amendment I have added to the Senate bill does."—*Congressional Record* (daily ed.), July 7, 1956, p. 10911.

[35] In 1947 the Arkansas House of Representatives, faced by different programs suggested by veterans organizations, adopted a resolution asking all the veterans groups to submit a "just, fair, reasonable and adequate consolidated veterans' legislative program" so that the General Assembly might enact laws that the former servicemen "so justly deserve."—*Arkansas Gazette,* January 17, 1947.

Group involvement in administration. Organized groups, as was noted earlier, may play a role of representation in relationships with administrative agencies. They advocate the cause of their members, provide information, encourage, and on occasion, intimidate. In another range of relationships they attempt to bring under their dominion administrative agencies of concern to them. One can only speak of recurring tendencies, for the realities differ from time to time and from situation to situation. Moreover, though the relationships often elude precise description because of their subtlety, they range from friendly collaboration, through virtual subjection of the administrative agency to the will of the organized group, to formal assumption of governmental powers by the private group.

Interest groups tend to share and advocate a similar fundamental philosophy about administrative role and organization. The doctrine recurs that the role of administrative agencies should be to function as advocates within the government of the interests within society with which they are concerned: the Department of Commerce should look out for business; Agriculture, for the farmer; the Bureau of Wildlife Management, for the sportsmen. Adherence to this doctrine by public officials, as often occurs, paves the way for harmonious relations between organized groups and their opposite numbers within administration.[36]

The philosophy of administrative representation of private interest carries with it the doctrine that administrative structure should be arranged to facilitate the exertion of group influences over administration, although rarely does a group make the contention so baldly. Thus, groups often advocate administrative arrangements that segregate into compact units governmental activities of concern to them. Such an arrangement facilitates the development of relations of mutual interdependence. For example, the teamsters union and truck transport associations urge that road transport regulation be handled by an independent agency and not by the Interstate Commerce Commission, an agency that also deals with railroads. The commercial fishermen hope for a separate bureau dedicated to their problems.

These administrative arrangements may create a relationship between agency and clientele in which the clientele, in the reality of politics, comes to control agency policy or at least have a veto over it. In state governments, for example, it is often difficult to tell at what point the state banking department ends and the state bankers' association begins. Pro-

---

[36] Consider the 1954 statement by Secretary of Commerce Sinclair Weeks: "I'm down in Washington pitching all the time for business."—*Boston Herald,* October 5, 1954.

fessor Fesler, after examining the situation in several states, concludes: "State banking departments are typically dominated by the bankers' association of the state." He finds that the control of state departments concerned with insurance and building and loan associations is "roughly analogous to that of banking departments." [37] Pieces of federal administrative machinery also at times come virtually under the control of private groups. In 1946 the Executive Committee of the American Legion had the effrontery virtually to summon General Omar Bradley, the Administrator of Veterans Affairs, to appear before it in Indianapolis to defend his policies. The General found it "impracticable" to attend and invited the committee to appear in his Washington office. The incident warrants attention only because it indicated that the usual plasticity of the administrator at the hands of the Legion did not prevail in this instance.

Formalized advisory and consultative relations between government agencies and those affected by its action provide a linkage that may closely approach group management of the agency. During World War II, the War Production Board built up an extensive system of industry advisory committees to aid in formulating policies concerning particular industries. These committees consisted of businessmen chosen by the board in a manner to be representative of all segments of industry: large and small, trade association and nontrade association.[38] Trade associations at times urge that such advisory committees consist of the board of directors of the association. In the National Recovery Administration of the New Deal, the directing groups of trade associations were assimilated into the governmental structure as code authorities to exercise governmental power over their respective industries. The code authorities attempted to enforce as law in large degree the practices that they had earlier sought, as private associations, to have their members follow.[39]

Authority is both elusive and mercurial and in these and other relations the determination of who is the boss at a particular time—government agency or private group—is often not easy. Private associations at times virtually take over an administrative agency by their control of the

[37] "Independence of State Regulatory Agencies," *American Political Science Review*, 34 (1940), p. 943.

[38] For a treatment of the practical and theoretical aspects of representation of interest, see Avery Leiserson, *Administrative Regulation, A Study in Representation of Interests* (Chicago: University of Chicago Press, 1942).

[39] The problems associated with private capture of government authority plagued the Eisenhower Administration in defense-connected activities. The normal difficulties were exacerbated by the disposition to rely upon affected industries to provide men to serve as government officials without compensation, a policy predictably productive of conflicts of interest.

appointment of its chief. The capacity to exert this control varies, but a private group almost invariably desires the chief of an agency of concern to them to be one of their own kind, a person who "understands" their problems. The following resolution by the American Federation of Labor indicates a spirit that pervades most organized groups:

WHEREAS, The various Government agencies dealing with the problems of labor and labor relations are headed and staffed with executives who are not trained in the Labor Movement, therefore, be it

RESOLVED, That the American Federation of Labor make known by way of official communication to all such Government agencies and to the President of the United States, its opposition to the appointment in executive and/or administrative position any person or persons who have not been trained in the Labor Movement and who are not themselves members of Organized Labor.

All these relationships between administration and private group produce varying results. The situation recurs in which the private group tends to convert public administration to group purpose. At the extreme, the power of the state is formally delegated to private organization and the line between public and private realms, often hazy at best, is erased.[40] Even when that point is not reached, private organizations, interwoven as they tend to be with the state's administrative apparatus, constitute to a degree an element of the machinery of government. Observation of the tendency of private groups to become assimilated into the apparatus of the state has led some political philosophers to advocate a formal incorporation of private groups into the governmental machinery. Such theories of pluralism once enjoyed considerable vogue, but the prevailing American view is that such aggrandizement of centers of private power would mightily complicate the problem of governing in the general interest.

Restraints on Particularism

We have seen that nonparty groups perform significant roles as virtual elements of the political system. Much public policy emerges from the

---

[40] To round out these summary observations the broad point should be repeated that private associations often perform, completely outside the formal governmental system, a function of governance. The formation and enforcement of norms of conduct occurs in labor unions, trade associations, churches, professional societies, and other groups. No small amount of public government flows from the weaknesses of private groups, unable to enforce their own norms, who appeal for state action to restrain, for example, the irresponsible sector of the trade. On occasion governance by private centers of authority extends beyond its own membership to control of of other elements in society. Consider how the Legion of Decency brought the movie industry to heel; in effect, one private group enacted laws to govern another and set up machinery, backed by powerful sanctions, to enforce them.

deliberations and experiences within private groups, as well as from friction, attrition, and agreement among groups. Private codes may be transmuted into statutes. Governance may be with the consent of the governed; it may also be at the initiative of the governed. The stuff of politics consists of these intricate and variegated group processes, as well as the great weighing of strength in a presidential election.

Probably, the political role of the nonparty group flows inevitably from social specialization and differentiation. If the system of organized groups did not exist, it would have to be contrived. Yet the operations of groups may endanger the general welfare—or more certainly the liberties and rights of members of other groups. While group objectives run from the selfless ambition to promote an unexceptionable cause to the most indefensible advancement of human greed, groups almost inevitably promote particularistic causes and partial interests. That endeavor need arouse no great concern until one partial interest collides with another or threatens a general interest. A major preoccupation of government is the policing of conflicts of interest.

Balancing of interest. To some extent, the outrageous demands of pressure groups are checked by the demands of other groups that may be equally outrageous. In situation after situation legislators and administrators are confronted by groups pushing in opposite directions, a state of affairs which permits government to balance one off against the other and to arrive more easily at a solution thought to represent the general interest.

Although the restraint of mutual antagonism is built into the group system, that check does not operate in many situations. The objectives of groups well disciplined and amply supplied with the materiel of political warfare often are countered by no organization of equal strength. The opposing interest may, in fact, be completely unorganized. The lobbyists for electrical utilities, for example, are eternally on the job; the lobbyists for the consumers of this monopolistic service are ordinarily conspicuous by their absence. The representation of these unorganized sectors of society becomes the task of politicians who, bedeviled by the group spokesmen on the ground, may succumb to the immediate and tangible pressures. In short, while group pressures often cancel each other out, this process restrains particularism erratically and uncertainly.

Overlapping group membership. Another restraint built into the group system arises from the limitations on group action from overlapping or multiple membership. Private groups rarely encompass all the interests or command the complete loyalty of their members. An upstanding citizen may be both a member of a parent-teachers association and of a taxpayers' association. He seeks both better schools and lower taxes. The leadership cliques of both groups may be limited by the risk that their members or at least some of them will not follow if they go too far. The sensitivity of the leaders of private organizations to such conflicting claims often is heightened by the fact that a goodly portion of their energies are consumed merely by the effort to keep the organization alive.

Overlapping membership may do more than dull the sharpness of group demands; it may immobilize a group on some issues. Thus, a recent Massachusetts campaign on a proposal to modify legislation prohibiting the dissemination of birth-control information saw the state medical society refrain from taking a position in deference to its minority Roman Catholic membership. In the same campaign the state federation of women's clubs took a stand in favor of liberalization and, when the rumblings began, hastily backed off. "We do have," an officer told the press, "people of many faiths and it's difficult when something controversial comes up. It's caused a lot of difficulty." Similarly, national labor organizations have adopted policies favorable to desegregation, although not without considerable anxiety about its effects on organizational unity. Many southern unionists belong also to white citizens' councils. On some questions members of business organizations have been torn between their loyalties to their trade association and their loyalties to the Republican party, a conflict that developed as the Eisenhower Administration asked business groups to turn off the heat on some questions in view of the exigencies it faced.

Regulation of lobbying. An old maxim of American political reform is that publicity is a powerful corrective of wrong-doing. If lobbyists work openly, the reasoning goes, their animus will be known to all and both legislator and public will be protected. Congress and over half the states require lobbyists to file financial reports which are available for public inspection. So mild a requirement may be of more significance than might be supposed, if one judges from the dodges employed to evade it.

The Federal Regulation of Lobbying Act of 1946 requires individuals, associations, corporations, and others seeking to influence legislation to register and file quarterly reports. These reports include an indication of specific bills in which the reporter is interested, a listing of publications issued in connection with legislative interests, receipts (including names of contributors of $500 or more during the quarter), and expenditures (including the names of recipients of expenditures of $10 or more). The reports, filed with officials of the House and the Senate, are assembled and printed quarterly in the *Congressional Record*. Although the Lobbying Act is ambiguous with respect to coverage and the facts to be reported, its operation has produced more comprehensive data than have hitherto been available on groups and individuals seeking to influence Congress.[41]

The requirement of periodic reports from lobbying organizations is supplemented by congressional investigations of pressure activities.[42] Such an inquiry may be instituted as an incident to a battle over a particular piece of legislation. Thus, in the 1935 debate over the Public Utility Holding Company Act inquiry brought out that utility people working to arouse opposition to the bill had let their enthusiasm run away with them. Wearied in their solicitation of telegrams to Congressmen, they began to sign to messages names selected at random from city directories. The timely revelation of such hijinks on the front pages presumably saps the potency of pressure. In 1956 a special inquiry into the gentle rain of $2,500 contributions to senatorial campaign funds at least made clear what sort of campaign was being waged on natural gas legislation even if it affected few votes in the Senate.

To be contrasted with such investigations in connection with individual bills are the occasional broad inquiries into the lobbying process generally. In 1949–1950 a House select committee, under the chairmanship of the late Frank Buchanan, a Representative from Pennsylvania, conducted a broad investigation that produced ten volumes of hearings, an invaluable source of information on lobbying activities. In 1956 the Senate set up a committee, under the chairmanship of Senator McClellan, to inquire generally into lobbying activities.[43]

---

[41] For an analysis of the act, see Belle Zeller, "The Federal Regulation of Lobbying Act," *American Political Science Review*, 42 (1948), pp. 239–271. See the McClellan Committee's proposed revision of the act, S. Rept. 395, 85th Cong., 1st sess. (1957), pp. 83–105. Whatever regulation of lobbying that occurs must not, to meet constitutional challenge, restrict the right of petition or abridge freedom of speech. In United States *v.* Harriss, 347 U.S. 612 (1954), the Supreme Court held that the federal act did not limit these rights but in so holding the Court interpreted rather narrowly the definition of persons to whom it applied. For a discussion of litigation under the act, see S. Rept. 395, 85th Cong., 1st sess. (1957), pp. 66–68.

[42] For a guide to such congressional inquiries and other related material, see D. C. Tompkins, *Congressional Investigation of Lobbying* (Berkeley: University of California Bureau of Public Administration, 1956).

[43] The power of Congress to inquire into the activities of those seeking to influence legislation has been challenged. In 1950 Edward A. Rumely, of the Committee for Constitutional Government, claimed that the guarantee of freedom of speech and press protected him from the demand of a congressional committee that he disclose the names of purchasers of publications of his committee. Instead of accepting "contributions" (which are required to be reported by the lobbying act), Dr. Rumely's

Registration and financial reports do not furnish information on the manner in which a group arrives at its legislative program, the representative or nonrepresentative character of the group, or other data useful to the legislator in appraising the statements of group spokesmen. In the routine course of committee hearings, legislators often seek such information from those who appear before them as legislative counsel.[44]

Statutory regulation of the activities of private associations presents questions both of constitutional power and of policy. Such control as is exercised must not abridge freedom of speech or restrict the exercise of the right of petition. Prohibition of lobbying would infringe the liberty of the citizen.[45] Special difficulties, both of constitutional power and of

---

committee accepted "orders" for books and other literature which were then distributed by the committee. The investigating committee's chairman called this a "phony sales dodge." Dr. Rumely wanted, he said, to avoid exposing the purchasers to "the pressure of the labor bosses or the smear of left-wingers." In 1951 Dr. Rumely was convicted for contempt of Congress because of his refusal to answer the committee's questions. The Supreme Court upheld a reversal of the conviction by the circuit court, but avoided the constitutional question by resting its decision on a finding that the investigating committee had exceeded the authority granted to it by the House. See U.S. *v.* Rumely, 345 U.S. 41 (1953).

[44] A new tactic in defense against high-powered activities has been developed by Pennsylvania truckers in their battles with the railroads. In their management of the railroad campaign against a bill to permit heavier trucks on the Pennsylvania highways, Carl Byoir & Associates had shown the uncanny capacity of public-relations experts to impart to their political work an aroma of crookedness and a texture of slickness. The firm's strategy in essence was not to show its hand as a railroad instrument but to make it appear that a grass-roots sentiment opposed the truckers which was accomplished by boring into existing organizations, by creating front organizations for propaganda, and by other such means. The truckers were not inactive themselves and finally in 1953 brought an unusual sort of suit under the antitrust act. They sought damages on the claim that the railroads had conspired to eliminate the truckers from interstate commerce in violation of the Sherman Act. To the astonishment of the railroads, which had done nothing more heinous than to exercise the ancient right of the citizen to try to flimflam the public and the legislature, a district court denied their motion to dismiss the suit.—Noerr Motor Freight Inc. *v.* Eastern Railroad Presidents Conference, 113 F. Supp. 737 (1953). While the litigation was in abeyance the truckers won passage of their legislation, but negotiations with the railroads to drop the suit failed. Whereupon in 1956 the railroads tried to file a counter action for $120 millions in damages; the truckers claim was for $250 millions. For a discussion of the case, see the note in *Harvard Law Review*, 67 (1953), pp. 354–5. For an account of the propaganda campaign, see Robert Bendiner, "The 'Engineering of Consent'—A Case Study," *The Reporter*, April 11, 1955.

[45] The possibilities in repression are suggested by the parallel actions of several southern states in 1956 and 1957 in harassment of the NAACP. Included were prosecutions for barratry, for activities tending "to create a breach of the peace," for doing business in the state without a permit, and investigations designed to make public membership lists to allow private coercion, economic and otherwise, of the

policy, attend the problem of controlling those group activities designed to "educate" the public rather than to deal directly with Congress. The question arises of the sorts of disclosures of contributions and expenditures that may be required of private groups without limiting freedom of speech and press.[46]

Pressure Groups and Political Parties

Organized interests constitute elements in the total political system and play significant roles in the political process as a whole. To account for the directions and content of public policy these groups, as well as political parties and the formal apparatus of government, must be brought into the picture. The earlier pages of this chapter set out the major types of relations between pressure groups and such elements of the formal institutional system as the legislative body and administrative agencies. In the description of the place of groups in the political system a question remains about the relations between pressure groups and political parties. Both types of organization are informal and extraconstitutional agencies that provide a good deal of the propulsion for the formal constitutional system. Unless some idea of the pattern of their relationships can be constructed, the mistaken notion may be left that they are independent and unrelated.

One broad proposition descriptive of the place of organized interests seems to fit, or to arrange in orderly fashion, a great many of the facts about their role in and linkage to the political system. At one extreme, along a scale of differentiation, the organized group pursues its objective in dealing with governmental functionaries—legislative and administrative—more or less independently of political parties. Its characteristics and the circumstances of its operation permit it more or less autonomously to function as a mechanism of communication between its membership and government. At the opposite extreme are organized groups which tend to operate in the closest communion with one [or the other] of the po-

---

members. See American Jewish Congress, *Assault Upon Freedom of Association* (New York, 1957).

[46] See the discussion of the matter in "Registration of Groups Tending to Influence Public Opinion," *Columbia Law Review*, 48 (1948), pp. 589–605. Federal income-tax regulations prohibit the deduction from gross income as a business expense of sums expended to "influence legislation." See "Tax Treatment of Lobbying Expenses and Contributions," *Harvard Law Review*, 67 (1954), pp. 1408–1417. The character of enforcement is an unknown quantity, but, after prodding by the McClellan Committee, the Commissioner of Internal Revenue in 1957 held that contributions to the "education campaign" of the Natural Gas and Oil Resources Committee were not deductible. The NGOR had spent almost $2 million to suggest the undesirability of federal regulation of gas prices.

litical parties. Their relationship may be one not only of parallelism of objective but of active collaboration. Between these two extremes are groups approaching in degree one [or the other] of the poles of the continuum. Such a conception amounts, in one of its dimensions, to the idea that a division of labor prevails between political parties and pressure groups; in another of its aspects it takes into account the collaboration that sometimes prevails between parties and pressure groups. The broad idea also implicitly recognizes that there are groups and groups; their size, composition, and objectives differ; so do their role and function in the political system.

Division of labor between pressure groups and parties. In the workings of the political system a division of labor occurs between political parties and pressure groups. This is not necessarily a clean-cut separation of functions. Parties perform some functions almost never undertaken by pressure groups; and some of the activities of groups—and perhaps most of the activities of many groups—concern matters that parties seldom take a position on. On the other hand, on some matters parties and at least some groups work either in collaboration or in opposition.

Among those functions most clearly assigned to parties is the nomination of candidates and the assumption of responsibility for the conduct of the government once an election is won. To be sure, a party may be, even in this activity, only a mask for a pressure group. On occasion a party within a state or a smaller jurisdiction may be the creature of a manufacturers' association, a farm group, or a labor organization. Yet by and large, the party does nominate candidates and does assume responsibility for running the government (although it is not to be denied that individual groups may run small pieces of the government).

Parties, too, make commitments on broad questions of public policy.[47] So do some pressure groups, but parties do not, and need not, take positions as parties on wide ranges of public policy and administration. To private organizations falls the task of formulation of recommendations and their advocacy in this sphere of government action that includes matters important to limited numbers of persons, quite technical matters, and the minutiae of government policy and operation as they affect particular interests.[48] To cite an instance: The American Glassware As-

[47] Parties and not pressure groups lead in the adoption of truly great measures. It is a custom of American politics that Congress enacts no heroic measure to remedy pervasive evils save over the violent protests of those to be immediately affected. The groups concerned predict dire consequences but ultimately learn to live with the new order. See the remarks of Mr. Sam Rayburn, *Congressional Record* (daily ed.), March 27, 1957, pp. 4032–33.

[48] Perhaps a line should be explicitly drawn between group action and individual

sociation urges the Census Bureau to tabulate imports of small shipments of glassware, a question that scarcely needs to be a matter of party policy. Or the American Beekeeping Federation opposes the "discriminatory part of the proposed prune juice order which prevents honey from being used as an added ingredient." Neither party need be regarded as derelict if it fails to become exercised about the question.

Furthermore, pressure-group staffs may perform a significant function of communication linking together government and the membership of their group. They may needle administrators into action—the functional equivalent of the action of the ward boss in taking care of a citizen's complaint about rubbish collection. They may advise; they may provide information; they may disseminate and explain rulings and regulations to their membership. Collectively this humdrum labor mightily relieves the party and the legislative representative. Congressmen must, of course, run an appalling number of errands and seek out the answers to a steady bombardment of inquiries. Their tasks would be even more formidable if the staffs of organized groups did not do a great deal of this work.

Partisan clusters of interest groups. Though a division of labor exists between political parties and pressure groups, it seems clear also that many pressure groups—perhaps most of the more important ones—have a partisan orientation. That proposition, which will be elaborated shortly, needs to be set against the traditional conception of pressure groups as nonpartisan organizations that pursue their objectives by building fires quite impartially under legislators of both parties. Since, so the reasoning went, major policy questions cut across both parties, their settlement required the construction of bipartisan legislative coalitions.

The old stereotype of pressure-group operation has been extended far more generally to group activity than the facts seem to warrant. It described quite well some of the great pressure-group campaigns. The Anti-Saloon League in its prohibition agitation built up a following that cut across party lines and pushed its measures through legislative bodies by building bipartisan coalitions. The organizations spearheading the movement for woman suffrage similarly recruited support wherever they could find it. While an occasional large-scale movement develops that cuts

action vis-à-vis government. Even in legislation, government continues to deal, more often than is commonly recognized, with the individual case rather than with the rights and duties of categories of persons. Thus, a bill to rehabilitate coastwise shipping turns out to be a bill to rehabilitate the finances of an individual shipping concern. Tax legislation is shot through with clauses designed for the advantage of a particular individual or firm, although they may be cast in general language. The advocacy of such individual actions raises, of course, a series of questions not covered by the group analysis.

across party lines, more often a group—at least a major group economically based—finds most of its friends in one party and only a few in the other. All pressure groups avoid formal affiliation with a political party and nurture their friends whatever party label they bear; nevertheless most of a group's friends are likely to have the same party label.

On the national scene certain major pressure groups cluster about each party. The policy orientations of the parties plough a furrow through the group system and most of the major groups—and some of the lesser groups—find one party far more congenial to their tastes than the other.[49] There should scarcely be dissent from the proposition that the leadership of certain peak organizations rests far more easily when the Republican party controls the national government. Included would be such groups as the Chamber of Commerce of the United States, the National Manufacturers Association, the American Iron and Steel Institute, the National Association of Electric Companies, and the American Farm Bureau Federation. This is not to say that all members of these organizations are Republicans or that the organizations get everything they seek from a Republican Administration. Yet they certainly enjoy easier access to points of authority and their own policies tend to converge with those of the Republican party. Nor is this to say that such organizations cannot do business under a Democratic Administration; they only believe that they do business with the government under those circumstances under less favorable terms.

A contrasting but less-imposing array of organizations runs with the Democrats. Perhaps most important is the AFL-CIO, which, like other groups, flies nonpartisan colors but seems to flourish must under Democratic rule. The Farmers' Union feels out in the cold when Republicans hold office. Importers' associations generally regard Democrats warmly as do the American Public Power Association and the National Association of Rural Electric Co-operatives.[50]

The contention is not that either party commits itself unreservedly to its camp followers among the pressure groups. Yet, given the drift of policy of either party, it attracts some groups and repels others. Democratic policy, for example, created no bond of affection between the party and the National Association of Manufacturers.[51] On the other hand, the AFL-CIO, while not enamored of all Democrats, began to encounter

[49] See E. E. Schattschneider, "Pressure Groups Versus Political Parties," *Annals of the American Academy of Political and Social Science*, 259 (Sept., 1948), pp. 17–23.
[50] For a thoughtful analysis which touches the several aspects of the relations between parties and farm groups, see C. M. Hardin, "Farm Price Policy and the Farm Vote," *Journal of Farm Economics*, 37 (1955), pp. 601–624.
[51] See R. W. Gable, "NAM: Influential Lobby or Kiss of Death?" *Journal of Politics*, 15 (1953), pp. 254–273.

rough sledding when Republicans won Congress in 1946 and its leaders after 1952 were consulted by the White House far less frequently than before. Similar differences in relations occur in the administrative departments; a change of administration tends to change the faces of the most influential lobbyists around the Secretary's office.[52]

The partisan orientation of large groups with a varied membership becomes more noticeable as these groups move from the advocacy of the narrow interests of their membership toward an attempt to represent the views of their members on almost the whole range of public questions. The resolutions of such organizations as the Chamber of Commerce, the AFL-CIO, and the American Farm Bureau Federation are not limited to matters of business, labor, and farming. All these organizations resolve on everything from atomic energy to public education. When groups expand their range of concern over the affairs of mankind they are bereft of cues to action in their immediate self-interest and grasp hold of whatever ideological rudder seems to suit their taste. Thus, in 1956 the board of directors of the American Farm Bureau Federation adopted a resolution supporting the position of the Eisenhower Administration on the development of hydro-electric power of Hells Canyon in Idaho. Farmers as farmers had no clearly defined concern about the matter, and the board of directors simply followed the ideological line of an organization generally as one with the Republican party and not indisposed to adopt a resolution at a strategic moment to aid their partisan allies.[53] Or when in 1955 the president of the CIO appeared before the House Committee on Agriculture to urge support of the Democratic-sponsored farm bill, he was performing a role different from that of the old-fashioned lobbyist who stuck to his own knitting.

Partisan and ideological differences may strain the unity of organizations based on common vocation or economic pursuit. Such differences may, indeed, provide the basis for groups of similar economic concern but of differing ideologies. For example, the policy differences between the Farmers' Union and the Farm Bureau Federation are probably much wider than are the economic circumstances of their membership. Farm Bureau control has been grasped in the main by persons with a long-standing conservative and Republican orientation. Evidently the Farmers' Union, perhaps by the accidents of history, attracts a membership tinged with old Populist rambunctiousness.[54] These ideological orientations guide

[52] See, for example, C. M. Hardin, "The Republican Department of Agriculture—A Political Interpretation," *Journal of Farm Economics*, 36 (1954), pp. 210–227.

[53] The Farmers' Union which also spoke for farmers but from a different ideological base regarded the Eisenhower power policy as "a total surrender to the electric company lobby."

[54] A small-scale study in Oklahoma found members of the Farm Bureau and Farmers' Union remarkably similar in economic circumstance and concluded that "the two

the organizations as they wander over the expanse of public questions and adopt resolutions purportedly reflecting membership preferences. Given the program or ideological choices organized groups face, they wind up generally on one side of the fence between the national parties.

Interweaving of party and group activities. Alliances of opinion and attitude between party and pressure group are supplemented by relations of mutual defense and offense in the legislative and electoral field. These relations invariably fall short of formal affiliation with the party; groups maintain a façade of nonpartisanism.

In the workings of legislative bodies, lobbying is often said to be destructive of party discipline and subversive of party leadership. At intervals, the legislative allies of an interest group do form a coalition cutting across party lines and wrest leadership from the parties. With the major economically-based pressure groups clustered around the Republican and Democratic parties, the broad tendency is that lobbying on many issues re-enforces the leadership of the party with which the group is allied. When Democratic leadership and the AFL-CIO are allied, the effects of pressure and party leadership operate in the same direction. The labor lobby may aid in holding in line a few wavering legislators. On the other hand, a lobbying organization, in so far as it exerts influence, may pull from the party generally opposed to it a few representatives whose circumstances are such that they can be weaned from their party leadership. Pressure groups cannot well assume the function of general legislative leadership. On the other hand, when party or presidential leadership is weak or indifferent, they may be extremely influential in the prevention of action.

The influence of private groups may be felt in the drafting of party platforms, in the making of nominations, and in the election itself. Here again a differentiation must be made between those private groups that maintain a fairly genuine freedom from involvement with political parties and those that approach the reality of alliance with Republicans or Democrats.

In the drafting of national platforms, resolutions committees, or their subcommittees, hear representations of the larger organized interests. The nature of the reception of the spokesmen for private interests depends largely on the broad relationship of their organization with the party. Labor leaders observe that they are received more cordially by Democratic committees and the party platforms tend to lean more to the labor viewpoint. Similarly business spokesmen have easier sledding with Republican resolutions committees. These differentials in access to the parties

organizations differ more in their ideologies than in their vested interests."—R. A. Rohwer, "Organized Farmers in Oklahoma," *Rural Sociology*, 17 (1952), pp. 39-47.

flow in part from the fact that the membership of private groups overlaps that of the party hierarchies. Labor leaders often sit in Democratic conventions as delegates and also occupy posts in the party hierarchy. Businessmen are not absent from Democratic conventions, but they occupy a position of considerably greater prestige in Republican gatherings.

Even in the making of presidential nominations private groups may exercise something of a veto, although it may be expressed by means far less formal than a resolution. An aspirant for a Democratic presidential or vice-presidential nomination is apt to have only gloomy prospects if he is opposed by the leaders of organized labor. Nor is a Republican a good prospect if he has earned the disfavor of the business community, although that disfavor is not apt to be expressed through formal actions by business organizations.

In the campaign itself organized groups vary from aloofness to complete involvement. What stance to assume involves a strategy question of considerable import for the group. A comparatively weak group whose objectives stir no great partisan issue may be far better advised to remain completely quiet during campaigns. They are strong enough to offend people who may win and with whom they will have to deal; they are too weak to create strong friends among those who win. On the other hand, the interests of some groups are so completely identified with those of a party that they might as well join in the fray and risk the consequences.

Private groups may engage in several types of campaign activity. The circulation of the voting records of legislators is a frequent practice. Those circulated by labor organizations ordinarily indicate that most of the legislators with "good" voting records from the labor standpoint are Democrats, while business sees statesmanlike qualities more frequently among Republicans.[55] The compilation of records may or may not be accompanied by a public endorsement of candidates. Not infrequently the public identification of a candidate with a particular group may be of negative value; the group endorsement drives away more votes than it attracts.[56] A group leadership sensitive to the proprieties consults a candidate before announcement of its support.

Endorsement may be backed up with active support. Labor organizations, working through their political subsidiaries, often help to get out

[55] This relationship may or may not hold with respect to state legislators, depending upon whether party lines mean anything in the state. The 1955 legislative report of the Associated Industries of Massachusetts listed 76 legislators with a zero record on measures of interest to industry during that year. All 76 happened to be Democrats. Another 82 legislators, all Republicans, scored 100 per cent in their votes on measures of interest to industry.

[56] H. E. Freeman and Morris Showel, "Differential Political Influence of Voluntary Associations," *Public Opinion Quarterly*, 15 (1951–52), pp. 703–714.

the vote and to man the polls. In a few states, especially those in which the Democratic party had been for a long time moribund, the labor movement in the 1930's virtually took over the Democratic organization. Manpower for the performance of party chores may also be supplemented by contributions to campaign funds. The role of labor organizations in party finance has been more or less open and aboveboard. Most of their political money goes to support Democratic candidates; and, in at least one union, the official who does the lobbying also doles out campaign contributions. If other national organizations, as organizations, contribute to campaign funds, it is not a matter of public record. In all sorts of organizations with a leaning toward this party or that a handful of ringleaders in the group often turns up under another guise as members of party finance committees or as fund solicitors. The association in form may not contribute but the relationships built up within the group can easily be converted to fund-raising purposes.[57] Short of actual campaign contributions, the general propaganda campaign of a pressure organization may incidentally promote the candidates of the party most in tune with its cause. During the 1950 congressional campaigns "not a single comment was made regarding the congressional campaigns" in the *Nation's Business*, the official organ of the Chamber of Commerce. In August, however, the magazine "began a series of articles entitled 'Seed Beds of Socialism' in which it characterized the Federal Security Administration as a blueprint for a totalitarian state, and the Department of Agriculture and Interior as more evidence of the destruction of American freedom." [58]

[57] Doubtless many pressure groups channel organization funds to candidates, but not much of this activity is a matter of record. Mr. Arthur H. Samish, once a noted California lobbyist, represented among other clients the California State Brewers Institute. Although in his appearance before Senator Kefauver's committee in 1951 Mr. Samish was somewhat evasive, the general drift of his story was that each campaign year he and his clients looked over the situation from the Oregon line to the Mexican border and decided which candidates to support for offices from city councilman up. An undetermined proportion of the institute's annual fund of around $150,000 for public relations went for political purposes. See *Investigation of Organized Crime in Interstate Commerce*, Hearings, Special Committee to Investigate Organized Crime, U.S. Senate, 81st Cong., Pt. 10, p. 1161ff.

[58] Joseph G. La Palombara, "Pressure, Propaganda, and Political Action in the Elections of 1950," *Journal of Politics*, 14 (1952), pp. 300–325.

Part Two | **THE PARTY SYSTEM**

In some respects a pressure group is a fairly simple entity. Brewers, for example, are threatened by a prohibition movement. They sense danger, recognize their common concern, and form an association to defend their shared interest. The group possesses a sharply defined membership, a concrete purpose with which all the members are psychologically identified, and the attributes of unity essential for concerted action. Not all pressure groups, to be sure, fit this simple pattern. As their membership increases, as they become less homogeneous, as the common interest dwindles, they become aggregates many of whose "members" identify themselves with the group only vaguely or intermittently. Nevertheless a relatively clear-cut sense of purpose tends to animate most pressure groups.

A political party, at least on the American scene, tends to be a "group" of a peculiar sort. Perhaps only by courtesy may a party be designated as a group. Among its members the sense of belonging, the awareness of shared concern, and the impulse to action in the same direction may be scarcely discernible.

A fundamental difficulty in talking about political party is that the term is applied without discrimination to many types of groups and near-groups. Discussion may be facilitated by some preliminary differentiations of the usages of the word "party." Within the body of voters as a whole, groups are formed of persons who regard themselves as party members. The Democratic group and the Republican group are mobilized only on election day but in the intervals between elections the members of each group—or many of them—react in characteristic partisan ways to public issues. Party in the sense of the "party-in-the-electorate" [1] is an amorphous group. It is not tightly knit like, say, a football team. Yet it is more than a statistically defined class of the population. It has a social reality not possessed by such statistical groups as "all" women, "all" men, or all persons between the ages 25–29.

In another sense the term party may refer to the group of more or less professional political workers. The Republican national committeemen, the Republican state central committees, the Republican county chairmen, and all the men and women who do the work of the political organization constitute a "group" more or less separate and apart from the "party-in-the-electorate," but not necessarily independent of it. In fact the professional political group usually consists of many subgroups, as does the "party-in-the-electorate," but for some purposes, and on some occasions, each may be regarded as a single great group.

At times party denotes groups within the government. Thus all Democratic Repre-

[1] The phrase is Ralph M. Goldman's. See his *Party Chairmen and Party Factions, 1789–1900* (Chicago: University of Chicago, Ph.D. dissertation, MS, 1951), ch. 17.

sentatives form a group within the House that acts with high solidarity on many matters. Similarly Republican Senators form a party group. At times there may be a "party-in-the-government" including the President, groups of his party in both House and Senate, and the heads of executive departments. We tend always to speak as if there were such a group which could be held accountable for the conduct of the government.

There are other senses in which the term party is used. Often it refers to an entity which rolls into one the party-in-the-electorate, the professional political group, the party-in-the-legislature, and the party-in-the-government. "The Democrats (or the Republicans) are to blame for the parlous state of the country." In truth, this all-encompassing usage has its legitimate application for all the types of groups called party interact more or less closely and at times may be as one. Yet both analytically and operationally the term party most of the time must refer to several types of group; and it is useful to keep relatively clear the meaning in which the term is used.

No attempt has been made to organize the entire book along the distinctions of the foregoing paragraphs. Though the chapters that make up Part Two include a great deal of data on the "party-in-the-electorate," their principal objective is to explain the function of the party system in the American governing process.

7 | The Party Battle, 1896-1956

A SKETCH of recent party history may serve as a bridge from our survey of the great interests within society to a detailed analysis of the party system. Political history is often sterile stuff, a collection of names, dates, titles, and events beaded on a chronological string. Yet a time perspective can yield an awareness of dimensions of the political system that otherwise escape detection. The wars of domestic politics, like those between nations, are not events of a moment but extend through the years.[1]

Modern political systems seem to be in a state of ceaseless unease. Social changes threaten their stability; external dangers jeopardize their exist-

[1] The best party history is by W. E. Binkley, *American Political Parties* (New York: Knopf, 1943). A more exhaustive treatment devoted principally to the period before 1910 is by Herbert Agar, *The Price of Union* (Boston: Houghton Mifflin, 1950). Another, older survey is E. E. Robinson, *The Evolution of American Parties* (New York: Harcourt, Brace, 1924). In addition to detailed election figures, brief discussions of each election are presented by W. Dean Burnham, *Presidential Ballots, 1836–1892* (Baltimore: Johns Hopkins Press, 1955) and by E. E. Robinson, *The Presidential Vote, 1896–1932* (Stanford: Stanford University Press, 1934) and *They Voted*

ence. Groups within the political system respond, defensively or offensively, to changes in their circumstances that develop with the march of history. Similarly the party system undergoes profound modification in its movement from the past into the future. The problems it meets are radically different from those of pressure groups. Political institutions must provide for the legitimate aspirations of group interests, a function partially met by toleration of organized groups. Yet a society built only of pressure groups would be a regime of incessant turmoil. Order must be imposed upon clashing particularisms; a semblance of national unity of purpose must be achieved.

To the political parties falls the task of keeping the peace among group interests. Political parties both comprehend and transcend the special interests of society: they must take into account the demands of interest groups; they must also consider aspirations not represented by organized groups; they must seek to speak for the nation as a whole—or at least for a substantial majority—and not merely for a small part of it. Their energies actuate the machinery of government, which is a powerful engine for the allocation of this world's goods among classes and groups. Yet parties must do more than combine interests for the satisfaction of mutually compatible greed: they must, at least in their American incarnation, implant a widespread belief that their policies promote the common weal.

Alterations in the party system from decade to decade result in part from changes in relative size, number, and relations of the underlying social interests. The rise of new groups and the disappearance of old compel readjustments in the coalitions formed by party leadership. Yet party leadership is more than a pawn of social forces. Party leaders seek to maximize their power by experimentation with formulas to bring together winning coalitions. Their most clever schemes for the cumulation of strength may be offset by a more skillful opposition leadership. Particular combinations of personality, political doctrine, and economic interest may gain great popular deference for a time. External danger, economic disaster, a competing idea may tear the combination asunder and set off frantic efforts to put humpty-dumpty together again.

In this process of maneuver to create combinations powerful enough to

for Roosevelt, *The Presidential Vote, 1932–1944* (Stanford: Stanford University Press, 1947). Other party histories include: W. S. Myers, *History of the Republican Party* (New York: Century, 1928); F. R. Kent, *History of the Democratic Party* (New York: Century, 1928); Malcolm Moos, *The Republicans* (New York: Random House, 1956). On earlier episodes in party development, see Claude G. Bowers, *Making Democracy A Reality* (Memphis: Memphis State College Press, 1954); Stuart G. Brown, *The First Republicans* (Syracuse: Syracuse University Press, 1954); Manning J. Dauer, *The Adams Federalists* (Baltimore: Johns Hopkins Press, 1954).

govern—in a manner to win the plaudits of the multitude—both parties have had to preoccupy themselves with the same problems. A major thread that runs through recent party history is a concern with problems born of industrialization. The decline of agriculture, the rise of manufacturing, the growth of a laboring class, urbanization, and the concentration of economic power created both the salient issues of political debate and the social groupings that were the building blocks of party coalitions. Amidst the confusion of new interests growing in importance and of old interests declining, party leaders strove to construct governing coalitions, as well as to contrive philosophies to justify their operations.

Though the problems associated with industrialization have dominated the tasks of party management, a second major strand of concern, that of foreign policy, has emerged which sharply modifies the problem of party leadership. World War I marked the arrival of the United States to a new status in world affairs, a role that the country sought for two decades to reject. World War II and the events afterward compelled the United States to meet its responsibilities as a world power. That necessity posed new problems for party leaders in the construction of coalitions to support a government both stable enough and vigorous enough to cope with the exigencies of our external politics. The new cleavages introduced by competing views about internal policy sometimes paralleled and sometimes cut across the old divisions created by the frictions of industrialization; always they posed perplexing tasks for party leadership as it attempted to maintain political support at home for what it had to do abroad.

Conservative Dominance Tempered by Insurgency, 1896–1912

With only a bit of poetic license, it may be said that the coalition constructed under Republican leadership after the Civil War controlled the country until 1932. The Democrats attacked the dominant Republican combination and from time to time gained control of the government for short periods, a control never firm enough to permit the establishment of policies diverging markedly from the prevailing pattern. The long period of Republican rule was based on the successful conduct of a domestic war for a high and noble purpose, which identified the Republican party with the Union, with patriotism, and with humanitarianism. Yet the inner strength of Republicanism did not rest on sentiment alone. Sentiment clothed bonds of substance. To the old soldiers—old Union soldiers— went pensions. To the manufacturers of the Northeast went tariffs. To the farmers of the Northwest went free land under the Homestead Act. To railroad promoters went land grants for the construction of railroads that tied together the West and the North—and assured that the flow of commerce would by-pass the South.[2] The synthesis of self-interest and glory formed a cohesive combination. The GOP represented a wonderfully effective contrivance not only for preserving the Union but for holding together East and West, magnate and factory worker, homesteader and banker, in the great enterprise of continental unification, development, and exploitation.

The postwar Democratic party, too, had its elements of strength, minority though it was. The political scars of war project themselves powerfully, through the generations, into peacetime antipathies toward old enemies and loyalties to old comrades in arms. National policies toward the South mightily re-enforced its Democratic predilections. Conquest and occupation by even a fraternal army place a durable imprint on political attitudes. By its defeat in war, the South also lost the old, old debate on the tariff, and had to reconcile itself to the status of a producer of raw materials exploited by manufacturing interests sheltered by a tariff wall. Yet its addiction to free trade gave it allies among those northern businessmen with a parallel outlook.

To a degree, Republicans and Democrats in national campaigns refought the Civil War for two decades. Republican orators waved the bloody shirt and Democrats struggled to overcome the handicaps from their identification with the cause of the South. The lines of cleavage seared into the electorate by the War and its aftermath persisted. Meanwhile industrialization proceeded apace and created the great political problems that were to put new strains on the party system. The rate and magnitude of the economic changes wrought by industrialization from 1850 to 1900 can be set out in statistical tables but their impact on people can only be suggested. From 1850 to 1870, railroad mileage grew from 8,700 to 54,000 and by 1900 to 193,000. The transportation network sucked the life out of little businesses in villages and hamlets over the land; it made farmers far less self-sufficient and far more vulnerable to the implacable fluctuations of the market; it created both an incentive for and the possibility of combination among manufacturing businesses. By 1890 farmers were outnumbered by workers in manufacturing, transportation, and related pursuits. And with the growth of large-scale factory employment, problems new in scale, if not in kind, emerged in the relations of employers and workers.

In short, in a brief period as time goes, the country underwent an economic revolution that posed radically new problems for the political system. The travail of adjustment set off political disturbances and discon-

[2] The above follows generally W. P. Webb, "How the Republican Party Lost Its Future," *Southwest Review*, 34 (1949), pp. 329–339.

tents which on the whole found expression outside the major political parties. In the 1870's and 1880's exotic new parties and movements appeared on the American scene, symptomatic of the growing pains of the economy. Among farmers the Grangers, the Greenbackers, the Farmers' Alliance, and eventually the People's party arose to protest the subjection of the agrarians to industry and finance. The Knights of Labor held their first national convention in 1878 and by 1886 had over 700,000 members. The grand master workman of the Knights, Terrence V. Powderly, had abjured the wage earner to join together with other men "in an effort to overturn existing conditions in the industrial world which made of him a serf in a land of liberty and sunshine." [3] In the same era trade unions, by a series of steps, merged into the American Federation of Labor. Socialist groups arose to advance the cause of the working classes. Workingmen's parties put forward candidates here and there. The anarchists urged the superiority of dynamite over ballots as a weapon against the oppressors of labor. The single-taxers, inspired by Henry George's *Progress and Poverty*, advocated their formula for social justice.

Of panaceas there was no end; and now and then workingmen rioted. Nor were anxiety and bewilderment restricted to farmers and workers. Businessmen, threatened by the rapid growth of combinations and trusts, feared the depredations of the industrial and financial buccaneers. Latter-day revisionists regard them as constructive pirates, but pirates they were, nevertheless. Upstanding citizens read Edward Bellamy, and middle-class humanitarians and reformers pondered what might be done to cushion the impact of the new industrialism. [4]

1896: Referendum on silver and a new alignment. No little time was to be required for the political system to digest the new industrial order. All the ferments and discontents of the 1870's and 1880's came to a head in the election of 1896 and led to a realignment of the old political cleavages by which the Republican combination gained new strength.

The election of 1892 had given the Democratic party simultaneous control of the Presidency and Congress for the first time since the Civil War. Its leadership had neither the capacity nor the disposition to annex to the party the smoldering elements of discontent. [5] President Grover Cleveland,

[3] Nathan Fine, *Labor and Farmer Parties in the United States, 1828–1928* (New York: Rand School, 1928), p. 119.

[4] For an account of the ideas of the leaders of protest, see C. A. Madison, *Critics and Crusaders* (New York: Holt, 1947).

[5] In 1892 division among the Republicans assured Democratic victory. Of Cleveland, A. W. Dunn says, "Big Business was behind him and there was no end of campaign money furnished to the national committee."—*From Harrison to Harding* (New York: Putnam's, 1922), I, p. 97.

by his use of troops in the Pullman strike of 1894, earned the animosity of labor. By his support of the gold standard he alienated the western silver faction of his party, mainly western debtor agrarians hard pressed by deflation.

Along with its other consequences industrialization brought the possibility of disastrous depressions. Financial panics were not new, but in the new industrialism contractions of economic activity struck both more sharply and more pervasively. Cleveland had the misfortune to be President when the depression of 1893 came along. Banking and commercial failures, urban unemployment, industrial stagnation, and low farm prices led to heavy Democratic losses in the 1894 congressional elections. Cleveland had pushed through Congress a revision of the tariff, which fact probably had no bearing on the panic but enabled Republicans to claim that low tariffs did not assure prosperity.

The forces of economic protest gained control of the Democratic convention of 1896, disavowed the policies of Cleveland, and set forth to unite all varieties of opposition to the established order. The Democratic platform declared for the "free and unlimited coinage of both silver and gold at the present ratio of sixteen to one. . . ." In debating this plank William Jennings Bryan stirred the delegates to a frenzy by his speech containing the famous passage:

We shall answer their demand for the gold standard by saying to them: "You shall not press down upon the brow of labor this crown of thorns. You shall not crucify mankind upon a cross of gold."

By their stand on silver and their nomination of Bryan, the Democrats appropriated the chief issue of the People's party, which had polled over a million votes in 1892. After some debate on the dangers of fusion, the Populists also nominated Bryan.

By its strategy in 1896 the Republican party not only turned back the first serious threat to the governing coalition it had built; it also added elements of enduring strength to the combination. That strategy involved, first, advocacy of the gold standard; thus they wrote off the silver-producing states and the advocates of the free coinage of silver. On its positive side, the strategy looked to the retention of the support of manufacturing interests, the solidification of the loyalties of financial groups, and the recruitment of a substantial vote from industrial labor. The nomination of McKinley, who had become in Congress the leading exponent of the protective tariff, assured the loyalty of the traditional hard core of Republicanism—the manufacturing interests. Banking and finance were terrified by the threat of inflation and contributed generously to the party committed to the maintenance of the gold standard.

Democrats sought to unite industrial labor and western farmers by making free silver the symbol of their joint protest against the depredations of the plutocracy. Republicans countered, successfully, with several appeals. The panic of 1893 enabled them to make the Democrats the party of depression, a label that stuck for a generation. The protective tariff became, under the ministrations of Republican campaigners, an assurance of employment to the factory worker as well as a boon to his employer. McKinley, pictured on the billboards as the "Advance Agent of Prosperity," promised a full dinner pail. Even the gold standard had its appeal for factory workers, who were educated about the effects of inflation on real wages, a process of instruction that included dire warnings by employers that factories would be shut down if the Democrats won. Beyond all these matters, both McKinley and his manager, Hanna, had a personal attractiveness to the industrial worker. Earlier in his career McKinley had, when it took courage, defended striking workingmen against prosecution and Hanna had earned the respect and affection of the workers in his own enterprises.[6]

The cumulative effect of the planks shaped for specific sectors of the population was a broad appeal to all those of conservative instinct. The crusading Bryan was pictured as the leader of a ragtag band of radicals that would upset the foundations of the Republic. The gold standard itself became a symbol of financial rectitude which titillated the moral sensibilities of men, especially of mortgagees. The oblique reference by the Democratic platform to the action that should follow a reversal by a reconstituted Supreme Court of a recent decision holding the income tax unconstitutional spurred the Republicans to greater effort and fed the anxieties of men of substance.

The usual interpretation of the election of 1896 is that the manufacturers and financiers of the East succeeded in persuading industrial workers to help them beat off the threat of the embattled agrarian debtors and radicals of the West. The reality seems to have been more complicated. The old Republican electoral following, inherited from the Civil War, was modified in several respects. Losses in the West were more than offset by gains in the manufacturing states of the East. Republicans enlisted in their cause large numbers of industrial workers. They carried the 10 largest cities of the country. Within the cities all types of neighborhoods

---

[6] The story is told that Hanna shocked his brethren of the Cleveland Union Club by the vigor of his comments about Pullman for his refusal to arbitrate the 1894 strike. The most moderate observation was said to be: "A man who won't meet his men half way is a God-damn fool." Hanna, a salty character, has been maligned beyond his deserts. On his career, see Herbert Croly, *Marcus Alonzo Hanna* (New York: Macmillan, 1912).

Table 7.1

Presidential Votes, 1896–1956

Year	Candidate	Electoral Vote	Popular Vote (in millions)	Per Cent of Two-Party Vote
1896	William McKinley (R)	271	7.1	52.2
	William J. Bryan (D)	176	6.5	47.8
1900	William McKinley (R)	292	7.2	53.1
	William J. Bryan (D)	155	6.4	46.9
1904	Theodore Roosevelt (R)	336	7.6	60.0
	Alton B. Parker (D)	140	5.1	40.0
1908	William H. Taft (R)	321	7.7	54.5
	William J. Bryan (D)	162	6.4	45.5
1912	William H. Taft (R)	8	3.5	35.6
	Woodrow Wilson (D)	435	6.3	64.4 [a]
	Theodore Roosevelt (Prog.)	88	4.1	
1916	Charles Evans Hughes (R)	254	8.5	48.3
	Woodrow Wilson (D)	277	9.1	51.7
1920	Warren G. Harding (R)	404	16.2	63.8
	James M. Cox (D)	127	9.1	36.2
1924	Calvin Coolidge (R)	382	15.7	65.2
	John W. Davis (D)	136	8.4	34.8 [b]
	Robert M. La Follette (Prog.)	13	4.8	
1928	Herbert Hoover (R)	444	21.7	58.5
	Alfred E. Smith (D)	87	15.4	41.5
1932	Herbert Hoover (R)	59	15.8	40.9
	Franklin D. Roosevelt (D)	472	22.8	59.1
1936	Alfred M. Landon (R)	8	16.7	37.5
	Franklin D. Roosevelt (D)	523	27.8	62.5
1940	Wendell L. Willkie (R)	82	22.3	45.0
	Franklin D. Roosevelt (D)	449	27.2	55.0
1944	Thomas E. Dewey (R)	99	22.0	46.2
	Franklin D. Roosevelt (D)	432	25.6	53.8
1948	Thomas E. Dewey (R)	189	22.0	47.7
	Harry S. Truman (D)	303	24.1	52.3 [c]
	Henry A. Wallace (Prog.)	0	1.2	
	J. Strom Thurmond (States' Rights)	39	1.2	
1952	Dwight D. Eisenhower (R)	442	33.8	55.8
	Adlai E. Stevenson (D)	89	27.3	44.5
1956	Dwight D. Eisenhower (R)	457	35.6	57.8
	Adlai E. Stevenson (D)	74	26.0	42.2

[a] Percentage division: Taft, 25.1; Wilson, 45.3; Roosevelt, 29.6.
[b] Percentage division: Coolidge, 54.3; Davis, 29.0; La Follette, 16.7.
[c] Percentage division: Dewey, 45.4; Truman, 49.8; Wallace, 2.4; Thurmond, 2.4.

—working class, middle class, and upper class—shifted from their 1892 vote toward the Republicans. Here and there wards returned Democratic majorities but there were fewer such wards and they were Democratic by smaller margins than in 1892. Moreover, in New England a marked rural shift to the Republicans occurred. Rural Yankee Democrats, who were more numerous than might now be supposed, moved over to the Republican ranks more or less permanently. Such gains as the Democrats made were in the silver-mining states; both mineowners and mine workers plumped for free silver with the same enthusiasm as the western farmer but for a different reason.[7]

1900: Imperialism. The Republican coalition, forged and tempered in the heat of the 1896 campaign, was to prevail in national affairs until 1912. That election, in effect, determined who was to govern for the next 16 years. It did not settle much else. The social strains and frictions emerging from industrialization remained to plague the Republican leadership as it sought to hold together a dominant coalition.

The McKinley Administration redeemed its tariff pledge by the Dingley bill of 1897, which tied the manufacturing interests of the nation even more closely to the Republican party. Before the campaign of 1900 the Spanish-American War intervened and furnished the new issue of imperialism. The upsurge of national fervor induced by war redounded to the advantage of the party in power, which also had the good fortune to have the currency problem eased through no effort of its own—new gold strikes increased the money supply. An upward movement of industrial production contributed to Republican popularity. McKinley had no difficulty in obtaining renomination by the 1900 Republican convention. The principal event of the convention, as it later turned out, was the nomination of Theodore Roosevelt, a person cordially distrusted by Hanna, for the Vice-Presidency. Matt Quay, Pennsylvania boss, who had a grudge against Hanna, joined with Boss Platt of New York, who wanted to be rid of Roosevelt as governor of New York, to bring about the nomination.[8] Western Republicans, still restive under control of the party by financial and manufacturing interests, welcomed the Roosevelt nomination.

[7] Marcus Daly, the Montana silver miner, backed the Bryan campaign by contributing more than $300,000, or so his son-in-law reports. See J. W. Gerard, *My First Eighty-Three Years in America* (Garden City: Doubleday, 1951), pp. 91–92.

[8] McKinley refused to permit Hanna to use the power of the Administration to control the vice-presidential nomination. Hanna is supposed to have remarked: "Don't any of you realize that there's only one life between that madman and the Presidency? Platt and Quay are no better than idiots!"—A. W. Dunn, *From Harrison to Harding* (New York: Putnam's, 1922), p. 335.

The Democrats again nominated Bryan, who contended that the campaign was only another episode in the battle of "Democracy against Plutocracy." The contestants were the same; only the issues were new, he argued. He viewed imperialism as merely another manifestation of plutocratic influence. The party platform asserted "that no nation can long endure half republic and half empire." Imperialism "abroad will lead quickly and inevitably to despotism at home." The Democracy declared monopolies to be "indefensible and intolerable." The charge was that "trusts are the legitimate product of Republican policies, that they are fostered by Republican laws, and that they are protected by the Republican administration, in return for campaign subscriptions and political support." The Democrats denounced the Dingley tariff as a "trust breeding measure," and reaffirmed the 1896 declaration in favor of the free coinage of silver. They opposed "government by injunction" and proposed the creation of a Department of Labor.

The Democrats were unable to crack the Republican coalition by these appeals. The Democratic percentage of the total popular vote fell only slightly, but the electoral vote was more favorable to McKinley than in 1896. Kansas, Nebraska, South Dakota, Utah, and Washington returned to the Republican fold, while Kentucky atoned for its apostasy of 1896 by going for Bryan.

Roosevelt the First. After McKinley's assassination Theodore Roosevelt succeeded to the Presidency as well as to the task of holding together the Republican coalition. He saw the potential rifts in Republican ranks and took steps to cut into the Democratic monopoly of championship of the underdog. He sought to shift Republican policies in the same direction that the Democrats had been moving, only not so far.

The party's conservative wing, under the leadership of Senator Nelson W. Aldrich, held firm control of Congress, and Roosevelt recognized the strength of these formidable opponents. For the duration of McKinley's incomplete term, Roosevelt did not challenge the conservative wing in Congress but acted in areas in which he did not need congressional collaboration. In 1902 Roosevelt's Attorney General instituted antitrust proceedings against the Northern Securities combination, a scheme to restrict competition between railroad titans for Chicago-Seattle traffic, and thereby lifted the spirits of those western Republicans who regarded trusts and railroads as the villains grinding down the poor and honest. In the same year the anthracite miners struck, and the operators stood on the God-given rights of property and refused to negotiate. Roosevelt intimated that federal troops might be used to take control of the mines, which would be operated by the government unless the mineowners arbitrated the dispute. Up to this time the use of troops in industrial disputes had been reserved for the benefit of employers. Roosevelt's action set off fine displays of profanity in the Union League clubs but renewed the Republican loyalties of workers and progressives.

1904: Democrats as reactionaries. Roosevelt's tactics helped hold to the party those recruited to its support in 1896, but they disturbed the manufacturing and financial interests. To them, Roosevelt was "unsafe," an estimate based on his actions in the coal strike, in the Northern Securities case, and on the muscular tone of his oratory critical of abuses in high places. Yet they had no alternative candidate and Roosevelt won the 1904 nomination.

As 1904 approached, Bryan argued that the Democrats, to retain their position as the party of protest, should take even more advanced positions, but the conservative wing triumphed in the nomination of Judge Alton B. Parker of the New York Court of Appeals. Southern Democrats, hopeful of victory and patronage, joined with the Northeastern conservatives in a nomination which squeezed the meaning from the platform's ringing denunciations of the trusts.[9]

Roosevelt's gestures to the West, to the progressives, and to labor held their support, and to the conservatives his bark, impressively ferocious though it was, seemed worse than his bite. The Democratic party's turn to conservatism pushed its percentage of the total popular vote down to 37.6, the lowest point it was to reach until 1924.

After he became President in his own right in 1904, Roosevelt took a somewhat stronger line in the fraternal differences among Republican factions. On some, but by no means all, issues he threw his strength to the progressive wing of the party. The battle was joined in the congressional dispute over railroad regulation; Aldrich led the eastern wing of the party against granting power to the Interstate Commerce Commission to fix rates to go into effect immediately. The western radical wing of the party, supported by shippers, recruited support from the Democrats to pass the Hepburn bill. Roosevelt stirred up popular enthusiasm for other measures that the conservative branch of his party viewed with alarm. The Pure Food and Drug Act thus became law, as did legislation providing for the inspection of meat-packing houses.

[9] The story circulated that the Democrats had been promised ample campaign funds if they nominated a safe and sane man but the arrangement fell through after the Democratic convention and after the moneyed interests had made peace with Roosevelt. See A. W. Dunn, *From Harrison to Harding,* I, p. 403.

1908: Taft and the progressives. As 1908 approached the coalition constructed by McKinley and Hanna and perfected by Roosevelt was subjected to growing internal strains. The business wing of the party became more reluctant to pay the price of power, that is, acquiescence in Roosevelt's leanings toward progressivism. Yet it was evident that the Democrats, disillusioned by the results of their conservative turn of 1904, would make capital of a resurgence of standpattism among the Republicans. Roosevelt exerted himself to unite the Republican party on William Howard Taft, an heir to carry on the Roosevelt tradition. In this endeavor he had to conciliate the party's conservative branch, which feared a continuation of his policies. He also had to persuade the progressive element of the party that Taft subscribed to the articles of progressive faith. The conservatives, oddly enough, swallowed Taft with bitter protest; the progressives took Roosevelt's word that Taft was one of the anointed.

Taft, victorious over the luckless Bryan, soon departed from the Roosevelt policies—and the fat was in the fire. Taft lacked Roosevelt's capacity to ride horses determined to veer off in different directions, but by Taft's time the elements of the Republican combination were becoming more difficult to manage. The progressive wing of the party had become stronger and the spirit of revolt within the party flourished. Into the progressive movement most of the old streams of protest had merged. That movement, whose temper is difficult to reconstruct, was a mixture of economic discontent, of middle-class protest against plutocratic influences, and of moral and religious fervor, as well as of more than a trace of sectionalism. It denounced special privilege and bossism, and fought for popular rule. It supported the direct primary, which was coming into use. Direct election of Senators was urged, and in some western states was becoming a reality although the constitutional forms were preserved. The Senate, the "millionaires' club" and a bulwark of property, was thus threatened. Conservatives became panicky as the initiative and referendum spread. The muckrakers uncovered graft and corruption in high places; the new cheap magazines disseminated their writings widely. State after state elected progressive governors, who drove through their legislatures tax and regulatory measures unpleasant for corporation executives to contemplate. Courageous men challenged the pillaging of municipalities by combinations of corrupt political organizations and special interests. City after city elected reform administrations, and municipal ownership of street railways became a favorite cause among reformers. Gambling houses were raided and houses of joy closed. Business enterprise of every kind quaked; the day of judgment apparently had come. The ordained institutions were said to be threatened and right-thinking men bemoaned the decay of our society, the rise of the proletariat, and the wickedness of demagogues, like Roosevelt, who catered to the masses.[10]

The progressive movement had, in addition to its moral overtones, some substantial economic foundations. Midwestern Republican farmers, as well as the Democrats, demanded a reconsideration of tariff policy. Agitation to that end had been noisy as early as 1903, when Mark Hanna took the position that, as things were, the Republican party should stand pat on the existing tariff law. He knew, said Herbert Croly, that "the tariff was the keystone of the whole Republican system. He knew that any revision upward would not be tolerated by public opinion, and any revision downward would tear the party to pieces." [11] From another quarter, the Republican coalition was threatened by labor. In 1906 the AFL, in its Bill of Grievances, asserted that the Congress had "been entirely preoccupied looking after the interests of vast corporations and predatory wealth." In the campaign of 1908 the Federation threw its weight, such as it was, to the Democrats, who had adopted platform planks favorable to labor.

Fate dropped the amiable and obese Taft into this situation. As he was at heart no crusader, his sympathies lay with the conservative wing of the party. Desirous of maintaining party unity, he lacked the adroitness to manage its warring factions. He had in his following Republicans like Aldrich of Rhode Island, high priest of protectionism, and equally genuine Republicans like La Follette of Wisconsin, hero of the progressives. Under Taft's heavy touch the Republican alliance began to disintegrate. His Administration got off to an inauspicious start in a battle over tariff revision. The 1908 platform, to placate Republicans of the corn and wheat producing areas, had declared "unequivocally for a revision of the tariff by a special session of Congress immediately following the inauguration of the next President." Taft called the special session and Aldrich led the high-tariff forces in Congress. Chided about his deviation from party promises, Aldrich responded that the promise was for "revision," not necessarily downward. Midwestern Senators—La Follette of Wisconsin, Dolliver of Iowa, Beveridge of Indiana, Cummins of Iowa, Bristow of Kansas, Clapp of Minnesota—opposed the Aldrich leadership, but the right wing of the party triumphed and passed a bill distinctly to the

[10] The spirit of the progressive movement can be sensed from the *The Autobiography of William Allen White* (New York: Macmillan, 1946).

[11] *Marcus Alonzo Hanna*, p. 418. Tariff legislation with specific rates on specific commodities—in contrast with a uniform *ad valorem* rate on all imports—constituted a wonderfully effective means for creating a lively sense of party obligation. Never could there be doubt about who received what benefits from whom. By the same token the making of tariffs required a skilled political hand to maximize the cumulation of obligation, for each specific action antagonized some people as it gratified others.

advantage of eastern interests. Taft's inept leadership on the tariff question brought disfavor which was compounded by his departures from the Rooseveltian conservation policies. He bobbled again in negotiating a reciprocity treaty with Canada which, had it gone into effect, would have subjected the western farmer to competition from Canadian farm products and have aided the eastern manufacturer. Finally, perhaps in an attempt to retrieve the favor of the progressives, the Administration initiated antitrust prosecutions which made enemies of some prominent Republicans of the industrial world.

The Republican coalition fell apart. In 1910 progressive Republicans joined with Democrats to cut down the powers of the Speaker of the House, a post that had become under "Uncle Joe" Cannon a symbol of standpat dominance of the Republican party. Taft failed in the primaries of 1910 to purge the Republican party of those of progressive bent, and the country returned a Democratic majority to the House. The remainder of his term was marked by further division within the Republican party and by the formation of the battle lines for 1912.

Democratic Interlude and the New Freedom

If a party is to govern, it must bring into mutually advantageous alliance an aggregate of interests powerful enough to win a presidential election. If it is to govern for long, it must see that the loaves and fishes are divided in a manner to command popular approbation. The alliance contrived by McKinley and Hanna and continued by Theodore Roosevelt amassed power to govern for a substantial period, but it could not solve the problem of the loaves and fishes. Roosevelt made gestures toward reform but in the main they were heroic verbalisms with a political function rather than an operational effect. Few indeed were the actions from 1896 to 1912 directed toward basic resolution of the dislocations associated with industrialization already apparent in 1896. Yet such problems do not take care of themselves and the campaign of 1912 set off a notable debate on their solution. Both shades of Republicanism had champions in the debate. The Democrats, under the leadership of Woodrow Wilson, put forward their program as they attempted to annex to their rock-bottom strength in the South and in the northern urban centers those elements of the people resentful of Republican policies.

Campaign of 1912. The campaign of 1912 stands out as one of the fabulous chapters of American politics. Roosevelt campaigned energetically to win the Republican nomination and to regain control of the party, but the Taft Administration controlled a majority of the delegates. Roosevelt was undoubtedly the choice of the mass of the party in so far as its wishes were expressed in those states choosing convention delegates by the direct primary. Taft, however, had early signed up the delegates of the southern states and was able to control a convention marked by controversy. The progressives, asserting that they had been robbed,[12] proceeded to bolt the Republican party and to found the Progressive party, with Roosevelt as its standard-bearer. It was a personal party, a party permeated with intense moral flavor, a crusade for righteousness or at least a movement rationalized in terms of righteousness. Progressive conclaves were wont to sing the "Battle Hymn of the Republic," and Roosevelt's speech to the Progressive convention was billed as a "Confession of Faith."

Roosevelt, with his doctrine of "New Nationalism," lifted political discussion to a new plane of sophistication. He attacked the virtues of weak government and expounded the idea that a government, as strong as it need be, should use its powers to promote the liberties of the weak against the greed of those in high places. For the traditional antitrust demonology that proposed to cure economic ills by jailing a few rascals, he substituted the idea of public control of more or less inevitable industrial combines. This idea was not unacceptable to Progressive men of wealth, who regarded some type of governmental control as in the cards. Roosevelt espoused all the progressive panaceas calculated to make government more responsive to the people: direct primaries, a nation-wide preference primary for candidates for the Presidency, the popular election of Senators, the initiative, referendum, and recall. The Progressives also pledged themselves to a long list of specific reforms: prohibition of child labor, minimum wages for women, the eight-hour day, regulation of security sales, social insurance, the establishment of a Department of Labor, and others.

The Democrats, still mindful of the electoral catastrophe that followed their conservative turn in 1904, determined to set a progressive tone for their own campaign. But this determination came after no little dispute in their national convention. Bryan, still the outstanding figure of the party, put the convention into an uproar—and the Democratic conservatives into a corner—by proposing the following resolution:

Resolved, That in this crisis in our party's career and in our country's history this convention sends greetings to the people of the United States, and assures them that the party of Jefferson and of Jackson is still the champion of popular government and equality before the law. As proof of our fidelity to the people, we hereby declare ourselves opposed to the nomination of any candidate for President who is representative of or under obligation to J. Pierpont Morgan, Thomas F. Ryan, August Belmont, or any other member of the privilege-hunting and favor-seeking class.

Be It Further Resolved, That we demand the withdrawal from this conven-

[12] Victor Rosewater, Republican national chairman in 1912, rebuts the charge of thievery in *Back Stage in 1912* (Philadelphia: Dorrance, 1932).

tion of any delegate or delegates constituting or representing the above-named class.

The conservative wing of the party fumed, but to have voted down the resolution would have been bad politics indeed. To accept it would make difficult the nomination of a conservative candidate. The second clause of the resolution would have compelled some eminent gentlemen to retire from the convention. After Mr. Bryan withdrew that clause, the conservatives manfully voted for the resolution. And the cartoonists pictured Bryan burning the progressive brand into the hide of the Democratic donkey.[13]

Woodrow Wilson won the nomination, after Champ Clark of Missouri had attained a majority but not the two-thirds then necessary to nominate. Wilson, a recent convert to progressivism, had been president of Princeton University and governor of New Jersey. His doctrines belonged to an older tradition than those of Roosevelt; his "New Freedom" stemmed from Jefferson. He sought to free men from restraints, monopolistic or otherwise, which restricted their liberties and prevented the full use of their talents. He regarded Roosevelt's "New Nationalism" with its powerful state as a threat to liberty. The Wilsonian doctrine, Roosevelt retorted, was "rural toryism," which would, if applied, lead to the repeal of all legislation for the protection of the social and industrial rights of man.

Taft could not compete in the campaign with men of the histrionic talents of Roosevelt and Wilson. He was a poor third in the running, polling 3,486,000 votes to 4,118,000 for Roosevelt and 6,296,000 for Wilson. The Republican split gave Wilson the victory. The electoral vote was: Wilson, 435; Roosevelt, 88; Taft, 8. The split within the Republican party was not sectional, although Roosevelt's popular vote was highest generally in the Middle and Far West. He won the electoral vote of Michigan, Minnesota, Pennsylvania, South Dakota, and Washington, and 11 of the 13 votes of California.

Wilson and the Presidency. Wilson brought to the Presidency both a program and a conception of presidential responsibility for leadership in the enactment of a party's legislative program. Supported by the spirit of progressivism abroad in the land, he pushed through Congress a remarkable program of legislation to cope with longstanding problems of the new industrial order.

The tariff had been debated for over a decade, but the Wilson Admin-

[13] For Bryan's account of the convention, see W. J. Bryan, and M. B. Bryan, *The Memoirs of William Jennings Bryan* (Philadelphia: United Publishers, 1925), Pt. I, ch. 10.

istration actually reduced the tariff—an action especially pleasing to the southern wing of the party. The tariff bill included an income tax; the Democrats came to power just as the income-tax amendment, proposed in 1909 by a coalition of Democrats and Republican insurgents, had finally been ratified. The currency problem—reflected in the agitation of the Grangers, the Greenbackers, the Populists, and the freesilverites of 1896 —was dealt with by the establishment of the Federal Reserve System. The solution differed from the panaceas proposed earlier, but the Reserve Act rectified shortcomings of the banking system that had plagued the country for decades. The Federal Trade Commission was created to attack the problem of restraints on competition in a manner different from the traditional antitrust procedures. The Clayton Act, in addition to its provisions regarding monopolies, exempted labor unions from the antitrust laws and contained other provisions that enabled Samuel Gompers, overoptimistically, to hail it as the "Magna Carta of Labor." Wilson approved an act safeguarding the rights of seamen. The Adamson Act fixed an eight-hour day for railroad workers.

After reversing his earlier views, Wilson urged the adoption of a statute prohibiting child labor, a law later to be held void. The Democrats also had something for the farmer: the Federal Farm Loan Act created banks to make long-term loans at low rates of interest. Governmental intervention on so many fronts amounted in its day to a bold assault on the problems of the time. Mild though it seems in retrospect, it aroused acrimonious opposition from those—mainly the business brass of the Republican party—who regarded themselves as injured thereby. By the same token the program strengthened the Democratic loyalties of those who had put Wilson into office.[14]

1916: "He Kept Us Out of War." The thinness of the Democratic margin of victory in 1916 indicated that Wilson had not yet constructed a new coalition capable of assuming a dominant role for long. His early legislative successes welded new support to the Democratic party, but perhaps the fact that war intervened prevented the completion of the task of weaving together a new coalition with lasting cohesiveness. At any rate war checked the tide of reform, and in the campaign of 1916 the conservative-progressive issue loomed less large than that of foreign policy. The Republicans, chastened by the experience of 1912, went beyond the ranks of the dedicated standpatters and nominated Charles Evans Hughes, who had gained renown for his work in the Armstrong investigation of life insurance and for his moderately progressive record as governor of New

[14] For a discussion of Wilson's ideas, see Richard Hofstadter, *The American Political Tradition* (New York: Vintage Books, 1954), ch. 10.

York. The regular Republican organization attempted in other ways to bring back into the fold those who had followed the Progressives out of the party in 1912. Roosevelt refused to accept the Progressive nomination again, and Hughes and Wilson fought a two-party battle in which Hughes' austerity evoked little enthusiasm; the Democratic record, with the aid of some ineptness in Republican campaign management, brought victory.

The Democratic organization emphasized the slogan, "He Kept Us Out of War," but the candidate refused to commit himself to a position that might later restrict his freedom of action. On foreign policy the issue was not clearly drawn; both parties were for American rights and adequate preparedness. They differed on who should be responsible for executing the policy. The polling resulted in an electoral vote of 277 to 254. Wilson carried the states of the Solid South and the West and broke into Republican territory to capture Ohio and New Hampshire. Professor Binkley attributes Wilson's victory in Ohio and California to the support of organized labor; railway workers were especially fearful that Republicans would repeal the Adamson Act, an inference from Hughes' attacks on the eight-hour day.[15]

Soon war came, and of war little can be said. Domestic politics was not adjourned, but the issues became different. Wilson's handling of foreign affairs aroused the animosity of Republican senatorial leaders. The senatorial cabal that defeated the League of Nations won control of the Republican party and removed from it the last taint of the progressive spirit of 1912. In the campaign of 1918 Wilson appealed to the country to return Democratic Congressmen who would support him in his policies; but it returned a Republican majority to the House—the period of normalcy had begun.

Normalcy and Its Aftermath, 1920–1932

When alarums and diversions distract the people, those with a steady eye on the main chance can make hay. In their energetic and unremitting pursuit of short-term gains, they may build up their accountability for a day of reckoning which, blindly, they believe will never come. Of alarums and diversions there was no lack in 1920. Disillusionment displaced the wartime spirit of idealism. Appeals for a return to isolation struck a responsive chord; the American people acted like an ostrich hell-bent for a sandpile. Voters of Irish and German extraction, in revenge for Democratic alliance with the British, were notably susceptible to isolationist oratory. Amidst this confusion, the business elements gained unchallenged control of the Republican party. The progressives by and large were dead

[15] *American Political Parties,* pp. 368–369.

and gone. The war had given a tremendous fillip to business expansion and a new generation of corporate leaders had come to power. The interests that had been dominant within the party before 1912 climbed back into the saddle. Yet this generation had neither the sagacity nor the restraint of McKinley and Hanna who took the elementary precaution of carefully tending their political fences outside the business community.

Harding and Coolidge. In the preliminaries to the Republican convention of 1920 the Republican senatorial leadership controlled the Republican organization. It was clear that the nominee would be a safe and sane man unlikely to challenge the primacy of the elder statesmen of the Senate. The mantle fell on Warren G. Harding, undistinguished in his record as a Senator and unmarked by any characteristic of greatness as an Ohio newspaper editor and publisher. In the convention maneuvers leading to his nomination, the principal leaders, says William Allen White, "wore unwittingly the collar of some commodity unit: steel, coal, oil, textile, banking, copper." The Republican platform reflected the views of the old guard, but made some genuflection to progressive principles. On the question of the League of Nations, the party stood for an "international association" to be based upon "international justice." The platform promised international agreements to "meet the full duty of America to civilization and humanity," but "without surrendering the right of the American people to exercise its judgment and its power in favor of justice and peace." In this language there could be found no germ of a strong international organization to promote peace.

Probably the Democrats had lost the election before the campaign began. The party chose James M. Cox, former governor of Ohio and another newspaper editor, as its presidential candidate. Franklin D. Roosevelt, then a young man of no great consequence who had been Assistant Secretary of the Navy, accepted the vice-presidential nomination. The Democratic party stood on Wilson's record, advocated entrance of the United States into the League of Nations, condemned the Republican party generally, and went down to inglorious defeat. Harding's promise of "normalcy" voiced the feelings of a nation weary of war, eager to restore things as they had been. Harding swept the nation with an electoral vote of 404 to 127. The western states moved back into the Republican column, and Cox carried only 11 southern states.

In the Harding and Coolidge Administrations finance and industry became dominant. No measure enacted by the Democrats for the control of business was repealed, but such laws were made harmless by tempered administration. Government by injunction prevailed, and labor was put in its place, a tactic that would have drawn corrosive comment from

Mark Hanna. Andrew Mellon, Secretary of the Treasury, preached the reduction of taxation of the rich in order that they might invest their money in employment-producing enterprise. Much of it, however, went into stock-market speculation. The Republican Administration, under the prodding of midwestern insurgents, expanded the farm credit system but this step was not enough to quiet the graingrowers, another anchor point in the old Republican combination. Even in Coolidge's first Administration the midwestern farmer was on a rampage, asserting that prosperity did not trickle down to him. The advocates of farm relief in forms ancestral to the Agricultural Adjustment Act, began to make themselves heard.

1924: Mediocrity vs. mediocrity. The New England rectitude of Calvin Coolidge and mounting prosperity carried the Republicans triumphantly through the election of 1924; so weak was the spirit of protest that the country paid little heed to the Teapot Dome scandals. The Democratic party, rent by internecine struggle, did little to encourage the public in the belief that it had the capactiy to govern. Its 1924 national convention was a savage bout beautiful to behold. The points of internal weakness in the coalition that is the Democratic party made themselves manifest; when urban Irish Catholics disagree with rural Protestants bitterness is bound to ensue. The New York convention fought over what, if anything, should be said in condemnation of the Ku Klux Klan, but most of all it fought over whether Alfred E. Smith or William G. McAdoo would be the party nominee. Behind Smith were arrayed the urban, Catholic, and "liberal"—by now some people were beginning to suspect that prohibition did not come up to forecast—elements of the party. McAdoo had the support of the southern, rural, dry, Protestant sectors. A hundred ballots could not break the deadlock and on the one hundred and third ballot the convention compromised on John W. Davis.

The Democracy, in its platform flayed the Republicans with might and main, but the conservative, though eminent, John W. Davis had neither the beliefs nor the manners of a leader of protest. He could give no punch to the platform charge that the Republican party believed "that prosperity must originate with the special interests and seep down through the channels of trade to the less favored industries, to the wage earners and small salaried employees." The resolutions' writers proclaimed: "A vote for Coolidge is a vote for chaos." They charged that the Mellon tax plan was "a device to relieve multimillionaires at the expense of other taxpayers"; they denounced the Fordney-McCumber tariff as "class legislation which defrauds the people for the benefit of a few." They announced that the "predatory interests" had, "by supplying Republican campaign funds, systematically purchased legislative favors and administrative immunity."

The oratory had little effect on the electorate. The Republican affirmation of "its devotion to orderly government under the guarantees embodied in the constitution" probably had no more effect. The Republicans pointed to prosperity, to the reduction of taxation, to the wise tariff provisions that had been enacted, to measures for the benefit of agriculture.

The Republican landslide gave Coolidge 382 electoral votes to 136 for Davis. The Democratic proportion of the total popular vote fell to an all-time low. Wise men predicted that the day of the Democratic party was done; but all was not well within the Republican party. Its midwestern wing was restive and limited secession occurred in 1924 in support of the Farmer-Labor candidacies of Robert M. La Follette and Burton K. Wheeler, who polled about one out of every eight popular votes in the nation. The Farmer-Labor platform proclaimed the great issue as "the control of government and industry by private monopoly."

After the election of 1924 the Coolidge Administration yielded no great legislative achievement. The midwestern agrarians of the Republican party became more vocal and succeeded in passing the McNary-Haugen bill, which Coolidge vetoed. The plaints of the farmer were drowned by the unprecedented prosperity of the speculators. Whether Coolidge was wise enough or whether he could have done anything to check the coming crash is problematic. William Allen White concluded that Coolidge perfectly expressed the dominant forces of the day.[16] However that may be, Coolidge rode the tide; but, apparently sensing what was coming, in 1927 he chose not to run in 1928. Mrs. Coolidge, at a family gathering, was reported to have explained: "Poppa says there's a depression coming." [17]

Hoover and the crash. With Coolidge's renunciation of the 1928 nomination, Herbert Hoover, his Secretary of Commerce, was soon in full cry after the nomination. Tagged by friend as the "Great Engineer" and by enemy as the "Wonder Boy," Hoover easily outdistanced other aspirants for the Republican nomination. He had to convince the Republican organizations that he could win; he did not belong to the inner circle of Republicanism as had Harding and Coolidge. By the nomination of Hoover, the Republicans yielded somewhat to the discontent within the party, for Hoover had accomplishments to his credit that placed him in a different category from the old-fashioned standpatter.

Northeastern elements of the party dominated the convention and easily overrode the demands of midwestern farm leaders for more positive promises to farmers. The prohibition issue aroused debate, but the party pledged itself to the vigorous enforcement of prohibition. The old Republican

[16] *A Puritan in Babylon* (New York: Macmillan, 1938).
[17] *Ibid.*, p. 366.

stand by, the protective tariff, was acclaimed as the source of all prosperity and as a boon to every section and to every class, although it was conceded that some revision of existing arrangements might be required in the light of the world situation.

The Democrats again essayed their role as the party of protest, but again demonstrated the incohesiveness of the elements that must make up such a party in comparison with the ties that bind a party whose ranks include the solid industrial and financial interests. The conditions were not ripe for a party of protest to win, but in making their nomination, the Democrats conspired with the forces working for their defeat. They chose Alfred E. Smith of New York as their nominee. A dripping wet, he renounced the party's dry platform plank. A child of the streets of New York, he could not induce the midwestern farmers to believe that the Democratic farm-relief plank meant what it said. A Catholic, he could not persuade many Protestants that the Pope would not make of the White House a branch Vatican.

Hoover later remarked that "the growing left-wing movement, embracing many of the 'intelligentsia,' flocked to Governor Smith's support," while Hoover committed himself to "the American system, as opposed to all forms of collectivism." [18] Such questions were pushed to the background by the tempest over religion and prohibition which operated to Republican advantage. In the South Smith's religion and his wetness were too much for dry, native-white Protestants. Hoover broke into the Solid South, and carried Florida, Kentucky, North Carolina, Oklahoma, Tennessee, and Texas. The electoral vote was 444 to 87. Had they studied the election returns more closely, the Democrats could have found cheer. Their proportion of the total popular vote jumped to 40.8 per cent from the 1924 figure of 28.8. They won the electoral vote of Rhode Island and Massachusetts, an omen of further growth of Democratic support in urban, Catholic, industrial centers. In every state north of the Ohio and east of the Mississippi their proportion of the total popular vote increased over the 1924 level. Hoover ran powerfully in the northern and eastern rural precincts but Smith boosted Democratic strength in the metropolitan and manufacturing centers.

In the cruelty of the polemics of politics Mr. Hoover became the symbol of the failures of an era, an attribution of responsibility far beyond the capacities of any individual, even though he may be President of the United States. Yet the governing coalition of which he had been a part had, it seemed almost as by an urge toward self-destruction, pursued policies that could only sap its own foundations. Nor did the crowd running the country have the will or the ingenuity to tackle any of the

[18] *Memoirs of Herbert Hoover 1920–1933* (New York: Macmillan, 1952), p. 202.

great problems of management of the new industrial order which were, by now, becoming more and more acute. That incapacity to act had its background in the long dedication of the Republican party to the belief that the economic system, if left alone, would take care of itself. "The abdication of responsibility revealed in 1929," says Professor Stromberg, "grew from the whole tradition of negativism ripening for upwards of fifty years. No group of men could have achieved such magnificent ineptitude spontaneously." [19] Whatever the explanation, the policies of the 1920's paved the way for national disaster and for a sweeping reconsideration of governmental policy.

The Democratic Era

The presidential election of 1932 marked a turning point in American party history. Under the impact of the Great Depression, the Republican following disintegrated and the circumstances were created for the formation of a new Democratic party. The new Democratic party built on its old foundations and enlisted much larger proportions of the economically less-favored groups. Under its leadership occurred the broadest governmental intervention in economic affairs that the nation had seen in times of peace and far-reaching measures of reform were enacted to cope with problems of the industrial order.

1932 and the New Deal. The campaign of 1932 presented no great uncertainties for the political forecaster. The Republican delegates who convened at Chicago to renominate Mr. Hoover exuded a synthetic enthusiasm in public but were privately appalled by the prospects. The Democrats, sure of victory, vied among themselves for the nomination and after a warm dispute agreed upon Franklin D. Roosevelt as their nominee.

The most clear-cut alternative of policy presented in the campaign was on prohibition: the Democrats were against it. Mr. Roosevelt appealed to all classes; he proposed a farm program, a labor program, a banking program, a business program, and stood for the theory of working in concert with all groups rather than of relying chiefly on industrial and financial leadership to lift the country out of the depression. Mr. Hoover was saddled with his record and with the impact of events and could scarcely obtain a respectful hearing in the campaign.

It is doubtful that the appeals of either candidate had much to do with the election results. All types of people had suffered deprivation; all were anxious for a change. Poor men, rich men, middle-class men, farmers, workers, all moved over into the Democratic ranks in sufficient number

[19] Roland N. Stromberg, *Republicanism Reappraised* (Washingon: Public Affairs Press, 1952), p. 40.

to give Roosevelt a resounding victory. All could identify themselves with the "forgotten man," and they could equally feel themselves deserving of a "new deal" without insisting on exact definition of what the "new deal" was to be. The electoral vote was 472 to 59; Hoover carried only Connecticut, Delaware, Maine, Pennsylvania, and Vermont.[20]

Washington was soon treated to a spectacle the like of which it had never seen, except on the occasion of Jackson's inaugural reception. The Democrats who assembled to take control of the government were a motley crew indeed. Southern statesmen of the old school mixed with the Bull Moosers, with suave and tough labor bosses, with intellectuals, with the Democratic contingent from big business, with bright young men from the Harvard Law School. Ghosts of the past were resurrected as former lieutenants of Bryan and Wilson emerged to take high places, and now and then an old Socialist who had been converted to the Democracy made a place for himself. Presiding over this assemblage was a man who, to the astonishment of all concerned, turned out to be a genius at the art of political leadership.

The country cried for action, and Roosevelt gave it action. After dealing with the immediate problem of restoring the nation's banks to operation, he proceeded to drive through a not unwilling Congress a series of measures for recovery and reform without parallel. Yet most of the measures stemmed from the American stream of reform agitation. The Democrats redeemed planks in their platforms of 1908 and later years; they put into law proposals in the Progressive platform of 1912; they breathed life into other long-past campaign promises.

The farmers were taken care of by the passage of the Agricultural Adjustment Act, which embodied means to control production, a step that Mr. Hoover's Farm Board had concluded to be necessary. Farm-mortgage moratoria were authorized to check foreclosures. The Grazing Act provided means for the regulation of the use of the public ranges; Mr. Hoover had appointed a commission to look into ways and means of preventing overgrazing. Banks received aid and were subjected to restraints. A major reform was the separation of banks from their security affiliates. The bank deposit insurance plan became law, albeit without Mr. Roosevelt's support. The Democrats in 1908 had plumped for a "guarantee fund" to pay off "depositors of any insolvent national bank." The dollar was devalued; thereby commodity prices were given a boost and the burdens of debtors eased. Horrendous results were predicted by spokesmen of the gold-standard cult. The Home-Owners' Loan Corporation was created and given $3,000,000,000 to stave off foreclosures of distressed homeowners, and relief funds were voted in huge sums.

[20] See Roy V. Peel and T. C. Donnelly, *The 1932 Campaign* (New York: Farrar & Rinehart, 1935).

A reciprocal tariff act, whose concept had earlier been vigorously opposed by the Republicans, was adopted. Also, a securities act became law, the objectives of which recalled the Progressive platform of 1912, which had pointed out that people were "swindled" out of millions every year by investing in stocks offered by "highly colored prospectuses" and that it was the duty of the government "to protect its people from this kind of piracy." The Tennessee Valley Authority Act settled the long dispute over the utilization of the Muscle Shoals Dam and the development of the water-power resources of the Tennessee Valley. Business leaders met in the annual session of the Chamber of Commerce of the United States and advocated a larger measure of governmental compulsion to aid business in its attempts at self-regulation. The National Industrial Recovery Act, one of the less well-advised New Deal measures, became law and was put into operation with great fanfare by General Hugh Johnson.

All these measures, and others too, left Congress a bit groggy; Congressmen who were inclined to balk heard from their constituents, and in 1934 the Democratic party gained congressional strength in the midterm elections, the first time a party in power had done so since the Civil War. There was more to come. The Social Security Act of 1935 provided, to meet immediate needs, a system of old-age assistance based on a means test and like arrangements for assistance to the blind and to dependent children. The same act, to meet the problem of the aged over the long pull, established a system of old-age insurance to be financed by compulsory contributions by employers and employees. The act also provided for unemployment insurance and for enlarged public health services. The National Labor Relations Act guaranteed to labor the right to organize and to bargain collectively.

Although the New Deal had its roots in earlier political discussion, it marked a sharp deviation from the policies of the preceding years, which had been dominated by the notion that the public good was promoted best by a government that restricted the sphere of its activities. One scholar concluded that "the New Deal represents the most zestful and thorough attack yet seen on those Whig principles which, with relatively minor exception, have dominated public policy since the days of the Federalists." [21]

1936: Referendum on the New Deal. In the election of 1932 all sorts and classes of people deserted the Republican party. In 1936 a reshuffling and sharpening of the lines of party battle occurred. As the New Deal took shape it attracted to the Democratic party even more completely

[21] T. P. Jenkin, *Reactions of Major Groups to Positive Government in the United States, 1930–1940* (Berkeley: University of California Press, 1945), p. 396.

than in 1932 voters of those classes that were its most immediate beneficiaries. On the other hand, the unfolding of the New Deal drove back
to the GOP many Republicans who had left their party in 1932.

As the campaign of 1936 approached—there was no doubt that the
Democrats would renominate Roosevelt—the Republicans gave thought
to the strategy of attack. They resolved upon a frontal assault upon the
New Deal whose principal planks ran diametrically counter to the doctrine of nonintervention in the economy. The big-business elements of the
party reacted with especial vigor to governmental restraint. The Republican party was not an adequate vehicle for the expression of their indignation; they formed the Liberty League to save the country and it conducted a vigorous campaign of protest. The Republicans nominated
Alfred M. Landon, governor of Kansas, and promulgated a platform
dedicating themselves to "the preservation of . . . political liberty." They
invited men of all parties to join them in defense of American institutions
and pledged themselves to maintain the Constitution and to preserve free
enterprise. They condemned unemployment insurance and old-age annu-
ities as "unworkable." They proposed that labor have a right to bargain
through representatives "of its own choosing without interference from
any source," a qualification reflective of the delusion of businessmen
that union members are held in bondage by their leaders. They pledged
themselves to "balance the budget," to maintain a "sound currency," and
not to devalue the dollar further. The Republicans offered the country
just about what it had had in the 1920's.

The country failed to be disturbed by Republican forecasts of disaster;
Roosevelt was returned by a larger majority than in 1932. He carried
every state save Maine and Vermont. By now the public opinion polls
had come into operation, and it was easier to discern the kind of coalition
that Roosevelt had built up. He had brought together the votes of traditional Democratic territory and the northern urban laboring vote. The
population dependent upon public relief overwhelmingly supported him,
and the Negroes had been wooed away from Republicanism. Businessmen
in the main remained Republican, but each successively lower-income
group voted Democratic in larger proportions.

The problem of holding this diverse coalition together grew more difficult after the President's 1937 proposal for the "rejuvenation" of the
Supreme Court. The Court had long been regarded as the great bulwark
of property rights. Supported by conservatives generally, it had often
been attacked by labor and protest groups. The Democrats in 1936 proposed, if necessary, a "clarifying amendment" to the Constitution to permit the enactment of laws necessary "to regulate commerce, protect public health and safety, and safeguard economic security." This declaration

followed Supreme Court decisions invalidating the Agricultural Adjustment Act and the National Industrial Recovery Act. Roosevelt went beyond the platform and proposed to "pack" the court and thereby set off a battle that solidified the conservative interests of the country and opened wider the split between his party's conservative and liberal factions. Defeated in his court proposal, Roosevelt won his primary objective. The Court itself soon altered the direction of its decisions, and retirements permitted him to name judges of a more acceptable political philosophy.

1940: Third Term and World War II. By 1940 the New Deal had run its course. The outbreak of the war in Europe and its potential effect on the United States commanded the attention of the public and of political leadership.

The coalition of interests cemented together by the New Deal held its main outlines in 1940, although the question of the United States' role in the emerging world crisis caused some erosion as well as some accretions. Italo-Americans and German-Americans moved to the Republican ranks in large numbers. On the other hand, gains accrued to the Democrats among pro-British sectors of the population. Substantial, but not noisy, new Democratic support came from those elements of eastern finance and industry deeply concerned about foreign policy questions.

Willkie, the Republican nominee, agreed in general with Democratic pronouncements on foreign affairs and it appeared that the foreign policy issue would be taken out of the campaign. Minor Republican orators, though, tried to pin the "war party" label on the Democrats and toward the end of the campaign Willkie, under the urging of the Republican professionals, began predicting war in a short time if the Democrats should win. "Don't Change Horses in the Middle of the Stream" became the Democratic slogan; Republicans attempted to raise the specter of dictatorship, attacked Democratic domestic policies, and appealed to the hallowed two-term tradition—but to no avail. Roosevelt won by 449 to 82 electoral votes. Willkie captured the loyalty of the mass of Republicans but was viewed coolly by the Republican machines as an amateur and a renegade Democrat. He carried only 10 states.

Of the politics of World War II it needs only to be noted that Roosevelt managed to hold together the antithetic elements composing the Democratic party. The party's internal strains made themselves more apparent in the events leading to the campaign of 1944. At the Democratic convention southern state organizations, conservative Democrats elsewhere, and the AFL succeeded in preventing the nomination of Henry Wallace, strongly backed by the CIO, for the Vice-Presidency. But the party closed ranks for the campaign and again defeated the Republican nominee, this time Governor Thomas E. Dewey of New York, by an electoral vote of 432 to 99. The Democratic proportion of the total popular vote again declined, but between 1940 and 1944 Roosevelt acquired additional support from business and professional groups, reflective perhaps of the Administration's swing toward the right and of the sense of responsibility of these groups in foreign affairs. Farmers, however, continued their movement toward the Republicans, resentful of Democratic policy toward labor and of Democratic policy calculated to keep food prices down.

Truman and the Fair Deal. With the death of Roosevelt, Truman inherited both the Presidency and the task of holding together the pieces of the Democratic party. Beset by adversity on every side, he confounded both his critics and his friends by winning the election of 1948. For the most part he followed policies initiated by Roosevelt and attempted to carry some of them somewhat further.

In forming their forces the Republicans had their own internal difficulties. The right wing of the party had by no means yet become reconciled to the New Deal. While the national conventions in 1944 and 1948 fell under the control of the Republican faction disposed to retain the New Deal—and manage it better—the tenor of the pronouncements of the right wing of the party created a popular suspicion that the Republican party, given authority, would liquidate the New Deal. That belief had some foundation in the actions of the Republican Congress, elected in 1946, in whittling down the position of labor by the Taft-Hartley Act. Dewey, the 1948 nominee, was called a "me-too" candidate, but Republicans of all hues rallied to his support.

Truman seemed to be defeated before the campaign began. Southern resentment over national civil rights policies ignited a revolt by the Dixiecrats, while Henry Wallace led another splinter into the so-called Progressive party. Yet these losses were more than offset by gains elsewhere, and Truman's campaign tactics—and circumstances—stirred the main elements of the old Roosevelt alliance to his support. Labor, in gratitude for Truman's opposition to the Taft-Hartley Act, exerted itself on his behalf. Rapidly falling farm prices—coupled with the failure of the Republican Congress to authorize actions to facilitate price support—renewed the Democratic attachments of midwestern farmers.[22] In the grain-growing areas of the Midwest Truman's vote exceeded that of Roosevelt in 1944, a rise probably accounted for in part by a return to the Democratic party of those who had voted Republican in 1940 and 1944 on foreign policy

[22] Corn dropped from $2.86 a bushel in January, 1948, to $1.37 in November.

grounds. Negroes turned out in record numbers to support Truman, a response to his civil rights position.

Roosevelt's New Deal and Truman's Fair Deal left a thick residue of legislation but they also introduced a new sharpness into American political debate. Although the Democratic program merely executed in many instances projects long considered in American politics, the total effect was to present in new form the broad issue of individualism versus collectivism. The New Deal emerged from the tradition of American progressivism, but it operated with a superior political leadership and applied its measures with a more sophisticated administrative technique. Instead of relying on moral castigation and the penalization of a few rascals to promote the public weal, it spent money, set up commissions and agencies, issued orders and rules and regulations, and generally used the powers of government. All these measures sharpened political conflict and raised broadly the question of the role of government in promoting the interests of its citizens. The overwhelming support of labor gave strength to the government, but it also solidified upper-class sentiment in opposition. Spokesmen for the more prosperous contended that the American way was threatened, that dictatorship was coming, that individual liberties were being bartered for a mess of pottage. This sort of discussion was not new: Theodore Roosevelt and Woodrow Wilson had been cursed with almost the same abandon as Franklin Roosevelt.[23] Yet the New Deal strained the capacity of the upper classes to accede to change, and right-wing predictions of leftist dictatorship were matched by leftist assertions that men of property and wealth had too little belief in democracy to stand idly by and allow the fulfillment of the logic of rule by the will of the masses.

General Eisenhower and the New Republicanism

Perception of the broad characteristics of political events improves with the passage of decades. Events of the moment, too, may only acquire their full significance in the light of their future repercussions. Interpretations of the Republican ascent to power in 1952 must, then, be tentative.

The sequence of elections before 1952 had, by their cumulative impact, made it plain that the Republican party could not win the Presidency if it seemed clearly to threaten the gains of the principal beneficiaries of the New Deal. The New Deal had to be accepted or victory had to be won

---

[23] In an article in *Forum* in August, 1918, Will Hays, the Republican national chairman, urged a "proper and just restriction of the present socialistic tendency in our government, to the end that while we fight to make certain forever the right of free government throughout the world we shall not forget that we have a Republic to preserve in North America." See his *Memoirs*, p. 187.

by diversionary tactics, by indirection, or by the rise of new circumstances which could be turned to Republican advantage.

The candidate, tactics, and circumstances necessary to dislodge the Democratic coalition converged in 1952. The candidate, General Dwight D. Eisenhower, brought to the party a great personal popularity and no offsetting liabilities in commitments to political beliefs likely to antagonize any major voting group. From his defeat of Robert A. Taft in the contest for the Republican nomination, the image emerged of a candidate who diverged from the prevalent popular stereotype of Republican leaders as isolationists and economic reactionaries. Mr. Taft had come to personify standpat Republicanism. Precisely what sort of Republican General Eisenhower was, nobody knew, but he was presumably different from Taft, an impression enormously helpful in the presentation of the General as a new Republican.

Eisenhower held the support of the upper-income classes which had to an extraordinary degree coalesced under the Republican banner, but even unanimity among these classes is not enough to win presidential elections. New support had to be recruited from those attached to the Democratic cause. That end was accomplished, but whether by the potency of Republican campaign appeals or by the circumstances creating discontent with the Democratic Administration one cannot say. The weariness of the nation with the Korean War and its concern about our position in world politics were exploited skillfully by Republican campaigners. Their candidate's experience, it could be contended, would assure competent management of military matters. Republican strategy blended an exploitation of anxiety about the Soviets abroad with the party's line on domestic policy. The party had been hammering for several years on the theme of "liberty against socialism," a propaganda tactic thought to be more promising than attack upon specific Democratic policies. In 1952 these themes became intertwined. In the more irresponsible Republican characterizations the Democratic Administration became a Communist-Socialist clique not to be trusted to defend American rights abroad and bent on the destruction of private enterprise at home. The supposed alternative of private enterprise or socialism was campaign hyperbole. The only state enterprise that had been developed or contemplated was in electric power and there the alternative was not socialism or free enterprise but public enterprise or private monopoly.

The Democrats nominated Adlai Stevenson, a candidate who lacked Eisenhower's personal appeal. To no small degree Democratic campaigners in 1952 were still running against Herbert Hoover as they recalled the days of depression and the benefits from Democratic actions. But memories are short and perhaps the new circumstances made the old appeals to important blocks of voters no longer effective. Workers feared that further inflation would reduce still more the worth of their wages. Farmers perhaps concluded that there was nothing more that Democratic agricultural policy could do for them. Further, the upward trend of family incomes, a most striking development of the Democratic years, had moved millions of people into those economic strata to which the traditional Republican orientation is most congenial.[24]

Whatever weight may be assigned to particular factors influencing voters in 1952, the total effect of the campaign was a movement toward the Republican party among people of all economic classes, all occupations, all geographic sections, and most religious and ethnic groups. Even in the South Eisenhower drew heavy support, especially in the middle- and upper-income brackets of the cities, perhaps a step toward a permanent Republican attachment among these groups.[25] The General polled slightly more than 55 per cent of the vote, enough to yield a landslide in the electoral college. To an unusual extent his was a personal victory rather than a party triumph; so thin were Republican margins in the House and Senate that a normal midterm sag in 1954 gave control of Congress to the Democrats.

Whether the Eisenhower victory created a durable new Republican coalition or inaugurated only a Republican interlude remained to be seen. The chances are that a single election does not form a new electoral grouping; it merely puts a party into office and gives it opportunity by its actions to weld together a cohesive following. Partisans of the Administration early heralded the arrival of a new Republicanism. Its creation required a reorientation of the party in both domestic and foreign policy. The fulfillment of the international necessities required management of the wing of the party intransigent in its opposition to Democratic foreign policies. That wing incongruously included both determined isolationists and bellicose individuals who wished to end the Korean stalemate by attacking Red China. The General's espousal and continuation of the broad outlines of the Truman-Acheson policies somewhat reduced the clamor against them from within the Republican ranks.

On the domestic front, a major problem in building lasting public support came from the fact that the business wing of the party was in the

[24] In 1939, 86.2 per cent of male wage and salary recipients had an income of under $2,000; only 4.5 per cent had an income of over $3,000. In 1951, 26.6 per cent had an income of under $2,000; 52.3 per cent had an income of over $3,000. In manufacturing the median income of male wage and salary workers in 1939 was $1,141; in 1951, it had become $3,393.—Herman P. Miller, *Income of the American People* (New York: Wiley, 1955), p. 99.

[25] See D. S. Strong, "The Presidential Election in the South, 1952," *Journal of Politics,* 17 (1955), pp. 343–389.

saddle, a fact about which its spokesmen, with the ineptness of political inexperience, publicly boasted. Although business itself had undergone radical alteration and presumably learned something since the 1920's it showed an overconfidence in its acceptability as a trustee for the national interest by its insensitivity to conflicts of interest as businessmen took office and in recurrences of the ancient Republican amiability on questions of protection of the national interest in natural resources. On the other hand, the Administration, without demonstrative public profession, swallowed the doctrine of governmental responsibility for the maintenance of employment, which had been embodied in the Employment Act of 1946. It was credited with skill in the practical application of Keynesian economics, a success which rested in part on high-level military expenditures.

The election of 1956 left no doubt that the country still liked Ike; whether it liked the Republican party was another question. The return of Democratic majorities simultaneously with the overwhelming re-election of a Republican President was an extraordinary occurrence. To a degree, the election reflected a recurrence of an old Republican ailment, western trouble. Its losses in House and Senate came in the farming areas west of the Mississippi and in the states of the Pacific Coast, perhaps reflective of discontent with Republican farm and conservation policies. On the other hand, Eisenhower gained over his 1952 vote in metropolitan areas and among industrial workers indicative of the weakening Democratic ties of these groups. The retention of southern support in 1956 made it clear that 1952 had marked a durable increase of Republican strength in the South.[26]

Morals of Party History

This sketchy account may activate enough of the student's knowledge of recent history to provide a chronological framework within which subsequent discussion of the party system may proceed. Apart from this mundane utility, even so condensed a tale points to a few observations about characteristics of the party system.

Party leadership and coalition formation. The great function of party leadership in the formation of governing coalitions obtrudes from the recital of the chain of major events. From the vantage point of time no doubt should remain that persistent contrasts prevail in the sorts of aggregates formed by the two major American parties. Since 1896, at any rate, the Republican party has, by and large, commanded the loyalties of the

[26] For an analysis of factors entering into voters' deliberations as 1956 approached, see Samuel Lubell, *Revolt of the Moderates* (New York: Harper, 1956).

great manufacturing, financial, and transportation interests and its leadership has endeavored, with varying success, to enlist in its support other blocks of the population sufficient to govern. On the other hand, the Democratic party has had, most of the time, a relatively small following within the economic elite. Usually stronger in the northern cities than in the northern rural sections, it has, from its southern base, competed with the Republican party for the margin of victory among northern workers, midwestern farmers, and the people of the mountain and coastal regions of the West.

The process of coalition, although described in the orthodox manner in the preceding pages, is not so simple as it might have seemed. The story may read as if farmers, businessmen, industrial workers, and other such categories were solid blocks to be won or lost to this party or that. That condition of solidarity is approached in some groups at some times, but more commonly the reality differs. In the 1930's, for example, well over a majority of industrial workers were Democrats but certainly not all such workers. In 1900 a larger proportion—how large nobody knows— of factory labor was Republican than in 1936. In 1944 more than a majority, but not all, midwestern farmers were Republican. In 1928 urban northern Catholics were predominantly, but not unanimously, Democratic; in 1952 a smaller proportion was Democratic.

Fluidity of electoral alignments. A look backward suggests something of the nature of the process of construction of partisan coalitions powerful enough to govern. It also makes clear that a fairly high degree of fluidity has existed in the partisan loyalties of the electorate. Over the short term, partisan attachments may seem to be rigid but over the long run, if a half century qualifies as the long run, wide swings in the division of party strength have occurred.

This quality of electoral inconstancy reflects, if it does not account for, significant characteristics of the American party system. The party battle might be a recurring test of strength between cohesive groups of voters, each seeking to recruit the narrow margin of support necessary to enable it to govern; but it is not on the American scene. Wide shifts in party support occur over the long pull. The breadth of the great fluctuations assures authoritative popular action at crucial moments rather than a decision on points, so to speak, which might carry no aura of authority.

Perhaps of greater importance than the amplitude of the fluctuations in party strength is the fact that voters of all classes, sections, and income levels participate in the great shifts from party to party. This enables each party to assert that its mandate to govern rests on the consent of all the people. Even though that fiction contains a variable admixture of fact, the possibility of its propagation has a significance in the process of governance. That significance may be divined if one considers the possibilities of a prolonged and bitter conflict for control of the government between highly disciplined groups of people defined along class, religious, or sectional lines. The fluidity of electoral attachments in a way limits the ferocity of political conflict; and there are limits to the extent and intensity of conflict a political system can endure.

These comments about the nature of the swings from party to party do not rest on as solid a body of fact as might be desired. Had Mr. Gallup's polls been in operation over this entire period, our knowledge of the political shifts of occupational, income, religious, national-origin, and other demographic categories would be more precise than it is. The suggestion that the wide swings are participated in by most elements of the electorate gains some support from the fact that voters in all sorts of states seem to move in the same directions as the great cycles rise and fall. In Figure 7.1 data appear to show the manner in which the broad fluctuations in party strength in the states occur in unison. One-half of the states, as the figure indicates, cluster in a quite narrow range in their Republican percentage of the presidential vote and move up and down together through time. The country as a whole, not just a part of it, tends to move

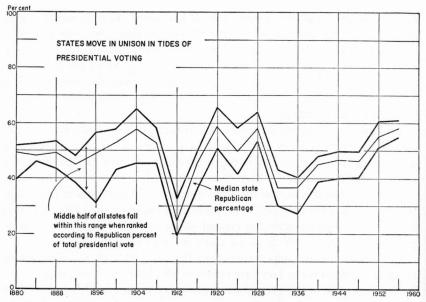

Figure 7.1. Middle Half of States According to Republican Percentage of Total State Presidential Vote, 1888–1956

toward this party and then toward that. The figure suggests that among persons of the most varying kinds there is a similar response to changing circumstances and party appeal, a characteristic of rather fundamental importance in the American party system.[27]

Cycles of party supremacy and intraparty conflict. The great swings in the partisan attachments of the country contribute to another notable characteristic of the party system, viz., the fact that many of the great battles of politics occur within parties rather than between them. Within each party, even when it has been driven back to its bedrock strongholds, bases exist for intraparty friction. The rural southern and northern metropolitan wings of the Democratic party have long lived in uneasy alliance. The eastern and western Republican wings never live for long in fraternity untinged by fratricide. Yet when the standpat wing of either party profits from the wide shifts in party support it attaches to itself elements that intensify the discord within the party. As a party enlarges its following and achieves a position to claim that it speaks for the country, it comes to include within itself the cleavages and conflicts that bedevil the country as a whole.

When the country has been "normally Republican," the Republican party has had its internal difficulties. The progressive-standpat battle of the first decade of the century became an outright party split; in the 1920's the western agrarians and progressives gave the Republican national leadership more difficulty than did the Democrats. In the era of Roosevelt and Truman conflict within the Democratic party took the center of the stage. When Eisenhower brought new adherents to the Republican party, he brought together a following far less homogeneous than had been the Republican minority.[28]

[27] The student should be warned that the data on this proposition also indicate that minor movements by sharply defined groups with the most specific interests occur in both directions at each election.

[28] Samuel Lubell bases his "sun and moon" theory of the American party system on this phenomenon of intraparty conflict. See *The Future of American Politics*, chs. 10–11.

8 | Nature and Function of Party

GOVERNMENT derives its strength from the support, active or passive, of a coalition of elements of society. That support may be rooted in interest, consent, fear, tradition, or a combination of these and other factors in proportions that vary from society to society. In one instance a comparatively small group with control of instruments of violence may cow the populace into submission. In other instances authority may stem in far greater degree from the consent of the governed. In some states those in power may claim the right to retain their places without challenge; in others, provision may be made for periodic changes in the personnel of government by orderly processes.

In times past, the right to rule was assumed—or grasped—by small groups who based their claim to authority on the rights of religion, birth, family, class, force, wealth. In modern times such narrowly based power has been challenged, if not swept away, by the demand that an ever-larger proportion of the people share in the process of governance. The party politician, rather than the prince, becomes the characteristic contestant for power. The political party becomes the instrument for the organization of support in societies founded on the doctrine of the consent of the governed.[1] Inherent in that doctrine is the idea of popular discharge of governments and their replacement by other rulers preferred by the people. The only way so far contrived by which such popular decisions may be made is through competition between political parties.

Within all sorts of human associations "political parties" exist, although they may not ordinarily be so designated. Affairs of a group—be it a nation, a church, a union, or a chamber of commerce—do not and cannot take care of themselves; small factions of men offer to assume responsibility for handling them. "Ringleaders" propose ways of dealing with group problems and vie for place; they exercise leadership. Although the germ of party may be observed in private clubs, societies, and associations, the party system in the nation possesses its special characteristics. The party system of a fraternity may be organizationally no more intricate than a back-room caucus. A party system for a nation includes means for the conduct of competition for control of the government in contrast with the more common existence in private groups of oligarchies infrequently challenged in their position. Moreover, a party system for the nation (or a state or a large city) must create organization to extend its leadership over considerable areas or over large numbers of people.

Party in the Governing Process

According to literary convention a discussion should be introduced by a definition of its subject. Pat definitions may simplify discussion but they do not necessarily promote understanding. A search for the fundamental nature of party is complicated by the fact that party is a word of many meanings. Indeed, the genus party comprehends many species. To define sharply one party may be to exclude another, for the role of party may differ from country to country. Moreover, even within the same political order the term party may be applied to different elements of the governing system. An approach more circuitous than the proposal of a two-sentence definition may lead toward a comprehension of the basic nature of party in the American system: the nature of parties must be sought through an appreciation of their role in the process of governance.

[1] See H. M. Clokie, "The Modern Party State," *Canadian Journal of Economics and Political Science,* 14 (1949), pp. 139–157. General political theorists have given scant attention to the party process. The most comprehensive theoretical analysis of the role of party in governance is the study by Avery Leiserson, *Political Parties* (New York: Alfred A. Knopf, 1958). See also R. A. Dahl, *A Preface to Democratic Theory* (Chicago: University of Chicago Press, 1956); N. A. McDonald, *The Study of Political Parties* (Garden City: Doubleday, 1955); A. Ranney and W. Kendall, *Democracy and the American Party System* (New York: Harcourt, Brace, 1956).

Genesis of party in democratization. Governments operated, of course, long before political parties in the modern sense came into existence. Men grasped power over their fellow men, maintained their position by a variety of techniques, and justified their authority by a variety of philosophies. Yet the regimes antecedent to modern democratic orders had in common the monopolization of power and authority by comparatively narrow social classes. Whether the mechanism of governance was a monarchy or a monarchy tempered by consultation with the aristocracy, authority rested in the hands of a few people who claimed to rule their subjects by right. Government might be ruthless or benevolent, but in neither circumstance did it concede a share in the governing process to its subjects; their duty was to obey their betters.

Political parties developed as these ancient practices were modified by the rise of democratic ideas, which undermined the foundations of the old order. The challenges to the privileged classes carried with them assertions, revolutionary in their day, of the right of the "people," or at least some of them, to be consulted, to give or to withhold their consent to the exercise of authority, or to participate in the governing process in other ways. Such doctrines, now commonplace, were subversive of the ordained institutions.

The proclamation of the right of men to have a hand in their own governing did not create institutions by which they might exercise that right. Nor did the machinery of popular government come into existence overnight. By a tortuous process party systems came into being to implement democratic ideas. As democratic ideas corroded the old foundations of authority members of the old governing elite reached out to legitimize their positions under the new notions by appealing for popular support. That appeal compelled deference to popular views but it also required the development of organization to communicate with and to manage the electorate. Thus, members of a parliamentary body, who earlier occupied their seats as an incident to the ownership of property or as a perquisite of class position, had to defer to the people—or to those who had the suffrage—and to create electoral organizations to rally voters to their support. In a sense, government, left suspended in mid-air by the erosion of the old justifications for its authority, had to build new foundations in the new environment of a democratic ideology. In short, it had to have machinery to win votes. The exact events of institutional development rarely fit precisely any such neat pattern, but such a theory of the genesis of political parties is suggestive of their basic function.

A variant of this broad explanation refines the theory to find the birth of political parties in virtual revolution. As democratic ideas spread, those dissatisfied with the old order rallied the masses, or at least many of those who had had no hand in government, against the established holders of authority. In effect, the outs played demagogue, lined up the unwashed in their support, and, at the elections, by superiority of numbers and organization they bested those dominant in government. Those who suffered such indignities were compelled in self-defense to defer to the people, no matter how distasteful it was, and to form organizations to solicit electoral support.

Rise of American parties. Early events in the development of American parties accord to some extent with these general patterns. Until after the adoption of the Constitution the gentry by and large ruled. They held office, not so much from their skill in swaying the multitude, but as a matter of generally recognized right associated with their status. The essence of the political system appears in the early processes of nomination. Members of the dominant political classes became nominees by individual announcement of their availability; or a friend of the candidate put him in nomination by an address published in the press. Leading personages, at least in the areas and in the times when the aristocratic influence prevailed most strongly, needed no party organization to nominate them or to campaign for them; gentlemen ordinarily regarded electioneering as bad form.

The Jeffersonian Republicans, who sought to oust the old order, developed party organization both to nominate candidates and to enlist voter support. A step was taken on the way to party organization in the formation of the Democratic societies, which flourished in 1793 and 1794. They provided channels for the expression of hostility toward the Federalists, friendship toward France, and antipathy toward "monarchical aristocratical" principles. Some of them did a bit of electioneering for candidates. The controversy they aroused indicated a significant transformation of attitude that had to occur before party government could exist. The notion that assaults on the government by the outs should be expected and could be tolerated had scarcely become established. In his message of 1794 Washington spoke of the commotions "fomented by combinations of men" who were "careless of consequences" and disregarded "the unerring truth that those who rouse cannot always appease a civil convulsion." The differentiation between criticism by the outs and the threat of revolution had not become understood by the ins—and perhaps not by the outs either.

The Democratic societies died out and the Jeffersonians took basic steps in the formation of a party system as they contrived a new political organization to throw the Federalists out of office. In Pennsylvania, New Jersey, New York, and Delaware they developed the delegate convention to nominate candidates upon whom their strength might be concerted.

The convention—in sharp contrast with the individual modes of nomination congenial to the gentry—provided a means for centering popular strength on candidates. Moreover, the convention permitted a combination of strength over large areas. Delegates from precincts gathered at the county seats, and those from the counties met at the state capital. To assemble delegates at the county seat—given the means of travel of the day —was an operation quite as great as gathering a state convention today. The political activists who shared in the nominating process in turn worked in their own territories to round up the vote for their candidates.

This new organization of political activity marked a profound change in the political system. Earlier, gentlemen of status offered themselves to the voters as candidates. The new system produced candidates whose nomination proceeded, in appearance at least, from the voters. It also provided an organizational apparatus reaching out into the electorate to rouse the voters. Often, as the system developed in this locality and that, the number of voters increased remarkably as political workers stirred the electorate to action. A party mechanism purporting to represent the generality drove the unorganized Federalists from power.[2]

Federalists saw the source of their woes but, outside of Delaware, they tended to bemoan rather than to imitate the new modes of political action. In 1806, for example, a Federalist journal in New Jersey spoke of the "combinations of men" who had "governed the elections of New Jersey." These combinations, or conventions of Republicans, had, in effect, decided "who should and who should not be voted" for by the people. "It is time to discountenance such proceedings. These combinations disgrace the state by appointing ignorant, weak and crazy men to go to Congress." Most Federalists of the old school were unable to bring themselves to adopt the low tactics of their opposition. Hamilton, however, defeated by Aaron Burr's concerted cultivation of the electorate, concluded that the Federalists "erred in relying so much on the rectitude and utility of their measures as to have neglected the cultivation of popular favor by fair and justifiable expedients."

In a broad sense party organization to nominate candidates, to rally electoral support, and to link officialdom to voters evolved as a means for consolidating the outs to capture control of the government. The technique amounted to a functional equivalent of revolution. When in his Farewell Message Washington warned against the spirit of party he was

[2] These remarks lean heavily on G. D. Luetscher, *Early Political Machinery in the United States* (Philadelphia, 1903). See also D. R. Fox, *The Decline of Aristocracy in the Politics of New York* (New York: Columbia University Press, 1919), and J. Charles, *The Origins of the American Party System* (Williamsburg: Institute of Early American History and Culture, 1956).

expressing the fears of the upper orders against those who would rouse the rabble.[3] He was also speaking for an era that had not yet seen the possibility of routinely conducting government in an environment of continuous partisan attack by a minority seeking to gain power.

After his review of these events Henry Jones Ford concluded that it was the "great unconscious achievement" of Jefferson "to open constitutional channels of political agitation." Into his Republican party flowed all the discontents that might otherwise have found expression in revolutionary strife or insurrection. By the channeling and the organization of these forces into a political party, change "became possible without destruction." [4]

These interpretations boil down to the argument that party organization and the associated practices of electioneering and deference to mass sentiments evolved to provide popular support for government as the old rationalizations of governmental authority were destroyed by democratic ideology. Party organization developed first among the outs who sought to replace the established holders of authority. Though the party process has an ancestral relation to revolution, in the descent a new means evolved for the displacement of governments from power.[5] The strivings of the outs for office become, by this reasoning, a sublimation of revolutionary movements.

These general ideas are further refined in the interpretation of party conflict as a competition by factions of the "governing classes" for the favor of the masses. Whether that conception has much validity today, it did have in the formative era of American parties. Jefferson and his associates, at odds with the Federalists, were equally of the gentry. In the view of the day, because "of party spirit gentlemen betrayed the interests of their order and menaced the peace of society by demagogic appeals to the common people." [6]

[3] "The very idea of the power and the right of the people to establish government presupposes the duty of every individual to obey the established government. All obstructions to the execution of the laws, all combinations and associations under whatever plausible character, with the real design to direct, control, counteract, or awe the regular deliberations of the constituted authorities, are destructive of this fundamental principle and of fatal tendency."

[4] See *The Rise and Growth of American Politics* (New York: Macmillan, 1898), chs. 7 and 8.

[5] One of the difficulties in detail of this sort of argument is that the caucus existed in cities such as Boston long before conventional party organization came into being. Luetscher emphasizes the difference between the delegate convention as the Republicans developed it and the old-time caucus. The delegate convention permitted a combination to develop over a state or other considerable area while the caucus was commonly restricted to a smaller unit.

[6] Ford, *op. cit.*, p. 90.

Institutionalization of party conflict. The party system gradually achieved what we now regard as its characteristic form, a process that occurred more rapidly in some states than in others. A major second phase in its growth was the establishment of organization among the opponents of the Republicans, the group that had first capitalized upon the possibilities of organized effort. As party practices took root, party conflict became institutionalized. That is, generally expected and accepted patterns of organization, of behavior, and of action developed. By the groping and halting processes by which human organization evolves, new habitual ways of governing came into being. Those new methods implemented the ideas of popular government; they provided a means for obtaining popular consent in keeping with democratic ideologies. But party did more than this. Party operations provided a substitute for revolt and insurrection and a new means for determining succession to authority. As the party process took form the workability of organized nonviolent conflict for control of government became established. Organized criticism and concerted efforts to replace those in power came to be regarded as routine. Once authority becomes subject to such challenges, and once sequences of elections occur, party government is extending its roots.

The institutionalization of party warfare marked a major innovation— or invention—in the art of government. Rituals, ceremonies, and rules of the game developed to guide the conduct of domestic hostilities which in an earlier day might have been fought out at the barricades.[7]

Elements of party apparatus. These comments on the broad function of parties have indicated some of the organizational precipitates of the development of parties. Yet it may be well to identify more specifically the various elements of party apparatus. Some of the confusion in the use of the term party flows from its application to different aspects of the system as a whole. When a group of members of a representative body work together for the achievement of common objectives, that group may come to be called a party. Or more generally when members of a government, executive or legislative, collaborate to achieve their aims, they may be said to constitute a party.

Other elements of party outside the governmental apparatus form the

[7] Children of the twentieth century may perceive only dimly the profound change involved in the subjection of government to partisan criticism and to the threat of partisan overthrow. Consider the assumptions about the place of government implicit in the fine of $100 assessed under the Alien and Sedition Acts against a Jerseyman named Baldwin "for expressing a wish that the wad of a cannon discharged as a salute to President Adams had hit the broadest part of the President's breeches."— Ford, *op. cit.*, p. 112. See J. M. Smith, *Freedom's Fetters: The Alien and Sedition Laws and American Civil Liberties* (Ithaca: Cornell University Press, 1956).

link between partisans in the government and the electorate. The term party may be applied to the organization that drums up electoral support and designates candidates. Commonly associated with this organization are the party leaders, candidates, would-be candidates, and campaign workers. To be differentiated from the electoral organization is the mass of partisans, the voters who are loyal "members" or followers of the party. While it may be useful for analytical purposes to focus attention on one or the other of these elements of party apparatus, if party is to be defined in organizational terms, it includes all these interrelated elements.

The Two-Party Pattern

A salient characteristic of the American party system is its dual form. During most of our history power has alternated between two major parties. Although minor parties have arisen from time to time and exerted influence on governmental policy, the two major parties have been the only serious contenders for the Presidency. On occasion a major party has disintegrated, but in due course the biparty division has reasserted itself. For relatively long periods, single parties have dominated the national scene, yet even during these eras the opposition has retained the loyalty of a substantial proportion of the electorate. Most voters consistently place their faith in one or the other of two parties; and neither party has been able to wipe out the other's following.

Concept of party system. Since many of the peculiarities of American politics are associated with the duality of the party system, the significant features of that system need to be set out concretely. An identification of its main operating characteristics will supplement the insights gained about the role of party in the governing process from the earlier excursion into the genesis of party. To speak of a party *system* is to imply a patterned relationship among elements of a larger whole. A pattern or system of relationships exists between, for example, two football teams. Each team has a role to play in the game, a role that changes from time to time. Within each team a subsystem of relationships ties together the roles of each player. Or, if one prefers mechanical figures, the components of an internal combustion engine combine and perform in specified relation to each other to produce the total engine, or system.

Similarly, a party system consists of interrelated components, each of which has an assigned role. The American party system consists of two major elements, each of which performs in specified ways or follows customary behavior patterns in the total system. To remove or alter the role of one element would destroy the system or create a new one. If one ignores for the moment the internal complexities of parties, the broad features of the system as a whole are quite simple. The major parties compete for electoral favor by presenting alternate slates of candidates and differing programs of projected action. It is a basic characteristic of the system that each party campaigns with hope of victory, if not in this election perhaps at the next.

In their relations to the electorate, another element of the system, the parties confront the voters with an either-or choice. Commonly the electoral decision either continues a party in power or replaces the executive and a legislative majority by the slate of the outs. The system, thus, differs fundamentally from a multiparty system which ordinarily presents the electorate with no such clear-cut choice; an election may be followed by only a mild modification of the majority coalition. The dual arrangement assigns to its parties a radically different role from that played by parties of a multiparty system.[8] The multiparty system may present to the electorate a choice ranging between extremes of the political spectrum but the dual system permits more extreme electoral decisions. The voters may throw the old crowd out of power and install a completely new management even if they do not set an entirely new policy orientation. The differences in the roles that their respective systems assign to them make a party of a multiparty system by no means the equivalent of a party of a two-party system.

To be distinguished from the roles of parties in electoral competition are the functions of party in the operation of government. The candidates of the victorious party assume public office. As public officers they may become more than partisans: they are cast in public rather than party roles. Yet the party role remains, for the government is operated under the expectation that the party may be held accountable at the next election for its stewardship. To the minority falls the role of criticism, of opposition, and of preparation for the day when it may become the government itself. These functions belong mainly to the minority members in the representative body but they may also be shared by the party organization outside the government. The minority role constitutes a critical element of the system. The minority may assail governmental ineptitude, serve as a point for the coalescence of discontent, propose alternative governmental policies, and influence the behavior of the majority as well as lay plans to throw it out of power.

In addition to the elements described, the party system includes customary rules which prescribe, often imprecisely, the manner in which the elements of the system shall interact. Of these, the most basic rule is that

---

[8] A party that may expect to gain complete control of the government must act far differently from one that may expect, at most, to become a component of a parliamentary coalition.

the government that loses the election shall surrender office to the candidates of the victorious party, a commonplace expectation which becomes significant only by contemplation of the relative infrequency of adherence to such a custom in the history of the government of man. Other rules and customs place limits on the conduct of party warfare. For example, the niceties of the etiquette of parliamentary conflict compel the attribution of good faith, patriotism, and even intelligence to the most despised enemy. Similar limitations, more poorly defined and less effectively sanctioned, apply to party warfare outside the parliamentary chambers.[9]

Such are the rough outlines of the American two-party system described in terms similar to those employed by social theorists in their conception of social systems generally. Real party life does not nicely fit any such neat system of patterned relations among sets of actors.Yet the conception of system alerts the observer to the interrelations of the elements of party institutions.

Why two parties? Foreign observers manifest the utmost bewilderment as they contemplate the American two-party system, and native scholars are not overwhelmingly persuasive in their explanations of it. The pervasive effects on American political life of the dual form make the quest for the causes of this arrangement a favorite topic of speculation. Given the diversity of interests in American society one might expect numerous parties to be formed to represent groups with conflicting aims and objectives. Yet that does not occur. In the less sophisticated explanations of why, the system is attributed to a single "cause." One commentator hits on this cause, another on that, and a third clings to his peculiar interpretation. A more tenable assumption would be that several factors drive toward dualism on the American scene. Whether one of those factors plays a determinative role remains problematic. Nor can one readily assign weights to the several variables.

Persistence of initial form. Human institutions have an impressive capacity to perpetuate themselves or at least to preserve their form. The circumstances that happened to mold the American party system into a dual form at its inception must bear a degree of responsibility for its present existence. They included the confrontation of the country with a great issue

[9] Hence, the deep bitterness aroused among Democratic politicians by the insinuations in the 1954 campaign and its antecedents by Messrs. Nixon, Dewey, and other Republicans that the Democratic party was a party of treason. Multiparty systems are able to accommodate parties opposed to the fundamental principles of the political order. The maintenance of a two-party competition—a winner take all system—must, over the long run, rest on a mutual recognition of equal loyalty to the political order.

that could divide it only into the ayes and the nays: the debate over the adoption of the Constitution. As party life began to emerge under the Constitution, again the issues split the country into two camps that corresponded roughly with the lines of division over the Constitution.[10]

The initial lines of cleavage built also on a dualism of interest in a nation with a far less intricate economic and social structure than that of today. Arthur Macmahon concludes that, in addition to other influences, the two-party division was "induced by the existence of two major complexes of interest in the country." [11] A cleavage between agriculture and the interests of the mercantile and financial community antedated even the adoption of the Constitution. This conflict, with a growing industry allying itself with trade and finance, was fundamental in the debate on the adoption of the Constitution and remained an issue in national politics afterwards. The great issues changed from time to time but each party managed to renew itself as it found new followers to replace those it lost. The Civil War, thus, brought a realignment in national politics, yet it re-enforced the dual division. For decades southern Democrats recalled the heroes of the Confederacy and the Republicans waved the "bloody shirt" to rally their followers. As memories of the war faded new alignments gradually took shape within the matrix of the pre-existing structure, with each party hierarchy struggling to maintain its position in the system.

Institutional factors. A recurring question in political analysis is whether formal institutional structure and procedure influence the nature of party groupings. Though it is doubtful that formal governmental structures cause dualism, certain features of American institutions are congenial to two-partyism and certainly over the short run obstruct the growth of splinter parties.

Some commentators, in seeking the influences that lead to two-partyism, attribute great weight to the practice of choosing representatives from single-member districts by a plurality vote in contrast with systems of proportional representation which are based on multimember districts. In a single-member district only two parties can contend for electoral victory with any hope of success; a third party is doomed to perpetual defeat unless it can manage to absorb the following of one of the major parties and thereby become one of them. Parties do not thrive on the certainty of defeat. That prospect tends to drive adherents of minor parties to one or the other of the two major parties. The single-member district thus

---

[10] For comments on the significance of early developmental factors for the form of British and French party organization, see C. J. Friedrich, *Constitutional Government and Democracy* (Boston: Ginn, 1950), ch. 20.

[11] Article on American political parties in *Encyclopedia of the Social Sciences*, XI, pp. 595–601.

re-enforces the bipartisan pattern. Each of the contending groups in such a district must formulate its appeals with an eye to attracting a majority of the electors to its banner.[12]

An essential element of the theory is its plurality-election feature. If, so the hypothesis goes, a plurality—be it only 25 per cent of the total vote—is sufficient for victory in a single-member district the leaders of a group consisting of, say, 15 per cent of the electorate, will join with other such groups before the voting to maximize their chance of being on the winning side. They assume that if they do not form such coalitions, others will. Moreover, concessions will be made to attract the support of smaller groups. If a majority, instead of a plurality, is required to elect, a second election to choose between the two high candidates in the first polling becomes necessary. Such a situation may encourage several parties to enter candidates at the first election, each on the chance that its candidate may be among the two leaders. Of course, under systems of proportional representation the incentive to form two coalitions, each approaching a majority, is destroyed by the opportunity to elect candidates in proportion to popular strength whatever the number of parties.

The validity of the single-member-district theory has not been adequately tested against the evidence.[13] Obviously, in those states of the United States in which third parties have developed fairly durable strength, the institutional situation has stimulated moves toward coalitions and mergers with one or another of the major parties. Yet the single-member-district and plurality election can at the most encourage a dual division—or discourage a multiparty division—only within each representative district. Other influences must account for the federation of the district units of the principal party groups into two competing national organizations.

The popular election of the Chief Executive is commonly said to be another institutional factor that exerts a centripetal influence upon party

[12] The single-member-district interpretation is presented in a comparative study by F. A. Hermens, *Democracy or Anarchy?* (Notre Dame: The Review of Politics, 1941). See also the analysis by E. E. Schattschneider, *Party Government* (New York: Farrar & Rinehart, 1942), ch. 5, and that by Maurice Duverger, *Les Partis politiques* (Paris: Armand Colin, 1951).

[13] Maurice Klain has pointed out that almost half of the American state legislators are chosen from multimembered districts, a practice of long standing in many states. See his "A New Look at the Constituencies: The Need for a Recount and a Reappraisal," *American Political Science Review*, 49 (1955), pp. 1105–1119. The chances are that the single-member district has a significant effect principally when it exists in conjunction with other factors that predispose the mass of the electorate to a dual division. Minor parties are obstructed (and encouraged to coalesce with a major party), for the system almost invariably reduces their share of the parliamentary seats below their proportion of the popular vote.

organization and encourages a dualism. The supposed effect of the mode of choice of the President resembles that of the single-member constituency. The winner takes all. The Presidency, unlike a French cabinet, cannot be parceled out among minuscule parties. The circumstances stimulate coalition within the electorate before the election rather than within the parliament after the popular vote. Since no more than two parties can for long compete effectively for the Presidency, two contending groups tend to develop, each built on its constituent units in each of the 48 states. The President is, in effect, chosen by the voters in 48 single-member constituencies which designate their electors by a plurality vote. The necessity of uniting to have a chance of sharing in a victory in a presidential campaign pulls the state party organizations together. The election of the President is paralleled by the popular election of state governors and municipal executives, who are chosen in a manner equivalent in its effects to the single-member district.

Systems of beliefs and attitudes. Certain patterns of popular political beliefs and attitudes mightily facilitate the existence of a dualism of parties. In turn, a two-party system, once in operation, may perpetuate and strengthen those beliefs and attitudes. These patterns of political faith consist in part simply of the absence of groups irreconcilably attached to divisive or parochial beliefs that in other countries provide bases for multiparty systems. Although there are racial minorities in the United States, either they have been politically repressed, as has the Negro, or they have been, as in most instances, able to earn a niche for themselves in the nation's social system. Nor do national minorities form irredentist parties. For example, the Germans of Milwaukee do not form a separatist party to return Milwaukee to the Fatherland as did the Germans of Alsace-Lorraine. Nor has any church had memories of earlier secular power and the habit of political action that would lead to the formation of religious political parties. Class consciousness among workers has been weak in comparison with European countries, and labor parties have made little headway. When one group places the restoration of the monarchy above all other values, that group regards the prerogatives of its church as the highest good, another places its faith in the trade unions, and perhaps a fourth group ranks the allocation of estates among the peasants as the greatest good, the foundations exist for a multiparty politics.

The attitudes underlying a political dualism do not consist solely in the absence of blocks of people with irreconcilable parochial faiths. A pattern of attitudes exists that favors, or at least permits, a political dualism. Its precise nature must remain elusive, but it is often described as a popular consensus on fundamentals. Powerful mechanisms of education and indoctrination, along with the accidents of history, maintain broad agreement upon political essentials if not a universal conformity. At times, it can be said, with a color of truth, that we are all liberals; at another time, it may be equally true that we are all conservatives. Breadth of consensus seems to be associated with a disposition to cope pragmatically with problems as they emerge. Standpatters, to be sure, remain who are attached irrevocably to an ancient formula for dealing with all questions, but they soon die off and seem never to be numerous enough to form the basis for a durable third party.

Political dualism is not a necessary result of wide consensus but a powerful, self-perpetuating consensus retards and discourages the growth of population splinters that might form the basis for a multiplicity of deviating parties. Within the context of the general consensus, perhaps dualism has been fostered by the occurrence of a succession of great issues, or complexes of issues, on which the voters could divide in two ways. Often these have not been issues of substance but of means or of timing. The simultaneous occurrence of burning issues that cut across the electorate in different directions might well strain the dual-party structure. A single great problem with a variety of solutions, each attracting the determined support of a sector of the population, could have the same effect.[14]

Explanations of the factors determinative of so complex a social structure as a party system must remain unsatisfactory.[15] It seems clear that several factors conspired toward the development of the American dual pattern. Whatever its origins, once the two-party system became established, the system itself possessed great durability and as a going system it exerted great influence in conditioning behavior. The system adapts new generations to its practices and new movements, new population groups, new causes tend to be assimilated into it.

Structure and Impact of Dualism

Whether an adequate explanation can be contrived why a people organizes its politics into a two-party pattern, the fact that it happens to do so has the most pervasive effects on the political system. The pattern of organization, once established and endowed with momentum, profoundly conditions the outlook and orientation of the top leadership of each party.

[14] The election of 1860 vividly illustrates the last proposition. Lincoln won the election with 39.9 per cent of the popular vote, but each of the four major candidates advocated a different solution of the slavery question and each attracted substantial popular support.

[15] On the problem of causation, see Leslie Lipson, "The Two-Party System in British Politics," *American Political Science Review*, 47 (1953), pp. 337–358. See also A. Downs, "An Economic Theory of Political Action in a Democracy," *Journal of Political Economy*, 65 (1957), pp. 135–150.

It affects as well the nature of the conflict and competition between the parties. A foundation may be laid for some observations about these consequences by an examination of a few of the more general features of the internal structure and composition of the major parties.

Inner structure of party. The inner structure of party represents a special case of the more general pattern of relationships between leaders and led. Those relationships involve an interaction between the inner core of leadership and the group membership. Leaders may carry along their followers, who also may mold both the tactics and objectives of the leaders. The echelons of leadership in both Democratic and Republican parties manage, within limits, the attitudes of their respective followers but, in turn, the attitudes of the loyal rank and file within each party may, again within limits, fix the orientation of the leadership. The broad outlooks peculiar to Democratic and Republican leadership structures tend to be associated with the characteristics of their respective followings.

The distinction between the inner core of party activists and the mass of membership leads some commentators to see the reality of party as the inner circle of party leaders and workers. Professor E. E. Robinson asserts that to comprehend the nature of a political party we must concentrate attention on the party's inner core or organization which comes

into being for the purpose of fighting and governing. It is not concerned with matters of fact, or doctrine, or even of principle, except as they bear upon the great cause for existence: success at the polls. Such organizations not only contain men of divergent views; they must also appeal to voters of differing opinions, prejudices, and loyalties. It is folly to talk of finding an actual basis [for political parties] in any set of principles relating to public welfare.

He sees party as a "comparatively small and compact body of men. Real power rests with them. They formulate appeals, direct campaigns, discuss in advance, and decide the nature of programs to be submitted to the voters." [16]

Emphasis on the inner group of leaders and workers centers attention on the main sources of party action, but the inner circle would amount to nothing without its following of faithful partisans. This is not to say that a more meaningful definition of party comes from defining it as a group consisting of those persons voting or registered as Democrats or Republicans. In many states membership in either major party is gained simply by a person's indicating the party with which he wishes to affiliate when

[16] E. E. Robinson, "The Place of Party in the Political History of the United States," *Annual Reports of the American Historical Association for the Years 1927 and 1928* (1929), p. 202.

he registers as a voter; affiliation is even less formal in other states. The process of gaining membership in the party is a different matter from affiliation with more tightly organized groups. The party member does not go through an elaborate ritual of induction into the group; in most instances he neither is acquainted with nor knows the name of the ward or county chairman of his party; he probably never supports his party in any way financially; the privileges and responsibilities of party membership rest lightly on his shoulders.[17]

Despite the informality of acquisition of legal membership in a party, the psychological attachment of the great mass of partisans to their party possesses remarkable durability. Even if the party member is an unfaithful attendant at party functions and an infrequent contributor to its finances, he is likely to have a strong attachment to the party heroes, to its principles as he interprets them, and to its candidates on election day. These loyalties, moreover, tend to persist. Even when he deserts his party's candidates, the voter may still regard himself as a good Republican or Democrat. The fairly stable party membership conditions the attitudes of party leaders, who must act in a manner to retain its loyalty.

The psychological attachment of voters to their party varies in intensity from the most unquestioning loyalty to the most casual sense of affiliation. The inner core and the mass of a party may be pictured as a set of concentric circles. A small hard core of leaders and workers, mostly the professionals, is surrounded by party members of intense devotion. As one moves from the center, successive circles may be taken to represent categories of persons with declining degrees of attachment to the party. This sense of belonging has been called party identification by Angus Campbell. A person regards himself as a Democrat or a Republican; he has a sense of identification with the party group and tends to regard its cause as his cause.

Campbell's studies establish the existence of these concentric circles of party adherents of varying party loyalty. At various times from 1952 to 1956 the respondents in national samples of the electorate rated the strength of their party identification in the proportions indicated in Table 8.1. The interviewees classified themselves in response to the question, "Generally speaking, in politics, do you usually think of yourself as a Republican, a Democrat, an Independent, or what?" If the answer was "Republican" or "Democrat," this question followed: "Would you call yourself a strong (Republican or Democrat) or a not very strong (Republican or Democrat)?" Independents were asked whether they regarded themselves as "closer to the Republican or Democratic party" and were

[17] See the analysis by C. A. Berdahl, "Party Membership in the United States," *American Political Science Review*, 36 (1942), pp. 16–50, 241–262.

Table 8.1

Distribution of Respondents in Four National Samples, 1952–1956, According to Strength of Party Identification [a]

Party Identification	October 1952	September 1953	October 1954	October 1956
Strong Democrat	22%	22%	22%	21%
Weak Democrat	25	23	25	23
Independent Democrat	10	8	9	6
Independent	5	4	7	9
Independent Republican	7	6	6	8
Weak Republican	14	15	14	14
Strong Republican	13	15	13	15
Apolitical, don't know	4	7	4	4
	100%	100%	100%	100%

[a] Angus Campbell and H. C. Cooper, *Group Differences in Attitudes and Votes* (Ann Arbor: Survey Research Center, 1956), p. 17.

classified accordingly as independent Republicans or Democrats. These admittedly crude measures of party identification have a validity in that those who called themselves "strong Democrats" (or Republicans) differ in their voting behavior and in other ways from those who regard themselves as weak or "not very strong" Democrats (or Republicans).[18]

The processes by which party identification is established and maintained are not well understood, but it is clear enough that the family is influential in building a sense of party identification. Commonly 75 per cent or more persons vote as their parents did and those whose parents were independents tend to be independents in high degree. Family influences are compounded by those of group, class, and community which by and large push in the same direction as does the family. However party identification may be created, it is, to a degree, independent of factors

[18] The flavor of the attitudes of the strong identifiers is illustrated by the observations of a pair of the respondents: "I was just raised to believe in the Democrats and they have been good for the working man—that's good enough for me. The Republicans are a cheap outfit all the way around. I just don't like Republicans, my past experience with them has been all bad." "I'm a borned Republican, sister. We're Republicans from start to finish, clear back on the family tree. Hot Republicans all along. I'm not so much in favor of Eisenhower as the party he is on. I won't weaken my party by voting for a Democrat." See the other similar quotations in Angus Campbell and others, *The Voter Decides* (Evanston: Row, Peterson, 1954), pp. 91–92, and their discussion of party identification in ch. 7. For an intensive analysis of variations in the activities and attitudes of partisans in a locality, see S. J. Eldersveld and others, *Political Affiliation in Metropolitan Detroit* (Bureau of Government, University of Michigan, 1957), especially chs. 4 and 5.

often thought to be determinative of partisan loyalty. Voters to some extent act as they do, not because they are workers or proprietors or farmers, but because they are Republicans or Democrats.[19]

Similarities and dissimilarities in party composition. The facts about party identification alone point to influences that condition the behavior of party leadership. The electorate does not divide itself neatly into two camps each consisting of voters deeply attached to one or the other of the parties. Rather each party has a basic following of strong supporters which is supplemented by a corps of weak partisans. Between these two party clusters is a block of voters—over one-fifth of the total—who have no sense of identification with either party but, when pushed, will often confess to a leaning toward one or the other.

A look at the social composition of the party followings will indicate other factors bearing on party behavior. The two sets of partisans differ in their social characteristics, and these contrasts are associated with the divergent orientations of the two party leaderships. The same data, paradoxically enough, reveal similarities in the composition of the two parties, a fact that also has a significant bearing on the operations of the party system.

The data support Charles Beard's conclusion that "the center of gravity of wealth is on the Republican side while the center of gravity of poverty is on the Democratic side." [20] The Democratic following consists in larger proportion of the lower-income groups, of the less-well educated, of the lower-status occupations, and of unionized workers than does the Republican following. The composition of party voters in the 1948 election, in which factors of party identification evidently played an especially significant role, reveals these differences in a marked form. In that year more

[19] The maintenance of a party attachment in conflict with other pressures often sets off psychological gymnastics within individuals. Thus, partisans whose policy beliefs diverge from that of the presidential candidate of their party may not see the conflict or may even perceive the candidate as in agreement with themselves.— B. R. Berelson and others, *Voting* (Chicago: University of Chicago Press, 1954), pp. 220-222. Or partisans may invent intricate rationalizations for a party attachment in conflict with their apparent objective interest. Even when he deserts his party the partisan may deceive himself. Of a sample of New Orleans voters who voted for Eisenhower in 1952, almost half either thought of him as an independent or declined to say whether they thought of him as a Republican or Democrat.—K. N. Vines, "Republicanism in New Orleans," *Tulane Studies in Political Science*, 2 (1955), pp. 119-120. On the acquisition of party loyalties in youth, see R. Centers, "Children of the New Deal: Social Stratification and Adolescent Attitudes," *International Journal of Opinion and Attitude Research*, Fall 1950, pp. 315-335; E. E. Maccoby, "Youth and Political Change," *Public Opinion Quarterly*, 18 (1954), pp. 23-39.
[20] *National Municipal Review*, 6 (1917), p. 204.

than twice as large a proportion of Truman voters as of Dewey supporters had had only a grade school education. Five times as many Dewey supporters as Democrats, relatively, were college trained. The proportion of professional and managerial persons in the Republican ranks was four times as great as their opposite numbers among the Democrats. The details appear in Table 8.2.

Table 8.2

Demographic Characteristics of Republicans and Democrats, November, 1948 [a]

Characteristic	Truman Voters	Dewey Voters
Education		
Grade School	48%	27%
High school	43	30
College	8	43
Not ascertained	1	
	100%	100%
Occupation		
Professional and managerial persons	9%	37%
White-collar workers	14	17
Skilled and semiskilled workers	40	14
Unskilled workers	13	7
Farmers	12	8
Other and not ascertained	12	17
	100%	100%
Trade-union affiliation		
Member	39%	11%
Nonmember	58	89
Not ascertained	3	
	100%	100%

[a] Source: Survey Research Center, University of Michigan.

The national leaderships of the Republican and Democratic parties see a different picture when they look over their shoulders at their followings, as Table 8.2 demonstrates. Yet the composition of the party supporters varies from election to election and the voters for either party always include a substantial representation from all income and occupational strata. The survey data on the presidential elections of 1948 and 1952 are compared in Table 8.3, which shows the partisan division of occupational groups rather than the occupational division of party groups. Eisenhower in 1952 drew more votes from the skilled, semiskilled, and unskilled workers than had Dewey in 1948. Yet in both elections the Republican party attracted the votes of substantial proportions of laboring groups and at both elections Democrats drew votes from all parts of the income and occupational spectrum. Accretions to the Republicans from among the skilled and unskilled workers from 1952 to 1956 were striking. It should be noted that the partisan divisions within occupational groups are not uniform everywhere. Southerners, for example, account for a disproportionate share of the professional and managerial and white-collar Democrats who show up in Table 8.3.

Table 8.3

Relation of Occupation of Head of Family to Voting Behavior, 1948 and 1952 [a]

Occupation	1948			1952		
	D	R	Nonvoter [b]	D	R	Nonvoter [b]
Professional and managerial	15%	57%	25%	27%	59%	12%
Other white collar	38	39	18	28	52	19
Skilled and semiskilled	52	15	29	39	34	26
Unskilled	33	12	49	40	19	40
Farm operators	25	13	54	24	42	33

[a] From Angus Campbell and H. C. Cooper, *Group Differences in Attitudes and Votes* (Ann Arbor: Survey Research Center, 1956), p. 30. The arrangement of the data to show the two-party division of those voting gives a clearer picture of the shifts within occupational groups in recent elections. The Republican percentages of those voting, according to the sample data of the Survey Research Center, for the years 1948, 1952, and 1956 were: professional, business, managerial, 81, 70, 68; white collar, 53, 65, 63; skilled and semiskilled, 27, 47, 56; unskilled, 33, 33, 46; farm operator, 41, 64, 55.—Survey Research Center, release of February 20, 1957.

[b] Democrats, Republicans and nonvoters do not in each instance total 100 per cent. The difference consists of supporters of other candidates and respondents whose vote was not ascertained.

The contrasts between the party groups indicated by Tables 8.2 and 8.3 are not the chance differences of a couple of elections: they reflect long-standing contrasts in party composition. Although voters shift from party to party from election to election, the facts, such as they are, suggest that at least in this century each party has had a fairly durable bedrock following. On the Republican side, the financial and manufacturing interests have been consistent sources of strength as have the upper-income groups generally. The Democrats, on the contrary, have—apart from their southern strength—tended to find their most marked support among industrial, urban, lower-income classes. This is not to say that Democrats invariably hold the support of a preponderance of these groups. The point is rather that even in their days of little hope, Democrats generally attracted larger proportions of such voters than they did of the typically Republican sectors of society. To a degree the party struggle could be described as a competition between the party leaderships for the support of workers. In their triumphs the Republicans may win even popular majorities in working-class wards, as they often did in 1956, but even at such times the Democrats draw their highest vote percentages, low though they may be, in such areas.[21]

Parallel to the differences and similarities in demographic make-up are differences in outlook on questions of public policy. Few public issues attract the opposition of most Democrats and the support of most Republicans, or vice versa. Some issues divide the parties scarcely at all; the issue cuts across party lines and splits both parties in about the same manner. Yet on contentious matters a common pattern is that the "center of gravity" of the opposition is to be found among the adherents of one party, whereas the larger proportion of the proponents will be found among the followers of the other party. In 1948, for example, seven of eight favoring the repeal of the Taft-Hartley Act voted Democratic; six of every seven persons opposing repeal voted Republican. In 1952, of those persons who thought that the government had been doing "too much" in "trying to deal with such problems as unemployment, education, housing, and so on," 85 per cent voted for Eisenhower. Of those who thought that the government had not done enough on these matters, 52 per cent supported Stevenson, a fact indicative of Eisenhower's inroads into groups of Democratic policy orientation. On the other hand, those who thought that what the government had done was "about right" split almost exactly 50-50 between the parties.[22] Those of conservative disposition, other analyses suggest, drift in higher proportion to the Republican banner and relatively more of the radicals find the Democracy politically congenial.[23]

[21] If the facts could be assembled, the chances are that the contrasts between the top level of activists and adherents—those who provide the money and the manpower for party work—would appear far more marked than are the differences between the masses of partisans. Sample surveys seldom chance upon a Democrat in the over-$10,000 income brackets. The prominence of heavy industry in the inner core of the Republican party has long prevailed. Thus, Will Hays, the Republican national chairman, said he was assured of "unanimous support" by the presidents of the "steel companies of America" at a lunch in 1918 with Judge Gary of United States Steel.—*Memoirs of Will H. Hays* (Garden City: Doubleday, 1955), pp. 158–159.

[22] Angus Campbell and others, *The Voter Decides*, pp. 117–118.

[23] See Richard Centers, *The Psychology of Social Classes* (Princeton: Princeton University Press, 1949). Other differentials exist in the composition of the major parties. Catholics, for example, lean toward the Democratic party; Protestants, toward Republicanism. See Wesley and Beverly Allinsmith, "Religious and Politico-Economic Attitude: A Study of Eight Major U.S. Religious Groups," *Public Opinion Quarterly*,

Interaction of party elite and mass. The contrasts and similarities between the partisans of the two major parties are, thus, paralleled by similar distributions of individual attitudes on issues between the parties. Do these characteristics of the followers help to account for the nature of the role of each of the parties in the dual system? The characteristics of the mass of a party result to a degree from the nature of the party leadership; every great presidential candidate leaves a heritage of devoted partisans. Yet, given a system in momentum, the characteristics of the mass of each party condition the behavior of its leadership and its role in the system.

If the broad record of this century may be taken as an index, the conclusion appears clearly enough that the leadership of each party has been anchored to its most reliable following. The record of party promise and performance contains a divergence parallel to the differences in party composition. The Democratic party in this century has elected Woodrow Wilson, Franklin D. Roosevelt, and Harry S. Truman. Their administrations were characterized by programs and proposals for economic reform and by an inclination to limit the power of business. Under the leadership of these Presidents, policies calculated to improve the lot of labor made far more notable headway than in Republican administrations. Democratic administrations promoted the cause of the farmer, especially the southern farmer, more vigorously than did Republican. Of the Democratic leaders who did not achieve the Presidency during this period, Bryan belonged to the same tradition as Wilson and Roosevelt, but Parker and Davis would have felt at home in the Republican party.

Over this period, the Republican party has had a fundamental policy orientation also in accord with the inclinations of its most faithful supporters. The campaign of 1896 cemented the bulk of the financial and manufacturing community to the Republican party. In the affairs of the party solvent citizens who feel that they can take care of themselves without government intervention, unless it is on a matter such as the tariff, have exerted great influence. Hence, the Republican party has been less disposed to advance the cause of labor by governmental action; it has felt that what is good for business is good for the country. In this century the

12 (1948), pp. 377–389. Moreover, although the evidence is limited, certain psychological differences may also prevail. Even when differences in income, education, and status are held constant, Republicans vote in higher degree than do Democrats; relatively more of them were "very much interested" in the election of 1952 than were Democrats; and a higher proportion of them felt themselves politically effective than was the case with Democrats. See Angus Campbell, "The Case of the Missing Democrats," *New Republic*, July 2, 1956, pp. 12–15. See also the perceptive observations by W. S. White, "How to Tell a Democrat from a Republican," *New York Times Magazine*, August 19, 1956.

Republicans have no great reform for the regulation of business to their credit, yet at times they have proceeded with vigor against business abuses, as under Theodore Roosevelt and Taft in the prosecution of combinations in restraint of trade. In so far as we have a "conservative" and "liberal" cleavage, that cleavage is along Republican-Democratic lines. Even this sort of distinction fails in many times and situations. Yet after discounting the statement to allow for campaign exaggerations, a residue of fact remains in Wilson's assertion that "the chief difference between the Democratic and Republican parties is that in the Republican party the reactionaries are in the majority, whereas in the Democratic party they are in the minority." [24] The troubled voter cannot use this as an infallible guide, for in each party sometimes the minority gains the upper hand, and always broad areas of agreement exist between the parties.[25]

The tug of the durable foundation of strong support within each party tends to fix the fundamental policy orientation of each party.[26] Yet the make-up of each party also restrains the zeal of the leadership in the advocacy of the cause of any single element within the party. Leaders in congressional districts may be extremists in the cause of organized labor, of suburban upper classes, of the Negro, of the Jew, of the wheat farmer, of the cotton farmer, of the manufacturers, or of some other element

[24] Quoted by Josephus Daniels, *The Wilson Era, Years of Peace, 1910–1917* (Chapel Hill: University of North Carolina Press, 1944), p. 11.

[25] One need not rely solely on the theory of interaction between leaders and followers to explain the contrasting modal outlooks of the activists of the two parties. The party leadership may take on the color of the mass of partisans; it is also apt to emerge from or to be of the mass. These assertions could be made more confidently if more data were available, such as the following table indicating the occupational backgrounds of candidates for nomination for county office in the party primaries in Vanderburgh, St. Joseph, and Marion counties, Indiana, in 1954:

Occupation	Republican		Democratic	
	Number	Per Cent	Number	Per Cent
Professional	23	25.8	17	17.7
Managerial	45	50.6	25	26.0
Clerical-sales	8	9.0	10	10.4
Manual workers	11	12.4	40	41.7
Others	2	2.2	4	4.2
	89	100.0	96	100.0

Source: Frank Munger, *Two-Party Politics in the State of Indiana* (MS, dissertation, Harvard University, 1955), p. 275.

[26] Relevant is the observation of the late Professor Anson D. Morse: "To sum up: the true end of party—the end, I would repeat, of which it is itself conscious—is, in ordinary times, to promote not the general interest, but the interest of a class, a section, or some one of the many groups of citizens which are to be found in every state in which there is political life, an interest which is always something less than the national interest."—*Parties and Party Leaders* (Boston: Marshall Jones, 1923), p. 22.

within each party; nevertheless, that segment of the party leadership with a national outlook—fundamentally those concerned with victory in presidential elections—must keep in view all elements within the party.

The diversity of the composition of a party operates thus to moderate the outlook of its national leadership. Those thrust—or who make their way—to positions of national leadership tend to be fundamentally sound on matters of concern to the party's inner core but they temper their devotion by an allowance for other interests within the party. Those with serious aspirations for a Democratic presidential nomination need to be sound on labor but they also must not unnecessarily frighten Democratic businessmen. No serious aspirant for a Republican presidential nomination can afford to be known as one who would put business in its place, yet he must have a somewhat benevolent regard for labor. On many other matters the national leadership is driven toward ambiguous stands by the conflicting elements within the party. The spectacle of a Democratic leader attempting to retain the support of both southern whites and northern Negroes exemplifies the matter as do the cross-pressures the Republican leadership undergoes as it is ground between the party's isolationist and internationalist wings. The top party leadership must try to restrain the extremists within the party ranks, search out areas of agreement and capitalize upon them, and, in general, attempt to hold together an unstable compound that often seems on the verge of disintegration.

In short, the diversity of pressures from within the party upon the leadership drives it toward moderation. Lower-level leaders may flourish by the fanning of extremist and particularist emotions, but the top echelons must seek to hold together divergent and often conflicting elements. The situation generates a radically different sort of imperative for the leadership than does the context in which party leaders of a multiparty system operate: they may be driven to accentuate the separatism of their electoral following.

Common influences on competing party leaderships. Still another aspect of the situation within which party leadership operates helps to account for additional characteristics of party behavior. Each party leadership must maintain the loyalty of its own standpatters; it must also concern itself with the great blocks of voters uncommitted to either party as well as with those who may be weaned away from the opposition. These influences tend to pull the party leaderships from their contrasting anchorages toward the center. In that process, perhaps most visible in presidential campaigns, the party appeals often sound much alike and thereby contribute to the bewilderment of observers of American politics.

The compulsions that pull the leaderships of both parties toward the center result in part from the simple arithmetic of presidential pluralities. To win a presidential election a party must both retain its traditional support and make gains among all sorts of people—farmers, laborers, white-collar workers, and the business and professional classes. While the competing appeals may stress differences in proposed modes of action, in competence to act, or in the timing of action, to antagonize any considerable class or group of voters is folly. The hearts of both Democratic and Republican orators may bleed, for example, with equal profuseness for the farmers, although what they propose to do for, or to, the farmers may differ in substantial detail. The practical necessity of appealing to all sorts of people and to all shades of opinion was emphasized by Thomas E. Dewey in his 1950 Princeton lectures. He spoke of impractical theorists who

want to drive all moderates and liberals out of the Republican party and then have the remainder join forces with the conservative groups of the South. Then they would have everything neatly arranged, indeed. The Democratic party would be the liberal-to-radical party. The Republican party would be the conservative-to-reactionary party.

The results would be neatly arranged, too. The Republicans would lose every election and the Democrats would win every election.[27]

Calculations of what is necessary for victory doubtless contribute to the tendency of both parties to make multiclass and multigroup appeals. Yet it seems evident that deep and subtle characteristics of American political culture also contribute to an explanation of the nature of the party battle. An expectation of that culture seems to be that the object of politics should be the maintenance of a concert of interests rather than the intensification of conflict of interest or the establishment of the dominance of a particular interest. No matter how devoted a party leadership may be to its bedrock elements, it attempts to picture itself as a gifted synthesizer of concord among the elements of society. A party must act as if it were all the people rather than some of them; it must fiercely deny that it speaks for a single interest. Selections from the campaign oratory of Franklin D. Roosevelt and Dwight D. Eisenhower have a remarkably similar ring. Both on occasion placed emphasis on the interrelations of the interests of farmers, workers, businessmen, bankers, all of whom had common cause in the achievement of great national purposes. And to a degree party victory represents the victory of a conception of national purpose, not the undiluted triumph of a particular interest.

All such partisan oratory contains, to be sure, an ingredient of campaign buncombe; it does not necessarily reveal the groups to which a

[27] *New York Times*, February 9, 1950.

party will be beholden if it wins. Yet the oratory doubtless also represents an obeisance to widely shared beliefs in the population. Generations of civic education have implanted an antipathy to "special" interests, a concern for the general interest. Each party must develop a conception of the general interest to mask its association with relatively narrow sectors of society. That necessity has consequences of profound significance, but one of the lesser results is that the parties are made to appear more alike than they actually are.

Dualism in a Moving Consensus

Although each party leadership tends to be anchored to the fundamental interests of the party, the total electoral situation and ideological climate pull both parties toward a point between the extremes. So flat a statement—and it is the essence of the argument to this point—may help to discern some of the order underlying the confusion of the American party system. Yet the proposition states only part of the reality. The process by which the parties move toward a point between the extremes is erratic, jerky, disorderly, and accompanied by no little friction and commotion. Moreover, the point of consensus or policy equilibrium toward which the parties move is itself not fixed: it moves as the parties approach it. In short, a conception of the party system must take into account its dimension of time. It may even be more useful to think of the party system as an historical process than as patterned institutional behavior.[28]

Foundations in consensus. If the time dimension is ignored, emphasis on consensus in the interpretation of American politics may convey a conception of a static politics and lead to the inference that the party battle is meaningless. If a differentiation is made between levels or types of consensus and if the party process is viewed through time, additional aspects of the workings of party dualism may be identified. Any competitive party system must rest on a consensus, an agreement among all concerned, about certain fundamental principles. In the United States, as in other working democratic regimes, such a consensus on fundamentals prevails, although no precise understanding may exist about what the fundamentals are. Obviously a significant area of agreement concerns the constitutional structure and procedure; no powerful element of society

[28] The following titles are pertinent to this discussion: J. R. Pennock, "Responsiveness, Responsibility, and Majority Rule," *American Political Science Review*, 46 (1952), pp. 790–807; Austin Ranney, *The Doctrine of Responsible Party Government* (Urbana: University of Illinois Press, 1954); Chester Bowles, *American Politics in a Revolutionary World* (Cambridge: Harvard University Press, 1956).

advocates the destruction of the constitutional order and the substitution of another. Beyond agreement on methods of government a vague area of substantive consensus concerns the acceptance in broad terms of the capitalistic system. Perhaps the more basic element of the consensus consists in the understandings and customs about how authority shall be exercised and in what manner changes shall be made rather than in agreement that certain matters shall not be changed.[29]

Without some such basic agreement party politics could scarcely exist.[30] A party system cannot be built in a society of irreconcilable sects, each of which proposes to install its own brand of political system. Those bent on mortal combat cannot practice a party politics. To affirm the necessity of a framework of shared beliefs as a basis for party politics is not to deny the possibility of the sharpest party conflict that does not strike at the foundations of the political order. The line between fundamentals, not to be questioned, and nonfundamentals, open to debate, may be illusory. That is, modification of the modifiable may, by insensible steps alter the basic nature of a political order. Nevertheless, in practice a range of debatable issues exists and its limits define the terrain over which the party battle rages.

Cumulative zones of consensus. It is within the limits of the arguable that the party battle occurs. It is in the adjustments to the settlements made within this range that it may be said that parties, in the long run, tend to move toward the same point between the two extremes. Innovation often meets the bitterest challenge; it is resisted; it may be accepted grudgingly; it may finally become conventional. It is in this process that another aspect of the nature of the party system becomes clear.

Triumphant parties that advocate great causes or that come into power at moments of great stress must contrive and enact measures that may be thought, even widely, to be destructive of the principles of the Republic.

---

[29] John Fischer has argued that among the unwritten rules is that each of the many groups of society "tacitly binds itself to tolerate the interests and opinions of every other group. It must not try to impose its views on others, nor can it press its own special interests to the point where they seriously endanger the interests of other groups or of the nation as a whole." By the arrangements of the party and governmental system each group can exercise an implied veto, but in its exercise, the group must "make every conceivable effort to compromise, relying on its veto only as a last resort."—"Unwritten Rules of American Politics," *Harper's Magazine*, November, 1948, pp. 27–36.

[30] Consider the comment by Sigmund Neumann: "Only where the specific interests of parties are imbedded in a common whole does the political struggle not lead to disintegration of the entire group. Only when essentials uniting the political adversaries are constantly reaffirmed can differences be balanced."—*Modern Political Parties* (Chicago: University of Chicago Press, 1956), p. 296.

Yet unless gradual acceptance of such innovation comes about, the cleavage between the parties could grow into a chasm unbridgeable by the compromises of party politics. Or alternations in party control and the accompanying changes of policy would jolt the social and economic system beyond the bounds of toleration.

In the interactions between the parties—which are spread over considerable time periods—what seems to occur is that to one party falls the lot of innovation. Its creative measures stir dissension and embitter the minority, although their more extreme aspects may be toned down in the process of enactment through the checks and restraints built into the governmental machinery. To the extent that new measures are both technically successful and evocative of popular support, they become embedded in the consensus by the impact of popular ratification in successive elections. The minority party eventually recognizes the inevitable and accepts the new order. Matters once contentious are relegated to the body of settled questions, and the growing edge of the political system moves on to new fields where new problems await solution and invite conflict.[31]

In this century the Democratic party has, perhaps both by chance and by the dynamics inherent in its make-up, been thrust into the role of innovator. Although the Wilson Administration put on the statute books a mass of new legislation, its product became relatively slight alongside the statutory accretion of the New Deal. Both by conviction and by its attraction for all those antagonized by the Rooseveltian program, the Republican party became a vehicle of resistance to the New Deal. In the 1936 campaign Alfred Landon, the Republican standard bearer, attacked even the Social Security Act. The bulk of the Republican leadership viewed the National Labor Relations Act with revulsion, and most of those who regarded themselves as affected adversely by each major Democratic measure found themselves in the Republican ranks.

Gradually the Republican party moved toward acceptance of the principal New Deal policies. This movement was accompanied by warm disputes among Republicans, and Republican candidates were long unsuccessful in persuading the electorate that their "me-tooism" was genuine. Perhaps the elections of 1946 and 1948 clinched the New Deal. The Republican Congress elected in 1946 made sounds as if it wished to dismantle the New Deal. The response of the country in 1948 persuaded even the most hard-shelled standpatters that the New Deal was here to stay.

[31] Such general remarks are suggested by the brilliant analysis by Arthur W. Macmahon, "Conflict, Consensus, Confirmed Trends, and Open Choices," *American Political Science Review*, 42 (1948), pp. 1–15.

The events of the 1952 campaign and of succeeding years brought more general Republican accord with the changes that had been wrought in both domestic and foreign policy. Eisenhower's convention victory over Taft represented a defeat of the isolationist and economically reactionary wing of the party. His election turned in considerable measure on his capacity to gain the confidence of erstwhile Democratic voters who continued to subscribe to Democratic views on public policy.[32] Once in office a goodly proportion of the crowd brought to power with the General seemed to interpret the election as a mandate to repeal the New Deal. Tentative steps in those directions with respect to farm policy, to housing, to TVA, to the REA, and in other fields brought sharp public reactions. "Even so stout a conservative as Mr. George Humphrey," the Secretary of the Treasury, observes Norton Long, "learned his Keynesian lesson, though not without a tight money fling that cost his party dear."[33] The congressional elections of 1954 reminded the Administration of the terms on which it could enjoy public confidence. Perforce, the Republican leadership became reconciled to the statutory precipitate of the New Deal. It could chip away at New Deal measures by inconspicuous administrative action; it could refuse to carry those policies further; but it could not reopen settled questions.

In the field of foreign policy a similar transformation occurred. Although Eisenhower had to contend with a determined rear-guard action by the isolationist wing of his party, the Republican leadership veered toward the acceptance of a larger role in world affairs than Republicans had traditionally contemplated with comfort. The new orientation by a Republican President brought a shift in the attitudes of rank and file Republicans.[34] Long in a state of disenchantment, they were brought to espouse policies that they had regarded as Democratic heresies.

Innovation, resistance, reconciliation. Although reservations may be made about the thoroughness of Eisenhower's renovation of the Republican party, the process described diluted the Republican nostalgia for the good old days and brought a semblance of reconciliation to the new order. Not all American party history can be neatly fitted into this pattern of innovation, resistance to innovation, and reconciliation. Though

[32] See Campbell, *The Voter Decides,* p. 174.

[33] "The Spectrum of Conflict," *Antioch Review,* Fall, 1956, pp. 265–277.

[34] While some persons become identified with a party because its leaders advocate policies pleasing to them, others adopt policy attitudes because they are identified with a party. The evidence seems to indicate that many Republicans, once the party leadership became perceptibly nonisolationist after 1952, changed their attitudes to accord with the new party line. See Angus Campbell and Homer C. Cooper, *Group Differences in Attitudes and Votes* (Ann Arbor: Survey Research Center, 1956), pp. 102–104.

some such process has recurred, each instance of a broad shift in the point of consensus has had its peculiarities. In each of the great episodes of our party history the political system gradually digested—or absorbed into the consensus—the consequences of far-reaching innovations.

If the parties are viewed in this temporal framework, one may better appraise the old saw that the parties offer the electorate only a choice between tweedledum and tweedledee. In fact, the differences between the parties vary from stage to stage in the conversion of controversy into new consensus as does the significance of the outcome of national elections. A Republican victory in 1936, for example, would have braked the New Deal to a halt and probably resulted in the repeal of its major measures. A series of Democratic victories demonstrated majority acceptance of the Rooseveltian reforms and time brought Republican recognition of that fact. By 1952 the policy differences between the parties had become far narrower, and the practical consequences of a Republican victory in 1952 differed radically from those of 1936. An election may abruptly check the growth of a new line of policy as did the 1918 and 1920 Republican victories in foreign affairs. It took another world war to set in motion again the drive toward reorientation of foreign policy vetoed by the elections of 1918 and 1920. By 1952 the spread between the parties on foreign policy had narrowed and the choice faced by the electorate more nearly approached one of tweedledum or tweedledee than it had been in the elections of 1920 or 1940.

For well over half a century, perhaps since the Civil War and certainly since 1896, the party orientations fixed by the upper echelons of each party have determined the fundamental role that each might play in the evolving consensus. With the liquidation of its progressive wing in 1912, the Republican party became so bound to its corporate constituency that it could take no major initiative in social and economic reform; perhaps the accidents of history that placed it in the minority in times of international crisis also induced within it a paralysis in the reconstruction of foreign policy.[35] Its internal dynamics and its place in the total system cast the Democratic party into a contrasting role.

---

[35] Perhaps the correct generalization is that neither party can well take drastic steps that may affect adversely its hard core of support. If so, the roles that the two parties may play in the workings of the system depend upon the nature of the cluster of interests and the characteristic skills of leadership that each brings to power. The utility of each party as an instrument for the service of the Republic, thus, depends somewhat on the circumstances of the time. Given their contrasting characteristics, the Democratic party has been in this century less handicapped internally than the Republican in the initiation of alterations in the domestic economic order. It is hazardous to forecast the sorts of broad problems that may arise in the future and the relative capacity of the parties to deal with them. Parties as well as problems change.

Role of the minority. To observe the party system through the sweep of time suggests an elaboration of the earlier analysis of the role of the opposition party's role in the dual system. The minority leadership, beyond the continuing function of reminding the majority that it is not really all the people and of assailing governments for their ineptitude, arbitrariness, and crookedness, has the task of promoting within its ranks an acceptance of modifications of the old order and of bringing its followers into accord with the dominant norms of the political community. Without the accomplishment over the long run of this sort of reconciliation, the two partisan camps could become so estranged as to paralyze the orderly processes of government.

This function falls by and large to the minority that has felt outraged by innovation and not to the minority that suffers no deprivation more serious than the disappointment of its hopes. Such a minority function, moreover, becomes perceptible only from a long-term view of the party process. Similarly, the minority from the same sort of time view has another major role in the system: that of consolidating sufficient strength to oust the government and to carry through the occasional thoroughgoing reorientation of the political order that circumstances and national conscience demand. The long look at the party system makes perceptible the significance of the availability of a minority force capable of making drastic adjustments of the political order when the occasion demands.

This is not, of course, to deny the importance for the dual system of the role of the opposition in more routine times. Without an opposition party there can be no dual system. The opposition makes possible the periodic presentation to the electorate of choices between governing cliques and of policy alternatives of a sort. The minority also must play a role in the conduct of government by maintaining a running fire of responsible criticism.[36] The American party system is singularly ill-adapted for the performance of this latter function, for the minority tends to be poorly organized for that purpose. Its titular leader, the de-

[36] In the field of foreign policy a special role falls to the minority leadership or perhaps more accurately to that sector of its leadership most sympathetic with Administration policies. The term "bipartisan foreign policy" is something of a misnomer yet at times the achievement of foreign policy objectives absolutely requires the concurrence of a substantial part of the minority senatorial group and appropriate interparty consultative relations have developed. The etiquette is suggested by the fact that in the midst of the presidential campaign of 1948 President Truman asked Arthur Vandenberg, Republican leader on foreign policy, to "slip in the back door" of the White House for a "private chat" in the course of which the President expressed his appreciation of the "judicial" tone of a campaign speech by Vandenberg and observed that the retention of the bipartisan foreign policy was more important than "who was elected President."—A. H. Vandenberg, Jr., *The Private Papers of Senator Vandenberg* (Boston: Houghton Mifflin, 1952), p. 452.

feated presidential candidate, may be without influence over his partisan colleagues in Congress to whom falls the day-to-day determination of party position. Given the fact that the congressional minority tends to speak only for one shade of the spectrum of party belief, odd sorts of minority views often predominate. For long the country shuddered at the image of the Republican party that emerged from the operations of its standpat leadership in Congress, and a minority Democratic party has its similar problems.[37]

Limits of partisan conflict. The breadth of the American political consensus keeps the party conflict within tolerable limits. "We cannot have," Pendleton Herring long ago observed, "a radical party standing for revolutionary change and a conservative standpat party. Such parties may exist only on the plane of discussion. Revolutionary communism can be tolerated by democracy as long as it remains an academic question." [38] On the other hand, the political system must have within it the means for substantial policy alterations from time to time. Such reorientations need to be managed so that over the long pull practically the entire society is carried along in what we have called a moving consensus. Otherwise the gradual accretions to the ranks of the irreconcilables would ultimately produce a bipolarization of antipathies hardly congenial to the existence of party government. Fundamental to the avoidance of the development of that sort of dual confrontation is the prevalence of a pragmatic outlook—as well as some self-restraint among the innovators. Yet the dual organization of politics, by the necessities it imposes upon those who would gain power, may contribute to the adjustment of the community to political change through time.[39]

[37] On the place of the opposition, see Norton E. Long, "Patriotism for Partisans: A Responsible Opposition," *Antioch Review*, Winter 1952–53, pp. 448–456; Paul T. David, "The Changing Party Pattern," *Antioch Review*, Fall 1956, pp. 333–350.

[38] "Political Parties and the Public Interest," *Essays in Political Science in Honor of W. W. Willoughby* (Baltimore: Johns Hopkins Press, 1937), p. 102.

[39] In 1955 midwestern, standpat, isolationist Republicans convened in Chicago on Lincoln Day for oratorical festivities devoted to belligerent criticism of Eisenhower, Dewey, and the eastern wing of the party generally. They regarded Eisenhower as a dangerous leftist, they despised Dewey, they were unhappy about American involvement in the United Nations. Even so the idea of bolting the party had little attractiveness. "While a lot of us get irritated with Eisenhower out here," concluded Gen. Robert E. Wood, "we still figure he's a lot better than anybody the Democrats can put in there."—*New York Times*, February 14, 1955.

9 | Sectionalism, Urbanism, and Party

AN EXTRAORDINARY characteristic of the American two-party system has been its continuity despite the most far-reaching changes in the underlying social and economic circumstances of the nation. From 1860 to 1955 the total population grew from about 31.4 million to 165 million. Over the same period vast areas of the West were settled and the great movement of people from farm to city took place. In more recent decades a restless mobility has carried people from section to section. Tens of millions of immigrants, most of them different in language and religion from the earlier settlers, found places for themselves in American life during the past century. In the same period industrialization proceeded apace. Withal a dynamic and changing social system has existed, a system quite unlike the systems of those in nations whose modern politics is restricted to the interstices of an ancient and rigid structure of status and class and rests on an economy of stagnation rather than of growth.

Through all these changes the major parties have maintained a continuous existence, at least since the Civil War, and the dual system has prevailed in its essence since the founding of the Republic. For a century, it may seem, the major parties have remained the same. In fact, only the system has remained more or less the same; the parties have changed. New wine has been poured into old bottles and old wine has been transferred from bottle to bottle. Old parties moved with the population into the newly settled territories. The parties managed to attract and to make places within their ranks for new Americans. They reached out to accommodate themselves to the consequences of industrialization. A remarkable feature of the party system has been its capacity to digest radical changes in the social and economic order while preserving its essential form and nature.

The ceaseless alteration in the composition and orientation of the major parties and in the character of the conflict between them makes problems for the political analyst. One era's classic treatment of parties obviously does not fit the facts of a later period although its clichés and generalizations may outlast the phenomena they describe. A full treatment of the process by which the parties have been molded by the changing social system and by which the parties themselves have perhaps molded the evolving society would be a formidable task. Yet some of the major elements of both continuity and change in the parties may be identified in broad terms.

Sectional interests have constituted important building blocks for the American parties. Each party has had its roots deep in sectional interest and each has sought to build intersectional combinations powerful enough to govern. While the sectional foundations of American parties have contributed mightily to the appearance of immortality of the parties, those foundations have for half a century been undergoing a steady erosion. Urbanization can serve as a shorthand term inclusive of a variety of tendencies destructive of sectionalism, such as industrialization, a sharpening of class consciousness, and immigration.

Sectionalism and Continuity of the Party System

For its two-party form and for the persistence of that form, American politics probably owes a considerable debt to an underlying dual sectionalism, which, for well over a century, contributed to a partisan dualism; and undoubtedly in the earlier decades of the Republic mightily aided in molding enduring political habits. The Federalists vied with the Jeffersonian Republicans; the Whigs and the Jacksonian Democrats competed for supremacy; the Democrats and the new Republicans fought a war, and they continued the battle later on the hustings.

Originally sectional dualism was associated with the advancing frontier. Among great nations of modern times the United States has been unique in possessing a sectional conflict growing out of the gradual spread of population over a continent. Long-established nations have their sectional issues, but the American westward movement caused a special type of political conflict. The areas settled first along the Atlantic seaboard furnished capital for the development of the western wilderness and thereby created a relationship of creditor and debtor between geographically differentiated groups; and, as James Madison observed, the clashes of interest between debtor and creditor have always been a "durable" source of faction. In other ways the interests of the East and of the advancing frontier were in conflict. A thinly populated agricultural West had interests that often ran counter to those of the more densely populated financial and industrial East. And the dominance of the East in all matters was threatened by the development of the West. Though the particular area constituting "the West" changed as the frontier advanced, there was always a West.

Sectionalism and the formation of the Constitution. Even the debate over the adoption of the Constitution took the form of a dual sectional conflict, a dispute between the frontier and the seaboard. Then, as is generally true, sectionalism masked underlying differences between territorially segregated interests. In his classic study, *An Economic Interpretation of the Constitution,* Charles A. Beard showed the importance of economic interests at stake in the adoption of the Constitution. In identifying the groups involved in the formulation and ratification of the document, Beard noted the existence of an important class of small farmers located mainly back from the seacoast, on the fringe of westward settlement, from New Hampshire to Georgia. This western inland section had interests antagonistic to those of the people of the seaboard. The small farmer was frequently in debt, often to a seaboard speculator, for his land; and he had to rely on the capital of the seaboard to develop the newly opened country. As a consequence of the difference of interests between the West and the East, there germinated from time to time legislative proposals disquieting to the East, such as easy-money schemes to alleviate the lot of the debtor and laws postponing the collection of debt, an early parallel to the modern "mortgage moratorium."

Quite different were the economic interests of the owners of personal property, concentrated principally along the Atlantic seaboard. Property in the form of money was endangered by western demands for inflation. Public securities sold at far below par, and ownership of the public debt was certainly not concentrated among the small farmers of the West. Manufacturing and shipping suffered from the tariff barriers between the individual states and from the absence of a strong central government to protect and promote their interests. Easterners owned large blocks of western lands that could not be profitably developed in the absence of a strong central government.

Opposition to the adoption of the Constitution came principally from "the agricultural regions, and from the areas in which debtors had been formulating paper money and other depreciatory schemes."[1] On the other hand, support for the new system of government came chiefly from the "regions in which mercantile, manufacturing, security, and personalty interests generally had their greatest strength."

The cleavages in the battle over the adoption of the Constitution projected into politics under the new government. Time was on the side of the growing West, which found its first great spokesman in Jefferson. The power of the Federalists depended primarily on the

. . . support of the wealthier classes of people and rested particularly on a combination of the commercial interests of the North Atlantic coast region, the tobacco planters of Virginia, and the rice planters of South Carolina. In 1801 Jefferson at the head of the Democratic-Republican party broke the power of this combination and obtained control of the federal government. There has been much discussion in recent years of the economic basis of Jeffersonian Republicanism. Out of the dust of controversy emerges the simple proposition that Jefferson succeeded in organizing the greater portion of the back-country grain growers from Maine to Georgia into a coherent "bloc," which formed the strongest element in his victorious combination.[2]

Jacksonian Democracy. Under the vigorous leadership of Jackson the western forces were again united against those of the East, or at least against the moneyed parts of the eastern population. Jefferson and Jackson built their fences on the solid soil of unity of the sectional interest of the then West. Says Professor Woodburn:

For fifty years after Jefferson's triumph the democracy which he promulgated found its support not only in the western parts of the original thirteen states but in all the oncoming new states of the West. Omit the South and think only of the states of the Northwest, Ohio, Indiana, Michigan, Iowa, Wisconsin. The party of Jefferson and of Jackson was able to carry these states, as also Pennsylvania, until close to the days of the Civil War, until the restriction of slavery had become the dominant issue in American history and the Democratic party had come largely under the control of southern slaveholders.[3]

The conflict between the seaboard and the frontier never arrayed all westerners against all easterners. The West had its allies in the East and the East by no means lacked support in the West. As people moved to the West they carried their partisan loyalties with them. Settlers from

[1] *An Economic Interpretation of the Constitution of the United States* (New York, 1913), p. 291. Quoted by permission of The Macmillan Company, publishers.
[2] A. N. Holcombe, *The Political Parties of To-day* (New York, 1924), p. 83. Quoted by permission of Harper & Brothers.
[3] J. A. Woodburn, "Western Radicalism in American Politics," *Mississippi Valley Historical Review*, 13 (1926), pp. 143–168.

Federalist and Whig and Republican areas retained their old attachments in their new surroundings, while Virginians, Kentuckians, Tennesseeans, and North Carolinians clustered in settlements that turned up as Democratic patches on the maps of election returns.[4] Even in the Pacific Northwest the settlers "were steeped in the Jeffersonian-Jacksonian tradition. Those from the slaveholding states of the upper and deep South may not have brought their slaves with them, but they did bring the principles of the Democratic party."[5]

As the slavery issue grew in intensity and salience, the old cleavage between East and West was replaced by a new sectionalism. The pattern of sectional politics became one of conflict between North and South. As the "solid West" disintegrated, "rival societies, free and slave, were marching side by side into the unoccupied lands of the West, each attempting to dominate the back country."[6] The outcome was the Civil War, which imprinted on American politics a new and lasting pattern of sectionalism.

Politics of Sectionalism After the War

The Civil War made the Democratic party the party of the South and the Republican party, the party of the North. That grand sectional division, which manifested a remarkable persistence, rested in part on a regional economic differentiation and the associated conflict in political objectives. Cotton growing and related agricultural pursuits dominated the South and contributed to a homogeneity of political outlook. A different, and more variegated, sectional interest generated the driving forces of the Republican party. So long as employing groups retained the confidence and loyalty of substantial numbers of factory workers the Grand Old Party had both votes and campaign funds. Yet the clashes of interest founded on economic geography did not alone provide the basis for the Democratic-Republican split. In the assessment of the strength of the sinews tying men of all classes of the North and South to the Republican and Democratic banners, heavy weight must be assigned to the regional patriotisms forged by war. Those loyalties were long sustained by the bloody shirt and the rebel yell. Of course, underneath the froth of sentiment substantial sectional economic interests prevailed after, as before, the war.

[4] Thus the politics of Indiana and to a lesser extent Ohio retained the marks of southern settlement in rural areas even in the middle of the twentieth century. Most of their areas of special Democratic strength turn out to have been settled by southerners.

[5] R. W. Johannsen, *Frontier Politics and Sectional Conflict* (Seattle: University of Washington Press, 1955), p. 14.

[6] Turner, *The Significance of Sections in American History* (New York: Holt, 1932), p. 27.

Nature of sectionalism. A more precise statement of the character of sectionalism ought to be interpolated lest the emphasis on its importance in American politics convey an erroneous impression. In an extreme form sectionalism might be taken to refer to a condition of absolute sectional solidarity in which the people of the South, say, were united on all issues against the people of the North, who were equally united in opposition to the South. Such a high degree of sectional cohesion and intersectional antagonism, it is scarcely necessary to say, rarely occurs within a working polity. Yet a sectional politics commonly involves a sharing of interests and attitudes by people of all sorts in a major geographical region against a similar clustering of interests and attitudes of the people of another region. Over long periods most people in each section may make common cause against the other over a single great issue or grouping of issues. Yet the friction along lines of geographic cleavage is commonly mitigated by a sharing of interests across sectional lines by at least some classes of people. Bankers, farmers, laborers of a wheat-producing section may unite on policies affecting wheat against all comers. On other matters, bankers of wheat-growing areas may join with bankers of other regions in common cause.[7]

Sectionalism tends to mask territorially separated interests. Sectional and regional loyalties—to the South, to the West, to New England—are not without strength. Differences in dialect, in social customs, and in history set off the people in one area from those of another.[8] Such differences furnish some basis for regional rivalries, but the concentration of cotton growing in the South and of manufacturing in the Northeast more persuasively explains decades of sectional political competition than does the fact that some people called themselves southerners and others regarded themselves as northerners. Perhaps the more homogeneous in interest the sections are, or the more complete the dominance of a single interest in each section, the sharper intersectional tension may become. On the other hand, the destruction of sectional homogeneity paves the way for political divisions along nongeographical lines.

Sectionalism, or conflict along territorial lines, may threaten national unity as sectional cohesion tightens and the lines of cleavage between sections deepen. The way of life of a region may lead its citizens to look

[7] Sectionalism is a matter of the degree of unity within sections. Many issues take a transient sectional form. The poultry raisers of New England, buyers of grain, may fulminate against midwestern grain growers over price-support policies. Yet most people of both sections have neither concern nor knowledge of the conflict. True sectionalism involves a greater salience of interregional conflict and a more widespread sense of mutual antagonism.

[8] See Merrill Jensen, ed., *Regionalism in America* (Madison: University of Wisconsin Press, 1952).

upon the "outsider" as an "alien"—a feeling not unlike that of the people of one nation towards those of another. Territorial differentiation and conflict in extreme form may pose for the politician the problem of manufacturing a formula for the maintenance of national unity. Only once did the American politicians fail in this endeavor, but we came to have, as the late Professor Turner said, "unlike such countries as France and Germany, . . . the problem of the clash of economic interests closely associated with regional geography on a huge scale. Over areas equal to all France or to all Germany, either the agricultural or manufacturing types are here in decided ascendency." [9] He likened the deliberations of party conventions and Congress and their results "to treaties between sections, suggestive of treaties between nations in diplomatic congresses."

Meshing of sectionalism and the party system. The sectional clusters of interest, founded on economics, hardened by the Civil War, and reenforced by subsequent events, formed the hard cores of the major parties. According to the more extravagant sectional interpretations, the South and the North competed for the support of the West in their battle for control of the national government. So forthright a view glosses over the confusing detail, but it fitted for many decades the broad contours of our politics.

Neither the hard core of the Democratic party, the South, nor the sectional bedrock of the Republican party, the North of 1861, consisted of peoples nicely homogeneous in attitude and interest as might be supposed from a simple sectional theory of politics. Rather within each of these sections, those interests associated with the leaderships of the Republican and Democratic parties managed to establish a position of sufficient dominance to maintain regional control over comparatively long periods.

Each great section inherited, to be sure, a pervading and durable sense of unity from the Civil War, but that unity had to be renewed and maintained by a composition of internal differences and by an exploitation of areas of common interest among different elements of each section. In the North the hegemony of the Republican party rested on the skillful maintenance of a combination of manufacturers, industrial workers, and farmers. The protective tariff, opposed by the South, provided a common bond for manufacturers and workers in protected industries. The same policy created difficulties in holding the grain growers of the Midwest in the Republican ranks. They could see the merit of a high tariff on cereals, but felt no enthusiasm for protective levies on farm implements

[9] *The Significance of Sections in American History* (New York: Holt, 1932), p. 36.

and supplies. The frequent nomination by Republicans of presidential candidates from Ohio, Indiana, and Illinois served, in Professor Holcombe's interpretation, to make the most "effective appeal to the farmers of the corn-growing regions." [10]

The Democratic party similarly, but with less difficulty, maintained its dominance in its southern hard core. Southern solidarity, as will be indicated shortly in more detail, rested on the common memories of military defeat, on the common interests of an agrarian region vulnerable to the fluctuations of the world market, and on the problems of race. Latent cleavages between commercial interests and poor farmers, manifest in such disturbances as the agrarian unrest of the 1890's, were suppressed by the stimulation of anxieties about the threat of the black rule. The combination of circumstances enabled the Democratic party to establish far more thorough control in the South than did the Republican party in the North. Substantial Democratic minorities challenged Republican dominance in the North, while in the South Republican voters were few indeed.

Within each party the sectional interests, which form the reliable and faithful core, gain a disproportionate influence in the party and thus assure that these interests will be amply represented in party councils. Democratic Senators and Representatives from the Solid South, re-elected term after term, gain positions of power in congressional committees under the seniority rules. Similarly, in national conventions and in the informal party councils these persons, through long service in party affairs, gain positions of vantage from which to defend and promote the interests of their region. Likewise, Republican leaders from the Northeast climb, through seniority, to positions of power in their party.

Neither the Old South nor the "Old" North, that is, the North of 1861, could alone control the nation. The party of each section had to seek support from outside to elect the President and a majority of Congress. In the process intersectional combinations were formed of South and West and of North and West. Their formation required either the existence of common or nonconflicting attitudes and objectives or the compromise or minimization of differences within the dominant multisectional alliance.

The nature of the patterns of competition and combination between sections may be made graphic by a few maps showing the division of electoral votes between the major parties in selected presidential elections. The election of 1896, the results of which appear in Figure 9.1, involved a sharp sectional conflict. The Democrats sought to join the agrarian South with the discontented debtor farmers of the West against finance and manufacturing of the Northeast. In the West silver-mining interests,

[10] Holcombe, *op. cit.*, p. 352.

Figure 9.1. Sectionalism: Electoral Vote in Presidential Election of 1896, by States

REPUBLICAN

DEMOCRATIC

TERRITORY

TERRITORIES

hopeful of disposing of their product at a high price, allied themselves with the Democrats. In the Northeast the Republicans succeeded in uniting the manufacturing classes and a substantial proportion of factory workers against the threat of lower tariffs and inflation. As Figure 9.1 indicates, the Republican strategy held together their bedrock support in the Old North and annexed to it the border states of West Virginia, Kentucky, Maryland. The Democrats added to their southern strongholds the electoral vote of most of the West but lost California and Oregon to McKinley by comparatively narrow margins.

In the presidential election of 1916 the pattern of intersectional combination took another form, as may be seen in Figure 9.2. The Republi-

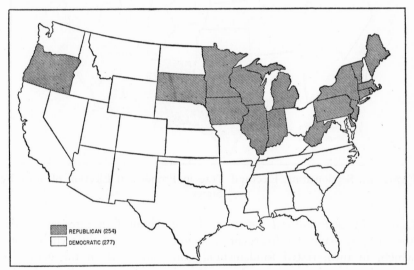

Figure 9.2. Sectionalism: Electoral Vote in Presidential Election of 1916, by States

cans were pushed back to their strongholds in the "Old" North, but managed to retain the support of Oregon, a state which, incidentally, took on a Republican coloration through its settlement by New Englanders. Wilson, the Democratic candidate, on the other hand, added most of the West to the Solid South and moved into Republican territory to take, by narrow margins, the electoral votes of Ohio and New Hampshire.

In the Republican landslide of 1920 the Democratic party fell back to its southern redoubt while the Republicans again extended their sway from the North over the entire West. Harding even managed to take the electoral vote of one state of the South, Tennessee.[11] The sectional pattern of 1920 appears in Figure 9.3. This map, as well as the others, gives an exaggerated impression of the sectional quality of the electoral decision. Each party polled a substantial minority vote in those states whose electoral vote went to the opposition.

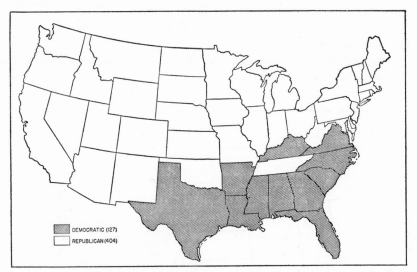

DEMOCRATIC (127)
REPUBLICAN (404)

Figure 9.3. Sectionalism: Electoral Vote in Presidential Election of 1920, by States

Geography and political behavior. These sectional disputes in politics arose largely from the divergent economic interests of different regions, which, in turn, rested fundamentally on differences in the nature of regional economic resources. This relation between geography and political attitude suggests a more or less parenthetical allusion to theories of the geographical conditioning of political behavior. The association of types of geographical environment with varying political attitudes has stimulated speculation about the geographical basis of politics. Most of this discussion, however, has centered on the geographical factor in international, rather than domestic, politics.

The writings of Montesquieu provide an early example of a geographi-

[11] The movement of the West away from the Democratic coalition began in the congressional elections of 1918. S. W. Livermore contends that an influential issue in the 1918 voting arose from Wilson's veto of a measure to increase the government purchase price of wheat. Cotton prices, not under regulation, climbed upward. Charges of favoritism to the South colored the Republican campaign of 1918 in the West.—"The Sectional Issue in the 1918 Congressional Elections," *Mississippi Valley Historical Review,* 35 (1948), pp. 29–60.

cal interpretation of politics. He placed emphasis on the influence of climate on human character and, in turn, on the nature of government. He believed, for example, that the colder climates produced a more restless and irritable people and a greater degree of political liberty; that the warmer climates produced an indifferent and lethargic people readily susceptible to subjugation and despotism. Similarly, plains people, without natural defensive barriers, were likely to live under a despot; those of broken and mountainous country were better able to defend themselves and to maintain political liberty.

Montesquieu's generalizations would not receive much credence today, but more refined correlations of the relationship between geography and politics aid in understanding political behavior. Such a relationship is most apparent in agrarian politics in which geographical factors condition, over large areas, the types of crops that may be produced and give the inhabitants of such areas common political interests and objectives. On the western margin of the plains wheat belt, with its uncertain and irregular rainfall, the clamor for various types of farm relief is usually loudest. The conditions of temperature and rainfall in Louisiana and Florida give us the politics of sugar cane, although it might be more accurate to say that politics gives us sugar cane in Louisiana and Florida, since the crop could not be produced without political protection. Conditions of rainfall, temperature, and soil limit the boundaries of the cotton belt and likewise the boundaries of one of the more formidable sectional blocs in American politics. The seat of political activity of the extractive industries—mining and petroleum production—is determined by the geographical location of those resources. The juxtaposition of the raw materials for steel influences the location of the metal industries and, hence, the sectional locus of the manufacturers.

At times the notion of geographical influence has been pushed to the form of an extreme geographical determinism, but more recently students have pointed out that man may affect geography as well as geography, man. The geography of the South did not predestine it to cotton culture and slavery; a complex of cultural factors—a demand for cotton, the availability of slaves, the existence of attitudes condoning slavery—brought about the utilization of southern soil by a slavocracy. Likewise, both the cotton and wheat belts have been pushed farther west by the breeding of plant strains that require less moisture and a shorter growing season; land geographically "destined" for grazing has been brought under cultivation. The textile industry, formerly concentrated in New England partially because of factors of climate and the availability of power, has moved southward with the development of new sources of power and new industrial techniques.

Man can to some extent offset the limitations imposed by the geographical environment. Yet within the framework of a given culture and technology the geographical endowments of different regions undoubtedly determine to a considerable extent the kinds of economic enterprise in which people can engage and thereby color their interests and ambitions in national politics. When technology, industrial or agricultural, overcomes geographical factors influencing the kinds of occupations people follow, geography ceases to "condition" political behavior. Nevertheless, the effects of climate and the geographical factors may be found at the basis of many of the interests whose influence and activity have persisted in American politics over long periods of time.

The South, the War, the Negro

Since the South has been our most cohesive section, the factors underlying its solidarity deserve special mention. For many decades it formed the bedrock of the Democratic party. It stood for the party and the party spoke for it. For 50 years changes in both the North and the South have been gradually undermining southern solidarity. Those tendencies came to a head in 1948 when several southern states declined to follow the northern Democratic leadership and bolted the party in the presidential election. In 1952 and 1956 the underlying developments predisposing some southerners toward Republicanism found expression in the vote for Eisenhower. Yet the intensity of southern reaction in 1955 and 1956 against moves toward the integration of schools for whites and blacks made it plain that southern solidarity of a sort would remain for some time.

Background of southern solidarity. The historic solidarity of the South arose from a combination of economics, of race friction, and of the events of history. Although the region long possessed an antipathy toward the tariff policies fostered in the North, that basis of unity did not alone suffice to solidify the South. An element of southern leadership succeeded in establishing a regional hegemony despite the existence of considerable economic heterogeneity. Even prior to the Civil War, marked cleavages of interest existed within the South and they found expression in competing parties. "The economic and political interests of the southern Whigs were the 'special interests' of the slavocracy. During the early 'forties the Whig party was frequently denounced as the aristocratic party of the slaveholders." The Democratic party drew on "the opposite side of the social scale—especially upon the small farmer of the back hill-country who could always be reached by the party's appeal to the agrarian spirit." [12] The South became a cohesive section when the slavocracy

[12] A. C. Cole, *The Whig Party in the South* (Washington: American Historical Association, 1914), pp. 69–72.

established its dominance in the region. In 1860 about 11,000 southern planters (about three-fourths of 1 per cent of the total free population) owned 50 or more slaves each. About 100,000 smaller planters owned from 10 to 50 slaves each. The small, slaveholding segment of the population, which had almost a monopoly of wealth, talent, and leadership, was able to impose its will on the South.

Great crises often mold political behavior into a durable pattern. Southern sectionalism bears the imprint of the trauma of history. The experiences of a war, an unsuccessful war, produced a regional cohesion with impressive qualities of persistence. A military occupation—known as Reconstruction—further solidified attitudes of hostility towards the outsider. Common resistance to the carpetbagger and Negro governments, no matter how much their misdeeds may have been exaggerated, further sharpened the sense of regional cause and further crystallized the determination to keep in his "place" the Negro, the more or less innocent cause of all the trouble.

The liquidation of the Reconstruction governments restored the Negro to his role of political subordination in the South, but the interracial equilibrium was threatened by the agrarian radical movement of the 1880's and 1890's. That movement promised a restoration of two-party politics in the South. The Populists and the Republicans of the southern highlands appeared as more or less lineal descendants of the pre-Civil War Democrats, while the conservative or bourbon Democrats functioned as successors of the pre-Civil War Whigs. The farmers' uprising in the South, unlike the Populist revolt in the Northwest, was slowed down, if not snuffed out, by the race question. Populists and bourbon Democrats bid against each other for support of the Negro. The danger that white disunity might restore carpetbagger or Negro government was harped upon, perhaps deliberately to frighten the discontented agrarians. Although the pattern differed in detail from state to state, the upshot of the agrarian crusade in the South was that the agrarians were quelled, the state constitutions were amended to record the *fait accompli* of the exclusion of the Negro from the vote, and the proposition was established that southerners should stand together in national politics.[13]

Indices of southern unity. The unity of the South is generally exaggerated, yet on one set of issues—those relating to the status of the Negro—a high degree of political cohesion prevails. Concern about the Negro may, in fact, be about all there is to southern solidarity, a proposition that may be illustrated by a few simple sets of data. Anthropologists tell us that in primitive cultures the cohesion of social groups is mightily promoted by

[13] See J. B. Shannon, *Toward a New Politics in the South* (Knoxville: University of Tennessee Press, 1949).

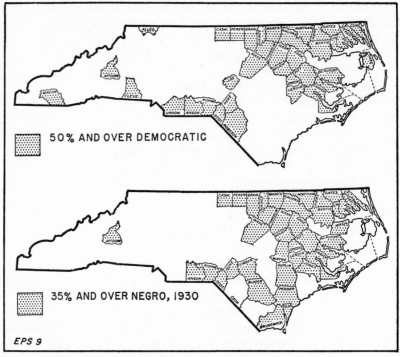

50% AND OVER DEMOCRATIC

35% AND OVER NEGRO, 1930

EPS 9

Figure 9.4. The Black Belt and The Die-Hard Democratic Vote: North Carolina Counties Over 50 Per Cent Democratic in 1928 Presidential Election and Counties with 35 Per Cent or More Negro Population, 1930

the proximity of unlike groups. If that phenomenon occurs generally, it would be expected that the strongest roots of southern unity would be found in those parts of the South in which Negroes constituted a large part of the population. On the other hand, it might be supposed that the bonds of southern unity would be weakest in those areas with fewest Negroes. The evidence supports the proposition that the whites of the black belt make up the backbone of southern solidarity.[14] In 1928 the nomination of Alfred E. Smith, a Catholic and a wet, strained the Democratic loyalties of the South. Several southern states went Republican. Although there were exceptions, the tendency over the South was for the areas with the highest proportions of Negro population to remain loyal to the Democratic party. Of 191 southern counties over 50 per cent

[14] The fact that the migration of Negroes from black-belt counties is reducing their Negro population proportions should not lead to predictions of a rapid softening of white attitudes towards blacks in these areas. H. D. Price demonstrates that white attitudes in such areas remain hostile long after a decline in Negro population proportions. See his *The Negro and Southern Politics* (New York: New York University Press, 1957), pp. 41-44.

Negro in population, 184 returned majorities for Smith. Of 266 counties less than 5 per cent Negro, only 79 gave him a majority. A map of North Carolina illustrative of the relation between the distribution of the Negro population and the 1928 Democratic vote appears in Figure 9.4.[15]

In 1948 the Democratic party espoused, through its platform and through the pronouncements of its presidential candidate, views on race relations that struck at the heart of the southern wing of the party. In every southern state rebellion against the national party leadership centered in the black belt. In the voting, although there were exceptions, the defections from the Truman candidacy were most marked in the regions with high Negro population concentrations. On the contrary, smaller proportions deserted Truman in the areas with few Negroes. An indication of the cleavage appears in the maps in Figure 9.5. The division

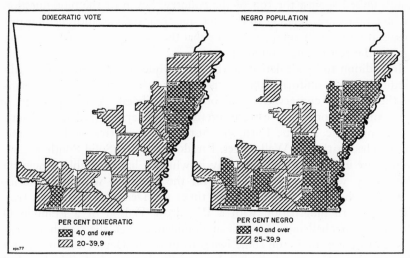

Figure 9.5. The Black Belt and The Thurmond Vote in 1948: The Case of Arkansas

between white-black areas could not, of course, be attributed solely to the race matter. In many southern states a vague sort of class politics finds expression through Democratic factions based in the fertile lowlands and in the less productive highlands. Moreover, elements of the party restive under its economic policies could express dissent by joining with the Dixiecrats with less inner conflict than support of the Republicans would have involved.[16] After several turns of the wheel, in 1956 the influence of the Negro question came to re-enforce southern Democratic loyalties.

[15] It may be advisable to note that it is in the areas of high Negro-population concentrations that relatively fewest Negroes vote.

[16] For a full treatment of the 1948 campaign, see Alexander Heard, *A Two-Party South* (Chapel Hill: University of North Carolina Press, 1952).

The states with the highest proportions of Negro population stood with the Democratic candidate, perhaps as the lesser of two evils from the regional viewpoint on the race question.

Another indicator of the fundamental basis of southern cohesion is provided by an analysis of the voting records of southern Senators. During the seven Senate sessions from 1933 through 1945, the Senate had 598 roll calls. On 85 of them at least 90 per cent of the southern Senators voted together. On 76 of the 85 roll calls the southerners voted with majorities of nonsouthern Democrats against majorities of Republican Senators. These were questions on which the solid South could make common cause with nonsouthern Democrats against the Republicans. On nine of the 85 votes, however, the southern bloc voted against majorities of both nonsouthern Democrats and Republicans. On these questions the South united against the rest of the country. Seven of the nine questions involved measures relating to the race question, such as antilynching proposals. It is primarily on the race issue that the South presents a united front against the rest of the United States.

In addition to its solidarity on the Negro question the South is usually credited with a uniform conservatism. In fact, on economic issues some southerners are conservative and others are liberal. A strong strain of agrarian suspicion of the eastern interest long characterized many southern Democratic leaders. Even so crusty a conservative as John Nance Garner had barbs for Wall Street. Paradoxically the Solid South has had to nurture liberalism. The only way in which it has been able to win the Presidency was by allying itself with the West or with the laboring masses of the North. At propitious times the Democrats emerged from their southern hibernation with a Woodrow Wilson or a Franklin D. Roosevelt to challenge Republican dominance. Yet the South has not wished to compromise on some issues to maintain Democratic unity. On the question of race relations it has stood adamant. It has had a dark streak of nativism, which found expression in the Ku Klux Klan and in anti-Semitic utterances. All these southern characteristics from time to time have driven deep fissures within the Democratic party. Withal, however, the northern wing of the party over the long run has been able to rely on southerners for greater support for policies of concern to it than can be recruited from Republican ranks.[17]

Impact of sectionalism on the party system. The broad patterns of intersectional rivalry and combination are obvious enough, but the strong sectional tinge in our politics also accounts for some other characteristics of our politics that puzzle native and foreign observers alike.

[17] For data on the range of southern congressional attitudes on liberal and conservative scales, see Chapter 24.

The notable element of traditionalism in our partisan attachments may hinge in considerable degree on sectionalism. In the South—and in the rural areas of the North—entire communities have remained overwhelmingly committed to the same party for generations. Sectionalism and stability of party loyalty may both rest on a continuing interest of a region. Yet beyond such conditioning factors, social and psychological features of sectionalism may contribute to persistence of party attachments. Economically based sectionalism in its more extreme form tends to be agrarian and rural. When a single interest dominates a huge area both economically and politically, the probabilities are that social pressures for political conformity result in a structure of partisan attitude with special powers of self-preservation. Even when sectional interests begin to change, the heritage of political faith may lag in its adjustment to the new state of affairs. The new technologies of transport and communication doubtless are reducing the durability of rural party attachments, but perhaps even yet rural communities retain a greater capacity to transmit and maintain party loyalties than do metropolitan communities.

A striking example of the phenomenon under discussion appears in Figure 9.6, which consists of a series of maps of Tennessee. At the time of the Civil War this state divided mainly between its western and eastern halves. In East Tennessee farmers of the highlands owned few slaves, whereas in Middle and West Tennessee the climate and topography favored the use of slaves. These regions differed over whether to secede from the Union. The people of East Tennessee who opposed secession later became Republicans. Those of Middle and West Tennessee became Democrats. This pattern of party division within the state remained relatively stable from 1860 to 1948, as the series of maps in the figure impressively shows.

Sectionalism also contributes to the multiclass composition of each of the major parties, a characteristic bewildering to those who regard only a class politics as "natural." A politics that arrays the people of one section against those of another pulls into one party men of all social strata. A common interest bound the southern banker, merchant, cotton farmer, and wage earner together against the northern combination of finance, manufacturing, and segments of industrial labor.[18] That latter coalition across class lines rested also on a presumed common concern about national policy.

[18] Even in 1952, by which time the old sectional solidarity had been strained, 46 per cent of the professional and managerial voters in the South were Democratic as against 28 per cent outside the South. Of other white-collar workers in the South 58 per cent were Democratic in contrast with 32 per cent outside the South. These percentages were derived from data provided by the Survey Research Center from its 1952 election study.

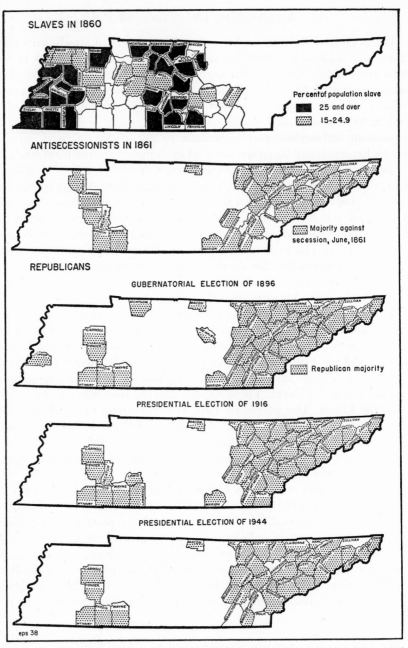

Figure 9.6. The Civil War, Traditionalism, and Tennessee Party Lines: Distribution of Republican Popular Strength, 1861–1944

Beyond the effect of common interest in uniting different classes of voters, the circumstances of rural and small-town sectionalism apparently facilitated the imposition on an entire society of the values of the dominant groups. Existence of all types of people in relatively close communion, in contrast with the class segregation inherent in the patterns of metropolitan residence, evidently tends to restrain the expression or development of latent cleavages. The structure of rural and small-town society thus apparently made for a higher degree of community unity across class lines than might be expected from the diversity in the objective characteristics of people of the small towns and the countryside.[19]

If agrarian sectionalism has had the effects assigned to it, the urbanization of the United States may have for the political order pervasive consequences that can, even now, be only dimly foreseen. The effects of urbanization have already been significant enough, but their full impact probably remains to be felt.[20]

Urbanization and the Growth of Class Politics

Sectionalism in American politics has always been to some degree a cartographic illusion. Representation on maps of regional voting blocs conceals the fact that within each region a minority exists which remains unmoved by appeals to the predominant sectional interest. Nevertheless, when a high degree of regional homogeneity prevails, political cleavages are apt to follow geographical lines. On the other hand, when sectional homogeneity declines—when a variety of interests exists in each region— and the differences between the various sections of the nation decline,

[19] The data on these points are limited but suggestive. See Duncan MacRae, Jr., "Occupations and the Congressional Vote, 1940–1950," *American Sociological Review*, 20 (1955), pp. 332–340, where he shows a positive correlation between laboring population and Democratic vote in urban congressional districts but an absence of such a correlation in rural districts. In Wisconsin, Leon Epstein shows that in the smaller towns the Democratic vote is less than might be expected on the basis of proportions employed in manufacturing. He suggests that perhaps "working-class consciousness is inhibited in the smaller as compared with larger cities by the more readily available personal and social channels for communicating middle-class values."— "Size of Place and the Division of the Two-Party Vote in Wisconsin," *Western Political Quarterly*, 9 (1956), pp. 138–150. Warren E. Miller shows that the minority party has special handicaps in rallying those voters predisposed to it in one-party areas.—"One Party Politics and the Voter," *American Political Science Review*, 50 (1956), pp. 707–725.

[20] Sectionalism, as has been noted, is a matter of degree, and no attention has been paid here to the variety of geographical groupings that appear from time to time as particular issues of sectional concern arise. See G. L. Grassmuck, *Sectional Biases in Congress on Foreign Policy* (Baltimore: Johns Hopkins Press, 1951); R. H. Smuckler, "The Region of Isolationism," *American Political Science Review*, 47 (1953), pp. 386–401.

political conflict is not so likely to be between geographically defined groups. So long as we were predominantly an agrarian nation it could be assumed that the great crop regions, founded on climate and geography, would act as sectional units. But when the dominance of cotton in the cotton belt and of corn in the corn belt is challenged, the economic basis for sectional unity becomes weaker.

Dilution of sectionalism. Diversification of interest dilutes sectionalism. The fading of the memories of the Civil War bears on the decline of sectional sentiment, but the weakening of sectional blocs comes fundamentally from the multiplication of interests within regions. Most of the alterations in the basic interests of agrarian sections are associated in one way or another with urbanization. Manufacturing, distribution, finance, and most other nonagricultural pursuits center in the cities. Moreover, most of the new ethnic groups disturbing to the old patterns of sectional unity have settled in the cities. Urbanization thus serves as an index of a complex of social and economic changes with political repercussions.

A simple set of figures portrays the moderation of sectional cleavages. Under a sectional politics the states of one section may be expected to give an overwhelming vote to one party; the states of the opposing section, a heavy vote to the other party. The net effect of the weakening of sectional solidarity has been a long-run tendency for the states to divide more nearly alike in their popular vote in presidential elections. As each party gains support in the ancient strongholds of the other, the dissimilarities among states dim. A rough measure of these tendencies appears in the graph in Figure 9.7. The presidential election of 1896 marked a high tide of sectional solidarity in mutual antagonism as the South and West opposed the North. When the states were ranked according to the Republican percentages of their popular votes in that year, the middle half of the states ranged from 56 per cent in North Dakota to 30.3 per cent in Texas. That wide difference among the states produced the 1896 peak in the graph. Gradually, and somewhat erratically as the graph reveals, the middle half of the states came to divide more and more alike and to be compressed into a narrower and narrower range. In 1952 the middle half of the states clustered between Oregon's 60.6 per cent Republican and Delaware's 51.7 per cent. This decline in the dispersion of the states crudely measures one dimension of the consequences of the erosion of sectional solidarity.

The processes of modification of sectionalism are most visible in the South, a region that long seemed monolithic. In its rapid urbanization of the past few decades, the South has undergone metamorphoses that occurred decades earlier in the North. These changes built within the southern cities neighborhoods of upper-income proprietors and managers with an economic base largely independent of the region's old agrarian interests. The new business classes, like the old business classes of the North, had little enthusiasm for the New Deal and Fair Deal. During the Democratic era a southern bloc often made common cause with Republicans in Congress to delay or to modify Administration proposals. After 1936 the Republican presidential vote began to increase in those neighbor-

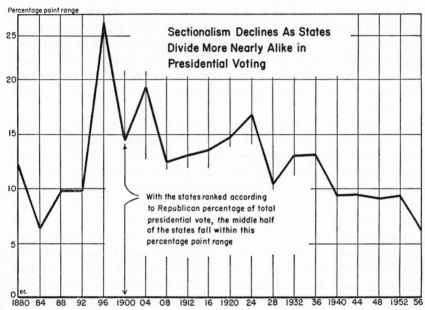

Figure 9.7. Interquartile Range of States When Ranked According to Republican Percentage of Total Presidential Popular Vote, 1896–1956

hoods of southern cities inhabited by the growing business groups. In 1952 Eisenhower's most marked strength fell in the upper-income residential areas of the major southern cities, while Stevenson drew his heaviest support in wards and precincts at the opposite end of the scale, a pattern that recurred in 1956.[21] In short, as the pulls of sectionalism have worn down, southerners come to divide politically more like the people of the remainder of the country. The slackening of sectional cohesiveness

[21] The high Republican percentage of the presidential vote in southern cities may be explained in part by the fact that southern urban labor is becoming politically activated at a much slower rate than the southern upper classes. In 1952, 51 per cent of southern skilled and semiskilled labor voted in contrast with 80 per cent voting outside the South. For the unskilled, the contrasting participation rates were 28 and 78.— Data from Survey Research Center, University of Michigan.

seems to be most notable in urban communities which are both most drastically affected by industrialization and somewhat less bound by anxieties about race.[22]

Extent and rate of urbanization. As the recent southern trends suggest, the changes associated with urbanization undermine the structure of historic agrarian sectionalism. A great area producing a major crop may be expected to carry along with it in national politics its small cities and villages that forage on the countryside, but a great industrial city has a political character of its own. It contains a variety of economic, racial, and social interests, often with little unity of purpose. It is possible to speak of wheat, say, as the dominant concern of several million people scattered over several states. But an equal number of people concentrated in the small area of a single city are not likely to be characterized by such a unity of interest.

It is commonplace that American cities have grown rapidly, yet it is difficult to grasp the magnitude of the change in our way of life and the almost cataclysmic political consequences of urbanization. In a period of less than a century a radical alteration in the way of life of a large proportion of the people has occurred. In 1870 only one out of four persons resided in an incorporated place of 2,500 or over; by 1940 almost three out of every five persons were urban dwellers. In 1870 only every tenth person lived in a city of 100,000 or more; by 1940 about three out of ten persons resided in such cities. Or, to look at the matter from the obverse view, in 1870 three out of four Americans were rural dwellers; by 1950 only about two out of five persons lived in rural territory and over half the rural dwellers were classified by the census officials as "rural nonfarm." These broad shifts in the rural-urban division of the population are depicted in Figure 9.8.

Of special significance has been the growth of the great urban agglomerations of population, for it is in the larger cities that the political consequences of urbanization manifest themselves most sharply. By 1950, 168 standard metropolitan areas (cities of 50,000 and their surrounding urban fringe) accounted for more than half, 56.1 per cent, of the entire population of the country. The trend may be illustrated in another way. In 1900 we had 78 cities of over 50,000 population; in 1950, 232 such cities.

[22] See the careful analysis by D. S. Strong, "The Presidential Election in the South, 1952," *Journal of Politics*, 17 (1955), pp. 343-389. See also the findings by Angus Campbell, *The Voter Decides* (Evanston: Row, Peterson, 1954), pp. 172-173, and C. A. M. Ewing and J. E. Titus, "Urbanism and Southern Politics" in R. P. Vance and N. J. Demerath, *The Urban South* (Chapel Hill: University of North Carolina Press, 1954).

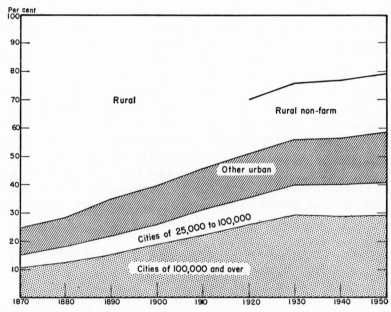

Figure 9.8. Urbanization: Distribution of Population of Continental United States Between Rural Territory and Cities of Specified Size Groups, 1870–1950

Or the new state of affairs may be suggested by the fact that in 1950 the three largest metropolitan regions—those of New York, Chicago, and Los Angeles—contained a larger total population than did the six states of New England plus Kentucky, Tennessee, Alabama, and Mississippi.

City, class, and party. Urbanization affects every aspect of the governmental process. It creates a host of new problems to be met by governmental agencies. It places on government the burden of the mediation of a vast number of new relationships associated with the interdependence of the components of an urban society. In its bearing specifically on the party system urbanization also has had a variety of consequences. It profoundly modified the sectional base of the party system which gradually adapted itself to the new state of affairs. Evidently as the population changes took place in the North the Democratic party became gradually more and more a party of the great cities. Democratic dependence on the urban vote began to increase long before the party became dominant in the cities in the 1930's. Simultaneously the Republican party became more dependent on rural and small-town support.

The growth of northern metropolitan influence in the Democratic party came to be symbolized by the conspicuous roles in national Democratic affairs of leaders of such centers as Chicago, Pittsburgh, New York, Providence, and Boston. The party was caricatured as a distrustful alliance of northern urban bosses and southern planters. From 1932 to 1948 the metropolitan centers contributed significantly to Democratic presidential victories, as has been demonstrated by Samuel J. Eldersveld. He analyzed in detail the bearing of metropolitan pluralities on the state-wide plurality of the winning presidential candidate in 10 of the most urban states containing in all 12 cities, each with a population of over 500,000.[23] The Democratic metropolitan pluralities in these 10 states accounted for the following numbers of electoral votes for the Democratic candidates in the elections of 1932–1948: 1932, 168; 1936, 142; 1940, 212; 1944, 193; 1948, 106. In the elections of 1920 and 1924 metropolitan pluralities favored the Republicans, but they won only eight electoral votes through such pluralities in 1920 and 39 in 1924. "In 1940, 1944, and 1948," Eldersveld calculates, "the Democrats would have lost the presidential election" without the urban pluralities they received from these 12 major cities. He opines that the "metropolitan vote may well have become the balance-wheel in our political system." [24]

The significance of urbanization for the party system does not come solely from the fact that the Democratic party developed urban bastions. Rather, the processes of urbanization created the raw materials for party cleavages more nearly along class lines than was the politics of sectionalism. Urbanization created new kinds of Republicans and Democrats. Those at the upper end of the income scale became more exclusively attached to the Republican party as a similar loyalty to the Democratic party developed in the lower-income brackets. Under American circumstances class attachments may not fix rigid partisan orientations, but the existence of an industrial society assures cleavages along class lines when class-relevant issues become salient. Evidently what has happened is that a sense of class politics and class solidarity remains stable at a high level among the upper-income groups while middle- and lower-income groups vary from time to time in the degree to which class and politics are associated. Perhaps in the election of 1936 the party division most nearly coincided with differences of income and occupation. That coincidence declined, as class-relevant questions faded from the forefront, and in 1952 and 1956 Republicans won substantial support in the lower-income groups.

Urbanization may have introduced a new element of volatility into

[23] The states are New York, Massachusetts, Pennsylvania, Maryland, Missouri, Illinois, Michigan, Ohio, Wisconsin, and California.

[24] "The Influence of Metropolitan Party Pluralities in Presidential Elections Since 1920," *American Political Science Review*, 43 (1949), pp. 1189–1206.

electoral behavior rather than a stable and continuing class cleavage. That is not to say that the electorate will over the short term—say, from election to election—necessarily swing erratically but that over a somewhat longer period an urban electorate may be susceptible to wider shifts in partisan attachment than would have been expected of the rural electorate of an earlier day.[25]

Urbanization has not completely dissolved sectionalism, and the blending of sectional and class interests in the party system helps to account for some of its peculiar characteristics. In the metropolitan areas party cleavages tend to follow class lines, although class and party vary in the degree to which they approach congruency. Each party, however, contains sectional interests which in a measure cut across economic class lines. The class and sectional composition of the Republican party makes for a higher degree of coherence than does the sectional and class make-up of the Democratic party.[26] Rural interests—at least under certain conditions—have a general outlook that can be reconciled with the upper-class orientation of the urban wing of the Republican party. On the other hand, the rural wing of the Democratic party often finds itself at loggerheads with the urban, laboring-class element. The rural Democrats often make common cause with the Republicans, some of whose leaders occasionally fondly contemplate a coalition with the Dixiecrats. Yet, when the Republicans annex sufficient support to win the Presidency, they bring into the fold enough urban workers to temper the position they take as a minority.

Suburbanization. After World War II suburbanization replaced urbanization as the most conspicuous type of population redistribution. The great central cities settled down to a fairly stable, or even declining, population

[25] It has been suggested that the middle classes, an imprecisely defined category, constitute the balance wheel in the new politics of urbanism. Those most imbued with middle-class values may play a special role in the long-term alternations in party position, but the evidence indicates that persons of all income and occupational classes participate in these movements from party to party. See A. N. Holcombe, *The Middle Classes in American Politics* (Cambridge: Harvard University Press, 1940).

[26] The nature of the inner bonds of the Republican party is suggested by a pronouncement of the executive secretary of the National Association of Real Estate Boards. He regarded cities as "populated for the most part with the mass-man, devoid of civic responsibility," who will "vote for anyone who offers him something." "Our one hope of survival as a free country," he gloomily predicted, "is that rural and semi-rural areas still dominate most of the state legislatures through their representatives and still dominate the House of Representatives in Washington." Urban real estate interests and rural representatives might make common cause against public housing for cities.—*Arkansas Gazette*, November 4, 1947.

as their suburbs mushroomed. Political observers saw in this demographic phenomenon the foundations for political changes of basic significance which were said to have made an initial appearance in the presidential voting of 1952. The interpretation ran to the effect that people, moving up the occupational and income scales, were making their way to the suburbs. There, surrounded by neighbors of unimpeachable respectability and Republicanism, the new suburbanites would gradually be absorbed into the GOP. This process of expansion of the middle classes would, sooner or later, mightily weaken the Democratic party.[27]

Comparison of the 1948 and 1952 presidential vote gives some support to the suburban interpretation. An analysis of the vote in 36 cities of over 300,000 population and in the surrounding voting units shows the usual Republican advantage in the suburbs. The Democratic percentages for these areas lumped together were:

	Central Cities	Suburbs
1948	57.9	41.9
1952	53.8	37.6

Eisenhower, thus, improved the 1948 Republican showing in central cities and in suburbs to about the same extent. The real suburban GOP gain came from the far more rapid growth of the total vote in the suburbs than in the central cities. The vote in these 36 cities increased by 16.8 per cent from 1948 to 1952; the total in their suburbs, by 46.1 per cent. In the suburbs a 1948 Republican plurality of 850,000 became a 1952 plurality of 1,905,000, sufficient in some localities even in 1952 to offset the Democratic lead in the central city.

Closer inspection of the suburbs raises some question whether suburbanization represents the most appropriate index of those fundamental changes of political import which are undoubtedly occurring in American society. There are suburbs and suburbs: working-class suburbs, middle-class suburbs, and doubtless a few of the old-fashioned, upper-class suburbs dedicated to gracious living. Some growing suburbs are becoming more Democratic; in others Republicans are holding their own or gaining. In central cities the changes said to be characteristic of suburbs are also taking place to some extent.

Those underlying social changes, which seem to be associated to some extent with suburbanization, are various. They include changes in the income level, alterations in occupational distribution, and the acculturation of the most recent waves of immigrants. Trends in the income level are almost startling in their rate and magnitude. The trends from 1939

[27] See Samuel Lubell, *The Future of American Politics* (New York: Harper, 1952); G. Edward Janosik, "The New Suburbia," *Current History*, August, 1956, pp. 91-95.

to 1954 appear in Table 9.1. In 1939, only 2.3 per cent of the income units (families and individuals living unattached to families) had annual incomes of $5,000 or more; that percentage had grown to 32.0 in 1954. Over the same period the percentages of income units with incomes of under $1,000 declined from 41.2 to 14.9. Though these changes in part reflect inflation, they are substantial. The data of the table should not be taken to mean that poverty has been abolished. One out of seven income units in 1954 had less than $1,000 income annually; almost four out of ten, less than $60 per week. Yet at the other end of the scale a many-fold increase had occurred in the proportions of families with incomes of more than $5,000, a sum sufficient to make them, at least in the 1950's, far more responsive to Republican doctrine than they had been in their less palmy days.[28]

Table 9.1

Percentage Distribution of Income Units, Families and Unrelated Individuals, by Income Levels, 1939–1954

Income Level	1939	1945	1949	1952	1954	1955
$1–999	41.2	18.3	12.7	14.5	14.9	14.0
$1,000–2,999	49.3	46.6	38.1	26.9	24.4	23.3
$3,000–4,999	7.2	26.3	32.3	31.0	28.5	27.7
$5,000 and over	2.3	8.8	16.8	27.7	32.0	34.9
Median Income	$1,231	$2,390	$2,959	$3,467	$3,730	$3,909

Source: *Statistical Abstract of the United States,* 1951, p. 269; 1956, p. 308.

Along with these income changes, gradual alterations in the occupational distribution are occurring. Perhaps most marked is the growth in the proportions of white-collar workers and other low-salaried workers. Such persons tend to develop identifications with upper-class norms and with the Republican party more frequently than do blue-collar workers at comparable income levels. For several decades the proportions of blue-collar workers has remained fairly constant, but it is probable that the statistical categories of skilled and semiskilled conceal changes in skill and outlook of some significance for political behavior.

In the great cities a notable process of acculturation has affected the

[28] These changes in income distribution did not impoverish the upper-income levels. In 1953 the top 5 per cent of families in income drew 20.7 of all family income before taxes, 18.2 per cent after taxes. Yet from 1939 to 1950 an extremely sharp decline occurred in the proportion of all income going to those in the upper 5 per cent. That decline resulted in large measure from increases in income of groups lower in the rank order rather than from absolute declines for the upper 5 per cent. It is not improbable that these losses of relative status (along with federal tax policy) contributed to an evident intensification of political cohesiveness in the top-income levels.

more recent immigrants. A generation or so of education, indoctrination, and adaptation reduces the differential between these groups and the older citizenry. These processes come to be associated with a residential dispersion which destroys the concentrations of persons both dependent upon and manageable by the old-fashioned city machine.[29] To some extent the immigrants of yesterday are replaced by the Negroes and Puerto Ricans of today, but the numbers available for ready mobilization by old-style organization methods have declined.

Directions of movement. The party system exists in endless flux. On the day after a presidential election the political pundits outline the new party system that has emerged from the campaign. Yet major alterations in the composition and orientation of the parties develop gradually over long periods in delayed response to the glacial alterations in the underlying social structure. A few of the social changes now under way have been identified and, if they continue, they may ultimately bring basic alterations in the party system. An economy capable of providing sustained employment, even without substantial reduction of income differentials, would radically alter the matrix within which the party system must operate. A labor force that included substantially larger proportions of white-collar workers, supervisory personnel, technicians, and managers would profoundly alter the conditions for the practice of politics.[30] A system of production and distribution that raised sharply the volumes of goods and services available to the lower-income groups would likely have an astonishing impact on the political system. Although progress has been made in this direction, a tempered skepticism may be in order about whether the differences between the haves and have-nots will soon disappear.

All such changes would affect the character of the conflicts, the issues, the frictions with which the party system would have to cope. The nature of the issues to be encountered as the nation moves into the future will fix the party lines. The parties will be nudged from their trajectories fixed by tradition as they respond to the impact of the large issues that come to be uppermost in the public mind. Historically those salient issues have been issues of domestic politics. The emergent issues and problems of international politics may well affect the party system in the most

[29] For a case study of the Italians in New Haven, see J. K. Myers, "Assimilation to the Ecological and Social Systems of a Community," *American Sociological Review*, 15 (1950), pp. 367–372.

[30] All the consequences might not be to the good. Morris Janowitz and Dwaine Marvick find that the lower middle class is particularly disposed toward authoritarianism.—"Authoritarianism and Political Behavior," *Public Opinion Quarterly*, 17 (1953), pp. 185–201.

unpredictable fashions. Unlike the issues of domestic politics, the common concerns of class or section provide no imperative cue for the citizen in the determination of political preference. Should the problems of foreign policy continue for long to be in the forefront—and domestic questions remain at a low priority—the party system might well undergo totally unexpected alterations.[31]

[31] An analysis based on the Survey Research Center's 1956 election study finds that since Center's 1945 study of class those who identify with the working class have become a larger proportion of the population while the proportion self-identified as middle class has declined. Yet from 1948 to 1956 the correlation of both policy attitudes and voting preferences with class status has declined. These changes are probably associated with the shifts in the relative salience of foreign and domestic issues as well as with other factors.—Philip E. Converse, "The Shifting Role of Class in Political Attitudes and Behavior" (unpublished manuscript).

10 | The Place of Minor Parties

THE MAJOR parties make up a system which amounts, in a sense, to more than the sum of its parts. The system consists not simply of the Democratic party *and* the Republican party: rather each party plays a role in a pattern of relationships involving both parties, the electorate, and the government. Moreover, through time the role of the individual party is transformed as it shifts from majority to minority, from governance to criticism. Neither party exists in isolation; each, whatever its role at the moment, is essential for the operation of the system and in turn the system gives meaning to the activity of the individual party. Perhaps all this amounts only to saying that a party can be best comprehended in the light of its place in the total political structure.

The earlier exposition conveniently ignored the fact that the two-party system never exists in pure form. A few odds and ends are left over after the major parties are assembled into a system. Minor parties also appeal to the electorate in every presidential campaign. Some of them have a long history; others spring to life, attract a heavy vote at one presidential election, and then disappear. The question now arises of the place, if any, of the minor parties in the system. Do they play a role, in their interactions with the major parties, in making the system as a whole what it is? Or should we dismiss the minor parties as embarrassing exceptions that do not happen to fit into the system? Are they merely fifth wheels that contribute nothing to the system as a whole?

The political scientist seeks uniformities of action to be able to describe political phenomena in general terms. When he follows that bent in an attack on the minor parties, he quickly finds that "minor party" is not a useful analytical concept, for such parties are most diverse. A meticulous student might well conclude that each minor party should be differenti-ated from all others. Each certainly has its unique qualities, but if each such party has nothing in common with others the analyst is hard put to discover any recurring role of minor parties in the system. One way out of the difficulty is to proceed on the supposition that different classes of minor parties exist. Those parties within each category may possess broad similarities of function, although each minor party may also possess unique characteristics.

A cursory look at the array of minor parties suggests a classification perhaps useful for analytical purposes. One group of minor parties con-sists of those formed to propagate a particular doctrine; most of them have nominated presidential candidates at election after election over fairly long periods. Their long duration may be more significant than is their doctrinal coloration in differentiating them from other minor parties. The Prohibition party and the Socialist party are illustrative of such parties that have been kept alive over long periods by little bands of dedicated souls.

To be contrasted with such standing minor parties are more or less transient third-party movements. American party history is marked by turbulences generated by the rapid rise, and equally rapid decline, of minor parties. Though they may move onto the political stage as a prairie fire running ahead of a strong wind, they die out after an election or so and are remembered principally by the historians.

Minor parties of these two broad types would be expected to play different roles in the party system. The continuing, doctrinal parties are in a sense outside the system. The recurring, short-lived, minor-party eruptions, on the other hand, are intimately connected with it. A sketchy examination of a few of the principal episodes of minor-party activity may help in our quest for a theory about third parties. For convenience, the short-lived third parties may be divided into parties of economic pro-test and secessionist parties, although the line is not always sharp between a party formed by secession from a major party and one that rises up more or less outside the major parties. That discussion will be followed by brief treatments of the doctrinal parties.[1]

Parties of Economic Protest

A minor party can expect to win the Presidency only if the party system is undergoing a radical transformation, with one of the major parties in process of dissolution. So drastic a reconstruction of the party alignment occurred most recently when the Republicans achieved major-party status. Since the Civil War, leaders of minor parties have doubtless from time to time nourished a belief that they had a chance to win, but that belief must surely have waned as in campaign after campaign the Presidency eluded their grasp.

Since the minor parties on the national scene do not win elections and do not campaign with any hope of success, they cannot be regarded as miniatures of a major party. They share the name party with the major parties but there the resemblance ends. If they play a role in the party system, it differs from that of the major parties. In our search for the function of minor parties, a plausible line of inquiry would be to determine whether their place in the system as a whole may not consist in their effects upon the major parties. Do third parties, and we have in mind at the moment the transient and sporadic upthrusts of minor-party dissent, contribute to the nature of the system by influencing the roles and positions of the major parties? The question is much broader than the usual speculation whether this or that 3 per cent of the vote polled by a minor party constituted a balance of power and swung the election in this or that state. The inquiry must go more broadly to the question whether these aperiodic departures from the two-party pattern affect significantly the orientations of the major parties at the next election and their roles in the system.

The Populist party. Several of the principal episodes of third-party activity have welled from serious economic discontent. In most of them agrarian distress has loomed large, although these parties have also often attempted to bring industrial labor into alliance with the farmer. The more spectacular farmer-labor movements have had their main strength in "the West." [2] The sequence of events leading to the fusion of the

---

[1] No recent comprehensive treatment of third parties is available. See the sketchy survey by W. B. Hesseltine, *The Rise and Fall of Third Parties* (Washington: Public Affairs Press, 1948), which contains a bibliography of the principal works. See also T. H. Greer, *American Social Reform Movements* (New York: Prentice-Hall, 1949) and M. S. Stedman, Jr., and S. W. Stedman, *Discontent at the Polls* (New York: Columbia University Press, 1950).

[2] Given the character of the system for the election of the President, a minor-party

Populist party, a party of western agrarian protest, with the Democrats in 1896 may be profitably examined for evidence on the role of minor parties.

After the Civil War a long-term deflation punctuated by occasional sharp, short-term dips in farm income generated a series of agrarian political movements. The Granger movement exerted enormous influence but did not take the form of a political party. As the Grange began to wane in the 1870's, the Greenbackers arose to attempt direct political action. Western farmers, a debtor class, responded with enthusiasm to the proposal that the currency be inflated. Their ills, they believed, could be cured by a generous dose of inflation. The Greenback presidential candidate in 1876 polled only a small vote, but in 1878 the voters sent 14 Greenbackers to Congress, including General James B. Weaver of Iowa who became the party's presidential candidate in 1880.

After 1878 the Greenback vote fell off and later agrarian discontent found expression through other channels. In the campaign of 1890, independent and "People's" candidates for state and local office, backed by the Farmers' Alliance and allied groups, met with considerable success in the southern and northwestern states. The leaders of these scattered movements gathered in Cincinnati early in 1892 and agreed to form a new political party to fight for reforms on a nation-wide basis. Later in the year the new party, the People's, or Populist, party nominated for the Presidency General James B. Weaver, the former Greenbacker.

Weaver's strong showing in the election of 1892 severely jarred the old party alignments. His party won a handful of seats in the lower house of Congress, placed its candidates in the governor's chair in three states, and elected hundreds of local officials. One of every 12 popular votes went to the Populist candidate who won 22 electoral votes. His strength was greatest in the western and southern states. In the western states the Populists often fused with the Democrats and at times in reality took over the Democratic party. The distribution of the Populist presidential strength by states appears in Figure 10.1. In the East the Populist party made little headway, although it caused shudders there. An impressive vote had been drawn by a party advocating unlimited coinage of silver at a ratio of 16 to 1, a graduated income tax, public ownership of the railroads, and other measures thought in the East to be destructive of the ordered course of things.

What impact did the Populist show of strength have on the party system generally? It seems evident that the Populist uprising contributed

---

movement with a sectional concentration of its strength is a factor much more to be reckoned with in national politics than is a movement with like popular strength distributed evenly over the country.

significantly to the marked realignment between the parties that jelled in the election of 1896. That realignment brought a sharper contrast in the policy orientations of the major parties, a contrast that was to persist long after the faithful few Populists last convened in 1908 to nominate a presidential candidate.

The strong Populist showing in 1892 set off a struggle within the Democratic party over the silver issue. The differences among Democrats were intensified by the policies of Cleveland, the President and leader of the conservative and sound-money wing of the party. William Jennings Bryan, who stood for about everything that Cleveland abominated, won the Democratic nomination in 1896. The fact that the insurgent wing of a party in power could control its national convention gives a measure of the extent of the Populist infection among Democrats. In its candidate and in its platform the Democratic party "swallowed the Populist party almost entirely (or vice versa!) and quite possibly saved itself from extinction in so doing." [3] Or as an old Populist leader remarked of Bryan: "We put him to school and he stole the schoolbooks."

The strong infusion of Populism within the Democratic party was accompanied by desertion by conservative Democrats and the party acquired a different policy orientation from the party of Cleveland. The new policy—broadly one of opposition to "the interests"—persisted after 1896, save for the experiment of 1904 which demonstrated that the Democrats could not win by outbidding the Republicans for conservative support. Bryan himself turned up in Wilson's cabinet and the strain of Populism persisted, may even still persist, in the Democratic party. On the other hand, the redrawing of party lines in 1896 drove from the Republican party many who were attracted by Populist doctrines and by the same token drew to it additional strength, especially in the East, from those groups fearful of the unorthodox doctrines proclaimed by the wildmen from the West. The exchange left the Republican party more homogeneous and able to pursue its policies with fewer internal differences.

The review of the Populist episode suggests that a minor-party movement, but not necessarily all such movements, may stimulate a widening of the differences in the policy orientations of the major parties and thereby deeply affect the party system. The minor party accomplishes this end in part by demonstrating the existence of a block of voters for whose support a major party may bid. To woo this support the major party must take a stand on the new issues insistently raised by the minor

[3] W. Dean Burnham, *Presidential Ballots, 1836–1892* (Baltimore: The Johns Hopkins Press, 1955), pp. 154–155. See also G. H. Knoles, *The Presidential Campaign and Election of 1892* (Stanford: Stanford University Press, 1942).

POPULIST
PER CENT

Under 20

20–29

30–39

40 and over

TERRITORY

TERRITORIES

Figure 10.1. Populist Strength in Presidential Election of 1892, by States party. Thus the minor party may serve as a bridge for the movement of people from party to party and in the process each party to some extent may lose its dissident elements to the other. Some such process seems to have been set in motion by the Populist movement, with marked effects on the major-party pattern.

The Populists also had an influence that extended beyond Democratic acceptance of their doctrines. Their energetic agitation in support of their cause gave currency to ideas which eventually gained wide support and became law. They preached the doctrine of popular government and demanded the direct election of United States Senators, the direct primary nominating system, the initiative and referendum, and woman suffrage. They agitated, too, for the adoption of new substantive policies. They criticized the inelasticity of the currency; the Federal Reserve Act coped with this problem by means different from that urged by the Populists. The germ of the idea of the present system of federally sponsored credit agencies for farmers was to be found in the Populist platform. The Populists were not solely responsible for the eventual adoption of these and other policies, but they did lead the agitation for many policies later put into law.[4]

Progressive campaign of 1924. Measured by electoral strength, the Progressive candidacy of Robert M. La Follette for the Presidency in 1924 was more impressive as a manifestation of economic discontent than the Populist crusade of 1892. One out of every six voters in the nation supported La Follette. Progressive agitation in 1924 was in part an intensification of the historic western insurgency, but it constituted more largely a response to the particular conditions of the early 1920's. Western agriculture, which had prospered during World War I, fell upon evil days with the sharp drop in farm prices in 1921. Labor had flourished under the Wilson Administration. The Republicans under Harding leaned toward the agricultural policy of eastern finance and set about to return business to its rightful place of pre-eminence. The restoration of normalcy struck railroad labor with special destructiveness. The Administration helped the railroads break the strike of 1922 by injunction proceedings and by encouraging the formation of company unions and the employment of strike-breakers. The eastern, industrial wing of the party, symbolized by Andrew Mellon, the Secretary of the Treasury, held sway in the Republican party, a party, William Allen White observed, "with no liberal flaw, spot, or blemish in its creed" which completely represented the "yearnings of a benevolent plutocracy." The Democratic party,

[4] The chief work on the Populists is John D. Hicks, *The Populist Revolt* (Minneapolis: University of Minnesota Press, 1931).

rent by internal struggle over the Klan-Catholic issue, did not offer a promising vehicle for the expression of the unrest in the land.

From among those disadvantaged by the events of 1921 and 1922 came the movement that led to La Follette's 1924 candidacy. In 1922, on the call of the railroad brotherhoods, the Conference for Progressive Political Action convened in Chicago. Its purpose was to "discuss and adopt a fundamental economic program designed to restore to the people the sovereignty that is rightly theirs, to make effective the purpose for which our government is established, to secure to all men the enjoyment of the gain which their industry produces." Important among the groups affiliated with the conference were the railroad unions, the Nonpartisan League and other agrarian groups, the Socialist party, and sundry reform leaders.

In 1924 the conference called a convention which, on July 4, endorsed La Follette for President. La Follette had long been a progressive Republican leader in Wisconsin and in the Senate, and his views expressed the demands of the forces of discontent. The convention delegated the selection of a running mate to a committee which later named Burton Wheeler, a Senator from Montana, who had a record as a Democrat opposed to the "interests." [5] La Follette's crisp platform was prophetic of the New Deal. It reiterated the old war cry against monopoly and privilege. It proposed to guarantee to labor the right to organize and bargain and to abolish injunctions in labor disputes. It asked that Congress be empowered to overrule decisions of the Supreme Court. It urged immediate tariff reductions and ultimate public ownership of railroads and water power. It supported measures to assure "fair prices" to farmers.

In its day the La Follette program was regarded as radical, and the campaign of 1924 was marked by bitter and demagogic charges by those who felt their interests to be threatened by his candidacy. Those who felt themselves most endangered were Republicans. It was "Coolidge or Chaos," and La Follette was pictured, in unrestrained terms, as a danger to the established order. The Progressives attempted to make monopoly and special privilege the great issue; the Republican orators wrapped themselves in the flag and propagated a caricature of the Progressives as advance agents for the proletarian revolution. There can be no denying that La Follette and his followers challenged the policies of those dominant at the time. Farmers felt themselves discriminated against by the eastern wing of the Republican party. Labor felt its status to be endangered and the executive committee of the American Federation of

---

[5] The convention did not "nominate" but "endorsed" La Follette's independent candidacy. For some of the groups concerned this gambit was important as a means of avoiding the issue of affiliation with a political party.

Labor endorsed La Follette. The railroad brotherhoods were out for revenge for what they regarded as acts of repression. The Socialists thought the time opportune to make no nomination of their own and to line up with the Progressives.

The Progressive campaign of 1924 continued the tradition of western dissent and the geography of the 1924 vote resembled that of the 1892 Populist vote. La Follette's heaviest support came from the West. He carried only Wisconsin, his home state, but in 10 other western states he ran ahead of Davis, the Democratic candidate. In California, the Demo-

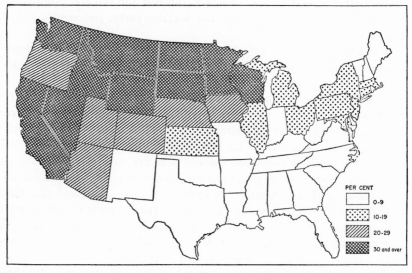

Figure 10.2. Popular Vote for La Follette and Wheeler Presidential Election of 1924, by States

cratic percentage of the total popular vote fell to 8.2; in Minnesota, to 6.8; in North Dakota, to 7.0; in Washington, to 10.2; in Iowa, to 16.5. From such figures it is usually deduced that La Follette drew most of his votes from the Democrats. It seems evident, however, that in the western states in which he was strong, many of his supporters also came from the Republican ranks. In most of these states the Republican percentage of the total vote dropped markedly from 1920 to 1924. In Idaho, to cite an extreme instance, the Republican percentage fell from 66 to 47 per cent. Although no detailed investigation has been made of the sources of La Follette's western strength, it is probable that he had a special attraction for farmers who had been touched by Nonpartisan League activities. Such was certainly true in North Dakota.[6] And the chances are that many old Populists were to be found in the Progressive ranks.

In two respects La Follette's strength differed from the 1892 Populist pattern. He drew little support in the South but he picked up strength in scattered industrial localities in the Northeast. In Cleveland, Ohio, he ran ahead of both major-party candidates and demonstrated strength in the industrial belt along the shore of Lake Erie. In Pittsburgh and the surrounding industrial counties he did well. Rochester, New York, and Passaic, New Jersey were other centers of notable strength. La Follette drew support, not in industrial areas generally, but in places in which local leaders had been active in progressive agitation and had prepared the way for their support of La Follette. In these localities his vote came by and large at the expense of the Democrats whose share of the vote declined sharply from 1920.[7]

La Follette's candidacy was a lost cause from the outset, but what can be said of the effects of the 1924 upheaval on the subsequent behavior of the major parties? Certainly the exact course of events differed in form from the 1892–1896 pattern of Populist revolt followed by fusion. Yet it may well be that the Progressive uprising had a somewhat similar influence in sharpening the alternatives between the parties and in preparing the way for a realignment within the electorate. The heavy La Follette vote in the West constituted both a warning and an invitation to Democrats and Republicans alike. In 1928 they responded differently and on the crucial issues of 1924 widened the gap between themselves in their campaign pronouncements. The Republicans in 1928 turned down a farm plank calculated to appeal to the West; they had won once without the Progressive vote and presumably thought they could do so again.

The Democrats in substance endorsed the McNary-Haugen bill, the remedy advocated by the agrarian radicals. Alfred E. Smith, who went into the campaign with a liberal record as governor of New York, sought to capitalize on agrarian discontent. The prominent Republican farm leader, George N. Peek, bolted to the Democrats as did Senators Norris

[6] In North Dakota, the 1924 Republican gubernatorial nominee, Sorlie, had been backed by the Nonpartisan League in the primary. In the general election the percentage of the three-party vote for La Follette tended to increase from county to county with the percentage of the two-party vote for Sorlie. The coefficient of correlation between the two sets of figures, with the Sorlie percentage as the independent variable, was +0.83. On the other hand, the Coolidge percentage of the vote tended to decrease from county to county as the Sorlie percentage increased. The correlation coefficient was −0.75.

[7] See A. W. Macmahon, "Political Parties and Elections," *Political Science Quarterly*, Supplement, 40 (1925), pp. 35–58.

of Nebraska and Blaine of Wisconsin. The *Madison Capital-Times,* the chief La Follette organ, endorsed Smith. Despite his best efforts, Al Smith, a Tammany Hall man in a brown derby, could not make himself plausible as the spearhead of a farmers' uprising.[8]

More compelling issues arose to divert attention from the discontents of 1924 and to postpone the consequences, if any, of that campaign on partisan alignment among the voters. In 1928 the questions of prohibition, of religion, of Tammany Hall outweighed whatever disposition existed among western voters to take the step from their Republican apostasy of 1924 to Democratic conversion in 1928. If support of La Follette was a way station for voters moving from the Republican to the Democratic party, they did not shift in large numbers until 1932. Nye says the Democratic party in 1932 "seemed to be the common rallying point for all the shreds of earlier progressive movements, for the 1912, 1924, insurgent, Wilsonian, and La Follette liberals."[9] Clearly many of the leaders clustered about La Follette became supporters of Franklin D. Roosevelt in 1932. Doubtless most of those Democratic voters who turned to La Follette in 1924 returned to the party in 1932. It is a fair guess, although the data are scant, that Republicans who followed La Follette in 1924 were especially prone to vote for Roosevelt in 1932.[10]

Secessionist Parties

Several of the principal third-party movements have emerged by secession from one of the major parties. The 1912 Progressive candidacy of Theodore Roosevelt sprang from a fatal cleavage in the ranks of Republican leadership. Similarly in 1948 the States' Rights or Dixiecratic

[8] The above treatment leans on the excellent study by K. C. MacKay, *The Progressive Movement of 1924* (New York: Columbia University Press, 1947).

[9] R. B. Nye, *Midwestern Progressive Politics* (East Lansing: Michigan State College Press, 1951), p. 354.

[10] The extensive studies necessary to support confident estimates of the electoral realignments induced by the 1924 episode have not been made. An inspection of vote shifts in Illinois counties suggests that the process was more complex than is commonly supposed. Evidently both Democrats and Republicans contributed to the 1924 La Follette vote. In 1924 the Democratic percentage of the three-party vote in 36 Illinois counties was higher than had been the Democratic percentage of the 1920 two-party vote; in 66 counties, the Democratic percentage declined from 1920 to 1924. A correlation, with the Republican percentage of the 1924 three-party vote as the independent variable and the Republican percentage of the 1932 two-party vote as the dependent variable, yields a coefficient of +0.84. The size of this coefficient and the slope of the line of regression would be consistent with the guess that 1924 La Follette voters (whether Democratic or Republican originally) tended to land on the Democratic side in 1932 along with 1924 regular Republicans amounting together to around one-quarter of the 1924 regular Republican proportion county-by-county.

movement originated in rebellion against the dominant Democratic faction, and other instances of party fission have occurred on a smaller scale. Such secessionist parties perhaps can be differentiated only formally from those grouped earlier as parties of economic protest. In their role in the party system as a whole the two sorts of parties appear to be fundamentally similar.

Progressive movement of 1912. The Progressive party, formed in 1912, was born of the ferment that agitated the country in the years before World War I. The Progressive movement included a strident populistic strain which manifested itself in agitation for the adoption of instruments of direct democracy such as the initiative, referendum, and recall. It also gave voice to a revulsion against the abuses, in both business and government, brought to light by the muckrakers. It probably reflected middle-class reaction against the growth in power of big business. Settlement-house reformers as well as millionaire reformers found places in the movement, which was characterized more by a hopeful but nebulous idealism than by a nicely wrought consistent creed.

Theodore Roosevelt, unhappy with the conservative leanings of William Howard Taft, his own choice to succeed himself in 1908, sought the Republican presidential nomination in 1912. In that endeavor he had support from his personal admirers and also from party organization men who feared that Taft could not ferry their state and local tickets into office. Some industrial leaders thought it inevitable that a progressive would be elected in 1912 and that Roosevelt was the safest of an undesirable lot. Others were attracted by his philosophy which might legitimize monopoly under a degree of public control. The Old Guard managed to hold firm control of the national convention, and Roosevelt's followers marched out to form the Progressive party, a coalition of discordant elements bound together by his personality.

Wilson, another progressive, with the aid of William Jennings Bryan, captured the Democratic nomination. From the outset of the campaign Taft's cause was doomed, and the canvass turned out to be a battle between Wilson and the picturesque Teddy. Roosevelt polled a larger popular vote than did Taft (27.4 per cent of the total against 23.2 per cent) and Wilson won the Presidency. Whether Roosevelt's candidacy threw the election to Wilson, as is often supposed, is questionable. The chances are that had Roosevelt not been in the race, many Republican voters of progressive inclination would have supported Wilson or, immobilized by the conflict between their Republican loyalty and their distaste for Taft, simply stayed at home on election day. Such a surmise gains some support, as Louis Bean has pointed out, from the fact that the voting in the 1912 congressional elections seemed to show that Wilson's party had enough popular support to win the Presidency without benefit of the Republican split.[11]

The effects of the Progressive bolt on the party system persisted long after election day of 1912. The more conservative, or at least less ebullient, Republicans had won unchallenged control of the Republican party machinery. The progressive Democrats were in the saddle in their party. The Progressive party organization was kept alive in the hope that the threat of another candidacy in 1916 would wrest from the regular Republicans platform concessions and an acceptable candidate. William Allen White, a leader in the move to exert this leverage, thought Charles Evans Hughes, associate justice of the Supreme Court who had made a reputation as a progressive when governor of New York, would be acceptable. Meanwhile Taft worked behind the scenes to checkmate the Roosevelt crowd; he, too, promoted Hughes. Taft calculated that the Progressives could "easily regard Hughes as a Progressive" but he also believed that Hughes had "learned a great deal since he was governor." In short, Taft thought Hughes had become a sound man with "more sense and a greater breadth of view." [12]

Taft's judgment seemed to be vindicated by Hughes' campaign. William Allen White wrote that Hughes gave the impression in the West that he was "one of those good men in politics—a kind of business man's candidate . . . always hovering around the status quo like a sick kitten around a hot brick!" [13] Although Roosevelt campaigned vigorously for Hughes, many of his Progressive followers dragged their feet in the 1916 campaign. The bulk of the 1912 Progressives returned to the Republican ranks in 1916, but it is quite evident that many also turned Democratic in 1916.[14] Wilson also doubtless gained through the new issues arising out of the European war which set off movements across party lines unlike those of 1912.[15]

[11] *How to Predict Elections*, ch. 7.

[12] H. F. Pringle, *The Life and Times of William Howard Taft* (New York: Farrar & Rinehart, 1939), II, 885-91.

[13] Walter Johnson, *William Allen White's America* (New York: Holt, 1947), p. 267.

[14] In California Hiram Johnson, undoubtedly a genuine Progressive, was on the ballot as the senatorial candidate in 1916. He polled 67 per cent of the vote against a Democratic candidate as Hughes lost by a narrow margin. In San Francisco Johnson drew 77 per cent of the vote; Hughes, 45 per cent. Hughes' loss of California (and the Presidency) has been attributed to his unintentional snub of Johnson during a swing through California, but the size of the margin between Hughes and Johnson makes plausible the supposition that Hughes simply had less appeal to the old Progressives of 1912 than did Wilson.

[15] A few exploratory correlation analyses yield no clear-cut evidence one way or

Of the effect of 1912 on the party leadership, George Mowry concludes that Roosevelt "contributed much to the conservatizing of the Republican party." [16] Many prominent progressive Republicans bolted to support Roosevelt in 1912. Of those in elective office, some lost out in the subsequent feuds between Republican progressives and standpatters. Others made their way back into the party but, Mowry says, "did not return to the powerful places" they had held in 1912.[17] By the same token, the episode bred within the Democratic party a generation of Wilsonians who, fired by the eloquence of their idol, long claimed for their party a monopoly of the tradition of progressivism.

Dixiecratic movement of 1948. The most significant recent secessionist party, the States' Rights or Dixiecratic movement of 1948, had as its hard core the controlling elements of the Democratic organizations of several southern states. Leaders of the movement, notably Gessner T. McCorvey, then chairman of the Alabama State Democratic Committee, developed a theory of the nature of party organization to support their refusal to be bound by the decisions of the party's national convention on nominees and platforms. Their theory grew from the strivings of the conservative wing of the southern branch of the Democratic party to restrain the policies of the party as a whole. A first, but abortive, step was taken in Texas in 1944 when the Texas "Regulars" attempted to carry the state for a Democratic slate of electors committed to vote against Roosevelt

---

another on the 1912–1916 movement of voters. A correlation of the Kansas county Democratic percentages, with the 1912 percentage of the three-party vote as X and the percentage of the 1916 two-party vote as Y, yields a coefficient of +0.51. So low a correlation indicates that Democratic gains in Kansas from 1912 to 1916 varied irregularly in magnitude from county to county. Since the 1916 Democratic percentage in most counties was higher than in 1912, it is a fair inference thass some of the 1912 Progressives became 1916 Democrats and others returned to the GOP. Yet it is also evident that other movements of voters occurred for reasons unconnected with the split of 1912. The coefficient of correlation for a sample of counties between the 1912 Progressive percentage and the 1912–1916 Democratic percentage point gain was only +0.207, indicating a very slight tendency for gains to be associated, geographically, with 1912 Roosevelt strength.

[16] *Theodore Roosevelt and the Progressive Movement* (Madison: University of Wisconsin Press, 1946), p. 378.

[17] No systematic analysis has been made of the reshufflings of political leadership associated with such cataclysms as 1912. Probably older leaders have special difficulties in moving from one major party to another. The major figures in 1912 Progressivism did not have much alternative but to return to Republicanism. On the other hand, an event such as 1912 may have a marked effect on younger men with leadership potential. For example, Dean Acheson records that, stirred by the bugle calls of T. R. and disillusioned by the triumph of the Old Guard, he eventually found himself to be a Democrat. See *A Democrat Looks at His Party* (New York: Harper, 1955), pp. 13–15.

but not instructed to vote for any specified individual. The assumption was that uninstructed electors, given a close electoral vote, could bargain with the leading contenders for the Presidency. A similar tactic also failed in Mississippi in 1944.[18]

By 1948 dissident southerners thought the time was ripe for a southern veto of Democratic national policies, particularly on the race question. The problem was how to revolt without seeming to bolt, how to support the Democratic party without supporting its presidential candidate. The theory now evolved that the national party was a confederation and that each state party could follow whatever course it might choose: it could, therefore, nominate on its Democratic ticket a slate of presidential electors pledged to support a candidate other than Harry Truman and the loyal Democrat could vote for these electors without committing the sin of bolting.

Unsuccessful in blocking the nomination of Harry Truman and in obtaining a satisfactory platform plank on the civil rights issue, a few southern Democrats walked out of the national convention. With other States' Rights Democrats, they met at Birmingham to consider lines of action. The Dixiecrats in 1948 rejected the idea of running uninstructed presidential electors; they preferred to name a candidate to "symbolize the cause." They recommended to the state Democratic organizations J. Strom Thurmond of South Carolina and Fielding Wright of Mississippi as nominees for the Presidency and Vice-Presidency. A struggle ensued within the southern states between the "loyalists" affiliated with the national leadership and the Dixiecrats for control of the state parties and for the authority to designate presidential electors to run on the Democratic ticket. Dixiecrats placed electors pledged to Thurmond and Wright on the ballot as Democrats in South Carolina, Alabama, Mississippi, and Louisiana. In these states where they were the "official" Democratic nominees, Thurmond and Wright won the electoral vote. Truman's name did not appear on the ballot in Alabama, but in the other three of the four states electors pledged to Truman were on the ballot, though not in the Democratic column. On the other hand, the Dixiecratic candidates did not win in a single state in which they had to run under a label other than that of the Democratic party.[19]

The Dixiecratic movement clearly illustrates some of the effects of minor parties on the party system. Some of those effects may be short-

[18] Alexander Heard, *A Two-Party South?* (Chapel Hill: University of North Carolina Press, 1952), p. 159.
[19] The total Dixiecratic popular vote was 1,169,000; the electoral vote, 39. One Tennessee elector, chosen on both the regular Democratic and States' Rights tickets, cast his electoral vote for Thurmond.

term; others may be felt only over a longer period. In the 1948 election itself the southern revolt was by no means a complete loss to the Democrats nationally. Truman chose to make a hard-hitting campaign on the issues of civil rights and economic policy. In effect, he wrote off the South in advance, and in the process he picked up much support in the North that would have been lost had he attempted to appease the southern rebels. Samuel Lubell has argued that no third party "is ever a complete liability. If it diverts votes, it also adds votes in counterattraction." [20] Northern Negroes went overwhelmingly for Truman.

The longer-term repercussions of the Dixiecratic movement included the stimulation of prayerful thought by the northern Democratic leadership on how to keep the South in the party. The national convention of 1952 gave extended, if somewhat inept, attention to the matter. While some southern Democratic leaders bolted the party in the presidential campaign, a southern third-party candidacy did not recur. In the prelude to the 1956 convention national Democratic leaders busily contrived lines of compromise and incessantly negotiated with their southern brethren on the terms of party unity. In short, the movement compelled in 1956 a weightier consideration of southern sensibilities in the deliberations of the national councils of the party.[21] The extent to which the Dixiecratic movement set up a conduit by which southern Democratic voters could make their way to the Republican party is problematic. The evidence seems to indicate that in some places the 1948 Dixiecrats became 1952 Republicans; in others, 1948 Dixiecrats returned to the Democratic fold. The 1952 movement to the Republican party in the South continued a longer-term trend for the conversion of upper-class, urban southerners to Republicanism, a process perhaps accelerated by the Dixiecratic revolt but largely independent of it.[22]

Into these observations there has crept an assumption that ought now to be made explicit. That assumption is that each minor-party episode should not be treated as an isolated event unconnected with what followed

[20] *The Future of American Politics* (New York: Harper, 1952), p. 203.
[21] An earlier party secession which probably contributed to a redirection of major-party policy was the 1872 Liberal Republican nomination of Greeley, who also received the Democratic nomination. The Liberal Republican movement had originated in Missouri and had there as a major objective the mitigation of the harshness of policies toward southern sympathizers and supporters in the Civil War. In its national aspect it also favored a more lenient policy toward the South, along with various reforms, and its actions in 1872 probably contributed to the eventual reconciliation of North and South. See E. D. Ross, *The Liberal Republican Movement* (New York: Holt, 1919).
[22] See the analysis by D. S. Strong, "The Presidential Election in the South, 1952," *Journal of Politics*, 17 (1955), pp. 343-389.

or preceded. Commonly the analysis of a minor party is restricted to the moment of its climax, with little inspection of its bearing on the stream of party life. The party system exists through time. Judgments of the place of minor parties in the system must be made in the setting of the temporal flow of the system.[23] Before formulation of such an appraisal, however, it is necessary to examine other, quite different, minor parties.

Marxist Parties

To be sharply differentiated from the aperiodic upsurges of nonrecurring minor party activity are the doctrinal parties with a long-continued existence. These groups can scarcely be regarded as political parties in an operative sense. Nor are they leading actors in domestic political crises as the one-shot parties have been. Rather they resemble sects only tenuously connected with the political system. Yet their members evidently derive profound satisfaction from participation in activities which have only the gentlest impact upon the course of events.

Most of these parties exist to agitate for one or the other of the many varieties of socialism. Although such American thinkers as Edward Bellamy exerted great influence in the early propagation of socialist ideas, American socialism is largely a transplanted growth that has failed to take political root in new soil. The great thinkers and philosophers of socialism have been Europeans; their ideas of objectives and of political strategy have been formulated from observation of European conditions. Almost all movements in European socialist thought have been paralleled by the formation of movements and organizations in the United States. The history of the fissions and internal battles of the socialist movement makes a complex story that is recounted with great solemnity by participants in the movement. Spokesmen for each faction and splinter acclaim themselves as the true apostles of Marx and denounce each other as traitors to the master, all with little effect on the American political scene.[24] Of the influence of socialist ideas there can be no denial, but

[23] Samuel Lubell, in somewhat different terms, makes this point in his analysis of the Union party of 1936. Its candidate was William Lemke, who polled 880,000 votes, and one of its principal leaders was Father Coughlin. The party made a powerful appeal to Roman Catholics with an anticommunist line including an attack on the Democratic Administration for its diplomatic recognition of Soviet Russia. Lemke drew especially heavy votes from some metropolitan Catholic precincts. Lubell's interviews persuade him that in 1948 the Lemke voters of 1936 returned to the Democratic fold on one side as Wallace and the left-wingers went out on the other. Truman attracted an especially heavy Catholic vote, a feat made possible partially by the absence of the Wallaceites. See Lubell, *op. cit.*, pp. 203-214.

[24] See, for example, J. P. Cannon, *The Struggle for a Proletarian Party* (New York: Pioneer, 1943); H. Kuhn and O. M. Johnson, *The Socialist Labor Party During Four Decades, 1890-1930* (New York: New York Labor News Co., 1931). Socialists are

that the socialist parties have had much of a hand in this influence is dubious.

Socialist Labor party. The oldest Marxist party in the United States is the Socialist Labor party. Although the party can be traced to the 1870's, it fixes 1890 as the beginning of its "real history." [25] That year marked the entry into its affairs of Daniel DeLeon who became its chief philosopher, its revered leader, and, after his death, its saint. The Socialist Labor party program provides "for the taking over, by the mass of the people collectively (the working class), the means of production, to administer these in the interests of the useful producers (which include all who labor, whether so-called manual or mental labor), through democratically elected representatives from the industries, chosen democratically by the mass of the people themselves who work in the industries." It regards itself as a revolutionary party which can by some way or another liquidate the capitalist system peacefully.

In its battle to promote working-class consciousness the SLP denounces the AFL and CIO as "preeminently capitalist weapons to bridle the working class," as "pro-capitalist" in philosophy, and as under the leadership of "labor-fakers." As for Stalinism, it is not true Marxism: "The only difference is that instead of being exploited by a capitalist class (as American workers are), the Russian workers are exploited by the State, and for the benefit of a privileged, bureaucratic caste." Norman Thomas' Socialist party is dismissed as a bourgeois party with no "program for dispossessing the capitalist class." Moreover the SLP charges that the Socialist party "is a fraud, a swindle perpetrated on the American workers, an organization that is up to its ears in capitalist politics." In rounding out the list of its antagonists, the Socialist Labor party includes the "international Vatican organization . . . a universal political machine, bent on world power, and less and less concerned about concealing its ends or disguising its means." [26]

The SLP makes strong medicine in its propaganda but polls few votes. In 1952 its presidential candidate, Eric Haas, drew 30,267 votes. In 1956

---

quite articulate and have produced an appalling quantity of literature on the cause. One volume of the two-volume work, *Socialism and American Life*, edited by D. D. Egbert and Stow Persons (Princeton: Princeton University Press, 1952), consists of a selective and critical bibliography.

[25] For an account of the complexities of American socialism from 1870 through 1901, see H. H. Quint, *The Forging of American Socialism: Origins of the Modern Movement* (Columbia: University of South Carolina Press, 1953).

[26] Quotations are from leaflets issued by the party and from its official organ, *The Weekly People*.

Mr. Haas was again nominated and proclaimed himself to be the only true socialist candidate in the race.[27]

Socialist party. The complex process of fission, mutual antagonism, and combination in the socialist movement yielded up in 1901 the Socialist party, the best known of the American socialist factions. As a right-wing socialist group, it has urged the achievement of public ownership of the means of production by parliamentary tactics. Along the road to the socialist state, the Socialist party advocates the ordinary liberal-democratic ameliorative measures, flavored perhaps with a dash of Christian socialism. All in all, the social democracy of the Socialist party has been characterized by a mildness that lent it a certain respectability in contrast with the doctrines of the more belligerent socialist sects.

First Eugene V. Debs, then Norman Thomas, led the Socialist group from 1904 to 1948. With two exceptions, one or the other of them was the Socialist candidate at the presidential elections during that period. In 1916 A. L. Benson headed the ticket and in 1924 the party supported La Follette. In 1904 and 1908 Debs polled almost 3 per cent of the total presidential vote and in 1912, in the high tide of the progressivism and reformism, his vote climbed to 900,000 or about 6 per cent of the total. In 1916 and 1920 the vote sagged back to the normal 3 per cent and in 1928 dropped to less than 1 per cent. The depression-fed protest boosted Thomas' vote in 1932 to 881,000, a bit over 2 per cent of the total, but afterwards the party's support again declined to well under 1 per cent.

The geographical distribution of the Socialist vote indicates a curious characteristic of the American socialist movement. With a program tailored for the industrial proletariat, the greatest Socialist strength in presidential voting was achieved in the western agricultural and mining states, areas in which the Populists had earlier made their best showing. In 1912, when the party polled its peak percentage of the total vote, the highest Socialist vote was in Oklahoma, where 16.6 per cent of the voters indicated a Socialist preference. States with more than 10 per cent of their vote Socialist were Oklahoma, Nevada, Montana, Arizona, Washington, California, and Idaho.[28]

From 1928 to 1948 Norman Thomas carried the Socialist banner in

[27] Not to be confused with the SLP is the Socialist Workers' party, a group of Trotskyites expelled from the Communist party in 1928. The SWP first nominated a presidential candidate in 1948, Farrell Dobbs, who denounced the Stalinists, the Norman Thomas Socialists, the Democrats, the Republicans, and the Wallaceites, as he portrayed his party as the "hope of the American working class." Again the nominee in 1952, Mr. Dobbs polled 10,312 votes.

[28] F. E. Haynes, *Social Politics in the United States* (Boston: Houghton Mifflin, 1924), p. 206.

presidential campaigns. His best vote came in 1932, but even under the conditions of 1932 the Democrats apparently got most of the votes of the downtrodden proletariat. In 1948 he attracted the suffrage of not much more than 100,000 voters. Perhaps wearied by his exertions in six futile presidential campaigns, Thomas proposed to the 1950 Socialist convention that the party conduct campaigns "only where circumstances make campaigns specifically and practically advantageous." He advocated that Socialists be encouraged to work within other groups and to support candidates of other parties when the Socialists had none. This policy, Thomas argued, would "release Socialist energy and funds for a more intensive campaign of organization and education for Socialism." The convention decisively voted down Thomas' proposal and decided to continue Socialist candidacies and to shun coalition with other parties. The members were adjured, even when the party had no candidate for an office, to avoid supporting candidates of "capitalist parties." The convention's rejection of Thomas' proposal was regarded as marking the end of his leadership of the party. Again in the 1956 convention he urged that energies be devoted to agitation rather than to the circulation of petitions to get presidential candidates on the ballot. Again his proposal was voted down as the convention nominated Darlington Hoopes, of Reading, who had been the 1952 standard bearer and polled about 20,000 votes.[29] To put a national ticket in the field is thought to help Socialist candidates for local office. Persistent patches of local Socialist strength exist in such places as Milwaukee, Wisconsin, Bridgeport, Connecticut, and Reading, Pennsylvania, where candidates who are regarded as essentially bourgeois reformers on occasion win office.

Communist party. The intricate steps leading to the establishment of the American Communist party would require a book to relate.[30] The main events began in 1919 when the left wing split off from the Socialist party. The left itself splintered into numerous Marxist groups, which paralleled the currents of schism within communist activity abroad and perhaps in some instances reflected only the ambitions of American leaders. In 1921, after a visitor from Moscow attempted to iron out differences among communist groups, the Workers' (Communist) party emerged as the American group with recognition from Moscow. In 1929 the name was

[29] For a single-volume treatment of the Socialist party, see David A. Shannon, *The Socialist Party of America* (New York: Macmillan, 1955). See also Ira Kipnis, *The American Socialist Movement, 1897–1912* (New York: Columbia University Press, 1952).

[30] See James Oneal and G. A. Werner, *American Communism* (New York: Dutton, 1947); Theodore Draper, *The Roots of American Communism* (New York: Viking, 1957).

formally changed to Communist party. The shifts in policy and strategy of the Communist party from 1921 on appear to have been governed either by the policy of Moscow or, when communications were imperfect, by what the local leaders thought to be the wish of Moscow. The party, thus, differs markedly from other parties on the American scene. It functioned by and large as an instrument of Soviet policy and it more or less consistently regarded itself as an instrument of ultimate revolution, although its expressions of policy ranged from gradualism to violence. None of these characteristics is compatible with existence as a party within the American constitutional framework.

The exigencies of Soviet foreign policy and the restrictions of federal legislation since 1940 further reduced the resemblance of the Communists to a conventional third party. In 1940 Congress by the Voorhis Act required organizations affiliated with foreign governments to register with the Attorney General and to file with him certain information about the organization. The Communist party, on paper, abandoned its affiliations with Moscow. The Smith Act of 1940 attempted virtually to outlaw the Communist party. That legislation made it a criminal act to "advocate, abet, advise, or teach the duty, necessity, desirability or propriety of overthrowing or destroying any government in the United States by force or violence." It also made it a crime to form a society to advocate such doctrines or "to be a member of, or affiliate with, any such society." [31] In 1951 the Supreme Court upheld the act as applied in a charge of conspiracy against 11 members of the national executive committee of the Communist party.[32] The Department of Justice proceeded then to obtain indictments and convictions of second-string party leaders. In 1957 the Supreme Court reversed convictions of West Coast Communists on the ground that the Smith Act did not prohibit advocacy of overthrow of government "divorced from any effort to instigate action to that end." [33] The same decision made it doubtful that persons could be punished on the sole charge of party membership unaccompanied by evidence of acts of incitement to revolution.

In keeping with its character as something other than a political party in the ordinary sense of the word, the Communist group placed little emphasis on electioneering. It ran candidates from time to time and in 1932 its presidential candidate polled slightly over 100,000 votes. Yet its major efforts were in other directions. By infiltration of disciplined cliques into other organizations, such as labor unions, it succeeded in using those groups to further its purpose of the moment. That purpose might be all-out support of national policy, as during the period of

[31] 54 Stat. 671.
[32] Dennis *v.* United States, 71 S. Ct. 857 (1951).
[33] Yates *v.* United States, 77 S. Ct. 1064 (1957).

Soviet–United States alliance. Or it might be simply the stimulation of confusion, division, and dissension.

Although not all the details are available, it is evident that Communists exerted great influence in Henry Wallace's Progressive party of 1948, if indeed they did not determine its major lines of action. At any rate the Communist national committee took credit for "the forging of the new political alignment and people's coalition," and the principal policies of the party paralleled the current Moscow line. Within the Progressive party Communists succeeded in isolating Wallace from non-Communist radicals and evidently influenced his policy pronouncements. After the campaign of 1948 a battle continued between the Communist and non-Communist wings for control of the shell of the party. In 1950 Wallace himself resigned from the party in protest against its pro-Soviet position on the Korean war. In 1952 the Progressive candidate, Vincent Hallinan, who happened at the time of his nomination to be in jail for contempt of court, drew 140,000 votes in contrast to Wallace's 1,150,000 in 1948.

The entire American experience with the Communist party in the 1930's and 1940's strained the capacity of a democratic order to cope with a group not committed to the constitutional principles of that order without abandonment of those principles. Although their loyalties were committed to the Soviet state, the Communists scarcely came under the proscriptions of treason or other conventional methods of self-defense of a national order. Unable to invent a satisfactory formula to cope cleanly with communism, the democratic order struck more or less blindly with crude instruments. In the process, native radicals, untinged by communism, suffered no little damage. And, indeed, those wielding anti-Communist weapons often aimed to discredit all political liberalism and radicalism, whatever its origin or hue. It requires a fine discrimination to repress one type of dissent and to refrain from repressing others.

Role of doctrinal parties. From these necessarily brief comments, it is evident that a doctrinal party is not the equivalent of the occasional outburst of short-term and relatively large-scale minor-party activity intimately connected with the conflicts of the major parties of the time. The doctrinal parties pursue their courses fairly independently of the major parties and can scarcely be said to affect the results of elections or to deflect the policy orientations of the major parties.[34]

[34] Perhaps for analytical purposes the Prohibition party could be classified with the ideological parties. It, too, lives a life largely apart from the determinative battles of politics. It has had presidential candidates at each election since 1872. The Prohibition vote was 72,949 in 1952. In 1956 the nominee was Enoch A. Holtwick who had been the vice-presidential nominee in 1952. See D. L. Colvin, *Prohibition in the United States* (New York: Doubleday, Doran & Co., 1926) and Roger W. Babson, *Our Campaign for the Presidency in 1940* (Chicago: National Prohibitionist, 1941).

Minor Parties in States

The conspicuous minor parties have been national parties with little substructure of state and local political organization. In a few cities the Socialist party contests municipal elections with success. A few of the powerful but transient third-party movements have been accompanied by considerable activity in state politics, as in 1892 and 1912. Yet the handful of minor parties of much consequence in state politics have existed independently on their local foundations rather than as branches or offshoots of one of the minor parties on the national scene.

Given the federal character of the American system, many state and local parties might be expected to develop from the special circumstances and needs of each state and locality. By and large the major parties nationally have demonstrated a capacity to accommodate themselves to considerable variety among their state and local affiliates as well as a capacity both to absorb and to discourage deviate groups. On occasion, coalitions, formal or informal, of Republicans and Democrats have crushed minor groups in state and local elections. Further, by their control of national patronage the major parties can create a special obstacle to independent state parties. Only in exceptional circumstances is a national administration disposed to nourish a minor state party, with patronage and policy, in competition with the "regular" state organization. Thus, the Farmer-Labor party of Minnesota elected governors, but the Democratic national committeeman distributed federal patronage within the state.[35] In due course, the state party joined with the Democrats to form the Democratic-Farmer-Labor party. The factors entering into the merger were numerous, but the maintenance of a state party unconnected with one of the major national parties presents no little difficulty.

When a state or local minor party has no hope of becoming a majority, its leaders are under temptation to fuse with one of the major parties in return for whatever concessions may be wrested from the major party. Usually the minor party finds itself swallowed up and digested in the process of fusion. The ordinary electoral procedures give no measure of the contribution of the minor party to the outcome of an election. The

---

In 1952 General Douglas MacArthur was put on the ballot in several states variously as the candidate of the Christian Nationalist party, the Constitution party, the America First party, and the American party. In 1956 T. Coleman Andrews of Virginia and T. H. Werdel of California carried the banner of isolationism and extreme conservatism as nominees of the Constitution party.

[35] See J. R. Starr, "Labor and Farmer Groups and the Three-Party System," *Southwestern Social Science Quarterly*, 17 (1936), pp. 7–9; G. H. Mayer, *The Political Career of Floyd B. Olson* (Minneapolis: University of Minnesota Press, 1951); D. R. McCoy, "The Formation of the Wisconsin Progressive Party in 1934," *The Historian*, 14 (1951), pp. 70–90.

leaders of, say, the Pro-Solvency party, may strain their diaphragms and stretch their vocal cords in support of the Republican candidate endorsed by their group; but, after the votes are in, only a seer can determine the number of Pro-Solvency votes, if any, delivered to the Republican candidate. And the Republican leaders, if they win, need not pay much heed to the importunities of the Pro-Solvency leaders, for it is a fairly safe bet that by the next election the Pro-Solvents will be dissolved.

Electoral procedures employed in New York have enabled minor parties to demonstrate precisely how many votes they contributed to a candidate. Under the laws of that state it has been permissible for a single individual to be the nominee of two or more parties. The candidate is listed on the ballot or the voting machine under the emblems of the several parties that have nominated him. Votes for him as the minor-party nominee are tallied separately. Minor-party leaders can thus point to their contribution to the vote of the victorious candidate. And they may also demonstrate that if their party had named its own candidate or endorsed the opposing candidate, the outcome would probably have been different. They may also hold out promises of what they propose to do or not to do when the next election rolls around.

The principal minor parties of New York have been the American Labor Party and the Liberal party. In 1936 labor leaders, at the instance of President Roosevelt, formed the ALP to garner labor and independent support for him in his campaign for re-election. David Dubinsky, of the International Ladies Garment Workers, and Sidney Hillman, of the Amalgamated Clothing Workers, and other union leaders associated with them in the ALP had long wished to see a labor party and had been unhappy with Samuel Gompers' "nonpartisan" policy for labor. They responded to Roosevelt's suggestion with alacrity and, after the campaign of 1936, were not disposed to regard the party, which had been supported by union funds and votes, as a one-campaign affair to be allowed to die.

Roosevelt's professional Democratic advisers in New York viewed the whole ALP venture with coolness; an ally today might become an enemy tomorrow. The flow of events justified their fears. In 1937 the ALP virtually compelled the Republicans to renominate LaGuardia for mayor, and, with ALP aid he handily defeated the Democratic candidate. In 1942 the ALP, unwilling to accept the Democratic nominee for governor, ran its own candidate and thereby helped Dewey to win.

As time wore on Communists filtered into the ALP and won control of local units of the organization. Hillman and Dubinsky, with the aid of upstate ALP units, only barely managed to induce the 1940 state convention to endorse Roosevelt for re-election. A battle for control of the ALP ensued that resulted in the withdrawal from the party of David

Dubinsky and his anti-Communist union to form the Liberal party. The Liberals in 1944 supported Roosevelt for the Presidency, as did the ALP, but they declined to support state and local candidates with ALP endorsement. After Hillman's death his union also withdrew from the ALP.

It gradually became apparent that in officiating at the accouchement of the ALP, Democratic leaders had helped to life something more than a mechanism by which labor could support the New Deal. When Democratic candidates received ALP endorsement, they were charged with being allies of communism. When the ALP or the Liberal party ran its own candidates, the election often went to the Republicans. Both the ALP and the Liberal party from time to time found Republican candidates for local and legislative office to be in accord with their principles and nominated them. Although such nominations attracted votes that would otherwise have gone mainly to the Democratic party, even the Republican professionals had no love for the labor interlopers in the great game of politics.

Old-line party leaders sought a way to free themselves from the gadfly splinter parties. They proposed to prohibit all dual nominations, but the legislature in 1947 compromised the matter by forbidding a person enrolled in one party to seek the primary nomination of another without the consent of the appropriate committee of the party whose primary he was invading.[36] Thus, Vito Marcantonio, ALP leader who had won Democratic nominations, could no longer run for a Democratic primary nomination without the consent of the Democratic county committee. The legislation also required that members of one party who were nominated by another should accept the nomination in writing.

Prohibition of dual nominations would probably sooner or later kill off third parties, but the 1947 New York law left open the possibility of their continuance and left to candidates and party authorities the question of coalition. Regular party leaders expressed general condemnation of coalitions but in practice the particular situation rather than principle seemed to govern. In 1948, Edward J. Flynn, Democratic leader of the Bronx, rejected ALP and Liberal alliance propositions in his own locality but conceded that outside his own county circumstances might be different. In negotiations participated in by the White House, coalition occurred on presidential electors. Dewey was highly critical of splinter

[36] In some states antifusion statutes prohibit the appearance of a candidate's name on the ballot in more than one place. In other states party-raiding statutes require that the candidate be a member of the party that nominates him. In the absence of either sort of act, a candidate may appear on the ballot several times as the nominee of several parties. For a survey of the legislation, see "The Constitutionality of Anti-Fusion and Party-Raiding Statutes," *Columbia Law Review*, 47 (1947), pp. 1207–1214.

alliances, yet many Republican legislative candidates accepted ALP endorsements.

The dissolution of the ALP in 1956 left the Liberal party as the principal minor party in New York. In most state-wide campaigns it makes the Democratic nominee its own and sometimes contributes the margin necessary for victory. In the 1949 senatorial race the percentage division of the total vote was:

Dulles, Republican		48.0
Lehman, as Liberal	8.6	
Lehman, as Democrat	43.4	
Lehman, Total		52.0

In the 1954 gubernatorial election Harriman's victory depended on his vote on the Liberal line. The percentage division of the three-party vote was:

Ives, Republican		49.9
Harriman, Liberal	5.2	
Harriman, Democrat	44.9	
Harriman, Total		50.1

Such election results regularly move the Republican legislature to attempt to modify the election laws to obstruct Democratic-Liberal coalitions. Measures that would have handicapped joint nominations were vetoed in both 1956 and 1957 by Governor Harriman.

New York minor parties have contrived, perhaps inadvertently, an electoral procedure favorable to the operation of minor parties, but it should not be supposed that New York's electoral laws alone produced these parties. Other conditions contributed to their vitality over a life longer than average for such parties. Perhaps of pivotal importance is the comparative indifference of their leaders to public office. With a leadership fairly solidly based in the trade-union bureaucracy, the principal party leaders can subsist quite well if they never win office themselves. They can afford to guide themselves by consideration of "principle" unlike the so-called "professional" politician who makes a living from his work. Moreover, the New York procedure circumvents the ancient dilemma of third parties—that if they nominate a candidate of their own, they might thereby contribute to the defeat of the major party candidate most nearly agreeing with their principles.[37]

Nonpartisan League. The Nonpartisan League provides another illustration of the problem more or less deviant groups face within the states in surviving in the face of the absorptive capacities of the major parties.

[37] For surveys of New York minor parties, see Warren Moscow, *Politics in the Empire State* (New York: Knopf, 1948), ch. 7; Hugh A. Bone, "Political Parties in New York City," *American Political Science Review*, 40 (1946), pp. 272–282.

The League remains influential only in North Dakota but in the years 1916–1922 it was a force to be reckoned with in the triangle from Wisconsin to Oklahoma to Washington. It demanded state ownership and operation of services thought to be controlled by exploiters of the farmer: grain elevators, flour mills, packing plants, mortgage banks, hail insurance. This was socialism for the other fellow. The League did not propose public ownership of farms and ranches.

The League chose to operate not as a political party but as a faction within the established parties. It early gained control of the government of North Dakota by supporting its candidates in the Republican primaries. In the states in which it operated from 1916 to 1922 it elected over 950 candidates to state and national office, usually by nominating its men in one of the major-party primaries. By "boring from within" it could sidestep the problem of weaning voters from their old party attachments; and by controlling the outcome of the primary of the dominant party in a state it could compound its own strength by the addition of the die-hard party voters who would stomach the League program rather than bolt the party.[38] After 1921 the League rapidly declined in strength outside North Dakota, but there it remained as a highly disciplined faction within the dominant party of a one-party state. In essence the League became a political party equipped with organization and with procedures for nomination of slates of candidates to be backed for nomination in the Republican primaries. Although the League's long persistence in North Dakota was remarkable, eventually the national party system's magnetism began to make itself felt. In 1956 the League began an attempt to move into the Democratic party and to leave the local Republican party to its conservative rivals in state politics.

Minor-Party Functions

The plainest moral of this tale of minor-party activity is that the language of politics is not a language of precision. The term minor party covers the most diverse sorts of political phenomena. A recognition of that diversity must be a first step in any effort to cope with the broad problem posed at the outset of the chapter, namely, what is the place of the minor party in the two-party system?

Perhaps the doctrinal parties can best be disposed of first. Their principal differentiating characteristics have been their long duration and their relatively exotic doctrinal positions. The position has been that they are

[38] For a discerning analysis of League tactics, see S. P. Huntington, "The Election Tactics of the Nonpartisan League," *Mississippi Valley Historical Review*, 36 (1950), pp. 613–632. See, for an able general review, R. L. Morlan, *Political Prairie Fire, The Nonpartisan League, 1915–1922* (Minneapolis: University of Minnesota Press, 1955).

not really operating elements of the party system. Rivulets alongside the main streams of party life, they maintain on the whole an isolated existence. Many an old Socialist might dissent from the application of this observation to his party, but it is difficult to see that even this party, both the most successful and the mildest of the doctrinaire parties, has had influences of perceptible significance on the workings of the party system.

Figure 10.3. Percentage of Total Presidential Vote Polled by Minor-Party Candidates, 1884–1956

On the other hand, the evidence seems to indicate that the rather large-scale, episodic, nonrecurring minor-party movements must be regarded, somewhat paradoxically, as integral elements of the so-called two-party system. They spring from the center of the political melee and in turn they affect the nature of the major parties and the relationships between them as they cumbersomely make their way from election to election. The remaining comments about minor-party functions will be limited to this type of third-party movement.

Commonly the significance of these minor parties is assessed in terms of the arithmetic of a single presidential polling. Hicks says, for example, that "in possibly half a dozen instances the third party vote has snatched victory from one major party ticket to give it to the other." [39] Perhaps so; perhaps not. Such calculations rest on assumptions not readily testable. At times, minor parties may, indeed, wield a balance of power and affect the outcome of an election.[40] Yet their larger role in the party system must be sought elsewhere.

[39] "The Third Party Tradition in American Politics," *Mississippi Valley Historical Review*, 20 (1933), p. 26.

[40] Such assumptions are often made by practical politicians. A major party may

The general role of the minor party can be discerned only with difficulty, for each of the principal third-party aberrations has had its peculiar characteristics. Yet each of these episodes appears to have had an impact, not only at the moment of the election, but subsequently on the character of the major parties of the system. That impact is uniform neither in degree nor in nature from episode to episode.

With respect to the policy orientations of the major parties, the minor-party eruptions in some instances nudge the major parties differentially and widen the policy gap between them. 1892, 1912, and 1924 appear to have been instances of this sort. In other cases, the policy impact of the minor party may bear chiefly on a single major party, as perhaps with the Dixiecratic movement.

As for the composition of the major parties, minor-party candidacies at times are but a step in the reshuffling of voters between the major parties. In the process each major party may gain by losing its most discordant elements to the other. On the other hand, on some occasions the minor party may serve only as a temporary haven for a strain of crackpots who find neither party congenial. The demonstration of the bearing of minor-party candidacies on the flow of voters from party to party is difficult because often the movement is concealed and confused by other types of movements of voters that occur from election to election. Hence, the full effects of third-party candidacies on voter alignments are at times postponed or offset or confused by the fact that "other things" do not always remain "equal."

When we attempt in this manner to specify in concrete terms the role of minor-party movements in the system as a whole, the integral connection of these disturbances with the system becomes apparent. In considerable measure, the minor parties develop because the major parties are as they are and in turn the major parties take the shape they do in part because of the operations of the minor parties. Minor-party activity tends to be a continuation of processes that are always occurring within, and between, the major parties. Factions within major parties continually strive to win the party to more complete commitment to their views. The opposing party, sensing discord in the enemy's camp, may put out bait to attract the wavering. Even in days of surface serenity, latent discord renders uneasy the life of a major party. That so few of these internal dissensions explode into minor-party candidacies is cause for astonishment.[41]

surreptitiously foster a minor-party candidacy in the belief that it will weaken the opposition. In 1948 in Indiana the States' Rights Democrats were denied a place on the ballot because of irregularities in the petition. In litigation on the matter it was revealed that the States' Rights petitions were printed in the Republican state headquarters without, the Republican state chairman blandly announced, his knowledge.

[41] The price that must be paid by secessionist leaders is perhaps a great deterrent

If these observations are correct, it follows that in its bearing on the major parties, the minor-party movement may be the functional equivalent of various inter- and intra-party processes. For reasons that are by no means self-evident, on some occasions an outburst of third-party activity occurs to realign the parties, to reorient their policies, or perhaps to redirect only one of the major parties. On other occasions, these consequences occur without the facilitation of third-party endeavor.

Students of the topic seem to agree that the day of the third party, at least in presidential elections, is done. Several justifications are advanced for this view. One of the less compelling, but nevertheless important, is that the procedural hurdles that must be negotiated by third-party candidates to get on the ballot have been made higher and higher. Another is that the general adoption of the direct primary has made it possible for dissident groups within the major parties, particularly when their membership is geographically concentrated, to nominate and elect their leaders as Senators and Representatives under the banner of a major party. Deviant opinion thus can ensconce itself within the duly accredited congressional ranks of a major party. Under these circumstances, to advance the cause there is, so the argument goes, no need to resort to the quixotic tactic of forming a third party.

A large-scale upthrust of minor-party strength is symptomatic of an incapacity of one or the other of the major parties to cope with the issues of the moment in a manner to maintain party unity. Third parties, Lubell argues, shed "penetrating light on the inner torments of the major party." [42] Those inner torments work themselves out sometimes through third parties, sometimes through other means. Perhaps the major parties, after a century of trial and error, have learned how to solve their "inner torments" without fission. A safer prediction would be that from time to time questions not soluble by the intraparty processes of the major parties will arise and spill out into third party movements. Such matters have arisen at least in 1872, 1892, 1912, 1924, and 1948. [43]

---

to major-party fission. They have little future if they try to cross to the opposition; they are regarded as suspect if they return to the fold. Hence, leaders of party rebellions often tend to be strongly entrenched in their own bailiwicks or otherwise in a position to assume the costs and risks of a politics of retribution.

[42] *Op. cit.*, p. 205.

[43] Minor parties now meet greater procedural difficulties than they once did. State legislatures have handicapped them by raising the number of signatures required to place a minor candidate on the ballot. In 1957 litigation was instituted in California with the object of determining whether inordinate obstacles to placing candidates on the ballot violated any federal constitutional right.

11 | State Parties

MANUALS on American government and politics commonly focus attention on the epic battles of Republicans and Democrats for control of the national government, on the interests clustered around the national party banners, on the grand policy issues that preoccupy Congress. Scholars, like most citizens, pay relatively less heed to the problem of political organization and leadership for the conduct of state governments. Yet state governments perform functions of no mean significance and determine policies of great concern to powerful social groups. The problem of party organization and function in the governments of the 48 American states is of corresponding import.

If the operations of state governments were not overshadowed by national affairs, the problem of state politics would appear of a magnitude to warrant the closest attention. Many American states could rank as substantial members of the family of nations. New York's population exceeds that of the Dominion of Canada, and California's is larger than that of Australia. The government of New Jersey serves slightly more people than does that of Switzerland, and Portugal is only a little more populous than Ohio. The Irish Free State and Minnesota have approximately the same population. Illinois' politicians must cope with as many people as do those of Belgium, and there are about as many North Carolinians as there are Finns. The relatively small state of Colorado almost equals Paraguay in population. The people of Pennsylvania outnumber those of the Netherlands, and the Virginia state machine should be able to man the government of Norway if the ratio of politicians to people is fairly uniform from culture to culture. Only enough Swedes remain in Sweden to give it a population not much larger than that of Michigan, and the citizenry of Massachusetts slightly exceeds that of Denmark.

Population provides no exact measure of the scale of governmental problems, but these comparisons suggest that the American states are political entities of respectable stature. Unlike independent states, they have no responsibilities in the field of foreign affairs, international trade, and the management of major defense forces. The Constitution assigns authority over such matters to the national government, yet there remains within the jurisdiction of the state governments a wide range of basic public functions. The construction of great public works, such as highways, the conduct of the mammoth American system of public education, the management of hospitals and other similar institutions, the adjudication of the bulk of private litigation, the creation and tutelage of the institutions of local government, the regulation of public utilities, the levying of taxes to support state activities—all these and other public functions are the business of the states.

Around the government of each of the 48 states a party system—or a factional system—develops to propel the machinery of government. Groups of men contend for control of the state government. Although state parties are intertwined with national parties and politics, in varying degrees the skirmishes for control of state governments are fought out on different issues and to some extent by different cliques of leaders than those involved in the federal battle. Political structures and practices differ widely from state to state, and it is feasible here only to set out a few major characteristics that suggest the variety in state party systems.

Varieties of State Political Systems

Political parties perform functions essential to the operation of a democratic order. They seek to build majority coalitions powerful enough to control the government. They advocate broad views on public policy; they designate candidates; and, once in power, they attempt to run the government in a manner to hold together the coalition that put them into office. The minority party maintains a critical vigil against the day when circumstances will permit it to oust the majority.

The institutions developed to perform these functions in each state often differ markedly in form from the national parties. It is an error to assume that the political parties of each state are but miniatures of the national party system. In a few states that condition is approached, but more often practices in the conduct of political competition only remotely resemble the national system. Each state has its own pattern of action and often it deviates markedly from the forms of organization commonly thought of as constituting party systems. It may fit neither the biparty nor the multiparty pattern. Moreover, the patterns of political action and organization differ widely among the 48 states.

The obvious contrast between the national and state party arrangements consists in the degree to which parties, as parties, compete for control of government. Within the national arena, Democratic and Republican parties vie for power on fairly even terms, at least over the long run, and present to the electorate a choice between broadly differing policy tendencies. In a few states that condition is approximated, but more commonly a single party dominates the government of the state. It may be ousted from control only infrequently. Under these conditions such political competition as occurs takes place within the dominant party of the state and departs drastically, at least in form, from the pattern of struggle for control of the national government.

Each state has, to be sure, its Republican party and its Democratic party. The organizing forces of national politics imprint their form and their names on state political systems. The state parties operate as affiliates of the national political parties in national politics. Even in that role, they possess a high degree of independence, but in their roles with respect to the state governments, state parties are autonomous in keeping with the constitutional theory of the federal system. That is, national party authorities do not make it their business to instruct a state affiliate to nominate a particular individual for governor or to take a particular line on policy.[1]

Deviations from the two-party pattern. Since a salient characteristic of most state party systems is their deviation from the two-party competitive pattern, states are commonly characterized as solidly Democratic, as strongly Republican, as leaning this way or that, or as competitive. None of these classifications describes state political systems with precision. One measure of the degree of attachment of states to the Republican or the Democratic party will group the states in one way; another, in another. At one time a particular measure will yield one result and at another time, another. Nevertheless, a few crude indices will indicate the range among the states in their balance of Republican and Democratic strength.

---

[1] If state parties were subject to national direction, a political unitarism would, of course, be superimposed over the formal federalism of the Constitution.

The office of the chief executive in the states, as in the nation, is a focus of party conflict. The extent to which a single party dominates this office provides a rough measure of the extent to which a state approaches or deviates from the pattern of bipartisan competition. An arrangement of states according to the number of years of Democratic control of the governorship in the years 1929–1956 appears in Table 11.1. The states of the Solid South had an unbroken series of Democratic governors during these years as did Oklahoma. At the other extreme, only New Hampshire

Table 11.1

Variations in Partisan Control of State Governorships, 1929–1956

Years Governor Democratic	State Groups
28	Alabama, Arkansas, Florida, Georgia, Louisiana, Mississippi, North Carolina, Oklahoma, South Carolina, Tennessee, Texas, Virginia
19–27	Arizona, Kentucky, Missouri, New Mexico, Rhode Island, Utah, West Virginia
14–18	Colorado, Connecticut, Indiana, Maryland, Massachusetts, Michigan, Montana, Nevada, New York, Ohio, Wyoming
7–13	Delaware, Idaho, Illinois, Nebraska, New Jersey, North Dakota, Washington
6 or less	California, Iowa, Kansas, Maine, Minnesota, New Hampshire, Oregon, Pennsylvania, South Dakota, Vermont, Wisconsin

and Vermont had a continuous chain of Republican governors. In nine other states grouped in the table Democratic gubernatorial victories were most infrequent. Among these strongly Republican states were the Great Plains states. In Oregon and California also Republicans managed to control the governorship most of the time despite the existence of goodly numbers of Democratic voters.

About a dozen states drop into a slot in the middle of the table reflective of the fact that Democrats and Republicans either alternated in power or held the governorship close to half the time during the period. Among these fairly competitive states were the Rocky Mountain states of Colorado, Montana, Nevada, and Wyoming and the older industrial states of Connecticut, Indiana, Maryland, Massachusetts, Michigan, New York, and Ohio. The table also identifies two other groups of states, one in which Democrats held the governor's office well over half the period and another in which the advantage rested with the Republicans.[2]

[2] The proportion of a period in which a single party held the governorship has its drawbacks as a measure of interparty competitiveness among different states. For

Another measure of party strength groups the states somewhat differently. Figure 11.1 shows the average Democratic percentage of the membership of the lower houses of the state legislatures in four groups of states over the period 1924 through 1956. In one group, as may be seen from the upper graph of the figure, the Democratic percentage of the legislators averaged around 90 per cent over the entire period, indicative of the practical nonexistence of the Republican party in these states.[3]

Figure 11.1. Average Democratic Percentage of Membership of Lower House of Legislatures in Four Groups of States, 1924–1956

At the other extreme are those strong Republican states in which the Democratic legislative representation is weak. In these states, whose averages appear in the bottom graph in the figure, Democrats win substantial legislative representation only under the most exceptional circumstances as in 1932, 1934, and 1936.[4]

example, in one state the Republicans might win a series of elections against a moribund Democratic party and then be replaced by an enlivened Democratic party for another series of elections. In another situation the parties might battle close elections and alternate in power so as to fall in the same pigeonhole as the first state. For an attempt to take both these factors into account in a comparison of the states, see J. A. Schlesinger, "A Two-Dimensional Scheme for Classifying States According to Degree of Inter-Party Competition," *American Political Science Review*, 49 (1955), pp. 1120–1128.

[3] The strong Democratic states averaged in the top graph of the figure were Alabama, Arkansas, Florida, Georgia, Louisiana, Maryland, North Carolina, Oklahoma, Tennessee, Texas, South Carolina.

[4] The states grouped as strong Republican, by the measure of strength in the lower

The two groups of states represented by the graphs between the strong Republican and strong Democratic groups in Figure 11.1 show considerably more variation from election to election in the party division of legislative membership. One of these groups leans toward Republican control of the lower house of the legislature, though on occasion Democrats may control.[5] The average of the other group leans toward the Democratic side of the fence, but Republicans can win the lower house in most of these states with varying degrees of frequency.[6]

The graphs in Figure 11.1 oversimplify the realities; they suggest that four clearly differentiated types of states exist. One could draw across the chart a graph for each state, an operation that would produce a complete but confusing picture. The group averages conceal some of the confusion but serve to make plain the variation in the balance of party strength among the states. The figure also draws to attention characteristics of the state party systems not revealed by our inspection of control of the governorships. The legislative figures often rank the states differently than do the gubernatorial data, a consequence in part of gerrymandering of state legislatures. The upper and lower graphs reflect the high degree of stability of legislative strength of the dominant party in the states at both the Republican and Democratic ends of the political spectrum. Even in the more competitive states, as the figure indicates, a most drastic set of conditions—namely, the Great Depression—must develop to bring about wide swings generally in the division of party strength, although the averages do conceal a few individual states with frequent shifts of considerable amplitude.

Secular shifts in party balance. One of the technical problems of classifying or describing the state party systems comes from the fact that over fairly long periods some of the states undergo marked realignments in their partisan loyalties. The classification according to periods of control of the governorship in Table 11.1 conceals such a secular shift in the party balance. Some of the changes, however, that have occurred in some states during the past three or four decades are reflected in Figure 11.1 on the

---

house of the state legislature, were Connecticut, Iowa, Kansas, Maine, Michigan, New Hampshire, New Jersey, North Dakota, Oregon, South Dakota, Vermont, Wisconsin.

[5] The states included in this group were California, Colorado, Delaware, Idaho, Illinois, Indiana, Massachusetts, Montana, New York, Ohio, Pennsylvania, and Wyoming.

[6] The states classified as leaning Democratic were Arizona, Missouri, Nevada, New Mexico, Rhode Island, Utah, Washington, and West Virginia. Obviously wide differences exist among these states and some of them, such as Rhode Island and West Virginia, have, during the period covered by the graph, undergone a political realignment.

division of legislative strength. Note there the curve of Democratic strength in the states that lean Democratic. In these states in the 1920's Republicans dominated the legislatures but after the upthrust in Democratic strength in the 1930's these states, as a group, settled down to a new plateau of much higher Democratic strength. A similar but less-marked shift occurred, as may be seen from the figure, in those states grouped as leaning Republican.

It is not entirely wrong to say that parties win elections in some states, not by the excellence of their candidates and the intensity of their campaign exertions, but by the slow cumulation of the effects of economic and demographic changes that make a state normally Democratic rather than normally Republican or vice versa. This process of realignment finds illustration in the conversion of Rhode Island from a stronghold of New England Republicanism to a normally Democratic state. The change is shown in the graphs in Figure 11.2. Before 1932 Democrats could win

Figure 11.2. Democratic Percentage of Two-Party Vote for Governor and of Membership of Lower House of State Legislature, Rhode Island, 1916–1954

the governorship and the lower house of the state legislature under such exceptional conditions as the little depression of 1921–1922. After 1932 the balance of power became reversed and the Republicans became able to win the state only at rare intervals.

In the past few decades similar secular shifts have gradually taken place in other states. The long-term growth of the Democratic party in Michigan has manifested itself in frequent control of the governorship, but the legislative apportionment enables Republicans ordinarily to hold control of the legislature.[7] Secular Democratic gains have occurred in Pennsyl-

[7] See J. K. Pollock and S. J. Eldersveld, *Michigan Politics in Transition* (Ann Arbor: University of Michigan Press, 1942), and Stephen and Vera Sarasohn, *Political Party Patterns in Michigan* (Detroit: Wayne University Press, 1957).

vania although not in sufficient magnitude to make Democrats dominant. In Maryland the drift seems to have been towards the Republicans. In some southern states, notably Florida, a long-term Republican growth has been far more evident in the presidential vote than in state politics.

National sectionalism and state one-partyism. Our measures indicate that the states range from those overwhelmingly Democratic in local affairs to those not quite so overwhelmingly Republican and that few states may be said to be equipped with party systems that are miniatures of the national party pattern. To a degree, state departures from the national pattern result from the fact that the states are segments of the nation. If state party systems were small-scale replicas of the national parties, the national system would differ radically from its present form.

Among one group of states apparently those factors that make them solidly one-party in national politics rebound, so to speak, upon state politics and mold it into a one-party form. This phenomenon has been most notable, of course, in the states of the South. The Civil War gave impulse to unity in national politics to defend the peculiar regional practices against assaults from the North. To support Republicans in national affairs was to support the sectional enemy. The maintenance of partisan unity in national affairs destroyed, or at least prevented the development of, Republican parties for the purposes of state politics. The necessities of unity against an external threat compelled a degree of unity at home. In time a technique developed by which external unity could be maintained and the conflicts of state politics could be fought out within the Democratic parties of the states. In the states of the North the war had a similar impact whose effects, although they were felt for decades, have by now largely worn way.

Another sort of interconnection between national and state politics may also push a state toward one-partyism. A state's social and economic characteristics may drive it toward one-partyism in both national and state affairs. To take an extreme hypothetical instance, a state dominated by industries organized by the CIO would have been in recent decades strongly Democratic nationally. It would also have probably been overwhelmingly Democratic in state affairs. Given the potency of the issues of national politics in shaping popular attitudes, the circumstances fixing the cleavages in national politics may incidentally form the divisions within state politics. Not often is a state so homogeneous in composition or attitude that it is driven to an extreme of one-partyism, although to some degree the predominant orientation on national politics operates in many states towards one-party dominance locally.

Nature of State Parties and Factions

The upshot of the foregoing analysis is that in about only a dozen states do the two major parties compete on a fairly even basis. The remainder of the states diverge in varying degrees from the two-party pattern. The net effect of the overwhelming attachment of many states to one or the other of the national parties means that, in reality, no party system exists within such states for state purposes. The great functions of parties—the construction of coalitions, the designation of candidates, the engineering of consent, the conduct of the government, and so forth—must be performed in these states in one way or another. But they are carried out by more or less amorphous institutions that are hardly the equivalent of party systems in the ordinary usage of the term. The general balance of power within the state—pro-Republican or pro-Democratic—fixes a framework within which factions, in a most bewildering variety of forms, struggle for supremacy within the state. A description of the ins and outs of all the 48 state political systems would fill a shelf of books, but the variation among them may be indicated briefly.

Variations in patterns of political competition. For purposes of analysis—and not necessarily for purposes of precise description—the state political systems may be regarded as occupying positions on a scale. At the center of the scale the Democratic and Republican parties compete for control of the state government more or less after the fashion of the national parties. As one moves from this central point in one direction the Democratic party becomes stronger and stronger and the functions of political parties are more and more performed by factions within the Democratic party. As one moves in the opposite direction toward the Republican end of the scale, the business of state politics comes to be carried on by factions within the Republican party. Toward the two extremes on the scale parties simply do not function in the sense of providing choices to the electorate between groups of men and sets of policies. In these states elections determine nothing; the essential decisions are made earlier in the nominating processes of the dominant party.

The predominance of a single party pushes back into the direct primary of that party the controlling electoral decisions of a state. In the primary battles of that party, leadership may be assumed by well-defined factions, by newspapers, by groups formed around the issues of a particular primary, or by other instrumentalities that develop to carry on the business of politics when the party system is estopped from doing so. The degree to which the conflicts of state politics become intraparty battles rather than interparty struggles differs from state to state. At the extremes of

Republican and Democratic strength no candidate of the lesser party has won a general election victory within the memory of any man now living. In states less thoroughly committed to a single party, the decisions of politics are commonly intraparty determinations, though occasionally the lesser party wins a general election.

These variations between the extremes of biparty competition and intraparty conflict are roughly reflected in the frequency of spirited contests within the party primaries for nominations.[8] In a general way in strongly Democratic states the primaries for nomination of Democratic candidates for the governorship are the occasion for warmly fought contests. In the same states the Republicans, if they nominate a candidate, ordinarily must draft some soul willing to make the sacrifice rather than choose from among eager aspirants. In contrast, in strong Republican states the Democrats must ordinarily exert themselves to dredge up a candidate while the fireworks explode in the contest for the Republican nomination.

These differences may be shown by data on the proportion of Democratic primaries warmly fought in different groups of states. If the leader in the primary draws less than half of the primary vote, a sharp contest for the nomination has usually occurred. Here are the percentages of Democratic gubernatorial nominations (in primaries not involving incumbent governors) made over most of the life of the primary system by less than 50 per cent of the primary vote:

Strong Republican states	6%
Competitive states	17
Strong Democratic states	61

In a state such as Vermont the Democratic nomination for governor goes by default. In the competitive states presumably the impulse is for party leaders to attempt to negotiate agreement on nominations and to maintain the maximum possible unity for the war against Republicans. In that group of states, as the figures show, close primary contests are infrequent. As one moves into the one-party Democratic states nearly all primaries (not involving incumbents) set off rivalry between contending candidates and factions, which is reflected in the large proportion of the primaries with less than half the primary vote to the leading aspirant for the nomination.

For the same groups of states the proportions of Democratic gubernatorial nominations made by 90–100 per cent of the primary vote present a reverse relationship. Those proportions were:

---

[8] Primary procedures and practices are treated in detail in Chapter 14.

Strong Republican states   56%
Competitive states   37
Strong Democratic states   0

To be matched up with these figures are the proportions of governors Democratic in these groups of states during the period covered by the primary data:

Strong Republican states   15%
Competitive states   49
Strong Democratic states   98

Republican gubernatorial primaries show a somewhat similar variation in the incidence of competition among different groups of states.[9] In states such as Vermont, Maine, South Dakota, Iowa, and Nebraska, Republican primaries commonly are marked by sharp rivalry for the nomination which ordinarily determines who will become governor. In the southern states, on the other hand, competition for the Republican nomination, whether made by primary or by convention, is usually not spirited.

Types of one-party factionalism. The foregoing analysis shows clearly that as states deviate from the two-party pattern intraparty competition intensifies. Yet it tells us nothing about the factions or groups that compete within the dominant party for the control of state affairs. The form and nature of those factions change from time to time within individual states and at a particular moment differ enormously among the states. Although the data do not suffice for a systematic classification of state political structures, a few examples will illustrate differing types of situations.

The factional systems of a few one-party states in reality seem to be party systems within the dominant party. That is to say, two groups develop, each with a recognizable policy orientation and each with an organizational hierarchy, which fight it out in the direct primaries much after the fashion of the parties in a two-party system. Moreover, in a few instances this informal party-system-within-a-party has maintained an existence over a considerable period of time.

Louisiana has had such a bifactional system. The battles between Huey Long and the conservative elements of the state precipitated the formation of the Long and anti-Long Democratic factions which have lived long after the circumstances of their origin. A major factor in their

---

[9] For the states included in the groupings in the text and for the measures used in defining the groups, see Key, *American State Politics: An Introduction* (New York: Knopf, 1956), p. 109.

longevity seems to be that they rest on durable differences of interest and attitude which might, in other places and circumstances, find expression through groups organized as parties rather than as intraparty factions. Huey Long, although treated in the national press as a buffoon and an ordinary southern demagogue, made an effective appeal to the less-favored classes and rewarded their loyalties with programs of concrete action. His successors continued that broad policy orientation, while the conservative interests of the state rallied around whoever happened to be the anti-Long leader of the moment. The two sets of factional leaders constructed popular followings with a relatively high degree of continuity from primary to primary. The popular cleavage resembled that between Republicans and Democrats in two-party states, and in presidential politics Republican support came predominantly from the conservative anti-Long faction.[10]

A factional system such as has existed within the Louisiana Democratic party presents to the electorate about as clear a choice between policy alternatives as does a two-party system. In effect, for the purposes of state politics, a bifactional system operates instead of a biparty system. Not often do intraparty factional groupings of one-party states have an equivalent degree of stability and differentiation. In North Carolina over a period of several decades organization and anti-organization factions competed for control of the state; each developed its strongest and most cohesive following in specific sections of the state. These followings had a fairly high degree of persistence and continuity through time as may be inferred from the maps in Figure 11.3, which indicate the areas of highest support for organization candidates in primaries from 1912 to 1948. The structure of the North Carolina organization following was probably fixed to a degree by the strength in county elections of Republicans in the western part of the state. Democrats in a minority locally or seriously threatened by the Republicans have an incentive to unite under central leadership in the intraparty struggles for control of the Democratic party and the state.

North Dakota for many years had a clear-cut bifactional system within the Republican party. The Nonpartisan League and the Republican Organizing Committee regularly held conventions, framed platforms, and designated slates of candidates to be supported in the primaries for the Republican nomination. The Nonpartisan League drew its heaviest popular support in the southern and western sections of the state, areas

[10] See Rudolf Heberle and A. L. Bertrand, "Factors Motivating Voting Behavior in a One-Party State," *Social Forces*, 27 (1949), pp. 343-350; A. P. Sindler, *Huey Long's Louisiana* (Baltimore: Johns Hopkins Press, 1956); P. H. Howard, *Political Tendencies in Louisiana: 1812-1952* (Baton Rouge: Louisiana State University Press, 1956).

on the whole of a less prosperous agriculture than the strongholds of the Republican Organizing Committee in the eastern section of the state. The ROC had urban commercial support and appealed to conservative people generally. The NPL-ROC cleavage also to some extent paralleled ethnic differences in the state with those of Germanic origin preponderantly aligned with the NPL, while Scandinavians tended more toward the ROC. Their economic outlook pulled many NPL followers towards the Democratic party nationally while their noninterventionist foreign policy views attracted them to the isolationist wing of the Republican party. In 1956 the NPL convention decided to enter its candidates for state office in the Democratic party, a move resisted by the older generation of the League. That step may, or may not, turn out to be a move toward the development of a dual party competition in state affairs.[11]

A state may be overwhelmingly attached to one party or another and yet lack well-organized, stable, and continuing factions. In such states the lines that divide the voters in one primary election may differ radically from the dividing lines in the next primary. The electorate appears to be fluid and amorphous and the leadership cliques poorly defined and certainly not perceived by the electorate as differentiated and competing groups. At widely separated moments of tension similar cleavages may recur in a mapping of the division of the primary vote, but these clusters of voters soon dissolve and are replaced by other groupings around the candidates of the day.[12] In such states it can scarcely be said that factions exist within parties that are the equivalent of political parties. Faced by confusing choices the electorate divides differently at each primary and the governing process itself may become erratic and unpredictable.

Still another type of factionalism tends to develop in the dominant parties of states that have a substantial minority party vote. These states are characterized by a pseudo-dualism; the parties compete on fairly even terms in the popular vote but only rarely does the minority party win. Pennsylvania, for example, has elected only two Democratic governors in this century. The high probability of Republican victory provides incentive for efforts to control the nominations of that party. In Pennsylvania the regular Republican organization has usually nominated its slate though at infrequent intervals struggles for supremacy occur between elements of the party in the Republican primaries. For several decades the regular organization has been closely associated with the Pennsylvania

[11] The best treatment of the Nonpartisan League is by R. L. Morlan, *Political Prairie Fire* (Minneapolis: University of Minnesota Press, 1955), although he carries the story only through 1922.

[12] See H. J. Doherty, Jr., "Liberal and Conservative Voting Patterns in Florida," *Journal of Politics*, 14 (1952), pp. 403–417.

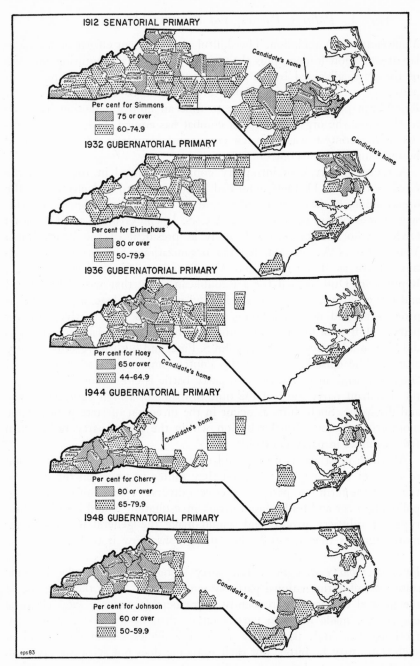

Figure 11.3. Persistence of Factions Within a One-Party State: Points of Highest Strength of "Organization" Candidates in North Carolina Democratic Primaries, 1912–1948

Manufacturers Association. The skillful and persistent efforts of the regular organization leaders, plus the support of the manufacturing interests of the state, all aided by an unsentimental utilization of the power of patronage created a faction almost invincible in its control of the state Republican party. Yet from time to time an unhappy faction has risen to challenge the organization and combat has ensued. In one notable instance the contest was between competing complexes of financial and business interests for control of the party.

A recent outbreak of intraparty conflict occurred in 1950 when the Governor, James H. Duff, who had been nominated and elected by the organization, broke with it and sought to control the designation of his successor as he ran for the Senate. Messrs. Joseph Grundy and G. Mason Owlett, who had succeeded Grundy as president of the Pennsylvania Manufacturers Association, led the organization. The propaganda pictured them as standpatters and Mr. Duff as a forward-looking, new Republican. Duff argued for a Republican party that would be "broad and not exclusive, a party of service and not of privilege, a party that is progressive and not backsliding, a party that is constructive and not petty." Duff won his primary campaign for the senatorial nomination as did his candidate for governor, John S. Fine, and both were subsequently elected. The episode serves in this context only to illustrate a type of "one-partyism" in which the two-party battle is close enough to compel the dominant party most of the time to maintain a high degree of unity and discipline. Such shifts as occur in the direction of state policy come more from the occasional rebellion within the major party rather than from changes in party control.[13]

All these illustrations do not add up to a comprehensive classification of types of one-party systems, but they suffice to underpin the proposition that the term one-party state covers diverse types of organization of political power and leadership. Further investigation would identify other types of subparty groups and would make the general impression far more complex than the preceding paragraphs show it to be.

Bases of biparty structures. The party systems of well under half the states resemble the national party system. In these states the outcome of the general elections is frequently unpredictable and the vital electoral choices are made between parties rather than between rival leaders of factions of a single party. The internal struggles within the parties of such states may be bitter, but their outcome does not settle the question of who is to control the state government.

[13] Wisconsin also has had a politics of Republican factionalism. See Leon D. Epstein, "A Two-Party Wisconsin?" *Journal of Politics*, 18 (1956), pp. 427–458.

Although some one-party states (in state affairs) tend to be competitive in presidential voting, by and large those factors that make a state competitive nationally also push toward the development of a dual pattern in state politics. The fundamental prerequisite is the existence of two complexes of interest with sufficiently divergent objectives to permit them to serve as the foundations for competing parties. Those "interests" need not be solely economic but may have an ethnic or religious tinge. The impulse to political division between such complexes within a state may, of course, be repressed by the heritages of history which happen to deter the formation of party cleavages paralleling those of the nation.

One of the most common foundations for two-party competition within individual states is that of the metropolis against the countryside. This is only a convenient shorthand description of a complex political pattern. Metropolis and country do not align solidly against each other. Ramparts are not erected where country meets city to divide the state sharply into two political groups. Rather, the typical pattern is that more than half the metropolitan electorate leans in one direction, whereas more than half the rural population leans in the other. Moreover, the urban-rural cleavage approaches in reality a group cleavage with urban-industrial wage earners opposing propertied groups both urban and rural. Often factors of religion and of ethnic origin also underlie the rural-urban differences. Yet the chances are that, independently of such factors, metropolitan and nonmetropolitan ways of life generate political differences.

New York State represents a party system built on metropolitan and nonmetropolitan bases, and also one that manifests in state affairs no small degree of independence from national political trends. In New York State campaigns the Democratic metropolitan stronghold yields well over half of the vote for Democratic gubernatorial candidates. On the other hand the Republican gubernatorial vote is similarly weighted by reliance on the faithful Republican vote of upstate towns, villages, and rural areas. The division of Democratic and Republican vote between New York City and upstate in gubernatorial elections during the period 1930–1954 is shown in Figure 11.4. The chart does not indicate the full extent to which the party cleavage approaches the rural-urban grouping, since both urban and rural upstate are lumped together.

New York's party structure illustrates some of the moderating influences built into the two-party system. Neither party can hope to succeed by advocating without restraint the cause of its own hard core. During a long period of Democratic control of the governorship by Alfred E. Smith, Franklin D. Roosevelt, and Herbert H. Lehman, the interests of New York City were not neglected. Yet to win the state these leaders

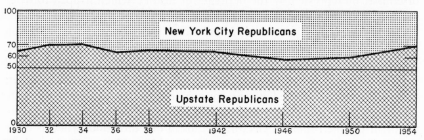

Figure 11.4. Metropolitan Base of Democratic Party and Upstate Base of Republican Party in New York: Percentage Division of Vote Polled by Gubernatorial Candidates of Each Party Between New York City and Upstate, 1930–1954

had to dissociate themselves from Tammany Hall sufficiently to allay upstate suspicion. To win they had to hold their own in the City and at the same time recruit upstate support. In the process the Democratic program became considerably more than a City program. In turn, Thomas E. Dewey had the strong upstate Republican vote to build on, but he also needed to wean City voters from their Democratic predilections. In the process of playing both ends against the middle, Dewey became a governor scarcely fitting the caricature of a reactionary Republican. In 1950 Dewey could boast of his program of rent control, public housing, fair employment practices, public health services, and other measures that Washington Democrats might claim as their own. Moreover, he interpreted his election that year as a mandate for state development of St. Lawrence power.[14]

In several other states the metropolitan-rural cleavage underlies a two-party competition for state control. In Illinois the Chicago and Cook County Democratic strength contributes disproportionately to the Democratic state vote, while the Republican vote has been more predominantly a downstate vote. In Massachusetts the Democrats of metropolitan Boston

[14] See Warren Moscow, *Politics in the Empire State* (New York: Knopf, 1948), chs. 5–6.

are pitted against the Yankee Republicans of the remainder of the state. In Michigan the somewhat imperfect bipartisan competition has its Democratic bastion in Detroit, while the Republicans draw more heavily on the outstate.

In some states the metropolitan-rural pattern is confused by the existence of two or more metropolitan centers, a factor that probably operates to make more difficult the management of the Democratic forces. In Missouri, the Democrats have had strong support in St. Louis and Kansas City, a metropolitan base diluted within the party by rural Democratic enclaves including "Little Dixie," a transplantation from the states further to the south. Connecticut represents an instance of a two-party state with no dominant metropolis but with a Democratic party that relies heavily on several major urban centers, as the rural and village areas remain preponderantly Republican.

Doubtless, in most states the apparent cleavage between the dominantly Democratic metropolis and the Republican nonmetropolitan areas conceals variations in partisan division among different types of nonmetropolitan communities. In Wisconsin, according to analyses by Leon D. Epstein, a fairly sharp difference exists between large- and medium-sized cities. Milwaukee and other urbanized places over 50,000 have had in recent years Democratic majorities in gubernatorial elections, while cities in the range of 10,000–50,000 turn in modest Republican majorities. The small cities and villages of under 10,000 are overwhelmingly Republican, while the voters of the farming townships are notoriously inconstant and swing from party to party.[15]

Significance of forms of political structure. What are the consequences of these variations among the states in the organization of political activity? The question cannot be answered with much confidence; the estimation of the effects of institutional arrangements belongs to the realm of art rather than precise measurement. Moreover, given the extreme variety in types of situations, generalization is most difficult. Yet a few more or less educated guesses may be made.

Although exceptions exist and the situation may differ from time to time even within the same state, as states deviate from the two-party pattern certain circumstances may tend to develop. First, the electorate may be presented with confusing and unclear alternatives as it is compelled to make the controlling decisions by choosing among individual leaders within the dominant party. A choice between party labels, each with a tradition and record behind it, may differ radically from a choice between

[15] "Size of Place and the Division of the Two-Party Vote in Wisconsin," *Western Political Quarterly*, 9 (1956), pp. 138–150.

aspirants for nomination identified with no policy tendency and running with no identifiable crowd of politicians.

The process of decision in the primaries of the dominant party also may introduce an element of pure chance into the electoral process. When three or more candidates seek a nomination, the peculiarities of their individual followings, the consequences of low electoral turnout, and the interactions among their candidacies may make the decision quite like a lottery. Election by lot may or may not be damaging in particular situations.

Another set of consequences may flow from the depressed condition of the minority party. So certain is it to be defeated, that it attracts an inadequate leadership, a circumstance that redounds to the general disadvantage when a landslide happens to throw it into office. By the same token, the second party becomes unable to perform effectively the vital function of criticism of the government. That activity may be carried on through internal squabbles within the majority, but greater effectiveness may be expected from an ably manned, institutionalized second party with a vested interest in exposing the weaknesses and abuses of the majority.

Legislative Apportionment and Party Government

State parties differ radically in the degree to which they approximate the two-party pattern. State political systems also diverge sharply from the national model in another respect. The institutional apparatus into which the state parties are fitted obstructs party government. Often Democrats win the governorship of a state but one house or both houses of the legislature may be beyond their reach. In fewer states the Republicans can on occasion place their candidate into office but are unable to capture majorities of both houses of the state legislature. This assurance of divided partisan control of state government flows in part from institutional factors such as the manner of distribution of legislative seats and, perhaps to a degree, from the nature of the party systems themselves. Whatever the cause, the consequence is that party government cannot operate in accord with the conventional conceptions in many states much of the time. The mechanism of government does not permit party government but puts teeth into the doctrine of checks and balances by, in effect, assigning different branches of the government to different parties.

Division of partisan control of state government. The hornbook theory of American parties runs to the effect that the party system overcomes the obstacles to governance in the separation of powers. A single party captures the executive and majorities in the legislative houses and extraconstitutional collaboration of fellow partisans directs the legislative and executive powers along the same path.

In the practice of state government this theory does not often nicely fit the facts. In one-party states the minority party is so weakly represented that the function of legislative organization and leadership falls to whatever factions develop a majority within the dominant party. In states with two-party competition the governmental machinery is so contrived that opposing parties often control the executive and the legislature. Or the party in opposition to the governor controls one house of the legislature. Legislation becomes a process of interparty negotiation or perhaps interparty warfare rather than one of the execution of a party program.

The tendency toward partisan division of control of the executive and legislature seems to be most marked in those states that most nearly approximate the two-party pattern in the organization of their politics.[16] In New York, for example, Republicans are virtually assured of legislative majorities by constitutional law. In Connecticut the overrepresentation of the small towns makes it certain that a Democratic governor will have to deal with a Republican lower house even though his party colleagues may control the senate.[17]

The extent of division of partisan control in state governments varies in the different stages of the political cycle. The imperfect meshing of party and constitutional system becomes most marked in eras when Democrats enjoy popular favor. Their gubernatorial candidates may attract sufficient popular support to go into office at such times, but the simultaneous elections of state legislatures yield Republican majorities for reasons to be explained in detail shortly. On the other hand, as popular sentiment shifts towards the Republican party its gubernatorial candidates are more likely to carry into office with themselves legislative majorities of their own party.

The extent of divided partisan control of state governments and the differentials in legislative opposition faced by Democratic and Republican

---

[16] In one-party states control of the governorship and the legislature rests nominally in the hands of the same party, but often there may be a situation equivalent to partisan division in two-party states. One party faction may control the governorship and another may be strong in the legislature. In many state legislatures the lesser party is too weakly represented to be much of a factor in the legislative process. After the 1954 elections, in 11 states the minority had no more than 10 per cent of the seats in either legislative house; in 13 states, no more than 20 per cent of the seats in either house; in 24 states the maximum minority strength was 30 per cent.

[17] For a more extended treatment of division in partisan control, see V. O. Key, Jr. and Corinne Silverman, "Party and Separation of Powers: A Panorama of Practice in the States," *Public Policy*, 5 (1954), pp. 382–412.

governors are shown for a group of 17 fairly competitive states in the panels in Figure 11.5. The curves in the upper panel reflect the marked spread between the numbers of states electing Democratic governors and the numbers simultaneously placing Democratic majorities into control of

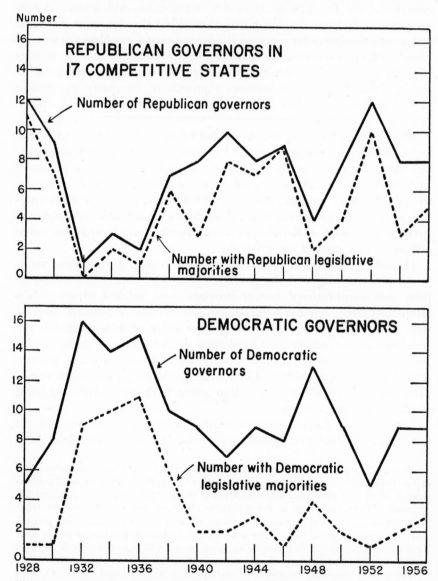

Number

REPUBLICAN GOVERNORS IN
17 COMPETITIVE STATES

Number of Republican governors

Number with Republican legislative
majorities

DEMOCRATIC GOVERNORS

Number of Democratic
governors

Number with Democratic
legislative majorities

Figure 11.5. Division of Governorship and Legislative Control Between Parties
in Seventeen "Competitive" States, 1928–1954

the legislature over the period 1928–1954.[18] The lower panel indicates the relative infrequency with which Republican governors in the same group of states have to cope with whatever problems arise from opposition majorities in the legislatures. Probably the sound general rule is that the lesser party, be it Democratic or Republican, may expect to be more successful in electing governors than in winning legislative majorities. Occasionally Kentucky, Maryland, and Tennessee elect a Republican governor but he commonly has to deal with a Democratic legislature. If there were more such states with Republican parties capable of winning the governorship only now and then, the differences in the frequency with which Democratic and Republican governors face opposition legislatures would not be so great.

Factors conducive to divided control. While the gerrymander accounts in large degree for split party control of state governments, other factors share responsibility for this condition. On rare occasions the electorate for good and sufficient reason deliberately chooses divided control. The general trend may be toward the Republican ticket, say, but the voters, or enough of them to control the decision, reject the Republican gubernatorial candidate. Over a long period of time in Ohio, Democratic gubernatorial candidates have succeeded in winning against Republican presidential and legislative tides. In the 1920's Vic Donahey and in the 1940's and 1950's Frank J. Lausche won majorities time and again as the rest of the Democratic ticket went down to defeat. It may be assumed that the voters knew what they were doing in these elections.

More commonly, divided control rests on a distribution of legislative seats that makes it impossible for a Democratic popular majority to elect a Democratic legislative majority. To some extent this consequence results from the concentration of Democratic voters in the metropolitan centers. There they may carry legislative seats by top-heavy majorities of 75 or 80 per cent of the popular vote. Were their strength more widely distributed, the same number of popular votes would yield a larger numbers of seats by smaller margins.

More significant than the incidental consequences of geographic concentration of Democratic voters is discrimination against cities in the allocation of legislative seats. In so far as Democratic-Republican lines parallel urban-rural lines, discrimination against cities in legislative representation falls on the Democratic party. Underrepresentation of cities comes about through several methods all of which are loosely described

[18] The states analyzed in the figure were Colorado, Connecticut, Illinois, Indiana, Maryland, Massachusetts, Michigan, Missouri, Montana, New Jersey, New York, Nevada, Ohio, Rhode Island, Utah, Washington, Wyoming.

as gerrymanders. Narrowly defined, the term gerrymander refers to the deliberate formation of legislative districts in such a way as to gain partisan advantage in the composition of the legislative body.[19] If district boundaries are drawn in the appropriate manner, one Republican (or Democrat) can be made to grow where two flourished before and at the same time district-equality in population may be maintained. Such ingenious exercises in political geography are not so significant as are applications of general rules of representation that give advantage to rural areas.

Some state constitutions explicitly recognize territory rather than population as the basis for representation. In New Jersey, for example, each county elects one senator, and a majority of the senate may be made up of senators from counties including only 15 per cent of the state's population. Equal representation of counties has been rationalized as a "federal" scheme by false analogy with the national Senate. A number of states employ a modification of the system of equal representation of territorial units; the constitution declares that representation shall be allocated among counties in accordance with population but hastens to provide that each county shall be entitled to at least one of a limited and fixed number of representatives. In North Carolina, to illustrate, the 120 members of the lower house are apportioned among the counties according to population, except that each county is entitled to at least one representative, a proviso that gives the populous counties less than a proportionate share of the legislative seats. Some state constitutions specifically limit the representation of the metropolis of the state. In Pennsylvania no city or county is permitted to elect more than one sixth of the senators, a provision adopted to limit the influence of Philadelphia.

However discrimination in representation is accomplished, the result is a restriction of the strength of the larger cities in the legislatures and, in most states outside the South, an artificial limitation of Democratic legislative representation. The dimensions of the discrimination are indicated by the 1938 finding of David O. Walter that the 96 metropolitan districts, as defined by the Census Bureau, had "on an average only three-fourths of their proper representation in each house of the legislature." [20] In 1955 Manning J. Dauer and Robert G. Kelsay found that from 1937 to 1955 the representativeness of the legislatures declined in about three-quarters of the states.[21]

[19] See E. C. Griffith, *The Rise and Development of the Gerrymander* (Chicago: Scott, Foresman, 1907).

[20] "Reapportionment and Urban Representation," *The Annals*, 195 (1938), pp. 11–20.

[21] "Unrepresentative States," *National Municipal Review*, 44 (1955), pp. 571–575. For a summary of the constitutional clauses governing apportionment of representation, see *Book of the States*, 1956–57, pp. 112–116. See also G. E. Baker, *Rural versus Urban Political Power* (Garden City: Doubleday, 1955).

Discrimination in representation and popular government. A consequence of the institutional systems that have been described is that in many states much of the time the political party cannot perform its supposed function of casting a net of unity over the separated organs of government. With one party in control of the legislature and the nominee of another in the governor's chair the legislative process may become stalemated; partisan bickering may be the rule; and action may be the result of negotiation between opposing party leaders, a condition that may or may not be conducive to the general good.

Yet the effects of institutional depressants of party government cannot be estimated solely from observation of the workings of state governments in which parties share control. The effects must to a high degree be surmised from guesses about what does not come about because of that condition. The course of politics in many states involves fairly regular victory for a single party. At intervals an exasperated public withdraws its favor from the dominant party, but its discontent finds only partial expression, for at least one house of the legislature remains beyond the reach of such movements of sentiment. In effect, the electorate cannot completely dislodge one crowd from control of the state government and replace it by another. Hence the occasional powerful movements for reform or for change tend to be frustrated by institutional blockades. Those interests committed to negativism gain advantage by the institutional rules of the game.[22] The phenomenon gains in significance when it is recalled that these obstructions to action are characteristic of most of the more populous states.

The high incidence of divided party control of state governments makes it essential that techniques be developed for the conduct of public business across party lines; otherwise states would be completely paralyzed. A wide range of state questions arouses no sharp partisan divisions and the degree of cohesion within party groups also differs greatly from state legislature to state legislature. Yet it is clear that the systems of representation and the divisions of party control dictate the nature of state action or inaction on a goodly number of basic issues. The constitutional or statutory apportionment of the legislative membership settles, or at least fundamentally conditions, the decision on those questions that divide the parties.[23]

[22] Alfred E. Smith, in the New York Constitutional Convention, charged that upstate Republicans, overrepresented in the legislature, had "opposed every progressive piece of legislation proposed in this State in the last generation."—New York State Constitutional Convention, 1938, *Revised Record*, IV, pp. 2881–2884.

[23] See W. Duane Lockard, "Legislative Politics in Connecticut," *American Political Science Review*, 48 (1954), pp. 166–73; W. J. Keefe, "Party Government and Lawmaking in the Illinois General Assembly," *Northwestern University Law Review*, 47 (1952), pp. 55–71; W. J. Keefe, "Parties, Partisanship, and Public Policy in the

States and the Tides of National Politics

Another broad factor powerfully conditions the operations of political systems within the states. The great tides of presidential politics tend to engulf the affairs of states and often to determine the results of state elections. The Democratic party may win control of a state as it rides into office on the coattails of a popular presidential candidate and through no merit of its program or its candidate. So may the Republican party gain state victory. Either party may be unceremoniously booted from office by the sweeps of national politics. Obviously the intrusion of extraneous factors into state politics obstructs the maintenance of a state politics with a focus on state affairs.

Cycles in party control of governorships. The interlocking of state and national politics is by no means complete. The one-party Democratic states of the South have a capacity in their local affairs to resist Republican landslides. In these states no Republican governors rode into office with General Eisenhower in 1952; nor did Herbert Hoover's coattails in 1928 have sufficient pulling power to upset Democratic governors in these states. At the Republican end of the spectrum only Vermont has shown an equivalent capacity to resist national Democratic tides.

With these major exceptions, a striking interlocking of state and national voting occurs, a relationship that appears most clearly from the behavior of state politics over a long period. When a region shifts its political preferences from Democratic to Republican, the presidential results, the elections to the House of Representatives, and the choices of governors tend to move in the same direction. Republicans replace Democrats, or vice versa, in about the same proportions. While both state and national voting may, in these great swings, be responsive to common causes, to some extent voting on state and local office represents a more or less automatic extension of strong preferences or dislikes in national politics. The pervasive effect of national politics becomes patent when inconspicuous state and local candidates, hidden away far down the ballot, ride into—or are ousted from—office with the movement of the national pendulum.

The graphs in Figure 11.6 picture the interrelation over one great swing of the political cycle between the results of elections to state governorships and to the national House of Representatives. The proportionate division of these posts between the two major parties varies with the

Pennsylvania Legislature," *American Political Science Review*, 48 (1954), pp. 450–464; M. E. Jewell, "Party Voting in American State Legislatures," *American Political Science Review*, 49 (1955), pp. 773–791.

ebb and flow of popular preferences. The actual shifts between parties of both House seats and governorships, of course, tend to be concentrated geographically in the areas of relatively close party competition. Given the division of states extreme in their partisan attachments, Democratic peaks in the cycle leave the Republicans in control of fewer governors than the Democrats hold when Republican strength nationally is at its highest point.

Correlation in state and national voting. The common subjection of state and national politics to the great fluctuations in the fortunes of the parties is made clear by the comparison of the results of state and national elections over long periods of time as was done in Figure 11.6. The interlocking of voting for candidates at the two levels of government may also be seen from an analysis of the voting at a single election.

A sample election chosen to indicate the character of this interrelationship is analyzed in the scatter-diagram in Figure 11.7, which shows the relationship between the proportions of the vote in each Ohio county polled by Harry Truman and by the Democratic candidate for governor, Frank Lausche, in 1948. A fairly close relationship prevailed from county

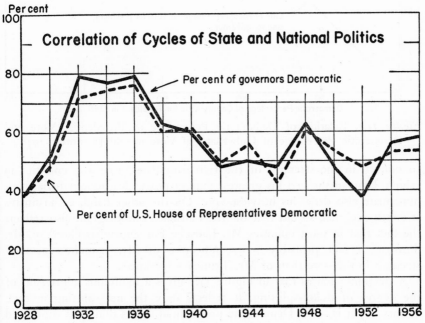

Figure 11.6. Percentage of U.S. House of Representatives and of Governors Democratic, 1928–1956

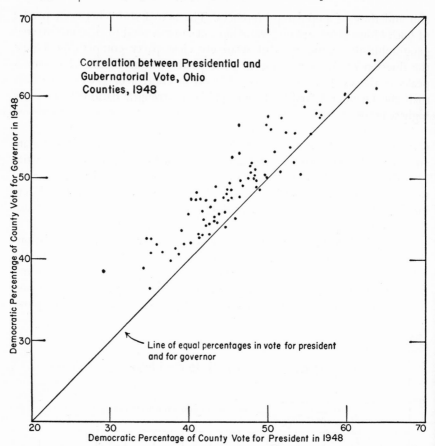

Figure 11.7. Relation of Democratic Percentage of Presidential Vote and Democratic Percentage of Gubernatorial Vote in Ohio Counties, 1948

to county in the strength of the two candidates. In those counties in which Truman showed his greatest pulling power his gubernatorial running mate also drew his heaviest vote. On the other hand, as Truman's strength declined, so did that of Mr. Lausche. The diagram also reflects the fact that in most counties Mr. Lausche ran somewhat ahead of Mr. Truman, a fact probably more indicative of Mr. Lausche's peculiar strength in the state than of Mr. Truman's weakness.

A diagram such as that in Figure 11.7 gives a minimum impression of the degree of ticket-splitting. It reflects only the net splitting in each county. That is, some Democratic presidential voters doubtless supported the Republican candidate for governor but they were exceeded by the Dewey voters who either did not mark their ballot for governor or supported the Democratic candidate. From the examination of many such diagrams, the impression builds up that presidential voting preferences are more volatile than are those in state and local elections. A presidential candidate may run ahead of his state ticket or he may fall behind, all depending on the trend of his party's fortunes nationally. The great movements of voters from one party to the other in national elections do not in the same degree dislodge people from their customary predilections in state politics.[24]

Separation of state and national politics. Designers of state governmental systems have on the whole held that some way ought to be devised to separate state from national politics. Their assumption has been that the settlement of the debates of national politics should not also fix more or less automatically the outcomes of state elections. Often the argument runs to the effect that there is no Republican or Democratic way to run a state government; the questions are mainly those of honesty and efficiency. It seems more correct to say that, at least in domestic matters, the great issues tend to divide people in roughly the same way on the broad issues of state and national politics. Straight-ticket voting in principle may make sense in many instances, although from time to time a worthy citizen may be well advised to vote against an incompetent who happens to win the nomination of his party for governor.

Despite the interlocking in the movements of party strength on both the state and national level, the electorate does manage quite often to make an effective separation of its choices of presidential and state candidates. The Democrats, under the leadership of Alfred E. Smith and Franklin D. Roosevelt, controlled the governorship of the state of New York during an era when Republican presidential candidates were rolling up big majorities in the state. Thomas E. Dewey and his Republican followers managed to control the state government during a period when Democratic presidential candidates usually carried the state.

In the strongly one-party states the outcome of the gubernatorial election almost certainly will be the same as in the presidential elections, but in states with a semblance of a two-party system split results are by no means uncommon. The narrower the popular margin by which a presidential candidate carries a state, the greater is the probability that enough votes will be split to give the gubernatorial victory to the opposing party.

[24] From the inspection of these relationships in many elections, the impression also develops that the interconnection between presidential and gubernatorial voting has been declining over the past half century. For many elections in the 1890's a diagram such as that in Figure 11.7 places most counties almost exactly on the line of identical percentage division in presidential and gubernatorial voting.

An analysis of gubernatorial elections over the period 1932–1950, presented in Table 11.2, demonstrates the point. In those states carried by Democratic presidential candidates by less than a 5 per cent margin, about one-half of the governors elected simultaneously were Republicans.

In the close states presidentially, the circumstances thus permit the electorate to discriminate effectively between presidential and gubernatorial candidates, or so it would seem from the relationships that appear in Table 11.2. In fact, probably what happens in the main is that the party entrenched in power in a state has, by virtue of the organization built up over a long period, a capacity to resist the effects of national tides. The more forceful the swing against it nationally, the less are the chances that the dominant party locally will survive the impact. Republican state organizations, although they might not be able to deliver the state against Roosevelt or Truman, could often manage to hold power themselves. Similarly, some Democratic organizations held state control in 1952 and 1956 although the General rode to an easy presidential victory in their bailiwicks. The capacity of the prevailing state organization to survive is suggested by the right-hand column of Table 11.2. The data there show that in the period covered by the table Republican candidates recaptured gubernatorial posts in the off years when there was no presidential campaign and when the national sweep was not running against them.

Table 11.2

Two-Year Governors Outside the South, Chosen in Presidential Years and in Off Years, 1932–1950, Related to Democratic Percentage of State Presidential Vote [a]

Democratic Presidential Percentage	Number of State Elections	Per Cent of Governors Democratic	
		Presidential Years	Following Off Years
Under 45	10	20.0 [b]	20.0
45–49	17	29.4	17.6
50–54	20	55.0	25.0
55–59	21	90.5	57.1
60 or more	15	93.3 [c]	80.0

[a] States and elections analyzed: Arizona, Colorado, Connecticut, Idaho (through 1946), Iowa, Kansas, Maine, Massachusetts, Michigan, Minnesota, Nebraska, New Mexico, New York (through 1938), North Dakota (except 1936–1938), Ohio, Rhode Island, South Dakota, Wisconsin (except 1932–1942), Wyoming (1932–1934).

[b] The deviate states in this cell were Maine in 1932 and North Dakota in 1940.

[c] The deviate state in this cell was North Dakota which elected Wm. Langer as its Republican governor in 1932.

The greater separability of state and national questions in the off years has led some states to schedule their gubernatorial elections in those years. The justification of this arrangement is that it permits the affairs of state politics to proceed unembarrassed by the considerations of national campaigns. In fact, the arrangement seems to give advantage in state elections to the candidates of the party that does not control the national government, as may be seen from the data in Table 11.3. That table compares,

Table 11.3

Four-Year Governors Outside the South, Chosen in Presidential Years and in Off Years, 1932–1950, Related to Democratic Percentage of State Presidential Vote [a]

Democratic Presidential Percentage	Presidential Years		Off Years [b]	
	Governors Elected	Per Cent Democratic	Governors Elected	Per Cent Democratic
45–49	5	40.0	6	33.3
50–54	10	40.0	13	23.1
55–59	15	80.0	4	50.0
60 and over	10	100.0	11	63.6

[a] The states electing governors in presidential years covered by the table were Delaware, Illinois, Indiana, Missouri, Montana, Utah, Washington, West Virginia. The off-year states were California, Idaho, Maryland, Nevada, New York, Oregon, Pennsylvania, Wyoming. Some of these states elected in the off years only for a part of the period 1932–1950.

[b] The off-year states are grouped according to their presidential vote in the preceding presidential election. The two groups of gubernatorial elections compared are thus, of course, elections in different states with similar Democratic presidential margins. Apart from the fact that few cases are involved, it should be kept in mind that factors in addition to the presidential division affect the results of the gubernatorial elections.

in relationship to the margin in the presidential voting, the results of gubernatorial elections in states choosing governors for four-year terms in presidential years and in another group of states electing governors for four years in nonpresidential years. In a Democratic era nationally off-year scheduling of state elections definitely gave advantage to Republican gubernatorial candidates.

On the other hand, Democrats gain advantage from off-year election scheduling in the days of Republican triumph nationally. Constitution makers have not invariably realized that off-year scheduling may have one effect at one time and another at a later time. During the years of Democratic dominance, Republicans in several states initiated movements for constitutional reform and managed to time gubernatorial elections so that their candidates were relieved, in effect, of the inconvenience of running against Franklin D. Roosevelt. Among the converts to the four-year term were Connecticut and New York. In the off year of 1954, Mr. Harriman in New York and Mr. Ribicoff in Connecticut eked out Democratic victories which would have doubtless been beyond their reach had they been running against a ticket with General Eisenhower at its head. In 1954 also the Democrats carried Pennsylvania, another four-year state, a feat which would have been most difficult to accomplish had the General been on the ticket.

While it seems evident that different results in the presidential and gubernatorial voting within states flow in part from the capacity of state party organizations to withstand the impact of the presidential swing, it should not be supposed that this is purely a mechanical braking effect. On occasion the people of a state may have ample provocation to rise up and indignantly and deliberately throw a governor out of office even though his party ticket as a whole rides to an overwhelming victory. Further, at times the voters of a state act consistently by splitting their ticket. For example, in Ohio, Mr. Lausche survived the Eisenhower tide, but he was a rather dilute Democrat, in many respects not unlike the General in the style and orientation of his politics.

Effects of isolation of state politics. Governmental gadgets designed to shield state politics from the blasts of the national political conflict have a superficial appeal. On its face, the theory that the electorates of states should be encouraged to focus their attention on state questions when voting in state elections is eminently reasonable. Yet to the extent that states can be isolated from national affairs, one-party dominance of states is probably facilitated. The minor party, deprived of the pulling power of its victorious national ticket, remains a minor party. The long-run strengthening of the lesser party would probably be aided by an occasional victory in a national landslide. Whether a strong second party in a state is desirable may be another matter. Yet in most states the lesser party sooner or later does win in a national landslide, and the better equipped it is with competent leadership perhaps the less disturbing are the consequences of these coattail victories.

Political Paralysis and the Role of the States

The analyses of the organization of state political systems cumulate into the conclusion that the states tend toward a structure of political leadership that is hamstrung if not paralyzed. The overwhelming commitment of many states to one or the other of the national parties is associated with a one-partyism within the states, a form of organization that confuses popular decision and handicaps political initiative. Many state elections seem to be decided by the more or less fortuitous impact of the external forces of national politics. When the foundations and impulses toward an effective party system exist, they are apt to be obstructed by institutional devices ingeniously contrived to make energetic government impractical.

One broad consequence of the ineffectiveness of state political organization and leadership appears to be an encouragement of federal centralization. Even though a matter may be within both the constitutional competence and the fiscal capacity of the states, unless adequate political initiative exists within the states no action may be taken. The fact that some groups are virtually blocked from winning control of a state government, even though they may command a popular majority, moves them to take their case to Congress. Those groups tend to be associated with the Democratic parties of the states, against which the institutional depressants operate with special rigor. To be sure, the characteristics of political organization within the states are by no means solely responsible for the march of authority to Washington. Given the national character of the organization of the economy, a broad range of matters is beyond the capacity of the states. Yet within that area in which state action remains feasible, political organization prone to inaction prevents a realization of the potentialities of state action and encourages movements for federal action.

Perhaps a federal system has inherent difficulties for the practice of popular government within the constituent units of the system. At least when national questions overshadow those in the competence of the states, one consequence may be, as has been argued, the warping of state political systems into forms not so well adapted as they might be to the necessities of popular government. Even beyond that infirmity, in the competition of two levels of popular government for popular attention and interest, that concerned with the more dramatic issues would be expected to be salient in public awareness. Questions within the national jurisdiction have come more and more over the decades to monopolize popular attention, a circumstance that probably affects the quality of state government and administration.

The consequences for state government of the types of organization of state politics that have been described may be most grave at moments of tension and crisis. Most of the time, state governments manage to perform their tasks more or less satisfactorily. Most of the time, no burning issues agitate the people. It is when crisis does develop, when serious questions demand attention, that the incapacity of the state political systems to act decisively and boldly has its most marked consequences for popular government. Those moments, fortunately, do not arise with great frequency.[25]

[25] The broad problems raised in this chapter have not been dealt with extensively, but several titles are relevant: Belle Zeller (ed.), *American State Legislatures* (New York: Crowell, 1954); Commission on Intergovernmental Relations, *Report* (Washington: Government Printing Office, 1955); Leonard D. White, *The States and the Nation* (Baton Rouge: Louisiana State University Press, 1953); William Anderson, *The Nation and the States, Rivals or Partners?* (Minneapolis: University of Minnesota Press, 1955); The American Assembly, *The Forty-eight States: Their Tasks as Policy Makers and Administrators* (The Assembly, 1955); V. O. Key, Jr., *American Politics: An Introduction* (New York: Knopf, 1956), and *Southern Politics* (New York: Knopf, 1949).

Part Three | # PARTY STRUCTURE
AND PROCEDURE

ATTENTION now shifts to another broad aspect of political parties. In the preceding chapters the major focus was upon their place in the process of governance, with emphasis on the American party system. In the development of the argument the broad, special characteristics of that system were set forth, as well as the policy orientations and composition of its individual parties. The picture needs to be rounded out by an examination of the machinery and procedures parties use in the fulfillment of their roles in the governing process. The chapters that follow will deal with the organizational apparatus of parties and with the procedures and rituals by which they designate candidates and formulate programs. The discussion, therefore, will be concerned more with the work of the party professionals than with the mass of party membership, with the apparatus for making party decisions rather than with voters. Such organizational apparatus, sometimes called "party-outside-the-government," is common to parties of all democratic orders, but the machinery of American parties includes features peculiar to this country—such as direct nominating procedures—to which special attention will be devoted.

12 | Party Organization

ORGANIZATION exists to facilitate collective activity. To understand party organization one must keep in mind the functions of party. A prime function consists in the nomination of candidates for office. When a crowd of people first foregathered and agreed to center their support on specified candidates in an election, "party" was born. As a corollary to nomination, party has the function of mobilizing electoral support. It may formulate policy proposals, or at least put into words the policy predilections of the group. Party may serve as a link between electorate and candidates and between people and government. It is a mechanism for the attainment of power; as such it may determine who gets power, and it may influence the exercise of authority as well.

These attributions of function imply that party is considered, for the moment at least, to be the comparatively small group of political activists —the "pros," the "politicians," the amateur politicians—those who devote time and effort to the business of politics. How many such persons there are can only be guessed; they surely do not number more than three or four million in an electorate of over 100,000,000.[1]

[1] George Gallup estimates that 5,180,000 persons claimed to have "worked" in the

How are the political activists, however large or small their number, to perform functions of the party? This is in essence the problem of party organization. What assignments of duties are to be made? What are the relations of authority, responsibility, leadership among the persons concerned? What are the rewards and punishments? Who makes what decisions? What procedures shall be followed in arriving at decisions for the party? In short, how are the activists to collaborate in carrying on the business of the party?

To cope in detail with such questions about American parties would require a treatment of encyclopaedic dimensions. Yet broad elements of party organization and some of its characteristics may be identified. Mechanisms for nomination are a basic element of the party apparatus. The national convention serves as the instrument for the designation of presidential and vice-presidential candidates. Through it the activists of each party select the candidates. The saying that the professionals choose the presidential candidates and the voters choose between them retains no little validity. For other offices, both state and national, the prevailing mode of nomination is the direct primary, a procedure that compels the professionals, to a greater or lesser extent, to share with the rank and file of the party in the nomination of candidates. The national convention and the direct primary will be treated in detail in succeeding chapters.

Beyond the nominating mechanisms are the party hierarchies—the "machine"—the organizations whose principal function is to mobilize voter support; they may also exert a controlling influence in the designation of candidates, whatever the formal procedure may be. The "party machine" is often described as if a military discipline prevailed from the national chairman at the peak of the hierarchy to the precinct captain at the base. That is by no means the reality. Perhaps the outstanding characteristic of American party organization, viewed from the national aspect, is its decentralized nature. In a sense, no nation-wide party organization exists, although each party, to be sure, has its national organs. Rather the national organization of each party consists of a working coalition of state and local organizations, which at times achieves a high degree of cohesiveness in action. The units allied together nationally differ widely among themselves in the form and manner of their organization and operation. Yet, without becoming bogged down in the variety of state and local organization, the general contours of the national party structure as a whole may be delineated.

1954 congressional elections: 3,020,000 for the Democrats; 2,160,000 for the Republicans. Projection of percentages in Angus Campbell's The Voter Decides suggests that around 2,000,000 of the Eisenhower voters in 1952 gave money or bought tickets to help the campaign as did about 1,600,000 of the Stevenson voters.

Formal Party Organization

The formal organization of the party is prescribed by the rules of the national convention and by state laws and rules adopted by state and local party authorities. As students of institutions assert, formal organization does not invariably coincide with informal organization. The man with the title of boss may not actually be boss. Nevertheless, formal organization has its functions and informal organization invariably is intertwined with it.

The form of party organization, like that of other organizations, is determined by the nature of the task to be accomplished. The major objective of party organization is the winning of elections. Hence party organization is built around the geographic divisions of the country for electoral purposes. The unit cell of the party is the precinct executive. The precinct is the basic unit of electoral administration and includes within its boundaries, on the average, several hundred voters. In the larger cities the next higher level of party organization is formed about the ward or district presided over by a leader whose jurisdiction comprises several precincts. From the wards or districts, councilmen or legislators are elected. More commonly the next higher level of party organization above the precinct is the county committee which may consist of precinct executives or of persons chosen by them. The county is an electoral unit for a variety of purposes: the choice of county officials, often the election of state legislators, and it may even be a congressional district. The party has a state committee or state central committee whose chairman is ordinarily a party figure of some importance. The next layer of party organization is the national committee, which includes representation from each state and whose chairman ranks high among the professional politicians of his party.

Although the party organization can be regarded as a hierarchy based on the precinct executive and capped by the national committee, it may be more accurately described as a system of layers of organization. Each successive layer—county or city, state, national—has an independent concern about elections in its geographical jurisdiction. Yet each higher level of organization, to accomplish its ends, must obtain the collaboration of the lower layer or layers of organization. That collaboration comes about, to the extent that it does come about, through a sense of common cause rather than the exercise of command.

National committees. The capstone of the formal party organization is the national committee. The Democratic national committee consists of one man and one woman from each state (plus members from territories and dependencies).[2] The same principle of representation governed the composition of the Republican national committee until the 1952 convention gave certain states a third member, the state party chairman. The state chairmen entitled to membership were those whose states (a) had cast their electoral votes for the Republican presidential candidate at the preceding election, (b) had a Republican majority in the state's congressional representation, that is, Senators plus Representatives, or (c) had a Republican governor. The enlargement of the committee encountered opposition from southern states, which expected to qualify less regularly for the third member on the committee than would the Republican strongholds, and from women, who lost their equality of representation on the committee with the addition of the state chairman.[3]

In form the national convention elects the national committee to serve for four years from the adjournment of the convention. In practice the delegation from each state proposes to the convention the national committee members from that state. In some instances a state's convention delegation has the actual power of nomination of the national committee members. In others, the actual decision is made by a direct primary in the state, by a state convention, or by the state committee of the party. Often the selection of national committeemen becomes entangled with the rivalries of aspirants for the presidential nomination since they are usually designated at the same time and by the same authority that chooses convention delegates. Thus, in the events leading to the 1952 Republican national convention, a goodly number of pro-Eisenhower men were chosen to replace pro-Taft committeemen.

Since membership on the national committee entails cost in both time and money, national committeemen tend to be men of both substance and political stature in their states. Most of them are either lawyers or businessmen; many mix law, business, and politics. The lawyer's shingle is often a cloak for a full-time dedication to politics, while some of the businessmen devote themselves to businesses peculiarly political, such as insurance. The national committeeman may be the real chief of his state party organization or his national power may be rooted in the leadership of a metropolitan center. He may be a lieutenant of the real leader of his state party or his membership on the national committee may be a recognition by the state organization for financial support or an accolade for an elder statesman.[4]

---

[2] On the infiltration of women into the national party organizations, see Marguerite J. Fisher and Betty Whitehead, "Women and National Party Organization," *American Political Science Review*, 38 (1944), pp. 895–903.

[3] *Proceedings*, 1952 Republican National Convention, pp. 278–289.

[4] These remarks may be illustrated by mention of a few members of the national

The duties of the national committee include direction of the presidential campaign, filling vacancies on the party ticket caused by death, maintenance and supervision of the national party headquarters, conduct of public-relations programs, raising funds, and making arrangements for the national convention. The committee fulfills many of its responsibilities either through committees or through the national chairman and his staff. Its decisions that attract most public attention are those on convention arrangements, for these actions often affect the interests of aspirants for the presidential nomination. The committee selects the convention city, issues the call for the convention, prepares a temporary roll of delegates, and recommends a slate of temporary officers. In addition, it has assumed the power to recommend permanent officers to the convention.[5]

The meetings of the national committees bring together party chieftains from over the country and furnish opportunity for consultation, combination, and maneuver concerning the party's next nominee. If the party is in power and the President is in line for another nomination, the committee may adopt a resolution commending his record and demanding that he accept renomination. In January, 1944, for example, the Democratic national committee expressed its confidence in Roosevelt and "earnestly" solicited "him to continue as the great world leader." If the party is out of power, the managers of contenders for the nomination will be on hand negotiating for support from the leaders assembled, but in such situations the national committee itself makes no formal endorsement. The Republican national committee introduced an innovation in January, 1952, when the major contenders were invited to appear, personally or by representatives, at its San Francisco session and put their case.

Since the national conventions meet only once every four years, significant issues of national policy arise between conventions on which an

---

committees in 1956. The Democratic committee included James M. Curley, former mayor of Boston, and governor of Massachusetts, long past his prime but not without influence; David L. Lawrence, Pittsburgh leader and a "pro" of the "pros"; Monroe Sweetland, Oregon publisher; Paul Chambers, president of several Arkansas retail enterprises; Thomas D'Alesandro, mayor of Baltimore and former U.S. Representative; Theodore F. Green, Senator from Rhode Island and former governor; George F. Rock, Denver banker; Jacob M. Arvey, Chicago lawyer and erstwhile Chicago boss; Carmine DeSapio, Manhattan Democratic leader.

The Republican committee included such men as: Harry Darby, manufacturer and former Kansas Senator; Albert K. Mitchell, New Mexico rancher; Clarence Brown, Representative from Ohio and publisher; H. J. Porter, Texas oil producer; Walter S. Hallanan, West Virginia Republican leader and president of Plymouth Oil; Ted Dalton, Virginia state senator and lawyer; Theodore R. McKeldin, governor of Maryland and former mayor of Baltimore; C. Wayland Brooks, lawyer and former Senator from Illinois; Guy Gabrielson, New Jersey lawyer and businessman.

[5] These matters are treated in detail in Chapter 15.

expression of party policy may be desirable. The national committee derives its authority from the national convention which gives it no mandate to function as a policy-maker between conventions. Nevertheless, on rare occasions the national committee issues pronouncements of party policy roughly analagous to platform planks. The Republican national committee, for example, in its April, 1942 meeting became embroiled in a battle between the isolationists, led by Robert A. Taft, and the international collaborationists, led by Wendell Willkie. The committee adopted a resolution to serve in effect as a platform for the 1942 congressional campaigns and in this resolution attempted to cleanse the party of its isolationism by recognizing an "obligation to assist in the bringing about of understanding, comity, and cooperation among the nations of the world." More commonly the national committee deliberations on policy matters result only in recommendations to the national convention. For example, the Democratic committee after a series of regional meetings and extensive consultations with party leaders, recommended to the 1956 convention that the loyalty pledge be abrogated and replaced by a milder formula acceptable to all concerned.[6]

A move toward a wider policy role for the Democratic national committee between conventions occurred after the 1956 defeat when its chairman, Paul Butler, set up an advisory council to issue policy pronouncements as occasion required. The national committee, in approving the creation of the advisory group, resolved: "The Democratic National Committee understands its function to be, during the interim between national conventions, the application of the party's platform to fast-moving events and the interpretation of party policies in the light of changing conditions." Within the "framework of the party's platform," the advisory committee would aid the national committee. The advisory council of about 25 members included prominent Democrats not on the national committee, such as Harry S. Truman, Adlai Stevenson, and Mrs. Franklin D. Roosevelt. By the work of this group the national committee leadership hoped to nudge the House and Senate leadership, predominantly southern, towards a program that would appeal to northern Democratic voters. Democratic House and Senate leaders declined to serve on the advisory council. Connection with a body outside the chambers that made

[6] Committee debates on policy may be mingled with the maneuvers of aspirants for the nomination. Thus, in January, 1932 the Al Smith forces sought to have the committee recommend a liquor plan to the national convention. The Roosevelt forces won the dispute and the committee "referred," instead of recommended, the plan to the convention. Farley, the Roosevelt manager in the episode, spoke of the "impropriety" of attempting to make the national committee the voice of the party in "matters of policy"—See Frank Friedel, *Franklin D. Roosevelt: The Triumph* (Boston: Little, Brown, 1956), pp. 238-39.

pronouncements on legislation could have embarrassed them in their parliamentary leadership, a consideration that probably coincided with a disinclination to accept leadership from the clique around the national committee.

National chairman: General position. The national committee, from its very size, cannot function as the working executive of the party. The kingpin of the national organization is not the national committee but its chairman. His most onerous responsibility is the management of the presidential campaign but other duties occupy him between elections. At the party's national headquarters in Washington he has under his supervision a staff of from 50 to 150 persons. During campaigns the national staff mushrooms as special units are created to care for phases of the campaign. After the campaign the electioneering machinery is dismantled and the national chairman is left with the direction of the party's day-to-day business. Not the least of his tasks is that of raising funds to support the normal activities of the national committee—and perhaps to pay off the deficit incurred in the last campaign.[7]

In form the national committee elects the national chairman, but he is in fact designated, ordinarily immediately after the national convention, by the party's presidential nominee. If a vacancy occurs between campaigns in the chairmanship of the party in power, the President customarily fills the vacancy.[8] If the chairmanship of the party out of power becomes vacant between campaigns, the national committee elects a new chairman.[9] These elections may be a test of strength between leaders or factions of the party and sometimes they reflect a dispute over policy. Thus, in August, 1949 the Republican national committee elected Guy Gabrielson as its chairman. He had the support of forces friendly to

[7] Cabell Phillips, "Party Chairman: Study in Feuds and Funds," *New York Times Magazine*, July 1, 1956.

[8] The nominee or the President may assure himself that his candidate for the chairmanship is not unacceptable to the leaders of important party factions. In 1953 both Taft and Dewey approved Leonard W. Hall before he was endorsed by Eisenhower for the Republican chairmanship. The committee, after Hall assured it that he would strive to give committeemen more of a hand in the distribution of patronage, elected him unanimously. In 1957 Eisenhower settled on H. Meade Alcorn Jr., to succeed Hall, a choice the committee ratified without dissent although some of its members would have preferred a chairman who was less of a "modern Republican."

[9] Ralph Goldman finds significant differences in the personal characteristics of Democratic and Republican national chairman. Although both parties tend to select men with long records of party service who live in pivotal states, the Democrats tend more to Roman Catholics than do the Republicans. Moreover, the only three national chairmen not native-born were Democrats.—*Party Chairmen and Party Factions, 1789–1900* (University of Chicago Ph.D. thesis, 1951, MS), pp. 45–55.

Senator Taft. The choice by the Democratic committee of Paul M. Butler in December, 1954 was regarded, perhaps erroneously, as a victory for the Stevenson wing of the party.

The broad position of the chairman may be inferred from the customs governing his designation. He is, in effect, a personal agent of the candidate, of the President if his party is in power; he may achieve a degree of independence if his party is out of power—a set of circumstances in which, however, he has little scope for action. Despite the limits of the office a few national chairmen have invested it with prestige and power; those who are credited with doing so happen to have been chairmen in palmy days of party victory. Mark Hanna, Will Hays, James A. Farley, and Leonard W. Hall are ranked among the great chairmen.[10] Farley's role as leader of the organization Democrats over the country has become legendary. The mass of professional party workers had a deep affection for him, a valuable asset to help keep the wheels of the organization turning. Yet the national chairman remains in a sense a hired man subject to the party's leader, the presidential candidate. No national chairman has built himself into a national boss. He is, in effect, a technician, a specialist in campaign management and machine tending, who holds his position by virtue of his relationship to the candidate.

The custom of designating the personal agent of the presidential nominee as national chairman has its disadvantages for the work of the national committee. The disruption of the committee's work is magnified by the fact that a new chairman often replaces most of the principal staff members with persons of his own choosing. In 1952 Clarence Budington Kelland, Arizona Republican national committeeman, attacked the custom of permitting the presidential nominee "to destroy a going organization on the eve of the campaign"; his pronouncements seem to have had no perceptible effect on practice. The parties would benefit from a well-managed headquarters staff with continuity of personnel, but they have not managed to create a "permanent undersecretary" for the national party staff.[11]

National chairman: Activities between campaigns. Between campaigns both chairmen are beset by the problem of raising money; otherwise the

[10] See James A. Farley, *Behind the Ballots* (New York: Harcourt, Brace, 1938); *The Memoirs of Will H. Hays* (Garden City: Doubleday, 1955); Herbert Croly, *Marcus Alonzo Hanna* (New York: Macmillan, 1912); Stewart Alsop, "Barnum of the G.O.P.," *Saturday Evening Post*, May 26, 1956 (on Leonard Hall).

[11] After his nomination in 1956 Stevenson did not replace the national chairman, Paul M. Butler, with James Finnegan, who had managed his campaign for the nomination. Congressional leaders came to the support of Butler and Stevenson acceded to their demand for his retention.

role of the chairman of the victorious party differs materially from that of the chairman of the losers. The custom used to be that the chairman of the victors became Postmaster General, a post that once controlled the largest single repository of federal patronage. The national chairmanship has become a full-time job, post-office patronage has become relatively less important than it once was, and, if two precedents make a custom, the positions have been separated. In the 1940's the Democrats made their chairmanship a full-time, well-paid position. Arthur E. Summerfield, when appointed Postmaster General by Eisenhower in 1953, resigned as Republican national chairman.

The post of national chairman of the ins takes on special importance either when a new President has been elected or when party control of the government has just changed. In either event a considerable reshuffling of top governmental personnel is in store. Applicants for patronage jobs must usually "clear" through the office of the national chairman, who must dispense patronage and favors in a manner to keep peace and harmony in the organization as well as to reward the truly deserving. Furthermore, he has to satisfy, in so far as practicable, those who hold liens on party action by virtue of their campaign contributions. By judicious and discreet intervention at troublesome points in the party organization over the country he seeks to strengthen the support of the Administration, to iron out local disputes, and to encourage state and congressional candidacies that may strengthen the party.

The President may call on his national chairman for aid in holding party lines in Congress on important votes. On occasion Jim Farley quietly aided Roosevelt in lining up congressional support. Under President Truman the Democratic national chairman's function with respect to policy expanded, or at least became more visible. His staff came to engage in more extensive propaganda in support of Administration policy and at times he attempted to stir up grassroots pressure to bring recalcitrant Democratic Senators and Representatives into line. In the unsuccessful endeavor in 1949 to obtain Senate confirmation of the reappointment of Leland Olds as a member of the Federal Power Commission, the national chairman, William M. Boyle, Jr., wired national committeemen and state chairmen for support in convincing the reluctant Democratic Senators that the rank and file of the party was with the President. Rejection of the nomination would be, he said, "a defeat for the millions of Americans who are entitled to fair power rates and a victory for the power lobbyists and the Republican party." The action was taken at the instruction of the President, who regarded the appointment as in execution of party pledges on utility policy.

Senators and Representatives, especially those in disagreement with the

President, do not take kindly to his use of the machinery of the national committee to attempt to maintain party discipline in Congress. Nor do they relish the propaganda activities of the national committee on controversial issues even though it may be merely supporting platform planks duly approved by the national convention. For example, Robert Hannegan, Democratic national chairman, in 1946 got caught in the crossfire between the conservative and liberal wings of his party. A series of pronouncements by him and by the editors of national committee propaganda sheets led to a caucus of southern Democratic House members who wanted Hannegan's scalp but agreed to be satisfied with apologies and retractions.

The national chairman of the party out of power is beset by different, if not fewer, worries than the chairman whose party holds the Presidency. Not long since, the national organization of the minority party was practically nonexistent between campaigns. In the 1920's Franklin Roosevelt observed that the Democratic national headquarters consisted of "two ladies occupying one room in a Washington office building." Over the past 30 years the national organizations of the minority have become far more active in the periods between presidential campaigns. After his defeat in 1928, Al Smith suggested that the minority party carry on a positive educational program rather "than sit by and adopt a policy of inaction with the hope of profiting solely by the mistakes or failures of the opposition." In 1929, with the appointment of Charles Michelson as director of publicity for the Democratic national committee, the minority party took the offensive. The publicity division prepared statements to be released mainly under the name of Democratic Senators and Representatives in criticism of majority policies. The minority obtained a wide hearing for its attacks on majority policy, irritated Republican leaders, and seldom failed to take advantage of an error by the majority. The barrage of publicity helped lay the basis for Democratic victory in 1932.[12]

. The national chairman of the outs has an opportunity to move into the vacuum created by the lack of a dominant party leader and to function as party spokesman. Yet the antagonisms between the congressional wing of the party and the presidential wing make it necessary that he tread warily. The congressional wing, even though it may reflect a special shade of opinion in the party, regards itself as authorized to make the record

[12] See T. S. Barclay, "The Publicity Division of the Democratic Party, 1929–30," *American Political Science Review*, 25 (1931), pp. 68–72; Charles Michelson, *The Ghost Talks* (New York: Putnam's, 1944), ch. 2. Probably reflective of the earlier intermittent character of the activities of the national committees is the fact that the records of both committees before 1928 have been either lost or destroyed. See D. R. McCoy, "The Records of the Democratic and Republican National Committees," *The American Archivist*, 14 (1951), pp. 313–321.

and the issues for the party. That sector of the party leadership with a national outlook points to the necessity of a program that will appeal to those areas in which the party congressional representation is weak.[13] The situation places the national chairman of the outs between conflicting forces. About the only safe course for him to follow is to limit his pronouncements to criticisms of the Administration and studiously avoid the enunciation of party position on new or controverted issues. Paul Butler, in the antecedents to 1956, developed the themes of the "give-away" of resources, the part-time Presidency, the capture of government by big business, all more or less noncontroversial propositions—at least within Democratic ranks.[14]

One of the incidental worries of the minority chairman is how to keep his job. As the designee of a defeated presidential candidate he may lack prestige in the party; then, too, he is likely to become the victim of maneuver for control of the party machinery by factions interested either in party policy or in the next nomination. During the long Republican minority era after 1932 that party's national chairmanship frequently became a bone of contention among party factions. Herbert Brownell, chairman designated by Dewey in 1944, for example, found it expedient to resign in 1946. One consideration was the fear by some of the party that Mr. Brownell might use his post to promote the renomination of Mr. Dewey in 1948. At a meeting of the national committee preceding Mr. Brownell's resignation one committeeman had expressed the view that there should be a new chairman "as pure as Caesar's wife, who does not have to determine whether his personal interest and his interest in Tom Dewey are more important than his interest in the Republican party and the United States of America."

Senatorial and congressional campaign committees. The party groups in both House and Senate maintain campaign committees. The National Republican Congressional Committee, the Democratic National Congressional Committee, the Democratic Senatorial Campaign Committee, and the National Republican Senatorial Committee exist independently of the national committees and are accountable to their respective legislative groups. The Democratic congressional committee, for example, according

[13] C. A. H. Thomson, "Research and the Republican Party," *Public Opinion Quarterly,* 3 (1939), pp. 306–313. Since the Congressional Reorganization Act of 1946 the minority in the Senate has had the services of the staffs of the Senate policy committees and in both chambers legislators have had more ample staff assistance.
[14] These themes can be traced in the *Democratic Digest,* a magazine published by the national committee. The official line of the Republican national headquarters is disseminated through *Straight From the Shoulder, A Journal of Political Fact,* a monthly publication.

to the party rules "has no organic connection with either the Democratic National Convention or the Democratic National Committee." It cooperates with the national committee and with the senatorial committee but "it has no official connection or fiscal relation with either." [15] Though the autonomous position of these committees parallels the separation of powers, the notion of an independent congressional campaign committee is said to have originated at a time of strained relations between President Johnson and the Republican majority of Congress in 1866. Lest the President use the national committee against it, the party in Congress formed an independent committee to campaign for the election of Republican Representatives in 1866. Later the Democrats created such a committee. With the adoption of popular election of Senators a need for senatorial committees arose.

The Republican congressional committee consists of one Representative designated by the Republican delegation from each state with Republican representation in the House. The Democratic national congressional committee likewise consists of a Representative similarly chosen from each state with Democratic representation, although the Democratic committee chairman may also appoint a woman member from each state on recommendation of the state's regular committee member, an option not often exercised. Thus each committee consists of from 35 to 40 members and each is equipped with a staff and several subcommittees.

In recent years the activities of the Republican congressional committee have been far more extensive than those of the Democratic committee, a difference reflected in their 1954 expenditures, $706,000 and $208,000. The staff of the Republican committee collects data about close districts, analyzes the records of incumbent Democrats, conducts general publicity, provides publicity and other campaign services for Republican incumbents and to a lesser extent to nonincumbent Republican candidates, and attempts to stimulate local organizations to put forward promising candidates. In 1954 a staff of about 30 persons dedicated its efforts to these activities. The Democratic committee has had a far smaller staff, not more than a half dozen, and has provided its candidates with fewer services. In addition to staff services, both committees make contributions, usually fairly small, to the campaigns of at least some of their House candidates.

The Democratic senatorial campaign committee exists independently of the congressional and national committees. An organ of the Democratic group within the Senate, it usually consists of approximately seven members appointed by the Democratic Senate leader. Members are chosen biennially from among those Senators not facing campaigns for re-election. Nor is a Senator with a senatorial colleague of his own party up for re-

[15] *Proceedings,* 1948 Democratic National Convention, pp. 548–549.

election in his own state eligible for membership. The Republican senatorial campaign committee, named by a chairman designated by the Republican Senate conference, varies in size from four to ten members.

Both senatorial committees maintain headquarters in the Senate Office Building in Washington and have small staffs—usually not more than five. The staffs engage in publicity work, dig up data for their party's candidates, provide campaign speakers, and generally make themselves useful. The committees allocate funds to candidates, again on a relatively small scale—in so far as the record goes.

The existence of the three national authorities—the national committee, the senatorial committee, and the congressional committee—for each party creates its administrative difficulties. The relationships among the committees vary from time to time and range from hostility to friendly collaboration. Special problems arise in raising money, since contributors become unhappy when approached by several solicitors from the same party. The Republicans maintain a combined financing operation, put the bee on contributors only once, and divided the proceeds among the committees. Democrats are in this respect, as in many others, less systematic and more variable in their practices.[16] Nor does the division of concern about national elections among the three committees simplify the conduct of campaigns, yet the existence of the independent senatorial and congressional committees enables the congressional wing of a party, or so it believes, to protect itself against neglect by the national committee.

State committees. The next layer below the national party organs, though by no means subordinate to them, consists of the state committees of the parties. Variety characterizes their composition, method of selection, duties, and even formal titles. They range in size from a handful to a group that can meet only in a convention hall. Their authority at one extreme amounts to that of a constituent body for the party in the state; at the other, it amounts to little more than the ministerial performance of duties minutely prescribed by statute.

Whereas the national committee exists as an extralegal creation of the national convention, state committees ordinarily are based on legislative act. State committees—sometimes called state central committees or state executive committees—are built on electoral subdivisions of the state. The Kansas state committee, for example, consists of the chairman and vice-chairman of each of the county committees, a total of 210 members. The voters of each of Alabama's congressional districts choose at the

[16] These paragraphs lean heavily on the admirable report by Hugh A. Bone, "Some Notes on the Congressional Campaign Committees," *Western Political Quarterly,* 9 (1956), pp. 116–137.

party primary eight members of the 72-member state committee. In some instances state legislative districts constitute the geographical base of the committee. The delegates to Texas state conventions from each of the state's 31 senatorial districts designate one man and one woman to membership on the state committee. Usually the state chairman occupies a position vis-à-vis the gubernatorial candidate like that of the national chairman in relation to the presidential candidate.

The method of selection, as these instances indicate, differs from state to state. Some state executive committee members hold their posts ex officio by virtue of their position in county units of the party. Others may be selected by county conventions, as in South Carolina where each county convention elects a member of the state committee. The direct primary is a common method of selection. In Illinois and in Ohio the party voters in the primaries elect state committee members in congressional districts; in Massachusetts the state senatorial districts are areas for the selection of state committee members. In some states the delegates to the state convention from the county or other representative district select a member of the state committee. In other instances a single committee may have members chosen in different ways. California's state central committee of over 600 members consists of delegates to the state convention, all county chairmen, and three appointees of each convention delegation. Such an institution provides a means for bestowing minor honors on the party faithful but can hardly be an agency for the conduct of party business which, thus, has to be handled through an executive committee.

Although the chief function of state committees is the conduct of campaigns through their officers and agents, they also exercise other duties in connection with the government of the party. The range of these functions and the degree of discretion vested in the committee are widest in the southern states and in a few other states in which the party has been subjected to least detailed statutory regulation. Included in the powers of state committees (but not necessarily within the powers of any single committee) are such matters as the following, when not otherwise regulated by law or party rule: issuance of the call for the state convention, selection of temporary officers for the convention, preparation of a temporary list of delegates, fixing the time of the primary, prescribing standards for party membership for participation in primaries, making nominations to fill vacancies by death or disqualification in the party slate of nominees, canvassing and certifying results of primaries, deciding primary contests, and generally supervising the party's primaries.[17]

[17] In some southern states the party organization could be called "nonpartisan" in state and local matters. The party organization does not need to conduct a general

The state committee may also exert a determining influence in the choice of delegates to the national convention, a factor that on occasion underlies struggles for committee control. The committee itself selects them in some states. In states that choose their delegates by convention the factional leader who has allied with himself most of the members of the state committee may enjoy great advantage. Even when the delegates are chosen by direct primary, control of the committee may be worth a battle. Thus, in California in 1954 a coalition including Senator William F. Knowland and Governor Goodwin J. Knight captured the Republican state central committee against forces allied with Vice-President Richard M. Nixon. The maneuver was not unconnected with the possibility that General Eisenhower would not run in 1956 and that Mr. Knowland might seek the nomination. Again, in Texas in 1956 Senator Lyndon Johnson and Representative Sam Rayburn fought successfully for control of the Texas state Democratic organization for objectives of national rather than state politics.

County committees. The county committee constitutes a unit of major significance in the party machinery and its chairman may be a local political potentate of considerable importance. Most commonly the county committee is an assemblage of the party's precinct committeemen, township committeemen, or party functionaries from other subdivisions of the county. The county committee concerns itself with campaigns for county offices; it is ordinarily tied into the state organization, formally or informally, through the county chairman. The 3,000 or so county chairmen of each party are the second lieutenants, or perhaps the non-coms, of the political army and have under their immediate direction and leadership the troops—the party workers who get out the vote.

The lowest, or perhaps the basic, layer of the party organization consists of the precinct captains or committeemen, sometimes elected by the members of the party in the precinct through the direct primary, sometimes selected by precinct conventions or caucuses, and in some instances appointed by higher authority. The precincts or election districts number more than 100,000.

Usually the statutes or rules also provide for party committees for districts not coterminous with counties from which officials are elected. The county chairmen of the counties included within a congressional district

---

election campaign. It tends to be obligated to neutrality among candidates in the primary. Often it conducts the primary, a role which also imposes an obligation of impartiality toward candidates and factions within the party. Control of the state committee is important in such states for its uses in the choice of delegates to presidential nominating conventions and in other phases of presidential politics.

may, for example, constitute a district committee. Similarly, committees may be provided for state legislative and judicial districts. Ordinarily these district committees play no significant role in party affairs and often remain dormant unless they are called upon to perform some statutory duty, such as filling a vacancy on the ticket.[18]

Interrelationships of organizational strata. The foregoing description suggests the bare contours of the formal party organization which has its roots in the electorate at the precinct level and reaches an apex in the office of national chairman. The entire structure is often likened to a military hierarchy, yet that conception is erroneous. County, state, and national party organs are each to a degree autonomous. So far as the formal authority goes the national chairman cannot issue directions to the state chairmen or the state chairman to the county chairmen. Though the levels of party organization are intimately interrelated, the linkage is from the bottom up rather than from the top down. This type of relationship appears strikingly in those instances in which precinct executives come together as a county committee which elects the county chairman; the county chairmen foregather as the state committee which chooses the state chairman; and now, on the Republican side, a great many state chairmen happen to be members of the national committee.[19] Even when the formal procedures do not provide such a pattern of interconnections, similar sorts of interrelationships often develop. Members of party committees, no matter what the committee's level, usually have a base of power in some geographical area smaller than the jurisdiction of the committee on which they sit. An influential county committeeman is apt

[18] The organizational apparatus of both parties includes various auxiliary groups, such as the Young Republican Federation and the Young Democratic Clubs of America. For several years Americans for Democratic Action functioned in effect as a progressive lobbying, agitational, and campaigning group auxiliary to the Democratic party. Its leadership consisted mainly of prominent New Dealers and Fair Dealers. In 1950, however, the ADA eliminated from its constitution a commitment to the Democratic party and asserted an intention to "continue to work for the nomination and election of candidates for public office of whatever party, when their records are consistent with the principles of ADA." In practice, the ADA rarely finds it necessary to endorse a Republican candidate. On its activities, see *Hearings*, House Select Committee on Lobbying Activities, 81st Congress, 2nd sess., Pt. 6 (July, 1950). To be differentiated from the standing auxiliary apparatus of parties are the organizations either activated or improvised at campaign time such as Citizens for Eisenhower.

[19] Before the 1952 Republican convention placed certain state chairmen on the national committee, midwestern and mountain state chairmen had complained of the weakness of the influence of the state organizations in the affairs of the national committee. The national committeeman does not invariably effectively link national headquarters and the state organization.

to be a power in his precinct, township, or election district. A member of the state committee to be reckoned with is usually a leader of note in his county. And those national committeemen whose word is paid much heed are men who have achieved prominence in their state organizations. Advancement in the political organization tends to be an expansion of influence from a geographical base rather than an ascent up a ladder.[20]

Unity and Disunity: National Party

Such are the broad outlines of the manner in which the party activists organize themselves to do the party's work. Viewed over the entire nation, the party organization constitutes no disciplined army. It consists rather of many state and local points of power, each with its own local following and each comparatively independent of external control. Each of the dispersed clusters of party professionals has its own concerns with state and local nominations and elections. Each has a base for existence independent of national politics. Each in fact enjoys such independence that more than a tinge of truth colors the observation that there are no national parties, only state and local parties.[21] Yet in one way or another the vast and cumbersome decentralized and dispersed party apparatus is brought to life as a national party organization. At the call of the national committee,[22] the state committees set into motion the processes for the choice of delegates to the national conventions (unless that function has been pre-empted by public authority), and the state party organizations bestir themselves to play a part in the choice of a presidential candidate.

[20] The interconnection of levels of organization is illustrated by the multiple roles in 1956 of the Hon. W. L. Dawson, Democratic Representative from Illinois. He was a precinct captain, a ward committeeman, vice-chairman of the Cook county Democratic committee, secretary of the Democratic congressional campaign committee, and vice-chairman of the Democratic national committee.

[21] President Eisenhower, when questioned in a press conference in October, 1956 about the somewhat doubtful "new Republicanism" of several Old Guard Senators, responded: "Now, let's remember, there are no national parties in the United States. There are forty-eight state parties, then they are the ones that determine the people that belong to those parties. There is nothing I can do to say that no one is not a Republican. The most I can say is that in many things they do not agree with me. . . . We have got to remember that these are state organizations, and there is nothing I can do to say so-and-so is a Republican and so-and-so is not a Republican."—Press conference of October 11, 1956.

[22] The call for the Republican national convention specifies that the secretary of the national committee shall promulgate the call by "sending a copy thereof to the two members of the Republican National Committee from each State, . . . and to enclose therewith copies of the Call for the Chairman and Secretary respectively of the State Central Committee or governing committee of the party therein, to be forwarded to said Chairman and Secretary respectively by the members of the Republican National Committee in and for said State."

Once the nomination is made the party apparatus becomes a mechanism for nation-wide electioneering.

National organization a combination or coalition. What holds the elements of the national party organization together? What gives it such unity as it has? What are the counter forces that create centers of autonomy within the party? If the organization is not strictly hierarchical, what is its character? These questions of the degree of unity and disunity within the national party organization usually arouse extensive comment about the lack of discipline rather than awe that at least a modicum of unity is achieved among political activists spread across a continent.

To explain the unity that develops within the national party organization one must look beyond the apparatus of party machinery itself and examine the social matrix within which the organization exists. The groups, classes, and sorts of people that attach themselves to each of the major parties have been identified in an earlier chapter. The geographically dispersed clusters of activists who make up the party organization are anchored, wherever they are, in those sectors of the community loyal to their party. These social interests, though scattered, may have parallel or common objectives. When Republican leaders gather in national conclave, they tend to share an outlook springing from their association with the business elements of their home communities. When the Democratic professionals convene, many of them, by virtue of their positions at home, will be oriented favorably towards organized labor; others will be bound together by a concern over the peculiar problems of the South. The social context of national party organization contributes to its internal cleavages as well as to its unity.[23]

All the factors that contribute to the grouping of sectors of the electorate into each of the party followings assure a degree of cohesiveness within the national party machinery. When it is said that national party is a coalition, the reference may be to the coalition or combination of social interests for which the party speaks. That combination induces unity within the political machinery, narrowly defined, and the combination may, of course, be to a degree a product of the workings of the party machinery.

It is well and good to emphasize the fundamental importance to na-

[23] From reflections such as these some observers leap to the conclusion that party organization is simply derivative of some more inclusive informal organization or power structure of society. That line of argument, to which sociologists seem to be especially dedicated, should be taken with reserve. Certainly at times a party machine acts clearly and devotedly as an agent for other interests in society. On the other hand, it always enjoys a sphere of independence and not infrequently becomes master of its own supposed principal.

tional party organization of the underlying coalition of social blocs and interests. Yet it remains for the politicians to work out the details and terms of the coalition. That process starkly reveals the nonhierarchical structure of national party organization. The party nationally tends to be an alliance of state and city leaders who work together most faithfully during a presidential campaign. The national committee is a gathering of sovereigns (or their emissaries) to negotiate and treat with each other rather than a staff conclave of subordinates of the national chairman. The basic coalition-forming process occurs in the national convention which nominates the candidate who succeeds in lining up a commanding block of state organizations. The nominee symbolizes the terms of the coalition at the moment; the platform may make them explicit. Or, on occasion, the decisions of the convention may leave gaping cleavages indicative of the inability of the politicians to bridge the differences among the elements of the party.

As party leaders in conventions and other conclaves maneuver to put together winning coalitions, "political" interests become involved that are quite separate and independent from the "social" interests underlying the party. Politicians, at least save in exceptional circumstances, want to win elections and they may be pulled together by a common "political interest."

Party discipline in presidential campaigns. Within the broad limits set by the composition of the party coalition, the national organization may be unified in greater or lesser degree by energetic and skillful leadership. During a national campaign the tethers linking the state organizations to the national chairman tend to be less slack than at other times. The hope for victory induces a willingness to accept leadership. The stronger that hope, the more cohesive is the national organization. If the presidential candidate seems to be a sure loser, the national chairman is apt to be as a sovereign without subjects.

In earlier times the national organization doled out sums from its war chest to state and local organizations and gained authority over the general conduct of the campaign. Although subventions from the national party to state parties have declined since the Hatch Act limited national committee expenditures to three million dollars in any one year, the national leaders are in contact with the sources of funds and can aid a local organization by steering contributions to it.

Some of the difficulties of whipping the state organizations together in a national campaign come from the administrative frailties of a huge organization, manned largely by volunteers and often at critical points by incompetents. In the campaigns of 1932 and 1936 James A. Farley,

Democratic national chairman, undertook to cut through the administrative layers to tie the local party committeemen more closely to the national committee. The national headquarters sent campaign literature in small quantities to each precinct committeeman in contrast with the previous practice of hopefully sending literature in bulk to state committees for redistribution to local workers. Mr. Farley observed that the

. . . fellow out in Kokomo, Indiana, who is pulling doorbells night after night and respectfully asking his neighbors to vote the straight Democratic ticket gets a thrill if he receives a letter on campaigning postmarked Washington or New York; and we made sure that this pleasure was not denied him.[24]

If the presidential candidate lends strength to the ticket, the state and local organizations can be expected ordinarily to work in harmony with the national leaders during campaigns. Without much urging from national headquarters, the state organization will agitate for Eisenhower and Stratton, or Eisenhower and Elmer Smith, or whoever the local candidate is. When the presidential nominee is thought to handicap the party's candidates for state and local office, the state and local organizations often keep quiet about the national ticket, endorse it in muted tones, or even quietly cut the head of the ticket. Though the national chairman lacks effective sanctions against such tactics of nonco-operation, a presidential candidate, unexpectedly elected, can even out old scores in the allocation of patronage. The manner in which local leaders adapt themselves to the expectation that the national ticket will lose is illustrated by a statement by a Philadelphia Republican leader concerning the 1936 campaign: [25]

The result was such an overwhelming repudiation of the Republican Party in our section that I have never seen the like of it, and hope never to see it again. In a normal Republican district of 9,000 votes Landon was able to get only 1,300, a little over 7,700 going to Roosevelt. I might say that as soon as I sensed the sentiment I considered it advisable to go easy in my efforts to push the candidacy of Landon and concentrated on the local ticket. In this I was successful to a degree, having a difference of nearly 500 votes in favor of the local candidates over the head of the ticket. Nevertheless I was not able to carry them because people were still afraid to split their vote on the machine.

State leaders who bolt the party to support the presidential candidate of the opposition party or of a third party place the ultimate strain on the national organization. Certain sorts of penalties, if not preventives, are available to the national committees. The Republican national committee may declare vacant the seat of any member who refuses to support the

[24] J. A. Farley, *Behind the Ballots* (New York: Harcourt, Brace, 1938), pp. 159–160.
[25] J. T. Salter, "Letters from Men in Action," *National Municipal Review*, 26 (1937), p. 422.

presidential nominee. The Democratic committee has exercised the same power, although its authority to do so did not become explicit until 1952. The Democratic committee in 1949 struck from its membership rolls the names of six Dixiecrats from four southern states—Mississippi, South Carolina, Alabama, and Louisiana. After the Texas national committeeman supported Eisenhower in 1952, the committee refused to recognize him as a member. In 1956, as a part of the compromise over the loyalty pledge for convention delegates, the Democrats adopted a requirement that every member of the national committee "declare affirmatively for the nominees of the convention." Failure to do so would be cause for expulsion by the committee. The same compromise expressed the "understanding" that by sending delegates to the convention each state Democratic party undertook to see that the voters of their state had an opportunity to vote for electors pledged to the convention nominees.

Such aggravated situations as the difficulties of the Democratic national organization with some of its southern state subsidiaries cannot be coped with by administrative sanctions. They are symptomatic of the existence in the party of an irreconcilable element rather than of defects of organizational arrangements. To maintain party unity the incompatible element must be driven from the party or ousted from control of the state organization. When in 1956 in several southern states Democratic leaders dedicated to Republicanism lost control of the party organizations to leaders committed to the support of the national party nominees, the problem of discipline disappeared. Although individuals may be dealt with to some extent by the application of sanctions,[26] when an entire state organization declines to go along with the national party the penalties are of little avail.[27]

Patronage: A cohesive factor? The party in power nationally has much greater opportunity and much greater resources than the party out of power to construct a truly national party organization. The patronage

[26] The party groups in House and Senate occasionally apply sanctions of a sort against their members who bolt the party in a presidential campaign. The House Democratic patronage committee, for example, cut off the patronage of Adam Clayton Powell, who supported Eisenhower in 1956. In a few instances Senators have been deprived of committee assignments, given undesirable assignments, or excluded from the caucus.

[27] The national organization, of course, has even less sanction against local organizations that may fail to support, or may even oppose, the presidential candidate. In 1948, for example, the Democratic organization of the third election district of Baltimore County, Maryland, formally resolved that no member of the executive committee would be ousted if he supported the States' Rights presidential candidate while working for the Democratic ticket locally.—*Baltimore Evening Sun*, September 21, 1948. In scattered instances in 1948, however, county and city committees did expel members who failed to support the national ticket.

in the hands of the national leaders is great enough to weld the state machines into a semblance of national unity. The power of patronage, among a great many other things, is reflected in the fact that a President can usually gain a renomination at the end of his first term. Patronage ties state organizations to the national leadership most effectively in those states in which the national majority is a weak minority locally. Southern Republican organizations historically have been beholden to the national leadership for favors received. Democratic organizations in Republican strongholds occupy, when Democrats control the national government, a similar relationship of dependency.

Serious limitations restrict the utility of patronage in the binding of state and local centers of power to the national leadership. In a measure, patronage distribution may be guided by commitments, tacit or explicit, made in the formation of the combination that won the nomination for the President. State organizations, moreover, demand their share as a matter of right and attempt to reduce the President's discretion in using patronage to strengthen his personal following. Furthermore, in the distribution of patronage, Senators and Representatives have an important voice, and they are not interested in building an organization with power centered in the hands of the national leaders. Instead, they wish to strengthen their own organizations or those state or district organizations with which they are affiliated. And when patronage appointments are made on the recommendations of Senators and Congressmen, the appointments will be such as to strengthen allegiances to the state and local organization.[28]

Senatorial courtesy may give state leaders quite as much control of some appointments as the President has. In 1950, for example, President Truman appointed Martin A. Hutchinson, of Virginia, to a post on the Federal Trade Commission, which required senatorial confirmation. Hutchinson had long been a prominent leader of the anti-Byrd faction in the Virginia Democratic party and had also led the 1948 campaign in the state for Truman while the regular Democratic organization remained neutral. At the urging of Senator Byrd the Senate refused to confirm the nomination. Thus the President was blocked in an attempt to recognize a Democratic faction loyal to the party nationally. In any event, patronage is of doubtful efficacy in the construction of an organization loyal to the national leadership against the opposition of a hostile state machine. The Indiana Republican state chairman, who did not much like Ike, remarked in 1957 to reporters: "I've told Alcorn [the Republican national chairman] that he better not hand out any patronage in this state

[28] See J. P. Harris, *The Advice and Consent of the Senate* (Berkeley: University of California Press, 1953).

without going through us. . . . I said that if there is anything like that, the national committee will not get a cent from Indiana."

Such power as patronage does give the national leadership was weakened by the passage of the Hatch Act in 1939. This act forbids federal employees—with the exception of the Chief Executive, heads and assistant heads of departments, and certain other policy-forming officials—to take any active part "in political management or in political campaigns." All persons employed in "any administrative position" are prohibited from exercising their "official authority for the purpose of interfering with, or affecting the election or the nomination of any candidate for the office of President, Vice-President, Presidential elector, Member of the Senate, or Member of the House of Representatives, Delegates or Commissioners from the Territories and insular possessions." Prominent among the congressional advocates of the legislation were Republicans supported by organizations built around state and local governments and Democrats fearful that their own political careers might be endangered by strong national party leadership built in part on patronage.

National party role in legislative elections. The centripetal influences of the presidential campaign induce a degree of unity in the party organization over the entire nation during a campaign. Yet that unity is the consequence of a coalition, a parallelism of interest, rather than of the power of national party headquarters. The role of the national leadership in the election of Senators and Representatives reflects the underlying nature of national party structure. A truly national party would have some influence over the designation of candidates for the Senate and the House; a slate of candidates would be supported for nomination consisting of persons with views generally in accord with national party policies. Instead, state and local leaders insist that the choice of party candidates for the Senate and House is a local matter.[29] They resent and generally defeat efforts by national leaders to participate in such nominations.[30] In turn, the national party leadership usually considers itself bound to support for election the local nominees bearing the party label whatever their views on party

[29] Congressional nominations are treated in Chapter 16.
[30] Contrast the situation in England: "In the matter of candidatures the Central Offices have control. The Labour Party in its constitution requires that before any parliamentary candidate can be regarded as finally adopted for a constituency as a candidate of the Labour Party, his candidature must be sanctioned by the National Executive. This requirement goes farther than that of either of the two other parties but the practice is quite the same in all parties. A Tory who is *persona non grata* is not likely to be nominated against the objection of the Central Office, and in normal times the same has been true of the Liberals."—J. K. Pollock, "British Party Organization," *Political Science Quarterly*, 45 (1930), pp. 164–165.

policy may be.[31] Thus, Eisenhower endorses a McCarthy, a Jenner, a Welker, men not conspicuous in their support of his policy inclinations. One of the prices of unity in support of the presidential nominee is a tolerance by the national leadership of the diverse shades of opinion within the party coalition. If politics did not make strange bedfellows, there could be no national party.[32]

Political bases of organizational decentralization. Both unity and disunity within the national organization have their roots in the diverse social, economic, and political interests in the party following. Yet another foundation of deconcentration of party leadership is the federal form of government. State and local party organizations are built up around the patronage of state and local government; and these organizations, particularly in cities and states dominated by one party, have a continuous life regardless of whether the party is in or out of power nationally. State and local patronage makes the local machine financially independent of the national headquarters and contributes to a spirit of independence. Federalism in our formal governmental machinery includes a national element independent of the states, but in our party organization the independent national element is missing. Party structure is more nearly confederative than federal in nature. The state and local machines, built on state patronage, are allied with or paralleled by machines built around the patronage controlled by Senators and Representatives; and owing to the method of dispensation of this patronage, the resultant machines are almost as independent of central control as are the purely local organizations. Federalism in government tends to encourage confederation in the party's government.

Informal Organization: State and Local

The discussion of the confederative character of national party organization has proceeded as if tightly organized party machines would be

---

[31] See C. A. Berdahl, "Party Membership in the United States," *American Political Science Review*, 36 (1942), pp. 16–18.

[32] National headquarters does support senatorial and congressional nominees with varying degrees of enthusiasm. In 1950 Howard Latourette, Democratic opponent of Wayne Morse in the Oregon senatorial campaign, submitted to national headquarters a campaign budget of $64,000. He received a check for $2,000 which he returned, with the charge that the national leadership preferred Morse, who often voted with Senate Democrats, over a genuine believer in "Democratic principles free from socialistic influence." In 1954 Democratic national chairman Stephen A. Mitchell refused to support, financially or otherwise, the House campaigns of James Roosevelt and Robert Condon in California. Mr. Condon had been labelled a "security risk" by the Atomic Energy Commission and Mr. Roosevelt had had his marital troubles.

found in the states and cities. In fact, behind the façade of the formal party organization the widest variety characterizes the actual organization of the political activists in the states and cities. The manner in which they manage to join forces to carry on the business of the party—the selection of candidates and the conduct of campaigns—varies greatly from place to place and from time to time in the same state or locality. Moreover, the extent to which the formal party organization—the formal mechanism prescribed by rule or statute—is the real organization differs from place to place. In some states it coincides with the working party organization; in other localities, manned by hacks, it is moribund, and groups of political workers completely outside the formal organization stir up candidates and advance their cause.

Types of organizational patterns. So few are the systematic analyses of the informal organization of parties that an attempt toward a typology of party structures would be hazardous. To suggest the range of variety, however, it may be useful to picture state and city organization as distributed along a scale from the highest degree of unity to complete fractionalization. The manner of the conduct of campaigns serves as a fairly reliable index to the nature of the organization of the professionals. A tightly knit clique of political activists ordinarily exists when campaign efforts are designed to promote the cause of the entire ticket, when the individual candidate usually says a good word for his running mates, when the canvassers work for the party cause rather than for individual candidates. Contrast with this the pulverization of the activists when it can scarcely be said that party organization exists. The gubernatorial candidate may have his own headquarters and his own campaign organization. Each other candidate on the ticket will have some sort of crew to prepare press releases, to mail literature, or to canvass the voters. Each candidate may carefully avoid involvement with other persons on the ticket and may even disassociate himself from his party label. Each may attempt to maximize his support from that sector of the electorate to which he presumably has the greatest appeal. This multiplicity of campaigns ordinarily reflects the existence, not of a cohesive stratum of political workers, but of a system of more or less allied clusters of professionals, each attached to the fortunes of an individual candidate.

The manner of nomination of candidates constitutes another index of the character of party organization. If a state or city committee endorses a slate of candidates for nomination in the primary and usually manages to bring about their nomination, often without even token primary opposition, a relatively cohesive organization probably exists. If on the other hand, the route to the primary nomination seems to be wide open and individual aspirants build their own organizations to fight for the nomination, a more fractionalized informal organization usually exists. Instead of a party organization, the actuality may be a congeries of personal and factional cliques.

Only the most impressionistic estimates can be made about the distribution of organizations along our scale. The common belief, whether right or wrong, is that party organizations east of the Mississippi and north of the Mason-Dixon line tend to be more cohesive than those of the West although conspicuous exceptions may be found on both sides of the River. Not infrequently a differentiation prevails between state and federal cliques: a cluster or clusters of activitists devote their efforts mainly to senatorial, congressional, and presidential politics; other clusters associate their fortunes with those of candidates for state and local office. Party structures are probably more tightly articulated in jurisdictions that nominate through the convention than in states with a custom of wide-open primary races.

Old-time reformers—and many Republicans—fondly believe that big city organizations tend more to dictatorial control than do those in the country. Probably city organizations are simply more conspicuous than rural and small-town machines.[33] Perhaps, too, state organizations tend to be less cohesive than city and county organizations. State organizations have the same problems of maintaining unity as does the national party organization. The state chairman, when he is more than a figurehead, may be only a moderator, a person acceptable to stronger men none of whom is powerful enough to control the state as a whole. County organizations go their own way and may or may not be well geared into state headquarters.

Party organization, old-style. Variety is the reality of party organization, but the stereotype of old-fashioned machine organization persists and is often regarded as more generally approximated than it actually is. Yet from place to place highly disciplined organizations continue to exist, chiefly with domains limited to counties and cities, much as they did in the past century.

The classic machine took a clearly hierarchical form, with a boss at the head of an organization of workers held together by the spoils of politics and capable of determining the party's nominations and of exerting a mighty influence in elections as well. In its most fully developed form the urban machine became the government in that many major decisions, as well as minor matters, were decided by the party functionaries who managed their puppets in public office.

[33] The Republican organizations of counties suburban to New York City appear to be much more firmly bossed than is the city Democratic organization.

Patronage is an important factor in building up lines of command and in establishing internal cohesion and discipline in the machine. Leaders who hire can also fire. In a machine-governed jurisdiction a large proportion of the officials of the party organization also hold public office, appointive or elective, and others may enjoy other perquisites or may be ambitious for public place. In a 1935 study of party committeemen in selected upstate New York cities, Professor Mosher found that 19 per cent of 3,618 committeemen had places on the public payroll. In Albany, 35 per cent of the Democratic committeemen were also public officials, and in Syracuse and Auburn the figure was 28.[34] In Chicago in 1928, 59.2 per cent of the precinct captains had public jobs.[35] "In the 689 districts in Pittsburgh," it was said in 1926, "all the outstanding district leaders, people that like to work at the polls and are interested in politics, are on the city or county pay roll."[36] Hugh Bone, in a 1952 study of a sample of Republican precinct committeemen in Seatttle, found 13.8 per cent to be public employees; the figure rose to 20 per cent when precinct committeewomen were classified according to their husbands' occupations.[37] How representative these cases are cannot be known. Certainly in many states and cities large proportions of party functionaries labor for the love of the game, for the recognition party posts bring them, and, frequently, because they are drafted by their fellow partisans to do a job they regard as a civic duty.

Patronage enables the organization leadership to weld together a cohesive group of workers animated by an appreciation of past favors and, even more, by an expectation of future rewards. The relationship is nicely illustrated by a noted statement by a Chicago ward leader to his precinct captains just before a 1926 party primary:

"I don't want applause; what I want first is pledge cards, but, more than that, votes. This is a real fight, and every man must do his share. Look at that chart—some of the precincts show no pledge cards at all. Who is the man from this precinct?"

"That's mine, Mr. ————. I have thirty cards at home and am just waiting to copy them before turning them in."

"You're expecting a raise in salary in your job, aren't you?"

"Yes sir."

[34] W. E. Mosher, "Party and Government Control at the Grass Roots," *National Municipal Review*, 24 (1935), pp. 15–18.

[35] H. F. Gosnell, *Machine Politics: Chicago Model* (Chicago: University of Chicago Press, 1937), p. 54.

[36] Testimony of Charles C. McGovern, Hearings before a Special Committee Investigating Expenditures in Senatorial Primary and General Elections, U.S. Senate, 69th Congress, 1st sess., pursuant to S. Res. 195 (1926), Pt. I, p. 109.

[37] Hugh A. Bone, *Grass Roots Party Leadership* (Bureau of Government Research, University of Washington, 1952).

"Carry your precinct or you not only won't get it, but you'll lose your job altogether.

"I don't want to scold, but I believe I've been as good to this ward as it has to me. . . . I want to say that if any man does not carry his precinct on the thirteenth of April, he'll be fired on the fourteenth. If a man means anything in his precinct, he can carry it. If he doesn't mean anything in his precinct, he has no business in politics and holding a job. The reason that _____ is on the ticket for municipal judge in spite of the fact that he is a new man in the ward is that he had the banner precinct. . . . I promise that whoever turns out the biggest vote in his precinct will be on the next county ticket, if I sit on the state committee, and I think I will.

"What is more, any of you that don't get out the vote and have jobs will lose them, and they'll go to those who do work and have no job. I'm looking at one right now that has no job, and he'll have one that someone else now has unless you get out the vote. Don't think I don't mean this. I've fired the ward committeeman and I've fired the president of this ward club, although he had a $6,000 job." [38]

Loyalty to the party machine depends by no means solely on the pecuniary tie. "In a few cases," Gosnell says in his study of Chicago precinct captains, "precinct captains were bound to their ward committeemen by personal ties of loyalty which grew out of crisis situations. When a ward boss could dramatically come to the rescue of some man who was in trouble with the police, he could count on that man for steady precinct work from that time on." [39] No less an authority than James A. Farley states that "those people who are inclined to imagine that patronage and patronage alone, is the only thing that keeps a political party knit together are off on a tangent that is about as far wrong as anything humanly could be. I am convinced," he says, "that with the help of a few simple ingredients like time, patience, and hard work, I could construct a major political party in the United States without the aid of a single job to hand out to deserving partisans." [40]

The ties of party loyalty, the obligations of individual to individual, the leverage of patronage, and the harnessed ambitions of men may create a compact and manageable group of party workers. Under ordinary circumstances, when the organization is not rent by dissension, it is almost futile to challenge it in the primaries. And if one controls the primary, he has gone a long way toward controlling all.

The organization is often pictured as a dictatorship, a description that fits in some localities at some times. More often the organization assumes

[38] C. H. Wooddy, *The Chicago Primary of 1926* (Chicago, University of Chicago Press, 1926), pp. 7–8.

[39] Gosnell, *op. cit.*, p. 67.

[40] *Behind the Ballots* (New York: Harcourt, Brace, 1938), p. 237.

the form of clusters of personal loyalties about nuclear individuals. The latter, in turn, are bound to persons higher up the hierarchy, often by materialistic ties, eventuating in a more or less effective control of the whole by a few individuals at the apex. Within this structure the more lowly offer a continuous challenge to the power of those higher up in the machine. Precinct captains seek to fight their way up the ladder. Ward leaders may look to the day when they may become city leader or, as a lesser achievement, extend their dominion over neighboring wards. In turn, the upper leadership occupies itself with purging the disloyal or rebellious by the withdrawal of patronage, by supporting a rival against the troublesome subordinate. By the continuing struggle within the organization those most fit for party warfare survive and a few men manage to climb to the top and establish themselves as upper-level leaders.[41]

In the orthodox accounts of organization potency prominence is given to the role of the precinct captain in rallying voters to the organization. The precinct executive "is the actual connecting link between the people and the organization, and he is the only connecting link—the only man in the machine who has any point of direct contact with the voters, who knows anything about them, who has any real influence with them." [42] In building a following the precinct executive can begin with his family, relatives, and friends. He can add the votes of those whose support can be recruited with election-day perquisites. He can usually designate two or three precinct election officials and thereby annex their votes and those of their families and friends.[43] On primary and election days he has at his disposal funds allocated to him for election-day expenses. He may have from $25 to $100 to hire watchers, runners, and other persons to get out the vote. With each accession to his payroll a vote or two or more is added to his little bloc.

The precinct captain, however, works throughout the year and adds

[41] The pros are not unaware of the natural processes of selection. In 1928, after the death of top Democratic leaders in Baltimore the lesser chieftains met and their decision was announced as follows: "We intend to work as a group for the harmonious carrying on the party affairs until a leader naturally develops. A boss cannot be selected, he must grow naturally. Some one in the group eventually will be recognized as having most power and as the wisest boss in the management of the party. Others will defer to that individual and he naturally will become the leader."—*Baltimore Evening Sun*, February 22, 1928.

[42] Frank R. Kent, *The Great Game of Politics* (Copyright, 1923, Doubleday, Doran and Company, Inc.), p. 1.

[43] The attractiveness of election-day jobs declines in periods of full employment. In St. Louis County in 1954 the county election board, to man the polls, had to summon about 75 persons to duty under its power to compel citizens to serve as precinct election officials.—*St. Louis Post-Dispatch*, August 3, 1954.

to his strength by continuous service to the voters of his precinct. Especially in the poorer neighborhoods he is likely to become a sort of social agency, distributing food to the needy and from time to time paying their rent and furnishing them with coal. W. S. Vare, Philadelphia Republican boss, boasted:

> In every precinct of the city there are two representatives of the Organization, elected directly at the Republican primaries and who are known as committeemen. They maintain contacts with the voters and are at their beck and call for 24 hours of each day of the year. In time of stress the poor or other unfortunates always turn to these Organization representatives to assist them. It is they that see that the sick are cared for and that the poor are provided for, and then even in death aid may be rendered. The Philadelphia Organization gives a real social service and one without red tape, and without class, religious, or color distinction.[44]

In addition to his social service work, the precinct executive serves as a buffer between governmental agencies and the voters of his precinct. He steers the alien through the naturalization procedure. He aids in obtaining private as well as governmental employment for the people of his precinct. He aids in contacts with public social agencies. He may see the judge and attempt to mix mercy with justice. In all these relationships he may obtain treatment for his friends that amounts to favoritism, but in a substantial proportion of these services he is primarily a guide. Governmental agencies are so numerous and complex that the average citizen is bewildered and does not know to whom to apply for any given service. The precinct executive "knows the ropes" and can be of service even when no question of favoritism is involved. Yet when he can have the traffic ticket "fixed" he can create a great obligation to himself.[45] By these means the working precinct executive can build a bloc of votes to be swung to the support of the organization slate in the primaries and mobilized for the party in the general election.[46]

Credulous students and Europeans subscribe to the view that the United States is blanketed by boss-led party organizations that subsist at the

[44] Quoted by D. H. Kurtzman, *Controlling Votes in Philadelphia* (Philadelphia, 1935), p. 29.

[45] See H. F. Gosnell, *Machine Politics: Chicago Model*, chs. 3 and 4; Roy V. Peel, *The Political Clubs of New York City* (New York: Putnam's, 1935); Sonya Forthal, *Cogwheels of Democracy, A Study of the Precinct Captain* (New York: The William-Frederick Press, 1946).

[46] Many are the tales of prodigious feats of precinct leaders in swinging the voters as they wish. Kurtzman, for example, tells of two Philadelphia committeemen who had been pardoned through the efforts of a man who subsequently became a candidate for a judgeship. Out of gratitude to this man they delivered to him 450 of the 460 votes cast in their division. For accounts of other like incidents, see Kurtzman, *op. cit.*, pp. 33–34.

public trough and command a following of voters attached to the party by a mixture of charity and chicanery. In some localities that sort of organization does exist. In others remnants of old-time organization remain. In still others the organization is most attenuated. The executive director of the Republican national committee reported that in 1948, 357 counties had no Republican chairman or vice-chairman and that 28,000 or almost one-fourth of all precincts had no Republican leadership. In the same year in Oregon the Democrats had operating organizations in only 13 of 36 counties. Nor are all of even the largest cities thoroughly organized. R. L. Morlan reported in 1949 that in no Minneapolis ward "is there a party organization adequately covering every precinct the year round." He says that "except in the weeks just preceding an important election, roughly 100 of the 634 possible precinct captaincies will be unfilled and not over half the remainder are filled by active party workers who can be depended upon all the time." [47]

Trends affecting party organization. Although we have no precise measures of the change, clearly over the past 50 years American party organizations have undergone radical alterations. Tightly managed state-wide party organization has become exceptional and has been largely replaced by a fractionalized system of personal and factional cliques of professionals within each party. Within cities and counties the same process of atomization has occurred, even though a few old-style machines remain. Along with these changes the capacity of the party organization to control nominations has declined markedly, and primary routs of famed old machines by upstarts recur. Politicians are not disappearing, to be sure, but the manner of their organization and operation are changing. Machines always have had their ups and downs but the American party machines have been undergoing secular changes rather than simply suffering periodic reverses. Moreover, the situations with which organizations must work have also undergone alteration, which, in turn, affects both the nature and effectiveness of the organization. All these trends, their exact nature and the magnitudes of their consequences, have not been carefully studied, but they may be taken into account here.

On the whole, the supply of public jobs to support organization workers has probably declined in the face of the rise of the merit system and the professionalization of the public service. The spoils system has not been eradicated and state and local services on occasion are shot through with patronage abuses, but for the country as a whole organizational cohesion born of a shared anxiety about job security is probably not what it was a half century ago.

[47] "City Politics: Free Style," *National Municipal Review*, 38 (1949), pp. 485–490.

Public welfare services now dwarf the old-time social services of the precinct captain and the ward boss. Some local machines have captured and converted the public welfare agencies to their purposes, but others have lost the battle to the professionals who man these new services. The voter now may not look to the district leader for a bucket of coal but may be concerned about how his Congressman votes on an amendment to the Social Security Act.

Dependent populations that once constituted bulwarks of organization strength have become far less numerous over the decades. After a generation or so education, cultural adaptation, economic advance create a new sort of population far less in need of the welfare services of the party and of its function of cushioning the relations of the group with a strange society. Pockets of manageable populations remain, Negroes in northern cities, for example,[48] but the characteristics of the population on which urban machines supposedly most depended have been substantially altered.

The people are different; so are the modes of communication with them. And the newer media of communication gain in importance as sources of political intelligence and as means of political manipulation in part because the people are different. Hence, to an extent startling in its degree in some jurisdictions, the doorbell ringers have lost their function of mobilizing the vote to the public-relations experts, to the specialists in radio and television, and to others who deal in mass communications.[49] A most striking illustration of the consequences of these changes occurred in the victory in 1951 of Rudolph Halley over the Democratic and Republican candidates for president of the New York City council. Halley's chief claim to fame was his service as counsel for the Kefauver crime committee whose dramatic hearings had been televised.

The general adoption of the direct primary opened the road for disruptive forces that gradually fractionalized the party organization. By permitting more effective direct appeals by individual politicians to the party membership, the primary system freed forces driving toward the disintegration of party organizations and the construction of factions and cliques attached to the ambitions of individual leaders. The convention system compelled leaders to treat, to deal, to allocate nominations; the primary permits individual aspirants by one means or another to build a wider following within the party. In some jurisdictions the revolt against the party organization associated with the introduction of the

---

[48] See John Madigan, "The Durable Mr. Dawson of Cook County, Illinois," *The Reporter*, August 9, 1956.

[49] See Norton Long, "Party and Constitution," *Journal of Politics*, 3 (1941), p. 203; H. S. Innis, "Technology and Public Opinion in the United States," *Canadian Journal of Economics and Political Science*, 17 (1951), pp. 1–24.

direct primary was so thoroughgoing that the party organs were forbidden to support candidates for nomination in the primary.

Counter-trends in organization. The recital of the long-term trends in
party organization should not be taken to mean that professional politicians are disappearing or that they will disappear. Rather, the manner
in which they organize to do their job is changing, the image they seek
to present to the public is changing, their mode of operation is changing,
and the sorts of people who function as professionals are also undergoing
modification.

Of the changes in the manner of organization, perhaps the most striking has been the fractionalization of integrated organization in the states
and localities and the substitution of complexes of cliques of professionals
grouped about individual leaders, a process which has proceeded in
differing degrees in differing localities. Where organizations retain a
semblance of unity greater attention is devoted to the promotion of programs of public action. The organization undergoes a face lifting; good
government is espoused as good politics, a transformation at times more
than skin deep.[50]

Beyond such changes, in a few states new-style organizations have
developed based more on common policy outlook and less on a common
ambition for patronage. These organizations seem to have a way of growing up outside the formal party organization, whose form and manner
of operation are closely regulated by law. They also have in common
an attempt to regain for the organized activists a determining voice in
nominations, a reaction from experience with the direct primary, whose
results often seem most erratic.

In Wisconsin the "Republican voluntary committee" arose to champion
the business outlook within the Republican party against the La Follette
leadership. It developed an apparatus, including a convention, outside
the formal, legally regulated organization which it controls. It controlled
most major direct primary nominations. Presently a similar informal
organizational structure developed among Democrats. Frank J. Sorauf
comments on these organizations:

Rising above all of the decentralizing forces in both voluntary committees
is a great unifier—the common ideology. Party leaders in both parties share a
common ideological allegiance that makes of them a homogeneous leadership

[50] For commentary in this vein, see Cabell Phillips, "Exit the Boss, Enter the Leader,"
New York Times Magazine, April 15, 1956; R. L. Heilbroner, "Carmine G. DeSapio:
The Smile on the Face of the Tiger," *Harper's Magazine*, July, 1954; Frank Hawkins,
"Lawrence of Pittsburgh: Boss of the Mellon Patch," *Harper's Magazine*, August,
1956; Harvey Wheeler, "Yesterday's Robin Hood: The Rise and Fall of Baltimore's
Trenton Democratic Club," *American Quarterly*, 7 (1955), pp. 332–344.

group within each party. And it is this unity that the voluntary committees provide so much better than the statutory organization could. Motivated by a loyalty to principles, the party leaders are commonly serving without anticipation of personal gain from patronage or election to office. The common ideology, therefore, provides a common goal, binds the various levels of the party together, and makes for a certain degree of centralization. To the extent that this unified party outlook fosters like-thinking party candidates, the ideology works toward a party responsibility.[51]

In California informal party organizations have developed outside the formal organization somewhat on the order of the Wisconsin pattern. Again a concern with nominations and a fairly high degree of policy homogeneity characterize the new organizations.[52] Whether these instances portend the shape of party reconstruction, they reflect experimentation among politicians in a quest for a mode of action appropriate to the new circumstances.

Popular Control of Party Organization

Party organization, as was suggested, may usefully be conceived as the problem of arranging collaboration among the political activists, those who carry on the business of the party—recruiting and designating candidates and promoting their election. Party organization does not encompass all activists nor are all holders of posts in the organization activists. Business leaders, labor-union officials, editors, advertising men, suburban housewives and all types of persons may actually be included in the thin rank of activists within each party.[53] Nor are the activists limited to any particular social class; they tend to be distributed over the spectrum of income and status. Yet among the activists the professional

[51] "Extra-Legal Parties in Wisconsin," *American Political Science Review*, 48 (1954), pp. 692–704, at p. 703.

[52] See Hugh A. Bone, "New Party Associations in the West," *American Political Science Review*, 45 (1951), pp. 1115–25; Currin V. Shields, "A Note on Party Organization: The Democrats in California," *Western Political Quarterly*, 7 (1954), pp. 673–683.

[53] Alfred de Grazia remarks that in the West ". . . the Republicans have a great many individual supporters who belong to real estate organizations, publishers' associations, insurance groups, Rotary, Kiwanis, and other fraternal organizations that function continually, and that, without breaking step with their routine operation, can convert themselves into political organizations. The transformation is often not a conscious one. Indeed it may not even be a transformation at all. But society is like a giant spider web of communication and contacts, and Republicans tend to be stationed at the centers of contact and communications with the society at large. As sparetime politicians, such contact-controllers and opinion leaders can easily bring to bear upon the political process their strong influences and political leadership."—*The Western Public* (Stanford: Stanford University Press, 1954), p. 184.

politicians, those holding office, those holding positions in the formal and informal party organization are most conspicuous.[54]

Legal regulation of party organization. It may be more or less inevitable that relatively small numbers of persons will make up the active elements of the party system. Perhaps in a democratic order, as in other orders, power and influence gravitate into few hands. That professional politicians, or a larger circle of activists, work together to put forward candidates, to proclaim their merits, and, often, to drag people to the polls to vote for them creates alternatives between which the electorate can choose. Paradoxically the operation of a democratic order depends on having some oligarchies about the premises seeking to grasp public office for one of their number.

The cliques of people who make up party organizations from time to time gained almost unlimited power in some states and cities. Such closely held power ran counter to the notions of popular democracy, and legislators set about to remedy the matter by bringing the party organization under popular control. By the adoption of the direct primary, the organization was stripped of its most important function, that of nomination. The party organization itself, consisting largely of self-appointed individuals, was made in varying ways popularly elective, on the supposition that this mode of choice would make the organization responsive to the rank and file.

With the conception that the Republican organization should act for all Republicans in the electorate or that the Democratic organization should serve as the agent for all Democrats, it perhaps followed that party officers should be chosen by the rank and file. That such a supposition represents the behavioral realities may be doubted, for no matter how the party functionaries are formally chosen they tend to be more or less self-appointed. Most people have no concern about the party organization. When party committeemen are chosen by popular vote few people bother to express a choice. Ordinarily no contest develops for the posts and when it does develop cliques of professionals test their strength with only limited involvement of the rank and file. Not atypical were the elections of 301 state committeemen in Massachusetts in 1944 and 1948. In 73 per cent of the elections only one name was on the ballot. In only two races were over 3,000 votes cast; in each district, judging by the general election vote, the potential partisan vote ranged to over 30,000. In two-thirds of the elections of committeemen less than a thousand votes were polled.

[54] See the study of organization in Elmira by Berelson and others, *Voting* (Chicago: University of Chicago Press, 1956), ch. 8.

On the whole, the introduction of procedures for the popular control of party organization has scarcely made the organization more of an agent of the rank and file. That does not mean that party organizations are not responsive to the rank and file. Many means exist, apart from popular election of ward committeemen, to bring party organization and mass sentiment into a rough harmony. It is the business of the party activists to estimate the intensities and directions of popular sentiment. Even though the organization may be internally dictatorial, it must win elections to remain alive. Perhaps the problem may be one not so much of popular control of party organization as it is of so arranging party structure that the activists can perform those functions essential for a well-ordered party government.

Democracy between rather than within parties. Against the viewpoint that parties must be governed internally in a "democratic" fashion is to be set the notion that "democracy" is achieved by popular choice between parties. The internal affairs may be, and perhaps have to be, oligarchical. To a degree this kind of situation prevails at the level of presidential politics. That there are presidential primaries must be conceded, but by and large the designation of candidates falls within the purview of the professionals and associated activists of each party. The electorate chooses between party candidates rather than among aspirants within each party, although the electorate is not without influence on the professionals even though its direct participation in nominations is limited.

One of the difficulties of the doctrine of interparty, as against intraparty, democracy is that its application requires the existence of two parties. That condition is not met in many states and localities. Unless intraparty democracy prevails the electorate has no choice. Yet it may well be that intraparty democracy tends to encourage the development of one-partyism and to make the politics of many states and cities, not a party politics, but a politics of factions, cliques, and individuals with amorphous popular followings.

13 | Party Machine as Interest Group

IN EARLIER chapters the idea was put forward that organized interests—business, labor, agriculture, religion, reform—are concerned with the acquisition of political power and influence in order that they may promote public policy favorable to their interests. Political parties are differentiated from pressure groups; they, unlike pressure groups, nominate candidates who seek formal control of the government. In doing so, parties must appeal to the entire community rather than to a single interest. Yet in one respect the inner core of the party—the machine or the party organization—may be considered to be in the same category as a pressure group: like the Chamber of Commerce of the United States, the party machine wants to bring about certain types of governmental action and to prevent others on questions of immediate concern to it. Though the party machine seeks many things from government, the end that excites the largest number of its members is public employment.[1] The

[1] Kurtzman reports that a Philadelphia ward leader remarked to a gathering of Republican committeemen: "Every vote should go to the Organization candidates. The Organization must exist if you want jobs for yourselves and your friends. Every city

organization may be considered, in effect, as a pressure group that desires to control the selection of as many public employees as possible and to control the distribution of other favors and perquisites in which members of the party hierarchy have an interest. The object of this chapter is to set out the principal matters with which the party machine is concerned as an interest group.

The Patronage System

The patronage system may be viewed in several ways. From one angle it may be considered as the response of government to the demands of an interest group—the party machine—that desires a particular policy in the distribution of public jobs. That policy is phrased by the more moderate party men in some such terms as these: "Other things being equal, a party worker in our party should be appointed to public appointive office." The more extreme adherent of the spoils doctrine would omit the phrase "other things being equal."

The patronage system may be considered, too, as a method of financing party activity. The operation of a party organization requires the services of many men and women. Its social and friendly functions go on the year round; during campaigns, when literature must be distributed, electors canvassed, meetings organized, voters brought to the polls, and many other campaign chores done, the work reaches its peak. Although much of this work is performed by unpaid volunteers, their efforts are not adequate. Indirectly, a considerable part of party expenses is met by the public treasury, and the chief means of devoting public funds to party support is through the appointment of party workers to public office.

From still another viewpoint the patronage system, with its rotation in office, has been considered as a means of filling offices that is peculiarly in keeping with democratic theory. Andrew Jackson was the great proponent of this conception of the system. He argued:

There are, perhaps, few men who can for any great length of time enjoy office and power without being more or less under the influence of feelings unfavorable to the faithful discharge of their public duties. Their integrity may be proof against improper considerations immediately addressed to themselves, but they are apt to acquire a habit of looking with indifference upon the public interests and of tolerating conduct from which an unpracticed man would revolt. Office is considered as a species of property, and government rather as a means of promoting individual interests than as an instrument

---

and county office from Mayor down should be occupied by Organization men. We must have the county offices so that we may be able to give jobs to the political workers and to our constituents."—*Methods of Controlling Votes in Philadelphia* (Philadelphia, 1935), p. 25.

created solely for the service of the people. Corruption in some and in others a perversion of correct feelings and principles divert government from its legitimate ends, and make it an engine for the support of the few at the expense of the many. The duties of all public officers are, or at least admit of being made, so plain and simple that men of intelligence may readily qualify themselves for their performance; and I cannot but believe that more is lost by the long continuance of men in office than is generally to be gained by their experience. I submit, therefore, to your consideration whether the efficiency of the government would not be promoted, and official industry and integrity better secured, by a general extension of the law which limits appointments to four years.

Because of his expression of this doctrine, Jackson is generally given more credit than he deserves for the introduction of the spoils system, whose roots antedated Jackson. "It is admitted now that President Jefferson removed about the same proportion of officeholders as did Jackson, and further that the principles governing his removals were essentially the same as Jackson's," says E. M. Ericksson. He concludes: "If one would be just in his estimate he must admit that the development of the spoils system was a gradual process for which no one man or administration can be blamed." [2]

Pressure on executives for appointments. However the system started, it has been the source of continued pressure on Presidents, department heads, governors, and others in executive positions to make appointments. President Polk, for example, in January, 1847 recorded in his diary that many persons had called to see him on "the contemptible business of seeking office for themselves or their friends." He felt that in making appointments he was unable to rely on the recommendations of Congressmen and others of "high station" who imposed on him and induced him "to make bad appointments." [3]

Succeeding Presidents were subjected to the same demands. In Cleveland's first Administration the demands on his time by office seekers was so great that he announced he would no longer "grant interviews to those seeking public positions or their advocates." A large part of his time during the first eight months of his term had been devoted to the consideration of applications for office. The public welfare, he thought, required that "the time of the President should be differently occupied." [4]

In the present century the pressure on the President for appointments

---

[2] "The Federal Civil Service under President Jackson," *Mississippi Valley Historical Review*, 13 (1927), pp. 517–540.

[3] Allan Nevins (ed.), *Polk, The Diary of a President, 1845–1849* (New York: Longmans, Green, 1929), pp. 183–184.

[4] Allan Nevins (ed.), *Letters of Grover Cleveland, 1850–1908* (Boston: Houghton Mifflin, 1933), pp. 88–89.

has been reduced by civil service legislation but it has by no means been eliminated. James A. Farley described the movement of would-be office-holders on Washington following the Democratic victory in 1932:

> I had anticipated quite a rush of deserving patriots who were willing to help F. D. R. carry the burden. But, to be frank, I had never had the slightest conception of what was about to happen. They swarmed in and flocked in by the hundreds and thousands until it seemed as though they must have been arriving by special trainloads. . . . For two or three months I was compelled to hand over the running of the Post Office Department to my worthy assistants.[5]

Customs in patronage distribution. Though the party seeks to control appointments to public place, party organization consists of dispersed and loosely linked centers of power. That internal skeleton of party becomes starkly apparent as one observes the distribution of jobs. Nice calculations of strength and status must be made in the allocation of patronage among claimants for recognition, and precautions must be taken to assure clearance with those whose status in the party suffices to command that they be consulted on particular appointments.

The statutes vest authority to make appointments in the President and heads of departments and agencies. The management of patronage requires that arrangements be established for consultation with party functionaries in the exercise of this authority. The problems of patronage administration revolve around the determination of whom to consult and around the allocation of patronage among those whose recommendations are entitled to be given weight. In large measure the problem of allocation distills down to one of division of the spoils among the party's Senators and Representatives.

Ordinarily the chairman of the national committee of the President's party serves as a center for the distribution of patronage.[6] In Eisenhower's first Administration, for example, the White House directed the Republican national chairman to receive applications sponsored by Republican Senators, Representatives, and state leaders and to transmit them to the appointing agencies. The departments and agencies were instructed to report to the committee each month on vacancies and to give it weekly

---

[5] *Behind the Ballots* (New York: Harcourt, Brace, 1938), pp. 226–227.

[6] National chairmen become annoyed when the President makes appointments without clearance through organization channels. Ed Flynn, Democratic national chairman in 1940, found that Roosevelt had made appointments of persons neither cleared with nor acceptable to state organizations. This, Flynn told the President, "caused great unhappiness and animosity throughout the party." The President did not always keep his promise to clear appointments with Flynn, which, Flynn says, caused him "a great deal of distress."—*You're the Boss* (New York: Viking, 1947), p. 162.

reports on positions filled.[7] The existence of such a patronage channel incidentally permits the maintenance of central records of appointments "charged" against individual Senators and Representatives, information useful in dealing with those who complain of their treatment in the distribution of patronage.

By custom certain classes of patronage posts have been assigned to Senators and Representatives of the President's party. Senators have asserted, under the prerogative of senatorial courtesy, control of appointments requiring senatorial confirmation to posts in their states, with certain concessions to Representatives. The Senators of the President's party, more usually the senior Senator if there are two, exercise a controlling voice in patronage appointments to other federal posts with responsibilities over the entire state. On the other hand, Representatives of the President's party may expect to be recognized in appointments to patronage posts within their own districts.[8] Thus, both Senators and Representatives seek to control those posts most closely connected with their own political fortunes, those in their own states and districts which they wish to be filled, if not by friends, at least not by their enemies. When the allocations have been made to Senators and Representatives of the President's party, there remain positions in offices located in states and districts represented in Congress by the minority party. For such places, the state and local organizations of the President's party most often make recommendations, although for such positions the President enjoys some discretion in the recognition of a patronage referee.[9]

In his recommendations the Senator or Representative may exercise his own discretion or he may be merely the terminal point of a chain of

[7] The White House memorandum to the agency heads observed: "A government position for a loyal Republican of proven ability to do a better job of government will thus earn votes of confidence next November and in 1956." The memo, issued in 1954, also stated that "Personal patronage resulting from highly personalized recruiting by certain uncooperative personnel people who are not in sympathy with this Administration has resulted in a terrific loss of opportunity to recruit qualified loyal Republicans."—Quoted by H. Hollander, *Crisis in the Civil Service* (Washington: Current Issues, 1955), p. 87.

[8] For an example of a precise formulation of the division between Senators and Representatives, see the agreement signed by the Democratic Senators and Representatives from Texas in 1933, which is quoted in the first edition of this book at pp. 306–307. The Senators controlled all posts requiring confirmation, judges, U.S. attorneys, marshals, internal revenue collectors, customs officers, and postmasters in their home cities. With these and certain other exceptions, to each Representative went control of all appointments in his district.

[9] See Harvey C. Mansfield, "Political Parties, Patronage, and the Federal Government Service" in *The Federal Government Service* (New York: The American Assembly, 1954). For practice under McKinley, see J. L. Bristow, *Fraud and Politics at the Turn of the Century* (New York: Exposition Press, 1952), pp. 36 and 63.

endorsement that reaches down the party hierarchy. An action of the latter type would be a recommendation for an appointment that originated with a county chairman, cleared the office of state chairman and that of the national committeeman, and eventually reached the state's Senator who processed it through the national committee. When this sort of procedure operates in its pure form, the power of appointment, for at least certain types of posts, in fact rests in the lower levels of the organization.

Although to a degree the distribution of patronage becomes bureaucratized with fairly clear understandings about who is entitled to what, vexing problems always remain for the President, the national chairman, and other national leaders. Save for a few renegades, the party's Senators and Representatives have to be taken care of, but in states and districts with no party representation in Congress decisions must often be made about which party factions or leaders to recognize as patronage referees. The Eisenhower Administration had to decide which Republican organizations in southern states to recognize and what to do for the Eisenhower Democrats. When the state chairman and the national committeeman become embroiled in disputes over who gets what, the problem reaches the door step of the national chairman.[10] Or the national leadership must make a choice between battling state factions, one of which may claim to be the true ally of the national Administration. Or special solutions must be contrived for special circumstances: during the first Eisenhower Administration, Thomas E. Dewey had a veto over federal appointments in New York State. Recommendations went up the organization ladder in the normal manner, but Dewey could block the appointment of any person unacceptable to him. The theory was that he was entitled to check appointments that might undermine his position as Republican leader in the state, an arrangement entirely unsatisfactory in Republican circles hostile to Dewey.

Patronage problems press most heavily upon the Administration of a party that has been out of power, and the management of patronage has wide ramifications both for the conduct of the government and for the nature of the party. Arrangements with Senators and Representatives may bear on the success of the legislative program.[11] Then, too, the system of

[10] For example, in 1949 the New Jersey state chairman and his faction of the state party importuned Democratic national chairman W. M. Boyle, Jr., to give "due recognition" to recommendations made through the state chairman and thereby to break the patronage monopoly of Frank Hague, the national committeeman and defeated mayor of Jersey City.

[11] A recurrent practice is for a new Administration to withhold patronage in the early stages until the legislative program is well underway, a technique calculated to enlist legislators in the Administration's cause.

clearances within the party organization over the country may be employed, within limits, to give aid and comfort to adherents to the President's faction of the party.

Pressure groups and patronage. In their strivings to control appointments to higher posts, Senators, Representatives, and party functionaries not infrequently serve as fronts for pressure groups with which their political fortunes are associated. The objective may be not so much to reward service to the party as to control future policy to the benefit of groups allied with the party generally or with a wing of it. The airlines have an interest in the members of the Civil Aeronautics Board; the natural gas and power corporations are not indifferent to the membership of the Federal Power Commission; the railroads have a concern about the Interstate Commerce Commission. Organizations with a varied membership, such as the NAM, may maneuver informally to influence even cabinet appointments. Organizations with a narrower and homogeneous membership have a direct interest in lesser posts. "So the mine workers concentrate on the chief of the Bureau of Mines, the real estate people on the FHA, the commercial banks on the Comptroller of the Currency and the Federal Reserve Board, the savings and loan league on the Home Loan Bank Board, the airlines on the Civil Aeronautics Board, and so on." [12]

State and city patronage procedures. The procedures for the allocation of patronage by city and state organizations vary, but, as with federal patronage, the pattern of operation tends to be influenced by the character of the organization and in turn affects the character of the organization. In a state or city with an atomized party the patronage of each department or agency is apt to be used to strengthen the personal following of the head of the agency concerned. As the organization becomes more unified, the tendency seems to be to bring all patronage into a single pool and to develop a systematic procedure for its allocation among the principal party functionaries. In Chicago, for example, the patronage appears to be largely in the hands of the ward committeemen, the number of jobs under the control of each varying with the population of the ward, with the ramifications of the committeeman's power beyond his ward lines, and with the esteem in which he is held by the higher party leaders.[13]

[12] Mansfield, *op. cit.*, p. 106.

[13] Patrick Nash, chairman of the Cook County Democratic Committee, made the following statement after the election of Edward J. Kelly as mayor of Chicago by the city council in 1933: "Before Mr. Kelly was definitely selected he promised that all jobs be filled through the ward committeemen. We all want jobs. But I know that

Cost of patronage. The stake of party machines in the game of politics through their control over patronage appointments has not been estimated in any accurate way, but certainly the annual cost runs into the millions. In 1932 Raymond Moley estimated that "roughly half" the cost of support of the magistrates' courts of New York City at that time went "either to political work or to utter waste and inefficiency." [14] In May, 1933 the New York Civil Service Reform Association found that the annual pay for positions exempt from civil service requirements in New York City "was only $7,000,000, but about half of this sum [represented] sheer waste of public funds." Most of the exempt positions were "passed around to the district leaders and their henchmen." [15] In 1937 Professor Pollock found that in Michigan the annual turnover of public employees, owing to the patronage system in the main, was 25 per cent. He estimated the annual cost of breaking in new employees at around half a million dollars.[16]

The cost of the patronage system is not to be measured by the salaries of inefficient employees alone. Their errors may be extremely costly. For example, a Chicago building inspector, appointed through party channels, inspected a water tank atop a building. The 40,000-gallon tank later collapsed and fell through six floors of the building, killing five men and injuring six others enroute. The inspector's testimony before the coroner's jury follows: [17]

Q. How long have you been a building inspector? A. Nine months.
Q. What were you before that? A. I was a malt salesman.
Q. When you were made a building inspector did you know anything about the work? A. No. I didn't know anything about it.
Q. When did you inspect the building and the tank? A. It was in January.
Q. Did you find anything wrong with the tank? A. No. It looked all right to me.

---

no ward committeeman wants a job at the expense of another ward committeeman or of the taxpayers. For that reason there will be no one chasing Mr. Kelly around. All applications will come through the ward committeemen."

[14] Raymond Moley, *Tribunes of the People* (New Haven: Yale University Press, 1932), p. 263.

[15] Efforts of the La Guardia administration in New York City to wipe out certain unessential county offices were blocked by the party organization. "The county offices contain 834 exempt positions which are used for the most part for rewarding political henchmen. The city pays to this group of 834 exempt employees $2,300,000 a year. Since they are nearly all chosen by the direct orders of county and district political leaders, the city is in effect sustaining the political machine by feeding its officers."—New York City Commissioner of Accounts, *Investigating City Government in the La Guardia Administration* (1937), p. 9.

[16] J. K. Pollock, "The Cost of the Patronage System," *The Annals*, 189 (1937), pp. 29–34.

[17] *Chicago Tribune*, June 2, 1934.

Q. Are you in a position to know whether it was all right or not? A. No, I'm just the same as you or anybody else who might inspect it.
Q. Did you inspect the anchor plates? A. Well, I looked at them.

It is not to be concluded that all appointees who owe their jobs to the party organizations are unfitted for office. Many persons of ability, industry, and loyalty to the public weal become public servants through party channels and remain permanently, to serve whatever party comes to power. They are overshadowed in public attention by such individuals as the building inspector whose disarming testimony has been quoted and by such rollicking cases as the minority registrar of the Baltimore Board of Supervisors of Elections. A patronage-starved Republican organization in 1941 and 1942 was so hard pressed for jobs that this $3,000 place was filled by a series of Republican ward executives. One would serve for a month, resign, and be replaced by another. Republican leaders defended the arrangement as a means of avoiding the evils of long continuance in office.[18]

Political Neutralization of the Civil Service

The existence of a large body of civil employees of federal, state, and local governments active in support of the party in power supposedly tips the scales in favor of the party that controls the electioneering activities of these employees. Often the party in power is tempted to improve on this advantage by increasing the number of patronage employees. Although the party out of power cannot support its workers from the public treasury, it commands the services of workers eager to obtain office as a result of future victory. And the hungry sometimes work harder than the well fed.

Whichever party wins, the public pays the cost of the patronage system. For this and other reasons there has been a persistent effort, to a degree successful, to remove the public employee from partisan activity. By political neutralization of the government service, technical merit may be established as the basis for the selection of public employees. The forces contending for political power will no longer need to form alliances with machines consisting primarily of public employees; and the control of government may be shifted from party to party without the disruption of the public service attendant upon large-scale turnover in subordinate administrative positions.

The neutralization of the civil service requires that the civil servant serve with equal loyalty whatever party is in power. Permanence of tenure of office is in one respect a condition of, in another, a consequence of,

[18] *Baltimore Sun*, April 13, 1942.

political neutrality. Political neutrality is an essential condition precedent to permanence of tenure, since no party can be expected to retain in the public employ individuals who have actively campaigned against it. On the other hand, when civil servants refrain from active participation in electoral campaigns, the government of the day may be stronger in its efforts to resist the demands of party workers that a clean sweep be made of the administrative services to provide places for those who have loyally served the party.

Pendleton Act of 1883. The principal type of public policy to neutralize politically the great mass of administrative employees of government has been so-called "civil service" or "merit system" laws. The Pendleton Act of 1883 created the Federal Civil Service Commission and provided for recruitment of persons to fill positions in the "classified service" by competitive examination. By classified service was meant the aggregate of positions covered by the legislation; those positions outside the classified service remain subject to the patronage system. In the excluded class of positions were such offices as United States marshal, collector of internal revenue, federal district attorney, and (with modifications from time to time) postmasters. Since 1883 the scope of the classified service has gradually been increased, with the defenders of the patronage system fighting a slowly losing battle.[19]

A corollary of appointment through competitive examination and tenure during good behavior is neutrality in political campaigns. In practice political neutrality has been difficult to enforce, but the tendency in the federal service has been to make more stringent the rules against partisan activity by employees in the classified service. The original rule of the Civil Service Commission provided: "No person in the said service shall use his official authority or influence either to coerce the political action of any person or body or to interfere with any election." Apparently this rule did not adequately cover the situation, for President Cleveland in 1886 issued an executive order exhorting federal officeholders to refrain from "obtrusive partisanship." When Theodore Roosevelt was a member of the United States Civil Service Commission, he observed excessive partisanship among federal employees and was moved to write for the 1894 annual report of the commission:

A man in the classified service has an entire right to vote as he pleases, and to express privately his opinions on all political subjects; but he should not take any active part in political management or in political campaigns, for precisely the same reasons that a judge, an army officer, a regular soldier, or a policeman

[19] For an account of the civil service reform movement, see F. M. Stewart, *The National Civil Service Reform League* (Austin: University of Texas Press, 1929).

is debarred from taking such an active part. It is no hardship to a man to require this. It leaves him free to vote, think and speak privately as he chooses, but it prevents him while in the service of the whole public, from turning his official position to the benefit of one of the parties in which the whole public is divided; and in no other way can this be prevented.

Almost the same language was used in 1907 when the rules under the Civil Service Act were amended to provide: "Persons who by the provisions of these rules are in the competitive classified service, while retaining the right to vote as they please and to express their opinions on all political subjects, shall take no active part in political management or in political campaigns." [20] In the application of the rule against taking "active part in political management or in political campaigns," fine distinctions have to be made between what is and what is not permissible behavior by a civil servant. He may express his views "privately" but not in public places or by the publication of a letter or article in favor of any party or candidate. He may make political contributions but only to persons not in the service of the United States and to them only "voluntarily." He may be a member of a political club but not one of its officers; he may not be a candidate for elective office; he may attend a political convention as a spectator but not as a member; he must not wear campaign badges or buttons.

Hatch Act. In 1939 Congress, in the Hatch Act, broadened the application of the rule of political neutrality. The rules under the Civil Service Act affected only the classified service and left a substantial number of unclassified employees free to engage in political activities. The Hatch Act declared it

. . . unlawful for any person employed in the executive branch of the Federal Government, or any agency or department thereof, to use his official authority or influence for the purpose of interfering with an election or affecting the result thereof. No officer or employee in the executive branch of the Federal Government, or any agency or department thereof, shall take any active part in political management or in political campaigns. All such persons shall retain the right to vote as they may choose and to express their opinions on all political subjects and candidates.

Specified policy-forming officials, such as the President, the Vice-President, the heads and assistant heads of departments, and other high officials whose business it is to make and defend governmental decisions are excluded from the prohibition of political activity. The effect of the

[20] For a full account of the evolution of federal policy, see Wei-kiung Chen, *The Doctrine of Civil Service Neutrality in Party Conflicts in the United States and Great Britain* (Chicago: University of Chicago Libraries, lithoprinted, 1937).

Hatch Act was to extend to most employees outside the classified service the rules that have long governed those in the classified service.[21]

Quite apart from legislative taboos on patronage, the assumption by the government of technical functions requiring the services of professional classes has made it "bad" politics for the party to apply the patronage system to many departments and agencies. Although Congressmen, for example, often bring pressure on administrative officers to appoint loyal party workers as clerks, stenographers, messengers, or other routine workers, they will keep hands off the professional and expert groups. Such a rule is not universally followed, but the extent of its observance indicates a recognition by political leaders that it is not to their interest to use a certain class of positions to reward party workers.

Federal patronage after 1952. When the Republican Administration came into power after the election of 1952, it faced a demand from the party ranks for patronage and was confronted by a public service that had been largely blanketed under the civil service laws by preceding Presidents. A favorite topic of discussion at sessions of the Republican national committee was the shortage of patronage, and the Republican Senate policy committee grumbled about appointments without consultation with the Senate and the imposition of requirements by the Administration that made deserving Republicans ineligible.[22] President Eisenhower met the situation by removing from the classified service about 134,000 positions. By no means all the holders of these positions were replaced by Republicans, but the list was combed for positions that might be transferred to Schedule C, a category of positions to be filled without regard to formal merit procedures. The contention was that certain types of appointments should be made at the discretion of the heads of administrative agencies in order that they might fulfill their responsibilities. That view had, to be sure, a degree of validity, but it could also be used to justify the replacement of competent and loyal career personnel by deserving Republicans.[23]

[21] For detailed interpretations and an impression of the types of violations proceeded against under the Hatch Act, see United States Civil Service Commission, *Hatch Act Decisions* (Washington: Government Printing Office, 1949). See also Ferrel Heady, "The Hatch Act Decisions," *American Political Science Review*, 41 (1947), pp. 687–699; F. D. Wormuth, "The Hatch Act Cases," *Western Political Quarterly*, 1 (1948), pp. 165–173.

[22] Senator Aiken of Vermont observed that he was getting "sick of" the Administration "setting up qualifications" for appointees "that only Democrats can meet."

[23] The National Federation of Federal Employees saw the existence of "a shocking willingness" in high quarters "to give an aura of sanctity to acts of outright spoilsmanship."—Quoted by Hollander, *op. cit.*, p. 6.

Limitations on state and local employees. Parallel to the federal enactments has been a trend toward the adoption of the competitive method for recruitment to state and municipal offices, along with accompanying limitations on partisan activity. State and local rules against the participation of civil servants in political campaigns have been less effective than the federal regulations.[24] In some states and municipalities stringent rules of neutrality in politics are consistently ignored. Only about a score of states have civil service commissions or like agencies that conduct competitive examinations for the selection of most state employees. Much less movement toward the substitution of merit for patronage has occurred in the counties, while about 40 per cent of the cities of from 10,000 to 100,000 population have no civil service system.

In all states and localities a large group of employees has been brought under the merit system by conditions attached to federal grants. The most significant group affected by such requirements consists of state and local employees in charge of state programs of public assistance and employment security. A 1939 amendment to the Social Security Act provided that after January 1, 1940 all state agencies in these fields should, as a condition of receiving federal grants, make provision for "the establishment and maintenance of personnel standards on a merit basis."

Congress has also, by its leverage through federal subsidies, extended the limitations on political activity of the Hatch Act to a substantial number of state and local employees. The relevant 1940 statutory provision reads as follows:

No officer or employee of any State or local agency whose principal employment is in connection with any activity which is financed in whole or in part by loans or grants made by the United States or by any Federal agency shall (1) use his official authority or influence for the purpose of interfering with an election or a nomination for office, or affecting the result thereof, or (2) directly or indirectly coerce, attempt to coerce, command, or advise any other such officer or employee to pay, lend, or contribute any part of his salary or compensation or anything else of value to any party, committee, organization, agency, or person for political purposes. No such officer or employee shall take any active part in political management or in political campaigns. All such persons shall retain the right to vote as they may choose and to express their opinions on all political subjects and candidates.

If the state authorities fail to remove from office a person found by the United States Civil Service Commission to have violated the act, a sum equivalent to two years' compensation of the violator is deducted from grants to the state concerned. The Civil Service Commission has made

[24] For a detailed description of practices in one patronage-ridden state, see H. O. Waldby, *The Patronage System in Oklahoma* (Norman: The Transcript Co., 1950).

findings and issued orders in a few such cases to the accompaniment of strident protests about states' rights and the constitutional privilege of the individual to participate in politics. Following the pattern of the federal legislation a goodly number of states and cities adopted laws and ordinances popularly known as "little Hatch Acts." [25]

There is some doubt about the efficacy of a limitation on political activity that is not accompanied by permanence of tenure and opportunity for a career in the administrative service. The affected state and local employees, Senator Thomas pointed out in the debate on the extension of the Hatch Act, "remain patronage employees. . . . Their tenure of office depends upon the success of their party at successive elections." Others may campaign, he said, "for the sole purpose of succeeding the Hatch mutes in office." When an employee knows that if his party loses the election he will lose his job, the temptation to engage in political activity in violation of the law is great.[26]

Long-run trends in patronage. During the past half century the proportion of the public service selected by patronage and the proportion of public employees active in party work have declined. The impact of merit system laws, the rise of professionalism in the public service, the increasing reliance on technical personnel have all taken their toll. Furthermore, the era of full employment after World War II and the changing conditions of private employment greatly reduced the appeal of public employment. Often the problem of the public administrator became one of attracting sufficient personnel to man the public service rather than one of warding off unqualified applicants carrying party endorsement.

Yet the patronage system remains, as it must, but to what extent is another question. A marked shrinkage of the patronage pool has occurred in the federal service. President Truman even succeeded, after a warm fight with the Senate, in transferring the collectors of internal revenue to the career service. Among states and localities the situation differs. In some

[25] The consequences of such legislation are illustrated by the following news story: "Mary Carrol . . . yesterday became the fourth municipal employee to resign from a post on the Republican Town Committee because of the 'little Hatch Act.' She has been vice chairman of the 27th Ward for 12 years. . . . She is matron in the women's comfort station in Church Street."—*New Haven Courier-Journal*, May 31, 1951.

[26] The prohibition of party activity by the public employees, it should be noted, by no means eliminates the party's patronage problems. A goodly number of posts must be filled as each party comes into power and the allocation of these jobs raises all the problems of due recognition of deserving partisans. A federal judgeship, for example, even though its occupant need never make another campaign speech, is highly valued both for its prestige and as a retreat from the uncertainties of politics. A vacancy on the bench excites the ambitions of those who have served their party well.

cities almost the entire municipal service consists of persons who gained their positions through party channels and who devote a portion of their time to the work of the party machine. In a few cities, at the other extreme, the number of patronage employees is extremely small. Some states have developed civil services that serve loyally and impartially whatever party is in power and refrain from partisan activity; other states have an almost completely new set of employees, outside the federally protected departments, when a new party comes into power.

Diverse Party Spoils

A loyal organization man may find ample reward in a public job. Yet the organization seeks jobs for more than the sake of the job itself. Control of place may bring also to the organization control of powerful sanctions in the administration of law to reward its friends or to penalize its opponents. The party as a whole must concern itself with broad questions of public policy; the party machine is more likely to worry about the thousands of decisions that may affect an individual for better or worse. Officials from a police patrolman to a cabinet member have within their discretionary decision questions of most immediate concern to the individual. Party organization leaders often take a lively interest in these decisions; they may be made to aid or injure members and friends of the organization.

To catalogue the types of decisions in which party organizations may interest themselves would require a listing of most activities of government. For the moment attention may be concentrated on types of public spoils that often serve about the same function as jobs in rewarding organization members and supporters. In the spending, managing, and controlling of public moneys and property many actions other than appointments to jobs may be converted to the purposes of the party organization.[27]

Judicial spoils. In all political organizations lawyers are to be found in prominent positions, and in some localities those affiliated with the dominant party machine are favored in appointments by the courts of masters in chancery, receivers, trustees, and other judicial functionaries. The board of managers of the Chicago Bar Association reported in 1934: [28]

[27] H. F. Gosnell reports, for example, that in Chicago: "Of the seven Democratic ward committeemen who were not employed by some governmental agency in 1928, three were in occupations which enabled them to have many dealings with public authorities. One was in the sewer contracting business; the second was in a law firm which had many political ramifications; and the third was in the insurance business."— *Machine Politics; Chicago Model* (Chicago: University of Chicago Press, 1937), p. 40.

[28] Report by the Board of Managers, Chicago Bar Association, February 1, 1934.

Recently, in exercising their discretion in the appointment of masters, certain judges have deferred to the wishes of politicians. The appointment of a master in chancery as one of the political spoils belonging to a successful party, regardless of the qualifications of the master, is a subversion of the judicial powers of the court. As a result of this system, many masters in chancery have been nominated by politicians and appointed by the courts, who are wholly unfit to perform the functions required of them.

Similar comments would be applicable to such appointments in many other localities; the federal district courts, too, have not been free from like practices. The large, sometimes exorbitant, fees drawn by receivers and similar officers acting in a fiduciary capacity under the supervision of courts make these appointments especially desirable to the legal lights of the party machine.

Political contracts. Urban machines are likely to have several contractors occupying important posts in the organization; frequently the contractor may not be a district leader or a ward committeeman but a silent and inconspicuous member of the organization. Contracts for public works may flow to the organization contractors, often at unreasonable figures. In turn, the contractor may use a part of his profits to aid the party machine in financing its campaigns.[29] The many jobs available on public works incidentally furnish an opportunity to allocate employment to the adherents of the machine. Supplies for public agencies may likewise be purchased from firms controlled by members of the organization. Firms providing services or materials on occasion pay a "commission" to an influential political leader, some of which may (or may not) benefit the party cause. Procurement officers may take special precautions lest contracts go to firms reputed to be associated with the opposition.[30] Almost every major locality has its contracting firms that are commonly regarded, sometimes correctly, as "Democratic" or "Republican" concerns. Modern reform movements and the general improvement in the quality of public administration have reduced greatly the grossness of spoils in contracts and purchasing. The "organization" contractor often has advantage in obtaining awards, but he is more likely to do approximately what he is paid for than he was a few decades ago.

[29] "This reputable firm of architects received $778,000 on four contracts awarded in the Walker administration, and in one case was so bold as to charge a $10,000 contribution to the Democratic organization on its books as an expense item for work on Riker's Island Penitentiary under the bookkeeping title 'Work in progress, job 394—Riker's Island Penitentiary.' "—New York City Commissioner of Accounts, *Investigating City Government in the La Guardia Administration* (1937), p. 132.

[30] On a contract award delayed until the Republican national chairman could be assured that the bidding firm was not a "New Deal outfit," see *Christian Science Monitor*, Oct. 19, 22, 1956.

Real estate purchase: "Honest graft." The purchase of real estate for public improvements has furnished opportunity for members of the upper strata of the party organization to enrich themselves. This practice, incidentally, contributed one of the classic phrases of the argot of politics, "honest graft." The late Senator Plunkitt, a godsend to the authors of textbooks, is reported to have said: [31]

There's an honest graft, and I'm an example of how it works. I might sum up the whole thing by sayin': "I seen my opportunities and I took 'em."

Just let me explain by examples. My party's in power in the city, and it's goin' to undertake a lot of public improvements. Well, I'm tipped off, say, that they're going to lay out a new park at a certain place.

I see my opportunity and I take it. I go to that place and I buy up all the land I can in the neighborhood. Then the board of this or that makes its plan public, and there is a rush to get my land, which nobody cared particularly for before.

Ain't it perfectly honest to charge a good price and make a profit on my investment and foresight? Of course it is. Well, that's honest graft.

A somewhat different light was put on the matter by Leonard Wallstein in an investigation of real estate purchases by the Tammany administration in New York City during the twenties. He found that persons with inside information on the land needs of the city acquired land in the names of dummies with "no apparent financial means, but who produce substantial sums of cash from safe deposit boxes or office safes, buy up property and turn quick profits, which are again immediately converted into cash and vanish. Clearly these operators have been merely the dummies of puppets for influential undisclosed principals." In short periods tremendous profits were made on a relatively small cash investment.[32]

Other proprietary operations. The examples cited involved the utilization of discretion in the management of public expenditures for the purpose of rewarding, supporting, or financing the work of members of the party organization. The annals of American administration abound with instances of similar abuses in connection with other activities of government that might be classed as proprietary. The purchase of insurance by public authorities has been in many times and places notoriously for partisan benefit, and a goodly number of political leaders operate as insurance agents. Commonly they also provide bonds for contractors and others required to give surety for performance. The word gets around that it is advisable for contractors to be bonded through a particular agency.

[31] Quoted in W. L. Riordan, *Plunkitt of Tammany Hall* (New York: McClure, Phillips, 1905), pp. 4–5.
[32] Leonard Wallstein, *Report on Law and Procedure in Condemnation Applicable to Proceedings Brought by the City of New York* (January, 1932).

Services, such as hospital care, may be provided without charge in appropriate instances. The disposition of public property may be governed by partisan consideration. Deposits of public funds may go to bankers supporting the organization.[33] All these and other such uses of authority over funds and property occur, although they are often individual misdeeds rather than systematic utilization of authority for the benefit of the organization.

The Shady Side of the Law

The common American belief seems to be that politicians are engaged in a dirty business. Although the belief usually caricatures the reality, it contains enough truth to warrant some attention. In the preceding pages emphasis rested on the expenditure of funds and the management of resources for the benefit of the party organization. At this point attention may be shifted to the application and misapplication of law to individual citizens in a way to reward party support, to recruit party support, or to penalize opposition. Such matters include anything from "fixing" a traffic ticket to an overly generous settlement of a disputed item of an income tax return, from overlooking the violation of a minor municipal ordinance to expediting an export license covering millions of dollars worth of goods.

Patterns of access to government. Democratic regimes possess no monopoly of favoritism and unevenness in the application of general rules of law to individual cases. Probably as long as man has governed man, fixers have sought to tamper with the scales of justice. The role of the political party in this process may be peculiar to democratic regimes, although one may well suspect that the parties—if they are parties—of dictatorial regimes are not above fixing a traffic ticket.

The pattern of relationships in which the party organization plays an intermediary role between citizen and government varies enormously. At one extreme might be placed the stereotype of the boss-ridden city in which the party boss and his aides in fact are the city government. To obtain almost any governmental action the citizen has to apply to the office of the boss. So thorough an envelopment of the formal administra-

---

[33] A report by the New Jersey state treasurer in 1954 quoted a letter from a banker to his county Republican leader asking that his bank be given an additional state deposit: "As I can't scurry around for business from private sources I should at least get some public funds to fill in." The banker had been diverted from his business by his activities as county campaign manager. In due course, his bank received a deposit from the state treasurer. This incident was reported by a Democratic state treasurer as he prepared to switch into government bonds $23,000,000 deposited in banks by his Republican predecessors.

tive apparatus by the party organization has become rare. In certain cities, to be sure, the situation approximates the old pattern. More often the ward committeeman or a similar party functionary is the person to see to obtain action on certain types of community services. At the other extreme one would place the role of the party organization as an "introducer" whose word insures a careful hearing and a responsible consideration of the problem of the person who approaches government through party channels.

Between the extremes of complete control of government by the party apparatus and the party as a channel of access lie all sorts of irregular patterns of relations between party and government. This district leader may have influence with a particular judge; that one may control the police department or parts of it. That ward committeeman may have an "in" with the prosecutor's office. This county committeeman may be the channel through which the tax assessor can be reached. The county chairman may have his lines into the governor's office. The state chairman or the national committeeman may be able to deal with the collector of internal revenue or the district attorney. Legislators frequently serve as channels to administrative agencies. Often the differentiation between party functionary and public official does not exist; a single individual may occupy both posts and may exercise his official authority to the advantage, or supposed advantage, of party in particular cases.

Underworld and party. Although a tortured interpretation of public policy may be served out for party advantage in any government activity, the most spectacular type of irregularity occurs in the relations between underworld and government, with party organization often as an intermediary. The industries on the shady side of the law—gambling, narcotics, prostitution, liquor in dry areas—must arrange with government either directly or indirectly through party for the privilege of operating. This necessity for "protection" in order to exist often results in a close communion between at least elements of the party organization and underworld bosses and leaders.

What conception to apply to the relation between party, government, and underworld to produce a meaningful description presents a puzzling problem. The simple conception seems to be that the gambling-syndicate boss bribes the holder of authority, against his will, to permit illegal operation. That picture usually errs on the side of naïveté. Another view is that illegal enterprise attempts to mold its environment, just as does the legal enterprise, to permit the most convenient and profitable operation. The circumstances require that the illegal industry employ peculiar methods for shaping its environment; behavioristically, however, such a group interacts with other groups and with government in an attempt to develop a *modus vivendi* in much the same pattern as does a group tolerated by formal law. Yet this conception implies more regularity, more of a "pattern," than seems actually to prevail.

The privilege obtained by the underworld syndicate amounts to a monopolistic license. It is usually accompanied by a policy of restraining competition through enforcement of the law against those not affiliated with the protected group. These "franchises" form the basis for profitable undertakings. The New York State Crime Commission, for example, found that profits from slot machines in the rooms of fraternal clubs and in veterans' halls in a one-horse town in upstate New York amounted to $500,000 in five years.[34] The largest manufacturer of punchboards amassed a fortune estimated at from 10 to 15 million dollars,[35] and the profits from the operation of punchboards amounted to fabulous sums. Estimates, necessarily with only sketchy bases, of the gross take of bookmakers for the nation as a whole run from three to ten billion dollars annually.[36]

The relation of the party organization to such enterprises is scarcely a matter of public record, and its description is fraught with difficulty. Often the party organization as such does not enter into the arrangement at all; even the patrolman on the beat may sell certain types of protection. Yet too often persons in the party hierarchy or their close associates have a hand in the fix. By no means all the enormous sums paid for protection go to party treasuries; yet, when campaigns have to be financed, underworld industries can be tapped for contributions. Moreover, in cities and parts of cities thoroughly organized by a gambling syndicate the runners, bookies, and other personnel can be converted into a formidable campaigning organization. The Chicago Crime Commission estimates that the handbook operators of that city can deliver 200,000 votes.[37] Rather than pay party functionaries for protection, gambling and racketeering groups at times take over party organizations or segments of organizations. Warren Moscow reports, for example, that underworld leaders in the 1940's installed their own men as district leaders in the New York City Demo-

[34] *New York Herald Tribune*, July 19, 1951.

[35] Gordon Schendel, "The Punchboard Racket," *Collier's*, February 10, 1951.

[36] The extent and variety of underworld enterprises are suggested by the findings of the Kefauver committee. See *Hearings*, Special Committee to Investigate Organized Crime in Interstate Commerce, U.S. Senate, 81st Cong., 2d sess., and 82d Cong., 1st sess., pursuant to S. Res. 202. See also the committee's final report, Senate Report 725, 82d Cong., 1st sess.

[37] See D. D. McKean, "Who Gets the Billion Graft?" *National Municipal Review*, 38 (1949), pp. 546–550.

cratic organization: "The late Albert Marinelli was made leader of the old Second Assembly District on the lower East Side literally by the guns of Luciano's gorillas, the first leader to be installed by the underworld itself." [38]

Businesses that operate near the boundary between legality and illegality appear to be especially dependent on pecuniary leverage in their dealings with government even when they are on the right side of the law. Legalized race tracks, for example, must have licenses—which may be revoked —to operate. Their stockholders seem to include an uncommonly large proportion of well-placed party leaders.[39] Such enterprises are also often vulnerable to demands that they hire their employees on the basis of party recommendations.[40] Similarly, the liquor business in all its phases from distilling to retailing puts large sums into politics. Not only must the legality of the industry generally be maintained; decisions must be assured on the rights of individual concerns to share in the business.

Penalties for opposition. Abuses of authority may penalize as well as reward. The powers of government may be utilized to bind individuals and groups to the support of the organization; they may also be used to penalize opposition and to intimidate those tempted to oppose. Corrupt party organizations over limited areas and for limited periods of time succeed in almost completely suppressing opposition. Those whose support cannot be obtained by fair means or foul may have life made miserable for them. Or the threat of reprisal may keep them mute. The annals of political irregularities contain endless examples, but the nature of the possibilities is suggested by the conclusion of Maurice Milligan concerning the Pendergast machine of Kansas City: "Make no mistake—this organization could do more than elect or defeat candidates for political office. It could make or break a business through tax levies, building permits, building

[38] *New York Times,* November 26, 1950. For data on the associations between New York district leaders, Republican and Democratic, and entrepreneurs in illegal undertakings, see New York State Crime Commission, *Second Report to the Governor,* March 9, 1954 (Legislative Doc., 1954, No. 40).

[39] Illustrative are the revelations coincident with the resignation of J. Russel Sprague as Republican national committeeman from New York in 1953. A goodly number of important Republican leaders had made fortunate investments in race tracks in the neighborhood of New York City. One investment of $2,000 yielded a profit of $194,000, after taxes, when sold after being held ten months. For a summary of the investigation into the matter, see *New York Times,* March 14, 1954.

[40] John Strohmeyer estimates that party leaders in Massachusetts, Rhode Island, and New Hampshire control jobs worth $1,000,000 a year at the tracks in their states. In 1955, 44 New Hampshire legislators worked at the Rockingham track.—See "Yankee Morals and the $2 Bet," *Harper's Magazine,* July, 1956.

condemnations by city inspectors, special favors, and in a hundred other ways." [41]

The Function of Spoils

The patronage system and various other types of spoils tend to be treated as an unfortunate manifestation of the innate perversity of man; and many specific instances of peculation, fraud, and nepotism in the public sphere are no different in motive or effect from departures from the code of proper conduct for persons in positions of trust in ecclesiastical, commercial, and labor associations. Yet the patronage system in the large is something more than a collection of unrelated cases of individual venality.

From one standpoint the patronage system and, to a certain extent, other types of spoils may be considered a means to aid in the financing of the elaborate party machinery that seems to be necessary under our form of government. With our innumerable offices filled by popular vote and our multiplicity of elections, it seems almost indispensable that many persons devote their time to party work. What men shall devote their time to this work? Only those who have adequate private means to permit them to dedicate themselves to the service of their party? That solution would hardly be in keeping with the spirit of American democracy. Carl Russell Fish argued that "the true cause for the introduction of the spoils system was the triumph of democracy." The work of the party "requires the labor of many men: there must be captains of hundreds and captains of tens, district chiefs and ward heelers. . . . It is an essential idea of democracy that these leaders shall be of the people; they must not be gentlemen of wealth and leisure, but they must—the mass of them at any rate—belong to the class that makes its own living. If, then, they are to devote their time to politics, politics must be made to pay." [42] Fish contended that the spoils system served in the period of its establishment "a purpose that could probably have been performed in no other way, and that was fully worth the cost." Without the inducement of public jobs and other perquisites, the formation of party organizations becomes difficult. Nevertheless, in some places effective local machines of a middle-class character have been constructed without benefit of spoils.

From another viewpoint the entire spoils system serves to maintain discipline within the organization or, more precisely, within segments of it. The preceding chapter emphasized the loose articulation of the elements

[41] M. M. Milligan, *The Inside Story of the Pendergast Machine by the Man Who Smashed It* (New York: Scribner's, 1948), p. 22.

[42] *The Civil Service and the Patronage* (New York: Longmans, Green, 1905), p. 156. Quoted by permission of the President and Fellows of Harvard College.

of the national organization as a whole. To some extent patronage helps hold together these elements, but the potency of patronage becomes more apparent in city organizations, state organizations, in the personal and factional followings of Senators, Representatives, and other leaders. The adroit allocation of rewards aids a party leader in holding his organization together. The usefulness of jobs for this purpose is obvious, but other types of spoils may be employed in the same fashion. A rebellious district leader or ward committeeman may discover that his printing contract or his fire hose business has been cut off by the higher-ups in the organization. The spoils system may, thus, serve as a method of consolidating into a cohesive group the persons constituting the machine. Yet one should by no means assume that the patronage system is invariably efficiently managed for party purposes. The fiction prevails that while party leaders may not always manage the public service well they are wizards in the conduct of party business. In actuality, patronage often goes to persons quite undeserving in terms of party service.[43] And the management of patronage may make enemies as well as friends. The saying is that a Senator, forced to endorse one of 10 applicants for a job, makes nine enemies and one ingrate.

The spoils of power are used to gain support of individuals and of groups under regimes in nondemocratic countries. Many commentators find the like use of spoils in the United States for this purpose to be monstrous and unparalleled, but the practice is as old as human government. Governors of all regimes use the perquisites at their disposal to command the support and loyalty of those susceptible to purchase in this fashion. The striking difference about American practice is the moral reprobation that accompanies it; conditions that elsewhere would be accepted as a matter of course are here considered not quite cricket.[44]

[43] Consider the following announcement from the official organ of the Philadelphia Republican organization. Steps were to be taken "to comb out of city and county offices the social and fraternal and 'pull' appointees, so that places can be made for the men who pull doorbells and produce majorities. . . . This is Senator Vare's idea and comes direct. Men who can't produce are to 'walk the plank.' This will be good news to the men who deliver."—Kurtzman, *Methods of Controlling Votes in Philadelphia*, p. 43. See also the analysis of the management of highway patronage in a Pennsylvania county by Frank J. Sorauf, "State Patronage in a Rural County," *American Political Science Review*, 50 (1956), pp. 1046–56. His findings indicate an ineffective management of patronage. Additional inquiries on the order of this by Professor Sorauf would be helpful in the assessment of the significance of the patronage system.

[44] On the use of patronage to maintain party discipline, the following comment by Professor J. K. Pollock is relevant: "It has often been contended that patronage is a necessary aid to political leadership in this country. But it is interesting to note that many of our greatest governors—Grover Cleveland, Robert Marion La Follette, Judson Harmon, Hiram Johnson and Albert Ritchie, to name a few—men whose

Nor can the spoils system be considered or understood in isolation. In a thoroughly machine-ridden city the observer, to comprehend the nature and function of the system, must look for the allies of the machine. "The major interests," says Odegard, "are content to leave minor spoils, such as jobs in the public service, to the party agents as long as these agents direct the affairs of state in a manner to promote the interests of the powerful oligarchies which control the economic and social destinies of the community." [45] If one examines a city corruptly governed at about the beginning of the century, he will observe a powerful political machine utilizing the spoils opportunities to the utmost. But allied with the machine probably would be found the telephone, traction, and power interests, which sought franchises and privileged treatment at the city's hands, underworld syndicates controlling gambling and prostitution, and perhaps other groups that required for their profitable existence a favorably disposed city administration. It was by the combination of the party machine, the utilities, and the underworld that control of the city could be gained, and by that control each segment of the power combination could obtain what it wanted.[46]

Thus it came about that important interests outside the party machine itself were content to leave unlimited spoils to the party organization in order that their own interests might be advanced. When all the franchises had been awarded, when privileges sought had been legally granted, the important business interests associated with the party machine were apt to become converts to the doctrine of economy and efficiency in government. Consequently a sharp decline in the scope of the spoils system has

political leadership was undoubted and of a high order, were not merely advocates of civil service but were responsible for its establishment in their respective states."— "The Cost of the Patronage System," *The Annals*, 189 (1937), pp. 29–34.

[45] "Political Parties and Group Pressures," *The Annals*, 179 (1935), pp. 69–81.

[46] The patronage-supported organization can, of course, become a unit of a constellation of interests whose elements differ from those of the classic American urban machine. In the hey-day of the New Deal, for example, the metropolitan machines were, at least in federal politics, by and large allied with the New Deal although in state and local matters they often continued to work with some of their associates of olden time. The power of patronage may be a counterpoise to business interests as well as an ally. Consider in this connection the remarks of Senator Paul H. Douglas in defense of senatorial patronage: "But I would like to have you consider just how long most liberals would be able to last in Congress if you stripped us of all patronage, as you desire. We who try to defend the interests of the people, the consumers and the taxpayers commonly face the powerful opposition of the special-interest groups which will spend enormous sums of money to defeat us. We are also commonly opposed by the political organizations at home and frequently by the national administration which all too often resents independence on our part. . . . If we are to survive we need some support rooted in gratitude for material favors which at the same time do not injure the general public."—*New Republic*, July 14, 1952, p. 2.

occurred in many American jurisdictions. Where the spoils system still exists unchallenged and unashamed, usually the power combination controlling the jurisdiction contains important elements in addition to the party machine itself—elements that seek to gain, through toleration of their machine allies, governmental action or inaction that might not readily be obtainable in any other way.

The interest of the party in patronage and in other perquisites encounters opposition from other social groups. The party hierarchy is in this respect like any pressure group: the unlimited prosecution of group interests may meet a countermovement from people adversely affected. In this process the long-term trend has undoubtedly been to limit more and more the perquisites of the party hierarchy. Merit system protection has been extended to most federal employees and to a substantial proportion of state and local employees. Many kinds of party spoils have been made illegal. Public services are manned to a higher degree by a professionalized personnel animated by a higher professional ethnic than prevailed in the past. Yet party machines resist encroachments on their ancient prerogatives, and movement toward weaning them away from their perquisites is slow and halting.

The truth is that we have contrived no system for the support of party that does not place considerable reliance on patronage. The party organization makes a democratic government work and charges a price for its services. Sometimes it becomes corrupt and levies an exorbitant charge. Fortunately not all political organizations are corrupt, and over the long run the spoils system has come to operate within narrower bounds. Yet until we invent some other system of political financing or new incentives for party service, the government, directly or indirectly, will contribute to the support of party activity.

14 | Nominations in the States

A BASIC party activity is the designation of candidates for public office. The American party system is characterized both by a variety of nominating customs and by modes of nomination peculiarly American. In most democratic countries other than the United States the choice of candidates rests in the hands of a relatively few party leaders and activists. The group that Americans would call the "party machine" selects candidates entirely without legal regulation. Our presidential nominating conventions approximate that pattern. They are extralegal bodies that commonly include the party chieftains, who, of course, operate in a glare of publicity. On the other hand, nominations of most candidates for state and local office as well as candidates for the national House and Senate are made in accord with detailed regulations prescribed by state legislatures. Moreover, the choice rests, in form at least, not in a few party leaders but in the mass of the party membership, which is entitled to participate in nominating primaries.

The American practice of mass participation in party nominations

points to a special characteristic of American parties, or at least to peculiarities of state and local parties. The classic conception of party assumes that a few, a manageable number, of individuals agree upon candidates who are advanced in the name of the party. A handful of men meets
in private and agrees to back a slate of candidates for county office. That
condition is approximated in some states and localities but more often the
party membership chooses the nominees after a campaign not unlike the
election campaign. This procedure makes a party itself an entity different
from the classical notion of a fairly coherent leadership corps with a more
or less identifiable popular following. Instead, the necessity for popular
appeal to win nominations tends to splinter the leadership into cliques,
factions, and even lone-wolf, individual aspirants for party power.

The bearing of nominating practices on the party systems of states and
localities may be suggested by a brief survey of the evolution of nominating procedures, by an indication of the relation between nominating customs and variations in party structure, and by some attention to more
technical aspects of the dominant form of nominations—the direct primary. Reserved for Chapter 16 is a consideration of special questions
associated with the nomination of candidates for the House and Senate.

Evolution of Nominating Practices

Through the history of American nominating practices runs a persistent
attempt to permit popular participation in nominations and thereby to
limit or to destroy the power of party oligarchies. The legislative caucus
fell before those who demanded that the people be given a voice in nominations. The new machinery, the nominating convention, itself became
an instrument of party leadership and was largely replaced by the direct
primary. These transformations of nominating procedures have not invariably taken control of nominations from the upper echelons of party
leadership, but the fact that they have occurred points to the pervading
belief that the mass of the people ought to have a hand in the management
of party affairs. Attempts to associate the party membership with nominating decisions affects significantly not only state and local politics but
also national politics.

Legislative assumption of nominating function. Soon after the Revolution
the legislative caucus became the means for the nomination of candidates
for state office. Legislators, however difficult travel might be, had to
gather at the state capital. Obviously these men of influence in their respective constituencies made up a group that could conveniently offer
party candidates to the voters. "This reflection occurred to the public,
and in particular to the members of the state legislatures themselves, and

they laid hands on the nominations of the candidates to the state offices." [1] The nominating caucus consisted of the party's members from both legislative houses meeting together. Its decisions were formulated as addresses by the participants as individuals and not in their capacities as legislators. By 1800 the legislative caucus was the prevailing mode of nomination in the states; it was also used in nominations for the Presidency, from 1800 to 1828.

The legislative caucus had hardly become established in the states when modifications began to be made to correct its shortcomings. It was unrepresentative in that those districts represented by the opposition party had no voice in the nomination. To remedy this defect, the "mixed caucus" came into use. In the mixed caucus special delegates sat to speak for the party members in those legislative districts represented in the legislature by the opposite party. In 1817 in New York, for example, a mixed caucus was held, "composed of the Republican members of the legislature, together with delegates chosen by the Republican voters in those counties represented in the legislature by Federalist members." [2] It was not devotion to the abstract notion of representation for all that led to the introduction of the mixed caucus; it was the practical fact that the pure legislative caucus might bring one result, the mixed caucus another.

Jackson and the congressional caucus. The abandonment of the legislative caucus in the states was associated with the overthrow of the congressional caucus, which fell before the onslaughts of Andrew Jackson, the hero of New Orleans, the idol of the West, the symbol of a rising spirit of democracy and egalitarianism. As an aspirant for the presidential nomination in 1824, Jackson could not hope to gain nomination at the hands of an unsympathetic congressional caucus. His backers set out to discredit "King Caucus," an instrument of the anti-Jacksonians. His friends boycotted the 1824 Republican caucus, which was attended by only about one-fourth of the Republican members of Congress. The defeat of William H. Crawford, the caucus nominee, was interpreted as a verdict against the caucus itself. Before the election of 1832 the national convention came into use.

The destruction of the caucus represented more than a mere change in the method of nomination. Its replacement by the convention was regarded as the removal from power of self-appointed oligarchies that had usurped the right to nominate. The new system, the convention, gave, or so it was supposed, the mass of party members an opportunity to par-

[1] M. Ostrogorski, "The Rise and Fall of the Nominating Caucus, Legislative and Congressional," *American Historical Review*, 5 (1900), p. 257.

[2] F. W. Dallinger, *Nominations for Elective Office in the United States* (New York: Longmans, Green, 1897), p. 28.

ticipate in nominations. These events occurred as the democratic winds blew in from the growing West, as the suffrage was being broadened, and as the last vestiges of the early aristocratic leadership were disappearing. Sharp alterations in the distribution of power were taking place and they were paralleled by these shifts in forms of nomination. The old order, as is usual, had its mourners. In 1843, for example, a Whig convention in Illinois offered a nomination to Governor Duncan of that state who rejected it with these words: [3]

> This convention system, if adopted by both parties, will make our government a prize to be sought after by political gamblers. It throws the chains of slavery and degradation around its votaries, prostrates the fine feelings of nature, extinguishes every spark of patriotism, creates jealousies, distrusts, and angry divisions in society, and will ultimately make us an easy prey to some fiend, or despot, at the head of an army or church, whose followers, like themselves, love the spoils of power better than the liberty of their country. . . .
>
> In fact, I look upon the convention system as designed by its authors to change the government from the free will of the people into the hands of designing politicians, and which must in a short time drive from public employment every honest man in the country. Is it not so to a great extent already?

Spirit of the convention system. In spirit the convention system, which was gradually installed over the entire country, marked a break with the tradition represented by the legislative caucus. The convention mechanism constituted in form a means for transmitting, from local assemblies, the wishes and impulses of the mass of party membership to a central point, where the selection of nominees was made. The convention was a means for the expression of the "popular will" of the party; it was a representative government for the party.

In practice the state convention consisted of delegates chosen either directly by the party membership in local units—towns, cities, or counties —or, more often, of delegates chosen by county conventions whose membership, in turn, had been selected by the party membership in the smaller local units. These basic gatherings of voters or party members to select delegates were called variously, "precinct conventions," "caucuses," or "primaries." In addition to the state conventions, other conventions were held to nominate candidates for offices filled by the voters of other areas: cities, counties, state legislative districts, congressional districts, and other electoral areas.

Disenchantment with the convention. The convention remained the dominant mode of nomination of party candidates until about 1910; eventually

[3] Quoted by C. E. Merriam and L. Overacker, *Primary Elections* (Chicago: University of Chicago Press, 1928), p. 256.

it fell into disrepute, as had the legislative caucus, and for much the same reasons. The convention came to be regarded as an instrument of organization control, as a means of boss rule, as an institution at war with aspirations toward "democratic" government.

After the Civil War the rapid growth of industry and finance made control of state governments a valuable prize for the seekers of legislative privilege. The expansion of cities laid the foundations for fortunes for those who could extract from city councils franchises and other rights. Those who sought control of government worked through the convention because it happened at the time to be a critical link in the governing process. The convention itself was blamed for their abuses.

At the "precinct convention" or "caucus" stage unfair practices often occurred. "Snap" primaries, those called without adequate notice, could be readily controlled by the party machine. On occasion, strong-arm squads in the cities intimidated the antimachine elements in the precinct caucuses. High-handed presiding officers might recognize only the members of their own faction. In the state or city convention itself the controlling faction might refuse to seat duly elected delegates and, instead, recognize contesting delegations affiliated with the machine. On occasion, money was used to manage the delegates.

Perhaps more important than such abuses for the downfall of the convention was the fact that it often came under the clear and open domination of a boss, of a city machine, of a state organization. Almost inevitably such an assemblage—even though it be an ecclesiastical convention—will be managed by a small clique. Yet the rings controlling nominating conventions consisted often of unsavory characters allied with both the moneyed interests and the underworld. The convention was a spectacle dramatizing the dominance of such combinations in states and cities. The impression conveyed by the convention may be suggested by Professor Charles E. Merriam's recollections of his experience as a delegate to a city convention:

I recall my last local convention under the old "deliberative" regime. The delegates had been chosen on the day before, and as soon as the returns began to come in the bosses gathered and began to appraise their strength in terms of the new battle. All night long the leaders counting their blocks of delegates had been sitting in high conclave, dividing the places on the ticket, trading back and forth, combining and recombining, bluffing and finessing. There were so many commissioners here and so many there, a county office here and another there, the patronage value of each carefully calculated in the bargain, sub-jobs, arrangements, understandings in regard to a wide variety of perquisites and privileges, all nicely calculatd in determining the equitable balance. Over all hung the shadow of possible war in the convention, possible combination for control between some two or more of the trading powers.

We assemble at high noon, a restless multitude of delegates; half-past twelve comes and nothing happens; one o'clock and we become impatient; but we are told that "They" have not arrived. "They" have not finished the slate. "They" will soon be here. "They" are coming and finally "They" arrive, and the convention solemnly opens. A motion is made here and there. A vote is called for and there is a murmur of voices. Many voices, for they must all be named by roll-call and the incantation continues. Another and another. Who was named then? And finally we hasten out, buying copies of an evening extra, and learn the names of the nominees. The ritual is over. And this is sometimes called "deliberation." [4]

Attempts were made to prevent convention abuses by law. Originally the party was a private association; it was no more illegal to commit fraud in the party caucus or primary than it would be to do so in the election of officers of a drinking club. Beginning in California in 1886, regulation of caucuses and conventions by law, at first optional with the party and later compulsory for all parties, was attempted. By the time that regulation became fairly general, the convention system was on the way out. Popular revolt against control by the groups that managed the conventions was directed also against the convention itself, an instrument of domination by the "interests."

Spread of the direct primary. Although the convention persists for the nomination of presidential candidates and in a few states for the designation of state candidates, the direct primary is now used for most nominations for state and local office. Under this system candidates are chosen through an election in which all members of the party, or in some instances any person qualified to vote, may participate. The voters act directly in contrast with their indirect choice through conventions made up of delegates one or two stages removed from the precinct caucuses or primaries.

The mechanism of the direct primary admirably suited the needs of the ideology of the progressive movement, which stirred American politics in the years following 1900. The leaders of that agitation demanded a restoration of government to the people and attacked the trusts, the interests, the seekers of special privilege, and the party machines. To them the direct primary constituted a means by which an enlightened people might cut through the mesh of organized and privileged power and grasp control of the government. They had a faith that the people, once equipped with the proper weapons, would throw from office the rascals in possession of the city halls and state houses. Although the primary had been experimented with elsewhere and had been used in the South, Wisconsin, under the leadership of Robert M. La Follette, enacted the

[4] *Ibid.*, pp. 259–260.

first state-wide direct primary law in 1903. Other states, mainly in the West where the progressive movement was strongest, soon followed. "In 1907 Iowa, Nebraska, Missouri, North Dakota, South Dakota, and Washington passed such laws; in 1908 Illinois, Kansas, Oklahoma, and Ohio followed; and finally, in 1909, Arizona, Arkansas, California, Idaho, Michigan, Nevada, New Hampshire, and Tennessee were added to the list." [5] By 1917 the direct primary had been adopted for most nominations in all save a handful of the states.

The spread of the direct primary is commonly attributed to its appeal as an instrument of popular rule, yet the probability is that the nature of the party structure in the areas of its origin stimulated its growth. In many states in the 1890's the party system had broken down in the sense that a single party dominated many states and localities. The lesser party not infrequently was under the control of the same interests that owned the principal party. In the South the destruction of the Republican party in the aftermath of Reconstruction left the Democratic party unchallenged. If governors and other officials were to be popularly elected, they had to be elected, in effect, by a direct primary within the Democratic party.

The direct primary first achieved fairly complete development in South Carolina, by party action rather than by statute. There the overturn of the convention system was also associated with drives against the ruling orders. Ben Tillman, the advocate of the primary system, led the back-country farmers against the so-called Bourbons.[6] The triumph of the Tillmanites in 1891 was followed by the installation of the direct primary. Concurrently in Georgia a movement for the direct primary led to its introduction for the nomination of candidates for local office and eventually to its use for state-wide nominations. Similarly, in Wisconsin and surrounding states the Republicans ruled without serious challenge. The ties of party—given the recency of the Civil War—made it simpler to advance popular government by introducing the direct primary to permit intraparty competition than to proceed by a realignment of parties.[7] The convention system in a one-party situation does not serve well to produce acceptable decisions on contests that stir and involve extensively the multitude.

In due course misgivings arose about the direct primary. It turned out that party organizations, party machines, and politicians had to manage the primary as they had always taken care of party affairs. Yet the direct primary created new conditions of work for party leaders, conditions that

[5] *Ibid.*, p. 62.
[6] J. D. Hicks, *Populist Revolt* (Minneapolis: University of Minnesota Press, 1931), pp. 143–144.
[7] The point of this paragraph is developed by Key, *American State Politics: An Introduction* (New York: Knopf, 1956), ch. 4.

affected their manner of operation and influenced the nature of party itself.

Nominating Processes and Party Structure

The evolution of nominating procedure has left the direct primary as the dominant method of nominating candidates for the thousands of state, county, and city offices, as well as for places in the United States Senate and House of Representatives. Parties continue to nominate through the convention in only a few places. New York, Indiana, Connecticut, and Delaware retain the convention for nominations for offices filled by the voters of the entire state.[8] Michigan parties nominate for the lesser state-wide offices through conventions. Other states retain the convention to choose delegates to the national presidential nominating convention or to adopt platforms and to settle other party questions. Yet direct primaries, held usually from April to September preceding the November elections, in most states settle the nominations of candidates.

Correlation between nominating forms and nature of party. Although the convention system of nominations seems to be associated with a general type of party system, the most bewildering variety of party structures exists behind the façade of the direct primary. In those jurisdictions employing the convention, "party" tends to approximate the old-time conception of it as a fairly cohesive crowd of activists—of professional politicians—who are able to settle their differences over candidates through the oligarchical processes of the convention. Aspirants for nomination at the hands of a convention must cultivate the good will of the comparatively small clique of persons who manage conventions. Agreement among a few leaders not uncommonly decides the nomination. Those leaders may have to choose among ambitious and powerful contenders or they may have to draft a promising prospect reluctant to make the race.[9] However the party leadership operates, nominations are made with precious little popular participation, although the leadership may take its decisions with an acute awareness of the probable popularity of their candidate at the general election.

The remnants of the convention system are mainly in states that retain

[8] Indiana's state convention delegates ballot secretly by voting machine, a practice that alters the nature of a convention. On the odd and wondrous practices of Delaware's conventions, see Paul Dolan, *The Government and Administration of Delaware* (New York: Crowell, 1956), pp. 35–36.

[9] Thus, in New York in 1954 Republican leaders drafted Senator Irving M. Ives to make the race for governor, while the Democratic convention chose Averell Harriman over Franklin D. Roosevelt, Jr. In 1956, the principal leaders of the Democratic organization induced Robert F. Wagner to accept the Democratic convention's nomination for the Senate.

a fairly even and continuous competition between the major parties for control of the state government. These states are also older states in which the party organizations have inherited and maintained a comparatively high degree of solidarity. The existence of two closely competitive parties probably made the propaganda of the enthusiasts for the direct primary less persuasive in these states; a "democratic" popular choice between parties existed even though the intraparty procedures for the designation of candidates were quite "undemocratic." At any rate, convention states usually have two relatively cohesive and competing party organizations. The states may retain the convention because the organizations are cohesive, or the organizations may give the appearance of solidarity because their states retain the convention system.

In contrast, the fact that a state uses the direct primary provides no indication of the underlying character of party organization. The direct primary procedure can accommodate itself to the most varied sorts of organization among the political activists. And perhaps the existence of the primary procedure itself gives encouragement to variety in forms of political organization. In some of the one-party states a two-party system, in effect if not in form, exists within the major party. In two-party jurisdictions both party organizations may be so well disciplined that their informal selections of candidates are ratified routinely in the direct primary; or political leadership in a state or community may be so pulverized that a myriad of personal factions compete in the primaries for nominations. In effect, party may not exist in the sense of organized leadership effort to capture the government by advancing candidates.

Situational consequences of the direct primary. A new institution of procedure may create a new situation in which candidates or officials must work. The new situation, because it involves new sorts of opportunities for action, may pave the way for, but not necessarily result in, new forms of behavior. The direct primary established a new set of circumstances within which political leaders concerned with nominations had to work. The character of these new circumstances encouraged the development of new forms of organization and disorganization of party leadership.

The fundamental alteration in the nominating situation brought by the direct primary was a broadening of popular participation in nominations. Although the mass of party members had had the privilege of participating indirectly in convention nominations by taking part in precinct caucuses or primaries, few took advantage of the opportunity. The convention process by and large involved either the ratification of the decisions of a handful of leaders or the settlement of conflicts among factions of the party leadership.

The adoption of the direct primary left the way open for all qualified voters to share with the party leadership in the designation of candidates. In fact, the extent to which popular participation in the primary occurs differs widely from state to state and from time to time. In over two-thirds of the primaries to nominate gubernatorial candidates in a group of non-southern states from 1926 to 1952 less than 35 per cent of the potential voters participated in one or the other of the major party primaries.[10] Although no data are available on popular participation in the choice of delegates to conventions, doubtless the primary brought a much wider participation in the nominating process.

Another measure of participation in nominating primaries appears in Table 14.1, which compares the total vote in party primaries to nominate gubernatorial candidates in all states with the vote cast in the general election for the primary nominee. Fewer than 60 per cent as many persons vote in most Republican primaries as vote for the Republican candidate in the general election. Outside the southern states the Democratic primary vote tends to be smaller in relation to the general election vote than is the Republican primary vote. In the southern states, however, the Democratic primary vote often exceeds the Democratic vote in the general election, a fact reflected in the distribution in the Democratic columns of the table.

Table 14.1

Contested Democratic and Republican Gubernatorial Primaries, 1940–1956 Distributed According to Percentage Total Primary Vote Was of General Election Vote for Primary Nominee

Primary Vote as Per Cent of General Election Vote	Republican Primaries		Democratic Primaries		Total	
	Number of Primaries	Per Cent of Primaries	Number of Primaries	Per Cent of Primaries	Number of Primaries	Per Cent of Primaries
10–19	6	4.8	6	4.1	12	4.4
20–39	17	13.6	41	28.1	58	21.4
40–59	55	44.0	18	12.3	73	26.9
60–79	28	22.4	20	13.7	48	17.7
80–99	8	6.4	13	8.9	21	7.8
100 and over	11	8.8	48	32.9	59	21.8
Total	125	100.0	146	100.0	271	100.0

Popular participation in nominations altered the situation confronted by the upper echelons of party leadership, by the party machine, by aspirants

[10] For the details of these figures, see Key, *op. cit.*, pp. 135–136.

for nominations. Rival factions and leaders now could fight out their differences in a campaign directed to the electorate—or a substantial segment of it—rather than be bound by the decisions of an assembly of delegates. Aspirants for nomination could likewise appeal directly to voters—or to those who voted in the primary—rather than be limited largely to the cultivation of the professionals who controlled the convention and constituted the operating core of the party. By the same token new elements of power were introduced into the nominating process. Prominent among them were newspaper publishers and others in control of channels to reach the public.

Competition for primary nominations. Clues to the ways in which the party leadership echelons adapted themselves to the new situation created by the direct primary may be found in analyses of the incidence of competition among aspirants for primary nominations in different sorts of circumstances. The frequency of contests in the primaries differs with the balance of strength between the two major parties in the general election voting. If the Republicans usually attract a small vote in a jurisdiction, their primary nomination tends to go to an unopposed aspirant who has taken the trouble to get his name on the ballot. As the usual size of the Republican vote increases, primary contests occur more frequently. When the Republican vote becomes so high that the Republican nominee invariably wins the general election, the frequency of contests for Democratic nominations varies among classes of constituencies with differences in the customary strength of Democratic candidates at the general election.[11]

These relationships in the division of strength between the parties and competition within parties for nomination were demonstrated by data on gubernatorial primaries at an earlier point.[12] Their existence in primaries to nominate candidates for the United States Senate and House of Representatives is shown in a later chapter.[13] Another illustration of the relationship appears in Table 14.2, which shows the incidence of competition in Republican and Democratic primaries for the nomination of

[11] Although the relationship between frequency of contests for nomination and the traditional balance of strength between the parties is fairly widespread, it should not be supposed that the party strength factor is the sole stimulant or depressant of rivalry for nominations. With a fairly high probability incumbents can, for example, look forward to renomination by the primary without serious contest. Yet there are exceptions to this rule and other customs and factors have a bearing. On some of these variations, see Julius Turner, "Primary Elections as the Alternative to Party Competition in 'Safe' Districts," *Journal of Politics*, 15 (1953), pp. 197–210.

[12] Pp. 319–20.

[13] Pp. 479, 488.

candidates for the Missouri House of Representatives. As that table makes clear, simultaneous contests in both party primaries in a single legislative district are exceptional in Missouri; contests tend to take place in the primary of the stronger party in a district. Another illustration of the variations in the incidence of party competition appears in Table 14.3. The data in that table on Republican nominations for the New Hampshire senate

Table 14.2

Balance of Party Strength and Competition for Primary Nominations: Contests for Nominations for Missouri House of Representatives, 1948–1950 [a]

Democratic Percentage General Election	Seats	Per Cent of Nominations Contested in—			
		Both Primaries	Neither Primary	Democratic Only	Republican Only
Under 40	66	0.0	47.0	0.0	53.0
40–49	63	7.9	44.4	7.9	39.7
50–59	72	11.1	56.9	18.1	13.9
60 and over	107	6.5	44.9	43.9	4.7
Total	308	6.5	48.0	21.1	24.3

[a] A contested nomination is defined for this table as a primary involving two or more aspirants for the nomination.

Table 14.3

Variations in Party Strength and Competition for Primary Nominations: New Hampshire Republican State Senatorial Primaries, 1910–1926, According to Number of Candidates Running in Primary in Relation to Republican Proportion of General Election Vote

Republican Per Cent of General Election Vote	Primaries According to Number of Candidates				Total
	Two or more		One		
	Number	Per Cent	Number	Per Cent	
Under 30	0	00.0	3	100.0	3
30–39	4	33.3	8	66.7	12
40–49	22	53.7	19	46.3	41
50–59	48	54.5	40	45.5	88
60–69	38	69.1	17	30.9	55
70–79	6	66.7	3	33.3	9
80 and over	2	100.0	0	00.0	2
Total	121	57.3	90	42.7	211

reveal the tendency for the frequency of primary competition to increase with the general election strength of the party.[14]

Varieties in leadership structure. As might be supposed, these variations in the incidence of primary contests reflect the existence of a variety of forms of organization of party leadership in states and in local electoral units. No satisfactory estimate can be made of the extent to which these different forms of organization prevail. Yet the nature of the major types may be roughly indicated.

In jurisdictions leaning strongly to one party or the other, as has been noted, contests for primary nominations in the primaries of the lesser party are relatively infrequent. Often a few leaders of the party agree upon a slate of candidates whose names are placed on the primary ballot. The problem usually is one, not of settling rivalries among would-be candidates, but of finding enough candidates to present a complete slate.[15] In other instances of uncontested nomination no concerted action to produce a slate occurs; scattered individuals, on their own initiative, circulate petitions or declare their candidacy and appear on the ballot. Under these circumstances often the party does not have candidates for all offices filled at the general election.

A radically different pattern of leadership at times stands behind an uncontested primary. The party organization, through its central committee or executive committee, endorses a slate of primary candidates. This committee action may be more or less customary and publicly known and accepted. Thus, in Chicago campaign leaflets may be circulated at the time of the primary under the title, "Candidates Endorsed by the Democratic County Central Committee and the Democratic State Central Committee," or "Regular Republican Candidates Recommended by the Cook County Republican Central Committee." If the organization is united and well fortified with campaign resources, challenge of its slate may be futile in the primary. The organization workers in each precinct marshal their following at the polls to win the nomination for the "regu-

---

[14] For an analysis of primaries for county offices in Iowa, see K. H. Porter, "The Deserted Primary in Iowa," *American Political Science Review*, 39 (1945), pp. 732–740.

[15] In some states the statutes give parties the option of nominating by convention or primary, and the lesser party often chooses to nominate by convention. The practice is especially notable among the Republicans in the southern states. An equivalent practice elsewhere is illustrated by the action of the Windsor County, Vermont, Democrats in 1954. A caucus, presided over by the Democratic county chairman, chose a slate of county candidates whose names were to be written onto the primary ballots by the faithful few Democrats to fulfill the legal niceties for nomination. The write-in method saved the trouble of obtaining signatures to petitions legally required for names to be printed on the primary ballot.

lar" slate.[16] No challenge occurs or other candidates for nomination make only the most perfunctory race and draw only a few votes.[17] The absence of a primary contest may, of course, also mean that extensive bargaining has occurred within the leadership ranks to quell incipient rebellion.[18] Some state laws prohibit endorsement of primary slates by party committees. Under these circumstances the leadership core of the party may act informally or may even create extralegal political committees that assume the function of slate-making and leadership in the nominating process.[19]

Serious contests within the primary may reflect a fractionalization of the leadership echelons of the party. Differences founded on rivalries of individual leaders, on ideological differences, or on other cleavages may be reflected in more or less continuing factional struggles within the party leadership. The existence of the primary opens the road for dissident elements of the leadership to carry their fight to the voters of the party and that road is often traveled.[20] A recurring characteristic of these confused

[16] In some jurisdictions a large number of signatures is required to place a candidate on the primary ballot, a requisite readily met for the organization slate but an obstacle to other aspirants. A candidate may place his name on the primary ballot in some jurisdictions by his own declaration of candidacy or by a petition signed by a nominal number of voters. The laws of some states require payment of a fee to obtain a place on the ballot. In southern states in which the party finances the primary the costs are assessed against the candidates; the individual fee may be several thousand dollars in a populous county. Michigan permits, as an alternative to a petition, a deposit of money to be made. The deposit is returnable if the candidate polls half as many votes as the nominee. Rural candidates, cannier about a dollar, choose the deposit alternative less frequently than the urbanites. See H. M. Dorr, "Nomination by Money Deposit," *National Municipal Review*, 43 (1954), pp. 288–292. These and many other features of the state primary laws are summarized in Sen. Doc. 116, 84th Cong., 2d sess. (1956).

[17] It may be that party organizations tend, other things equal, to agree upon a slate and repress their internal differences, most often when the electorate customarily divides near the 50-50 mark. Groups, when threatened by a dangerous enemy, may tend to cohere more strongly.

[18] For example, the concession of patronage appointments by one party faction to another to ward off the threat of a primary challenge against an aspirant for, say, a senatorial nomination. Or, a skillful allocation of places on the primary slate has satisfied all concerned. Or ambitious men have been promised that their turn will come next time.

[19] See Frank J. Sorauf, "Extra-Legal Political Parties in Wisconsin," *American Political Science Review*, 48 (1954), pp. 692–704.

[20] Bitter primary fights consume campaign resources and often leave scars that make it difficult to unite the leadership against the opposition in the general election campaign. The statutes often place obstacles in the way of the loser of a primary so unreconciled that he proposes to run as an independent in the general election. State laws at times prohibit an independent or third-party candidacy by a primary loser. Others achieve the same end by requiring that petitions for independent candidacy in the general election be filed before the party primaries.

factional conflicts is that the voters often have no notion of the nature, composition, orientation, or objectives of the leadership factions that struggle for control of the nominations. Instead of finding on the ballot a well-advertised "organization" slate and perhaps an "anti-organization" slate and a few volunteer candidates, the voter finds names of individual candidates backed by anonymous or the most nebulous groups or cliques. A handful of party officials, of associated interest group leaders, and of other political activists may have agreed upon a man to back for governor, say, in the primary, but their deliberations may never be a matter of general public knowledge. Another clique of professionals and their associates with access to enough money to finance a primary campaign may place another man in the race. Or the moving force in forming leadership cliques may be the aspirants for the nomination. Whatever the process, the primary voters may have only a glimmering of the nature of the leadership squabble they are called upon to decide.

At times the direct primary operates without the help of more or less durable groupings of party leaders who advance persons for nomination. Instead a large number of individuals may attempt to build little followings to win the nomination for a particular office at a primary; the general rule of nomination by a plurality of the votes may enable the most unlikely aspirants for the nomination to win and may make the nomination a decision by chance. Or, given the large numbers of offices filled by election, little leadership clusters may be constructed at the time of each primary by the many individuals who seek to be candidates for the various offices. The professionals do not unite behind a slate; nor do they divide into a pair of groups. Rather the process of struggle for primary nominations generates many small clusters of "pros" and "semi-pros" about aspirants for individual offices. And, in truth, at times it is utterly unreal to speak of the existence of any sort of party leadership group with any capacity to steer or influence the nominating process. Individuals, for example, with the "right" name may poll heavy votes without the aid of any support among the professionals, a circumstance that reflects the existence of an unbossed, unled, and usually uninformed electorate.[21] Under these conditions the voters in the primary are often guided by religious or eth-

---

[21] Thus, the nominee of the Wisconsin Democratic primary for attorney general in 1956 was one Robert La Follette Sucher, who was reported by the press to be "an unknown" but he had a name politically attractive in Wisconsin. In 1954 Massachusetts Democrats nominated for state treasurer one John Kennedy, another unknown who happened to have the name of Kennedy, a name made both popular and familiar by the junior Senator from the state. In Boston in 1956 one of the 12 candidates for nomination for sheriff was one William P. Foley who polled 8,879 votes; he had earlier run for the city council under his former name, William P. Intraversato, and attracted

nic preferences, by the recommendations of newspapers, or by their recognition of a name that seems to them to be familiar and of good repute.[22]

Primaries as elections. In many states and in many units of local government the winner of the primary almost invariably wins the election. In
these one-party jurisdictions it can hardly be said that a "party" system
exists. Nor can it be said that the primary is a method of nomination; it is
the election.

The real "parties" in these jurisdictions are the factional groupings that
compete for electoral favor within the primary of the dominant party.
The "party systems" in such jurisdictions take a variety of forms. In some
southern states the competing factions within the Democratic party have
a continuity, a solidarity, and an identity in the public eye that make
them not unlike the major parties in a two-party state. In other states the
factional groups in the dominant party may be amorphous, ill-defined,
and kaleidoscopic. In counties, cities, towns, villages, and other one-party
units the forms of intraparty factions are doubtless varied but information
about them is scarce.

In these one-party jurisdictions, though the "nominations" are technically made by primary, the nominating process actually occurs at the
stage when the "organization" puts candidates into the primary, when
cliques rally behind an aspirant for the nomination, or when other preprimary maneuvers occur to sift out and designate the more formidable contenders for the formal nominations.

A substantial proportion of American state and local elections are held
merely to ratify the nominations of the primary of the dominant party.
An analysis by Cortez A. M. Ewing suggests the degree of the finality of
the primary. He finds that from 1896 to 1946 slightly more than half (53.5
per cent) of the elections to the national House of Representatives were
by a 20 per cent popular plurality; that is, the winner had at least a 60-40
lead in the election. Thus in half the contests the outcome was rarely
much in doubt; the decision fell to the voters in the major-party primary.
As would be supposed the states in which the largest proportions of con-

---

far fewer votes. A Boston politician not born a Foley finds it advantageous to become
one.
[22] The unbossed primary electorate which acts on a minimum of information permits some politicians to engage in a genteel form of extortion. In some districts an
Irish name, or a Jewish name, or a Yankee name, or even any sort of name is good for
a substantial number of primary votes. A name may be entered in the primary and
used as leverage for the extraction of cash or other valuable consideration from the
front-runner most apt to be injured. On appropriate settlement, the name is with-
drawn before the ballot is printed.

gressional elections were won by pluralities of more than 20 per cent were in the South.[23]

In most states the party nomination goes to the candidate with the highest number of votes in the primary even though he may lack a majority of the votes. In two-party states minority nominations occur fairly frequently but create no widespread dissatisfaction. Most of the one-party states, however, have sought to assure majority nominations by requiring a second, or runoff, primary, if no candidate receives a majority at the first primary.[24] At the second polling the contest is between the two persons polling the highest vote at the first primary. The runoff primary seems to have been adopted, not on the basis of the abstract majoritarian principle, but as the result of the rise of multifactional systems productive of frequent minority nominations.[25]

Primary and Party Responsibility

The direct primary procedure seems in general to make more difficult the domination of the nominating process by the party organization and the interests affiliated with it. That result comes about in part because the primary encourages cleavages among the political professionals and careerists by permitting them to carry their differences to the primary voters for settlement. The selection of candidates may even become the fortuitous result of the interaction among many centers of influence.

[23] "Primaries as Elections," Southwestern Social Science Quarterly, 29 (1948-49), pp. 293-298. See also Professor Ewing's Primary Elections in the South (Norman: University of Oklahoma Press, 1953).

[24] Some states both within and outside the South sought to avoid minority nominations by preferential voting but they abandoned that system. See O. Douglas Weeks, "Summary of the History and Present Status of Preferential Voting in State Direct Primary Systems," Southwestern Social Science Quarterly, 18 (1937-38), pp. 64-67.

[25] The runoff primary for state-wide offices exists in Alabama, Arkansas, Florida, Georgia, Louisiana, Mississippi, North Carolina, Oklahoma, South Carolina, Texas, and Virginia. Tennessee requires a runoff in the unlikely event of a tie vote. The systems in Arkansas, North Carolina, and Virginia diverge in detail from the pattern described in the text. Kentucky and Utah at one time or another have used the runoff. In contrast with the attempt to assure majority nominations, Maryland and Georgia have systems that permit minority nominations. In these states the nomination is technically made by conventions but delegates are bound, after the fashion of presidential electors, by the primary vote in their constituencies. The apportionment of convention delegates follows that in the state legislatures and thus discriminates against larger urban communities. A candidate may, as did Eugene Talmadge in Georgia in 1946, lead in convention votes but trail in the popular primary vote. In 1950 John M. Butler won the Maryland Republican senatorial nomination and W. P. Lane, the Democratic gubernatorial nomination without a popular plurality. See F. L. Burdette, Election Practices in Maryland (College Park: University of Maryland, 1950).

And at times the party leadership may seem to disappear as it disintegrates into picayune cliques.

Such tendencies, it is often asserted, destroy party responsibility. The concept of party responsibility is most ambiguous, but those who employ it in this context seem to mean that the weakening of the influence of party organization in the designation of candidates tends to produce irresponsible, that is, ill-considered, choices. The inner core may find its choice for nomination defeated in the primary by a banjo player, a demagogue who really ought to be in the other party, or some other bizarre person whom the party wheelhorses cannot support with enthusiasm in the general election campaign.[26] From another angle the destruction of party responsibility may mean that discontented elements in the party may determine the nomination on issues that should have driven them to the opposite party. The complaint is made, for example, about the occasional nomination of Fair Deal Republicans in Republican primaries. From another aspect, the notion of weakening party responsibility may mean that most voters are attracted to the primary of one party and there fight out the issues that would otherwise be settled in the general election campaign, with the result that whatever consistency of attitude party candidates might otherwise have over a period of time is broken. In the process the minority party may be weakened or virtually destroyed.

Preprimary convention. To offset some of the less happy results of the primary nominating process and to permit an open and accepted role by the party organization in the choice of candidates, a few states have enacted legislation authorizing conventions to designate a slate of candidates before the direct primary. Ordinarily the primary ballot indicates that these candidates have the endorsement of the party convention. If the convention arrives at decisions acceptable to the major elements of the leadership, its choices may not even be challenged in the primary. Or if the convention leaders also have at their command an adequate electioneering organization, their slate can readily triumph over independent candidates. In effect, the preprimary convention procedure in some instances brings into the open and gives official blessing to the function of the party leadership in building organization slates for the primaries.

[26] The characterization by Boyd A. Martin of the situation in Idaho undoubtedly applies in some other states: "Many Republican politicians were afraid of insurgent groups within their own ranks, as well as of outside groups like the Non-Partisan League. The more conservative elements wanted a bottleneck at the top of the state party organization. This feature of control from the top was what the conservative leaders called *party responsibility.*"—*The Direct Primary in Idaho* (Stanford University: Stanford University Press, 1947), p. 76.

Some of the results attributable to the primary, as well as some of the considerations involved in the preprimary convention, are suggested by the Massachusetts preprimary convention. In that state the Republicans in 1948 and 1950 had slates for state offices composed entirely of Yankee Republicans. Some Republican leaders surmised that their misfortunes might have come from their failure to take into account in their slates the ethnic realities of Massachusetts. Yet to nominate in a free primary anybody other than a Yankee was difficult. Under Republican leadership, with some aid from Italo-American Democrats restive under Irish domination of their party, the 1951 legislature voted to authorize preprimary conventions. The Democratic governor vetoed the bill, but the Republicans proceeded to hold an extralegal convention to endorse a primary slate. A nicely balanced slate emerged from the convention deliberations: three Yankees, two Jewish-Americans, an Italo-American, and an Irish-American woman. The convention slate, which had the overwhelming support of the party leadership, won handily in the primary.

With the election of a Republican governor and legislature in 1952 the way was cleared for adoption of legislation on preprimary conventions which occurred in 1952. Under the law, if a party exercises the option to hold a preprimary convention, those endorsed are placed first on the ballot and are identified as holders of convention endorsement. By working through a convention which permits a consolidation of strength behind a slate and the recognition of different elements in the party, the organization may be able to offer a group of candidates more formidable in the general election than those produced by a pure primary. One of the oddities of the direct primary in state affairs is that because of differentials in primary participation from place to place a particular segment of the party—for example, the Democrats of the major city—may gain a preponderant voice in the primary. Candidates capable of popular triumph in the primary under such circumstances may not be strong candidates before the larger electorate in the general election.

Preprimary conventions are used, or have been used, in other states. For a time New Mexico had a preprimary convention. In that state the Republican party is especially handicapped in operating through the direct primary which tends to favor nominees from a handful of Republican counties, persons who often have a weak state-wide appeal even though they may be popular in their own party.[27] Nebraska also has abandoned the preprimary convention. Given the predominance of the Republican party in Nebraska in recent years, that state's action suggests that the conditions most favorable for the preprimary convention include the

[27] See Jack E. Holmes, *Problems Relating to Various Nominating Procedures in New Mexico* (New Mexico Legislative Council Service, 1955).

existence of a fairly even competition between two parties. Peril probably moves the leadership of a party to seek party unity through convention or negotiation. The dominance of one party almost insures that the conflict for popular favor will be fought out in its primary; the deliberations of a preprimary convention are not apt to produce agreement among all factions and potential candidates.

Usually the preprimary convention statute provides for the identification of the convention slate on the primary ballot but also permits other aspirants for nomination to gain a place on the ballot by petition. Under the Colorado variant the name of any person receiving 20 per cent of the convention vote goes on the ballot. If several persons so qualify, their names are placed on the ballot in the order of the size of their convention vote. Usually each party convention endorses only one person for nomination for each office; the dominant group of each party in effect names a slate that is ratified in the primary. Other individuals may be placed on the ballot by petition. Utah's preprimary convention designates two candidates for each nomination—if there are two convention aspirants— and no provision exists for other candidates to enter the primary by petition.[28]

In several states the equivalent of the preprimary convention has grown up in extralegal form in reflection of attempts to consolidate party leadership on nominations. California's development of informal preprimary assemblies is one of the more striking instances. The convention of the Republican Assembly endorses primary candidates, and when no suitable aspirant turns up under his own power the Assembly may search out a prospect and induce him to seek the primary nomination with its endorsement. The Democrats followed the precedent of the California Republicans and formed the California Democratic Council in 1953 to make preprimary endorsements. After the 1954 primaries, it could be said that "although the direct primary election remained the formal method of nomination in both parties, the actual decision was made by extralegal groups, with few other aspirants entering the primary." [29] Similarly, in

[28] See R. N. Ballard, *The Primary Convention System in Utah* (Institute of Government, University of Utah, 1947). Brief accounts of the preprimary convention systems may be found in *A Model Direct Primary System* (New York, 1951), being a report of the National Municipal League's Committee on the Direct Primary, of which Joseph P. Harris was chairman.

[29] Thomas S. Barclay, "The 1954 Election in California," *Western Political Quarterly*, 7 (1954), p. 597. See also Hugh A. Bone, "New Party Associations in the West," *American Political Science Review*, 45 (1951), pp. 1115–1125; Currin V. Shields, "A Note on Party Organization: The Democrats in California," *Western Political Quarterly*, 7 (1954), pp. 673–683; Dean R. Cresap, *Party Politics in the Golden State* (Los Angeles: The Haynes Foundation, 1954), ch. 7.

Wisconsin, party associations have grown up outside the formal, or legally prescribed, party apparatus to hold conventions in order that the principal leaders of the party may agree upon and endorse candidates to support in the direct primaries.

Other modified primary systems. Another variation on the pure direct system is exemplified by the statute adopted in 1955 by the legislature of Connecticut, a state which had been most steadfast in its adherence to convention procedures in nomination. The 1955 law provided for postconvention primaries by which candidates rejected by the convention might appeal to the party voters in the primary. Persons who received at least 20 per cent of the convention vote were permitted to challenge the convention nominee in a subsequent direct primary. The primary could be set in motion by filing a petition and making a deposit to be returned if the challenger polled at least 15 per cent of the primary vote. The Democratic state chairman opined at the time of the passage of the law that the new procedure would pose a problem for political leaders in that they would have to choose candidates who could overcome a primary challenge. A candidate with good prospects at the general election, he thought, might not necessarily do well in a primary. Conceivably the procedure for appeal from convention to primary will splinter the party leadership, although the full effects, if any, of the new situation on the cohesiveness of the party organization will materialize only gradually.

Open and closed primaries. Another characteristic of direct primaries that bears upon the role and influence of the party leadership in the nominating process concerns the question of what persons are entitled to vote in the primary. Participation in a "closed" primary is limited to party members. Under an "open" primary system the voter may decide when he goes to the polls whether he will vote in the Democratic or the Republican primary. The details of the administration of these systems, in reality, either obstruct or facilitate the movement of voters from the primary of one party to that of the other.

The most common mode of determination of party membership and, hence, of eligibility to vote in the closed primary of the party is by enrollment at the time of registration. At that time the voter "enrolls" as a member of the party of his choice or asserts an affiliation which is indicated on the registration record. On primary day he is given the ballot of the party shown on the registration record. In some jurisdictions the party preference for entry on the records is expressed on the occasion of the voter's first primary vote. Whatever the procedure for enrollment, the voter is put to some inconvenience if he wishes to change his enrollment from one party to another, a step which must be taken some time before the primary. Furthermore, the registration lists commonly include the names of persons who have chosen to affiliate with no party and thereby are ineligible to vote in the primaries.

Some versions of the closed primary system include no enrollment procedure. Rather a test of party membership may be applied at the polls at the time of voting in the primary. Only infrequently is the right of persons to vote in such primaries challenged. The test of party membership is prescribed either by law or by party rule or by state action supplemented by party rule: it is usually in terms of past partisan allegiance, present affiliation, or future intention, or a combination of these. Past allegiance may be determined by the elector's assertion that he supported the party's nominees at a preceding election. Present affiliation consists ordinarily in the elector's assertion that he is a member of the party. Future intention consists in an intention to support nominees of the party in the general election. The Texas primary ballot, for example, contains the following pledge to meet the test of present affiliation and future intention: "I am a Democrat and pledge myself to support the nominees of this primary." Such "tests" become almost a matter between the individual voter and his conscience. Hence, the difference between the open primary and some forms of the closed primary at times becomes less than sharp.[30]

The essential idea of the open primary appears in the manner of conduct of primary elections. In some states the primary ballot contains several party columns. Each party column includes the names of aspirants for the party nomination, grouped by offices, and the voter may make his choices for candidates for the several offices in whichever party column he chooses. If he votes in more than one party column, the ballot is invalidated at the count. Some states staple different party primary ballots together and permit the voter, in the pooling booth, to detach and mark one which he deposits in the ballot box while he drops the unused ballot or ballots into a box for discards. Under either system, the voter's decision about which primary he is to participate in remains secret. Wisconsin, Montana, Michigan, and Utah have employed variations of the second form of open-primary ballot, while Minnesota, Idaho, and North Dakota have used the single ballot with separate party columns.[31]

[30] Thus, in Texas in 1952 the friends of Senator Taft claimed that many "Democrats" had entered Republican caucuses and precinct conventions to support Eisenhower in the contest for the Texas Republican delegation to the national convention. The Texas legislature in 1957 gave consideration to a bill to require that party preference be stamped on poll tax receipts, an equivalent to enrollment under registration systems, in order to keep Republicans out of Democratic primaries and vice versa.

[31] The most comprehensive treatment of the open-closed primary question is by C. A. Berdahl, "Party Membership in the United States," *American Political Science*

Washington in 1935 carried the open-primary principle to its logical conclusion by adopting the "blanket" primary, under which a voter can split his vote by voting in different party primaries on different offices. The ballot is arranged in an office bloc form, with the party affiliation of each aspirant for a nomination indicated after his name. The voter may skip back and forth from party to party as he moves down the ballot from office to office.[32]

The ease with which voters may move from party to party under the open primary doubtless creates uncertainties for the party leadership in its efforts to control nominations as well as in tests of strength between leadership factions. The primary of one party may be raided by the voters of another in order to assure the nomination of a weak candidate who can be defeated in the general election. That maneuver requires, of course, the existence of a disciplined and tight organization for its execution.[33] Or at times a battle between two strong candidates in the primary of one party may attract enough voters from the other party to govern the outcome. Thus, in 1956 Glenn R. Davis, who had the support of the Wisconsin regular Republicans, lost in the primary to Senator Alexander Wiley, an Eisenhower Republican. Whether rightly, the outcome was attributed in part to an invasion of the Republican primary by Democrats. In other states Republicans have at times moved into a Democratic primary to support a conservative Democratic aspirant for a nomination. On the basis of an analysis of Michigan experience under the open primary, Professor Pollock concludes that party lines are crossed in the primaries, not to vote for a weak person to defeat in the elections but "almost always to vote for a strong candidate whom" the primary invaders expect "to support in the final election." [34]

While the consensus among students of party government appears to be that party would be better able to perform its role in the advancement of candidates if the open primary were abandoned, it must be conceded that systematic knowledge of the practical consequences of the open primary is limited. Yet it seems fairly clear that the open primary makes difficult the maintenance of orientations differentiating the two parties

---

Review, 36 (1942), pp. 16–50, 241–262. See also Illinois Legislative Council, Research Department, *The Direct Primary Ballot* (Publication No. 25, July, 1940).

[32] See C. O. Johnson, "The Washington Blanket Primary," *Pacific Northwest Quarterly*, January, 1942, pp. 27–39. See D. M. Ogden, Jr., "The Blanket Primary and Party Regularity in Washington," *Pacific Northwest Quarterly*, 39 (1948), pp. 33–38.

[33] In fact, even under the closed primary occasionally an organization in a small area may have such a surplus of voters that it can enroll enough persons as members of the minority to control its nominations.

[34] James K. Pollock, *The Direct Primary in Michigan, 1909–1935* (Ann Arbor: University of Michigan Press, 1943), p. 60.

and probably handicaps the lesser party in those jurisdictions in which one party holds a substantial advantage. The voters of the lesser party may find it more attractive to exercise a balance of power in the primary of the major party than to engage in the troublesome task of building up their own party.[35]

Cross filing and related practices. Closely related to the question of what voters are to be permitted to participate in a primary is the question of what tests shall be met by persons who seek the party's nomination in the primary. In most states a person may run for nomination in only a single primary, and ordinarily he must meet a test of party membership to enter the primary. Eligibility is usually established routinely without controversy. The exceptions tend to arise at times of internal party crisis accompanied by desertion to the opposition. In some southern states, for example, the tests for primary candidates exclude individuals who campaigned against Democratic candidates at the preceding general election. Thus, some persons who bolted the Democratic party to support Herbert Hoover for President in 1928 found themselves ineligible to run for Democratic nominations in the primaries of 1930.[36]

In a few states a person may seek nomination for the same office in the primaries of both parties. If he wins both primaries he goes on the general election ballot as both the Democratic and Republican nominee. The best known "cross-filing" or "double-filing" system is that of California, although a few other states permit the practice. A major consequence of the practice of cross filing on a large scale seems to be to handicap or retard the growth of the lesser of the two parties. A party that has long dominated an area has among its leaders many well-advertised names and its candidates, given the low level of information of the primary electorate, can often capture the nominations of the lesser party as well as those of its own. That effect is well demonstrated by the experience of California. In 1944 in 90 per cent of the state senate districts a single can-

---

[35] The point is illustrated by the experience of 1954 under the Texas primary, technically a closed primary but in fact open. Conservative leaders of the Democratic party urged Republicans to vote in the Democratic primary for Governor Allan Shivers. So long as Republicans can move into the Democratic primary and aid in electing one of their own sort, the incentive to build a Republican party may be weak.

[36] The requirement of party loyalty for primary candidates had a curious consequence in Alabama in the 1948 election. In that state Democratic presidential electors are nominated in the party primary; persons voting in the primary pledge themselves to support the nominees in the general election. In 1948 presidential electors pledged to oppose Truman were chosen in the primary. Senators, Representatives, and other prominent officeholders favorable to Truman could not oppose Dixiecratic pledged electors without disqualifying themselves as candidates in future Democratic primaries.

didate won both party nominations in the primaries; and well-known Republicans have in several instances won both nominations for state-wide office.[37] As the Democratic registration increased gradually over a long period the proportions of dual nominations increased; evidently Republicans found it expedient to neutralize the drawing power of the Democratic label at the general election by seeking Democratic as well as Republican nominations. In the quest for dual nominations Republicans had on the whole an advantage over the Democrats whose primary candidates were, on the average, less well known than the Republicans.

Democrats made efforts to repeal the cross-filing statute, but succeeded only in obtaining a requirement that the party affiliation of aspirants for nomination be indicated on the primary ballot. If a Republican sought a Democratic nomination, "Rep." would appear after his name on the Democratic primary ballot. This change in ballot form, which occurred as the Democratic organization itself was gaining strength, produced a marked change in primary results in 1954 and 1956. Democratic primary voters, now able to know whether they were voting for a Republican or a Democrat for the nomination, favored their fellow partisans and far fewer dual nominations were made.

In New York a variation of cross filing exists. It serves mainly to facilitate coalition between the Democratic and Liberal parties. For those candidates nominated by convention in that state, parties may combine by nominating the same candidate. For offices for which nominations are made by primary, candidates for nomination must be enrolled members of a party unless the appropriate party committee grants an exception to the rule. That arrangement, given the fact that New York party organizations usually control the outcome of their primaries, permits negotiations between a third party and a major party for coalition by dual nomination.

In New Hampshire primary candidates have been able to obtain dual nominations by write-in. Since most county offices in the state have been far beyond the reach of Democrats, often no Democratic candidate appeared on the primary ballot for at least some offices. The leading candidate in the Republican primary could also often readily win the Democratic nomination by encouraging a few friends to write his name in as the Democratic nominee. During the 1920's usually less than 10 per cent of the county offices in the state were won by persons nominated in both the Democratic and Republican primaries. In the 1930's and 1940's an upsurge in Democratic popular strength occurred; with it came also a sharp rise in the proportions of county officers elected with both party nominations. Evidently it became worth while for Republicans to make

[37] W. W. Crouch and D. E. McHenry, *State and Local Government in California* (Berkeley, University of California Press, 1952).

some effort to capture Democratic nominations, lest they be faced by general election opponents made formidable by the general drift of sentiment toward the Democratic party. The chances are that the availability of a procedure for boring from within and capturing the nominations of the lesser party tends to obstruct or delay a secular buildup of minority strength. Perhaps the moral is that a party must be able to protect itself from capture by the opposition if it is to fulfill its role in the system as a whole. Party leaders and activists who can be routed in their own camp by the majority can scarcely be expected to lead a militant minority.

Reform of nominating procedures. As may have been surmised from the preceding discussion, debate and contention over nominating procedures did not end when the direct primary generally superseded the convention system in the states. The direct primary came in on a wave of belief that here was a means by which the "people" might rule without much interposition by "politicians." Second thoughts have tended toward the view that ways and means should be found by which party organization might play a legitimate and effective role in nominations, a recognition of the elemental necessity for organized leadership in a democratic politics. Indicative of this broad shift in emphasis is a report by the National Municipal League's Committee on the Direct Primary which recommends that the party organization, acting through committees or conferences, should be authorized to propose organization slates that would be so designated on the primary ballot. The committee also advocates that individual candidates be allowed to seek the nomination of only one party, a proposal that would abolish cross filing.[38]

The Committee on Political Parties of the American Political Science Association has taken a similar position on these points and goes further to express a preference for the closed over the open primary on the ground that the closed arrangement "tends to support the concept of the party as an association of like-minded people." [39] The general drift of such recommendations is toward a revitalization of party organization, a process most feasible in jurisdictions with a fairly evenly balanced two-party competition. The chances are that in the heavily one-party jurisdictions, state and local, the direct primary will long survive in a relatively pure form. The primary procedure provides the foundation for a brand of

---

[38] The committee's report has been issued by the National Municipal League under the title, *A Model Direct Primary Election System* (1951). See the analysis by the committee's chairman, Joseph P. Harris, "A New Primary System," *State Government,* 21 (1948), pp. 140–143.

[39] The committee's report, "Toward a More Responsible Two-Party System," was published as a supplement to the *American Political Science Review,* September, 1950.

popular government in one-party areas that differs in form and structure from the two-party system but nevertheless seems to be deeply rooted in the areas in which it exists.

Nominations and the Nature of Party

This survey of nominating procedures serves to outline the main features of a significant segment of political practice. The data, moreover, provide additional insight into the nature of party itself. Observation of the permutations of nominating procedures leads to the conclusion that whatever the form of the procedure, relatively small, more or less cohesive groups tend to take the lead in organizing support for candidates. Under the system of the legislative caucus the party leaders in the legislative body took the initiative. Under the convention system the party organization, with its precinct, county, city, and state functionaries, constituted the group that guided and managed conventions. Under the direct primary the party organization remained and adapted its methods to the new machinery of nominations. Whatever the form of nominating procedure, its operation has required the collaboration of men working in concert toward common ends. And they are usually professional politicians, who perform a task that has to be accomplished to operate government. In speculation about the workings of the nominating process, the following comment by H. J. Ford is relevant:

One continually hears the declaration that the direct primary will take power from the politicians and give it to the people. This is pure nonsense. Politics has been, is, and always will be carried on by politicians, just as art is carried on by artists, engineering by engineers, business by businessmen. All that the direct primary, or any other political reform, can do is to affect the character of the politicians by altering the conditions that govern political activity, thus determining its extent and quality. The direct primary may take advantage and opportunity from one set of politicians and confer them upon another set, but politicians there will always be so long as there is politics.[40]

Although the tendency toward leadership and control by the closely knit inner core of the party may prevail, the conditions under which that core works may be seriously altered by changes in the nature of the nominating process. The adoption of the convention system marked a revolt against the "autocratic" character of the caucus system. The tendency toward democratization found expression in a new nominating form. Under the convention system there would be, it was thought, a means for the ready expression of the wishes of the mass of party membership. As it developed, the convention system itself was soon branded as "bossism."

[40] "The Direct Primary," *North American Review,* 190 (1909), pp. 1–14.

The direct primary was turned to as a means of obtaining a direct expression of choice of the party membership on nominations. Although the machine remained, in the formation of its slate for the primary it apparently has had to be more solicitous of the sentiment of party membership than it was under the convention system. Under this scheme the machine candidates have to run the gantlet of the primary, and this obstacle in the road to election may be quite serious. The conditions created by the primary may even pulverize the machine into little cliques or perhaps, under one-party conditions, stimulate the creation of two or three submachines or organizations within the major party.

Yet each major step in the development of the nominating process has marked a further obeisance to the doctrine that the will of the rank and file of party membership should prevail. Although a change in the system of making nominations does not eliminate the function of the organized minority in leading party opinion, it may enable a different minority to prevail. "We are always pulling down bosses," Ford observed, "because transient combinations of would-be bosses and reformers may develop strength enough to overthrow a particular boss or a particular machine. But while bosses and machines come and go, the boss and the machine are always with us." [41]

[41] *Ibid.*, p. 4.

15 | National Conventions

THE NATIONAL convention represents the solution by American parties of the problem of uniting scattered points of political leadership in support of candidates for the Presidency and Vice-Presidency. As such, the convention is the basic element of national party apparatus. The parties of other democratic nations have their assemblies and conferences but none of these bodies approximates in its role the American national party convention. The convention is unique among national party authorities because it nominates the candidates for the Presidency and Vice-Presidency. In turn, the Presidency owes some of its fundamental characteristics to the fact that presidential nominations emerge, not from the deliberations of party groups in Congress, but from the national convention.

The national convention did not come into being in a day: it evolved over a considerable period of time. Early presidential nominations were made by congressional caucuses, that is, gatherings of members of the party in Congress. When the Federalist representation in Congress was sharply reduced by Republican victories, the Congressional caucus could not speak for the party as a whole. The Federalists had to devise other means for agreeing among themselves on a candidate whom the party would support. In 1808, at a secret meeting of Federalist leaders in New York, Pinckney and King were nominated for the Presidency and Vice-Presidency. "This was," says S. E. Morison, "the original national nominating convention." [1] Again, in 1812 Federalist leaders met privately in New York to agree upon nominations.

These early cabals did not lead immediately to the full-fledged national convention. The congressional caucus fell before the onslaughts of Andrew Jackson. As an aspirant for the presidential nomination in 1824, Jackson could hardly hope to gain the nomination at the hands of an unsympathetic congressional caucus. His backers inaugurated a campaign to discredit the caucus itself. They boycotted the 1824 Republican caucus, which was attended by only about one-fourth of the Republican members of Congress. The caucus decision was accorded little respect by the party over the country. William H. Crawford, the caucus nominee, received fewer electoral votes than did Jackson. If the party was to act as a unit in presidential elections, an authoritative mode of presidential nomination had to be contrived.

By a series of steps the national convention developed to nominate presidential candidates. The model of state nominating conventions was at hand, but its extension to national nominations required both time and the displacement of the congressional caucus.[2] In 1828 state conventions, state legislatures, and state legislative caucuses made presidential nominations, that is, they nominated Andrew Jackson.[3] In 1831 the Anti-Masonic party held what is commonly regarded as the first national convention, and later a Democratic convention assembled in Baltimore to nominate Van Buren to run as vice-presidential candidate with Jackson in 1832.

The Democratic convention of 1831 amounted to little more than a body to ratify Jackson's choice of Van Buren as his running mate. Nor did the National Republican Convention held in the same year do more

---

[1] "The First National Nominating Convention, 1808," *American Historical Review*, 17 (1912), pp. 744–763.

[2] In 1824 the Democrats of Lancaster County, Pennsylvania, resolved that the "most unexceptionable" method of nominating would be a national convention but they thought it "entirely impracticable, from the immense extent of our country, and from the great expense necessarily incident to an attendance from the extreme parts of the United States."—Edward Stanwood, *A History of the Presidency from 1788 to 1897* (Boston: Houghton Mifflin, 1898), p. 130.

[3] The Jackson Convention at Harrisburg, Pennsylvania, in 1828, nominated a slate of presidential electors and required from each candidate for elector a written pledge to vote for Jackson.—Florence Weston, *The Presidential Election of 1828* (Washington: Catholic University, 1938), p. 105.

than execute a foregone conclusion, the nomination of Clay.[4] Only gradually did the convention become a body capable of reconciling factional differences and of commanding the acquiescence in its decisions of party leaders over the country. In 1832, for example, Pennsylvania's Democratic electors gave the state's electoral vote, not to Van Buren, the convention vice-presidential nominee, but to Wilkins, one of that state's senators. Similarly, in 1836 the Virginia electors bolted the party on the vice-presidential nominee, and the choice of Vice-President devolved upon the Senate in the absence of an electoral majority. In 1840 the Democratic convention renominated Van Buren but could not agree upon a vice-presidential nominee and resolved to "leave the decision to their Republican fellow-citizens in the several States." The Democratic electoral vote for Vice-President went largely to Richard M. Johnson, but South Carolina, whose legislature continued to choose electors, cast its electoral vote for another candidate.

The Democratic convention of 1844 by its nomination of Polk was the first, says Goldman, to create "an original synthesis" that reconciled factional differences and produced unanticipated party unity.[5] Earlier conventions had in their presidential nominations chiefly proclaimed foreordained designations and had been unable most of the time to produce party unity on the vice-presidential candidate. In 1844 Polk was so dark a horse that he had no support on the first ballot. His nomination marked the coming of age of the convention as an institution capable of creating as well as of ratifying consensus within the party. Simultaneously with the development of the convention, presidential electors came to be chosen by popular vote and the supremacy of the convention in party affairs became evident as party candidates for presidential elector were brought under the discipline of the national convention.

Thus there developed a mechanism through which party leaders, dispersed over a nation of continental proportions, could negotiate sufficient agreement to maintain parties capable of governing through the presidential system. The creation of the convention as a route to the Presidency independent of Congress was congenial to the doctrine of separation of powers. Yet the establishment of the supremacy of the convention in the choice of presidential candidates had other consequences. The convention, diverse in its composition and unpatterned in its ways, remains free to chose presidential candidates from a range of alternatives. Had the congressional caucus prevailed, the chances are that the old war horses of the

[4] S. R. Gammon, Jr., *The Presidential Campaign of 1832* (Baltimore: Johns Hopkins Press, 1922), p. 71.

[5] Ralph M. Goldman, *Party Chairman and Party Factions, 1789–1900* (University of Chicago dissertation, MS, 1951).

party organization in Congress would have had the edge in the race for the Presidency. A Taft would have won over an Eisenhower, a Garner over a Roosevelt. Those factors conducive to advancement in hierarchies would have governed in the successive screenings on the way to the Presidency. An institution so transient as a national convention can be unconventional in its choices, a circumstance that is sometimes frightening; yet it permits the occasional choice of great leaders who probably could not have made their way up a tighter party hierarchy.

Preconvention Maneuvers

The process of nomination of a presidential candidate begins long before the convention in campaigns to sell a potential candidate to the party and to obtain the selection of delegations instructed to support him at the convention. These preconvention maneuvers fit no set pattern and cannot easily be described in general terms. Yet they may be better understood if they are observed with an awareness that the task of the convention is to unite the party in support of a presidential candidate. That may be accomplished by a compromise of the conflicts within the party or by a test of the strength of competing factions leading to a settlement on terms not beyond acceptance by the losers.

The character of the preconvention campaign to round up support for aspirants for the nomination thus becomes a function of the tensions and cleavages within the party. Durable bases for conflict exist within each party. Regional or sectional objectives diverge, as between the southern and northern Democrats or between the coastal and interior Republicans. Within each party class and group ambitions may collide. Yet the latent internal differences are activated in varying degrees at different times. At one time a balance of forces may have found a formula for unity that maintains relative calm within the party; at another, the most exacerbated relations may develop. These variations in the intensity of internal party conflict reflect themselves in the preconvention campaigns of would-be nominees.

Continuation of dominant coalitions. In one type of situation the preconvention campaign tends to be relatively uncontroverted. A dominant coalition controls the party and proceeds in the preconvention period to the routine selection of delegates committed to a continuation of the existing leadership. Most commonly these circumstances exist when a sitting President seeks renomination. If the President wants a renomination, the preconvention campaign is likely to be a prosaic affair. By custom a President is "entitled" to a second nomination and he has the advantage of controlling the party machine in obtaining it. Although it is quixotic to challenge him, some small but noisy dissident faction not infrequently attempts a revolt, proclaiming itself the true custodian of the party gospel.

In part, the President's capacity to win renomination comes from his control of the patronage and perquisites of government. More fundamentally his renomination reflects an expression of the power of the coalition he has constructed within the party. Thus, the 1956 Republican preconvention campaign generated no great suspense. Although beset by anxieties about whether the President would be able to run again, the leaders of the Eisenhower coalition proceeded to obtain the designation of delegates committed to him without much opposition. The remnants of the old Taft wing of the party muttered a bit but they were powerless against superior forces. On occasion the nomination by the party out of power may constitute a reassertion of the power of a coalition formed at the preceding convention, yet such a renomination is not ordinarily made without challenge. Dewey's renomination in 1948 represented a continuation of the leadership he had achieved in 1944, a reaffirmation won, however, against strong opposition.

Factional competition. When no coalition has working control of the party, factions within the party battle for delegates to the convention. Although the groups that struggle for ascendancy may be vaguely defined, on occasion fairly sharply defined factions compete for favor in presidential primaries and vie for support from state conventions as they choose their delegations to the national convention.[6]

The spirited competition between the Eisenhower forces and the Taft faction in the preliminaries to the 1952 Republican convention clearly reflected the major policy differences within the Republican leadership. At one extreme were those most critical of Democratic foreign policy, a group that coincided fairly closely with those Republican conservatives most critical of Democratic policy on economic issues. Senator Robert A. Taft and his associates attempted to bind these elements of the party to the support of his candidacy. In opposition were those Republican leaders more disposed to favor the Democratic foreign policy or at least who were prepared to accept a role of American leadership in world affairs. The same group regarded itself as "progressive" on domestic policy.

These lines of party division in preconvention maneuvers differ from time to time in the same party. In his campaign for the 1932 Democratic nomination, for example, Franklin D. Roosevelt carefully cultivated the

[6] For a classification of nominations, see Paul T. David and Ralph M. Goldman, "Presidential Nominating Patterns," *Western Political Quarterly*, 8 (1955), pp. 465–480.

South and the West, regions whose leaders had a long-standing antagonism toward the conservative and so-called Wall Street crowd in the Democratic party of the time.[7] Decades later, in 1952, another set of factions developed in the preliminaries to the Democratic convention. Averell Harriman sought the nomination as a gilt-edged and undiluted New Dealer while Senator Russell of Georgia rounded up delegates committed to the southern viewpoint on civil rights. Somewhere in between these positions was Senator Estes Kefauver. The nomination went to Adlai Stevenson, who had not campaigned for delegates, but whose characteristics were such that his supporters could align behind him the center and uncommitted elements of the party.[8]

The clarity with which factional lines are drawn in the preconvention maneuvers differ from time to time. Aspirants for the nomination often straddle issues and thereby muffle or avoid conflict. Often they also pull their punches in their encounters lest the basis for collaboration in the campaign be destroyed. At times the policy differences between competitors for the nomination may be negligible and the conflict becomes largely one of personalities.

Favorite sons and other bargainers. Although some sort of factional cleavage is often perceptible prior to an open convention, many aspirants for the nomination scarcely fit into the factional pattern. Delegations from particular states may, for example, be instructed for a "favorite son" of the state: a man who usually has the support of his own delegation and no other. He is put forward to hold the delegation free for negotiations at the convention; bargains may be struck with a leading contender who needs the votes to win the nomination. The second place on the ticket may go to a favorite son, or there may be promises of other sorts of preferment if the party wins the election.[9] Uninstructed and uncommitted delegations enjoy the same freedom of negotiation. The presence of delegations not irrevocably committed to any of the leading aspirants gives the convention flexibility as it strives toward a consensus on a candidate.

[7] For a comprehensive and perceptive account of the Roosevelt preconvention campaign, see Frank Freidel, *Franklin D. Roosevelt: The Triumph* (Boston: Little, Brown, 1956), chs. 10–19.

[8] See Walter Johnson, *How We Drafted Adlai Stevenson* (New York: Knopf, 1955).

[9] In speaking to the Kentucky Democratic convention which had instructed its 1956 delegation for him as a favorite son, Governor A. B. Chandler observed that there were "no second-class citizens in Kentucky and that we know how to help each other so that there is equal opportunity for all." The commentators thought that the Governor was putting himself forward as a vice-presidential possibility who might appeal to both southern and nothern wings of the party.

Tactics of preconvention campaigns. The tactics employed by aspirants and their supporters in building strength within the party before the convention are by no means stereotyped, though certain recurring problems have to be met. Ordinarily a small headquarters organization is established to handle publicity and to manage all the chores connected with building a bloc of delegates in advance of the convention. The manager of the campaign publicizes his candidate, negotiates with the party leaders in various states, arranges speeches at appropriate times on major issues, and attempts to make it appear that his man is the person who can win for the party. At times the preconvention campaign is on a scale that makes it a rehearsal of the presidential campaign itself, and costs of well over a million dollars may be incurred.

A tactical problem confronted by all aspirants is the timing of the announcement of their candidacies. One maxim is that a candidacy announced too soon may be blighted like an early-blooming flower; too late an announcement may give an advantage to other contenders. In October, 1951 several Republican governors vowed a strong preference for Eisenhower as the 1952 nominee but expressed their fears that unless the General soon made his availability plain the nomination would go to Taft by default. Often candidates occupy a public office and make a great virtue of tending to their knitting as governor, say, as they await the most propitious moment to announce their candidacy. Their managers meanwhile busily engage themselves in promoting movements to "draft" their man whose eagerness for the nomination is hardly a well-kept secret. A candidate may even succeed in avoiding an announcement. In 1944, Tom Dewey, who had made a strong showing in the 1940 Republican convention, maintained the fiction that he was not a candidate although his managers were active in recruiting delegate support.[10] In 1952 Adlai Stevenson made no campaign for delegates and consistently denied that he was a candidate. Nor did he agree to accept the nomination until after the first convention ballot.[11]

A major aspect of a preconvention campaign consists of enlisting the support of state and local leaders. Their influence may be decisive in the actions of state primaries and of conventions in the selection of national convention delegates. The manager for the candidate early attempts to impress on these men that his candidate would make a strong head of the

[10] Senator Pepper, Democrat, observed: "The heir-apparent to the Republican throne, that gilded, public-relations-advised candidate, the Governor of New York in his best and most studied pose of the coy maiden who is so diligently sought, the one who says 'no' with lisping lip, but with the dark lashes of her inviting eyes says 'come on.' "—*Washington Post*, February 16, 1944.

[11] J. M. Arvey, "The Reluctant Candidate—An Inside Story," *The Reporter*, November 24, 1953.

ticket; the candidate himself usually meets with small groups of these leaders in order that they may look him over.[12] A candidate who has gained the leadership of one shade of opinion of the party is likely to obtain commitments from state and local leaders of like beliefs. Another candidate may mobilize the leaders of a different hue of party faith.

While in a sense the preconvention campaign is both a campaign for the favor of a few thousand party leaders as well as perhaps a conflict among factions of those leaders, the preconvention rituals include appeals to the wider public. The leading candidates seek to build up a public image of themselves that accords with their judgment of the dictates of sound strategy. They usually make speeches on important current issues at widely separated points in the country to let themselves be seen and heard and to gain national attention. No little calculation enters into the decisions about what speeches to make and what to say. A forthright stand may make enemies as well as gain recruits. One speech may be enough to demonstrate that a man cannot capture popular favor, and his boom is deflated early in its career.

A question of strategy that vexes managers of would-be nominees is whether to enter the presidential primaries that are held by about half the states from March to May to select convention delegates. An early victory in a pivotal state may win the delegation and impress the party in other states with the aspirant's vote-pulling power. On the other hand, a defeat may bring the boom to a premature end. Yet a refusal to enter the primary may be interpreted as a manifestation of lack of confidence. Since the primary choice is to a large extent governed by the wishes of the state organization, it would be rash to enter a primary unless the candidate has the support of the organization or of an important faction, or felt that he could defeat the state machine.

As the preconvention campaign unfolds a few serious contenders emerge, and they are faced by the necessity of deciding what to do about "favorite son" candidates. Should a leading contender challenge a favorite son in his own state? To do so might antagonize men who will control delegates in the convention. One tactic is to ask for second-choice support after the favorite son. In 1939 this was the strategy of the McNutt managers, who said, "In no State that has a favorite son are we asking for more than second choice." By such an approach leading candidates hope to keep on good terms with the lesser contenders and perhaps gain their support in the convention. By the same strategy lesser contenders may avoid antagonizing a leading candidate. In 1952 Governor Earl Warren, of California,

---

[12] In 1952 one of Taft's managers said that many prominent men had accepted invitations to go to Paris to talk with General Eisenhower. "A few have," he said, "insisted on paying their own expenses."

announced that he would not enter the Ohio primary: "Ohio is the home state of Senator Taft, and he is certainly entitled to the delegation of his home state if he wants it."

The candidate who early develops significant strength is sometimes faced by a combination of other candidates who desire to prevent the settlement of the nomination prior to the convention. If a leading contender can be "killed off," the way is left open for a negotiated nomination in the convention, and other contenders will at least have a chance. One technique is not to oppose openly the prominent aspirant in his fights for delegates but to ask for the selection of uninstructed delegates. The state leaders then will also be in a better bargaining position in the convention. In 1932, to illustrate, the Smith forces desired to head off the Roosevelt movement, and Jouett Shouse, a Smith supporter, suggested that "it would be wiser not to instruct delegates to the Democratic convention in favor of any candidate save where such instructions are necessary under the law. The convention should be unfettered by instructions." [13] By this means the Smith faction hoped to stop Roosevelt. The strategy is by no means new. In 1892 those opposing Harrison for the Republican nomination sought the selection of uninstructed delegations with the hope that such delegations could be united around some other candidate at the convention.

"Availability" of candidates. The lore of American politics includes suppositions about tests that would-be presidential nominees must meet in order to be "available." Although the notion of "availability" is useful for feature stories every four years, its content lacks precision. Yet certain characteristics of the party system do operate negatively to make some eminent men "unavailable." A man with a record of antagonism toward an important sector of his party—as an antilabor Democrat—would probably be regarded as "unavailable." Or a person irrevocably committed to narrow ranges of policy—a Republican Asia-firster in 1952, for example— might not be expected to have a party-wide appeal. On the positive side, to be available a man must be a well-known public figure, a person with no disqualifying blemishes on his record, and he must have about himself the aura of a potential chief executive. Residence, too, is a significant factor. A party leader from a state with a large electoral vote that might be thrown one way or the other in the election is in a much better position to fight for the presidential nomination than one from a state traditionally attached to one party. Moreover, with the large delegation from his own state he has the beginnings of a bloc of convention votes. A governor

[13] Peel and Donnelly, *The 1932 Campaign*, p. 66.

of New York, of Ohio, or of California may hope to be among the availables.

At the present stage of American politics a man must be a Protestant of good "American stock" and name to be available. He should not be too closely affiliated with any particular interest or group, nor should he have committed himself on a great and contentious issue before the time is ripe. Yet he must stand for something or a complex of things—a general point of view—in public life. To go from the ranks of the availables to those of the nominees a man also needs a certain amount of luck. He must come on the scene at a moment when his particular combination of traits suits the temper of the times. In 1936, for example, an Eisenhower probably would have had rough sledding. Or, only a Roosevelt could have had the good fortune to strive for the Presidency at a moment when his qualities fitted the needs of his party and the spirit of the times so well.

Preconvention sifting. The maneuvers that precede the convention narrow its range of choice. The candidate may be nominated in fact before the convention meets; the delegates may convene only to ratify an accomplished fact. A true "dark horse" nominee whose selection is a complete surprise is rare. Hence, in a consideration of the nominating process great emphasis must be placed on the events antecedent to the convention. These processes are not easily described in general terms. Each instance is likely to have its own peculiarities, and the most unpredictable developments may occur in the competition to get to the White House. That competition involves a complicated process of weighing, testing, rejecting, and admission into the circle of serious competitors. One boomlet may be killed by the demonstration that the aspirant simply has no vote-getting ability. Another would-be President may be vetoed by his failure to gain the confidence of an important bloc in the party. Another may be unable to attract enough financial support to make much of a preconvention showing. Others find their way at least partly through the maze of obstacles to the White House and go to the convention with substantial backing.

Apportionment and Selection of Delegates

The delegates whose support aspirants for the nomination seek are chosen within the states. The manner of their choice and the method of determining the number of delegates to which each state is entitled are of basic importance in the determination of the character of the convention as an institution.

During most of the history of the national conventions votes have been apportioned among the states in accordance with their strength in the electoral college, a principle adopted by the Democratic convention in 1831. Each state was at first entitled to one vote for each of its two Senators and one vote for each member of the House of Representatives from the state; later the number of votes was doubled.[14] This rule remained in use in unmodified form by the Republicans until their convention of 1916 and by the Democrats through the convention of 1940.

Apportionment: Special problems of the Republicans. The original rule of apportionment presupposed a more or less even spread of party strength over the entire country. As a matter of fact such a distribution did not exist, and solidly Democratic areas had relatively as great strength in Republican conventions as states with heavy Republican majorities. The application of the rule created no serious difficulties in the Democratic party, but its use led to party disaster for the Republicans and eventually to its modification by them. Until recent times the Republican vote was extremely light in the South; the rule of apportionment gave to the states of this region a far greater convention strength than their party vote warranted. In the southern "rotten boroughs" the Republican organization existed to distribute patronage—when the party controlled the national government—and to deliver delegates in the national convention, a pair of operations not unrelated.

Although the equity of the apportionment system had long been questioned, it was not until 1912 that a combination of circumstances occurred to bring about an alteration of the rule. In that year the system, which was partly responsible for Taft's control of the convention, led to a split in the Republican party, with Taft as the regular nominee and Theodore Roosevelt as the standard-bearer of the rebellious Progressive faction. The split gave the election to the Democrats, and the Republican national committee in 1913 took steps to reduce the inequities in the apportionment of delegates by submitting a new plan of apportionment for approval by the state conventions. The rule, approved by them and first used in 1916,

---

[14] In the textual discussion "delegate" is used synonymously with "vote." The Republicans allow only one delegate for one vote and the rule is enforced. The Democrats have been troubled by the designation of delegates in excess of the number votes, a way to "recognize" the party faithful and to assure them good seats in the convention. In 1940 one Mississippi district, entitled to two votes, sent 54 delegates to cast them. The 1940 convention attempted to cope with the problem by resolving that in future conventions no "fractional distribution" should be permitted that would give any delegate less than a half vote. Within the general rule the convention call permits a state delegation to include delegates at large equal to twice the number of votes at large (those votes allotted for each Senator and Representative at large). The convention call instructs states to send one delegate for each district vote; this limit is not rigidly enforced. In 1952 with 1,230 votes the Democrats had 1,642 delegates.

provided that the national convention should consist of "four delegates-at-large from each State; two additional delegates-at-large for each Representative-at-large in Congress from any State; one delegate for each Congressional District in each State; and one additional delegate for each Congressional District in each State in which the vote for any Republican elector in the last preceding Presidential election, or for the Republican nominee for Congress in the last preceding Congressional election shall have been not less than 7,500," plus certain delegates from the territories. The change decreased the representation of the Solid South by 76 votes.

The new rule left the weak Republican areas still overrepresented in relation to their Republican voting strength. A series of subsequent modifications, either by or under the authority of the national conventions of 1920, 1940, and 1952, made further adjustments designed to penalize those areas with relatively few Republican votes and to increase the relative strength of those states with heavier Republican popular strength. The cumulation of these changes produced the following rule of apportionment under which the 1956 convention was chosen:

Delegates at Large

1. Four delegates at large from each state.

2. Two additional delegates at large for each representative at large in Congress from each state.

3. Four delegates at large for Alaska; six delegates at large each for the District of Columbia and Hawaii, and four additional delegates if the delegate to Congress elected at the last preceding election was the Republican nominee; [15] three delegates at large for Puerto Rico, and one for the Virgin Islands.

4. Six additional delegates at large from each state casting its electoral vote or a majority thereof for the Republican nominee for President in the last preceding presidential election. If any State does not cast its electoral vote or a majority thereof for the Republican nominee in the last preceding election, but at that election or at a subsequent election held prior to the next Republican National Convention elects a Republican United States Senator or a Republican Governor then in such event such state shall be entitled to such additional delegates at large.[16]

District Delegates

1. One district delegate from each congressional district casting two thousand votes or more for any Republican elector in the last preceding presidential

---

[15] The bonus of additional delegates was granted by the 1940 convention.

[16] The 1940 convention gave a state the additional opportunity to gain its bonus of delegates by electing a Republican Senator at the election following the presidential election. The 1948 convention extended the opportunity to win bonus delegates to include the gubernatorial election and to the elections covered in the last clauses of the quoted rule.

election or for the Republican nominee for Congress in the last preceding congressional election.[17]

2. One additional district delegate from each congressional district casting 10,000 votes or more for any Republican elector in the last preceding presidential election or for the Republican nominee for Congress in the last preceding congressional election.

Under these rules the number of delegates fluctuates from convention to convention; in 1936, the total was 1,003; in 1940, 1,000; in 1944, 1,057; in 1948, 1,094; in 1952, 1,206; in 1956, 1,320.

Apportionment: Democratic practice. The Democratic party has been more fortunate than the Republican party in the matter of apportionment. It has been able to follow the practice of allowing each state a delegation twice the size of its congressional representation without serious controversy because of the lack of a problem such as the Solid South presents to the Republicans. Yet the 1936 Democratic convention, to offset southern sentiment against the abrogation of the two-thirds rule, directed the national committee to submit to the next convention "a plan for improving the system by which delegates and alternates to Democratic National Conventions are apportioned." The committee was ordered, in formulating this plan, to "take into account the Democratic strength within each State, District of Columbia, and Territory, etc. . . . ." The 1940 convention adopted a rule to grant to states that go Democratic in a presidential election an additional two votes in the next convention. The national committee in 1947 increased this bonus to four votes. The application of these rules, with some minor modifications, resulted in a 1952 convention of 1,230 votes, a 1956 convention of 1,372.

Methods of choosing delegates. Two methods are employed in the selection of state delegations to the national conventions. About a third of the state governments conduct presidential primaries in which the voters may choose delegates directly and usually may also express a preference among the aspirants for the presidential nomination. In the remainder of the states the political parties designate delegates through conventions or committees. In a few instances district delegates are chosen by primary; the delegates at large, by the state convention.

[17] This section contains significant changes made by the conventions of 1940 and 1952. Before the action of 1940 each congressional district was entitled to at least one delegate in the convention. The 1940 convention set a requirement of 1,000 Republican votes to qualify for one delegate and the 1952 convention raised this figure to 2,000.

Conventions and committees. A handful of states permit state committees of the parties to choose delegates to the national convention. More usually, in the absence of a public primary, the state parties act through conventions, which vary considerably in their form and mode of selection. Most commonly they are built on a system of indirect election beginning with precinct meetings of voters which choose delegates to county conventions from whence go delegates to the state convention. Yet in a few states the state conventions consist of delegates chosen by precinct committeemen and other party functionaries. The state convention may choose the entire delegation, or district conventions may choose district delegates and the state convention the delegates-at-large. The Republican rules express a preference for state and district conventions separate in time and place from the state convention. The equivalent result is at times obtained by district caucuses at state conventions; the convention chooses a slate of delegates built up of nominees of the district caucuses.

Ordinarily the convention procedure does not permit extensive participation by the rank and file of the party in the choice of delegates. Although the convention may not be bossed, the selection of delegates becomes a matter handled almost exclusively by the party professionals. Yet on the whole the convention processes produce delegations representative of the general tenor of sentiment of the party in the state. The principal difficulties with selection by convention seem to occur when the character of the state party is such that the modus operandi of the convention cannot produce a decision regarded as fair and acceptable to all concerned. In several southern conventions in 1952 the old-guard professionals who had been managing party affairs for years dealt roughly with the influx of "new" Republicans who wished delegations instructed for Eisenhower. Under more normal conditions party managements seem to be generally able to guide the work of conventions toward decisions accepted as authoritative on all sides.

Presidential primaries. In 1956, 19 states conducted a presidential primary of one sort or another and in most of them all or nearly all of the national convention delegates were chosen by primary vote. The presidential primary came into existence at about the same time and for the same reasons that the direct primary was substituted for the convention method of nomination of candidates for state offices. Conventions were thought to be susceptible to manipulation by party leaders and a widespread faith existed that more popular participation would have a cleansing effect on politics.

Although Wisconsin in 1905 and Pennsylvania in 1906 adopted laws providing for the direct election of delegates—all delegates in Wisconsin and district delegates in Pennsylvania—the birth of the full-blown presidential primary is usually traced to an Oregon law adopted by popular vote in 1910.[18] That law provided for a preference vote by the voters on presidential aspirants, as well as the direct election of all delegates to the convention. Between 1910 and 1916 the presidential primary spread so rapidly among the states that it was predicted that within a short period the national convention would become, like the electoral college, a mere mechanism for recording decisions already arrived at by the electorate. The drive for the presidential primary, however, was soon spent, and since its peak in 1916 several states have abandoned it.

Types of presidential primaries. The enthusiastic early advocates of the presidential primary hoped to short-circuit the indirect convention procedures and give to the party voter an opportunity to express effectively a preference between aspirants for the presidential nomination. Some of them believed that the national convention would eventually merely express a popular choice previously made. In fact, the extent to which the vote at the primary affects the votes of the delegates at the convention differs greatly from state to state with the form of the state primary as well as with variations in local custom and tradition. The primary laws involve, in varying combinations: (1) presidential preference voting, as between Stevenson and Kefauver, the so-called "beauty contest," and (2) direct election of delegates to the convention. The manner in which these questions are presented to the voter on the ballot varies greatly and affects the clarity of the expression of voter sentiment, a proposition that may be made plain by mention of the principal forms of the primary.

(1) Presidential preference vote with election of national convention delegates by state convention. The primary ballot permits an expression of preference between aspirants for the nomination, but the state convention continues to choose the delegates who may or may not turn out to be supporters of the candidate who wins the "popularity" contest. This arrangement has been on the books in Maryland for some time, and Indiana used it first in 1956.

(2) Combined expression of preference and vote for pledged convention delegates. By a single mark on the ballot the voter may express his preference for a presidential aspirant and vote for a slate of delegates

---

[18] Louise Overacker, *The Presidential Primary* (New York: Macmillan, 1926). For a summary of primary statutes, see R. D. Hupman and S. H. Still, Jr., *Manner of Selecting Delegates to National Political Conventions and the Nomination and Election of Presidential Electors* (Washington: Government Printing Office, 1955).

pledged to support his preference. In South Dakota in 1952, for example, the Republican ballot included a column headed "Candidates Preferring Robert A. Taft for President." An X at the head of the column, in effect, combined an expression of a preference for Taft for the nomination with a vote for candidates committed to his support in the convention. California employs this form of primary with the election at large of the entire state delegation; the winner of the preference vote wins all the delegates. In Minnesota and Wisconsin the combined ballot form is used but since delegates, save the at-large delegates, are chosen by congressional district, the state delegation can be split among competing candidates. The winner of the state-wide preference vote does not necessarily win all the delegates.

(3) Separation of preference vote and delegate election. Another group of states complicates matters by requiring the voter to mark his ballot twice, once to indicate his choice among presidential aspirants and again to vote for convention delegates. In some states the ballot contains no indication of the presidential preference of the delegate candidates, and the voter may even support delegates actually opposed to his presidential preference. The New Hampshire ballot in 1956, to illustrate, contained a presidential preference column headed: "I hereby declare my preference for candidate for office of President of the United States to be as follows." Other columns contained the names of candidates for delegates-at-large and for district delegates and alongside their names were indications of their presidential preference: "Favorable to the nomination of William Knowland for President," and so forth.

(4) Direct election of unpledged delegates, with no presidential preference vote. In a few states delegates are chosen by direct primary but the ballot permits no expression of preference for presidential aspirants nor does it indicate the intentions of the candidates for delegate. New York employs this arrangement and from time to time it has been used in Pennsylvania, Illinois, West Virginia, and Nebraska. In some campaigns slates committed to competing candidates may be in the field but the absence of ballot identification makes the expression of voter preference difficult. In New York and Pennsylvania the primary commonly attracts little interest since by custom about all that it amounts to is a ratification of the slate of delegates chosen by the state organization, which operates very much as if the presidential primary did not exist.

Role of presidential primary. The primary has introduced a considerably higher degree of popular participation in the choice of presidential nominees. That participation may not be determinative of the candidates, but those who would be nominees must ordinarily conduct campaigns directed to the voters to a greater degree than when the nominations were more exclusively in the hands of the party professionals. The primary probably makes some men presidential hopefuls who would not have been in an earlier day. Thus, Estes Kefauver, with a reputation developed through the televising of his crime investigations, became a far more serious contender for the nomination in 1952 and in 1956 than he would have been in the days before the presidential primary.

On occasion it seems as if the effect of the primaries is to kill off candidates rather than to determine which of the two or three aspirants who reach the convention with considerable blocs of delegates will be nominated. In 1944 Wendell Willkie withdrew from the race for the Republican nomination after an early defeat in the Wisconsin primary. He lost to a slate of delegates pledged to Dewey, who had disavowed the slate and not even bothered to campaign. Or in 1956, Stevenson's victory in the California primary was regarded as the death blow to the Kefauver candidacy. On the other hand, a spectacular performance in a primary may give a candidate a powerful boost and bring leaders to his bandwagon. In the 1952 "Minnesota miracle," when over 100,000 persons took the trouble to write in the name of Eisenhower in the primary, Republican leaders all over the land could see that a vote-getter had arrived on the scene.

Although the primary has modified nominating practices, it has not produced conventions of automata that mechanically record the preferences expressed by the voters at home. Party organizations in many states retain a fairly high degree of autonomy despite the primaries. Candidates for the presidency choose not to enter many primaries. State delegations often retain their freedom of choice by commitment to favorite sons through the primary as before; the voters may even vote for uncommitted delegations. Indeed, for the convention to be capable of achieving its broad objective of developing party consensus on a candidate, delegations must possess a range of discretion.

Proposals for a nation-wide primary. When the memory of the Republican convention of 1912 was fresh, numerous proposals were made for the establishment of a nation-wide preference primary, which perhaps would have required a constitutional amendment. President Wilson, in his first message to Congress, urged a national system in these words: "I turn now to a subject which I hope can be handled promptly and without serious controversy of any kind. I mean the method of selecting nominees for the Presidency of the United States. I feel confident that I do not misinterpret the wishes or the expectations of the country when I urge prompt enactment of legislation which will provide for primary elections throughout the country at which the voters of the several parties may choose the nominees for the Presidency without the intervention of nominating conventions." Congress did not act on the recommendation. From time to time renewed flurries of interest in the matter develop. In 1952 a Senate committee even reported a bill to encourage the states, by financial assistance, to hold presidential preference primaries, although the proposal died at that stage.

The invention of the straw poll has introduced a sort of nation-wide preference primary. In recent conventions the nominations and the rankings of candidates for the nomination have followed fairly closely the sentiments of party members as revealed by the polls. It is doubtful that the polls control convention actions, though they may establish that convention actions do not deviate nearly so far from popular sentiment as some advocates of the presidential primary would have us believe. It has been contended that during the past half century the convention has become, in fact, the captive of the forces of mass democracy. It is limited in its deliberations to consideration of those who have achieved, by one means or another, the status of a celebrity. When one person is clearly the national favorite the convention has, or so it is argued, no choice but to nominate him.[19]

Organization of the Convention

On the appointed day [20] the delegates convene to play their parts in our great quadrennial political drama. The city fathers of the convention city [21] deck out the town in bunting and flags as if a huge county fair

[19] See W. G. Carleton, "The Revolution in the Presidential Nominating Convention," *Political Science Quarterly*, 72 (1957), pp. 224–240.

[20] In 1956 the Democrats met in Chicago on August 13; the Republicans, in San Francisco on August 20. These conventions met later than the usual dates in June or July. Moreover, the Democratic convention preceded the Republican, the first time since 1888. The timing of the conventions assures a long campaign in comparison with other great democracies and consideration is given from time to time to proposals to schedule the conventions later. One rebuttal has been that in such countries as Great Britain the candidates for prime minister are known long in advance and the parties are engaged in continuous campaigning. On the other hand, an American party that nominates a relatively unknown candidate needs time to make his qualities known.

[21] The place of the convention is designated by the national committee. Esoteric considerations of party advantage are said to have a part in the selection. It is doubtful that the location of the convention affects the popular vote, but that possibility is urged by the advocates of specific cities. Aspirants for the nomination often attempt to influence the choice of location to avoid cities that would pack the galleries with hostile crowds and to seek the designation of cities where the gallery and newspaper atmosphere would be favorable or at least neutral. Prime considerations are that the convention city have adequate travel and hotel facilities and that it possess a suitable auditorium. Beyond these requirements the bonus offered by the local citizenry may be influential. Thus, San Francisco paid $250,000 to bring the Republican convention

were in progress. Banners identify the headquarters of the presidential aspirants. Their managers issue optimistic predictions of their first-ballot strength and work frantically behind the scenes to try to approach in fact their predictions. By badges, arm bands, and buttons the delegates and visitors proclaim their allegiance. The convention gathers in a great auditorium—such as the Chicago International Amphitheater, the San Francisco Cow Palace, Madison Square Garden in New York—the main floor of which seats the delegates and their alternates, more than two thousand in all; the galleries take care of the overflow of alternates from the main floor and of thousands of spectators. The scene presents a spectacle of confusion and disorder astonishing to foreign observers. The convention hall is equipped with amplifying apparatus so that the officials and delegates may make themselves heard. The radio and television chains have their equipment set up to report the happenings to tens of millions of people listening and looking throughout the nation, and hundreds of newspaper reporters are on hand to record their impressions of the proceedings.

Temporary organization. The convention is opened by the chairman of the national committee, who presides until the temporary officers are elected.[22] The national committee presents to the convention a slate of temporary officers, of which the temporary chairman is the most important.[23] The preconvention maneuvers of the aspirants for the nomination include efforts to gain sufficient votes in the national committee to assure a neutral, if not a friendly, temporary chairman. Usually the nominee of the national committee is approved by the convention, but at infrequent times the election of the temporary chairman becomes a test of the strength of contending factions within the party. In the Republican convention of 1912, for example, the national committee and the Taft forces successfully backed Elihu Root for the temporary chairmanship over the opposition of the Roosevelt delegates. In the same year Bryan and the

to that city in 1956. In some recent conventions the leadership has felt constrained to prolong the session in order that local innkeepers and tippling-house proprietors might recoup their contributions to bring the convention to the city.

[22] Each session of the convention is opened with prayer, by clergymen selected with an eye to the representation of the leading faiths. Thus at the 1940 Republican convention prayers were offered by a rabbi, a Lutheran, a Christian Scientist, an Archbishop, an African Methodist bishop, a Presbyterian, the Chancellor of an Archdiocese, a Baptist, a Protestant Episcopal bishop, a Methodist, and the Chaplain of the Connecticut State Senate, a divine of unspecified denomination.

[23] The other temporary officers—who are usually made permanent—include the secretary, sergeant-at-arms, parliamentarian, chief tally clerk, chief reading clerk, doorkeeper, and various other assistants and officials necessary for the operation of the convention.

Wilson delegates unsuccessfully opposed the national committee nominee for the Democratic chairmanship, Judge Alton B. Parker, who had the support of delegates pledged to Harmon and Underwood. In 1952 the Eisenhower forces made much propaganda about a rigged convention when the national committee proposed Walter S. Hallanan, a partisan of Taft, but they did not oppose his designation at the convention.

The temporary chairman presides until the permanent organization is effected. He may have opportunity to make rulings of critical significance for the results of the convention. He also has traditionally delivered the keynote speech, a custom from which the Republicans departed in 1952 and 1956. Their keynoters in those years, General Douglas MacArthur and Governor Arthur B. Langlie, were not incumbered with the duties of temporary chairman. The keynoter inveighs against the opposition, recites the great achievements of his party, invokes the memory of the great party leaders of the past, and generally attempts to set a stirring theme for the convention. The old-fashioned keynoter has probably become a casualty of television. Rip-roaring political oratory, a hybrid of elocution and calisthenics, seems not to be well suited for television, or so opined some observers after the performance of the 1956 Democratic keynoter, Tennessee's Governor Frank G. Clement, a master of a classic but dying form of rustic political declamation.

An early step in the convention is the designation of its four great standing committees: (1) credentials, with the function of examining credentials, hearing challenges against the right of delegations to sit, and recommending a permanent roll of delegates to the convention; (2) permanent organization, with the function of recommending a set of permanent officers for the convention; (3) rules, with the duty of reporting to the convention a set of rules to govern its procedure; and (4) resolutions, with the task of drafting and presenting a platform to the convention. In practice each state and territorial delegation names a person to sit on each of these committees except that one man and one woman are designated by each delegation for membership on the resolutions committee. The Democrats adopted the innovation of female representation on the resolutions committee in 1940, and the Republicans followed in 1944.

Permanent organization: Rivals maneuver for advantage. The first committee report disposed of by the convention is usually that of the committee on credentials, but, for convenience, the report of the committee on permanent organization may be mentioned first. The item in the report of this committee that may give rise to controversy is its recommendation for the post of permanent chairman. The factions aligned behind each aspirant for the presidential nomination desire the selection of a permanent chairman who is at least not hostile to their candidates. A minority report from the committee on permanent organization may furnish the occasion for a test of strength between candidates for the nomination. In 1932, for example, the majority of the committee on permanent organization nominated Jouett Shouse, affiliated with the anti-Roosevelt bloc, for the permanent chairmanship; the Roosevelt forces were able to rally a majority of the convention to support the late Senator Walsh of Montana as permanent chairman.[24] Usually, however, the suspense over who will be permanent chairman is not great. He is ordinarily "chosen" long before he is "elected" by the convention. The national chairman in consultation with other party leaders or a subcommittee of the national committee acts on the question usually several months before the convention which ratifies the choice. Each party has in recent conventions relied on its ranking member of the House of Representatives. Joseph W. Martin, Jr. served as permanent chairman of the Republican conventions of 1944, 1948, 1952, and 1956, while Sam Rayburn chaired the Democratic conventions of 1948, 1952, and 1956. When he takes the gavel from the temporary chairman the permanent chairman delivers a speech that may be a smaller edition of the keynote speech.

The formal organization of the convention consists of the permanent chairman, the standing committees, and the functionaries necessary for the work of the assembly; in addition, as with congresses and parliaments, there tends to be also an informal organization of the blocs and factions seeking to steer the deliberations of the convention. Before the 1932 Democratic convention, for example, the Roosevelt leaders held a caucus at Hyde Park to agree on how to run the convention. It was decided that Walsh would be permanent chairman, Arthur Mullen the floor manager for the Roosevelt forces, Senator Hitchcock chairman of the committee on resolutions, and that Judge Mack would nominate Roosevelt. At the 1952 Republican convention Thomas E. Coleman, of Wisconsin, served as floor manager for Senator Taft; Senator Henry Cabot Lodge, for the Eisenhower forces. Lodge directed the strategy that struck with the "fair play" resolution relative to the seating of delegates, a move which, along with the accompanying propaganda, pictured the Taft forces to the country in the embarrassing position of opposing "fair play."

On occasion the informal organization of the leading candidate plans the convention in great detail. When a convention meets to renominate a sitting President, his leaders may have the convention proceedings so thoroughly under control that practically every item of procedure is laid out in advance, even to the allocation of the honors of seconding motions

---

[24] For an account of this affair, see Charles Michelson, *The Ghost Talks* (New York: Putnam, 1944), pp. 4–8.

for adjournment and of proposing resolutions of gratitude to the committee on local arrangements. When a stentorian voice echoes through the hall, "The chair recognizes delegate Jones from Wisconsin to offer a resolution," the script is merely being followed. The 1956 Republican convention, operating under the stimulus of television and the guidance of persons experienced in show business, provided an extreme example of the extent to which the entire proceedings of a convention could be staged and built up of speeches and actions tailored to a general theme.[25]

Credentials: Contested delegations. The national convention is the judge of the qualifications of its own members. In the early history of the convention, the review of delegates' credentials was casual. When no formally elected delegates appeared to represent a state, chance visitors from the state might be allowed to cast its vote at the convention. With the regularization of convention procedure, practices developed for the determination of the right of delegations to convention membership. The question of the right of a delegation to sit commonly arises when a contesting delegation appears and claims to be the legitimate spokesman for the party in the state. Assertions may be made of irregularities in the choice of a delegation.[26]

Prior to the opening of the convention, the national committee of each party prepares a temporary roll of the delegates entitled to sit in the convention. To do so, it must make a preliminary decision on challenged delegations, if any, and to that end it hears the parties to such contests. The Republican national committee is required by party rule, however, to place on the temporary roll the names of those delegates certified by appropriate state officials as having been designated in accordance with state law. Some delegations, of course, go to the convention under certification of party officials rather than of public functionaries.

When the convention of each party meets, the documents used by

---

[25] It may well turn out that the urge to look good on television may drive more of the business of conventions into smoke-filled rooms.

[26] In 1952 a contesting Louisiana delegation to the Republican convention (pledged to Eisenhower) asserted that the Taft delegation had been chosen by arbitrary management of parish mass meetings and the state convention. One parish mass meeting was said to have gone something like this: "Gentlemen, the purpose of the meeting is to elect delegates to the District and State Conventions. I nominate myself as Permanent Chairman, I second the nomination, I close the nominations, I declare myself the Permanent Chairman. I nominate myself as a delegate to the District and State Conventions, I second the nomination, I close the nominations, I declare myself the delegate to the District and State Conventions. Good evening, Gentlemen."—*Original Brief on Behalf of Louisiana Delegates Representing New Republican Leadership in Louisiana* (by John Minor Wisdom and others as counsel), p. 49. See also L. V. Howard and D. R. Deener, *Presidential Politics in Louisiana, 1952* (Tulane Studies in Political Science, 1954).

the national committee in preparing the temporary roll are delivered to the committee on credentials.[27] It hears the claims of the contesting delegations anew and reports to the convention, which accepts or rejects the recommendation.

The importance of the decision on contests arises from the fact that each delegation that claims to be duly authorized to represent a state may be pledged to a different candidate for the presidential nomination. In some circumstances the convention, in deciding which delegation to seat, may be deciding which candidate will be nominated. Hence the managers for each candidate take a keen interest in the contests and marshal their forces to assure a decision to their advantage, occasionally without much regard to the equities of the contest.

At almost every convention a contest or so develops, whose resolution often indicates which candidate for the nomination is in control of the convention. The most spectacular battles over credentials occurred in the Republican conventions of 1912 and of 1952. The national committee, in the preparation of the 1912 temporary roll, seated delegations pledged to William Howard Taft rather than the contesting delegations supporting Theodore Roosevelt. The committee on credentials and the convention itself followed in general the decisions of the national committee. The temporarily seated delegations, even though contested, were entitled to vote on all contests save their own; the action of the national committee and of the convention in seating Taft rather than Roosevelt delegates gave Taft the nomination.

The rule of 1912 to permit temporarily seated delegates to vote on the settlement of contests except the one affecting their own right to sit rose up to plague the Republicans in 1952. In their management of the regular Republican organizations in several southern states the partisans of Senator Robert A. Taft had operated in a high handed fashion to obtain control of the convention delegations against the protests of "new" Republicans, that is, mainly Democrats, who demanded the selection of delegates pledged to General Eisenhower. The Eisenhower managers advanced on the convention behind a smokescreen of outraged virtue; they had been robbed. The Texas state convention, Taft-controlled, had perpetrated a "steal." The offensive led off with a convention motion, a so-called fair-play motion, to prohibit delegates on the temporary roll

[27] The 1952 Republican convention, as an aftermath of the battle over credentials in that year, adopted a rule directing the chairman of the national committee to appoint prior to each convention a "contest committee" to review the records and briefs submitted by contesting delegations and to report to the national committee the issues of law and fact raised by the contest. The national committee then proceeds to a hearing and decision on the issues posed by its contest committee. For the Republican rules on contests, see *Proceedings*, 1952 Convention, pp. 292–294.

from Texas and Georgia and most of those from Louisiana from voting in the convention on any question until their right to sit had been finally settled. The Taft forces opposed changing the rules in the midst of the game and argued that by simply contesting enough delegations the convention could be made powerless to act. The Eisenhower forces won the adoption of their proposal.[28] They then induced the convention first to reject the southern delegations that had been given temporary seats by the Taft-controlled national committee and then to seat delegations favorable to the General.[29]

Democratic conventions in 1952 and 1956 had warm disputes on the question of seating delegations from the South. In these instances the debate hinged, not on whether the delegations had been chosen in accord with regular procedures, but on the loyalty of the delegations to the party and on their willingness to be bound by the action of the convention. The decision of such matters thus went beyond the technical validity of credentials and to the question of the authority of the convention in the party as a whole, a question to be explored later.

Platforms

The resolutions committee presents to the convention a recommended platform, which states broadly the party program. The platform of the party in power makes resounding and prideful references to its record of performance and to the magnificent qualities of its leaders. The out party usually includes in its resolutions caustic criticisms of the record of the ins.[30] The adoption of the platform does not occur in isolation from the other activities of the convention but is ordinarily integrally related to the other major decisions by that body. Usually the group that controls the nomination also controls the resolutions committee. Commonly the questions of policy that are intertwined with the nomination will also vex the platform drafters.

---

[28] Subsequently the convention amended its permanent rules to bring them into accord with the fair-play motion. The change prohibits voting in the convention by delegations under contest except those placed on the temporary roll by the vote of at least two-thirds of the members of the national committee. The latter proviso presumably limits the possibility of hamstringing the convention by frivolous contests.

[29] For a survey of the 1952 conflict over credentials, see Paul T. David and others, *Presidential Nominating Politics in 1952* (Baltimore: Johns Hopkins Press, 1952), I, pp. 68–88. On the Texas Republican convention whose delegation was challenged, see O. Douglas Weeks, *Texas Presidential Politics in 1952* (Austin: The University of Texas, 1953).

[30] The Democratic convention of 1840 is said to have adopted the first full-fledged platform.—G. S. P. Kleeberg, *The Formation of the Republican Party as a National Political Organization* (New York, 1911), p. 63.

Platform sources. A sitting President seeking renomination is likely to guide the deliberations of the resolutions committee of his party's convention. The sources of drafts and suggestions for the resolutions committee of an open convention or of a convention of the outs tend to be more diverse. In 1932, although James Garfield was chairman of the Republican resolutions committee, "Secretary of the Treasury Ogden Mills brought the entire platform from Washington, with the exception of the plank on prohibition, which was written in Chicago by men who knew" Hoover's desires.[31] The Democratic platform of 1936 was written by Roosevelt and sent to the resolutions committee which approved it after the alteration of one sentence.[32]

The resolutions committee of a convention not controlled by an incumbent President receives from a variety of sources drafts of proposed planks or of entire platforms. A leading candidate for the nomination may have had a draft platform prepared by his associates in advance of the convention. A dominant personality in the party may exercise a controlling voice in the content of the platform.[33] A recognized specialist of the party may draft the plank on his specialty.[34] On occasion a study committee accumulates data and proposals for the resolutions committee.[35] In short, the resolutions committee suffers from no lack of advice about what ought to go into the platform.

Committee proceedings. The resolutions committee or a preliminary drafting committee designated by the national committee ordinarily begins its work a week or more in advance of the opening of the convention. It holds hearings for the benefit of pressure-group representatives, party personages, and others who wish to expound and to publicize their proposals for the platform. This parade of pressure-group representatives is principally ritualistic, but the views of those interests most closely associated with each party tend to find their way into its platform.

While the actions of the resolutions committee may be determined in varying degrees by the wishes of the sitting President or by a dominant clique of convention leaders, its work is rarely mere formality. Com-

---

[31] Peel and Donnelly, *The 1932 Campaign*, p. 86.

[32] Raymond Moley, *After Seven Years*, pp. 346–347.

[33] Thus, Bryan is said to have controlled the content of the 1912 Democratic platform. A. W. Dunn, *From Harrison to Harding* (New York: Putnam's, 1922), II, p. 195.

[34] Senator Vandenberg contributed a working paper which became, in essence, the 1948 Republican foreign policy plank.—*The Private Papers of Senator Vandenberg* (Boston: Houghton Mifflin, 1952), pp. 428–430.

[35] Ronald Bridges, "The Republican Program Committee," *Public Opinion Quarterly*, 3 (1939), pp. 299–306; E. F. Cooke, "Drafting the 1952 Platforms," *Western Political Quarterly*, 9 (1956), pp. 699–712.

monly no controversy exists on the major part of the platform, yet, at least in a convention without clear centers of control, the committee itself must accomplish, through subcommittees and drafting committees, the considerable task of piecing together a platform. Its deliberations usually center on one or two questions that are currently points of deep differences within the party. The accepted strategy is to attempt to compromise these differences in order to arrive at a platform draft that will not provoke a debate on the floor of the convention.

The negotiations to bring about concurrence among the major factions of the party on contentious issues ordinarily involve the principal interested party figures even though they may not be members of the resolutions committee. In 1952, for example, the Democratic resolutions committee succeeded in negotiating agreement upon a civil rights plank, a perennial source of dissension among Democrats. Similarly, in 1956 some Republicans demanded that their platform include a strong assertion on civil rights; a group of southern Republicans threatened to take the question to the floor of the convention if inadequate consideration were given to the peculiar southern situation. A moderate, that is, a compromise plank, bridged the gap and, with the re-enforcement of Administration endorsement, served to avert a floor fight.

Appeal to the convention. When efforts to reconcile differences at the committee stage fail, the minority may submit a separate recommendation to the convention on the bitterly contested items in the platform. Convention leaders invariably attempt to avoid such a test of strength. In a sense, national party rests on coalition and compromise; when platform questions arise that are not susceptible of compromise, the limits of action by the national convention have been reached. A floor fight may deepen cleavages rather than settle controversy. Nevertheless, a minority of the resolutions committee may make a dissenting report to the convention. In the 1928 Republican convention, for example, a minority plank on agriculture, proposed by Earl C. Smith, a delegate from Illinois, was supported by 15 states in the committee on resolutions. The minority foresaw a defection of midwestern farmers from the Republican party: "We come to you within these four walls pleading with the delegates not to drive the farmers of the Republican States out of their party." [36] The minority plank was rejected, but it was not until 1932 that the midwestern farmers rebelled.

In the 1948 Democratic convention attention was focused on the civil rights plank. In a vain effort to bridge the differences within the party the Truman leadership in the convention developed a plank that the

[36] *Proceedings*, 1928, p. 150.

southerners thought too forthright and the northerners regarded somewhat belligerently as too weak. Both the southern and northern factions
expressed their dissatisfaction with the resolutions committee's recommendation by proposing their own views on the floor of the convention
and defending them with an impressive volume of torrid oratory. The
triumph of the northern liberals—and the rejection of the southern plank
—contributed to the split in the Democratic party. The entire incident
demonstrated, at least negatively, the uses of platform ambiguity in holding together party groups of divergent views. Again, in 1956, the civil
rights question produced a minority report: the dissenters were northern
Democrats who were under the necessity of making a demonstration
to forestall losses among Negro voters.

Nature of the platform. No tightly reasoned or succinct manifesto of
party doctrine emerges from the convention. The platform tends to be
wordy and to be cast in the rhetoric of political declamation.[37] Platforms
become objects of cynical regard, yet their qualities mirror the characteristics of the party system itself: the platforms are as they are because the
party system is as it is.

The platform may speak with boldness and forthrightness on a range
of issues, usually settled issues or matters on which the party maintains
a traditional position. On such matters, the platforms of the two parties
often differ, contrary to general belief. The differences may be in emphasis, degree, detail, or timing, but these are, in the main, the differences of
American politics. The contrasts between the party platforms also vary
in degree from time to time with the alternating intensification and reduction of conflict between the parties.

On highly contentious questions the platform may be—but not always
is—ambiguous. The fundamental nature of the American party dictates
the vagueness of its pronouncements on some controversial issues. The
construction of a coalition with a chance to win an election may require
the suppression or the subordination of divisive questions. The maintenance of unity in support of a presidential candidate may be facilitated
by the platform's escape clauses for some sectors of the party and by its
silence on other matters. All this is not to glorify obfuscation, but merely
to suggest that the platform is conditioned by the political system as a
whole. A desideratum of the system is the maintenance of coalitions inclusive enough to contend for the presidency; platforms must conform
with that necessity. No simpler way exists to destroy an electoral coali-

[37] The 1956 Democratic platform ran to about 15,000 words; the Republican, 13,000.
For the platforms, see K. H. Porter and D. B. Johnson, *National Party Platforms,
1840–1956* (Urbana: University of Illinois Press, 1956).

tion than for its majority to insist on precise, forthright, and advanced policy positions unacceptable to other elements of the coalition.

Platforms are electioneering documents, not blueprints for action. They may indicate the general direction of movement sought by the dominant elements of the party, but from both practical and theoretical necessities they ordinarily leave wide latitude for discretion once the election is won. Lines of action can rarely be spelled out in detail in advance of the time of action. Furthermore, a national convention with power to bind its nominees for President and the congressional candidates on the party's ticket to specific courses of action would become, in effect, the government. The President and the party in Congress can hardly be reduced to this subordinate role; they become the government and, for the welfare of the nation as well as of their party, must act as the government and not as the rubber stamp of a party organ. In England, where a much sharper distinction is drawn between the party in Parliament and the party organization outside the government, the parliamentary party has refused to be bound and has demanded that it not be embarrassed by specific and binding instructions—or platforms—adopted by the national organs of the party outside the government. Probably a similar fundamental tendency—that is, a cleavage between the extragovernmental party organization and the party as government—has operated in this country, although there has been no systematic rationalization of that factor.[38]

Candidates "amend" the platform. The generalities of the platform are amplified by the presidential candidate in his speeches during the campaign. The platform is open to interpretation and, as Sherman Adams said of General Eisenhower in 1952, the candidate "is the one who has to interpret it" if he "has a different view as to the shading or meaning of words." Occasionally the candidate proceeds to amend the platform before the convention has adjourned. In 1904 the Democrats, still suffering from their espousal of the free coinage of silver in 1896, nominated Parker, a conservative easterner, and said nothing about coinage in the platform. Parker telegraphed the convention to inform it of his firm attachment to the gold standard and asked that the nomination be declined for him if this stand was not satisfactory to the convention. The convention stated that since the platform was silent on coinage, Parker's views should not preclude him "from accepting a nomination on said

[38] Ford observes, however: "The Whigs, a party of political odds and ends, did not formally present a platform either in 1840 or in 1848. The prepossessions in favor of parliamentary control which clung to the Whig party made the laying down of platforms in connection with presidential nominations a disagreeable duty."—*Op. cit.*, p. 205.

platform." In 1928 the Democratic convention pledged "its nominees to an honest effort to enforce the Eighteenth Amendment." As the convention was about to adjourn, it received a telegram from Alfred E. Smith in which he made clear his belief that "fundamental changes" should be made in the "provisions for national prohibition."

Governor Landon, in 1936, telegraphed the Republican convention before it nominated him expressing his views on several planks of the platform. The platform favored state laws on child labor and on hours, wages, and working conditions of women; Landon favored, if it was found necessary, a constitutional amendment to permit federal action. The platform, too, promised "a sound currency to be preserved at all hazards." Landon interpreted that to mean "a currency expressed in terms of gold and convertible into gold," with certain hedging sentences. The convention pledged the party to "the merit system"; Landon concretized the generality by promising to include within the merit system "every position . . . below the rank of assistant secretaries of major departments." Every candidate in one way or another finds it necessary to "interpret" ambiguous platform planks during the course of his campaign.

Nominations

After the platform has been disposed of, the convention reaches its main job: the making of presidential and vice-presidential nominations. Meanwhile, the leaders for each presidential contender have been engaged in interminable conferences, in maintaining the morale and loyalty of the faithful delegations, in trying to induce the wavering to join their ranks, and in angling for promises of second-ballot support from delegations pledged to favorite sons and other long-shot candidates. Each campaign manager has his espionage agents to ascertain the strength of the opposition, to gain advance knowledge of their strategy, to avoid being taken by surprise.

Placing the candidates in nomination. The states are called in alphabetical order for nominations. A state near the beginning of the list may yield to a state farther along the line that has a serious contender. For example, Alabama may yield to New York to permit it to place its candidate in nomination. The nominating speeches traditionally maintain a high standard of extravagance, although connoisseurs of political oratory contend that recent conventions have produced no really fine performances. A noted speech was that of Franklin Roosevelt nominating Alfred E. Smith in 1928 which concluded:

America needs not only an administrator but a leader—a pathfinder, a blazer of the trail to the high road that will avoid the bottomless morass of gross materialism that has engulfed so many of the great civilizations of the past. It is the privilege of the Democracy not only to offer such a man but to offer him as their surest leader to victory. To stand upon the ramparts and die for our principles is heroic. To sally forth to battle and win for our principles is something more than heroic. We offer one who has the will to win—who not only deserves success but commands it. Victory is his habit—the happy warrior, Alfred E. Smith.

In 1928 John McNab nominated Hoover at the Republican convention:

I nominate him for his lofty character as a man and citizen; for his broad and kindly human sympathies; for his wholesome heart that rejoices above all things else that he has been useful to the people of his native land.
And now, engineer, practical scientist, minister of mercy to the hungry and the poor, administrator, executive, statesman, beneficent American, kindly neighbor, wholesome human being, I give you the name of Herbert Hoover.

The custom is, as in the quotations, to describe some mythical character, to extol his virtues, to demonstrate that he can be victorious, and, at last, to reveal what everybody knew all through the discourse, his name. The naming of the candidate is the signal for bedlam to break loose. Supporters of the candidate start processions through the aisles; bands play the campaign song; delegates and spectators yell themselves hoarse. These demonstrations are, of course, only most infrequently spontaneous; they are merely synthesized in varying degrees. The length of the demonstration and the intensity of the applause may give a rough index of the strength and popularity of the various candidates, but no votes are changed by the noise. The pageantry and the demonstrations give the delegates something to do while their leaders are negotiating behind the scenes.[39] And delegates may be relieved of the chore of parading about the convention hall by the employment of professional demonstrators.

After each nominating speech several seconding speeches follow; they are shorter but of the same tenor as the nominating speeches. Politicians highly prize the opportunity to make such a speech before a nation-wide television audience, and assignments to make speeches sometimes become counters in the game of politics. State delegations have been delivered in gratitude for an invitation to make a nominating speech.[40]

[39] Edward J. Flynn, one-time Democratic national chairman and long-time Bronx leader, concludes that "there are probably considerably less than one hundred men in any convention who really dictate what occurs. These men meet in the so-called 'smoke-filled' rooms."—*You're the Boss* (New York: Viking, 1947), p. 97.
[40] The 1956 Republican convention deviated from practice in that its managers arranged for short seconding speeches to be made by nondelegates chosen to suggest that traditionally Democratic groups had allied themselves with Eisenhower. A labor union official, a member of the Farmers' Union, a Jew, a Negro, a southerner, and

Balloting for the candidate. With the completion of the seconding speeches the convention is ready to vote, and the roll of states is called. The chairman of each state delegation announces the vote of the state; the announcement may be the occasion for huzzas or boos. Usually the vote is simply announced; in earlier and more flowery days the announcement was the occasion for a short speech more often than now. Thus, in 1868, when Montana was called: "The mountains of Montana, from whence flow the waters of the Columbia and the Mississippi, are vocal with the name of Grant, to whom she gives two votes."

If the first ballot fails to produce a majority, other ballots are taken until a decision is reached. The lack of a majority on the first ballot intensifies efforts by the managers of the leading aspirants to attract additional support on succeeding votes. As the balloting proceeds, state delegations may march out of the hall to caucus to determine what they will do as the political winds shift, or they may go into a huddle on the floor of the convention hall. From time to time the correctness of the chairman's report of a state's vote may be challenged by a member of the delegation, and the convention chairman orders the delegation to be polled. Each delegate from the state then announces his vote. The demand for a poll of a delegation may be a dilatory tactic to play for time as managers negotiate.[41] The switch of a pivotal state in the balloting may mark a turn of the tide toward a particular aspirant. In 1932, when McAdoo cast California's vote for Roosevelt on the fourth ballot, the nomination was in fact made and other states rushed to the bandwagon.

The nomination is often made on the first ballot; the convention merely records the victory of the aspirant who has gathered the support of a majority of the delegates before the voting started. In the 1944 Republican convention Dewey's managers were able to assemble a majority before the balloting; and when the time came to vote, the other aspirants bowed out of the race. Dewey received all the votes on the first ballot except that of a lone delegate from Wisconsin, who held out for MacArthur. In 1956 Stevenson, in part because of Kefauver's withdrawal shortly before the convention, won on the first ballot in the Democratic convention.

The Republicans have had fewer prolonged convention struggles than the Democrats. Since the Civil War two-thirds of the Republican presi-

other such persons made speeches directed more to the television audience than to the convention. The Farmers' Union member, it turned out, had dropped by the Union office to join on the way to the convention.

[41] The demand for a poll of a delegation may also be a move to place the face of each delegate in front of the television camera. The Democrats in 1956 adopted the rule that a state's delegation would be polled only upon demand by one-third of its members.

dential candidates have been nominated on the first ballot. Only half the Democratic candidates during the same period were nominated on the first ballot. The Democrats set the record in 1924 when they took 103 ballots to break the deadlock between Smith and McAdoo and to nominate Davis. The Republican peak of 36 came in 1880, when Garfield was nominated as a compromise candidate after a deadlock among the supporters of Grant, Blaine, and Sherman.

Composition of party differences in the nomination. The function of the convention is to settle the conflict among factions of the party for the presidential nomination. Yet the task of the convention leaders amounts to considerably more than this. They must seek to guide the convention toward a decision on a nominee who can be supported by all factions of the party. At times that result comes about by the concentration of strength on a candidate who personifies the terms of consensus among the party factions. At other times the etiquette of political combat operates to sooth the wounds of those who suffered undeniable defeat. At still other conventions, animosities reach such intensity that deadlock ensues and whatever parity unity is achieved by the convention is façade and nothing more.

The process of negotiation toward agreement was well illustrated by the Republican nomination of Dewey in 1948. As the delegates arrived in Philadelphia spokesmen for Dewey, Taft, and Stassen issued the routine predictions of victory. It was apparent that Dewey had the largest bloc of delegates but not a majority. The decision rested with the leaders of uninstructed delegations and delegations committed to favorite sons. These leaders made their estimates of the situation perhaps not without consideration of the probable effect of alternative courses of action on their own political fortunes. Before the balloting began Senator Edward Martin of Pennsylvania withdrew as a "favorite son" to support Dewey. Charles A. Halleck, a Representative from Indiana, took a similar step and his prospects of becoming the vice-presidential candidate were regarded as improved. On the other hand, Governor Green of Illinois plumped for Taft and thereby made himself a possible vice-presidential nominee if Taft won.

With the first ballot whatever doubt remained about the strength of the respective aspirants was erased: Dewey, 434; Taft, 224; Stassen, 157. On the second ballot the vote stood: Dewey, 515; Taft, 274; Stassen, 149. The convention recessed at about five o'clock to reconvene later. The negotiations of the intervening two or three hours do not appear on the record. When the convention reconvened, Senator Knowland of California read a statement from Governor Earl Warren, California's favorite son, who declared it obvious that Governor Dewey was the favorite and that no useful purpose would be served by prolonging the balloting. Governor Stassen withdrew; the leader of the Michigan delegation withdrew the name of Senator Vandenberg; Senator Baldwin of Connecticut, who had been supported by his delegation for two ballots, announced for Dewey as did the leader of the MacArthur bloc. The convention voted unanimously for Dewey. The leaders who had been engaged for months in mortal combat buried the hatchet, rallied round the winner, and made a great show of unity. Doubtless in the process of negotiation commitments, contingent upon victory, had been made, some expressly and others tacitly.

In a contested convention the groping of leaders toward agreement by no means extinguishes conflict among factions led by determined and ambitious men. The most diverse factions may unite to hold their lines in the balloting in an attempt to "stop" a leading contender for the nomination. At times when contentious issues drive deep fissures through the party whatever decision the convention yields may leave elements of the party in an abiding mood of dissent. Even so, the etiquette of the old "pros" dictates that even if an opponent is defeated, his nose need not be rubbed in the dirt as well. Amateurs quickly learn the code. In 1952, before the chairman of the Republican convention had announced the results of the final roll call, General Eisenhower had made his way to Senator Taft's hotel to say a word to the vanquished aspirant for the nomination.

Peculiarities of the convention constituency. The nomination and the platform represent an attempt to unite the party and to present to the country a ticket that will win the elecion. The consensus that emerges from the national convention tends to present to the nation an image of the party that diverges notably from the impression built up by its congressional branch. That contrast rests perhaps fundamentally on the fact that the convention represents, at times overrepresents, sectors of the party whose views do not find adequate expression in Congress. When the Democrats are the out party, for example, the Democratic congressional contingent tends to be in large degree southern; its votes and the pronouncements of its leaders over time create a picture of a party dedicated in exceptional degree to the peculiar interests of the South. The national convention, on the other hand, includes delegates from districts with substantial numbers of Democratic votes but no Democratic congressional representation. As Westerfield puts it: "Between 1943 and 1954 the Southerners consistently held around 45 per cent of the Democratic seats in the Senate and around 50 per cent of those in the House—

but only about 25 per cent of the votes at national conventions." [42] The conventions nominate a Roosevelt, a Truman, or a Stevenson—men who give the party a policy outlook in contrast with that held by most of its congressional leaders.

Similarly the Republican convention gives to the presidential politics of that party a hue quite unlike the policy coloration of its standpat congressional wing. The midwestern areas in recent decades have contributed disproportionately to the party's congressional contingent, and the region's isolationist and conservative spokesmen painted the prevailing picture of the party in the public mind. Yet the national convention in 1952 could nominate Eisenhower rather than Taft, who had unquestioned leadership of the congressional wing of the party. In the convention the coastal states—both Atlantic and Pacific—had a far stronger voice than they had had in the party's congressional councils.[43]

Democratic two-thirds rule. Two features of nominating procedure peculiar to Democratic conventions need to be mentioned. The national convention follows the unit rule and until 1936 required a two-thirds vote to nominate. In the first Democratic convention, that of 1831, the nomination of Jackson for the Presidency was a foregone conclusion, but the two-thirds rule was adopted to govern the decision on the vice-presidential nomination. In the convention of 1835 the committee on rules recommended that "a majority of two-thirds shall be required to elect the candidates for President and Vice-President." The proposed rule was defended as calculated to produce "a more imposing effect." [44] Though its adoption may have assured this "imposing effect," the rule also generated difficulties and stimulated attacks based on the majority principle.

The continuance of the rule was debated from time to time, but not until 1936 was a convention able to consider the rule on its merits. The question of its continuance had always been tied up with the fate of particular aspirants for the nomination. Furthermore, the two-thirds rule was

---

[42] H. Bradford Westerfield, *Foreign Policy and Party Politics* (New Haven: Yale University Press, 1955), p. 47.

[43] *Ibid.*, pp. 39–45. The bearing of representation on the tenor of convention decisions is affected by the types of winning coalitions that are formed in conventions. Paul T. David finds that in Democratic conventions since 1928 the South has provided a proportion of the winners' votes smaller than its percentage of the convention membership. In the Republican conventions the Midwest has had the same sort of below-par record. In both parties the Northeast provided a share of the winning votes greater than its proportion of the convention total. See P. T. David, "The Changing Party Pattern," *Antioch Review*, Fall, 1956, pp. 333–350.

[44] Stanwood, *A History of the Presidency from 1788 to 1897*, p. 182.

associated with the unit rule by which the entire vote of a state delegation may be cast for the candidate supported by a majority of the delegation. The vote of a few large states, when almost evenly divided but cast as a unit, could give the nomination to a person actually supported by only a minority of the convention. The two-thirds rule made such a result less likely.[45] Moreover, the Solid South regarded the rule as a means by which it could veto candidates displeasing to the region, a view that came to have less and less foundation as the South's proportion (24.3 per cent in 1956) of the convention votes declined.

In 1932 an attack, destined eventually to be successful, was begun against the two-thirds rule by the forces seeking the nomination of Franklin D. Roosevelt. The Roosevelt managers made a hasty retreat when it appeared that their proposal to change the rules of the game to favor their candidate would backfire and the question was postponed until 1936. In that year the report of the committee on rules, presented to the convention by Bennett Champ Clark, whose father had lost the nomination in 1912 because of the operation of the two-thirds rule, recommended its abrogation. With Roosevelt the certain nominee, the requirement of only a majority to nominate could be adopted without affecting the interests of any aspirant for the nomination. Southern Democrats continued in later years to complain of the 1936 action and from time to time proposed, without much hope of success, a return to the old rule.

Democratic unit rule. The Democratic unit rule requires that the entire vote of a state delegation shall be cast as the majority of the delegation desires, if the state delegation has been so instructed by the state convention. The national convention, however, recognizes state laws that do not subject delegates chosen within congressional districts to the operation of a unit rule imposed by the state convention.[46] For example, if the Virginia state convention instructs its delegates to the national convention to abide by the unit rule the convention will recognize the instruction as binding upon it. The unit rule, then, is not imposed on the state delegation by the national convention; the convention merely enforces the instruction of the duly constituted agencies of the party within the states. The Republican national convention, on the other hand, does not

[45] Carl Becker, "The Unit Rule in National Nominating Convention," *American Historical Review*, 5 (1899), p. 62.

[46] This exception was introduced by the Democratic convention of 1912 at the instance of delegates chosen by presidential primary and pledged to Wilson. The majority of the Ohio delegation, operating under a unit rule, desired to cast the votes of such delegates for Governor Harmon. *Proceedings*, 1912, pp. 59–60; A. S. Link, "The Baltimore Convention of 1912," *American Historical Review*, 50 (1945), pp. 691–713.

recognize as valid a state instruction to its delegation to operate under the unit rule.

During this century, with the increase in the number of states failing to instruct their delegations to act as a unit, the importance of the unit rule in Democratic conventions has considerably diminished. As an indication of the practical degree of departure from that rule, it may be noted that on the first ballot for the vice-presidential nomination at Chicago in 1956, the votes of the delegations from 22 states were divided among two or more candidates. Additional states, too, may not have been bound by the unit rule but merely happened to be unanimous in their choice.

Naming the vice-presidential candidate. Energies and enthusiasm are exhausted by the strain of the nomination of the presidential candidate; the convention, in a state of emotional deflation, then proceeds, often hurriedly and without much relish, to finish its business with the nomination of a candidate for the Vice-Presidency. The factors governing the selection of the running mate for the head of the ticket are numerous but a few patterns recur. The presidential nominee ordinarily can, in fact, make the choice, although the range of his discretion may differ with circumstances. A limiting consideration frequently persuasive is the supposed necessity of "balancing" the ticket. It is usually thought advantageous to recognize a party faction or a geographical section other than the one represented by the presidential candidate. In 1912 the Democrats nominated Wilson of New Jersey and Marshall of Indiana; the Republicans, Taft of Ohio and Sherman of New York. In 1928 the Democratic convention selected Senator Robinson of Arkansas as the running mate of Alfred E. Smith. "Robinson was a Southerner, a Protestant, and a Dry, and his selection was dictated by the northern Democracy's desire to divide honors with the South and hold it in line for Al Smith. Thus, as one writer remarked, 'The Democratic donkey with a wet head and wagging a dry tail left Houston.'" [47]

The nomination for the Vice-Presidency occasionally is determined by the maneuvers leading to the nomination for the Presidency. In the 1932 Democratic convention the California delegation, pledged to Garner, swung the presidential nomination to Roosevelt. The convention the next day unanimously placed Garner in second place on the ticket.[48] In the

[47] Peel and Donnelly, *The 1928 Campaign*, p. 34.

[48] Arthur F. Mullen says that the shift of the California delegation appeared to give the nomination to Roosevelt but that the deciding factor was an agreement between him and Tom Connally, leader of the Texas delegation, that the vice-presidential nomination would go to Garner. See A. F. Mullen, *Western Democrat* (New York: Wilfred Funk, 1940), p. 276.

Republican convention of 1944 a similar sequence of events occurred when Governor Bricker yielded the presidential nomination to Dewey without a fight and subsequently received the second place on the ticket.

Commonly the convention ratifies the choice of the presidential candidate or his managers as a matter of routine but on occasion the Vice-Presidential nomination sets off a battle. In 1948 the Republican convention cheerfully accepted Dewey's recommendation of Warren.[49] In 1940, in contrast, the Democratic convention reluctantly and with loud manifestations of displeasure ratified Roosevelt's choice, Henry Wallace. In 1944 the Democratic convention had, at first, no clear guidance from Roosevelt; several aspirants believed that he had given them the green light. The right and left wings of the party checkmated each other. The left vetoed James Byrnes of South Carolina but was unable to win for its candidate, Wallace. The nomination of Harry Truman provided a classic instance of the maintenance of party unity by the nomination of a candidate not zealously supported by any wing of the party but also not entirely unacceptable to any major faction of the party.[50]

Conventions depart from their off-hand consideration of the Vice-Presidency chiefly when the presidential nominee is obviously not in the best of health. Such a circumstance explained to some extent the warmth of the contest in the 1944 Democratic convention. In 1956 Eisenhower's health made the question of the vice-presidential nomination a potential source of controversy among Republicans, but skillful management of the steam roller by party leaders forestalled effective challenge of Nixon.[51] Stevenson, the Democratic presidential nominee, sought to make capital of the Republican situation by inviting the Democratic convention

[49] Senator Vandenberg related that Dewey, after his nomination, assembled about 20 Republican leaders to consider the vice-presidential nomination. The group, in a discussion lasting from 11 P. M. to 4 A. M., arrived at unanimous agreement on Warren.—*The Private Papers of Senator Vandenberg* (Boston: Houghton Mifflin, 1952), pp. 439–441.

[50] Edward J. Flynn records the survey to find a vice-presidential candidate as follows: "We went over every man in the Senate to see who would be available, and Truman was the only one who fitted. His record as head of the Senate Committee to Investigate the National Defense Program was excellent, his labor votes in the Senate were good; on the other hand, he seemed to represent to some degree the conservatives in the party, he came from a border state, and he had never made any 'racial' remarks. He just dropped into the slot."—*Op. cit.,* p. 181.

[51] The role of Eisenhower in the renomination of Nixon should be of great interest to students of political technique, once the memoirs are all in. By a series of actions that seemed both to endorse Nixon and to leave the door open for other candidates the convention arrived with no competing candidate in sight yet with the fiction of a door still open. If the General wanted a renomination of Nixon from the outset, his actions must be set down as a remarkably adept management of a situation; if he did not, a contrasting judgment would prevail.

to make a free choice for the second place, a step that set off a wild scramble for delegates among aspirants for the nomination. That an "open" convention on the vice-presidential nomination should have attracted widespread comment serves to mark it as an exception to the more general practice in which the wishes of the presidential nominee govern.

Notification of the nominees. It used to be the custom for the convention to appoint a committee to notify both the presidential and vice-presidential candidates of their nomination. A committee journeyed to the home of the nominee. Its chairman made a speech of notification and the candidate responded with a speech of acceptance. The notification was often an important political ceremony and the speeches significant campaign documents. In 1932 Roosevelt flew to Chicago to appear before the convention to accept the nomination and broke, as he called it, "the absurd tradition that the candidate should remain in professed ignorance of what has happened for weeks until he is formally notified." The Roosevelt precedent seems to have established a new custom, which, incidentally, enables the candidates to avail themselves of some free television and radio time. In 1940 Wendell Willkie, however, adhered to the old practice and made a major campaign event of his acceptance speech at Elwood, Indiana, his childhood home.

Role and Function of the Convention

How is the national convention to be evaluated? A favorite critique of the national convention is that by Ostrogorski, who called it a "colossal travesty of popular institutions"; the platform "a collection of hollow, vague phrases." He quoted with approval the saying: "God takes care of drunkards, of little children, and of the United States!" [52] Other observers, both imported and indigenous, remark on the hilarity and unseemly demeanor of delegates gathered together for the solemn business of nominating a candidate for the Presidency of the United States. It is indeed true that the conventions are rarely august assemblages. They partake of the more robust features of American character. Yet such critiques go only to appearances and do not touch the function of the national convention in the American party system.

In a fairly real sense, the national convention is the national party. When means develop for uniting people in support of a nominee, the essence of party comes into being. When the national convention was contrived to designate presidential nominees, viable national party came

[52] See his complete statement in *Democracy and the Party System in the United States* (New York: Macmillan, 1910), pp. 159–160.

into existence. The national convention thus is at the heart of the national party system. Without it or some equivalent institution party government for the nation as a whole could scarcely exist.

The position of the national convention reflects both the strength and the fragility of the national party. The convention casts a net of party unity over party leaders scattered through the counties, the cities, and the villages of the 48 states and brings them to the support of its nominee. The convention provides a means for the contending candidates, factions, and interests within a party to consult and agree upon the terms on which they will work together in the presidential campaign. The resulting concert of interests exerts a formidable power throughout the nation. The national convention, a body unknown to the laws or to the Constitution, brings its affiliated organizations in 48 states to the support of electoral candidates who, if they win in their states, cast their votes without question for the nominees of the convention.[53]

The binding quality of the convention's decision derives more from consent than from any sanction available to the convention or to its agents. The Democratic convention of 1948 demonstrated the limits of the convention's authority when it found itself unable to make a nomination that all the state organizations regarded as binding. The Democratic parties of Mississippi, South Carolina, Louisiana, and Alabama had a "Democratic" candidate other than that of the national convention. Because Mr. Truman's views on race policies were unacceptable, these state organizations, in effect, seceded from the party and named a candidate of their own to whom their electors were pledged, J. Strom Thurmond, the Dixiecratic or States' Rights candidate. The 1948 southern bolt had its reverberations in the 1952 Democratic convention when the liberal wing challenged the right of Dixiecratic leaders who had not supported the nominee in 1948 to sit in the convention. After an historic donnybrook, the 1952 convention adopted a rule requiring that all delegates, as a condition of sitting in the convention, give an assurance that they would use every "honorable means" to see that the nominees of the convention were placed on their state ballots as the Democratic nominees.[54] Even in the 1952 con-

---

[53] The exceptions only "prove" the rule. In 1948 a Democratic elector of Tennessee voted for J. Strom Thurmond, the States' Rights candidate, although Truman had won the popular vote in the state. In 1956 an Alabama elector, despite Stevenson's victory in the state, voted for Walter B. Jones, an Alabama judge. In so doing the elector, W. F. Turner, violated the pledge to support the nominee of the national convention he had been required to take by the Democratic state executive committee to become a candidate in the primary for the post of elector.

[54] "No delegate shall be seated unless he shall give assurance to the Credentials Committee that he will exert every honorable means available to him in any official capacity he may have, to provide that the nominees of this Convention for President

vention the assurance was not uniformly required.[55] Yet the convention nominees did appear on the ballots of the southern states in 1952, although not all southern Democratic leaders supported them in the campaign.

In the preliminaries to the 1956 Democratic convention the problem of the "loyalty pledge" arose in a new form. Should the pledge as adopted in 1952 be required of all delegates in 1956? What should be done about those who had participated in the 1952 convention but had campaigned for Eisenhower? Most of the more prominent southern Democrats who had supported the General were not chosen in their states as delegates and the convention did not have to decide whether to seat such "Republicrats" as Governor Shivers of Texas, James F. Byrnes of South Carolina, or Robert F. Kennon of Louisiana. Moreover, national leaders in an endeavor to heal the breach between the South and the North agreed well in advance of the convention to abandon the loyalty pledge adopted in 1952.[56]

Despite the inability of the national party, through the convention, to bind all elements of the party all the time, the total performance of the national convention as an instrumentality for weaving together the diverse and geographically scattered elements of each party into a national whole constitutes an impressive political achievement. In another respect, the national convention makes a special contribution to the American political system. Had the congressional caucus by some chance survived as the means for nominating presidential candidates, the odds are that Presidents and the presidential system itself would have been radically different. The convention provides a channel for advancement to the

---

and Vice President, through their names or those of electors pledged to them, appear on the election ballot under the heading, name or designation of the Democratic Party. Such assurance shall be given by the chairman of each delegation, and shall not be binding upon those delegates who shall so signify to the Credentials Committee prior to its report to this convention."

[55] For an account of the 1952 convention actions on the 1948 bolters, see David, *Presidential Nominating Politics in 1952*, I, pp. 112–142.

[56] The formula adopted by the Democratic national committee in its call for the 1956 convention was: ". . . it is understood that the Delegates to the Democratic National Convention, when certified by the State Democratic Party, are bona fide Democrats who have the interests, welfare and success of the Democratic party at heart, and will participate in the convention in good faith, and therefore no additional assurances shall be required of Delegates to the Democratic National Convention in the absence of credentials contest or challenge." The proviso on contests left open the possibility that the party loyalty of a delegation might be challenged by another delegation claiming to be the true representatives of the state party. For a discussion of the adoption of the formula, see "The Democratic Party's Approach to Its Convention Rules," *American Political Science Review*, 50 (1956), pp. 553–568.

Presidency independent of the Congress, a channel that can probably be navigated by men who could not make their way to the top through Congress and that probably is closed to others who can achieve leadership in Congress.

If these estimates are correct, the convention profoundly conditions the character of the American governmental system. It does not limit access to the Presidency to those who climb the ladder within the narrow confines of the inner circles of the representative body; nor does it restrict competition to those who gain the deference of their fellows within any narrowly defined group of party notables. The convention operates flexibly with a range of freedom that enables it to elevate to leadership men it judges to be suited to the needs of the time rather than merely to promote those who have worked their way up the bureaucratic ladder of party status. So broad an avenue to executive authority, it may be argued, leaves the way open to the "man on horseback." Yet so far the convention system and the associated modes of election have worked within the limits of the basic tenet of party government, namely, that no election shall foreclose the opportunity for another election.[57]

[57] The most comprehensive analysis of any set of national conventions is that of the 1952 conventions by Paul T. David, Malcolm Moos, and Ralph M. Goldman, *Presidential Nominating Politics in 1952* (Baltimore: Johns Hopkins Press, 5 v., 1954).

16 | Congressional Nominations

An incidental moral of the preceding chapters is that the term nomination covers the most diverse phenomena. The grand compromises negotiated in a national convention result in the nomination of presidential and vice-presidential candidates. The spirited primary contest of a pair of fledgling lawyers in a South Carolina county settles, subject to the formalities of the general election, which one will go to the legislature. In a well-organized congressional district, the deliberations of a handful of leaders determine the nomination, whether the formal action is by convention or by direct primary. In another, the erratic interplay of personal ambitions, pressure-group efforts, and newspaper favor or disfavor eventuates in an unpredictable nomination by a free and unfettered primary. In view of the varied practices in nomination, as well as of the significance of the nominating process in fixing the characteristics of the national parties, the selection of candidates for Congress warrants special attention.

Observation of the nomination of candidates for the House and Senate brings forcibly to attention at least two peculiar characteristics of the American party system. First, is the odd mixture of centralization and decentralization in the organization of the American parties. The presidential nominating convention makes a decision that is accepted—at least most of the time—as authoritative by the state units of the party. The state's presidential electors, if they win the election, serve as rubber stamps for the party's national convention. The most extreme decentralization prevails, too, for each state and each congressional district exercises complete autonomy in the designation of nominees for Senate and House. No national party office, either Democratic or Republican, asserts the right to control nominations made by the party subsidiaries in the states or districts.[1] In the national conventions a consensus is sought among the divergent interests within the party; in the nominations for House and Senate those same interests are free to impose their special policy coloration on the local candidates of the party. The differences compromised in the national convention are perpetuated, even accentuated, in the party's congressional slate.

A focus on nominations also brings to the fore another feature of the American system, namely, the fact that much of our politics is intraparty, not interparty, politics. Given the existence of many states and districts strongly attached to one or the other of the parties, the actual choice of Senators and Representatives is often made at the nominating stage. The reality of the nominating process thus differs greatly from district to district and from state to state. "Nomination" may mean that alone or it may be the equivalent of election.

Senatorial Nominations

Senators are the great panjandrums of American politics. The special role of the Senate elevates its members to positions of great power within the government and among them are to be found conspicuous spokesmen for the chief shades of opinion within each party. Their control—formal and informal—over appointments in the executive branch always gives them great influence in administration and sometimes enables them to become *de facto* heads of departments or agencies—without any of the inconveniences of accountability. Elected to represent their states, Senators often become in effect spokesmen for interests spreading across state lines—the steel makers, the labor unions, the Farm Bureau, the China lobby, the National Manufacturers Association, the liberals, the isolationists, even, on occasion, the crackpots. Their long tenure—a couple of re-elections gives them 18 years—aids them in building their power. Even one Senator can make a nuisance of himself; a handful of them in a wrecking mood can bring the executive branch into a cowering state of contemptible paralysis. A President must come to terms with the Senators

[1] On British practice in this respect, see Allen M. Potter, "British Party Organization, 1950," *Political Science Quarterly*, 66 (1951), pp. 65–86.

of his own party—or outmaneuver them. In the minority party, given the lack of an acknowledged national leader, Senators are apt to become the party spokesmen most prominent in national attention. One of them may even become the recognized chieftain of the party, as was the late Senator Taft, although more commonly a few of them share leadership.

Commonly nominations for the Senate go to men who have achieved eminence in the party in their state. By their performance in other public offices and by their ascent up the ladder of party status, men make themselves "available" for the senatorial nomination. Of those Senators who served between 1920 and 1956, about a quarter had been state governors and almost a third members of the national House of Representatives. A third of them had been members of state legislative bodies and about one out of ten had been elected to a state-wide office other than governor, such as attorney general. The southern Democratic bloc of Senators included an especially large proportion of former Representatives, while the Republican group from strong Republican states included a much larger proportion of ex-governors than did the entire roster of Senators.[2] These facts suggest that the natural processes of leadership selection tend to narrow the range of eligibles for senatorial nominations. In only a few states can the party organization cast the mantle of its nomination upon an unknown and thereby convert him into a potential Senator.

Convention nominations. The parties in the states select their candidates by either the direct primary or the convention. Only a handful of states retain the convention system, although the realities concealed by the direct primary are at times its equivalent. New York, Delaware, Indiana, and Connecticut nominate senatorial candidates by convention. In most of the southern states the Republican party acts through conventions, but these nominations are only accolades to Republican worthies and not choices of serious political consequence.

Although the workings of the convention system in the states has not been extensively analyzed, the procedure of choice resembles that of the presidential nominating conventions. Often the nomination is settled in advance of the convention by negotiation among party leaders. Since a campaign for the Senate in a populous state is both expensive and strenuous, the problem may be one of drafting a candidate from among the

---

[2] Of the southern Democrats, 44 per cent had served in the House. Of the Republicans from a group of 12 strongly Republican states, 40 per cent were ex-governors. Incidentally, Democrats draw a higher proportion of their Senators from the legal profession than do the Republicans, about three-fourths against one-half, a fact probably reflective of the contrasting composition of the leadership corps of the two parties.

few individuals with sufficient status to make them promising candidates. In New York in 1956, state Democratic leaders, aided by the head of the national ticket, Adlai Stevenson, induced Mayor Robert F. Wagner of New York City to accept the senatorial nomination. In other instances organization leaders are divided and the nomination is settled only when the convention votes are counted.

Senatorial nominations, by whatever method, are made by state authority without formal interposition of national leaders. Yet the circumstances surrounding the convention procedure permit, when the will is there, a degree of collaboration between national and state leaders. Quite often New York conventions, both Democratic and Republican, have nominated candidates for the Senate and for the governorship whose designation has been favored by the party's President or presidential candidate. This has been not a matter of coercion by the national party leadership but rather of agreement about lines of action most likely to be of mutual benefit in specific campaigns.

Direct primary nominations: Democratic. Most states nominate their senatorial candidates through the direct primary, a formal procedure of popular choice that may conceal the location of real power to designate candidates. The actual choice may be that of a well-knit party hierarchy which is routinely ratified in the primary. Or the primary may involve a genuine test of popular strength between leaders supported by party factions, pressure organizations, newspapers, church groups, or other such centers of influence. Then, too, an aspirant for the nomination may campaign with no asset other than his own belief that he is called to lead the people.

Careful inspection of Table 16.1 will suggest the variety in the reality underlying the forms of primary nominations. That table analyzes only those Democratic primaries of the period 1920–1954 in which no incumbent Senator sought renomination. The nominating process differs radically when the sitting Senator seeks renomination, a matter to be touched on shortly. One broad point that the table reveals is that the frequency of spirited primary competition for nomination varies among the states with the strength of the Democratic party. In states in which the probability of Republican victory was high, most of the time only a single name appears on the Democratic primary ballot. On the other hand, in the states in which Democratic nomination virtually assures election, nomination without opposition occurs rarely, and sharply fought contests for the nomination are far more frequent.

Even though the frequency of competition for nomination increases

Table 16.1

Frequency and Intensity of Competition for Senatorial Nominations in Democratic Primaries Involving No Incumbents, Related to Democratic Percentage of General Election Vote for Senator, 1920–1954 [a]

Democratic Percentage of General Election Vote	Number and Per Cent of Primaries According to Percentage of Primary Vote to Nominee				Total Number of Primaries
	Under 60 Per Cent		90–100 per Cent		
	Number	Per Cent	Number	Per Cent	
10–19	0	0.0	5	83.3	6
20–29	3	14.3	15	71.4	21
30–39	11	25.0	28	63.6	44
40–49	41	40.2	35	34.3	102
50–59	25	46.3	18	33.3	54
60–69	9	56.2	2	12.5	16
70 and over	13	54.2	3	12.5	24
Total	102	38.2	106	39.7	267
In South [b]	21	61.8	3	8.8	34
Elsewhere	81	34.8	103	44.2	233

[a] This table includes only those primaries in which incumbent Senators were not seeking renomination. Senators serving under appointment who sought nomination were treated as nonincumbents for the purposes of this table. The coverage of the table is fairly complete for the primaries of the period.
[b] This line includes the Confederate states plus Oklahoma.

with the expectation of general election victory, not all nominations for sure seats are contested. Nor do all nominations for seats certain to be lost go by default. It is evident that factors in addition to the prospects for victory help determine whether primary contests will occur. Examples pulled more or less at random from the cases hidden away in Table 16.1 will indicate types of nominating situations.

About half of the Democratic candidates included in the table who were eventually elected won their primaries in a walk or had been nominated unopposed. Francis J. Myers, for example, was unopposed for the Pennsylvania nomination in 1944. Presumably the principal leaders of the Democratic organization of the state concurred in his nomination; at least none of them felt disposed to back a challenger in the primary. Similarly the 1948 unopposed nomination of Paul H. Douglas in Illinois reflected the fact that his support by the Illinois Democratic organization settled the matter. Some unopposed nominees operated from positions of personal prestige, such as Joseph C. O'Mahoney of Wyoming in 1954. After long service in the Senate, he had been defeated in the Republican landslide of 1952. His unopposed nomination in 1954 came in recognition of his position as a Democratic leader in the state.

Other eventual winners of the general election had to fight for their nominations. Thus, in Idaho in 1944 Glenn Taylor, the singing cowboy, proved that a wandering minstrel could win the Democratic nomination in that state by polling 33 per cent of the primary vote in a field of four candidates, a fact indicative of the existence of a fractionalized and impotent Democratic hierarchy. Hidden in the same cell of the table is the 1932 Colorado primary, won by Alva B. Adams with only 53 per cent of the primary vote in a field of two contestants, symptomatic of a warm primary contest.

The peculiarities of the southern political regime, by now familiar, also affect the figures in the table. Fairly close contests for nominations occur about twice as frequently in the South as elsewhere, as the subtotals of the table show. Only rarely does a southern state nominate a candidate for a Senate vacancy without some sort of primary fight and often the outcome is close. In these states the primary is the election and the battles in the primaries tend to resemble those between party candidates in the rest of the country. The southern nominating process—that is, the determination of what two or three persons will contend in the primary— occurs in the combinations of factional and local leaders, in the decisions of those in a position to finance a primary campaign, in the endorsements by major newspapers, and in other such informal ways.

Direct primary nominations: Republican. Variations in the process of nominating Republican candidates for the Senate through the direct primary resemble those demonstrated to exist for Democrats by Table 16.1. Spirited contests for nominations, when no Republican incumbent is seeking renomination, occur more frequently as the probability of Republican victory in the general election increases. Yet even when the chances of Republican victory are high, by no means are all Republican senatorial primaries marked by factional fights for popular favor. In some states some of the time and in others most of the time sufficient unity exists in the Republican organization to bring substantial agreement among party leaders on the nominee in advance of the primary. In New Jersey in 1954 the Republican organization drafted Clifford P. Case to run for the Senate and he was not opposed in the primary. In the same year Colorado Republicans designated Gordon Allott as their candidate without primary opposition. Probably, other things being equal, this organizational solidarity on nominations is most apt to develop either when the chances of election are slight or when the strength of the opposition imposes internal discipline. Yet other things are rarely equal, and about two-thirds of the Republicans elected to the Senate for a first term between 1920 and 1954 had had to win a hard primary fight.

National party leadership and nominations for vacancies. Quite apart from the tradition of local autonomy in the determination of nominations, popular participation in the nominating process prevents extensive participation by national party leadership in the designation of senatorial nominees. When nominations are popularly determined, a President or a national chairman cannot very well negotiate with a handful of leaders for a nominee attuned with the national leadership. Moreover, the popular character of nominations itself drastically limits the range of the availables. At times the natural processes of leadership selection make a single individual the "logical" choice before the primary: that is, his standing with the party following is judged by all concerned to make him the strongest man for the nomination. Or perhaps those processes have produced only two or three men sufficiently known to the electorate to be serious aspirants for the nomination. The actual designation of a nominee is only the end point of a process of leadership selection; in only a few states can the controlling clique of the organization settle on a relatively unknown person and by giving him the party nomination invest him with sufficient status to make him a strong candidate.

Yet the national party leadership on occasion takes a hand in the choice of senatorial nominees. It can do so advantageously and effectively only under a limited set of circumstances. When a seat is held by the opposition, the national party leadership may help to recruit and support for the nomination a strong candidate to challenge the incumbent. Even this sort of intervention is fraught with hazard. The problems and possibilities are suggested by the role of the Eisenhower Administration in building the Republican slate of senatorial candidates in 1956. In that year the President persuaded John Sherman Cooper, Ambassador to India, to run for the Senate in Kentucky, and the Republican state committee, in dire need of a strong candidate, nominated Cooper with cheers. For the second Kentucky seat, the Republicans nominated Thruston B. Morton, who had resigned as Assistant Secretary of State to make the race, apparently with the blessings of the Administration. The White House aided Washington state leaders in bringing Arthur B. Langlie into the race against the incumbent Democrat Warren Magnuson. Langlie's position in the state assured him of the primary nomination. In Colorado, ex-governor Dan Thornton, evidently with White House encouragement, was nominated to succeed a retiring Republican, a designation easily arranged because of Thornton's prestige in Colorado as well as of the comparatively unified status of the Republican organization in that state. When the state party organization itself is fairly united and sees eye to eye with the President, the national leadership may participate in the recruitment of senatorial candidates to fight campaigns against opposition incumbents. A radically different situation presents itself when the choice is made by a wide-open primary campaign. In 1956 Douglas McKay resigned as Secretary of the Interior to seek the Oregon Republican senatorial nomination. He went into the campaign with White House commendation, apparently on the assumption that the national Republican headquarters had paved the way by inducing the other aspirants for the nomination to withdraw from the primary. The way had not been paved and, in consequence, McKay had to campaign vigorously for the nomination against Philip S. Hitchcock, a liberal Republican, to the accompaniment of considerable grumbling about the meddling of national headquarters in Oregon affairs.[3] McKay won the primary. The chances of losing such a contest and of finding on the party slate a candidate who had bested the forces of the national leadership in the direct primary usually suffice to discourage national intervention.

These instances of national intervention in senatorial nominations are exceptional. More commonly the national party leadership, at least publicly, does not involve itself in primary contests. The more typical situation is illustrated by the 1954 Illinois Republican primary, won by Joseph T. Meek, a lobbyist for Illinois retail merchants. Meek took a strong stand against Eisenhower's foreign policy and his nomination was interpreted as a victory for "Midwestern Republicanism." No strong spokesman for the Eisenhower wing of the party ran in the primary; nor did the national leadership express a preference among the aspirants. If the victor in such a primary gets to the Senate, he owes nothing to the national party organization and may, with some correctness, regard his nomination and election as an expression of popular dissatisfaction with the national policies of the party.

Senatorial nominations: Incumbents. When an incumbent Senator seeks a renomination, the problem is not one of determining succession to party leadership in the state; it is simply whether to continue the existing leadership. Commonly the Senator holding office has constructed a following

---

[3] *The Oregon Statesman*, a Republican journal, objected "to the commissioning of a candidate by the Republican national chairman or by the White House as was done with McKay, to the extent of having a special letter of commendation written by the President. . . . We think Hitchcock should stay in the race both because of his splendid qualifications and to repudiate the notion that Oregon is a province of the GOP GHQ."

that virtually assures him of nomination for another term if he wishes it. Only about 10 per cent of the incumbents who seek renomination in direct primaries are denied it. Yet the regional variations in their degree of success and in the frequency of strong opposition to them point to important characteristics of the party system.

While almost 90 per cent of the Democratic Senators who sought renomination over the period 1920–1954 were successful, only outside the South could a Democratic incumbent expect renomination either with no opposition or with token opposition. (Of course, in prospect any challenge is apt to appear formidable and only in retrospect does it become trifling.) In the South Democratic incumbents were compelled frequently to fight a strenuous campaign to obtain renomination, an endeavor in which they were by no means uniformly successful. In the South (the Confederate states plus Oklahoma), 42 per cent of the primaries involving incumbents, 1920–1954, gave less than 60 per cent of the vote to the winner. In the remainder of the country only 15 per cent of the primaries were marked by so sharp a contest. In the South, 30 per cent of the incumbent Senators received 80 per cent of the primary vote; in the rest of the country, 55 per cent of the incumbents polled over 80 per cent of the vote. Of the 20 incumbents who lost in their bids for renomination, 18 were southerners.[4] The probability of defeat of a southern incumbent was about 30 out of 100; in the remainder of the country, less than 2 out of 100.

Given the inclusion of most shades of opinion within the Democratic party of the South, primary campaigns between Democrats tend to take on the tone of contests between Democrats and Republicans elsewhere. In 1934, for example, Theodore Bilbo, an heir to the Populist tradition, upset in the primary Hugh Stephens, a southern statesman of the more conservative school. In Florida George Smather's primary triumph in 1950 over the incumbent Claude Pepper was regarded as the equivalent of a Republican victory. In 1954 John Sparkman, an Alabama liberal, turned back the challenge of Laurie Battle, no adherent of the Fair Deal. In Arkansas in 1954 John L. McClellan, a conservative, won renomination against Sid McMath, former Arkansas governor who had been a prominent partisan of the Truman policies. Although not all southern senatorial primaries are marked by such clear-cut factional alignments, the incumbent southern Democratic Senator may expect, with far higher frequency than his northern colleague, a powerful challenge in the primary.

Incumbent Republican Senators win renomination at about the same rate as the Democrats: about 90 per cent of the time. While the defeated

---

[4] In these counts those Senators who were serving by appointment and seeking their first nomination were excluded.

Republican aspirants over the period 1920–1954 were geographically widely scattered, they tended to be, like the defeated Democrats, from states relatively sure for their party. About a third of the Republican upsets were in North Dakota and Wisconsin, states in which a dual factionalism prevailed within the Republican party not unlike that in the Democratic party in southern states.

National party leadership and the renomination of incumbent Senators. The lack of influence of national leadership in the renomination of incumbent Senators highlights the decentralized structure of the national parties. When the problem is to draft a strong candidate to fight an opposition Senator, the national leadership in a restricted category of situations may take a hand in building the senatorial ticket. Yet when a sitting Senator seeks renomination, the prevailing etiquette demands nonintervention by the national leadership. He has made a record in the Senate either as a supporter of the President or perhaps as a thorn in the side of the Administration. Or, if he is a member of the minority, he has either worked with the party leadership or he has given free play to his own policy eccentricities.

By and large, the sitting Senator who is at odds with the national leadership of his party need fear no attempt by the national party authorities to undercut him in his campaign for renomination at the state party primaries. Nor, if he has gone down the line for the party leadership, can he expect much help if he encounters a serious challenge in the primary. Only infrequently do national party leaders attempt to purge the party of the disloyal, and their success is invariably slight. In 1910 President Taft and the conservative wing of the Republican party attempted to drive the progressive element out of the party by defeating its legislative leaders for renomination in the primaries and conventions that year. Under the leadership of President Taft and Senator Aldrich, the eastern standpat Republicans campaigned against the renomination of western progressive leaders. The Republican campaign committee propagandized the western states against progressives, such as Dolliver, Cummins, and Beveridge, and urged the nomination of true Republicans. Eastern money flowed into these areas to finance the fight, and Taft withheld patronage from progressive Republicans. Patronage referees from the other wing of the party had the distribution of local jobs. Conservative leaders traveled to the West and opened fire against La Follette. Even in some eastern states the insurgent wing of the party was strong enough to merit the opposition of the regular party organization. When the returns were all in, the national party leadership had almost completely failed. State after state renominated progressives, who were as thorns in the flesh of the national party leaders. Taft failed to make the party a simon-pure conservative party.[5]

Republican national leadership failed in efforts to upset state organizations of a progressive tinge; the Democratic national leadership has also failed to upset that party's conservative state machines. In the senatorial primaries of 1938 President Roosevelt sought to exert his influence as the party's national leader. Battles in Congress over the President's proposal to revamp the Supreme Court, over the administrative reorganization bill, and over the wages and hours bill had indicated sharp cleavages within the Democratic party. The first primary of the year occurred in Alabama, where J. Thomas Heflin was opposed by Lister Hill, a New Dealer, in a contest for a Senate vacancy. "The support of all three branches of labor," Professor Shannon concludes, "and the inferential blessing of the President, who allowed Hill to ride on his train across Alabama, together with the aid of Governor Bibb Graves' political organization seemed to have been decisive in Hill's victory." [6]

In Florida the sitting Senator, Claude Pepper, who had supported the President on all his major measures, was opposed by Representative Wilcox, an anti-New Dealer, and by former Governor Sholtz who professed friendship for the President. James Roosevelt, son of the President, announced that "we" desired the return of Pepper to the Senate, and the victory of Senator Pepper was followed by a bold declaration by the President:

As President of the United States, I am not asking the voters of the country to vote for Democrats next November as opposed to Republicans or members of any other party. Nor am I, as President, taking part in Democratic primaries.

As the head of the Democratic party, however, charged with the responsibility of carrying out the definitely liberal declaration of principles set forth in the 1936 Democratic platform, I feel that I have every right to speak in those few instances where there may be a clear issue between candidates for a Democratic nomination involving principles or involving a clear misuse of my own name.

Do not misunderstand me. I would certainly not indicate a preference in a state primary because a candidate, otherwise liberal in outlook, had conscientiously differed with me on any single issue. I should be far more concerned about the general attitude of a candidate toward present-day problems and his

[5] G. E. Mowry, *Theodore Roosevelt and the Progressive Movement* (Madison: University of Wisconsin Press, 1946), chs. 4 and 5. On the surreptitious attempt by officers of the Republican national committee to defeat George Norris in the 1930 Nebraska primary, see *Fighting Liberal, The Autobiography of George W. Norris* (New York: Macmillan, 1945), ch. 28.

[6] J. B. Shannon, "Presidential Politics in the South: 1938," *Journal of Politics*, 1 (1939), p. 150.

own inward desire to get practical needs attended to in a practical way. We all know that progress may be blocked by outspoken reactionaries and also by those who say "Yes" to a progressive objective, but who always find some reason to oppose any specific proposal to gain that objective. I call that type of candidate a "Yes, but" fellow.

In pursuance of this policy the President intervened in Democratic primaries in Oklahoma, Kentucky, Georgia, South Carolina, and Maryland. The upshot seemed to be that the influence of even so popular a President as Roosevelt could not defeat a Senator running for renomination with the support of the state organization.[7]

Large-scale intervention by the national leadership in senatorial primaries has occurred only at intervals of sharp internal conflict within the party. Usually the national leadership remains silent, even when its staunch supporters face opposition. In 1956, for example, the Wisconsin Republican organization denied its endorsement to Alexander Wiley, a principal spokesman for the Eisenhower Administration, as he sought renomination in the primary. It backed instead Representative Glenn R. Davis, a dissenter from the Administration especially on foreign policy. So far as the record goes, the Administration turned not a hand in support of Wiley in the maneuvers before the action of the Wisconsin organization. Nor did the President in the primary campaign that followed indicate to the Republicans of Wisconsin a preference for Wiley. The President stood on the view that he should take no "part in any Republican primary." Mr. Wiley won on his own.

Local autonomy in nominations, however they are made, gives a firm anchorage in the grass roots to Senators with views that diverge from the national party line. Moreover, reliance on popular modes of nomination lends special legitimacy and authority to the position of the deviant Senator. He can feel that his renomination amounts to a popular ratification of his views, although it may only reflect the fact that his name is well known. Yet primary nomination may even give advantage to the Senator of unorthodox views. Popular participation in the primary tends to be quite low, and apparently, too, those who vote in the primary tend to be disproportionately persons of a particular shade of opinion within the party.[8] In any event, the sitting Senator who builds popular support

[7] Jim Farley regarded the purge as a violation of the "rules of the game" which treated nominations as "local matters." He traced all the woes of the "Democratic party, directly or indirectly, to this interference in purely local affairs. In any political entity voters naturally and rightfully resent the unwarranted invasion of outsiders." See *Jim Farley's Story, The Roosevelt Years* (New York: Whittlesey House, 1948), chs. 13–14.

[8] In a little over half (56 per cent) of the senatorial primaries, 1948–1954, the total vote in the party primary ranged between 25 and 70 per cent of the vote for the

often can win renomination over the opposition of a state party organization that would prefer a candidate more in harmony with the national leadership. In the 1920's, for example, Smith W. Brookhart, an agrarian radical of the day, won renomination in Iowa as the state Republican organization, assembled in convention, refused to endorse him for election and declined to invite him to speak to the convention. Few are the state organizations that can deny renomination to a Senator. Yet instances occur. In 1948 the New Jersey Republican organization, under the leadership of Governor Alfred E. Driscoll, decided not to support Senator Albert W. Hawkes for renomination. The Senator's conservative views were out of line with the outlook of the younger, liberal element of the party. Senator Hawkes, probably certain of defeat, did not choose to run in the primary.

These consequences of the decentralization of nominations have been dwelled upon at length by persons interested in contriving ways and means to convert the party groups in Congress into cohesive entities more capable of meeting the tasks of government. Considerably less attention has been given to the fact that the process of nomination also produces those Senators—commonly more than a majority of each party group—who hold together in the advancement of the party's national viewpoint. The conspicuous deviates from the party line tend to be from the states without sharp interparty competition, although, of course, not all Senators from such states are party rebels.

Nominations of Representatives

The process of nominating House candidates resembles in its broad outlines that of senatorial nominations. The choice is made independently within each district. The nomination of Representatives is also often in fact the election, given the existence of many districts comparatively sure for one party in the general election. The predominant mode of nomination is the direct primary; the principal exception consists in southern Republican use of conventions to nominate candidates who run for glory rather than for office.

Nominations in primaries involving no incumbents. As with the nomination of Senators, major differences exist between primaries in which incumbent Representatives seek renomination and those in which the party must select a candidate either to replace a retiring member of the party

---

party's candidate in the general election. About one-third (31 per cent) ranged in participation between 25 and 50 per cent of the candidate's general election vote. In about 15 per cent of the primaries, mostly southern, primary participation exceeded the general election vote for the candidate.

or to run for a seat the party does not hold. The analysis of primaries involving no incumbents provides clues to the varieties of actual practice under the primary procedure. Table 16.2, in a familiar pattern, relates the frequency of competition among aspirants for primary nominations to the subsequent general election vote.

Table 16.2

Intraparty Competition for House Nominations and the Prospects of General Election Victory: Proportions of Nominees Winning Primaries Involving No Incumbents by Wide and by Narrow Margins Related to Subsequent General Election Vote, 1952 and 1954[a]

| Candidates' Percentage of General Election Vote | Total Number of Primaries | | Proportions of Candidates Nominated with Indicated Percentages of Primary Vote | | | |
| | | | Democratic | | Republican | |
	D	R	Under 60 Per Cent	90–100 Per Cent	Under 60 Per Cent	90–100 Per Cent
0–29	19	17	10%	90%	23%	53%
30–39	97	42	19	70	36	36
40–49	104	54	34	41	46	31
50–59	21	24	38	23	67	4
60–79	6	8	83	0	62	12
100	12	1	100	0	100	0

[a] The 1952 coverage of the table includes Ariz., Colo., Fla., Ga., Idaho, Ill., Iowa, Kans., La., Me., Md., Mass., Mich., Minn., Mo., Mont., Neb., N.H., N.J., N.C., N.D., Ohio, Okla., Ore., S.D., Tenn., Texas, Utah, Vt., Vir., Wash., W. Va., Wis., and Wyo. The 1954 coverage includes the same states with the exceptions of Iowa, Mont., Neb., Wash., Wisc.

One broad class of primaries, it may be inferred from the table, consists of those in districts in which the candidate will have only a slight chance of victory in the general election because the district ordinarily goes to the opposition by wide margins. In such districts rivalry for the minority nomination is not ordinarily marked. Close primary contests are relatively infrequent and often only a single name appears on the primary ballot. In such districts the problem may be to seek out a candidate willing to make a hopeless race.[9] At times, however, as the table shows, close pri-

[9] Newbold Morris relates that Fiorello LaGuardia entered politics in a Tammany controlled district. The Republican district leader remarked in the clubhouse as petitions for nomination were being prepared, "We haven't got a candidate for Congress, boys. Who wants to run?" LaGuardia immediately volunteered. "O.K. What's your first name?" "Fiorello," he replied. "Hell, let's get somebody whose name we can spell!" By vigorous argument, LaGuardia won the nod but he lost the election.— *Let the Chips Fall* (New York: Appleton-Century-Crofts, 1955), pp. 75–76.

mary contests occur in hopeless districts. Even though he has no chance to go to Congress, the winner of a nomination may gain prestige in the party organization and put himself in line for advancement in other directions.

Different circumstances prevail, as the table suggests, when the winner of the nomination has a good chance for general election victory. Broadly, the frequency of warmly fought contests for primary nominations increases with the rise in the certainty that the nominee will be elected.[10] In those districts overwhelmingly committed to one party the winner of the nomination of the chief party ordinarily has had to beat a strong primary competitor.

One type of difference among districts that obtrudes from the table does not explain itself. Among the fairly close districts in the primaries of both parties some nominations result from close popular votes in the primaries, while in other districts candidates are designated without a primary contest. These differences probably reflect, among other things, underlying variations in the organization or structure of party in the constituencies. In some districts, in tightly organized cities, for example, the party organization may be able to crush opposition to its primary slate. The normal road to nomination may be through organization endorsement.[11] The aspirant who does not gain organization support usually regards his cause as hopeless and does not enter the primary. In such districts if an independent candidate does run, the organization usually piles up an imposing majority against him.[12]

More often the congressional district is so loosely organized that genuine primary competition occurs in the districts fairly evenly balanced between the parties. The congressional district is not ordinarily of much importance as a unit of party organization; congressional district committees, usually provided for by statute or by party rule, are more often

[10] Table 16.2 employs the general election vote after the primary as a measure of the prospects of victory, a measure not entirely satisfactory. The vote at the preceding election may be a better measure of expectations about the next. Of those seats won by Democrats by from 50 to 55 per cent of the vote, competition within Democratic primaries tends to be more frequent in those districts that had been held by a Democrat than in those districts that had been held by a Republican.

[11] For 39 years, or so it was said in 1956, no organization Republican had been defeated for the primary nomination for Representative from Westchester County, New York.—*New York Times,* May 13, 1956.

[12] Sol Bloom related the circumstances of his choice for the nomination in a Tammany district in New York: "I knew a lot of people, and I had no serious known enemies. That was one of the reasons for picking me. . . . I was also comfortably situated financially and could afford the expense of the campaign. Briefly, I had been chosen to run because I was an amiable and solvent Jew."—*Autobiography of Sol Bloom* (New York: G. P. Putnam's Sons, 1948), p. 200.

moribund than not. Outside of those areas in which strong city or county organizations incidentally encompass congressional districts, the organization tends to be more an informal and personal organization of the incumbent Representative than a party organization. When the incumbent dies or retires, his organization falls to pieces and a free-for-all contest for the nomination may ensue.

To estimate the relative frequency of the occurrence of these differing patterns would require more extensive investigations than have been made. The most clear-cut differentiation that emerges from the available data is between the South and the remainder of the country. In Democratic primaries in the South not involving incumbents the man who would be a candidate for the House almost invariably has a tough primary fight on his hands. Elsewhere that may be true in only about half of the primaries.[13] This contrast reflects, of course, the peculiar nature of the southern political regime.

Outside the South fewer Democratic than Republican primaries are characterized by sharp competition, and more Democratic than Republican candidates win nomination without even nominal primary opposition.[14] The reasons for this differential are not apparent; it appears, too, fairly consistently in primaries for nomination of candidates for other types of offices. Possibly the Republican party outside the South simply has a larger supply of persons who combine an ambition for office with the time and means to make primary races.[15]

The process of nomination for the House of Representatives is in some ways more notable for what does not occur than for what happens. The high degree of local autonomy in the selection of candidates for vacancies reflects both the decentralization of national party organization and the popular character of the nominating process. Such national intervention as occurs seems to be limited chiefly to an occasional attempt to induce a potentially strong candidate to run for the nomination for a close seat not

[13] In the Democratic primaries in the districts in Table 16.2 in which the Democratic candidate subsequently won the election, one-fifth of the nominations outside the South were made without a primary contest; in the South, none. In only half the primaries outside the South did the nominee poll less than 60 per cent of the primary vote; in the South (the Confederate states plus Oklahoma), 94 per cent of the nominees had that small a primary vote.

[14] Of the Democratic primaries in Table 16.2 outside the South followed by a Democratic general election victory, 20 per cent involved no competition; of the Republican primaries, 6 per cent.

[15] For a more detailed consideration of the incidence of competition in House primaries, see Julius Turner, "Primary Elections as the Alternative to Party Competition in 'Safe' Districts," *Journal of Politics*, 15 (1953), pp. 197–210. See also C. A. M. Ewing, "Primaries as Elections," *Southwestern Social Science Quarterly*, 29 (1948–49), pp. 293–298.

held by the party.[16] Unless their tracks are well covered, this limited initiative by national leaders does not extend to all such districts in which the party might have a chance to win a seat from the opposition.

Incumbent Representatives and the direct primary. Once elected, a Representative usually wants to stay in Congress. To remain he must win renomination from his party in his district. Once renominated an incumbent Representative's fortunes may be governed by the national trend of sentiment in the election. If the drift is against his party and he comes from a marginal district, the odds against his re-election may be high no matter how strenuous his own campaign exertions may be. On the other hand, if the trend favors his party, even though his district is normally close, he is almost certain of re-election.

The existence of a large number of congressional districts sure for one party or the other, coupled with the fact that nominations are commonly made by popular procedures, gives to the nominating process a special importance. In the many sure districts the direct primary becomes the principal occasion on which a Representative may account to his constituency, although the participating primary constituency may be a caricature of the entire constituency. Even when a Representative faces a real threat from the opposition at the general election, he may have to make an electoral campaign against rivals within his own party who challenge him for the nomination. This double jeopardy constitutes one of the oddities of the American party system.

The Representative in office who seeks renomination enjoys great advantage over those who would challenge him. Extremely few Representatives—usually no more than eight or ten—are defeated in the direct primaries at each two-year interval. Furthermore, their primaries involve close contests less frequently than do those in which no incumbent seeks renomination. Of the Democrats or Republicans running for renomination, from 5 to 15 per cent may be involved in primary races in which the winner receives less than 60 per cent of the vote. One-half to three-fourths of the Representatives who seek renomination win without primary opposition. Democratic incumbents in the southern states meet formidable opposition more frequently than do Representatives elsewhere in the country.[17]

[16] In 1956 Eugene Farnum won the Republican primary nomination in the 8th Massachusetts district. Regarded as a potentially strong candidate, he had been urged to seek the nomination by Leonard W. Hall, the Republican national chairman, as well as by state Republican leaders, who hoped to capture the seat which had been wrested from a Republican in 1954 by Democrat Torbert H. McDonald.

[17] These remarks are based on analyses of the primaries of 1948, 1952, and 1954. In the primaries in which Democratic incumbents sought renomination in these years,

The relative infrequency of the defeat of incumbents as they run for renomination probably provides no adequate measure of the significance of the popular nominating procedure in sensitizing the Representative to demands within his constituency. Although the odds may favor him, an individual Representative never knows when he will be among those who must make a hard primary fight. He must keep his fences mended and to antagonize even the smallest interest within the district may be to encourage it to support an entry against him in the primary, an entry who may be defeated but with some trouble and at some cost.

At the nominating stage the Representative is on his own in marked contrast with his position at the general election when the direction of movement of the national sweep may be determinative. The Representative must fight a lonely battle for renomination. Even if he has supported the Administration regularly, he cannot look to the national party authorities for aid if he is challenged in the primary in his district. Perhaps he can wheedle from the White House an encouraging word, but neither the national nor the congressional committee can be relied upon for substantial financial aid in his campaign for renomination. If he is not of the Administration party, he is apt to be even more completely on his own resources as he fights for renomination.[18] On the other

---

the winner had less than 60 per cent of the vote in the following proportions of the primaries: 1948, 16 per cent; 1952, 12 per cent; 1954, 7 per cent. The corresponding figures for Republican incumbents were: 14, 4, 4. In primaries involving Democratic incumbents, the winner had 90–100 per cent of the vote in the following proportions of the primaries: 1948, 56; 1952, 48; 1954, 64. The corresponding figures for Republican primaries were: 53, 66, 70.

[18] The policy of hands off primaries by the national party authorities is violated from time to time but evidently Representatives, no matter how loyally they support the party line in Congress, may not routinely expect aid when they meet primary challenges. National leaders may steer contributors to beleaguered colleagues. Senator Barry Goldwater, once chairman of the Republican senatorial campaign committee, remarked in the 1956 hearings of the McClellan Committee: "Many, many people come to me, some Democrats even, I am happy to say, and say, 'I would like to get some money into Senator X's campaign.' We tell them that it is a primary problem and we are not interested in the primary, and we keep out of it. But . . . we suggest that he see so-and-so, who will be very glad to handle it. That comes up on both sides of the aisle, and it is one of the ways that money is channeled around into the primaries, and it will happen in general elections, too." How important this routing function is in primary finance and the degree to which it is used by the national leadership to aid those friendly to it remain unknown.

In a pair of celebrated cases in 1950 Senator Owen Brewster, chairman of the Republican senatorial campaign committee, advanced from his personal funds $5,000 each to the primary campaigns of Richard Nixon of California and Milton Young of North Dakota. The committee had a firm rule not to aid in primaries; for these two men, though, Senator Brewster said, "we had high regard." Nixon and hand, the incumbent need have little worry that the national leadership will instigate opposition to him in the primary. In a few instances Roosevelt and Truman gave support to primary opponents of incumbents who had been conspicuous dissenters from the party line in the House. Such cases of national intervention are notable by their rarity.

A Representative who manages to stay in office for several terms has opportunity to become known in his district, to do small favors for many voters, to strengthen his position with the party workers in his district, and in general to crystallize his following. He gains experience and builds up seniority, a fact of which he reminds his constituents, and he ordinarily engages in more or less continuous campaigning for renomination and re-election, partially at public expense.[19] Certainly it makes sense for a party to renominate a Representative who has served his party and his district well. Under these circumstances the explanation of the extent to which incumbents encounter primary opposition may present more of a problem than the explanation of why so many are named without opposition.

Inspection of primaries involving incumbents suggests that certain types of circumstances stimulate primary challenges of incumbents who seek renomination.[20] One type of situation, not uncommon, is that of an aging Representative who, after long years of service, begins to let the reins slip or becomes simply the victim of an aggressive younger candidate not

---

Young won nomination and became entitled to a grant of $5,000 each from the committee, the receipt of which enabled them to repay Senator Brewster.

The Republican congressional campaign committee provides services to Republican incumbents—aid in preparing newsletters, photographic services, and the like—which incidentally help the incumbent who happens to have to fight a primary campaign. In 1954, Hugh Bone records, the Republican committee gave $1,000 to each of 16 Republican Congressmen and $500 apiece to another 36 in April, a date which preceded the primaries, but officials of the committee indicate that they do not provide such aid when there is a primary contest. See Bone, "Some Notes on the Congressional Campaign Committees," *Western Political Quarterly*, 9 (1956), pp. 116—137.

[19] The congressional frank happily saves outlays for postage in the circulation of "reports" to constituents which have appeared in the *Congressional Record* and been reprinted at cost by the Government Printing Office. Such essays appear with profusion in the *Record* as the primaries approach. For example, extensions of remarks by the Hon. Clifton (Cliff) Young, of Nevada, appeared in the *Record* of August 13, 1956, under the following headings, among others: "Congressman Young Supports Small Business," "Congressman Young Active in Wildlife Improvement," "Congressman Young Aids Nevada Workingman," "Congressman Young Supports Civil Rights."

[20] Save for a somewhat higher frequency of challenge in southern primaries, the frequency of close contests in primaries involving incumbents does not vary with the balance of strength between parties as was shown by Table 16.2 to be true for primaries with no incumbents running. The incidence of primary contests is fairly evenly distributed over the range of districts arrayed according to party strength.

disposed to wait his turn until the old man dies or retires.[21] A first-term Representative who has not had time to establish himself in his district may be regarded as vulnerable by other ambitious politicians who may challenge him in the primary. When district lines are altered in a reapportionment, the structure of support patiently built up by a Representative becomes disorganized and he often must defend his position against those who judge the new situation to be favorable to themselves.[22] A Representative, too, may come from a state or district in which the battles of politics are normally fought out in the primaries between well-defined factions of the dominant party. He, more frequently than other Representatives, must defend his position in primary battles, although he does not suffer the inconvenience of a general election campaign.[23] Somewhat similar are the occasional challenges to incumbents in metropolitan districts that arise as an incident to battles for control of the party organization.

An incumbent may be challenged in the primary on broad policy grounds. Given the infrequency of serious contests of any sort, intraparty ideological cleavage cannot often be the basis for a primary challenge against an incumbent. Yet contests so rooted do occur. In 1956, for example, several Republican Representatives had to cope with primary competitors who contended that the incumbent had shown himself to be no Eisenhower Republican.[24] Or an incumbent may have found himself in trouble in the primaries on the charge that he had become too much

---

[21] For example, in the 21st Ohio district in 1952, Robert Crosser, age 80, lost in the primary. In the same year, 79-year-old Homer D. Angell lost in Oregon's 3rd district as he sought nomination for a ninth term. In 1956 in the 13th Massachusetts district, Richard B. Wigglesworth, a Republican with 28 years of House service, had to fight a primary campaign against a young challenger. In the same year, W. F. Norrell, who had had a stroke, managed to win nomination for a tenth term from Arkansas' 6th district against aspirants who made his health an issue.

[22] The marked lack of enthusiasm of legislators toward proposals to shift the boundaries of their district may stem as often from fear that change would make their lot difficult in the primary as from anxiety that the opposition party might gain advantage.

[23] Thus, in North Dakota in 1954 Representative Otto Krueger, a candidate of the Republican Organizing Committee, was challenged in the Republican primary by Orris Nordhougen, who had the support of the Nonpartisan League. Or, in Louisiana in 1956, Representatives T. A. Thompson and Otto Passman had opposition in their campaigns for renomination from aspirants supported by Governor Earl K. Long.

[24] In 1956 in New York's 27th district Representative Ralph W. Gwinn, 71, faced primary opposition from Christian H. Armbruster, who attacked Gwinn's lukewarmness in support of Eisenhower. Gwinn regarded Armbruster as a "New Deal Republican" too young to comprehend the "evils" of the New Deal and Fair Deal. Similarly, in Massachusetts' Cape Cod district Representative Donald Nicholson, candidate for

of an Eisenhower Republican.[25] Similarly, in Democratic primaries at times an incumbent has to meet the charge that he is or is not a Fair Dealer.

On these matters of intraparty ideological cleavage the party's voters in the primary must ordinarily act on the basis of singularly inadequate information. Only rarely does the national party leadership give the voters guidance by indicating either approval or disapproval of the incumbent's record, which becomes the subject of conflicting assertions more confusing than enlightening to the electorate.[26] The nominating stage is the point at which party discipline can be most effectively applied. Yet the direct primary is a procedure not easily usable, either by the national leadership or by the voters of a district, for that purpose.[27]

Legislative Nominations and the National Party System

Focus on the process of nomination of candidates for the House and Senate highlights the decentralized character of each of the major parties. In a sense national party exists only in the nomination of the President and in the campaign for his election. Each of the constituent units, the states and the congressional districts, of the party acts independently in the designation of candidates for Congress. To the extent that they put forward like-minded candidates, the result is a consequence rather of a parallelism of outlook and interest than of a managed articulation of action.

---

nomination for a sixth term, had to counter a challenger who asserted that the district needed a Congressman who "acts like a Republican—an Eisenhower Republican."

[25] For example, in 1954 Representative Stuyvesant Wainwright of New York's 1st district met primary opposition from one William P. Shea who urged withdrawal from the United Nations, backed Senator Joseph McCarthy, and advocated the return of control of the Republican party to genuine Republicans.

[26] At times the record of the incumbent presents a policy issue apparent to the primary voters. In North Carolina in 1956 three Representatives who had not signed the "Southern Manifesto" on integration were opposed in the primary on that ground. Only one of them, Harold D. Cooley, won renomination.

[27] It may well be that more disciplining occurs in the primaries than is commonly supposed. In 1954 Republican primaries, those incumbents with quite low scores in support of Eisenhower proposals (under 60 per cent) met fairly stiff primary opposition about three times as frequently as did incumbents with higher scores of party regularity. The numbers involved were small and the factors stimulative of primary contests are numerous. The question whether Representatives who deviate from the party line, other things being equal, need have special anxiety about primary opposition would be worth further investigation. Julius Turner presents some evidence to indicate that the deviate Representative has a relatively low survival capacity. See his *Party and Constituency: Pressures on Congress* (Baltimore: Johns Hopkins Press, 1952), pp. 174–178.

In decentralization of nomination is to be found a basic characteristic of the American party system. Localization of nomination assures both a representation of local peculiarities in the party groups in Congress and, by the same token, a magnification of the difficulties of action by the party as a whole on many types of legislation. That this decentralization of power within the parties should remain, as almost all other facets of American life have fallen prey to centralizing processes, reflects the stubborn persistence of informal political customs.

Signs of centralization in the legislative nominating process are not lacking, but national initiative seems to be effective only within a limited range of circumstances. The presidential candidate and other national leaders may intervene to aid in drafting candidates thought to be strong enough both to win a House or Senate seat from the opposition and to lend strength to the ticket as a whole. Even such limited intervention may be fraught with hazard unless most leaders of the constituency see eye to eye with the national leadership. Moreover, aid and encouragement in the enlistment of a candidate to challenge an incumbent of the opposition party is a far more feasible type of national intervention than is the attempt to defeat or replace a candidate of one's own party who deviates markedly from the legislative policy of the national party. Only infrequently have Presidents attempted to purge their party of such persons and then without notable success.

Reliance on popular nominating procedures in most states and districts may anchor the power of decision in the localities and make difficult the participation of national leadership in legislative nominations. Nomination rests not in the hands of a few leaders with whom agents of the national headquarters might consult and reason; it rests rather in the free and unfettered vote of those who participate in the direct primary and produce its unpredictable results. A national party agent cannot negotiate with a constituency itself susceptible to agitation by the cry of external intervention from candidates opposed to the national leadership.

It is commonly said that the direct primary also tends to increase the frequency of deviation from the national party line by legislative nominees. The argument rests on the assumption that the convention mode of nomination facilitates the maintenance of a degree of consistency of outlook through control of nominations by a self-perpetuating clique. The primary, on the other hand, destroys that consistency and, in so doing, robs the opposition of the opportunity to take advantage of popular dissatisfaction with the stronger party in the state or district. As shifts in outlook occur, the views of the dominant party's nominees may change. Such variability of leadership is thought to be facilitated by the open primary through which Democrats may help nominate a Republican candidate or vice versa. In any event, when the leadership of the stronger party shifts like a weather vane, voters of a state or district are under no compulsion to send a candidate of the lesser party to Congress. Instead, they send a man who may deviate from the national line of the stronger party. That the primary procedure facilitates these deviations from orthodoxy seems plausible, although it may well be that they would find expression through whatever nominating procedure happened to be used. It is certain enough that in most districts not much by way of cohesive inner organization exists to serve as guardian, either independently or in collaboration with the national leadership, of the party creed.[28]

A major consequence of the decentralization of nominations probably is that neither party mobilizes its maximum potential in legislative contests. Most of the senatorial and congressional incumbents of each party normally seek re-election, but the recruitment and designation of candidates to fight for seats held by the opposition is left mainly to the fortuitous workings of local initiative. The result is that in many districts the minority fails to put up strong candidates even though it has a chance to win. Many districts are unnecessarily conceded to the opposition. National party leaders in quest of a point for leverage to strengthen their party might well give thought to spending a few hundred thousand dollars a year in drumming up and supporting able House and Senate candidates for seats held by the opposition. The effects over the long run in the workings of the party groups in House and Senate might be startling.[29]

[28] Americans probably on the whole find it more congenial to alter the policy of their party than to shift their party allegiance. The system is so marvelously flexible that this reorientation of party outlook need not involve an overturn of party leadership. In 1950 the Hon. Usher L. Burdick, a Representative from North Dakota, opened a circular to his constituents with these sentences: "The Primary Election will soon be on and I have deemed it advisable to outline some of the issues which I think should be discussed in this campaign. I have outlined my views without equivocation and those views will be my continued views unless the people at meetings and through cards and letters give evidence of the voters' opposition."—*Burdick's Magazine*, May–June, 1950.

[29] One hears rumors from time to time of the activities of nonparty groups that move in to stimulate primary candidacies of persons favorable to their interests. A pro-tariff group may, for example, do missionary work over the country; or a labor group; or a representative of the railroads. The extent to which such groups seek, sub rosa, to fill the vacuum left by party inactivity has never been fully explored; the data would be most difficult to unearth.

Part Four | # PARTY AND THE
ELECTORATE

THE PARTY apparatus, by posing alternative candidates and programs, arranges the situation to permit the electorate to play its role in the system of party government. Competitive appeals by party spokesmen to the electorate for authorization to govern dramatize the fundamental characteristic of government by the people. Yet it requires, as the preceding chapters have shown, a great deal of party machinery and activity to set the stage for the voters' part in the governmental process.

The question of central interest in the chapters that follow is the function and nature of the actions of the electorate in party government. The great and determinative actions of the voters occur in the presidential and congressional elections. For their treatment it will also be necessary to consider other related or relevant topics, such as campaign management, conditions for the exercise of the suffrage, mechanics of the conduct of elections, and participation of voters in elections.

17 | Campaign Techniques

A CRITICAL phase of the process of party government is the battle for ballots. Through the national conventions the party system poses for the electorate alternatives in leadership and in policy orientation. At the nominating stage each party attempts to iron out frictions among its elements, to reassure the interests traditionally associated with it, and, by other means, to form its battalions for the assault against the opposition. In the campaign the candidates, the activists, the professionals of each party carry their cause to the electorate as they vie for the popular verdict. In these recurring clashes of electioneering armies in verbal combat is found one of the distinctive processes of popular government. The capacity of its electorate to undergo the tumult of an electoral campaign and still make wise decisions may determine whether a popular government survives.

An American presidential campaign is one of the most awesome spectacles known to man; the fate of a nation may hinge on the outcome of what seems to be a donnybrook among demagogues and Madison Avenue types. Yet our verified knowledge of what goes on in the minds of the voters as they move toward decision is limited; our knowledge of their response to different types of appeals is equally thin. Campaigns are likened to the appeals of opposing counsel to a jury. They are said to be a means of educating and informing the people about candidates and issues. They are classed along with soap-selling operations as systematic manipulations of the mass mind. They are treated as a ceremony by which a party obtains popular consent to govern. They are cynically dismissed as a ritual through which politicians, tools of the interests, profess a love for the people and humbug them. A presidential campaign may contain all of these elements, but whatever its precise nature, it moves the electorate to a determination of who shall govern the country.

Campaign Organization and Management

A presidential campaign may be thought to be the work of a tightly knit organization spread over the entire country and directed by cunning men wise in the ways of managing the multitude. In truth, the campaign organization is a jerry-built and makeshift structure manned largely by temporary and volunteer workers who labor long hours amidst confusion and uncertainty. Assignments of responsibility and lines of authority are likely to be hazy. The army of campaign workers is loosely articulated and some of its regiments may be sulky, if not actually insubordinate.

Top management of campaigns. A prime necessity in the management of a presidential campaign is the achievement of sufficient unity of command at the top level of the party organization to permit the execution of a coherent and considered campaign strategy. Otherwise, different elements of the party pursue contradictory propaganda lines, ill-considered and off-the-cuff tactics are developed from day to day, resources are dissipated, and disorder prevails. Yet the attainment of a modicum of unity even at the top organizational levels seems to be frustrated by recurring obstacles.

Ultimately perhaps the presidential candidate must be his own manager, though his effectiveness in that role depends in large measure on his capacity to construct an effective team of top-level associates. No matter what his skill in that respect, he may be either hamstrung or favored by circumstances. Traditionally the chairman of the national committee has managed the presidential campaign. That pattern prevailed in 1956 when Eisenhower relied principally on Leonard Hall, the national chairman. In 1952, because of the jealousies between old-line Republicans and the Eisenhowerites, considerable backing and filling occurred before Eisenhower settled the rivalries at the top levels by stationing Sherman Adams in Washington as his personal agent to deal with the national committee, a move that left the national chairman in a secondary role. In 1952 Stevenson maintained a personal headquarters at Springfield, supposedly to dissociate himself from the Truman Administration, while the national committee operated in Washington. This "two-headed" monstrosity caused much muttering among the professionals, yet in 1956 it reappeared in diluted form when Stevenson designated James A. Finnegan as his personal campaign manager while Paul Butler remained as national chairman.

The tasks of the top-level campaign leadership, in varying degrees of association with or subordination to the candidate, include planning the broad lines of campaign strategy. At this level also co-ordination needs to be achieved among the national committee, the senatorial and congressional campaign committees, and the nonparty committees supporting the candidate. The diverse propaganda activities of the national committee staff must be kept in line with general campaign strategy. An adequate basis of understanding and system of communication must exist so that the candidate, as he tours the country with his own speech-writing entourage, will not conduct a campaign independent of that of the other elements of the organization. To attempt to cope with such problems the national headquarters commonly includes some sort of co-ordinating committee, board of strategy, or advisory committee. The candidate, too, keeps a close watch on detail as well as on broad strategy, although it is an exceptional candidate who can both stand the strain of campaign tours and take much of a hand in the management of campaign organization.

National committee operations. Whatever his relation to the top command the work of the national chairman becomes more onerous as the national committee goes into action for the campaign. The committee must intensify its fund-raising efforts. It must enlarge its permanent staff units and create new, temporary operating units as well. Most of these staff divisions of the national committee are concerned with propaganda in one way or another. A publicity division may prepare press releases, pamphlets, leaflets, comic books, and other such campaign materials. An advertising agency may be employed to arrange for radio and TV time, to advise on the mysteries of these media, and even to prepare substantive campaign materials. A research division may dig up data and write speeches for the candidate and for lesser speakers. A speakers' bureau may recruit orators and route them over the country. Divisions may be created to appeal to groups, such as labor, ethnic minorities, women, Negroes, medical men, or whatever groups seem to deserve, or be susceptible to, attention at the moment.[1] To manage all these and other

[1] See T. M. Black, *Democratic Party Publicity in the 1940 Campaign* (New York:

units so that their work builds into a consistent propaganda campaign strains the administrative capacity of the national chairman; his skills are by no means invariably equal to the task.[2]

The new technology of communications may be laying the basis for a much tighter top control of campaigns. Party propaganda for the entire nation may be fed into a single TV camera. This funneling of communications lays the basis for a thorough-going enforcement of campaign strategy, for an insistence upon adherence to common themes, for a complete co-ordination of party appeals. Instantaneous communication over the nation also makes less tolerable the disunity that often prevails at the top level of party organization. The picturesque professional politician and the hard-bitten newspaperman who predominated around the old-fashioned campaign headquarters may be yielding to the advertising man and to the public-relations expert. These sorts of developments occurred to an especially notable degree in the Republican campaigns of 1952 and 1956.[3]

Mobilization of state and local party machinery. The integration of state and local party machinery into the national campaign presents its special problems. Given administrative firmness and skill, the top command may fit into a campaign strategy the lines of attack by the candidate, the propaganda themes of the national committee, the efforts of speakers under the control of the national committee, and the work of other elements of the national apparatus. The extension of national leadership and direction to state and local organizations, however, requires both diplomacy and good fortune. These organizations enjoy an independence of the national committee and they also have their own fish to fry as they work for their local candidates.

The factor most conducive to effective involvement of state and local organizations in the national campaign is a belief that the head of the ticket will help float local candidates into office. In 1948, for example, all hands expected Mr. Dewey to win the Presidency, and Republican state and local organizations implored him to speak in their localities. At

Plymouth, 1941), chs. 2, 3; John Stanton, "The GHQ's of the Two Political Armies," *New York Times Magazine,* October 8, 1944.

[2] For an example, see Ralph D. Casey, "Republican Propaganda in the 1936 Campaign," *Public Opinion Quarterly,* April, 1937, pp. 27–44.

[3] In some states and localities the public-relations man has almost completely superseded the professional politician in the management of campaigns. When he accepts a commission to manage a campaign he needs to insist upon complete supervision of campaign propaganda, an insistence that both protects him in his responsibility for his undertaking and produces a far higher degree of unification of campaign management than often prevails under the professional politician.

the same time Mr. Truman was thought to have no future, and many Democratic state and local organizations scarcely exerted themselves on behalf of the man from Missouri. In 1956 Republican state and local organizations could work with zeal for Mr. Eisenhower; they placed a high estimate on the supportive power of his coattails. Some Democratic organizations sat on their hands, for they regarded Mr. Stevenson's cause as hopeless and identification of their candidates with him as injurious. An incumbent President, of course, has ways and means of encouraging the loyalty of state and local leaders. They are obligated by past favors and, unless the President's prospects for re-election seem slight, they usually have a lively sense of the potential embarrassment of dealing with a President who owes them nothing.[4]

Although the sense of common cause and the stimuli of common interests that affect dispersed state and local organizations induce a modicum of participation in the presidential campaign, the national chairman has few sanctions against the state organization that drags its feet. In an earlier day, before the Hatch Act limited national committee expenditures, the national committee often subsidized state organizations. Now, the national chairman may steer contributors from the financial centers to deserving state organizations. He may advise and encourage. He may hold out hope for reward after victory. He may, as James A. Farley did, cut through the organizational layers and provide literature and other campaign aids directly to precinct workers. When worst comes to worst, the national chairman may encourage friends of the candidates to establish a state campaign headquarters separate from those of an inert regular party organization in order that at least a show of activity may be made.

The capacity of the candidate to appeal directly to the voters by radio and TV has reduced or at least changed the significance of local party organizations in presidential campaigns. Precinct workers, or so it is supposed, once performed yeoman service in rallying the faithful, in propagating the party gospel, and in converting the wavering. Although the data on the point are limited, probably the local organization makes its major contribution by getting out to the polls those voters who might be expected to be favorable to the candidate rather than in winning the undecided. Precinct workers can bestir the laggard to register, arrange for absentee ballots, distribute literature, remind the voter that election day has arrived, furnish baby sitters, provide transportation to the voting

---

[4] Grover Cleveland in 1892 observed that there was "nothing in the world" that would make the New York Democratic organization "hearty and honest in the campaign as surely as the conviction that the country can be carried without them."— Allan Nevins (ed.), *Letters of Grover Cleveland, 1850–1908* (Boston: Houghton Mifflin, 1933), p. 296.

place, and occasionally deliver a vote. The new votes won by doorbell ringers in a presidential campaign must be few indeed. Yet electronic communications have not made party organization obsolete. The relative success of the parties in mobilizing their workers to get out the vote may determine the winner of the electoral vote in a close state.[5] Party organizations may play a broader part in the determination of the outcome of party primaries in which voters are few and the candidates relatively unknown.

Nonparty organizations. Nonparty organizations often powerfully supplement the work of the regular party organization. Given the widespread negative attitude towards "politics," these groups can attract the support of prominent citizens not disposed to associate themselves with a purely party endeavor. They can also tap financial support that the party cannot and recruit election-day workers who cannot be readily mobilized under the party banner. The Associated Willkie Clubs, the Volunteers for Stevenson, and the Citizens for Eisenhower illustrate the type of nonparty group that can bring to the cause the labors of a candidate's admirers whose amateur status as politicians may be counterbalanced by their zeal and enthusiasm. Such an organization, if prominent in the public prints, may by its existence convey an impression that the candidate's following extends far beyond the party ranks as "plain citizens" of all types spontaneously enlist in the holy cause.

Nonparty groups also create problems in campaign direction. Often these groups grow from the organization that won the nomination for the candidate and are peculiarly his personal organization. As such they are regarded with suspicion by the old-line professionals, and jealousies and discord develop between the amateurs, starry-eyed in their devotion to the candidate, and the professionals, who have seen candidates come and go. Quite practical problems of co-ordination of effort also arise. Under whose auspices will speeches be made in this locality? Who will raise money from whom? How are conflicts in TV scheduling to be avoided? How is a division of labor in canvassing to be accomplished? Will the amateurs fight for the local ticket as well as the presidential candidate? Friction may occur at all levels from the national headquarters to the precinct.[6] Yet such organizations seem to be fairly standard ad-

---

[5] For a case study of the work of local organizations, see Bernard Berelson and others, *Voting* (Chicago: University of Chicago Press, 1954), pp. 163–181.

[6] On the troubles of the Associated Willkie Clubs, see H. O. Evjen, "The Willkie Campaign: An Unfortunate Chapter in Republican Leadership," *Journal of Politics*, 14 (1952), pp. 241–256. For a study of a more effective independent committee, see D. R. McCoy, "The Progressive National Committee of 1936," *Western Political Quarterly*, 9 (1956), pp. 454–469.

juncts to the regular party apparatus; they permit the enlistment of both workers and voters who hesitate to identify themselves with the party.

To be differentiated from the nonparty groups closely associated with the candidate are those committees set up as fronts for the national committee. Most committees of independents, of labor leaders, of farmers, of lawyers, of businessmen, and of others that spring up during the campaign are unacknowledged subsidiaries of the national committee. Propaganda may be issued in the name of such subsidiary organizations and endorsement and support of the candidate may be gained from persons unwilling to appear under straight party auspices. The supposition underlying the establishment of these adjuncts to the regular party organization is that their appeal will be more effective with the groups concerned than a straight party appeal. By the multiplication of such groups the notion may be gotten across that the candidate draws impressive support from a wide range of social groups.

Campaign Strategy

Commentators on politics have borrowed from the military the concept of strategy. A presidential campaign, as a military campaign, may be conducted in accord with a broad strategy or plan of action. That general plan may fix the principal propaganda themes to be emphasized in the campaign, define the chief targets within the electorate, schedule the peak output of effort, and set other broad features of the campaign. The strategic scheme then provides a framework to guide the detailed work of the party propagandists, the labors of the speechwriters, the decisions of those who parcel out the campaign funds, the schedulers of the itineraries of the principal orators, and the day-to-day endeavors of all the subordinate units of campaign organization.

Often the outlines of a campaign strategy are scarcely visible amidst the noise and confusion of the campaign and, indeed, campaigns often rest on only the sketchiest of strategic plans. The preparation of a reasoned and comprehensive strategy requires more of a disposition to think through the campaign in its broad outlines than often exists around a national headquarters. Once the plan is made, its execution requires an organization sufficiently articulated to respond to general direction in accord with the plan, a requisite that is not always met. And even when a campaign is blueprinted in advance, a flexibility must be built into it to take advantage of the breaks and to meet unexpected moves by the opposition.

Situational limitations on strategy. The characteristics of the situations within which presidential campaigners operate set limits on, or condition, the kinds of strategy that may be employed in the battle for the voters' affections. These limitations are not discerned by those who regard campaigns as occasions on which unprincipled men in their quest for power may exploit without limit the prejudices of the masses as they play upon the inherent wickedness and perversity of man. While campaigns have their unlovely aspects, the mores of the democratic order as well as the particular circumstances of individual campaigns place bounds on the types of strategy that may be profitably pursued.

The political culture sets continuing, though vague, standards of campaign etiquette. The content of the political culture cannot be readily defined but it includes the firmly embedded modal expectations of the electorate about what is and what is not proper in the realm of politics. The predominant attitudes, for example, make futile those campaign appeals that extend beyond or deviate clearly from the constitutional consensus. Campaign objectives that would be both feasible and proper in a different political culture would in the United States appear outlandish and to be sought, if at all, by splinter parties not hopeful of gaining power. The drive toward conformity with the basic values and objectives of the society discourages appeals looking toward basic innovation, although it needs to be remembered that the content of these unwritten limitations on political debate change through time.

Other more apparent determinants of broad strategy emerge from the characteristics of the immediate situation in which the campaign occurs and from the candidate's position in it. The candidate of the party out of power thus tends to follow a strategy of attack upon the record of the party in power. The public-relations specialists who worked out the general strategy for the Eisenhower campaign in 1952 concluded their presentation: ". . . the recommended strategy is: *Attack! Attack! Attack!*" [7] The circumstances permitted heavy emphasis upon criticism of the record of the party in power and required no intensive merchandising of an alternative program.

The candidate of the ins, also by virtue of the circumstances of his situation, tends to be driven toward a strategy of defense of his party's record. Adlai Stevenson in 1952 was thrust into a posture of defense of the Truman Administration. In 1956, after four years of Eisenhower, the Republican strategists were denied the simple strategy of attack and had to point with pride to their record. Supposedly a defensive strategy is disadvantageous, but whether it is depends on the nature of the ground the candidate is defending. The ins may be able to picture their campaign as a continuation of a great crusade in which they had won only a

[7] S. Kelley, Jr., *Professional Public Relations and Political Power* (Baltimore: Johns Hopkins Press, 1956), p. 155.

skirmish at the preceding election, a strategy open to the Democrats in the campaigns after 1932 and to the Republicans in the campaign of 1956. In 1952 the Democrats were still running against Herbert Hoover and in 1956 the Republicans fired many a barrage at Harry Truman. The ins, unless disaster or ineptitude has overtaken them, enjoy a considerable advantage.[8]

Another broad factor that conditions the strategies of campaigns consists of a bundle of circumstances that might be labeled the temper of the times. In eras of general complacency and economic well-being assaults against the interests and crusades against abuses by the privileged classes seem to pay small dividends. Periods of hardship and unrest move campaigners to contrive strategies to exploit the anxieties of people—or to insulate themselves from public wrath.

Group targets. The customs of American campaigning dictate that the presidential candidate make it appear that he speaks for all the people, all classes, all races, all religions. He seeks to become the embodiment of all aspirations in a grand harmony of interests which denies conflict and even rises above partisanship. Yet beneath the obligatory façade of universality of appeal, party strategists give thought to ways and means to design appeals calculated to inflame, to attract, to enlist particular groups. The contrivance of a group strategy involves the hazard that gains by an appeal to one group may be offset by losses from another group antagonistic to the first.

An important target group consists of the voters traditionally attached to the party. The party's foundation in interest rests among these voters who also provide its most consistent electoral support. Save in exceptional circumstances, the campaign strategy fixes a course calculated not to strain the loyalties of the party diehards, although they may be relied upon to view tolerantly at least for a time gambits antagonistic to them but designed to bring unbelievers to the true faith. The 1952 Republican strategy, for example, assumed that to win the election the party should begin with those who had stuck "with the party through thick and thin." These voters, the campaign strategists asserted, "must not be alienated." High priority was assigned to the task of renewing and maintaining the

---

[8] The separation of powers and the possibility of nominating presidential candidates without a clear party background gives the American party battle an odd characteristic. The outs may escape accountability for their record in Congress. In 1952 Eisenhower's nomination enabled the Republican party to disengage itself from the performance of its congressional wing during the preceding years. A different strategic situation would have been created by the nomination of Senator Taft, a man indubitably associated with the party record.

loyalties of this segment of the party.[9] In 1956 Adlai Stevenson gave sedulous attention to the southern Democrats, a policy not without its offsetting disadvantages, given the composition of the Democratic following.

While all ethnic, religious, and economic groups must receive a minimum of ceremonial deference, the party strategy may provide for powerful drives for the support of particular groups or classes within the electorate. These group appeals may be merely a part of the strategy calculated to retain the support of groups long attached to the party. Or they may be designed to draw voters from groups traditionally attached to the opposition. The circumstances may make it probable that such groups have become especially susceptible to special appeals. In 1956, for example, Republicans sought to weaken Negro attachment to the Democratic party—a strategy facilitated by developments in segregation policy that enabled Vice President Nixon to refer to Earl Warren as a "great Republican Chief Justice." In 1948 Mr. Truman, faced by desertion in the South, wound up his campaign with specific commitments and powerful appeals to groups outside the South: Negroes, Jews, and industrial workers. In 1956 the Democrats, aided by the impact of both drouth and Republican farm policies, were encouraged to make a strong play for western farm support.

Geographical targets. Another element of strategy consists in schemes for the geographical distribution of campaign effort. The system of voting for President traditionally has encouraged both parties to devote little effort to those states strongly attached to one party or the other and to concentrate campaigning in the close states. Moreover, the fact that the winner in a state takes all its electoral votes makes concentration of effort in the larger, close states rational; a given amount of effort may yield far more electoral votes in one state than in another. The formation of a geographic strategy requires educated estimates of the closeness of sentiment in the various states as well as judgments about which of the supposedly close states might respond most readily to the appeals open to the party in the particular situation. A geographic strategy may be merely a strategy directed towards certain classes or groups of voters that happen to be concentrated in close states. Perhaps a geographic strategy is most available when the electorate is not exercised about broad national questions that concern people all across the country. Then local issues and local questions may be most advantageously emphasized.

The execution of a geographic strategy requires that campaign themes, the assignment of major speakers, and the concentration of money be

[9] Kelley, *op. cit.*, pp. 151–152.

handled in accord with the general plan. In the closing days of the 1940 presidential campaign the Democrats sent into Ohio—a state thought to be slipping toward Willkie—President Roosevelt, Henry Wallace, Mayor LaGuardia, Senator Norris, and various other Democratic bigwigs. In the same campaign the Democrats-for-Willkie focused a large-scale mail circularization campaign in states that could be converted to Republicanism by a slight shift. In 1944 Dewey made a 6,700-mile swing to the Pacific Coast with only seven scheduled speeches, most of them in supposedly doubtful states. The principle of concentration of fire is further illustrated by the selective purchase of radio time. In 1936 the Republicans excluded southern stations from their network deals; dissemination of Republican propaganda in that area then would have been an unfruitful effort. In 1952 Republican strategists worked out and executed a plan for "an all-out saturation blitz radio-TV spot campaign" concentrated in 49 counties in 12 states during the closing week of the campaign.[10]

Campaign timing. An element of campaign strategy is the timing of the output of campaign efforts. The supposition is that if all resources are thrown into the campaign too early, the campaign may reach its peak long before election day and exhaust the campaign chest and the party personnel before the moment when greatest exertion is needed. The campaign should be timed to produce the greatest effect just before the election. Managers of campaigns are by no means completely free in their decisions on timing. They must pay some heed to the strategy followed by the opposition. Candidates not widely known may need to conduct a long campaign simply to make their name familiar to the voters as did Stevenson in 1952. The challenger of an incumbent President may be compelled to begin his attack long before the President feels it necessary to take to the hustings. In 1936, for example, Franklin D. Roosevelt went on a cruise and yielded the stage to the Republicans in the early weeks of the campaign. He resisted pressure from his uneasy advisers to answer Landon's opening volleys and waited until late October to mount his offensive.[11] In 1956 Eisenhower's strategists settled on a short campaign to begin with weekly television appearances by the President and to wind up with a burst of effort by all hands in the closing weeks. They calculated that Stevenson would "talk himself out," make mistakes, and arrive at the home stretch both physically exhausted and without anything to say that he had not said earlier.

[10] *Ibid.*, pp. 187–190.
[11] See J. M. Burns, *Roosevelt: The Lion and the Fox* (New York: Harcourt, Brace, 1956), pp. 271–288. See also H. F. Gosnell, *Champion Campaigner: Franklin D. Roosevelt* (New York: Macmillan, 1952).

The general notion among the professionals seems to be that a campaign should be managed so as to culminate in a peak of enthusiastic effort a few days before the election, an outburst that generates the impression of confidence, that seems to indicate an overwhelming tide of support for the candidate. On occasion that pattern is approximated as one or the other of the campaigns seems to dominate the radio and TV, to pre-empt the headlines and the advertising columns, to fill the billboards, as it reaches a climax of shrill intensity that blankets out the opposition in the days just before the voting. How much of an effect all this has on the voting is another question.

Campaign themes. A prime problem in campaign strategy is the creation of a dominant theme or themes for the campaign. This problem goes beyond the simple choice of issues to emphasize or the selection of aspects of the opposition's record for attack. It extends to the creation of a tone or a spirit for the campaign, an aura that envelops the entire operation and gives a distinctive character to the undertaking in all its details. Thus, in 1956 the Republican campaign appeared to be pitched to a lofty line of sincerity, morality, and piety, a theme or tone that seemed to permeate most aspects of the campaign. Or in 1936 the Democratic campaign evidently was calculated to build a total impression of Roosevelt as the leader of a crusade to crush the selfish interests that had resisted a new deal for the common man. In 1948 Truman created a different sort of total impression, a cocky little man who ran a "give-em-hell" campaign as he took the fight to the grass roots. In 1952 the Republican attack distilled down to an assault on the "mess in Washington," a convenient phrase under which all varieties of dissatisfaction might be amalgamated. In the same year Stevenson sought to set a distinctive campaign tone with his proposal "to talk sense" to the people. In 1948 Dewey, confident of victory, waged a high-level campaign designed to avoid the creation of animosities embarrassing to him as he floated into office on a cloud of universal good will.

Art and Artifice in Campaigning

One may speak of grand campaign strategy, rationally formulated and executed with precision, but a great deal of campaign management rests on the hunches that guide day to day decisions. The lore of politics includes rules of thumb that are supposed to embody the wisdom of political experience as guides to action. Whether the maxims of the practicing politician have any validity, they do have an interest as an element of the art of politics, an interest frequently capitalized upon by the writers for the Sunday supplements.

Front porch, swing around the circle, or whistle stop. An old problem of campaign tactics is the question of the extent of the speaking and traveling schedule of the head of the ticket. Should the candidate make an extensive swing around the country and speak at as many places as practicable or should he make a "front-porch" campaign? The decision on this question may depend on the qualities of the candidate. In 1920 the Republican strategy was to keep Harding at home in Marion, Ohio. "Keep Warren at home," the Republican leader Penrose is reported to have said. "Don't let him make any speeches. If he goes out on a tour, somebody's sure to ask him questions, and Warren's just the sort of damn fool that'll try to answer them." "The Front Porch campaign," according to Samuel Hopkins Adams, "was determined upon. The role assigned to the candidate was that of the modest, simple, sagacious, home-loving, home-staying statesman. He was to be 'just folks.' To the Mecca of Marion would come the devout, and the Prophet would edify them with the sound doctrine of orthodox Republicanism." [12] Another Ohio Republican, William McKinley, had earlier made the classic front-porch campaign. He set out for the nation his views on the issues of 1896 in his responses to speeches by the leaders of delegations that came to Canton by special train to pay homage to the candidate.

In the 1932 Democratic campaign James Farley says that a vexing question was whether Franklin Roosevelt should stay at home and issue statements on the occasion of the visits of party dignitaries or travel about the country "flinging bold challenges at the Republican foe." Leading Democrats, such as John N. Garner, advised that the front-porch technique be used; all Roosevelt had to do to win the election was to stay alive until election day. Roosevelt, however, chose to make a swing to the West Coast, an action that incidentally rebutted opposition insinuations about the state of his health.

Television has made the vine-clad front porch obsolete. The choice becomes one of whether the candidate is to travel about the country and mingle with the multitude or stay at home near a television camera. In 1956 Mr. Eisenhower's managers intimated in the early stages of the campaign that their candidate would limit himself to a few television speeches from Washington. An appearance or so by the General in a television studio quickly persuaded those concerned that the General's talents could be better employed on the stump.

Picturing the candidate to the public. Given the bearing of the personal qualities of the candidate on electoral decision, the outcome of an election may be determined by the image of the candidate implanted in the

---

[12] Samuel Hopkins Adams, *Incredible Era* (Boston: Houghton Mifflin, 1939), p. 170.

minds of the voters. The nature of the image to be propagated depends on the strategy and circumstances of the campaign. Within limits, skillful propagandists can convert a candidate into a mythical character possessing in distilled form the qualities thought to be advantageous for the campaign. Television, instead of obstructing this process by making the candidate's qualities perceptible to all, may aid in the transformation—so long as the candidate can find his way through the speeches that have been ghosted for him. "In our day," says Mosca, "sects and political parties are highly skilled at creating the superman, the legendary hero, the 'man of unquestioned honesty,' who serves, in his turn, to maintain the luster of the gang and bring in wealth and power for the sly ones to use." [13] Before Charles Michelson became director of publicity for the Democratic national committee he commented on the process of making imaginary characters of the candidates, thus:

> The American people will elect as President of the United States in November a nonexistent person—and defeat likewise a mythical identity.
> They will vote for and against a picture that has been painted for them by protagonists and antagonists in a myriad of publications, a picture that must be either a caricature or an idealization.
> Herbert Hoover, the miracle man, the perfect human machine, destitute of error, with a vision beyond cosmic bounds, who resolves every problem into its mathematical elements; who has on tap all the wisdom of the universe; who plots his tasks with unerring curves and discharges them by rule and measure; who has not time for mirth or diversions; no thought but of duty before him.
> Alfred E. Smith, the ingenuous child of the New York sidewalks, simple beyond belief, but with that simplicity is combined a knowledge beyond that given in books; a demigod to whom all the complexities of government are clear as day; a paragon of wisdom, gentleness and righteousness, whose facile mind fathoms automatically every depth of economics and politics.[14]

Senator Watson of Indiana records that prior to the 1920 convention Penrose of Pennsylvania attempted to persuade him to accept the Republican presidential nomination. Penrose met Watson's modest, though correct, denial that he was of presidential stature by the remark: " 'Well, Jim, we'll have enough votes to nominate you, and always after a man is nominated they bring out the royal robe and put it on him, and that covers up all the cracks and nail-holes.' A wise remark, for it always happens just that way." [15]

[13] *The Ruling Class* (New York: McGraw-Hill, 1939), p. 194.
[14] Quoted by Casey, "Party Campaign Propaganda," *The Annals*, 179 (1935), pp. 96-105.
[15] James E. Watson, *As I Knew Them* (Indianapolis: Bobbs-Merrill, copyright, 1936), p. 208. Quoted by special permission of the publishers.

The fictional picture of the candidate expedient and profitable to propagate varies with circumstances and, to some extent, with the talents of the candidates. In 1932, for example, Franklin Roosevelt thought it desirable to "dramatize himself as a breaker of custom, a daring, resolute champion of action, establishing a bold contrast with the country's picture of Hoover as timid, hesitant, irresolute." [16] Immediately after his nomination, he went by plane to Chicago to accept the nomination before the convention itself rather than await the customary formal notification of the nomination weeks later. By action, then, rather than by words, he created the desired impression. In the 1944 Republican campaign the accent was on youth: Dewey and his entourage were pictured as young, aggressive, forward-looking men; Roosevelt and other Democratic leaders were attacked as tired, old, quarreling men. In 1952 Eisenhower's managers sought to merchandise him as a man who embodied the homely virtues, a simple and sincere man of unmatched integrity, yet possessed of an experience and wisdom beyond compare that would enable him "to go to Korea" and bring peace, order, and security to a troubled world.

On occasion it becomes in order to renovate the public image of a candidate, an endeavor that strains the capacities of the propagandist but is not beyond achievement. The 1956 tactics in the reconstruction of the public perception of the Republican vice-presidential candidate, Richard Nixon, provide a striking illustration. By his record in his campaign for the Senate in California and by his performance in the national campaigns of 1952 and 1954, Nixon had created the impression that he was a slick debater, not above low tricks of campaigning, a man whose convictions veered from day to day with the winds of expediency. As 1956 approached Democratic campaigners contemplated this target with glee, but Nixon disarmed them by manufacturing a "new Nixon," a man who had grown almost to presidential stature, a thoughtful and restrained man, a man dedicated to Eisenhower, to moderation, to the Republican party and, above all, to the welfare of the nation. Nixon's achievements, *Time* concluded at the end of the campaign, promised him "a new and impressive stature in his party and in his country." [17]

The creation of an etched image of the candidate may reduce to a single, appealing symbol the party's position on intricate and complex issues. The candidate may personify a general approach to public questions or a general spirit in public policy. Consider: Bryan, a fearless crusader attack-

[16] Raymond Moley, *After Seven Years* (New York, 1939), p. 26. Quoted by permission of Harper & Bothers.

[17] The Survey Research Center found that of its 1956 national sample, 23 per cent held strong anti-Nixon opinions. The comparable 1952 figure was 7 per cent.

ing the strongholds of special privilege; Harding, the easy-going, pleasant embodiment of the yearning for normalcy; Coolidge, the conservative, shrewd, safe, New Englander; Wilson, the militant battler for a new freedom; Franklin Roosevelt, the champion of the forgotten man; Eisenhower, the good and sincere yet superhuman man; Jackson, the champion of the common man. To fill such roles requires a modicum of histrionic skill; great politicians must be actors of sorts and politics has its elements of make-believe. Not all candidates succeed in achieving a sharply defined image in the minds of the voters; even when they do, people's perceptions of them may differ from the strategist's designs. Thus, in 1948 a considerable number of voters viewed Dewey as smug, complacent, patronizing, noncommittal, foppish, overdressed, and antagonizing in appearance.[18]

The lofty, nonpartisan pose. If a presidential candidate has attained great popularity, it may be possible for him to assume a position above the battle. His lofty eminence makes attack difficult; it may create an impression of assurance of victory, of a great figure who rises above his petty associates, of a man above politics, of a giant beyond reach of quixotic sallies by the pygmies of the opposition. Perhaps the popular expectation that Presidents should be something more than partisans contributes to the beatification of presidential candidates, but some of them succeed in becoming more saintly than do others. Franklin D. Roosevelt demonstrated some skill in this respect, as various candidates who challenged him learned to their dismay, but Eisenhower undoubtedly demonstrated greater genius in disentangling himself from the ruck and the muck of the political battle. He managed to disengage himself so completely from politics, even from his own Administration, that he provided a target beyond range. From this point he could in the campaign of 1956 look down on the "locust-swarm of partisan orators" in the Democratic ranks, he could belittle the moans of a "few politicians," he could dismiss criticisms of his farm policy as "drivel" concocted by "partisan orators" and "anguished politicians." This disengagement from politics also permitted him to disassociate himself from the dubious tactics of his allies. Republican literature referring to "Democratic wars" brought from him the indignant comment: "I don't believe when America gets into war we can afford to call it anything but 'our war.'" Democratic tacticians never managed to identify Eisenhower with his party or with his fellow campaigners, so skilled was he in constructing and maintaining an image of himself as a sincere man of integrity

[18] Angus Campbell and R. L. Kahn, *The People Elect A President* (Ann Arbor: Survey Research Center, 1952), p. 50. On popular images of the candidates in 1952, see Angus Campbell and others, *The Voter Decides* (Evanston: Row, Peterson, 1954), ch. 4.

apart from the wickedness of politics. The most finished partisanship under some circumstances is to appear to be no politician at all.

The silent treatment. Some campaigners are so circumstanced that they may be correct in regarding it as sound policy never to mention the name of the opposing candidate. He may be referred to as our opponent, as the gentleman from New York, or he may be completely ignored. Roosevelt explained this policy on the theory that many people could not remember names. They voted for names they knew. To name the opponent was to advertise his name and to impress it on the public mind. Roosevelt knew that there would be no lack of mention of his own name by his enemies.[19]

A candidate can give the silent treatment to the opposing standard bearer only under favorable circumstances. Roosevelt could run as if Landon or Dewey were not in the race; Eisenhower could pay little heed to Stevenson. On the other hand, a candidate opposing a popular leader almost of necessity must attempt to cut him down to size. Democratic strategists in 1956, for example, struggled with the question of what to say about General Eisenhower. After the General's heart attack, it seemed advisable to moderate criticism of him lest, by arousing sympathy, more be lost than gained.

Defensive strategy: Reply or ignore? As a presidential campaign moves along the question recurs of what to do about the opposition's attacks. Should a candidate answer them or should he ignore them? "There's an old bromide in politics that goes something like this: 'If your opponent calls you a liar, do not deny it—just call him a thief.' " [20] The same rule on the proper response to an attack has been put by Murray Chotiner, public-relations adviser to Vice-President Nixon, in this way: ". . . when you answer it, do so with an attack of your own against the opposition for having launched it in the first place." By far the most adroit handling of a dangerous attack in recent American politics occurred in 1952 as Richard Nixon dealt with the revelation of a fund to which a number of his supporters had subscribed to aid him in paying the incidental expenses of his senatorial office. In the politics of an earlier day the episode would have been regarded as a handful of businessmen buying themselves a Senator. Not so, as Nixon fielded the play under the coaching of his public-relations advisers. A few southern California patriots had contributed to help the Senator get his message to the American people. That message exposed the Democratic Administration, "the Communism in it,

[19] Frances Perkins, *The Roosevelt I Knew* (New York: Viking, 1946), pp. 115-116.
[20] "The ABC's of Political Campaigning," *New York Times Magazine*, September 22, 1940.

the corruption in it." The publicity about the fund had been a smear, "to silence" him, to make him "let up." He dared to continue to fight: "Because, you see, I love my country. And I think my country is in danger." [21] The Senator emerged as a clean-cut, young hero, poor but honest, smeared by conspiring Commies who sought to block his devastating blows—a recovery acclaimed by connoisseurs of such matters as without equal in the history of humbuggery.

Another gambit in coping with an attack is to have it answered, not by the head of the ticket, but by a lesser political figure, a move that conveys the impression that the charge scarcely merits the attention of the top man but nevertheless puts an answer into circulation. In 1936, says Charles Michelson, "Governor Landon's acceptance speech put us somewhat on the spot. It did not seem fitting that the President should answer it—for he could not take a defensive attitude. We finally decided on an hour's program in which a chain of four Democratic Governors participated, chiming in, each from his own State House." [22]

The basic difficulty in answering attacks is that the enemy chooses the terrain of battle, which is favorable to his cause. For that reason it may be preferable to ignore an attack altogether. Or an unwise attack by an irresponsible member of the opposition may be chosen for reply, a tactic that shifts the initiative to the defense. In the 1940 campaign, for example, Roosevelt chose to answer the charge of an obscure Republican campaigner that the President's supporters were "paupers, those who earn less than $1,200 a year and aren't worth that, and the Roosevelt family." The discovery of this remark occasioned high glee on the Roosevelt campaign train; a quick estimate put about half of the American population at the time into this definition of pauper. Roosevelt responded: " 'Paupers,' who are not worth their salt—there speaks the true sentiment of the Republican leadership in this year of grace. Can the Republican leaders deny that all this all-too-prevailing Republican sentiment is a direct, vicious, unpatriotic appeal to class hatred and class contempt? That, my friends, is just what I am fighting against with all my heart and soul."

Campaigners, as they avoid or parry charges, naturally place emphasis on what they regard as their strong points; likewise they say little about the weaker elements in their record or program. The opposition follows a like policy of speaking endlessly of the popular features of what it has to offer and of minimizing mention of the less attractive aspects. In consequence the issues seem never to be joined in the campaign oratory. Thus, in 1940 the Republicans spoke frequently and vociferously on the third-term issue; the Democrats scarcely mentioned it. They spoke of the de-

---

[21] See the treatment of the incident by Kelley, *op. cit.*, pp. 177–184.
[22] *The New York Times*, November 15, 1936.

sirability of an experienced Administration at a critical time in foreign affairs, a proposition difficult for the Republicans to challenge. In 1952 Democrats pointed with pride to the achievements of their foreign policy in Europe; the Republicans did not talk much about Europe but said a great deal about Asia.[23]

Driving a wedge between the opposing candidate and his followers. An old campaigning maxim is that "a candidate should always separate his opponent from the rank and file of the party." Willkie in 1940 strove to draw a line between Roosevelt and the Democrats. The "New Dealers" (not the Democratic Administration) had, he argued, departed from the precepts of Democratic heroes and saints. "So if there is any Democratic disciple of Thomas Jefferson in Dubuque he ought to vote for me. Surely any Andrew Jackson Democrat should vote for me and not for my opponent. . . . No Cleveland Democrat should vote against me." He talked to the Democrats as if they had been betrayed by Roosevelt and the "New Dealers." In turn, Roosevelt avoided attacks against "Republicans" or the "Republican party." Instead, he concentrated his fire on "Republican spokesmen" or "Republican leaders." Republican voters with Democratic inclinations could then say to themselves, or so Roosevelt thought, "he doesn't mean me." [24] Similar is the direction of intense criticism against minor figures rather than the chief of the opposite party. A campaigner may concede the greatness of the rank and file of the opposition, admit that the opposing standard bearer is an honorable man, but, sadly and reluctantly, point to the petty scoundrels who surround him.

Ridicule: A two-edged sword. A subtle art of campaigning is the use of ridicule, sarcasm, scorn. Few presidential candidates are masters of this art. A classic of the type was Roosevelt's speech to the International Teamsters Union in September, 1944, in which he skillfully poked fun at the opposition. In this speech the President rose to the defense of his dog Fala. The President's wife, the President's sons, and the President could ignore attacks on themselves, but Fala's "Scotch soul was furious." Listeners laughed raucously before millions of radios: "I think I have a right to object to libelous statements about my dog." The speech, however, had far-reaching effects. A rip-roaring declamation, it was calculated to arouse the voters from their apathy. Perhaps it was also designed to anger the opposition candidate. The next day Dewey promised "unvar-

---

[23] For examples, drawn from senatorial campaigns, of the tendency of campaigners to talk past each other, see L. C. Ferguson and R. H. Smuckler, *Politics in the Press* (East Lansing: Michigan State College, 1954), pp. 32–41.

[24] Burns, *op. cit.*, p. 286.

nished candor"; and his next speech, thrown together in haste, did not reflect the same sober consideration as earlier speeches and paved the way for campaign boners, or so the political writers opined.[25]

The art of the smear. Although presidential campaigns may be cleaner than they were a century ago, fine specimens of the smear turn up now and then.[26] A smear is a charge regarded as not quite cricket. Most smears are lies, nothing more, nothing less, but they also include lines of attack that attribute unpatriotic or selfish motives to the opposition or that raise questions no honorable man would raise. A simple falsehood must, of course, be presented in a manner to appear to be the truth. Thus, in 1932 a photograph of a sign before a "Hoover Ranch" reading "No White Men Wanted" was widely circulated; the enterprising photographers had hung a placard prepared for the occasion alongside a sign in front of a California ranch named for Mr. Hoover by one of his admirers. Or in a Maryland senatorial campaign in 1950 opponents of Millard Tydings published a tabloid which included a faked photograph showing Tydings in a friendly conversation with Communist Earl Browder. The supposedly damaging falsehood merges over into the smear that questions the patriotism or motives of the opposition, e. g., that Truman carried the nation into the Korean affair to avoid depression.

In some circles the art of smearing without seeming to smear is regarded with high esteem. That may be accomplished by innuendo, which leaves absolutely no doubt about what is being said yet in cold print the language does not technically say what was said. Thus, in the campaigns of 1952 and 1954 various Republican orators left the indubitable impression with their auditors that the high Democratic leadership was tinged with treason, Communism, and corruption. Yet so nicely worded were these speeches that Democrats who cried "Foul" could not point to the phrase that designated them as traitors. There is some indication that one of the contributions of the advertising profession to politics consists in newer techniques of communication by suggestion, intimation, or indirection.

Obviously the head of a ticket cannot be associated with the dissemination of the more obvious sorts of smears. At times lesser leaders may make a public smear but the more personal smears travel by word of mouth; sometimes the movement of stories is deliberately expedited; sometimes they originate spontaneously and travel under their own power. The an-

[25] On the speech about Fala, see R. E. Sherwood, *Roosevelt and Hopkins* (New York: Harper, 1948), ch. 31.
[26] See Hugh A. Bone, *"Smear" Politics* (Washington: American Council on Public Affairs, 1941).

cestry of a candidate, his extramarital exploits, his meanness, his disposition
to rob his fellow man, his association with doubtful characters, his wife's
alcoholism, the peccadillos of his children, and a variety of other matters
are dealt with in yarns that find their way across the country during a
campaign. A few men traveling out of national headquarters can spread
a story a long way in a few days.[27] About the only sure defense open to
a candidate is a good espionage service to ferret out opposition intentions
and the hardihood to threaten to disseminate an equally outrageous tale
about his opponent.

Communications Media

The appeals determined upon by the campaign strategists must be gotten to the voters. The candidate in a small rural county may have a word
with and shake the hand of every voter in the jurisdiction before election
day. The conditions of national politics differ radically from the suppositions of democratic theorists who see the entire citizenry assembled under
a spreading chestnut tree to settle the affairs of state. A presidential candidate, save through the shadows of television, can show himself to only a
few voters. Nor can he, given the looseness of national party organization, depend exclusively upon party workers over the nation to carry his
message to the people. He must utilize the media of communication—
press, radio, television—to project his image and to transmit his appeals to
the people.

Campaigning and the communications revolution. The revolution in
communications technology has profoundly altered the character of campaigning and perhaps changed as well the fundamental bases of political
power. These technological innovations began scarcely more than a century ago and multiplied rapidly in recent decades; their full effects have
doubtless not yet been felt. In Andrew Jackson's day the facilities for
reaching the mass of the people were meager indeed. In the campaign of
1828 Jackson's chief means for circulating his views was the United States
Telegraph, a partisan newspaper with a circulation of 40,000 weekly. Its
successor, the Washington *Globe,* by 1834 had a daily circulation of
12,000. Democratic doctrine proclaimed in the leading articles of this

---

[27] An act of Congress of 1944 requires that campaign literature include the names
of the persons responsible for its publication or distribution, a requirement calculated
to discourage the publication of smears. The act was also intended to reach such
tactics as the circulation among Detroit Negroes in 1956 of a letter that urged the ad-
dressees to vote Democratic "because the Democratic party keeps the colored in their
place." The letters came, or so the indictment later charged, from a volunteer worker
for the Minute Men for Eisenhower.

paper was reprinted by local newspapers over the country but only after the Washington newspaper had been conveyed to their offices by the primitive transport of the day.[28]

The communications system of Jackson's time made it essential that the national party have allied with itself local newspapers; it also left a place of great importance for party workers. The trend of technology over a century shortened the lines of communication between the national leadership and the electorate. The invention of the telegraph permitted the simultaneous publication of an item in every city of the land. Parallel improvements in printing machinery and newspaper merchandising brought newspapers within the reach of practically everyone. Later the introduction of movies made it possible for the candidate to be seen and heard by millions of people. The inauguration of network broadcasting after 1920 brought the entire nation within earshot of the campaigner. Television, first used extensively in the campaign of 1952, added another thread to the direct linkage of presidential candidate and voter.

These developments in communications made it possible for national leaders to reach and influence mass opinion directly without heavy reliance on an intermediate network of party workers or of party newspapers. The same developments probably also tend to elevate to power different persons, those with skills in the use of mass communications; at least they require some mastery of those skills. And campaigners must staff their organizations with specialists in the various communications media.

The press: Reporter and partisan. American political parties have fewer and fewer newspapers openly allied with them as partisan journals. The decline of the partisan press, often supported by public advertising or other patronage, has affected the Democratic party far more than it has the Republican party.[29] The independent or nonparty press tends by and large to be Republican in sympathy. Yet the managers of both parties must deal with a press that professes to function as a more or less neutral conduit through which news of events flows. Campaigners must contrive ways and means to inject their propaganda into the channels of the press.

The candidate cannot afford to be ignored by the press; his entourage, as well as the national headquarters, includes men whose job it is to facilitate the work of the newspapermen and to feed materials to the press. The politician believes that unfavorable treatment by the press is better than no coverage. Frank R. Kent put the maxim: "It is better to

---

[28] E. M. Eriksson, "President Jackson's Propaganda Agencies," *Pacific Historical Review*, 6 (1937), pp. 47–57.

[29] On the decline of the party press, see W. P. Beazell, "The Party Flag Comes Down," *Atlantic Monthly*, March, 1931.

be roasted than ignored." The late Claude A. Swanson phrased it: "When they stop writing about you in politics, you are dead." [30] Candidates strive to keep in the headlines; every day there must be a story for the press. When the presidential candidate goes on tour, provision is made for correspondents to accompany him; they are furnished advance copies of speeches and facilities to aid them in covering the campaign.

Apart from the coverage of party meetings and speeches, campaign managers funnel their message into the editorial rooms by other means. In the 1936 Republican campaign, for example, the publicity department made arrangements to furnish its press releases in mat, plate, and proof form to weeklies and small dailies. "At their own request 7,000 weeklies and 280 dailies received W.N.U. plate service; 430 weeklies and 557 dailies got mat service, and proof service was supplied to 25 weeklies and 780 dailies." [31] The total number of press releases distributed during the campaign was estimated at 361,000. The publicity divisions of both parties are diligent in furnishing partisan argumentation to the press, and column after column in small dailies and country weeklies is filled with material supplied from party headquarters in the form of "editorial suggestions." The foreign language press historically has presented a special problem to party managers, but its decline in importance has doubtless reduced this drain on campaign coffers.

Newspapers, despite their avowal that they are common carriers and little more, may give advantage to one candidate or the other in their news columns by allotting their favorite more space, by prominent placement of stories about him, by misleading headlines, and by other means observed in any campaign. Although some newspapers give fair coverage to both candidates during campaigns, the preponderance of editorial support tends to go to the Republican side along with whatever bias prevails in the treatment of news. In newspaper editorial support in 1952 Stevenson enjoyed an advantage in only Georgia, Kentucky, and North Carolina and he "had no daily newspaper support in nine states—Connecticut, Delaware, Maine, New Hampshire, North Dakota, Rhode Island, South Dakota, Utah and Vermont." [32]

About the only weapon a candidate has against newspaper bias is to scream to high heaven about the iniquities of the one-party press, a gambit which may help keep the press a bit more in tune with its pro-

[30] Frank R. Kent, *Political Behavior* (New York: Morrow, 1928), pp. 252–253.

[31] Casey, "Republican Propaganda in the 1936 Campaign," as cited, pp. 27–44.

[32] N. B. Blumberg, *One-Party Press?* (Lincoln: University of Nebraska Press, 1954), p. 16. Blumberg finds that of the total newspaper circulation in 1952, 80.24 per cent was pro-Eisenhower; 10.88 per cent pro-Stevenson, in the editorial columns. In that year 14.5 per cent of the newspapers editorially preferred Stevenson, a decline in Democratic support from 38.7 per cent in 1932.

fessed aim of fair reporting whatever its editorial stand may be.[33] The advertising columns of the newspapers are usually open to party committees but normally at a higher rate than is charged to commercial advertisers. Politicians place no high value on newspaper advertising, yet when one side advertises the other feels that it must do so too. In presidential campaigns the national committees place little newspaper advertising but provide mats for local groups that wish to do so, a means by which national headquarters can maintain some control over what is said in advertisements paid for by enthusiastic local committees.

What of the influence of newspapers? Do people vote as their favorite editors recommend? Do slanted news columns win votes? Do the great publishers swing elections? The evidence on such matters is extremely limited, although it is evident that newspaper influence differs enormously from situation to situation. Roosevelt won four presidential elections over the opposition of most of the press; Truman enjoyed no widespread newspaper support. Eisenhower, on the other hand, had the support of the bulk of the daily press. With newspaper support Roosevelt might have won by wider margins; without newspaper support Eisenhower might have won by narrower margins. The chances are that newspapers exert greater influence in state and local matters than in presidential campaigns. Voters in jurisdictions that elect obscure candidates to fill inconspicuous positions may rely to a greater extent on the press for guidance. In party primaries the press may, other things being equal, exert more influence than in general elections, but in some jurisdictions newspaper opposition is said to be a positive advantage. In turn, newspapers themselves may to some degree be under the same sorts of influences as is the electorate; some newspapers do cross party lines from time to time.[34]

The effect of the press is not to be measured solely by its impact on the fortunes of the candidates during the course of a campaign. By steadily hammering their policy predilections, campaign or no campaign, newspapers over the long pull affect the attitudes of their readers, an influence that may be reflected in the voting when an election rolls around. The cumulative educational effect of the press in individual communities may

[33] The weekly newsmagazines, of which *Time* is the most important, evidently do not regard themselves as bound by the canon of full and fair reporting to which daily newspaper publishers give at least lip service. In these weeklies, most notably in *Time*, editorial and news materials are so blended that they tend to be indistinguishable.

[34] For materials on press influence in local campaigns, see R. D. McKenzie, "Community Forces: A Study of Non-Partisan Municipal Elections in Seattle," *Social Forces*, 2 (1923–24), p. 271; H. F. Gosnell and M. J. Schmidt, "Factorial Analysis of the Relation of the Press to Voting in Chicago," *Journal of Social Psychology*, 7 (1936), pp. 375–385.

become both pervasive and durable. A community dependent, for example, on a Hearst newspaper for a generation or so may develop into a quite different place than one blessed with a more responsible press.

Party literature. During a presidential campaign the national headquarters of the parties publish large quantities of pamphlets, leaflets, and circulars. By such means the party can deliver messages tailored to the interests—and prejudices—of special groups of voters, furnish ammunition to its friends, and present arguments and material that would not be printed by newspapers or transmitted by the radio stations. A 1940 Republican leaflet, "A Third Term?," gave in parallel columns pictures and statements of pro- and anti-third-termers. Among the former were, according to the leaflet, Earl Browder, "Boss Edward J. Kelly," "Boss Frank Hague," and Harold Ickes; among the latter, George Washington, Thomas Jefferson, Andrew Jackson, and Woodrow Wilson. A 1948 Democratic leaflet was entitled, "The G.O.P. Congress that Pigeonholed Progress!" The Republicans issued one under the simple banner, "High Tax Harry." The campaign comic book, a relatively new form of campaign literature, lends itself to a most graphic expression of partisanship. Even the most partisan newspaper rarely puts the partisan message as bluntly as it can be stated in campaign literature.

Of the millions of pieces of literature printed in each campaign—some estimates run into the hundreds of millions—a great deal probably never reaches the voters. Its distribution is both a wearisome and costly task. If it is mailed, a large outlay for postage and clerical labor is required. If it is entrusted to party workers for distribution, it may not be distributed, for the party organization is seldom as efficient as it is reputed to be. Shipments of literature in bulk to state committees often stop at state headquarters. Louis Howe, secretary to Franklin Roosevelt, found that only about 3 to 5 per cent of the literature distributed to state committees by national headquarters ever reached the voters. In the 1932 Democratic campaign the national committee sent a few pieces of each kind of literature to each of about 140,000 local committeemen instead of depending on state committees to distribute bulk shipments to precinct workers. In 1952 the Republican national committee distributed to state and local committees catalogs in which items of literature were listed along with indications of where to buy it. If local committees buy their literature, they should be more disposed to exert themselves to distribute it.

Radio and television. Television and radio have reduced the press to a secondary role in the calculations of the managers of presidential campaigns. These new communications media give the candidate direct access to the people of the nation. He can speak to the voters with no fear that his remarks will be misrepresented by the headline writers or buried on the back pages. If he is a skilled TV performer and the party war chest allows, he can use TV and radio to counterbalance newspaper opposition. Moreover, radio and TV are, in their capacity as reporters of the news, under more of a compulsion than the press to give an even-handed account of events.

As they have supplemented and to a degree supplanted the older modes of communication, TV and radio have imposed new requirements upon campaigners and campaigning. Doubtless the radio or TV presentation reaches a far larger proportion of the electorate and brings into the political audience a far wider variety of people than ever came within earshot of the old-time political orator. Radio and TV speeches must be far more simply put and far shorter than the old-fashioned long-winded political speech if the attention of the audience is to be held and if the message is to be put across. The new media also require for their best use a mastery of speaking techniques and practices unlike those of the bellowing orator with windmill arms. The persuasive affirmations of the seductive radio voice are more likely to be accepted than are the same words in print.[35] Television has also brought experimentation with propaganda presentations in forms other than the traditional political speech. Spectacles involving the participation of drum majorettes, Hollywood starlets, bogus farmers, and file clerks from the model agencies, with an occasional word by the candidate, are produced for the edification of the multitude. Even the lowly singing commercial has been impressed into the service of politics.

Obviously the new media require at campaign headquarters technical specialists in addition to speech writers. They pose also new problems of tactics as well as new opportunities to reach the people. In 1952, for example, the Democrats made extensive use of television beginning early in the campaign in order to overcome the handicap from the fact that Stevenson was comparatively unknown. Eisenhower, on the other hand, had not yet developed a TV technique and the calculation was that barnstorming would be advantageous to enable as many voters as possible to see the General's folksy manner at first hand. Beyond such questions that grow out of the circumstances of specific campaigns are numerous problems of technique in the use of TV and radio, such as the timing of presentations, the relative emphasis on spot announcements and set speeches, and the minimization of interference with popular programs of entertainment.

Although television even by 1956 had had a powerful impact on cam-

[35] Note the comment of an Illinois farmer: "Sometimes when I listen to Roosevelt I even get to thinking he's right and all the time I know he's wrong."—Lazarsfeld and Stanton, *Radio Research 1941* (New York: Duell, Sloan and Pearce, 1941), p. 267.

paigning for the Presidency, its full effects have probably not been felt. They certainly have not been systematically identified. One consequence that seems indisputable is that individuals can by dramatic television performances attain a national recognition and attract a national following much more rapidly than by reliance on older communications media. Through the televising of his crime investigations, Senator Estes Kefauver became a national figure almost overnight and a contender for the Democratic presidential nomination in 1952 and 1956. Whether television facilitates the manipulation of the electorate by campaigners remains open to doubt, although its existence compels campaigners to adapt their styles to it.[36] Nor has television supplanted other media as a source of information. The evidence indicates that reliance on television as a source of information about campaigns declines with increase in educational level.[37]

Political rallies: The personal touch. The radio and TV are no substitute for the old-fashioned political rally where the candidate can be seen and heard; the tactical problem in campaigning has been to contrive ways and means of combining the personal touch of the rally with the marvels of electronic communication. The psychological evidence indicates that individuals in crowds are rendered suggestible. The applause picks up the doubters in the audience and carries them along. Listeners to a radio speech lack the emotional stimulus of the crowd; one or a handful of persons may be listening. Television adds the bearing, the gestures, the smiles of the speaker to the voice of radio, but the "personality" of the candidate may not make its way to the image on the television screen.

The campaign of 1956 provided a test of some of these considerations. Republican campaign planners early hoped to limit Eisenhower to a few high-level speeches from television studios. This sort of presentation turned out to be deadly. A revision of tactics substituted telecasts of the candidate as he spoke to rallies. In this way the cheers of the throng go out over the air and perhaps give televiewers the illusion that they are themselves in the audience and subject them to some of the emotional impact of audience participation. Yet the speaker before a great rally must adapt his delivery to the fact that most of his auditors are not in the hall but are in small groups before receivers scattered over the country.

The experience of 1956 confirmed an earlier judgment of James A.

[36] An analysis of Iowa counties with high television density and of counties with little television coverage in 1952 indicated that no significant difference either in voting turnout or in party division of the vote existed between the two sets of counties.— H. A. Simon and F. Stern, "The Effect of Television Upon Voting Behavior in Iowa in the 1952 Presidential Election," *American Political Science Review*, 49 (1955), pp. 470–477.

[37] Angus Campbell and others, "Television and the Election," *Scientific American*, 188 (1953), pp. 46–48.

Farley who conceded that radio was a "tremendous factor" in the Roosevelt political fortunes, but, he said, "to my way of thinking, there is no substitute for the personal touch and there never will be, unless the Lord starts to make human beings different from the way he makes them now." [38] The participation of the candidate in parades and rallies permits great numbers of people to see him and probably also helps maintain the zeal and enthusiasm of party workers. At any rate, party managers work on the theory that TV has not made barnstorming obsolete. The airplane and the TV have only modified the conditions of campaigning.

Effects of Campaigns

Presidential campaigns culminate in the great decisions of the American democratic order. The spectacle of a campaign—with its hullabaloo, its nonsense, its fabrications, its exaggerations—raises doubts among the faint hearted whether the Republic can long survive, whether the electorate can make these decisions in the national interest. Do clever rhetoricians manipulate and deceive the voters? Do special interests as they work through the parties manage to induce voters to tolerate intolerable privilege, to vote against themselves? Do charismatic candidates flimflam the public? Do appeals to ignorance, to prejudice move the electorate to decide on the basis of considerations irrelevant either to its own interest or to the public weal? Are voters swayed by promises of unattainable achievements to be forgotten no sooner than the crowd of glib rascals gets into office?

All such questions go to the heart of the democratic process, and their answers are by no means obvious. Certainly on occasion propaganda artists bunco the voters into electing both scoundrels and incompetents. Privileged groups have successfully defended almost interminably positions seriously detrimental to great numbers of citizens. Reckless campaigners have even poisoned the minds of the people against policies necessary for national security. Such occurrences generate anxieties about the capacity of people for self-government, which are not to be allayed entirely by the observation that despite all these things the Republic has survived. Yet the actions of voters may be better appraised if they are placed in a broader context than the campaign itself. People make the great decisions of self-government by choosing among alternatives put forward by the party system. Those decisions can be no better, no wiser than the choices put to the voters. Their record of decision may be quite as good as the record of the national leadership, the so-called wiser and better people in the proposal of alternatives. Furthermore, a limited government provides a hedge against popular folly—as well as a check on

[38] *Behind the Ballots*, pp. 301–302.

wisdom. A government so complex as the American system, with its built in checks against action, tends to restrict the consequences of individual elections.

All such judgments about the quality of the popular electoral decision rest in high degree upon intuitive judgment. The hard knowledge about the interaction between campaigner and voter is thin, yet enough systematic inquiry has been done to help put the role of campaigning in perspective.[39] The effects of the campaign are limited by the loyalties of the party faithful. Perhaps three-fourths of the voters remain loyal to the same party's candidate from one presidential election to the next. This persistence of attachment means that a varying but large proportion of the electorate behaves in a manner viscous rather than volatile, at least over the short run.

The blandishments of the campaigner are also often outweighed in their influence upon the voter by the impact of events. In some presidential elections more votes are won or lost before the campaign begins, even before the nominations are made, than are affected by the campaign itself. In an intensive study of Erie County, Ohio, a sampling of the electorate indicated that the change in sentiment from November, 1936, to May, 1940, accounted for twice as many votes as did the impact of the 1940 campaign. The events that impel the voter in one direction or another may be remote or immediate. People experience or observe at first hand immediate events; remote events have their impact through the mass media. Large-scale economic deprivation, for example, may be immediately perceptible to many people and have its effects on their voting. Remote events —the "mess in Washington," the diplomatic ineptitude of John Foster Dulles—are perceived through the mass media and in such matters the slant given the picture of the world by the media may govern the effects, if any, of events upon voting.[40]

Diehard partisans may remain unmoved by opposition oratory and events may fix many voting decisions, yet campaigns undoubtedly have their effects. Lazarsfeld has identified three of them: re-enforcement, activation, and conversion. Re-enforcement is the effect of the campaign in strengthening the loyalties of the devoted partisans. The campaign helps

[39] The major studies that throw light on the matter are: Paul F. Lazarsfeld, Bernard Berelson, and Hazel Gaudet, *The People's Choice* (New York: Duell, Sloan and Pearce, 1944); Angus Campbell, Gerald Gurin, and Warren E. Miller, *The Voter Decides* (Evanston: Row, Peterson, 1954); Bernard Berelson, Paul F. Lazarsfeld, and W. N. McPhee, *Voting* (Chicago: University of Chicago Press, 1954); Morris Janowitz and Dwaine Marvick, *Competitive Pressure and Democratic Consent* (Ann Arbor: Bureau of Government, University of Michigan, 1956).

[40] See Bernard Berelson, "Events as an Influence Upon Public Opinion," *Journalism Quarterly*, 26 (1949), pp. 145-148.

keep up the courage of those whose minds are already made up. The staunch Republican (or Democrat) exposes himself largely to propaganda favorable to his viewpoint and thereby reassures himself of the soundness of his judgment. A substantial decline in the number of dedicated partisans in the electorate might, by increasing the proportions susceptible to campaign propaganda, alter the character of American politics. Activation consists in arousing the interest of persons indifferent at the outset of the campaign and inducing them to vote. They tend to vote in the direction that might have been predicted on the basis of their personal characteristics. Crystallization of the views of the indifferent and undecided may determine the outcome of an election.

The numbers of voters converted by the campaign may be small but sufficient to swing the election one way or the other. Sample surveys provide some measure of the magnitude of shifts in voter affections during campaigns; the essence of the knowledge on the point is that the size of the shifting group of voters differs from campaign to campaign. In 1940, the evidence seems to indicate, the results of the presidential election would have been the same had it been held in August rather than in November. In 1948, on the other hand, the campaign apparently won the election for Truman. The net effect of the shifts of voters during the last weeks of campaign moved the Democrats ahead of the Republicans, who led in the early stages; possibly the more the voters saw of Mr. Dewey the better Harry Truman looked. In 1952 General Eisenhower led in the sample surveys as the campaign began, and all the ballyhoo had no substantial net effect on the division of the electorate.

These kinds of analyses that identify with fair precision some effects of campaigning may lead to a complacent view of the state of the practice of democracy. It may well turn out that the capacity of people to govern themselves and of popular institutions to shape questions for popular decision will in the future be subjected to far more severe tests than they have been in the past. The increasing salience of problems outside the immediate experience of the voter tends to increase his dependence on the media. The controllers of the media, as well as political campaigners, come to be equipped with both instruments and propaganda techniques more suited to manipulation of the mass from central points of power. These and other tendencies will doubtless make the maintenance of civic intelligence a problem of profound continuing significance.[41]

[41] This chapter has been directed toward presidential campaigns. An additional range of practice and probably sharply differing patterns of electoral behavior prevail in many state and local campaigns. See, for example, Paul F. Lazarsfeld and Morris Rosenberg, "The Contribution of the Regional Poll to Political Understanding," *Public Opinion Quarterly*, 13 (1949–50), pp. 569–586; C. E. Parker, "Polling Problems in State Primary Elections," *Public Opinion Quarterly*, 12 (1948–49), pp. 728–731.

18 | Party Finance

To MAKE a respectable showing a campaign manager must have at his disposal substantial sums of cash. The raising of funds to support the party headquarters and to finance the extraordinary costs of the presidential campaign is one of the most vexing tasks confronting the national chairmen. State and local party executives and managers of candidates seeking nominations must likewise devote considerable effort to solicitation of funds.

The nature of our parties makes the problem of financing American political activity especially worrisome. No major party in the United States rests on a base of dedicated dues-paying members who regularly remit their bit to support party work. Instead of being able to rely upon a steady flow of funds from the faithful, as happens from time to time in other countries,[1] the American party manager must organize heroic efforts to raise large sums as each campaign rolls around. He may be able to tap a goodly number of reliable partisans who contribute from campaign to campaign but he must also search out new prospects who may be responsive to the appeals of his party under the circumstances of the moment.

[1] See J. K. Pollock, *Money and Politics Abroad* (New York: Knopf, 1932).

Fund raisers, whatever worthy cause they promote, share the vicissitudes common to their calling, namely, the difficulties of separating the solvent citizen from his cash. Those who endeavor to fill the party coffers must cope, in addition, with the special problems of financing political activity. They work in a society in which the cynical view is that every man has his price. The collection of funds to meet the campaign costs may readily be made to appear to conflict with the democratic tenet that in some way or another political leaders should be beyond purchase. Fund raising becomes, then, a suspect operation and those who participate— either as contributors or as receivers—must make a show of adherence to an involved etiquette. Its rules often find their way into the law of the land, at times in forms which, if followed literally, would make it virtually impossible to finance campaigns.[2]

Magnitude and Nature of Campaign Costs

Although the data on campaign finance suffice to support some observations about trends in total campaign costs, about costs of particular sorts of campaigns, and about the purposes for which the money goes, perhaps the most significant conclusion from the data is that it takes a lot of money to elect the representatives of the people. Large sums are required to meet the legitimate costs of presenting on even a modest scale the cause of a presidential candidate to an electorate of a hundred million people. Campaigns for lesser offices cost less, yet the candidates and managers concerned face a formidable task in raising the necessary money.

Total outlays for campaigning. So numerous are the committees making campaign expenditures and so incomplete are the reports on their finances that figures on the total cost of political activities in the United States must be estimated rather than compiled. Alexander Heard, after the most thorough examination of the data that has yet been made, estimated that

---

[2] On the subject of this chapter, see Louise Overacker, *Presidential Campaign Funds* (Boston: Boston University Press, 1946) and her *Money in Elections* (New York: Macmillan, 1932). An earlier study is J. K. Pollock, *Party Campaign Funds* (New York: Knopf, 1926). On regulatory measures, see E. R. Sikes, *State and Federal Corrupt-Practices Legislation* (Durham: Duke University Press, 1928). Congressional Quarterly News Features assembles after each election data from reports of expenditures filed by candidates and campaign committees; the resulting analyses may be found in the *Congressional Quarterly Almanac* or in the Quarterly's *Weekly Reports*. Congressional committees usually investigate the financing of presidential and congressional elections, and their hearings and reports may be examined with profit. On the 1956 campaign, see U.S. Senate, 84th Cong., 2d sess., Subcommittee on Privileges and Elections of the Committee on Rules and Administration, *Hearings on 1956 Presidential and Senatorial Campaign Practices* (1956) and the report of the same committee on *1956 General Election Campaigns* (1957). These items are cited hereafter as Gore Committee, *Hearings* and *Report*. The Gore Committee's report constitutes

in 1952 the cash expenditures "for nominating and electing all public officials in the United States was around $140,000,000." [3] In addition campaign managers receive the volunteer services of workers and contributions of other things of value—space, the use of automobiles, and the like. Professor Heard says that these noncash donations "probably amount to more than 5 per cent of the cash outlay." This estimate excludes the value of part-time volunteer services.

While this overall estimate may be in error by several million dollars in one direction or another, checks against expenditure reports known to be fairly complete provide basis for some confidence in it. The estimate of $140,000,000 spent in the year of a presidential election works out to about $1.42 per potential voter in the nation or to about $2.27 per voter in the presidential election. The plausibility of these figures may be checked by any voter who takes the trouble to guess what it cost to get to him the assortment of campaign literature he receives by mail from candidates for all types of offices during the year of a presidential election. In some jurisdictions that cost, which represents only a part of campaign outlays, would approach two dollars, although it should not be supposed that per capita campaign expenditures are uniform over the country.

Another way to judge the plausibility of estimates of the size of political expenditures is to look at the costs of commercial advertising. In 1956, according to *Printers' Ink*,[4] Procter & Gamble spent $55,400,000 for network TV and advertising in magazines and Sunday magazine sections. For the same purposes Colgate Palmolive paid out $29,500,000; General Motors, $48,900,000; and Chrysler, $26,900,000. Two soap makers and a pair of automobile manufacturers, thus, spent far more for advertising in 1956 than is estimated to have been spent in campaigns for nomination and election to all public offices in 1952.[5]

Costs by level of government. The question, what does it cost to get elected to office, is, given the organization of American politics, if not a

the most comprehensive analysis of campaign finance made under official auspices. Part 2 of the *Hearings* also includes extensive analyses of data on 1952 campaign finance prepared by Alexander Heard, whose forthcoming study, *The Costs of Democracy*, will report the most thorough analysis of American party finance that has been made.

[3] *Money and Politics* (Public Affairs Pamphlet No. 242, 1956), p. 2.

[4] March 29, 1957.

[5] Another interesting comparative figure is the $1,300,000 spent by Robert R. Young and his associates in their proxy fight for control of the New York Central Railroad Company in 1954. In 1955 Mr. Young asked the Central stockholders to reimburse the Alleghany Corporation, which had advanced the campaign costs. He explained that "it would be a discouraging precedent to owners of other non-owner-directed companies for us to defray our own expenses when the benefits redound to all Central shareowners, pro rata."

nonsense question, a nice problem in cost accounting. The simultaneous conduct of interrelated campaigns for many offices makes it impossible, even if all the expenditures by all campaign committees were known, to allocate costs among the campaigns for individual offices. Expenditures by the national committees are devoted primarily to the presidential campaign, but the presidential candidate may be expected to use a little television time to say a good word about the congressional and senatorial candidates on the ticket. The state committees of the parties usually make substantial expenditures in support of the party slate as a whole. County committees conduct campaigns in support of candidates for national, state, and local office. Individual candidates often spend large sums to get themselves elected but their activities may benefit their running mates on the party ticket as well.

Though the cost of a particular campaign may be impossible to ascertain, estimates may be made of expenditures by campaign committees and agencies at different levels of government. Professor Heard estimates that 14 per cent of the $140,000,000 spent during the entire year of 1952 consisted of expenditures by the national party committees and other national committees; 48 per cent, of expenditures by party and nonparty committees operating on a state-wide basis; and 38 per cent, of outlays for local and district activities. These proportions are for the nation as a whole; among the states the division between state and local costs varies on both sides of the national average.[6]

These figures give us no notion of the magnitudes of the tasks confronting the chairmen of individual committees in financing the activities for which they are immediately responsible. A few figures on the expenditures of individual campaign committees in 1956 may serve that purpose. Disbursements by major national-level Republican committees from January 1 to November 30, 1956 were as follows:

Republican National Committee, $2,768,519
Republican Senatorial Campaign Committee, $1,469,822
Republican Congressional Committee, $2,778,285
National Citizens for Eisenhower-Nixon, $1,510,194

On the Democratic side disbursements by the principal spenders for the same period were:

Democratic National Committee, $2,619,746
Democratic Senatorial Campaign Committee, $266,885
Democratic Congressional Committee, $245,741
Stevenson-Kefauver Campaign Committee, $1,092,110
Volunteers for Stevenson-Kefauver, $493,492

[6] Heard, *Money and Politics*, p. 4.

Indicative of the financial problems faced by senatorial candidates are figures on a few 1956 campaigns. They include expenditures reported by candidates and outlays by some, but probably not all, committees operating on their behalf. They include no allocation to the senatorial races of a share of outlays by the state committees. The sample figures follow:

California: Richard Richards (D), $181,915
          Thomas H. Kuchel (R), $374,248

Idaho: Frank Church (D), $41,189
      Herman Welker (R), $50,484

Illinois: Richard Stengel (D), $132,054
        Everett M. Dirksen (R), $111,088

New Hampshire: L. M. Pickett (D), $350
              Norris Cotton (R), $8,280

Oregon: Wayne Morse (D), $149,104
        Douglas McKay (R), $214,775

The division of campaign costs between state and local party committees and special committees supporting individual candidates differs widely among the states. A few figures on direct expenditures by party committees (excluding their disbursements to other committees) in the period September 1 through November 30, 1956 will suggest the magnitude of the operations of these committees:

Arizona Democratic State Central Committee, $18,218
Arizona Republican State Committee, $36,937

Cook County, Illinois, Democratic Committee, $511,367
Illinois Republican State Central Committee, $199,470

Michigan State Democratic Committee, $150,773
Michigan Republican State Central Committee, $386,330

New York State Democratic Committee, $265,092
New York Republican State Committee, $670,417

Oklahoma Democratic State Central Committee, $148,492
Oklahoma Republican State Committee, $79,648

Allegheny County, Pennsylvania, Democratic Committee, $158,103
Allegheny County, Pennsylvania, Republican Committee, $311,538

These figures should not be regarded as measures of the relative sizes of party expenditures in the localities concerned. Each party spent additional sums through other committees.[7]

[7] All the 1956 figures are from the Gore Committee, *Report*. In addition to the sums indicated for the national-level committees, most of them had accumulations of unpaid bills on November 30.

These 1956 figures may be supplemented by instances chosen more or less at random to illustrate further the altitude of the financial hurdles on the way to public office. In 1926 Frank L. Smith won the Illinois Republican nomination for Senator in a primary that involved the expenditure of slightly more than $1,000,000 about equally divided between Smith and his opponent. In the 1926 Republican primary in Pennsylvania $2,265,000 was spent in the fight for the nominations for governor and United States Senator. At the time such sums were thought to be scandalously large, but expenditures of quite imposing totals are now commonplace. In 1948 about $500,000 was spent on behalf of Fuller Warren as candidate for governor of Florida in two Democratic primaries. The 1950 New York City mayoralty campaign involved outlays of about $800,000. The 1950 Ohio senatorial election cost well over $2,000,000, the bulk of which went for support of the late Senator Taft.[8] In 1954 New York Democrats spent over $1,000,000 in support of Harriman in the gubernatorial race as the losing Republicans reported an outlay of $884,000. The 1952 Massachusetts Senate race by John F. Kennedy cost at least $350,000.[9] In the 1952 preconvention campaign for the Republican presidential nomination Citizens for Eisenhower spent $1,200,000 and other committees also made outlays on behalf of the General. In 1956 in a California campaign on an initiated proposal to control oil production, opponents and proponents spent a total of over $5,000,000. In the same state in 1950 Governor Warren's campaign outlays were $400,000, while his Democratic opponent, James Roosevelt, reported expenditures of about $100,000.[10] All these races involving large sums may be matched by examples of campaigns conducted at modest cost. In the New Hampshire Republican senatorial primary of 1954 the three contestants reported expenditures of slightly over $20,000 each. These costs, small as senatorial races go, were said to be the largest ever spent in a senatorial campaign in that state. From time to time a Senator or a Representative avers, probably truthfully, that he has obtained renomination and re-election without the expenditure of over a hundred dollars.

Variations in total expenditures. Total expenditures doubtless vary from election to election both within the nation and within individual states and districts from time to time. Doubtless also these differences are associated

---

[8] See Senate Committee on Rules and Administration, Subcommittee on Privileges and Elections, 82d Cong., 1st and 2d sess., *Hearings on Investigation into the 1950 Ohio Senatorial Campaign* (1951 and 1952).

[9] See Hugh Douglas Price, "Campaign Finance in Massachusetts," *Public Policy*, VI (1955), pp. 25–46.

[10] J. P. Harris, *California Politics* (Stanford: Stanford University Press, 1955), p. 48.

with varying characteristics of the campaigns involved, although the data are too fragmentary to demonstrate those relationships conclusively. Yet certain factors seem to be responsible for gross differences in outlay. The perceived stakes of an election and the intensity of the feelings it arouses may bear on the level of expenditure. When a popular candidate threatens to upset applecarts, those who are fearful about their applecarts are likely to be generous in their contributions to his opponent. The presidential campaign of 1896, for example, excited both the anxieties and the generosities of the corporate interests. On the other hand, if feelings are not intense or if the outcome of the election seems to be foreordained, party treasurers may have much greater difficulty in raising funds and perhaps not so much will be spent. Often members of the House and less frequently members of the Senate win re-election with relatively small campaign costs. Their secure position assures that no campaign of consequence will be mounted against them and they are not compelled to spend heavily.

The chances are that per capita expenditure varies with the character of campaign organization, other things being equal. In some jurisdictions the party conducts a unified campaign in support of all the candidates on the ticket. In others, it is every man for himself, with each candidate having his own campaign organization and publicity program. The odds are that a common campaign can be carried on at a lower cost than can a series of independent campaigns for every man on the ticket. Whether party committees conducting unified campaigns invariably take advantage of the economies of consolidation is another question.

The character of party organization may also bear significantly on the costs of campaign for nomination. In jurisdictions with weak or divided party organizations warm primary contests tend to be the rule and they may be quite costly for the contenders. On the other hand, when the party organization unites behind candidates, whether nominations be by convention or by primary, outlays for campaigns for nomination tend to be less. Nomination costs also differ widely with circumstances. The spirited contest for the Republican presidential nomination in 1952 involved outlays of perhaps several million dollars; Mr. Eisenhower's renomination in 1956 was not expensive.

The character of the constituency may affect campaign costs, again with other things being equal. To reach the voters in a metropolitan district may be more expensive than in a rural district. Urban politicians meet powerful nonpolitical competition for the attention of the public; probably a congressional or senatorial campaign is more salient in the field of attention of a rural than a metropolitan constituency. Or, the candidates for mayor in a small town may have been known for years to most of the voters in the town; the mayoral candidate in a metropolis ordinarily has to spend a good deal of money to make his name, as well as his merits, known to his fellow citizens.

In some instances the availability of funds rather than the necessities of the campaign lead to exceptionally heavy expenditures. At best campaign managers must judge the wisdom of expenditures by hunch and they are beset on every side by proposals to spend. When they happen to have a candidate of great means, or a candidate who has access to large resources, they find ways to spend whatever is available.

Objects of expenditure. Though the sums known to have been spent by individual candidates and committees may seem enormous, inspection of the costs of types of campaign activity makes it clear that campaign managers must incur large obligations to meet even the minimum necessities. The chances are also that over the past 50 years changes in the nature of political activity have increased the relative importance of campaign activities that have to be paid for in hard cash.

A major item in the budgets of national and state campaign committees consists of outlays for publicity in its many forms. The long-term trend in the distribution of campaign expenditures has probably been toward the use of a larger and larger proportion of the available funds for publicity. This development has paralleled the rise of new media for propaganda, such as radio and television.

Radio and television expenditures bulk especially large in the expenditures of committees operating at the national level in a presidential campaign. Almost one-third of the outlays of national level campaign committees in 1956 went for radio and television. It requires little ingenuity to run up a big bill for radio and television time. In 1952 the Citizens for Eisenhower paid $267,000 for an election-eve broadcast that lasted an hour and a half. By 1956 to hire the complete radio and TV facilities of NBC for half an hour would use up most of $100,000.

The most complete data on radio and TV costs during a campaign were compiled by a Senate committee in 1956. The committee, instead of relying on the reports of campaign committees, obtained reports from the networks and from radio and TV stations of their sales of time during the period September 1 through November 6. They sold almost $10,000,000 worth of time during this period. This total thus excluded the expenditures for time in the primaries and in such general election activity as occurred before September 1. Some of the details of the data collected by the committee are presented in Table 18.1.

State and local campaign committees place heavier emphasis on newspaper advertising than do national committees. A survey of political advertising in 410 newspapers from July 1 to November 30, 1956, produced

Table 18.1

1956 General Election, Payments for Radio and Television Broadcasts,
September 1–November 6 [a]

Campaigns	Democratic	Republican
Presidential	$1,949,865	$2,739,103
Senatorial	691,031	788,280
Congressional	330,247	509,552
All other offices	1,149,569	1,344,956
Total	$4,120,712	$5,381,891

[a] From Gore Committee, *Report.*

an estimate that political committees spent $4,280,000 for newspaper advertising during that period. Payments to lesser newspapers are sometimes said to be for editorial support. The foreign language press and the Negro press especially have gained the reputation of susceptibility to offers of advertising in exchange for editorial endorsement.[11]

Other forms of publicity account for smaller proportions of the campaign budget, yet their use requires substantial sums. During the 1956 campaign 25 outdoor advertising companies sold over $500,000 worth of billboard space to campaign committees. Use of direct-mail publicity can become costly. The postage cost alone on a first-class mailing to 100,000 voters would be $3,000. Printing, addressing, and other costs would doubtless be double or triple the postage cost. Lithographs, photographs, and campaign novelties add to publicity costs. In 1940 the Republican National committee spent $48,000 for Willkie buttons.

Overhead expenses include a variety of miscellaneous costs. The staff of the party committee, maintained year in and year out, must be augmented at campaign time. Nonparty committees recruit staffs for the duration of the campaign. The costs of special trains for the presidential candidate, of chartered planes, and of travel for field workers and for speakers must be covered. Postage, rental of quarters, equipment, telephone, telegraph, and express add to the overhead. Seemingly inconsequential items can account for large sums. A campaign year postage outlay of a quarter of a million dollars by a national committee is not uncommon.

Election-day expenses are heavy for city and county organizations. The polls must be manned with watchers; runners are needed to bring out the

[11] In 1944 practically all expenditures for newspaper advertising by the Democratic national committee went to newspapers of racial groups. The major portion went to the Negro press.—C. W. Smith, Jr., "Campaign Communications Media," *The Annals,* 259 (Sept., 1948), pp. 90–97.

voters; men and women must be stationed near the polling places to distribute literature and sample ballots; automobiles must be on call to transport voters to the polls. Lavish expenditures for election-day work at times closely approach bribery; the worker traditionally has been expected to vote right and to induce his family, friends, and relatives to do the same. The level of election-day outlays differs widely from place to place. In some communities the party committee may need $100 or more per precinct for primary or election day. In others this sort of expense may be negligible. In some types of precincts volunteer workers may readily be enlisted for the chores of election day; in others, greater reliance is placed on paid workers.

The financial transactions of many party and campaign committees include sums that the committee itself does not spend directly but disburses to other committees. These payments from committee to committee usually serve the purpose of transferring money to those points where the need is presumably greatest. State and local committees often make payments to the national committee. A national level committee will make subventions to state committees, to senatorial committees, or to House candidates. Labor committees usually collect funds and make transfers to party and campaign committees. Some committees, particularly on the Republican side, exist primarily to collect funds and then parcel out the proceeds among operating committees.

Trends in costs. Even though the data on party finance are too thin to show trends accurately it seems plain enough that over the past half century the problems of financing political activity have changed in nature. The rapid growth of the electorate, not only in the nation as a whole but within states, congressional districts, and other campaigning units, has increased total costs. Beyond this increase in the absolute size of expenditures, the changes of recent decades in style of campaigning probably increase the per capita cash outlay necessary to get the message of the candidate to the voter.

The most striking change in the mode of campaigning is the increased reliance on the media of communication. In an earlier day speeches by presidential candidates and aspirants for lesser office as well were more noteworthy events than they now seem to be. Voters assembled from miles around to listen to the interminable oratory of their political idols. Nowadays the campaign treasurer still has to finance the travels of his candidate over the country, but he must also raise the money to put the show on the TV and radio networks.[12] Probably the communications

[12] Richard L. Neuberger quotes the reminiscence of a former governor of Oregon: "I was elected with $3,000. All the money came from my own bank account and that

revolution has had less of an impact on congressional campaigning than on the budget of presidential campaign committees. The same probably applies to many campaigns in smaller electoral units. A mayoral candidate in a great city may find TV an efficient way to speak to the voters but the candidate for a state legislative post from a district within the same city would ordinarily get more for his money by spending it in other ways.

Other changes have also created new needs even if they do not invariably create readily identifiable new items in the campaign budget. The long-run decline of the avowedly partisan press has deprived campaigners of that assured channel to the electorate; to achieve an equivalent impact on the voter other species of propaganda need to be used.

Changes in party organization itself have created new problems of campaign finance. The odds are that over a half century the party organizations have declined in vitality. In place after place, the coverage of the city with precinct executives, often supported by the public payroll, has become quite incomplete. Although the character of the standing party organizations differs greatly from locality to locality, probably for the country as a whole its functions have come more and more to be performed in ways that require cash outlays.[13] Moreover, the rise of the direct primary has introduced an important new element of cost into politics. Campaigns for delegates to nominating conventions were doubtless at times costly, but certainly the modern primary campaign has made the process of nomination more expensive.

Raising the Money

Few unsolicited contributions arrive at party headquarters. A handful of devoted souls send their checks at campaign time without prompting. Many others give regularly but they must be reminded to do so. Still others must be cajoled into doing their financial duty to their party.

In reflection about raising money to support political activity it needs to be kept in mind that the problem is not entirely one of party finance but in large measure one of financing individual candidates. In this county and that, one or the other of the parties may succeed in monopolizing the

---

of one friend. Today $3,000 would just about buy you half an hour on a state-wide radio hookup. Folks once came from miles around by horse and buckboard to attend a political rally. Now they wait for you to go into their homes by radio and newspaper advertising or direct mail. That takes a lot of money."—"It Costs Too Much to Run For Office," *New York Times Magazine*, April 11, 1948.

[13] The testimony also seems to be that the election-day expenditures that approach bribery, i. e., the hiring of "workers" who were expected to deliver their vote and a few others, has declined. Full employment and inflation reduce the persuasive power of a ten-dollar bill.

collection of funds; the party committee conducts a party campaign and doles out funds as it wishes for the separable costs of individual candidates. In substantial degree, however, American politics is atomized and each candidate must in some way or another cover his own campaign expenses. The problem of the individual candidate is perhaps most marked in campaigns for nomination; there funds must be raised not to support the party but Elmer Snodgrass in particular. The ability to raise the money to finance a primary campaign thus may become an absolute requisite for a serious fight for a contested nomination. At the general election appeals for funds may be made in the name of the party and that appeal has some effect. Yet so individualized is American politics that in most states each candidate for an important office usually operates a substantial campaign effort independently of that of the party organization.

Partisan contrasts in sources. Given the variety of candidates for whom committees and managers raise funds, many kinds of sources are tapped for contributions. This candidate for the Senate may be able to draw on labor funds; that candidate may have a special appeal to oil men. Another may have a following among merchants. One candidate for governor may draw heavy financial support from the liquor interests. One candidate for the House may have banking support; another may have had a wealthy father. Commonly a candidate relies upon many sources. The element of personal friendship may be of great importance in the raising of money for a candidate, especially in primary campaigns.

Little or no systematic information is to be had about the sources of contributions to most campaigns. Considerable analysis has been made of the sources of contributions to national committees. The findings, in essence, seem to be that each party draws heavily on those elements of society traditionally associated with it. Although party spokesmen, both Democratic and Republican, love to discourse upon the universality of the appeal of their party, the hard financial fact seems to be that the money comes in the main from those whose interests are thought to be tied to the party's cause. Probably the same general rule holds for contributors to the funds of candidates for House and Senate and for other offices, although the data have not been put together to demonstrate it. All this is not to aver that donors make gifts uniformly with the expectation of a specific quid pro quo; it is rather that in presidential politics some groups find one party's general position congenial and others move in the opposite direction.

Differences in the sources to which the parties have access appear in a dramatic form from an analysis of the contributions of officers and directors of the great corporations during the 1956 campaign. Gifts of

$500 or more known to have been made by such persons aggregated more than $1,900,000, of which more than $1,800,000 went to Republican campaigns and around $100,000 to Democrats, the latter scarcely enough to cover the postage bill of the national committee. Table 18.2 shows the approximate percentage division between Democratic and Republican campaigns of the yield of contributions of $500 or over by officers and directors of various types of business enterprises.

Table 18.2

Division between Republican and Democratic Campaigns of Yield of Reported Contributions of $500 or More in 1956 from Officers and Directors of Types of Business Enterprises [a]

Type of Enterprise	Republican	Democratic
225 largest corporations	94.6%	5.4%
29 largest oil companies	95.9	4.1
10 leading radio and TV stations	97.4	2.6
17 certified airlines	80.7	19.3 [b]
37 advertising agencies	100.0	0.0
47 underwriters of bonds	99.2	0.8

[a] Derived from Gore Committee, *Report*.
[b] Most of the deviation of the airline category from the general pattern was accounted for by Democratic contributions by R. J. Reynolds, a director of Delta Airlines. Air transport is one of Mr. Reynolds' lesser business interests.

Democratic fund raisers make little headway among the industrial elite as represented by the officers of the great corporations, but this should not be taken to mean that they receive no financial support from business. Their generous givers simply tend to be different from those whose financial affections lean Republican. These contrasts are brought out by the data of Table 18.3, which indicates the proportion of the yield of gifts of over $1,000 for each party derived from broad types of contributors. In 1940 and 1944 a far larger proportion of the Republican collections in sums of $1,000 or more came from bankers, brokers, manufacturers, utility men. Democrats obtained a larger proportion of their funds from a varied array including brewers, distillers, contractors, merchants, officeholders, and men connected with the building materials industry. The metropolitan wing of the Democratic party has long had its affiliations with the liquor business. Any party in power becomes attractive to contractors and it is, of course, in a position superior to that of the outs in the solicitation of officeholders. The table shows, too, the sharp relative decline in Democratic reliance on bankers, brokers, manufacturers, and the like after 1932. Contributions by persons in these categories to the Democratic cause dropped abruptly between 1932 and 1936 as the New Deal drew more clearly the lines of political battle.

Table 18.3

Percentages of Total Contributions from Gifts of $1,000 or More to Democratic and Republican Presidential Campaigns from Persons Identified with Various Economic Pursuits, 1932, 1940, and 1944

Source	1932 [a]		1940 [b]		1944 [c]	
	D	R	D	R	D	R
Bankers, brokers, manufacturers, oil, mining, utilities, real estate, insurance	45.2	60.6	21.1	57.0	24.3	59.4
Brewers, distillers, soft drinks, contractors, builders, building materials, publishers, radio, advertising, amusements, professions, officeholders, merchants	21.7	11.0	46.8	9.2	46.2	15.6
Others and unidentifiable	33.1	28.4	32.1	33.8	29.5	25.0

[a] Derived from data presented by Louise Overacker, "Campaign Funds in a Depression Year," *American Political Science Review*, 27 (1933), p. 776. The percentages are based on gifts to the national committees.

[b] Derived from data presented by Overacker, "Campaign Finance in the Presidential Election of 1940," *American Political Science Review*, 35 (1941), p. 723. In this table the gifts from organized labor included in the original tabulation were omitted to obtain comparability with the 1932 and 1944 figures. The figures for 1940 are based on contributions to the national committees.

[c] Derived from data presented by Overacker, "Presidential Campaign Funds, 1944," *American Political Science Review*, 39 (1945), p. 916. These figures include gifts of $1,000 or more to the national committees and to certain related organizations as well.

Contributions from labor groups go to support Democratic campaign efforts in about the same degree that funds from corporation officials go to the Republicans. Seventeen national labor organizations reported political expenditures of $2,156,000 from January 1 to November 30, 1956. Of this sum, $540,000 was spent directly, chiefly for publicity, and the remainder went as contributions to national, state, and local campaign committees, chiefly Democratic. A Senate committee obtained reports from 171 state and local labor organizations whose expenditures from September 1 to November 30, 1956 amounted to $830,000. About one-half of this sum was spent directly while the remainder was transferred to other campaign committees most of which were Democratic.[14]

Big and little givers. Both Democrats and Republicans rely upon large gifts for the bulk of their campaign funds. In 1952, according to Professor

[14] Gore Committee, *Report*, pp. 45-48.

Heard's analysis, gifts of over $500 comprised 68 per cent of the receipts of 18 national-level Republican committees and 63 per cent of the funds of 15 national-level Democratic committees.[15] In 1936, 1,945 contributors of over $1,000 furnished almost half the total receipts of the major-party national committees. Probably state and local campaign committees depend to a lesser degree on large gifts, although instances occur in which a handful of donors provide most of the substantial sum required to run for the Senate or for a governorship.

Scraps of evidence suggest that dependence of national campaigns on an extremely few extremely large contributions is not so marked as it once was. Thus, in 1918 Will Hays needed $300,000 to get the Republican congressional campaign under way. He went to New York to have a word with William Boyce Thompson who, Hays says, responded without hesitation: "Tell Senator Smoot you have the money. I will underwrite the $300,000. I will get two or three others, but I will be responsible for the whole." [16] The Democratic national committee ended its 1904 campaign with a deficit of $900,000, and, it is said, Thomas Fortune Ryan and August Belmont picked up the tab.[17]

Reliance on a few fat cats may be less than it once was, but trustworthy information on the numbers of persons who contribute and the size of their donations is lacking. Certainly an extremely small proportion of the voters contribute. The Survey Research Center in 1952 asked a national sample of voters living in households: "Did you give any money or buy tickets or anything to help the campaign for one of the parties or candidates?" Four per cent of the respondents said that they had done so: 6 per cent of the Eisenhower voters, 4 per cent of the Stevenson voters, and a smaller percentage of the nonvoters.[18] Projection of these ratios to the entire electorate indicates that in 1952 about 3,000,000 people made some sort of contribution. The same question produced in 1956 a somewhat higher percentage of contributors.[19]

[15] *Money and Politics*, p. 13.

[16] *Memoirs of Will H. Hays* (Garden City: Doubleday, 1955), p. 127.

[17] The story goes that Urey Woodson, secretary of the Democratic national committee, told his callers, Ryan and Fortune, the size of the deficit. "'That's very reasonable,' said Ryan. . . . Then he turned to Belmont. 'Gussie,' he suggested casually, 'you send your check for $450,000 and I'll send mine for $450,000. We'll pay these bills and let Mr. Woodson and the boys go home.'" Belmont protested that he already had $200,000 in the campaign. "'Yes, Gussie,' Ryan replied quietly. 'I know that. But remember—Parker was your candidate.' Gussie paid, and so did Ryan."—Joseph F. Guffey, *Seventy Years on the Red-Fire Wagon* (1952), pp. 30–31.

[18] Angus Campbell and others, *The Voter Decides* (Evanston: Row, Peterson, 1954), p. 30.

[19] The percentages of respondents in occupational groups who claimed to have given money or bought tickets in 1956 were: professional, 19; business and managerial, 18; white collar, 7; skilled, 8; unskilled, 7; farm operator, 6; retired, 6; housewife, 6.

The evidence clearly supports the conclusion that national-level committees obtain most of their money from contributors of large sums, that is, if one regards $500 as a large sum. The evidence on the sizes of contributions to other sorts of campaign committees is much less satisfactory. Professor Heard estimated that in 1952 some 20,000 persons contributed at least $500 to one type of campaign committee or another. The Gore committee staff assembled a list of slightly more than three hundred individuals, married couples, and firms making political contributions of $5,000 or more during 1956: $2,894,000, to various Republican committees; $860,000, to Democratic committees. The data available to the committee did not include the records of many campaign agencies active during the year in state and local campaigns and was doubtless incomplete for committees concerned with presidential and congressional candidates.

Who the little givers are and how much they give are unknown. A sizeable group consists of candidates themselves. Tens of thousands of candidates for town, city, and county offices pay their own campaign expenses, which are nominal or amount to only a few hundred dollars. And a candidate may from time to time move into the ranks of the big givers as he finances his own campaign. A larger number of little givers is accounted for by those public employees who make more or less voluntary gifts. They too, in some jurisdictions, may be regarded as candidates: if their side loses they may be replaced.

Another numerous group of little givers, perhaps the largest, consists of trade unionists who are tapped for a dollar or more by the political education committees of their unions. Trade unions may use union funds accumulated from dues in some jurisdictions and in some campaigns. The extent to which unions engage in this practice makes their members contributors to political activities. The more conspicuous union political activities are carried on by special political action committees with funds that must be solicited especially for this purpose from individual unionists. Union officials do not themselves know how many individuals contribute. An estimate of 1,500,000 in a presidential election year would probably be high.

On the face of it, the party dinner would seem to be a way of enlarging the base of contributors. The Democratic national committee in the 1930's began systematic use of Jackson Day dinners to raise funds. The Republicans soon took up the $100-a-plate dinner; they made a most spectacular application of the technique in 1956 when they raised $4,000,000 in one evening by dinners over the country which were linked by closed-circuit television to hear the President speak. Although dinners may bring in a

Among income groups, the proportions ranged from 1 per cent for the under $1,000 group to 33 per cent for the $10,000 and over group.

fringe of new contributors, the chances are that in the main the same people who contribute directly buy the tickets. Ordinarily the party's fund-raising machinery manages the dinners and pushes the sale of tickets. Not many people turn up unannounced to buy tickets at the door. The $100-a-plate dinner incidentally has some happy features. The contributor may remain anonymous, at times advantageous both to the party and to the contributor. Probably a good many tickets also appear in one guise or another as items on corporate expense accounts.

Although the polls indicate that millions of persons would donate $5 to their party if they were solicited,[20] the hard fact is that the American parties do not have an organization that can be turned to large-scale canvassing for funds. Few county or city organizations could man a community-wide fund-raising drive; to the extent that they could, they would be reluctant to collect funds for the state committees. Few state committees can enlist county and city organizations in a collecting drive; when they can do so, the state committees would prefer not to share the proceeds with the national committee. And few state committees will respond with enthusiasm to national leadership in the organization of a drive for small contributions. All these problems and more were encountered by Beardsley Ruml when he set out to collect a million $5 contributions for the Democratic campaign in 1952. Many state organizations would have nothing to do with the campaign. Others insisted on keeping all the proceeds from the sale of the $5 certificates. Others left such work as was done to volunteers and the professionals then complained that the volunteers were tapping their regular contributors. An estimate of the total yield of the drive was $600,000.[21] Large sums could be collected in driblets, but it would require an almost revolutionary reformation of party organization to do so.

Organization for fund raising. The types of organizations for raising funds are almost as numerous as are campaigns. The candidate himself may have to touch his friends and acquaintances for cash. In another instance a single individual may be given the job of raising money. Often, however, the larger campaign units create specialized units to solicit contributions—a finance committee or division. Party finance committees follow a pattern of operation characteristic of the financing of nongovernmental collective

---

[20] The Gallup poll in September, 1956 asked the question: "If you were asked, would you contribute $5 to the campaign fund of the political party you prefer?" The responses were: 35 per cent, yes; 50 per cent, no; 15 per cent, don't know. On this basis, door-to-door canvassing could yield around 17,000,000 $5 contributions.

[21] See John Van Doren, *Big Money in Little Sums* (Chapel Hill: Institute for Research in Social Science, 1956).

endeavor ranging from the support of the county fair to the endowment of colleges. That is, a committee of men of prestige in the group concerned turns a modicum of heat on those able to contribute. For convenience in solicitation, if for no other reason, men of means find themselves the least neglected target of the fund-raising committee.

The Republican party has developed a far more effective money raising apparatus than have the Democrats. In most of the states and in some subdivisions of states a Republican finance committee collects funds which are in turn allocated to the national committee, to the state committee, and to other campaign committees according to their relative need. This mode of operation reduces, although it has by no means entirely eliminated, the multiple solicitation of the same individual for contributions to different party committees. The finance committees usually include in their membership business leaders and others not professionally active in politics. In some instances the volunteer members of the committee operate with the advice of experts in the conduct of fund-raising drives. These specialists have developed methods for the conduct and management of philanthropic fund raising through volunteer solicitation and those methods may be transferred to party financing.[22]

A finance committee with the proper membership can be most persuasive with prospective contributors. In 1956, for example, John Hay Whitney served as chairman of the United Republican Finance Committee of New York, which had jurisdiction over New York City and environs. "We try to make all our solicitations personal," Mr. Whitney said. They tried to see to it, he said, that "our fund raisers get out and visit, and talk, and meet the people who contribute." [23] A committee chaired by Mr. Whitney, a man of more than moderate standing among men of means, could raise money for almost any cause. In 1952 the chairman of the New York committee was Winthrop W. Aldrich, chairman of the board of the Chase National Bank. In that year the committee raised $2,385,000. Committees composed of such persons have ready access to people with money to give. And people with money to give may hesitate not to give to such committees. In fact, many of the members of such committees and their prospects spend a good many of their days each year soliciting each other for one worthy cause or another.

Democratic fund-raising efforts are more erratic, less systematic, and less effective. This comes about in part from the fact that the Republican party has a larger and perhaps more homogeneous following of solvent prospects available for solicitation. More fundamentally, however, there

[22] The most active of these specialists in Republican finance is Carlton G. Ketchum, of Pittsburgh. See his testimony in Gore Committee, *Hearings*, Pt. 2, pp. 445–454.

[23] See Mr. Whitney's testimony, Gore Committee, *Hearings*, Pt. I, pp. 38–44.

is a higher degree of organizational disunity within the Democratic party, a factor which in turn may derive from the diverse social composition of the party. Nevertheless the Democrats have made no impressive attempt to apply the more systematic methods employed to some extent by the Republicans.[24]

Indirect contributions from the public treasury. Private contributors provide the bulk of political funds, but the government itself, in one way or another, finances a not inconsiderable share of campaign activity. This source of support naturally is available only to the incumbent official or party except in Oregon and North Dakota which states publish pamphlets made up of information about the candidates furnished by them.

Sitting Senators and Representatives enjoy perquisites that can be turned to use in campaigns. Their official staffs usually labor diligently in their campaigns for re-election. One of the more innocent aids available to an incumbent is the use of the congressional frank for the distribution of campaign literature. A Congressman may extend his remarks in the *Congressional Record;* that is, he may have printed in the *Record* remarks never delivered orally, obtain copies at cost from the Government Printing Office, and frank them to his constituents without postal cost. In some instances the use of the congressional frank on campaign literature is simply a means by which a party committee, by agreement with a Congressman, transfers to the government the postage cost on huge quantities of campaign literature. In other instances the frank is used in a purely individual campaign endeavor by a member of Congress. The Honorable Joachim O. Fernandez of Louisiana, for example, early in 1940 extended his remarks under the heading, "I Am a Candidate for Re-election." [25]

The greatest contribution of the public treasury to party finance is made through the public employment of persons who devote part of their time to the work of the party organization. Although it doubtless runs into millions of dollars annually, the contribution of federal, state, and local governments to the maintenance of party organizations through the patronage system cannot readily be estimated. It is expected, of course, that Presidents, governors, Congressmen, and legislators shall defend and advocate policies before the electorate, but the electioneering activities of the lower-ranking administrative employees are on a different plane. Of the latter employees, some devote a large proportion of their time to precinct work; others may spend only a few days immediately prior to

[24] See the comment by Heard, *Money and Politics*, pp. 22–25.
[25] *Congressional Record* (daily ed.), March 11, 1940. It has been proposed that "outs" running for Congress be given the benefit of the frank to offset the advantage enjoyed by sitting members.

the election. Some are competent and able public employees; others are on the public payroll only because they have special skills in the management of the electorate.

The returns from the assessment of public employees for party purposes may be regarded as an indirect contribution by government itself. The collection of funds from administrative employees of government is a practice almost as old as the Republic. Its present extent cannot be accurately known. At the federal level, the outright assessment of classified civil service employees has apparently become negligible. Incidents occur sporadically, but they are made to appear as "voluntary contributions," a response to legislation prohibiting assessments. Among states and cities assessment seems to occur more frequently than in the federal service. Given the size of modern government payrolls, systematic collections can yield substantial sums. Assessments of 3 per cent of the annual salaries of Jersey City employees by the Hague organization were said to have netted $174,000 in 1948 and $167,000 in 1949.[26] Somewhat akin to assessment is the collection by party committees of more or less customary amounts from nominees on the ticket to help cover the general costs of the campaign. In fact, party organizations frequently nominate persons who are able to contribute liberally to the party war chest.[27]

Public funds are more or less indirectly channeled into campaigns by such means as have been mentioned. Incumbent officials and parties have at their command the apparatus of government and can often put official action into a form or time action for immediate campaign advantage. The incumbent always has the advantage, or the disadvantage, of his record, but some actions seem to be made with an eye to the campaign immediately ahead. Tax reductions seldom occur save in election years.[28]

---

[26] Private employers occasionally "assess" their employees for political contributions. In 1952 persons in the Ford Motor organization raised funds from Ford dealers, although it was insisted that no "pressure" was involved. The same practice occurred in General Motors. In 1956 an official of J. Walter Thompson Company, an advertising agency, circularized the top employees of the company and suggested that a Republican contribution was in order: "What would happen to the growth of our own company if we faced an extended period of business uncertainty?" Now and then instances come to light of persuasive solicitation of corporate personnel at the executive and supervisory levels; how widespread the practice is cannot be said.

[27] Expenditures by candidates, incidentally, are not deductible as a cost of doing business in the computation of federal income taxes.—McDonald *v.* Commissioner of Internal Revenue, 65 S. Ct. 96 (1944). A Minnesota statute of 1955 permits candidates to charge specified sums as business expenditures under the income tax law of that state.

[28] In 1952 and 1956 Senator John J. Williams, of Delaware, charged that rulings by the Commissioner of Internal Revenue with respect to unpaid loans to the New York State Democratic Committee constituted "an indirect way of financing the Demo-

The nether side of party finance. Campaign finance has its seamy aspects, which create special problems for fund raisers. Finance committees have to work to get most contributions but they need also to fend off some persons eager to give money. Entrepreneurs engaged in economic pursuits on the shady side of the law, as well as others on the edge of trouble with the prosecutor, may approach headquarters hopefully with bags of greenbacks. James W. Gerard, treasurer of the national Democratic finance committee for many years, recorded that he had often declined large "contributions because of their suspicious source." A contribution from "a notorious gambler or bootlegger" might, he said, "seriously embarrass the party." [29] R. Douglas Stuart, 1952 Republican treasurer, said: "We guard against unwelcome contributions by requiring that every contribution carry the name of the donor. . . . Where contributions are in cash we require that the contributor be identified." [30] A contribution from a more or less legitimate source may be declined because the candidate wishes to be under no obligation to the donor.[31] Another class of donor whose motives may well be suspect are those persons who rush to volunteer to help pay off the deficit of the winning candidate. National committees regularly receive unsolicited contributions after their candidate wins. The flow is especially heavy if the outcome was unexpected. In 1948, for example, an inexplicable delay in the mails brought to Demo-

---

cratic campaign of 1948 out of the Federal Treasury." The committee offered to settle its debts at 10 cents on the dollar and the 90 per cent loss was held to be a nonbusiness bad debt that could be offset against capital gains in fixing income tax liability. For Senator Williams' charges and the relevant tax rulings, see *Congressional Record* (daily ed.), June 14, 1956, pp. 9357-62. At least two of the lenders whose loans turned sour—Marshall Field and David S. Schulte—did not take advantage of the Treasury ruling.—*New York Times* and *New York Herald Tribune*, April 30, 1952.

[29] *My First Eighty-Three Years in America* (Garden City: Doubleday, 1951), p. 325.

[30] Stories circulate of campaign treasurers who tell bearers of suspect money to bring it back in the name of a respectable donor, a practice that may account for inclusion in the lists of contributors the names of persons who never in their life had as much ready cash as they are credited with having given to the party cause. Stories also abound of campaign treasurers who put dubious money in the safe and returned it after the campaign, a gambit that at least denies the cash to the opposition and avoids antagonizing the giver. Another type of practice appeared from the 1953 testimony of the New Jersey Republican state chairman. He explained that the custom was to report only those contributions in the form of checks; cash was never reported.

[31] A. W. Dunn says that in 1904 the Republicans rejected only one corporation check, one for $100,000 from the tobacco trust. Antitrust proceedings were to be initiated against it, and the Administration wanted to avoid "any entanglements through a contribution from that source."—*From Harrison to Harding* (New York: Putnam's, 1922), p. 401.

cratic national headquarters in the days after the election a gentle rain of checks dated several days before Truman's unexpected triumph.

One broad type of contribution may result from virtual extortion. From time to time vulnerable persons may contribute under the threat of damaging government action. This kind of collection procedure is most likely to occur in corrupt, bossed communities. Thus, a newspaper comment on advertising in the program of an athletic event sponsored by a Chicago ward club noted that most of the buyers of space were neighborhood saloons. A saloonkeeper never knows when he is violating the law but they do know, it was said, "that violations by those who are not right-minded means license revocation." [32] Contributions may also be exacted from contractors and other suppliers of goods and services to public agencies. Often such persons make contributions at their own initiative since they may believe that they would make themselves quite conspicuous by failing to do so.[33]

Regulation of Party Finance

The finances of American party committees, candidates, and campaign managers are regulated by state and federal law. Legislation purports to require publicity of campaign finance, to limit the amounts spent, to prohibit certain types of contributions to campaigns, and to limit the size of contributions. In general, the laws do not in fact limit expenditures, substantially affect the size of contributions, or assure full publicity. The statutory ambivalence reflects a legislative deference to the popular opinion that the power of money ought to be restricted and a simultaneous recognition of the hard fact that rigid limitations probably would be unenforcible. Nevertheless loopholes in finance statutes are not explicable solely in terms of legislative hypocrisy. The organization of campaign activity presents almost insurmountable technical obstacles to the control of finance. In a federal politics of simultaneous but related campaigns any

[32] *Chicago Daily News*, December 5, 1935. In 1936 the Democratic National Committee is said to have netted at least $250,000 from its *Book of the Democratic Convention of 1936*. The revenue came principally from the sale of advertising. The Hatch Act amendments of 1940 make it unlawful for any person or corporation "to purchase or buy any goods, commodities, advertising, or articles of any kind or description where the proceeds" directly or indirectly inure to the benefit of candidates for any federal elective office.

[33] Fund solicitors can exert leverage over banks with deposits of public funds. A candidate for state treasurer in Illinois, for example, approached a bank with large deposits of public funds but was told he did not have "a Chinaman's chance" to win. The improbable winner won. He withdrew $10,000,000 in state funds from the bank, but he testified that he "tried to be easy with them." He gave 30 days notice and started withdrawals at the rate of $500,000 a month and then went up to $1,000,000 a month.—*Congressional Record* (daily ed.), March 14, 1957, pp. 3301–3302.

attempt to limit expenditures is almost inevitably doomed to failure. When the candidate for the Senate, say, approaches his expenditure limit, outlays in the name of the candidate for governor—or for sheriff—may help the cause just as well as expenditures in his name. Yet, as will be shown, the laws regulating campaign finance have had some effects—many of them bad.

Requirement of publicity. A common type of party-finance regulation is the requirement of publicity of the amounts of contributions, the names of contributors, and the nature of expenditures. The underlying assumption is that wrong-doing does not flourish in public. The legislation grew from the belief that secrecy of party finance facilitated purchase of government action. In 1904 Alton Parker, the Democratic candidate, made an issue of the secrecy of funds by the assertion that corporations were furnishing funds to the Republican campaign to purchase the favor of the Republican party. The Democratic campaign treasurer of 1904, Perry Belmont, led a movement to obtain appropriate legislation.[34] The first fruits of the work of Belmont and his allies were not publicity laws but laws prohibiting corporate contributions. By 1908, however, public sentiment moved both parties to make their financial records public and in 1910 Congress required candidates for Congress and political committees to report their campaign receipts and expenditures.

The federal law requires candidates for Senator and Representative and political committees to file at set intervals statements with the clerk of the House of Representatives. The term "political committee" includes organizations accepting contributions or making expenditures to influence the election of candidates "in two or more states," or in a single state if the committee is a branch or subsidiary of a national organization (other than a state or local committee of a political party). The reports must include the name and address of each person who has contributed more than $100, the names and addresses of persons to whom payments of $10 or more have been made, and certain other information. Most states also have legislation requiring candidates, committees, and campaign managers to file similar statements with appropriate public officials.

Although the reports filed under federal and state law make public much information about party finance, that information is both fragmentary and incomplete. The statutes themselves are often defective. The federal law, thus, does not apply to primary campaigns, an omission attributable to the earlier view that nominations were beyond federal purview. Some laws require only that reports be filed after the election. The

[34] Perry Belmont, *An American Democrat* (New York: Columbia University Press, 1950), ch. 17.

coverage often does not extend to all who may spend in support of a candidate. Some states require reports by only the candidate and exclude party committees. The federal law requires that a candidate for House or Senate report money received and expended by himself "or by any person with his knowledge." This provision, coupled with the exemption of intra-state committees, assures incomplete reporting. Candidates often manage to have no knowledge of sums spent by others in their behalf. Expenditures by lobbying and "educational" organizations may fall outside the statutory definition of reportable expenditures. In 1944 the Committee for Constitutional Government spent $250,000 in the first nine months of the year. A volume it distributed widely began: "This book shows how the New Deal is taking America into national socialism." The inference might have been that the committee opposed Mr. Roosevelt, but it refused to disclose the names of its contributors. It averred that it supported no candidate or party: "We support the Constitution and free enterprise." [35]

In addition to the defects in the laws, noncompliance and the form of the data submitted help to keep party finance out of the goldfish bowl. Failure to file is rarely followed by prosecution, although the omission of a report in some jurisdictions makes a candidate conspicuous. Reports may put some contributions in the names of dummies: some donors fear reprisals if they have backed the losing candidate. Moreover, the most detailed information may be unrevealing; extensive analysis is required to get at the significance of the data.[36] Hurriedly prepared newspaper stories rarely reveal the inner meaning of the reported facts. Often it requires efforts beyond the capabilities of a newspaperman to ascertain from the reports even so simple a fact as how much money has been spent in a campaign.[37]

[35] Senate Report 101, 79th Cong., 1st sess., p. 10. Certain constitutional questions concerning the extent of the power of Congress to compel reports were answered in Burroughs *v.* United States, 290 U.S. 534 (1934). In 1928 the Anti-Smith Democrats, an organization led by Bishop James Cannon, Jr., collected and expended funds in a campaign against Al Smith. In defense against an indictment charging failure to report, Cannon and his secretary, Burroughs, contended that Congress had no power to regulate presidential elections, and therefore no authority over the campaign activities of individuals. (The Constitution provides that presidential electors of each state shall be appointed "in such manner as the legislature thereof may direct.") The Supreme Court held that Congress had acted within its power. The requirement of reports might be said to limit freedom of speech, a contention that has not been authoritatively settled. See the discussion of the point in the note, "Statutory Regulation of Political Campaign Funds," *Harvard Law Review*, 66 (1953), pp. 1259–1273.

[36] The analyses of reports under the federal law by both congressional committees and private persons doubtless have contributed over a long period to the building of the image of the Republican party as the party of wealth.

[37] If all funds for each campaign had to be funneled through a single official, respon-

Limitation of sources of funds. Contributions from certain types of sources have been prohibited or otherwise limited. The basic explanation for statutes with these purposes has been that the classes of persons affected have been thought to be especially attached to a crowd other than that which controlled the legislature, but other considerations have also been influential. Certain business interests have been thought to be especially prone to the political exertion of their pecuniary power. In other instances the statutes protect those vulnerable to solicitation—for example, public employees.

The federal government and about three-fourths of the states restrict corporate contributions. The federal legislation, enacted in 1907, was an outgrowth of the efficiency with which Mark Hanna assessed corporations for the support of the Republican campaign of 1896 and of the revelations by the "muckrakers" of corporate corruption of state and local politics around the turn of the century. The 1907 act made it unlawful for "any national bank, or any corporation organized by authority of any law of Congress" to contribute "in connection with any election to any political office," or for "any corporation whatever to make a contribution in connection with any election at which presidential and vice presidential electors or a Senator or Representative . . . are to be voted for." The more inclusive limitation on national banks arose from the fact that Congress had broad power over corporations chartered by itself. The narrower limitation on other corporations was based on the authority of Congress over the election of presidential electors and over the election of its own members. In 1947 the prohibition was extended to contributions in connection with nominations for the offices tied by the earlier legislation to the two classes of corporations. Another group of corporations—utility holding companies and their subsidiaries—was brought under federal control by the Public Utility Holding Company Act of 1935, which forbids companies to contribute to federal, state, or local campaigns.[38]

---

sibility for reporting could be much more clearly fixed. A recent Florida statute requires that all funds go through a single campaign treasurer's hands and be deposited in a bank depository. The terms of the statute made it illegal for a citizen to buy newspaper space or radio time without clearance with the candidate's campaign treasurer. The statute, which has evidently brought about fairly complete publicity, was attacked as an unconstitutional limitation of freedom of expression but was upheld by the Florida Supreme Court. See E. E. Roady, "Florida's New Campaign Expense Law and the 1952 Democratic Gubernatorial Primaries," *American Political Science Review*, 48 (1954), pp. 465–476.

[38] The practices that the legislation sought to prevent may be deduced from the case of the Union Electric Company, which was in 1942 found guilty of violation of the act. During the 'thirties it made contributions to candidates and party committees in Missouri, Illinois, and Iowa. It accumulated a fund of $591,000 for these purposes by obtaining rebates from persons to whom it made payments and by the use of false

Although campaign treasurers no longer accept corporation checks, corporations find ways and means of spending money in campaigns. Campaign literature may be sluiced through the corporate postage meter; the corporate printing bill may include items that have no relation to the corporate charter; corporate personnel may be assigned to campaign duty. Apart from such concealed contributions, quite open propaganda may be conducted to influence elections. Costly campaigns of so-called institutional advertising and of trade association propaganda have become the fashion in big business circles. What effect, if any, expenditures for these purposes have cannot be known, but the outlays have evidently been, if not pro-Republican, at least anti-Democratic in motive.[39] Moreover, the statutes prohibiting corporate campaign contributions do not extend to expenditures for lobbying or for propaganda for or against legislation. Corporate influence may work through these means quite as well as through electoral campaigns.[40]

Congress has placed limitations on trade unions analogous to those on corporations. In 1936 the United Mine Workers, the Amalgamated Clothing Workers, the International Ladies' Garment Workers, and other labor organizations gave $770,000 to the Democratic campaign.[41] For the first time labor had become a major source of campaign funds and an agitation

expense accounts, and thus concealed the political use of its funds. See Egan *v.* United States, 137 F. (2d) 369 (1943), certiorari denied, 320 U.S. 788.

[39] Illustrative is an advertisement published in September, 1956 by the Guaranty Trust Company of New York under the title, "The Real 'Giveaway.'" It began: "It is during political campaigns that the cry of 'giveaway' reaches its greatest intensity. This is the cry raised by advocates of 'public' power whenever it is proposed to allow private enterprise to develop a waterpower site. The implication is that natural resources rightfully belonging to all the people are being 'given away' to favored groups." The president of Guaranty Trust was asked: "Is it your view and the view of the Guaranty Trust Co., sir, that this is nonpolitical material?" He replied: "Yes, sir," and explained that neither "in the advertisement nor in the article from which it is taken is there any mention of any candidate or any political party." He indicated that the company had in its income-tax accounts treated the cost of the advertisement as an ordinary business expense. See Gore Committee, *Hearings*, Pt. 2, pp. 344–351.

[40] Some discouragement to the expenditure of funds for lobbying, propaganda to influence legislation, or voting is furnished by the legal provision thas such outlays are not deductible as a business cost in the determination of income-tax liability. The determination of precisely what expenditure falls within the regulatory inhibition presents recondite questions, and the impression prevails that the Internal Revenue Service is not draconian in its quest for violations. The Federal Power Commission, through its control of the accounting of its licensees, may require that political expenditures be charged to surplus rather than to operating expense and thus compel the stockholders rather than the customers of the utility to pay the cost of propaganda.

[41] Louise Overacker, "Labor's Political Contributions," *Political Science Quarterly,* 54 (1939), p. 59.

began for restrictive legislation, in which Republicans were far more active than Democrats.

The Smith-Connally Act of 1943 restricted union contributions for the duration of the war, and in 1947, in the Taft-Hartley Act, Congress placed corporations and labor organizations permanently on the same footing. It was made unlawful for

. . . any corporation whatever, or any labor organization to make a contribution or expenditure in connection with any election at which Presidential and Vice Presidential electors or a Senator or Representative in, or a Delegate or Resident Commissioner to Congress are to be voted for, or in connection with any primary election or political convention or caucus held to select candidates for any of the foregoing offices.

The language of the statute is not so restrictive as it may seem.[42] The most clear-cut effect of the act is to prohibit contributions from union treasuries—from funds built up from union dues—to campaigns for President, Senator, and Representative. Even that proscription may be violated from time to time directly or indirectly. Campaign literature can go through union as well as corporate mailing rooms.

A major consequence of the statute has been the use of specially created political affiliates of unions; the campaign funds of these organizations come from contributions solicited from union members for political purposes rather than from dues. The peak labor political committee is COPE —the Committee on Political Education of the AFL-CIO. It represents an amalgamation of the Labor's League for Political Education of the AFL and the CIO Political Action Committee. COPE and its related units in the national unions, the locals, and the state federations are not labor organizations as defined by the federal statute. They are free to solicit funds and to make contributions and expenditures in national elections. Yet the necessity of raising special political funds rather than using regular union revenues limits labor. The collection of large sums in small amounts is no easier for labor organizations than it is for political parties.[43]

While the prohibition of union contributions is unequivocal, a good

[42] For a treatment of the history and interpretation of the legislation, see Joseph Tanenhaus, "Organized Labor's Political Spending: The Law and Its Consequences," *Journal of Politics*, 16 (1954), pp. 441-471.

[43] Charges recur that union political education committees extort contributions from unionists. That may happen from time to time, but it is doubtful that such coercion is either more effective or more prevalent than the pressure that can be brought by a finance committee headed by the town's leading banker on businessmen or by the president of a corporation on his vice-presidents. For a discussion of practices in raising funds among businessmen, see Duncan Norton-Taylor, "How to Give Money to Politicians," *Fortune*, May, 1956, pp. 113-117.

deal of logic-chopping goes into the determination of what is and is not permissible under the proscription of expenditures. The Supreme Court's interpretation of the term has left some leeway for the expenditure of funds from union treasuries. It held that the statute did not apply to expenditures in the publication and distribution of issues of *The CIO News* containing endorsements of candidates for Congress. Purchase of newspaper advertising and radio time by a small union lacking a newspaper of its own has also been held to be beyond the statutory prohibition.[44] Such rulings encouraged extensive use of the labor press in campaigns.

Unions interpret the statute to permit expenditures for "educational" purposes from general union funds.[45] Such activities include the conduct of registration drives, the publication and distribution of the voting records of members of Congress, and general education about public affairs. The union contention is that expenditures for such purposes are not in connection with the election of any candidate and thus are not prohibited by the law.[46]

The federal statute does not reach contributions from union treasuries to campaigns for state and local office. Some states prohibit such use of union funds, but their laws do not affect labor committees in their solicitation of voluntary contributions.[47] In a few states unions have been a major source of Democratic funds, and Republicans have sought prohibitory legislation, which is justified on the ground that union membership is often, in fact, compulsory and that political financing from union treasuries amounts to compulsory levies against Republican unionists to support Democratic candidates. In 1955 the Wisconsin legislature, by a strict party vote in both houses, enacted prohibitory legislation. In the course

[44] United States *v.* Congress of Industrial Organization, 335 U.S. 106 (1948); United States *v.* Painters Local Union No. 281, 172 F. (2d) 854 (1949).

[45] In 1957 litigation was in process on the constitutionality of the prohibition of union expenditures. The United Auto Workers was charged with making expenditures to pay for television programs supporting Democratic candidates for Senate and House. The lower court threw out the indictment but the Supreme Court sent the case back for trial before ruling on the constitutional questions. In a dissent Justices Douglas and Black argued that the statute as applied was "a broadside assault on the freedom of political expression guaranteed by the first amendment."— United States *v.* United Auto Workers, 77 S. Ct. 529 (1957). In the subsequent trial the lower court acquitted the UAW and thereby prevented consideration by the Supreme Court of the constitutional issues posed by the case.

[46] See the testimony of Jack Kroll and James L. McDevitt, of COPE, in Gore Committee, *Hearings*, Pt. I, pp. 45–65.

[47] The Alabama statute was held unconstitutional because a like prohibition had not been applied to employers' associations.—Alabama State Federation of Labor *v.* McAdory, 18 So. (2d) 810 (1944).

of the debate it was said that the law would cut off 40 per cent of the revenues of the Democratic party in the state.[48]

Another control of the source of party revenue is the prohibition of the assessment of public employees. Legislation to prohibit assessments is designed to protect government employees as well as to deny this source of revenue to those in power. The defenders—and there are defenders—of the practice of assessment contend that by raising funds in this fashion the party is able to maintain an independence of wealthy contributors and vested interests. The Federal Civil Service Act of 1883 forbade the solicitation or receipt by any officer or employee of the United States of any "assessment, subscription or contribution, for any political purpose whatever" from any other federal officer or employee. Persons not employees of the government may solicit voluntary contributions from employees so long as the solicitation does not occur on government premises; occasionally these collections amount to assessments. Federal legislation also prohibits assessments of state and local employees paid wholly or in part from federal grants or loans, a provision that covers large numbers of state and local workers. Less than half the states prohibit assessments against state and municipal employees generally.

Contractors, suppliers, and other persons having financial transactions with the government have been important donors to campaign funds. In corrupt situations contractors may be virtually compelled to contribute to the party treasury. The 1940 amendment to the Hatch Act attempted to prevent contributions from persons dealing with the federal government. The act prohibits contributions by contractors and the solicitation of contractors for contributions "during the period of negotiation for, or performance" of a contract with a federal agency.

Limitation of amounts spent. A persistent objective of the regulators of party finance has been to limit the amounts spent in campaigns. The electorate may be overwhelmed by extravagantly supported propaganda, or

---

[48] Public policy toward the use of union funds in politics has been a warm issue in Great Britain. Until 1927 unions could use dues for political purposes unless the dues-payer had "contracted-out," that is, specified that he did not wish to pay dues for that purpose. The Conservative government in 1927 enacted legislation requiring that members "contract-in," that is, agree specifically and individually to pay dues for political purposes. In 1946 the Labor government restored the pre-1927 rule. The Georgia Supreme Court in 1957 adopted, in effect, the "contract-in" rule in a decision in which it held unenforcible mandatory union membership under the Railway Labor Act when the union used dues "to promote ideological and political issues and candidates" opposed by the worker. That interpretation may or may not prevail when the issue reaches the United States Supreme Court.

plutocratic elements may prevail—conditions scarcely compatible with popular government. The statutes express the moral judgment of legislators that excessive sums should not be spent in campaigns yet they do not actually restrict expenditures. If the laws in force have any effect, they probably contribute to the disorganization of the parties, help conceal the size and sources of campaign funds, and bring about a more immediate sense of indebtedness of candidates to donors.

In the Hatch Act of 1940 Congress laid down this rule: "No political committee shall receive contributions aggregating more than $3,000,000, or make expenditures aggregating more than $3,000,000 during any calendar year." Before this enactment national committees had on occasion spent more than $3,000,000 in presidential election years. The consequence of the limitation was the creation of committees, more or less independent of the national committee, each of which could raise and spend $3,000,000 and keep within the law. Citizens for Eisenhower-Nixon or Volunteers for Stevenson-Kefauver serve to help the parties comply with the Hatch Act as well as to campaign.

A multiplicity of committees has always existed, but often independent committees were but fronts for the party's national committee. The existence of several national-level committees, each with its own funds, complicates the task of campaign management and tends to divide party leadership at the top. Moreover, the limitation on the national committee reduces its earlier importance as a fund-raising agency which disbursed funds to state committees and to individual House and Senate candidates. These national subventions gave some leverage to national headquarters in its leadership of state committees and enabled the national headquarters to do more than is now legally possible to aid its congressional candidates. Central collection incidentally permitted contributions to be pooled in a common fund from whence they flowed to congressional candidates, a procedure that permitted to some degree the creation of an obligation by the candidate to the party rather than to the individual donor.

By the Corrupt Practices Act, which long antedated the Hatch Act, Congress limited the amount to be spent by "a candidate" for the House or Senate in his election campaign, and thereby excluded from the restriction expenditures in the primary campaign and those made by other persons in behalf of the candidate. The federal limits, unless the law of the state sets a lower maximum, are $10,000 for a senatorial candidate and $2,500 for a House candidate. For the larger states and districts the limits are variable, depending on the size of the vote cast in the last election but in no case may they exceed $25,000 for the Senate and $5,000 for the House. Expenditures for certain purposes, for example, postage, are not included within the limitation. The restraining effect of the federal law is purely illusory.

Most states also have laws placing limits on the size of expenditures in campaigns for state and local offices. Limits set in specified sums are most common although they are sometimes related to the size of the salary of the office or to the number of voters. Whatever their form, the laws ordinarily fix unrealistic limits but contain loopholes commodious enough to permit the business of politics to proceed without violation of the terms of the statute.

Statutes limiting the size of campaign outlays are declaratory of righteous indignation about huge expenditures rather than restrictive of behavior. Yet the technical obstacles to limitation are formidable. What size must campaign funds be to enable candidates and party committees to reach the voters with the minimum essential information? That basic question has never been examined. Instead nice round figures have been pulled from the air and written into the law. Another major problem arises from the organization of campaigns themselves. Enforcement of a limitation can rest only on a centralization of authority for expenditure in the campaign. With an exception or so, no American legislative body has been able to bring itself to require that all campaign expenditures go through a treasurer or manager designated by the candidate. Such a centralization of authority would provide a basis for limiting outlays only in those situations in which individual campaigns are conducted without much relation to other simultaneous races, as in the primaries of some one-party states. When the party committees, committees for federal, state, and local candidates, and other committees campaign side by side for a ticket of candidates whose fortunes are interrelated, restriction of the level of expenditure becomes almost impossible.

Limitation of size of individual contribution. Large contributions carry the risk that individual campaign donors will provide so large a share of the costs of a campaign that the party committee or the official concerned will be owned by the big giver. In 1940 in the Hatch Act amendments Congress prohibited gifts of over $5,000 in any one year to the campaign of "any candidate for an elective Federal office" or to any committee campaigning on behalf of candidates for federal office or on behalf of a national party. The law explicitly excluded state and local committees from the restriction. Another sort of big gift not affected by the law is a transfer from one committee to another. A labor committee may pool voluntary collections of a dollar and convert them into gifts that are large proportions of the budgets of some campaigns.

The obvious route for avoidance of the limit has been followed. Persons who wish to give over $5,000 make gifts within that limit to each of several committees or to the campaigns of several candidates for the House and Senate. Or they may make gifts of any size to state committees and keep within the federal law. At times several gifts from the same family, each within the legal limitation, bring the charge that the old patriarch has given sums of legal size in the names of his nieces and nephews.[49] The gift tax probably is more effective in keeping down the size of contributions than is the Hatch Act. The tax is complicated but the practical effect for exceptionally wealthy—and generous—individuals is that political contributions of over $3,000 to any single donee in a single year are taxable.[50]

The restriction on the size of gifts—combined with the restriction on the level of expenditures by the national committee—probably encourages wealthy individuals to spread gifts to the campaigns of House and Senate candidates over the country. In the absence of the Hatch Act an alternative which could, but not necessarily would, be followed would be a single large donation to the senatorial, congressional, or national committee, which in turn could aid individual candidates. The alternative mode of financing should create a less-intimate financial nexus between the big giver and the candidate.

Limitation of purpose of expenditure. Expenditures for specified purposes are prohibited chiefly by state legislation. The earlier tendency in legislative drafting was to prohibit expenditures thought to be corrupt. Bribery of voters, for example, is everywhere unlawful. In various states expenditures are prohibited for treating, for conveying voters to the polls, and for election-day workers. The more recent legislative technique has been to specify the objects for which money may legitimately be spent. Well over half of the states have legislation enumerating lawful items of expenditure, which items vary from state to state. Whatever the form of the legislation, the limitations do not hamper campaigning.

[49] A favorite pastime of the analysts of campaign reports is the identification of members of the same family who contribute. Thus, in 1956 the records showed that members of the du Pont family contributed $248,000; of the Rockefeller family, $152,000.—Gore Committee, *Report*, pp. 65–66. Such figures do not in themselves indicate any intent to take advantage of the loopholes of the Hatch Act. About all that they prove is that a du Pont or a Rockefeller would be astonished if he lived through a campaign without being solicited by a Republican finance committee.

[50] For an analysis of the gift tax, see the testimony of Justin F. Winkle, Assistant Commissioner of Internal Revenue, Gore Committee, *Hearings*, Pt. 2, pp. 352–362.

What the Money Buys

The cynical view that a campaign contribution is equivalent to a bribe at times indubitably matches the facts. Yet the significance of money in politics can be grasped only by a view that places party finance in the total context of the political process. It is probably fair enough to conclude that men of wealth on the whole use money in politics to protect what they regard as their interests. Their votes are few in a regime of popular government and they build their political defenses by the use of money. Others have votes; they have money. The two are, if not in perpetual conflict, always potentially at loggerheads.

Such statements about the concern of moneyed interests in politics may be generally correct. The difficulty comes in filling in the details, the shadings, the rights and wrongs. That the unbridled dominance of money would run counter to the tenets of a democratic order may be indisputable. On the other hand, a democratic regime that tyrannized men of wealth would both commit injustice and perhaps destroy its instruments of production. The pragmatic question about the power of money in politics may come down to one of how much power and how that power is used. The abuse of that power may generate disharmonies among the elements of the political order or produce intolerable oppression. On the American scene in some eras the power of wealth has seemed to be without check, but days of reckoning also seem sooner or later to arrive. A considerable body of social and regulatory legislation, enacted over the determined opposition of most men of wealth, serves as evidence of the strength of the counterpoises against wealth. Money has its power in politics but that power has its limits.

Certain practices and customs in campaign finance mitigate or at least gloss over the role of money. Not all the money, not even all the big money, is on the same side. Competition and conflict among those of wealth seep over into the party battle and the general public is sometimes the beneficiary. Moreover, on the national scene the etiquette seems to be that large contributions are made not in expectation of a specific quid pro quo for the individual contributor. The giver rather supports the party whose general outlook seems both most congenial to him and most likely to further his interests. Once the victory is won the contributor can certainly expect to have access to government, to have his views heard sympathetically if not invariably heeded.[51] The power of money may, thus,

---

[51] Consider a statement by Senator John L. McClellan, of Arkansas: "I don't think anybody that gave me a contribution ever felt he was buying my vote or anything like that, but he certainly felt he had an entree to me to discuss things with me and I was under obligation at least to give him an audience when he desired it to

come as much from the fear that the contributor of today may contribute to an opponent at the next election as from the recipient's gratitude for past favors. Even as powerful a Congressman as John Nance Garner in 1928 had to fight opposition financed from outside his district to punish him for his support of the federal estate tax, or so he charged. And, in 1957, the Republican national chairman saw fit to report to the President that the Administration's budget policy was slowing up income from the big givers.

All this is not to deny that from time to time—how often, nobody knows—campaign contributions purchase specific action. A party or a candidate that encounters great difficulty in raising the money absolutely necessary to meet campaign expenses may be under an especially strong pressure to make concrete commitments in exchange for financial support. It may be—and there are scraps of evidence to support the view—that the party or candidate least dedicated to the cause of wealth tends more to put itself under obligation to do specific favors for contributors somewhat beyond the fringe of respectability. Dog-track operators do not let their ideology warp their political judgment; they can do business with either a liberal or a conservative; their chief concern is that they deal with a winner.

No rigorous examination has been made of the bearing of the size of campaign funds on the outcome of popular elections. A census of all races for all offices—congressional, state, local—would probably show that most, but by no means all, winners had had the longer campaign purses.[52] Even so, the question would remain whether money had turned the trick. Winners have a habit of attracting money. Yet it seems equally clear that in the really great elections, the presidential sweepstakes, the size of the campaign chest does not in itself control the outcome—although big donors may not be neglected after the election. The string of Democratic victories from 1936 to 1948 was accomplished against superior Republican financial resources. Money is not the sole currency of politics; Roosevelt held counters in the game that outweighed money. Nor can it be convincingly argued that superiority in campaign funds had a controlling influence in the Eisenhower victories of 1952 and 1956, although an ample supply of cash was a great convenience to the campaign managers.

The problem raised by the size of campaign funds has not been so much that the longer purse would prevail but that the less-well financed party

hear his views."—U.S. Senate, 84th Cong., 2d sess., Special Committee to Investigate Political Activities, Lobbying, and Campaign Contributions, *Hearings*, pursuant to S. Res. 219 and S. Res. 47 (1957), p. 1046.

[52] See George Lundberg, "Campaign Expenditures and Election Results," *Social Forces*, 6 (1928), pp. 452–457.

could not get its case before the public or make an effective challenge. In presidential politics in recent campaigns this has been essentially a problem of Democratic finance. The managers of the Democratic campaigns of 1948, 1952, and 1956 struggled with recurring financial crises. Hours before a scheduled broadcast the money would not be available to pay the bill—which the broadcasters prudently insist shall be paid in advance. Or the till would not contain enough to move the candidate's special train more than a couple of hundred miles up the track. Votes may outweigh dollars, but a tribune of the people who aspires to be President needs enough money to meet the rockbottom campaign necessities. To some extent labor organizations have replaced the men of means who moved away from the Democrats in 1936, yet the party on the national level has chronic financial difficulties.

For two decades after 1936, regularly after each presidential campaign, a congressional committee recommended revision of the federal legislation, and with equal regularity no action was taken. The preponderant opinion developed that statutory limitations of the size of campaign funds were futile and that perhaps the most effective regulation would be an insistence upon full publicity of campaign receipts and expenditures. While the most stringent efforts to ferret out and punish the grosser forms of campaign corruption are always in order, probably the cures of the problems of finance are not regulatory. By the expenditure of energy and ingenuity in the raising of funds parties could broaden the base of contributors and thus both reduce their obligation to a few big contributors and meet the bills. Success in these directions would require heroic efforts, and proposals have been made for government aid in various forms. Direct public subsidy to the parties, the public provision of fixed amounts of radio and television time to the principal candidates, and the encouragement of many small contributions by provisions for small income-tax credits are some of the proposals that have been made.[53]

[53] A special Senate committee under the chairmanship of John L. McClellan recommended in 1957 a thorough revision of the statutes governing campaign finance. See Senate Report No. 395, 85th Cong., 1st sess. (1957). Some experimentation has been attempted in the states. A 1955 Minnesota law permits certain deductions of political contributions under the state income-tax law. California has a similar statute. In 1957 Puerto Rico enacted legislation to grant government subsidies to the parties of the island.

19 | Presidential Elections

To THE electorate falls a crucial role in the democratic process. The nature of that role is fixed by the choices presented to the electorate by the party leaderships. Thus the electoral role in a biparty system differs radically from that in a multiparty order. In one instance the voters decide which party is to govern; in the other, the election may be only a census of shades of opinion within the electorate.

The place of the electorate in the political system has been described in many ways. Perhaps only in a biparty regime can the electorate be likened to a jury and its vote to a verdict. Less persuasive is the frequent personification of the electorate as a giant of a man who speaks at times in commanding tones, at times in riddles. Again, the electorate is compared to groups of sports fans, to spectators cheering for their favorite teams. Or it is pictured as built of antagonistic groups battling for economic self-interest or for ideological causes. Students of electoral behavior seek to identify factors guiding the individual voter to decision: his political inheritance, his friends, his associates, his group affiliatons, his sources of information among the media. All these and other ways of viewing the electorate have their merits—and their limitations. The anthropomorphic erection of the great person of "the people" represents organismic fiction. On the other hand, concentration of attention on the individual voter pulverizes the electorate and diverts attention from its collective role in the process of governance.

Another approach toward an understanding of the function of the electorate is to regard elections as great collective decisions. What is the nature of the popular verdict in a presidential election? True, a thousand different "reasons" may explain the votes of individuals. But can a broad meaning be plausibly attributed to the results of a presidential election if it is examined in its total situational context and in its place in the stream of events? By such a view the nature of great popular decisions in presidential elections may possibly be divined. A rough categorization of presidential elections according to the dominant character of the popular decision may be attempted. Each election, to be sure, is unique; elections cannot be grouped neatly into pigeonholes. Nevertheless an attempt to identify types of elections may suggest clues to the nature of collective electoral decision.[1]

[1] American students are familiar with the mechanics of the election of the President. For others it should be explained that the mode of election is, in form, indirect. The President is chosen by an electoral college for a term of four years. To constitute the electoral college each state appoints, "in such manner as the legislature thereof may direct, a number of electors equal to the whole number of Senators and Representatives to which the State may be entitled in Congress."—Constitution, Art. II. The electors meet in each state and vote by ballot. The votes are counted by the President of the Senate. A majority of the electoral votes is necessary for election. In the absence of a majority, the House of Representatives chooses from among the three persons with the highest number of votes. The House votes by states, each state having one vote.—Constitution, Amendment XII.

In practice the state legislatures have directed that the electors be chosen at large by popular vote within each state. The candidates for electors are nominated, through various procedures, by the parties within the states. The voters of a state may have a choice between slates of electors nominated by the Republican and Democratic organizations within the state. Each slate of electors, if it wins, is bound, chiefly by custom, to cast its electoral votes for the presidential candidate nominated by the national convention of its party. Violations of the customary obligation are most infrequent. The Supreme Court has held that a state legislature may permit state parties to require of their nominees for elector a pledge to vote for the party's candidate.— Ray *v.* Blair, 343 U.S. 214 (1952). Despite his commitment by a pledge under the statute under which this case arose, one Alabama Democratic elector in 1956 cast his vote not for Stevenson but for Walter B. Jones, an Alabama judge. See Ruth C. Silva, "State Law on the Nomination, Election, and Instruction of Presidential Electors," *American Political Science Review*, 42 (1948), pp. 523–529; Robert G. Dixon, Jr., "Electoral College Procedure," *Western Political Quarterly*, 3 (1950), pp. 214–224.

Proposals for a modification of the method of election of the President received ex-

Landslides: Votes of Lack of Confidence

One category of elections appears quickly from an inspection of presidential elections in the quest for an understanding of electoral decision. On occasion the electorate votes a party out of power in a decisive manner; it expresses clearly a lack of confidence in the crowd that has been in charge of affairs. The mandate to the incoming party may be vague, and, indeed, it may be difficult to read into the vote a bill of explicit dissatisfactions with the party that has been cast out of office. Yet the election clearly expresses a widespread unhappiness over past performance. To this sort of election the term landslide may be applied, although that word in common usage means, unhappily, any election won by a large plurality. In those landslides that express a lack of confidence, the party in power, in comparison with the preceding election, loses voting strength in most counties of the country. Although the data are lacking, the odds are that the decline in strength also permeates most social and economic classes.

In a landslide the might of the electorate in a democratic order appears in a most spectacular fashion. The people may not be able to govern them-

---

tensive attention by Congress in the 1940's and 1950's. Among the agitators for change were southern politicians who believed that Negro and labor groups in politically close nonsouthern states with large numbers of electoral votes were able to compel presidential candidates to cater to them. Other groups were moved by a desire to adopt procedures that would make impossible the victory of a candidate with fewer popular votes than another as well as by other motives. The principal proposals for reform were:

1. To substitute a direct popular vote by a national constituency for the present system.

2. To require the choice of those electors corresponding in number to the state's Representatives, from congressional districts rather than by general ticket at large. The fact that the congressional districts, as drawn by the state legislatures, give advantage to Republicans attracted support for this proposal from that party.

3. To retain the present allotment of electoral votes among the states, but to abolish the electors and to provide for the division of the electoral votes of each state among the presidential candidates in the same proportions as the state's popular vote is divided among them.

Various combinations of the second and third proposals as well as varying formulations of all three proposals have been considered by Congress.—See Ruth C. Silva, "The Lodge-Gossett Resolution: A Critical Analysis," *American Political Science Review,* 44 (1950), pp. 86–99, and her "Reform of the Electoral System," *Review of Politics,* 14 (1952), pp. 394–407. See also Lucius Wilmerding, Jr., "Congress Faces Electoral Reform," *National Review,* March 7, 1956. Extensive analyses of the proposals appear in *Nomination and Election of President and Vice President,* being Hearings before a Subcommittee of the Committee on the Judiciary, U.S. Senate, 84th Cong., 1st sess., on S.J. Res. 3 and other resolutions (March, April, 1955). Useful also are the analyses appearing in speeches by Senator Paul H. Douglas in the *Congressional Record,* March 26 and 29, 1956. For a chronology of presidential elections, see E. H. Roseboom, *A History of Presidential Elections* (New York: Macmillan, 1957).

selves but they can, through an electoral uprising, throw the old crowd out and demand a new order, without necessarily being capable of specifying exactly what it shall be. An election of this type may amount, if not to revolution, to its functional equivalent.

The election of 1932. The characteristics of the presidential election of 1932 correspond closely to those of the model of a landslide marking a general withdrawal of popular confidence in the party in power. The Great Depression brought injury not only to farmers and industrial workers but to employers, financiers, merchants, and all classes of people. The Republican Administration floundered as disaster piled upon disaster, and Mr. Hoover became the symbol of the many ills that beset many people. The polling of 1932 expressed unmistakably discontent against Mr. Hoover and his party; his proportion of the two-party vote declined from 58.8 per cent in 1928 to 40.9 per cent in 1932, an exceptionally wide movement of voters.

The shift away from the Republican party between 1928 and 1932 occurred almost everywhere. An analysis by counties according to the increase in the Democratic percentage of the vote appears in Table 19.1. In

Table 19.1

Landslide Elections: Distribution of Counties According to Percentage Point Shift in Popular Vote, 1928–1932 and 1948–1952 [a]

Percentage Point Shift	Per Cent of Counties with Democratic Gains, 1928–1932 [b]	Per Cent of Counties with Republican Gains, 1948–1952 [c]
0–9	8.4	31.3
10–19	28.0	42.0
20–29	36.5	16.6
30–39	17.6	4.9
40–49	4.6	2.6
50 and over	3.9	1.6
Counties moving counter to trend [d]	1.0	1.0
	100.0	100.0

[a] For each election the proportions of counties rest on a sample of every tenth county alphabetically listed by states.

[b] The shift is measured by the difference in the Democratic percentage of the two-party vote.

[c] The shift is measured by the difference between the Republican percentage of the three-party vote in 1948 and the Republican percentage of the total vote in 1952.

[d] The widest movement counter to the trend among the counties in these cells of the samples was six percentage points.

99 per cent of the counties of the country Mr. Hoover's proportion of the popular vote declined from 1928 to 1932; in over one-fourth of them the Republican strength dropped by more than 30 percentage points. Although sample surveys were not then in operation, other evidence suggests that declines in Republican strength occurred in all income and occupational groups. The election was not a revolt of the downtrodden; rather an antipathy toward the Administration and a yearning for something different penetrated all social strata.[2]

Other landslides. The 1932 election may be regarded as a prototype of the electoral decision that expresses a lack of confidence in the party in power. When one seeks to identify other elections that fit nicely into the same category, the limitations of any typology of elections become embarrassingly clear. The presidential election of 1952, however, in certain ways resembled that of 1932 and may be placed in the same general class. Although different groups of people were animated by different motives, most classes of people shifted in some degree away from the Democratic party between 1948 and 1952. The total effect was a clear-cut withdrawal of majority support from the Democratic party. The spread of that shift in sentiment over the country is suggested by the data of Table 19.1. In 99 per cent of the counties the Republican proportion of the presidential vote increased between 1948 and 1952. The survey data indicate that the movement to the Republicans occurred also in almost all demographic groups. Republican gains were least marked in upper income and occupational groups, presumably in part because by 1948 Republicans had enlisted almost their maximum possible support among these categories of people. The data of the Survey Research Center on the partisan divisions of income levels in 1948 and 1952 appear in Table 19.2.

The election of 1952 may have been a vote of lack of confidence in the Democratic party, but the results provided no explicit policy directives for the incoming Administration.[3] The electorate may make unequivocal judgments on past performance or between candidates but its prescriptions for future action are blurred. The surveys indicated that the new

[2] See Roy V. Peel and T. C. Donnelly, *The 1932 Campaign* (New York: Farrar & Rinehart, 1935).

[3] Hyman and Sheatsley, on the basis of polls in the fall of 1947 and 1948, consider it probable that "Eisenhower could have been elected President on either major party ticket, in either 1948 or 1952." They surmise that "the issues of Communism, corruption and Korea, over which the 1952 campaign was fought, were of decidedly less importance than was the simple candidacy of Dwight D. Eisenhower."—"The Political Appeal of President Eisenhower," *Public Opinion Quarterly*, 17 (1953–54), pp. 443–460. See also J. C. Davies, "Charisma in the 1952 Campaign," *American Political Science Review*, 48 (1954), pp. 1083–1102.

Table 19.2

Partisan Divisions in Presidential Elections of 1948 and 1952 by Income Levels [a]

	Voted:			Did Not Vote
	Republican	Democratic	Other	
1952				
Under $2,000	30%	23%	b	47%
$2,000–2,999	36	31	1	32
$3,000–3,999	40	35	1	24
$4,000–4,999	41	41	1	17
$5,000 and over	59	28	1	12
1948				
Under $2,000	16%	28%	2	54%
$2,000–2,999	17	38	6	39
$3,000–3,999	35	34	5	26
$4,000–4,999	36	33	6	25
$5,000 and over	53	25	4	18

[a] From Angus Campbell and others, *The Voter Decides* (Evanston: Row, Peterson, 1954), p. 73.
[b] Less than 1 per cent.

Republicans tended to adhere to Democratic policies; the major foundation of the Republican victory consisted of persons who had voted Democratic in 1948, who had a Democratic policy orientation, and who continued to regard themselves as Democrats.[4]

The policy shadings of the electoral decision had to be discovered as the new Administration felt its ways along diverse courses of action. The Republican party had won a mandate to govern, but the limits of that mandate were fuzzy. Old-guard Republicans gleefully concluded that they had been instructed to repeal the New Deal. As the Administration probed to locate the limits of its mandate in field after field it found it prudent to pull back from positions taken initially and to maintain substantially the status quo in policy. The obstructions encountered in Congress, the congressional elections of 1954, the protests of pressure groups, and popular attitudes communicated to government by other means contributed to the definition of the terms of popular support of the Administration.

These remarks suggest some of the limits of the role of elections in the American democratic process. Elections measure only one dimension of public sentiment. The details of the electoral verdict have to be filled in

[4] On these points, see Angus Campbell and others, *The Voter Decides*, ch. 12.

by other modes of consultation of the public. Elections are only one of the means by which popular influence plays upon government in a democratic order.[5]

Reaffirmation of Support: Votes of Confidence

In another type of presidential election substantially the same coalition of voters prevails as provided the majority in the preceding election. Such an election may be regarded as a vote of confidence in the general course of action the Administration has followed. Not all re-elections of Presidents or all instances in which the President succeeds another of the same party can be placed in this category. In some elections the Administration is returned to power but with substantial losses among one or more groups of voters and perhaps compensating gains among other groups. An ideal type of election as a simple vote of confidence would be one in which the party lines within the electorate had remained stable since the preceding polling.

Elections of 1900, 1904, and 1908. No election completely meets the specifications for a vote of confidence as it has been defined. Invariably from one election to the next some voters cross party lines in both directions. Others become disillusioned and decide to stay at home on election day. Yet in their broad context the elections of 1900, 1904, and 1908 may be regarded as reaffirmations of the vote of confidence won by the Republican party in the decisive election of 1896.

It seems probable that elections that build up social tension to extremely high peaks are followed by a let down in the intensity of antagonism. The frenzied exertions of campaigners in such an election sharpen cleavages, produce a high turnout of voters on both sides, and perhaps mobilize the maximum strength of the minority. The outcome of the battle clearly establishes the supremacy of the victors, and the vote of the minority sags at the next election as it becomes apparent that all is lost anyway. Even the winning party, confident of its position, may drop strength here and there as its campaign efforts do not suffice to bring out its potential strength.

This sort of pattern seems to fit roughly the elections of 1896 and 1900. The silverites in the election of 1896 fought a losing battle but in so doing

[5] The election of 1920 probably also belongs in our category of landslide elections. From 1916 to 1920, the Democratic percentage of the two-party vote declined from 51.7 to 36.1. Examination of the 1920 returns also suggests that one might form a category consisting of elections that mark a restoration of an equilibrium established at an earlier, landmark election. The county by county vote in 1920, for example, in some states closely resembled that of 1896, with the notable exception of Republican gains in some counties populated by ethnic groups antagonized by Democratic foreign policy.

they exerted themselves mightily in their own domain to produce a maximum vote for Bryan, the Democratic candidate. The election statistics make it look as though in the mining states every prospector voted and perhaps twice. The plebiscite of 1896 clearly settled the silver question and in 1900 McKinley easily won re-election. The most marked differences in the voting in 1896 and 1900 were in the western mining states. The mine owners did not pour money into the campaign this time; their cause was clearly lost. McKinley polled a markedly higher vote in the mining states than he had in 1896 while in many of the northeastern and southern states his strength dropped slightly.[6]

The candidacy in 1904 of the picturesque Theodore Roosevelt on the Republican ticket and of the conservative Democrat Alton B. Parker created a set of choices different from those presented to the voters in 1900. Yet the election of 1904 may be fitted into our general category of votes of confidence. The flamboyant Roosevelt with his progressive oratorical flourishes attracted new Republican support west of the Mississippi.[7] Eastern Republicans tolerated the forensics and supported him in slightly higher degree than they had McKinley in 1900. These contrasts in the shifts in the West and in the East between 1900 and 1904 are illustrated in detail for California and Indiana by the scatter-diagrams in Figure 19.1, which compare the Republican percentage of the vote, county by county, in the two elections. In Indiana, a state with a long history of tightly organized two-party politics, Roosevelt made gains over McKinley in most counties, but in California this gain was far more marked.

William Howard Taft in 1908 lacked Teddy Roosevelt's special appeal to the West but he managed to hold together the main elements of the coalition that had supported Roosevelt in 1904. The vote for Taft resembled more closely the 1900 vote for McKinley than it did the 1904 vote for Roosevelt. Most of the states with marked Republican losses from 1904 to 1908 were western states in which Roosevelt had drawn heavy new support in 1904.[8] By and large in the East Taft held the Republican support of 1904. Comparisons by county of the vote in 1904

[6] From 1896 to 1900 Republican proportion of the popular vote increased by more than 10 percentage points in Colorado, Idaho, Montana, Nevada, Utah, Washington, and Wyoming.

[7] All the states, save one, in which the Republican percentage of the total presidential vote increased more than 10 percentage points from 1900 to 1904 were west of the Mississippi. They were Colorado, Idaho, Kansas, Michigan, Minnesota, Montana, Nebraska, Nevada, North Dakota, Oregon, South Dakota, Utah, and Washington.

[8] The states in which the Republican proportion of the total presidential vote declined by more than 8 percentage points were Colorado, Idaho, Kansas, Minnesota, Nebraska, Nevada, North Dakota, Ohio, Oregon, Pennsylvania, South Dakota, Washington, Wisconsin, and Wyoming.

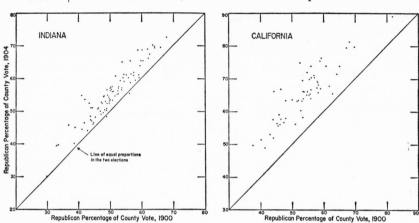

Figure 19.1. Presidential Elections of 1900 and 1904 in Indiana and California: Comparisons of Republican Percentage of Vote by Counties

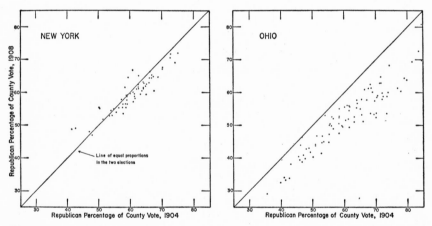

Figure 19.2. Presidential Elections of 1904 and 1908 in New York and Ohio: Comparisons of Republican Percentage of Vote by Counties

and 1908 for the states of New York and Ohio, which appear in Figure 19.2, contrast the situation in a state in which the party lines held with a state in which the Republican strength declined.

1948: Reactivation of the New Deal coalition. In important aspects of the electoral behavior involved, the election of 1948 deviates from our model of a pure vote of confidence; yet in its broad context that election amounted to a vote of confidence in the Democratic Administration. Since 1932 the Republican party had been attempting to crack the new Democratic coalition. That combination held together against attack with the notable exceptions of the defections of 1940 and 1944 on foreign policy questions. In the congressional elections of 1946 Republicans won majorities of Congress and proceeded to act as if they had a mandate to reverse New Deal policies.

In his forthright campaign of 1948 President Truman unequivocally championed the principal elements of the New Deal and Fair Deal. In contrast Governor Dewey followed a statesmanlike course; that is, his ambiguous utterances left doubt about his party's position on measures of interest to the component blocs of the Democratic coalition. In the voting those groups of voters who had constituted the backbone of New Deal support rallied to the Democratic banner and confounded Republican expectations.

Mr. Truman's espousal of civil rights legislation yielded especially strong support among Negroes; the rebellion of the States' Rights Democrats aided in the retention and recruitment of Negro support. Industrial workers concurred with Truman's opposition to the Taft-Hartley Act and gave him their vote in high degree. Those Catholics who had been alienated by the wartime alliance with the Soviets found their return to the Democracy simplified by the defection of the Wallaceites. Midwestern farmers, antagonized by Republican congressional policy on agriculture, also made their way back to the Democratic party, a movement facilitated by the end of the war and the temporary lull on the foreign front. Metropolitan consumers were held in line by Truman's defense of controls over rents and prices.[9]

Group Alienation and Attraction: Realignments

A third type of presidential election usually involves a return of the Administration to power and in that sense might be regarded as a vote of confidence. Yet in this sort of election the Administration wins with the support of a coalition different from that comprising its majority at the preceding election. Large numbers of voters have been alienated and the support of others has been gained. The causes of these shifts are various. The Administration's policies may have repelled important groups of voters who desert its candidates in disenchantment; the same policies may well have also attracted new support. Or the movement may be in response to some characteristic of the candidate or feature of the pro-

[9] On the 1948 election, see Angus Campbell and Robert L. Kahn, *The People Elect A President* (Ann Arbor: Survey Research Center, 1952). The election of 1944, held in the midst of war, showed a remarkably small change in the aggregate vote since the preceding election, and would be classifiable as a vote of confidence or a popular decision to stand pat for the time being.

gram of the party challenging the ins. Thus, this sort of vote records a realignment among the groups supporting the parties, which may be either transient or durable. A specific policy or event may drive large proportions of a particular group of people from their traditional party attachment for a single election. Or the impact of policy or events may produce a durable realignment of the party loyalties of particular groups or classes of people.

Always from one presidential election to the next some voters meet each other as they cross party lines. Hence, all elections might be classified in the category of those that involve an attraction and a repulsion, a realignment. Nevertheless, some elections reshuffle voters on an extremely large scale. In other instances the magnitude of the realignment may not be so great but the electoral consequences of quite specific policies are readily identifiable and occur on a substantial scale: analysis of the voting makes it clear that fairly large numbers of voters have moved across party lines, apparently in response to the movement of events or to policy actions.

1928: Mixture of durable and transient realignment. The combination that put Herbert Hoover into office in 1928 differed from that which supported Coolidge in 1924. The issues of the campaign drew heavy new support to the Republican ticket from certain sectors of the population, drove 1924 Republicans to the Democratic banner, and attracted to it also the support of many persons who had probably not voted in 1924. In large measure the new Republican support was transient in character, while the accretions to the Democratic ranks were far more durable. The election marked the recruitment to the Democratic party of large numbers of voters who were to remain staunch supporters for at least two decades.

The issues of the campaign activated latent animosities that cut across old party loyalties. The candidacy of Alfred E. Smith, a Catholic with a progressive record as governor of New York, drew heavy, new Democratic support in the metropolitan, industrial, foreign-born, and Catholic populations. This growth in Democratic strength was also associated with exceptionally high rates of increase in voter turnout, which suggested that the Democratic appeals tapped elements of the population not politically active in the preceding election. Especially notable were the Democratic gains in the New England states, where Rhode Island and Massachusetts went Democratic. Smith's opposition to prohibition as well as his Catholicism redounded to the advantage of Hoover in the rural, dry, Protestant areas of the nation. While the Republican share of the vote increased over that of 1924 in most rural areas predominantly Protestant, the campaign yielded the greatest Republican dividends in the southern states. Hoover carried several states of the Solid South and in others the normal Democratic majorities were sharply reduced.[10] Illustrations of these contrasting movements within the electorate from 1924 to 1928 appear in Table 19.3.

Table 19.3

Realignment of 1928: Changes in Democratic Proportion of Presidential Vote, 1924–1928, in Selected States

Roman Catholic States			Protestant States		
State	Per Cent Catholic [a]	Democratic Gain, 1924–1928 [b]	State	Per Cent Catholic	Democratic Loss, 1924–1928
Rhode Island	47.3	13.7	Virginia	1.6	16.5
Massachusetts	38.3	25.5	Alabama	1.4	16.6
Connecticut	34.7	18.3	Tennessee	1.0	8.2
New Hampshire	31.5	6.5	Georgia	0.6	7.6
Vermont	24.9	17.3	S. Carolina	0.5	1.4
Maine	21.8	9.2	N. Carolina	0.2	13.8

[a] Number of Roman Catholics reported by 1926 census of religious bodies as a percentage of total 1930 population.

[b] Percentage point difference between 1924 Democratic percentage of three-party vote and 1928 Democratic percentage of two-party vote.

Although the Republicans triumphed in 1928, the campaign had the significant long-run result for the Democrats of creating abiding Democratic loyalties among metropolitan groups that had been either Republican or indifferent to politics. In its impact especially in the northeastern states the election might be called a critical election in the sense that it froze into the electorate cleavages that were to prevail, at least in their main outlines, through 1948. The widened differences of 1928 between the cities and the countryside of New England persisted in subsequent presidential elections. On the other hand, over most of the country, the Republican gains of 1928 were wiped out in 1932.[11]

[10] By an analysis by partial correlation of the 1928 vote in 173 randomly chosen counties in Massachusetts, New York, Ohio, Illinois, Wisconsin, Colorado, Montana, and California, W. F. Ogburn and N. S. Talbot found that the vote for Smith was more closely associated with antiprohibition sentiment than with Catholicism.—"A Measurement of the Factors in the Presidential Election of 1928," *Social Forces*, 8 (1929), pp. 175–183. See also E. A. Moore, *A Catholic Runs for President* (New York: Ronald, 1956).

[11] For a statement of the concept of a critical election and for a detailed examination of the 1928 election in New England, see Key, "A Theory of Critical Elections,"

1936: Ratification of the New Deal. In the realignments in the voting of 1936 the coalition built by the New Deal jelled. The 1932 voting had been characterized by accessions to Democratic strength among all classes of people. The unfolding of the Rooseveltian legislative program cemented additional support to the Democratic party and simultaneously drove back to the Republican party many who had voted for a change in 1932.

No survey data are available for 1932 and statements about the movements of voters between 1932 and 1936 must necessarily be guarded. Yet, on the basis of extensive analysis of the election returns, educated guesses are possible. The policies of the New Deal brought in 1936 substantial new support from their beneficiaries. Metropolitan, industrial workers turned in heavy Democratic majorities. The unemployed, and those who feared that they might become unemployed, voted Democratic in higher degree. Organized labor moved more solidly into the Democratic ranks. These movements amounted to a continuation and confirmation of the trends that began in 1928.

Defections from the Democratic ranks were most notable in the business groups and in some rural areas. The Republican campaign against the New Deal voiced the resentment of business groups at new government regulations, expressed anxieties about the new role granted to organized labor, and assaulted welfare policies, such as the Social Security Act and unemployment relief. In area after area the voting statistics reveal an upsurge of Democratic strength in 1932 followed by a decline in 1936.[12] The departure of the business elements from the Democratic party manifested itself graphically in party finance. Contributions by manufacturers and bankers to the Democratic war chest in 1936 aggregated less than half the sum from those sources in 1932. The 1936 Republican take from these classes of contributors more than doubled that of 1932.[13]

The return of a party to power under circumstances of the 1936 cam-

---

Journal of Politics, 17 (1955), pp. 3–18. This discussion of the 1928 election illustrates some of the difficulties of categorizing presidential elections. That election was critical in the sense that for some areas and groups the realignments of that year turned out to be quite durable. Yet in other parts of the country the Republican upsurge was only a momentary phenomenon. Probably the election of 1896 could be characterized more generally as critical. The Republican gains in 1896 turned out to be extraordinarily durable, although the western Democratic gains were more transient.

[12] Gallup poll estimates of the Democratic percentage of occupational groups in 1936 were: professional, 49; businessmen, 47; farmers, 59; white-collar workers, 61; skilled workers, 67; semiskilled workers, 74; unskilled workers, 81.—See E. G. Benson and Paul Perry, "Analysis of Democratic-Republican Strength by Population Groups," *Public Opinion Quarterly*, 4 (1940), pp. 464–473. On the 1932–1936 shifts in Iowa, see H. F. Gosnell and Norman Pearson, "The Study of Voting Behavior by Correlational Techniques," *American Sociological Review*, 4 (1939), pp. 809–815.

[13] See the chart at p. 545 of the third edition of this book.

paign gives such an election a special significance. Drastic innovations in public policy aroused the most bitter denunciation by the outs; the ins had to stand on their record. The electorate had before it the question whether to ratify these innovations, few of which had been clearly foreshadowed in the 1932 campaign. The result could only be interpreted as a popular ratification of the broad features of new public policy.[14] Yet the defections among some groups of voters measured dissent to the new line of policy and could have been regarded as a warning that these pockets of discontent might grow. In any case they had to be reckoned with.

1940: Ethnic response to foreign policy. The existence in the United States of large blocs of immigrants and their immediate descendants with ties of sentiment and loyalty to their homelands has provided bases for a type of voting behavior perhaps peculiar among the great democracies. A line of foreign policy favorable to the old country may attract the zealous support of those psychologically attached to their fellow countrymen abroad. The same policy may drive from a party other groups whose ancestry runs to nations not favored by the Administration's foreign policy.

The events preceding the 1940 election activated the primeval loyalties and hatreds of various nationality groups, and the 1940 election returns recorded marked Democratic losses among groups that had given Roosevelt strong support in 1936, as well as gains among other groups. The Administration policy of hostility toward fascist aggression in Europe drove those of Germanic origin in large numbers into the Republican camp.[15] In city after city over the country wards with large proportions of voters of Italian origin shifted away from the Democratic party. In county after county with large concentrations of persons of German origin a like response to events occurred. That shift is illustrated by the analysis of the movement of voters from 1936 to 1940 in the counties of North Dakota, which appears in Table 19.4. The higher the proportion of persons of Germanic origin in North Dakota counties, the wider was the shift away from the Democratic party between 1936 and 1940. Whether this movement rested on a pacifism, especially notable among the Volga Germans, or a dislike of Roosevelt's strong language about Hitler and the old country may be debatable, but that it occurred there can be no doubt.

The policy of friendship toward Britain and France attracted new support among the voters of areas inhabited by people of British origin. In

[14] It is a nice question whether such an election records a majority approval of a party's past program or reflects only the addition of minorities each of which approves those measures of immediate concern to it.

[15] These shifts have been treated in detail by Samuel Lubell, *The Future of American Politics* (New York: Harper, 1952), ch. 7.

Table 19.4

Foreign Policy and Ethnic Voting: North Dakota Counties According to Percentage Point Decline in Democratic Percentage of Presidential Vote, 1936–1940, Related to Percentage of County Population of German or Russian Origin, 1930

Per Cent of Population German or Russian [a]	Number of Counties Declining Specified Number of Percentage Points, 1936–1940				
	0–9	10–19	20–29	30–39	40–49
0–9	12	3			
10–19	5	10	2		
20–29		3	2		
30–39		3	3		
40–49			1	2	
50–59				3	1
60–69			2		
70–79					1
Total	17	19	10	5	2

[a] Proportions of county population born in Germany or Russia or of German or Russian parentage. Those of Russian birth or parentage were principally "Volga" Germans.

the rural sections of Maine, New Hampshire, Vermont, and Massachusetts Roosevelt polled a higher proportion of the vote than he had in 1936, and doubtless over the entire country he attracted new support from persons sympathetic to the British cause. Administration criticism of German anti-Semitism renewed and strengthened the Democratic loyalties of Jews.[16]

1956: Mixed verdict. The Eisenhower victory could be regarded as a straight vote of confidence. That appraisal, however, must be modified by

[16] See L. H. Fuchs, *The Political Behavior of American Jews* (Glencoe: Free Press, 1956). From time to time the political orientation of religious groups is influenced by the foreign policy of the administration in power. Thus, in 1914 and 1916, Roman Catholic lay societies waged a campaign of criticism against the Wilson Administration for its policy towards disorders in Mexico that had injured the church in that country. See J. M. Blum, *Joe Tumulty and the Wilson Era* (Boston: Houghton Mifflin, 1951). Such injections of religion into politics are to be differentiated from those resting on simple domestic antagonism among religious groups. Thus, Theodore Roosevelt wrote in 1908 that he had received hundreds of letters from clergymen, "the more narrow-minded evangelical Protestants," protesting against Taft chiefly because he was a Unitarian.—Anson Phelps Stokes, *Church and State in the United States* (New York: Harper, 1950), II, p. 405.

recognition of the contrasting trends within the electorate between 1952 and 1956. Broad areas of the country, mainly east of the Mississippi, increased their Republican presidential pluralities. West of the Mississippi a movement away from the 1952 high mark of Republican strength occurred.[17] That shift was far wider in the congressional voting than in the presidential polling. The resurgence of Democratic strength kept control of Congress from the Republicans, even though they handily won the Presidency.

Although in some urban centers the Republican gains in 1956 over 1952 were of astonishing magnitude, for most demographic groups in the country as a whole the shift was comparatively small. A party in power has the opportunity to expand the bases of its support or to make new enemies. Republican cultivation of the Negro, combined with the unattractiveness of the Democratic appeal to this group, yielded an exceptionally wide gain among colored voters. Similarly workers, both skilled and unskilled, moved across to the Republican column. The Republican percentages of the two-party vote, as indicated by the 1952 and 1956 samples interviewed by the Survey Research Center, for selected demographic groups were as follows:

	1952	1956		1952	1956
Professional, business,			Negro	21%	36%
managerial	70%	68%	Grade school	52	59
Other white collar	65	63	College	74	69
Skilled, semiskilled	47	56	Union	44	48
Unskilled	33	46	21–34 years old	55	59

These national figures doubtless conceal movements in contrary directions within each group. Nor do they indicate variations in behavior from place to place. The most marked Republican defections occurred among farm operators. The Survey Research Center samples showed the divisions among farm operators in 1948, 1952, and 1956 to be:

	1948	1952	1956
Democratic	59%	36%	45%
Republican	41	64	55

As these figures suggest the farm vote has become extremely volatile. Doubtless in the Great Plains states the Republican defections from 1952

[17] States with smaller proportions of the two-party vote Republican in 1956 than in 1952 were California, Colorado, Idaho, Iowa, Kansas, Minnesota, Mississippi, Missouri, Montana, Nebraska, Nevada, North Dakota, Oregon, South Carolina, Washington, and Wyoming.

to 1956 were much wider than among farm operators generally. Farmers in that region were hard hit by both drouth and price declines as well as antagonized by Republican farm policy. In the farming states between Mississippi and the Rocky Mountains, however, Republicans generally picked up strength in the cities and towns which offset to some extent the sag in farm support. This tendency for the Republican losses to be concentrated in farming areas and for their gains to come from the small cities and towns finds illustration in the map of Montana in Figure 19.3. Republican losses in the Pacific Coast states seemed to be associated in part with the policy of Republican partnership with the private utilities in the development of water resources.[18]

DECLINE IN EISENHOWER'S RURAL SUPPORT

Counties with 6 point or more decline in Republican vote percentage, 1952-1956

○ Counties with towns or cities of 4000 or more

Figure 19.3. Montana Counties with Republican Losses of Six or More Percentage Points, 1952–1956, and Location of Towns of 4,000 Population or More

Realignments and public policy. As these sketchy remarks make plain, a variety of sorts of broad electoral decisions are grouped in the category of realignments. Their common characteristic is that blocs of voters move in opposite directions. The kinds of problems that these elections raise for the Administration put in office vary. In some instances the election may

[18] On the 1956 election in the 11 far western states, see "Western Politics and the 1956 Elections," *Western Political Quarterly*, 10 (1957), a symposium by F. H. Jonas, N. D. Houghton, T. J. Anderson, Curtis Martin, Boyd A. Martin, Thomas Payne, A. E. Hutcheson, D. W. Driggs, F. C. Irion, J. M. Swarthout, Hugh A. Bone, and Herman H. Trachsel.

mark a stage in the dissolution of an old governing coalition. In another the election may provoke a reconsideration and perhaps a modification of Administration policy. It is as if substantial numbers of people were saying, "When we elected you before, we did not mean for you to do what you have done." In another instance the Administration may regard the election as a ratification of past actions by a new majority so strong that the defections may be viewed with equanimity. In still another the Administration may be alarmed by its losses but believe that the pursuit of its fixed policy course is warranted in the national interest.[19]

Political Cycles and Secular Trends

Our categorization of presidential elections according to the nature of the broad electoral decision in the context of events may convey the impression that such elections are isolated, disconnected, or independent episodes in our political life. On the contrary presidential elections are but quadrennial readings of the public temper which undergoes continuous change. Each election is a prelude to the next and each bears a greater or lesser resemblance to the preceding election. Each may be affected by gradual changes affecting particular groups of the electorate, changes that proceed steadily over long periods. Systematic knowledge of the processes of alteration of party attachments through time is most limited. Had Mr. Gallup's polling organization been in operation for half a century or so one could speak of these processes with greater confidence. Nevertheless their effects are hidden away in the voting in every presidential election, and over the long run they may change significantly the general framework of attitude pattern and population composition within which indi-

[19] These analyses of the shifting of blocs of voters from election to election makes relevant mention of the independent vote. One of the pleasant fictions of American politics is that substantial numbers of voters are independents who take a disinterested view of the political struggle and, after mature deliberation, cast their ballots as they deem the general interest dictates. They may split their ballot or move from party to party in response to the cues of conscience. The findings of the preceding pages suggest that in the movement of voters from party to party in presidential elections independence probably consists in high degree of group responses to events or to issues. The voter gains freedom from party by his subjection to class or group interest. The extent and character of voting independence becomes a function of the strength and nature of cross pressures. As circumstances develop in which some powerful competing group claim commands the loyalties of individuals, they become independent of party and cross party lines or split their tickets. Doubtless presidential elections illustrate only some of the types of independence. The concept of the independent voter encompasses so great a variety of behaviors that it is almost useless for analytical purposes. See the discussion by S. J. Eldersveld, "The Independent Vote: Measurement, Characteristics, and Implications for Party Strategy," *American Political Science Review*, 46 (1952), pp. 732–753. His article contains a bibliography of studies of the independent voter.

vidual campaigns occur. Despite the difficulty of identifying these changes, some indication of their probable character is in order.

Acculturation and partisanship. The American political system has absorbed wave after wave of immigration. As each new influx of migrants arrived peoples of like national origin, language, and culture formed political blocs attached to this or that party as circumstances, immediate self-interest, or a strategy of self-protection dictated. In most eastern seaboard cities the Irish adhered to the Democracy. Scandinavians tended toward the Republican party. Germans in some areas became Democrats; in others, Republicans. These groups were used by the parties and in turn they used the parties.[20]

Although from time to time specific events or issues activate memories linked to the homeland even across several generations, over the long run the cohesiveness of national-origin groups declines. Group ties weaken as English replaces the native language. The public schools place their stamp on the children. The next generation begins to find its way up the business ladder and into the professions. The slums are depopulated as people make their way by stages to the suburbs. A sense of resentment of exploitation of the group by professional Irish, Poles, or Italians develops. The old country culture gradually comes to be modified, if not displaced, by the American "culture."

Over the generations the gradual weakening of the cohesion of ethnic groups is paralleled by changes in voting behavior. A secular decline in the partisan solidarity of the group occurs as members of each generation become more susceptible to the political appeals to which people generally respond rather than to group-directed appeals. Individual elections may, to be sure, reactivate the ancient solidarity of particular groups. The secular decline in solidarity by no means follows a smooth curve. The rates of change may differ among different groups and even within the same national-origin group from place to place.

The data on these processes are almost nonexistent, but the evidence on geographically isolated pockets of settlement probably reflects changes that have been taking place in various groups in the electorate. Consider, for example, the record of Dubois County, Indiana, which appears in Figure 19.4. That chart shows the division of the presidential vote of a rural German Catholic community since 1892.[21] Over this period the Demo-

[20] See Oscar Handlin, "The Immigrant and American Politics" in D. F. Bowers (ed.), *Foreign Influences in American Life* (Princeton: Princeton University Press, 1944).

[21] See Elfrieda Lang, "German Immigration to Dubois County, Indiana, During the Nineteenth Century," *Indiana Magazine of History*, 41 (1945), pp. 131–151.

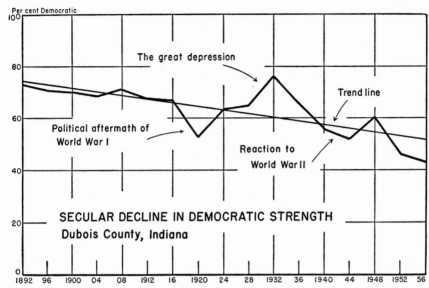

Per cent Democratic

The great depression

Trend line

Political aftermath of
World War I

Reaction to
World War II

SECULAR DECLINE IN DEMOCRATIC STRENGTH

Dubois County, Indiana

1892 96 1900 04 08 1912 16 1920 24 28 1932 36 1940 44 1948 1952 56

Figure 19.4. Democratic Percentage of Presidential Vote in Dubois County, Indiana, 1892–1956

cratic proportion of the vote within this county rose and fell with variations in Democratic fortunes nationally, but these fluctuations occurred around a declining trend line over the long term.[22]

The trend line on Dubois County shows a long-term change affecting a relatively isolated rural community, but the chances are that some such gradual processes of alteration affecting many groups not territorially segregated are hidden away in the election returns. Such secular changes do not, of course, have marked short-term effects on elections. From one election to the next the total change may be quite small, or movements in both directions may offset each other in the presidential voting. Yet over the long run this area or that is gradually transformed from a Democratic stronghold to a competitive area or even into a Republican stronghold, or the movement goes in the reverse direction. The processes of conversion cumulate over the decades and alter the "normal" balance of strength between the parties in cities and in states.

Changes in structure of the economy. Over the long sweep of time the gradual changes in the structure of the economy are reflected in the presidential voting as well as in the kinds of problems with which legislators have to wrestle. Exploitation by the Democratic party in this century of

---

[22] For other data on partisan changes through the generations, see Berelson and others, *Voting,* ch. 4, and Campbell and others, *The Voter Decides,* ch. 5.

the opportunities built up by industrialization provides a striking example. Yet even over shorter periods of time than that covered by the industrial revolution drastic alterations occur in particular states and regions. The gradual growth of Republican strength in the South has been principally the response of a growing urban middle class to the issues presented by the party system since 1932. In the campaign of 1952 this process accelerated and, along with other circumstances, brought enough of a Republican vote to carry some southern states.

A long-time Democratic state may abruptly cross the 50-50 line, but that jump may have been preceded by accretions to Republican strength over many years. The chances are that political effects lag behind economic changes. Indeed, those changes perhaps do not automatically project themselves into the political arena but await stimulation and exploitation by the political leadership. The nature of this temporal process may be inferred from Figure 19.5, which shows the extent to which the Republican and Democratic parties in New Hampshire have relied upon support from the industrial towns and cities since 1888. Before the turn of the cen-

Figure 19.5. Percentages of Democratic and Republican Presidential Vote in New Hampshire from 25 Industrial Towns and Cities, 1888–1952

tury, each party drew about the same proportion of its strength from these areas. After 1896 a secular trend set in by which Democrats came to draw larger and larger proportions of their vote from the industrial towns and cities. The trend undoubtedly reflects factors other than the gradual activation of the Democratic potential among urban mill workers. Persons of French-Canadian origin increased both in number and in their degree of attachment to the Democratic party. Whatever the factors involved, the chart suggests that many such currents may flow within the electorate over the decades.

Internal migration. In the nineteenth century the pattern of distribution of the great streams of internal migration were of basic significance in the fixing of the partisan attachments of newly settled areas. Even now movements of people from place to place alter the politics of individual communities and states. They may not materially affect the balance between the parties in the nation as a whole, but they may make a one-party state a competitive state or otherwise alter the normal partisan division. Though the consequences of these movements cannot be measured with exactitude, the direction of their effects is often clear enough.

The gradual growth of Republican strength in Florida can be traced in large part to the continuing movement to that state of aging Republicans in quest of sunshine. Of the people who have been taking up residence in Arizona in recent years, about one-third, it is estimated, "do not need to earn their living." [23] World War II brought to Oregon shipyard workers from the South and East and subsequently lumber companies imported woodsmen from the South. The Georgia drawl is heard in the lumber camps and mills. "With the southern accent has come a built-in inclination toward Democratic politics." [24]

The migration of the southern Negro to northern cities has had its consequences for the receiving states and localities in both local and national politics. The exodus of metropolitanites to the suburbs has its effects, although they are somewhat obscure. In some instances Democrats take over the suburbs; in other instances suburban Republicans are re-enforced by new recruits from the city. In still others new suburbanites transfer their allegiance from the Democracy to the Republican party. Probably of greater significance in conversion than physical movement to the suburbs is the fact that many new suburbanites are also going up the income scale.[25]

[23] N. D. Houghton in *Western Political Quarterly*, X (1957), p. 97.
[24] J. M. Swarthout in *ibid.*, p. 145.
[25] For further discussion of internal migration, see ch. 9.

Political cycles. The ubiquity of cyclical phenomena in nature has stimulated search for cyclical patterns in electoral behavior. Some speculators opine that the body politic undergoes a pulsating behavior. Movements of sentiment toward one extreme create their own corrective when a weariness of a politics of intensity sets in motion a swing back toward serenity. Arthur M. Schlesinger, for example, finds broad shifts in the nature of governmental policy and parallel changes in the general mood of the nation. The nation alternates between eras of conservatism and liberalism or between eras of emphasis on the rights of property and of emphasis on human welfare. These periods do not coincide with shifts in party control; the predominant mood of an era envelops Presidents and Congresses whatever their party complexion may be.[26]

Others identify cycles in the division of strength between the parties. Elections come to be determined by the stage in the cycle at which they occur. So long as two parties alternate in power a graph of party strength through time must assume a rough cyclical form. Whether the underlying behavior is "cyclical" may be another question.[27] Still others regard voting cycles as derivative of economic cycles. An analysis of presidential elections from 1828 through 1944 shows that the people tend to continue an administration in power during prosperous times and to vote against an administration "when depression marks the approach of election time." Over that period when prices were rising or at a high level of stability, the party in power was returned to power in 16 out of 18 elections. Changes in administration tended to occur when prices were declining or were stable at a low level. Among the exceptions to these general rules were the election of Hayes in 1876, when the official outcome may have differed from the popular verdict, and that of 1912, when Theodore Roosevelt split the Republican party.[28]

To picture presidential elections as episodes in a cyclical fluctuation of party divisions dependent on business cycles assigns to economic factors a predominant place in voting. Of their importance there can be no question. Yet on occasion other considerations, such as foreign policy, may produce an outcome at variance from what might be expected from the general state of the economy. Moreover, the supposition of derivative cycles assumes a popular disposition to put in office whatever party is out of power, Republican or Democratic, after a downswing. Neither of these assumptions is as valid as it may have been in the past century. Nor is the evi-

[26] A. M. Schlesinger, "Tides of American Politics," *Yale Review* 29 (1939), pp. 217–230.
[27] See Louis H. Bean, *How to Predict Elections* (New York: Knopf, 1948).
[28] F. A. Pearson and W. I. Myers, "Prices and Presidents," *Farm Economics* (New York State College of Agriculture), No. 163, September, 1948, pp. 4210–4218.

dence persuasive that cyclical behavior of a "political" nature exists, such as that assumed in the idea of recurrent spurts of innovation which breed their own ebb in periods of calm.

Elections in the Democratic Process

Presidential elections constitute decisions of fundamental significance in the American democratic process. The trooping of millions of voters to the polls symbolizes self-rule and legitimizes the authority of governments. But beyond such mystical functions of the electoral process, elections are pivotal decisions which in turn control many lesser determinations made in the name of the people. Our explorations have been in quest of some understanding of what the electorate does decide or of its role in the democratic process. Obviously the voters decide which party is to govern. That choice tends to bring in its train predictable consequences in direction if not in detail of governmental action, given the contrasting composition and policy orientations of the competing party leaderships. But what beyond the choices of governors do elections decide? Nothing, it may be said. Or a theorist with rationalistic inclinations may picture the party platform as a program of action which the winners are, by their solemn compact with the majority, bound to execute. Neither of these views satisfactorily reflects the reality. Considered in the framework of the flow of events and of the available alternatives it seems clear that elections decide more than simply who shall govern. Yet the scope and nature of the decision may not be apparent until some time after the election. Nor can it be contended that the voters in the prevailing majority invariably sense the broad meaning of their collective action.

Some elections, it has been argued, express clearly a lack of satisfaction with the performance of the crowd that has been in charge. The possibility of so efficacious an expression of discontent underlies the discipline of a democratic people over its government. Elected officials must live under the threat of defeat or disavowal. Other elections may be plausibly interpreted as a vote of confidence. More commonly the electorate may bring in a mixed verdict; some voters are happy with the course of affairs and others are deeply dissatisfied. Even these confused elections may, in their situational context, be meaningful decisions. Thus the election of 1896 rejected the upsurge of western silver-agrarian radicalism and gave popular blessing to a coalition which governed until at least 1912. The election of 1936 ratified a sharp turn in public policy and successive Democratic victories clinched the reforms of the New Deal. The terms of the electoral decision of 1952 brought Republican acquiescence in the new order. A series of elections may fix the contours that guide the broad flow of public policy. Specific elections may give an unmistakable mandate for a change of direction. Others may approve a newly instituted order of affairs. Still others may record a majority support for the status quo but the rumblings of the minority may be a portent of a growth of discontent.

Retrospective judgments by the electorate seem far more explicit than do its instructions for future action. An approval of the continuation of the prevailing course of action may be clear enough. Or a rejection of past performance may be resounding. Yet the most acute ear attuned to the voice of the people can sense only the vaguest guidance for innovation to cope with the questions that must be met day by day as an Administration governs. The efficacy of self-government thus depends on party and governmental leadership with the initiative and imagination necessary to meet the public problems that develop and with the courage to assume the political risks involved. The vocabulary of the voice of the people consists mainly of the words yes and no; and at times one cannot be certain which word is being uttered. On occasion it seems that assiduous but myopic dedication to the doctrine of self-rule brings governmental stagnation or paralysis as timorous politicians listen vainly for positive instructions from the voice of the people. Popular government demands that politicians be accountable but it does not relieve them of the duty of initiative.[29]

These explorations provide a general conception of the limits and nature of the role of the electorate. As one attempts to see national elections in their place in the governing process—in their relation to the party system, in their bearing on the operations of government—it is well to ponder about the mores, the understandings, the customs, the conditions that make feasible these interpositions by the mass of the people in affairs of state. For a political order to withstand periodic electoral clashes, the electorate itself must possess appropriate expectations and inner restraints. Party leaderships in their relationships to the electorate and to each other must keep party warfare within tolerable limits. Governing officials must be bound by an intricate set of norms which, if they do not absolutely limit governmental action, fix procedures and forms of action that maximize acceptance of authority and thereby make contemplation of the consequences of elections bearable, if not invariably comforting.[30]

[29] The prediction of public reaction to new courses of action is so primitive an art that thoughtful politicians remark that the only course to follow is to take the action that seems right, on the assumption that it will be defensible at the next election.

[30] This chapter has been directed solely toward national elections. Elections in smaller jurisdictions reveal a far wider variety of electoral phenomena, much of it of a droll nature. The battles of the Smiths and the Jones' over which clan will name the county supervisor involve matters of a different order than presidential elections. Or a competition of three Irishmen and four Italians for a nomination in a mixed district may combine civic training and a lottery.

20 | Congressional Elections

Essential to the American system of separation of powers is the mutually independent election of President and Congress. Vitality is breathed into the constitutional separateness of their positions by the fact that each owes its election and its allegiance, more or less directly, to the voters. Yet the separation of the choice of executive and legislature vastly complicates the task of the electorate as it attempts to make those broad decisions that are its responsibility in a scheme of popular government.

The electorate must choose, not an assortment of unrelated functionaries, but a government. Yet on the day of a presidential election not one but around 500 elections occur. Forty-eight states choose presidential electors, 435 districts elect Representatives, and a third of the states designate Senators. The problem of choice becomes manageable through the workings of the party system, which allies in common cause candidates for the Presidency and for the Senate and House. By the partisan linkage of candidates, Democratic and Republican, from California to Massachusetts, from North Carolina to Montana, great decisions on the general direction of governmental action can be made by the voters.

Despite the capacity of the party system to confront the nation's electorate with great alternatives, the independence of the choice of executive and legislature assures that elections will produce a mixed mandate. To some extent the affairs of senatorial politics in each state and of congressional politics in each district are governed, not by the great considerations of national politics, but by questions more or less peculiar to the locality. A state may return a Democratic candidate to the Senate on the same day that it gives its electoral vote to the Republican presidential aspirant. A landslide may carry a President and congressional majorities of his party into office. Yet simultaneously local and parochial considerations may be influential in the choice of individual Senators and Representatives. One Senator may be invincible whatever the direction of movement of the tides of national politics. Another may owe his election indubitably to his unequivocal association with the policies advocated by his party's presidential candidate.

This mixture of nationalism and parochialism in elections contains the roots of the conflicting tendencies of amalgamation and cleavage in executive-congressional relations. That mixture also makes it difficult to discern what a national election decides. Yet, by patient analysis of congressional voting, recurring patterns can be identified, patterns that disentangle to some extent the components of nationalism and parochialism in a national election. The sharper identification of these factors ought as well to promote an understanding of some aspects of the party system that remain obscure when attention centers solely on presidential politics. In this analysis the Senate and the House will receive separate consideration, since the roles and manner of election of these bodies differ.

Electoral Bases of Senatorial Roles

Among parliamentary bodies of the world the American Senate is unique. As it has grown in prestige and authority, other upper chambers have evolved into debating societies or havens for superannuated politicians. The basic circumstance that permits the Senate to flourish is the existence of presidential government; the presidential system makes possible a genuine bicameralism. Other factors also contribute to the position of the Senate. The freedom of discussion enjoyed by its small membership makes it a forum for full, if not always elevating, debate. The popular election of Senators by constituencies that are often truly great commonwealths endows Senators with an authority not enjoyed by members of upper houses designated by appointment or by accident of birth.

Beyond such factors the manner in which the Senate as an institution meshes with the party system profoundly influences its behavior. Forces of localism and of party compete for the loyalty of Senators, and the relative weights of these forces are rooted in the characteristics of the party system. Further, both the timing and the vigor of the expression of these forces are affected by the electoral system. With a six-year term, a Senator may, and at times does, bombastically represent the temper of his constituency as of four or five years earlier. The six-year term also puts many senatorial elections in the off years when the nation seems to speak with a different voice than it does in the years of presidential voting.

Senators and variations in party competition. Observation of the American Senate may yield an impression of chaos and disorder, of an arena in which strong men—be they honorable men or scoundrels—can construct for themselves positions of great power and influence and indulge in the most eccentric individualistic politics. Yet not all is anarchy within the Senate. Good and sufficient reasons inherent in the situations in which Senators find themselves account by and large for their differences of behavior.

The variations in the degree to which the parties are competitive within their respective states condition in a major way the policy inclinations of Senators. Those from one-party states may be untouched by the great tides of national politics. On the other hand, Senators from close states may live under the strongest compulsions to collaborate among themselves in the promotion of the cause of their party nationally. These variations in party competition are an index of other differences among the states. A Democratic Senator from Georgia, secure in his position, works in a different field of influence than does a Democrat from Illinois. A Republican from New York, uncertain in his tenure, confronts a different world than does the Republican from Kansas, almost certain of re-election until dotage or death overtakes him. The conditions of election in sure states tend to separate the Senator from the fortunes of his party nationally. The weakness of party competition often reflects the existence of a special regional interest or issue to which the Senator must devote himself undeviatingly.

The proportion of Senators from sure states and from competitive states varies somewhat from time to time. For long periods a state may elect Senators by overwhelming majorities and then a major shift in presidential politics will bring the state's senatorial seats into the contested category. A gross conception of the extent to which senatorial choices result from closely fought battles may be derived from Table 20.1, which groups senatorial elections from 1920 to 1956 according to the closeness of the vote. If an election won by less than 60 per cent of the vote is regarded as contested—a generous definition of contested—about one-half of the elections over the period were warmly fought. A more realistic estimate would be that one-third of the senatorial elections were closely contested. By the same token no overpowering uncertainty existed about the results of perhaps one-half of the senatorial elections.

A larger proportion of Democratic than of Republican Senators is elected without serious challenge. Over the period, 1920–1956, slightly more than one-half of the Democratic winners carried their states by more than 60 per cent of the popular vote, while only slightly over one-third of the Republican Senators polled as large a vote. Around 35 per cent of the Democrats, mostly southerners, won with more than 70 per cent of the vote.

Table 20.1

Sure and Close Senate Races: Distribution of Senatorial Elections, 1920–1956, According to Democratic Percentage of Two-Party Vote [a]

Democratic Percentage of Vote	Number of Elections	Per Cent of Elections	Distribution by Winning Party	
			Per Cent of Republicans	Per Cent of Democrats
0–9	5	0.8	1.9	
10–19	6	1.0	2.3	
20–29	28	4.7	10.7	
30–39	51	8.5	19.5	
40–44	69	11.5	26.3	
45–49	103	17.2	39.3	
50–54	89	14.8		26.3
55–59	72	12.0		21.3
60–69	56	9.3		16.6
70–79	27	4.5		8.0
80–89	25	4.2		7.4
90–100	69	11.5		20.4
Total	600	100.0	100.0	100.0

[a] Includes only elections for a full six-year term; excludes eight elections at which independent or third-party candidates won.

Articulation of senatorial and presidential election. The character of the Senate itself, as well as the nature of the broad decisions made by the electorate, is affected by the constitutional scheme for the election of Senators. A different situation prevails in the election of Senators in presidential years and in off years. In presidential years a fairly close articulation prevails in the voting for President and for Senate. The winning presidential candidate tends to carry into office with himself senatorial candidates on his party ticket. It is absurd to speak of this phenomenon as a simple coattail effect.[1] Both presidential and senatorial candi-

[1] Warren E. Miller, "Presidential Coattails: A Study in Political Myth and Methodology," *Public Opinion Quarterly*, 19 (1955–56), pp. 353–368.

dates are propelled into office by a trend, or a burst, of sentiment favorable to the winning party. Yet the constitutional system also cushions these trends and limits their impact, for only a third of the Senate is renewed at the time of a presidential election. The other Senators remain, if not untouched by the political winds of the moment, somewhat sheltered from their blast.

To understand more precisely the relationship between senatorial and presidential voting in presidential years requires attentive study of Table 20.2, which analyzes the senatorial elections of 1920, 1924, 1928, 1952, and 1956, years of Republican presidential victory. Observe, first (from the right-hand column), that the wider the margin of victory of the Republican presidential candidate in a state, the greater were the chances that the Republican senatorial candidate would also carry the state. As the parties within the states become more competitive, the presidential candidate, in years of Republican victory, demonstrates greater popular strength than that of his senatorial running mates. If the winning presidential candidate does not carry a state, the chances that the Republican senatorial candidate will win become slight indeed. In the elections analyzed, only three Republican senatorial candidates won as their states went Democratic presidentially.[2]

Table 20.2 highlights another set of relations between the presidential plebiscite and the senatorial sweepstakes. The capacity of a drift to the Republicans to carry senatorial candidates into office with the presidential candidate depends on whether seats have been held by Republicans or Democrats. Almost certainly a Republican will replace a Republican in those states carried by the winning Republican presidential candidate. In the elections analyzed only a handful of Republican seats were lost to the Democrats in states carried by the Republican presidential candidate. Most of these losses occurred in 1952 when Republicans Ecton of Montana, Cain of Washington, Kem of Missouri, and Lodge of Massachusetts were defeated as General Eisenhower led in their states. With the exception of Lodge, who met formidable Democratic opposition, these candidates were notable exponents of policies opposed to those supposedly fostered by the General. It may not be politically profitable, in a close state, to be conspicuously out of harmony with the head of a ticket who happens to gauge the popular mood correctly. Other factors, too, may account for loss of a senatorial seat as the presidential candidate wins. In 1956, for example, Democrat Joseph Clark replaced James H. Duff of Pennsylvania as Eisenhower carried the state, a result, among other things, of division in the Republican organization.

In their years of presidential triumph Republicans have greater success

[2] Pine in Oklahoma in 1920; Hebert in Rhode Island in 1928; and Ernst in Kentucky in 1920.

in retaining senatorial seats than in wresting seats from Democrats. The wider the Republican presidential margin, the greater are the odds that the Democrats will lose senatorial seats that they occupy. Here again the data of Table 20.2 are instructive. The exact nature of the phenomena underlying the capacity of Democrats to retain seats in the fashion indicated by the table must remain speculative. Perhaps the amassing of popular strength behind a winning presidential candidate may be likened

Table 20.2

Articulation of Presidential and Senatorial Voting in Years of Republican Presidential Victory, 1920, 1924, 1928, 1952, 1956

State	Republican Seats [a]			Democratic Seats			All Seats	
Republican Presidential Percentage	Number	Number Held	Per Cent Held	Number	Number Lost	Per Cent Lost	Number	Per Cent Republican
0–19				5	0	0.0	5	0.0
20–29				4	0	0.0	4	0.0
30–39				8	0	0.0	8	0.0
40–49				13	3 [b]	23.1	13	23.1
50–59	28	21	75.0	33	12	33.4	61	54.1
60–69	32	30	93.8	12	8	66.7	44	86.4
70–79	17	16 [c]	94.1	4	4	100.0	21	95.2
80–100	3	3	100.0	0	0		3	100.0

[a] Republican seats include those for which Republican incumbents sought re-election and those seats to which a Republican had last been elected. The same rule defined the Democratic seats. The tabulation covers only those elections for full six-year terms.

[b] These are the three seats, mentioned in the text, won by Republicans despite the loss of the states by their presidential candidate.

[c] The only Republican seat classified as lost was that of Smith W. Brookhart of Iowa whose 1924 certificate of election was successfully contested before the Senate by his Democratic opponent.

to a tidal wave that destroys those structures nearest the point of initial impact and does less and less damage to other structures as it moves inland. The resistance of Democratic state organizations to the impact of a Republican presidential victory varies similarly among the states. Senatorial posts are lost most frequently in those states in which the Republican presidential candidate is strongest, and as his appeal declines, from state to state, the chances that Democrats will hold senatorial places increase.

Democratic survival of Republican presidential victory appears most marked in the years of Republican landslides. In 1928 Hoover carried state after state in which Democratic Senators retained their posts. Among them were King of Utah, Dill of Washington, Kendrick of Wyoming, Pittman of Nevada, Wheeler of Montana, Ashurst of Arizona, and Copeland of New York. In the same year several southern Democratic Senators, less surprisingly, won re-election as Hoover carried their states. The Eisenhower sweep of 1952 similarly accounted for several of the instances in the table in which Democrats held Senate seats against the Republican tide: Byrd of Virginia, Chaves of New Mexico, Pastore of Rhode Island, Holland of Florida, Daniel of Texas, Gore of Tennessee. Obviously a factor contributing to capacity to maintain control of a seat is the political potency of a well-established incumbent Senator with a large personal following.

In years of Democratic presidential victories, the prospects of senatorial candidates, Democratic and Republican, are the reverse of those prevailing in years of Republican triumph. Table 20.3, which analyzes senatorial elections in Democratic years, is almost a mirror image of the preceding table. In Democratic years the chances for election of Democratic senatorial candidates increases, from state to state, as the popular margin of the presidential candidate widens. The exceptions to this rule that appear in the table were elections of Democrats in 1948 in southern states that

Table 20.3

Articulation of Presidential and Senatorial Voting in Years of Democratic Presidential Victory, 1932, 1936, 1940, 1944, 1948

State Democratic Presidential Percentage	Democratic Seats [a]			Republican Seats			All Seats	
	Number	Number Held	Per Cent Held	Number	Number Lost	Per Cent Lost	Number	Per Cent Democratic
0–29	3 [b]	3	100.0	0	0		3	100.0
30–39	1 [b]	1	100.0	1	0	0.0	2	50.0
40–49	4	0	0.0	24	4 [c]	16.7	28	14.3
50–59	38	35	92.1	27	19	70.4	67 [d]	80.6
60–69	16	16	100.0	12	8	66.6	29 [d]	82.8
70–79	12	12	100.0	1	0	0.0	13	92.3
80 and over	18	18	100.0	0	0		18	100.0

[a] Seats for which Democratic incumbents were candidates for re-election or seats to which a Democrat had last been elected. The tabulation covers only those elections for regular six-year terms.

[b] These deviate seats were southern seats filled, as usual, by Democrats in 1948 as their states went Dixiecratic presidentially.

[c] These are the seats, mentioned in the text, won by Democratic candidates despite the inability of the Democratic presidential winner to carry the states involved.

[d] These totals include independent and third-party seats.

went Dixiecratic presidentially. If the Democratic presidential candidate does not carry a state, the Democratic senatorial candidate has little chance to win. Only four instances occurred in the five presidential election years analyzed in Table 20.3.[3]

In their years of presidential triumph, Democrats can expect to retain virtually all those seats they hold in the states their presidential candidate carries. Such seats tend to be lost only under exceptional circumstances.[4] On the other hand, Republicans manage to hold a goodly number of senatorial seats in states that their presidential candidate loses. The stronger the Democratic presidential candidate, from state to state, the smaller is the probability that Republicans will retain their seats. Yet most striking instances occur of capacity to stand against the Democratic tide. The most marked case among those in the table was the 1932 North Dakota election when Republican Gerald Nye went back into office with 72 per cent of the vote as 71 per cent of the Dakota voters marked their ballots for Franklin Roosevelt.[5]

These analyses resolve themselves down to the proposition that the fortunes of presidential and senatorial candidates are fairly closely articulated in presidential years. The party that wins the presidency manages to retain most of the seats it holds from states whose electoral vote it captures. It makes inroads on the seats held by the party losing the Presidency although that party manifests considerable capacity to withstand the presidential tide. Individual senatorial candidates have a keen awareness of these relationships and often choose their campaign tactics accordingly. In Iowa in 1948, when the prospects for Mr. Truman were on the dark side, Guy Gillette, Democratic candidate for re-election to the Senate, sought to avoid a close tie-up with the Truman candidacy. Some of his campaign literature did not identify him as a Democrat or mention his party. On the other hand, in 1952, in Wisconsin Joseph McCarthy made energetic efforts to get aboard the Eisenhower bandwagon. In the same year in Massachusetts, Democrat John Kennedy, perhaps unim-

---

[3] In 1932 George H. Moses, of New Hampshire, lost to Democrat Fred H. Brown, and Hiram Bingham, of Connecticut, was defeated by August Lonergan. In 1944 John Moses replaced Gerald Nye in North Dakota and in 1948 J. Allen Frear won over C. Douglass Buck in Delaware.

[4] Illustrative was the 1936 victory of Henry Cabot Lodge, Jr., heir to a famous Massachusetts political name, over James Michael Curley, a Democrat strong in Boston but weak elsewhere in the state, who sought to win a seat to which a Democrat had last been elected.

[5] Other instances of Republican senatorial survival of the disaster that befell their presidential candidate in their states include the victories of McNary in Oregon in 1936, of Borah in Idaho in the same year, and of Norbeck in South Dakota in 1932.

pressed by the chances for Stevenson, did not strive to associate himself sharply in the public mind with the head of the ticket.[6] A presidential candidate, too, may believe it advantageous to separate himself from a senatorial candidate of his party. In 1957 President Eisenhower observed that it was important that Republicans control Congress "and to that extent," he said, "I am for whoever the Republicans of any particular state or district nominate. But when it comes down to who I am for enthusiastically, and who I am for merely because they are Republicans, is a very wide difference."

Off-year senatorial elections. The victorious party amasses support behind its presidential candidate whose strength its senatorial candidates seem never to match. Yet the direction of the movement of public sentiment tends to be unmistakably clear. It is toward one party—in both executive and senatorial spheres—and against the other. The significance of the articulation of senatorial and presidential voting, however, must not be overestimated. Only a third of the Senate seats are filled in a presidential year. In the off years the conditions of electoral decision are different. Each senatorial race becomes to a degree an autonomous event, though the cleavages of presidential politics project themselves to some extent into individual senatorial contests in the off years. Each race occurs within the framework of the balance of power in presidential politics and the off-year races collectively may even amount to a referendum on the conduct of the national administration. In senatorial, as in House elections, the candidates of the President's party are at a disadvantage in the off years. Nevertheless the off-year results are closely related to the presidential voting of the preceding presidential year.

Close inspection of Table 20.4, which analyzes senatorial elections in the off years of Republican administrations, reveals the character of the midterm decision. From that table it is plain that the probability of loss of Republican senatorial seats in the off years of Republican administrations increases, from state to state, as the strength demonstrated by the Republican President in the preceding election declines. Perhaps the less strong the current Republican predisposition of a state, the greater are the chances that general dissatisfaction with the national administration, unpopularity of a particular Senator, or peculiar local factors will result in

---

[6] In Connecticut in 1952 the percentages of senatorial candidates' advertisements and news items about them that associated the state race with the presidential campaign were for Ribicoff, the Democratic candidate, 7; for Bush, the Republican, 98.—L. C. Ferguson and R. H. Smuckler, *Politics in the Press* (East Lansing: Michigan State College, 1954), p. 57.

the loss of a Republican seat in the off years. Whatever the factors producing the outcomes of the individual elections, the total effect is a party oriented action by the electorate.

In a few instances Democrats lost seats at the midterm election. Even these losses fit the interpretation of midterm results as party oriented. Republicans picked up seats at the midterm only in states in which their

Table 20.4

Advantage of the Outs in Off-Year Senatorial Elections: Results of Senatorial Elections in Off Years During Republican Presidential Administrations, 1920–1954

State Republican Presidential Percentage in Preceding Election	Republican Seats [a]		Democratic Seats [b]	
	Number	Number Lost	Number	Number Lost
Under 40	0	0	14	0
40–49	6	4	7	0
50–59	16	11	21	0
60–69	25	5	11	5 [c]
70–79	18	4 [d]	0	0

[a] Seats to which Republicans had last been elected.
[b] Seats to which Democrats had last been elected.
[c] These are the exceptional instances, mentioned in the text, in which Democrats, from states with extremely strong Republican presidential preferences, lost in the off years of Republican administrations.
[d] All these seats were lost in 1922.

presidential candidate had shown extremely great strength at the preceding elections. In at least some of these states a sharp shift in presidential preference of the state had occurred since the incumbent Senator of the outs was elected. Thus, 1922, a year of generally good fortune for Democratic candidates, saw the defeat of Gilbert M. Hitchcock of Nebraska who had been elected in 1916 when Wilson drew 57 per cent of the Nebraska vote. By 1920 the Democrats could muster only 33 per cent of the state's vote in the presidential polling, and Nebraskans in 1922 elected Republican Robert B. Howell to bring their senatorial representation into line with their changed presidential preference. Similarly, in 1954, Iowans declined to return to the Senate Guy Gillette, who had won, along with Truman, in 1948. By 1952 Democrats could attract only 35.8 per cent of the Iowa presidential vote and the overwhelming Republican preference persisted sufficiently in 1954 to defeat Gillette.

Yet it should not be supposed that all midterm senatorial elections are precisely alike. The tendency of the President's party to lose a few seats and only under exceptional circumstances to take seats from the outs appears quite uniform. On occasion, however, the reaction against the President's party is so marked as to indicate a sharp loss of public confidence. Such an instance turns up neatly in Table 20.4, which shows a handful of Republican seats lost in 1922 despite the fact that Harding had carried the states concerned in 1920 with over 70 per cent of the vote. So extreme a shift in popular sentiment indicated the depth of discontent generated by the sharp economic downswing early in the Harding administration.

During Democratic presidential administrations the pattern of off-year senatorial elections is, in principle, the same as that prevailing in Republican administrations: that is, Republicans usually capture some Democratic Senate seats. The chances of an overturn are related to the Democratic presidential strength in the preceding polling. The wider the Democratic margin, the less hopefully may a Republican candidate eye a seat occupied by a Democrat. The stronger a Democratic President has shown himself to be in a state, the more confidently may a Democratic Senator from that state expect re-election.

The details of these relationships are set out in Table 20.5, which also contains data to re-enforce the earlier observation that not all midterm elections are alike. Commonly the President's party can have only the most slender hope in its midterm campaigns to capture Senate seats held by the opposition. Yet Table 20.5 turns up a goodly number of instances in which Democratic candidates replaced Republicans at the midterm of Democratic administrations. Most of them occurred in the 1934 elections, when

Table 20.5

Advantage of the Outs in Off-Year Senatorial Elections: Results of Senatorial Elections in Off Years During Democratic Presidential Administrations, 1932–1950

State Democratic Presidential Percentage in Preceding Election	Democratic Seats [a]		Republican Seats [b]	
	Number	Number Lost	Number	Number Lost [c]
40–49	10	6	21	2
50–59	37	20	22	6
60–69	26	3	7	3
70–79	11	0	1	0

[a] Seats to which Democrats had last been elected.
[b] Seats to which Republicans had last been elected.
[c] Of these 11 losses of Republican seats at midterm elections, 10 occurred in 1934.

the electorate expressed an overwhelming approval of the New Deal by voting Republicans out of office on a large scale, contrary to the usual midterm pattern.

Patterns of senatorial elections and the party system. The combination of party institutions, patterns of electoral behavior, and electoral procedures that has been described contributes to the powerful resistance of particular areas and interests to the nationalizing tendencies within the parties—that is, to the decentralization, or perhaps the fractionalization, of power within the political system. Mass sentiment which crystallizes in support of a winning presidential candidate cannot be converted into an equivalent control over the Senate. Even within the President's own party, Senators are elected, often from sure states, without relation to the outcome of the presidential voting. The force of the winning presidential coalition is also splintered by staggered Senate terms.

By and large, resistance to the power of the winning presidential coalition expresses itself in party terms, in the capacity of some minority candidates to withstand the surge of the presidential campaign itself, and in the capacity of others to win election in the off years. The minority, Republican or Democratic, fights from bastions of strength not readily reducible by the triumphant majority. Whether the provision of bulwarks for the minority invariably redounds to the general weal may be debatable, but there can be no doubt that our arrangements include such bulwarks. Their significance can perhaps be surmised by consideration of the probable results of electing the entire Senate for four-year terms in the years of presidential elections. Minority representation in the Senate might, in time, be reduced to miniscule proportions. Moreover, the fortunes of the Senators of the President's party would become more closely bound to those of the President and perhaps vice versa. A marked transformation of the character of the Senate would probably occur.

Party, Presidency, and House of Representatives

While the House of Representatives is constitutionally as independent of the executive as is the Senate, the timing and circumstances of its election bring it more strongly under the nationalizing influences of party. The renewal of the entire membership of the House at the time of the presidential election associates the political fortunes of House candidates more closely with their party ticket. Even the midterm elections, a consequence of the two-year House term, tend to reflect shifts in national sentiment toward the parties as a whole, although peculiar local factors often determine the results of individual races.

Co-ordination of elections of Representatives and President. The simultaneous election of the President and of all House members enables the
electorate to place control of these two organs of government in one or
the other of the major parties. Furthermore, it permits, although it does
not assure, a maximum unification of party campaign effort behind both
presidential and congressional candidates and subjects most races for Representative to the influences that play upon presidential voting.

In consequence of these interrelations the winning presidential candidate ordinarily carries into office with him a House majority of his own
party, and partisan balance in the House fluctuates with variations from
election to election in the division of the presidential vote. Figure 20.1

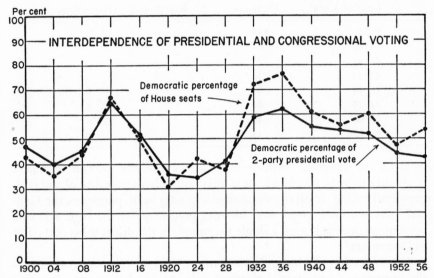

Figure 20.1. Democratic Percentage of Two-Party Vote for President and
of Membership of House, 1900–1956

shows this relationship for the elections since the turn of the century. As
the figure suggests, the correlation between presidential and congressional
voting is by no means perfect. A given division of the popular presidential
vote is not invariably associated with precisely the same division of House
seats. A presidential candidate may be somewhat weaker than his party
generally, as was probably true of Tom Dewey, the Republican candidate
in 1948, and Adlai Stevenson, the Democratic candidate of 1952 and 1956.
Nevertheless the figure highlights the broad association of presidential
and congressional voting in the years of presidential elections.

Even the extraordinary election of 1956 in which Republicans failed to capture a majority of the House as Eisenhower won re-election fits the pattern of association between presidential and House voting. In that election some Republican House candidates triumphed over sitting Democrats, chiefly in districts Democrats had won by narrow margins in 1954. On the other hand, Democrats replaced enough Republicans to hold their

Table 20.6

Party Shifts of House Districts in 1956 Related to 1954 Vote

1954 Election		1956 Election	
Republican Per Cent of Vote	Number of Districts	Shifted to Republican	Shifted to Democratic
0–34	145	0	
35–39	28	1	
40–44	27	2	
45–49	32	6	
50–54	61		6
55–59	62		3
60–64	56		2
65–100	24		0

majority. In all of the shifting districts save one, the drift of sentiment from 1952 to 1956 was in the same direction in both presidential and congressional voting. In all the districts newly won by Republicans, the General increased his strength over his 1952 percentage of the vote. His vote percentage declined, with a single exception, in the districts his party lost to Democrats.[7]

The subjection of House elections to the tides of sentiment that govern the outcome of presidential elections helps to account for the fact that the House is more responsive than the Senate to presidential leadership. The impact of presidential landslides may, in fact, be so great as to reduce the House minority to a corporal's guard. Only 132 House Democrats, about 30 per cent of the membership, survived the Harding victory of 1920, while a mere 89 Republicans, only 20 per cent of the House, went to Washington after Roosevelt's sweep of 1936. Such elections yield embarrassingly large and often unmanageable, majorities for the President's party.

Despite the articulation of presidential and congressional elections a

[7] The exception was the 2nd district of Maine. The General gained in 1956 over his 1952 percentage in the district. Had the congressional voting been in November, the Republicans would have had a better chance to retain the House seat.

goodly number of House members may confidently expect election, once they win nomination, come what may in the presidential plebiscite. A bloc of almost 100 southern seats is ordinarily quite safe for Democratic candidates, and certain metropolitan districts are almost as surely Democratic.[8] Republicans control fewer sure seats. Those districts in which the division of the vote is normally near the 50-50 point are most apt to swing from party to party with the presidential vote. The number of such districts changes from time to time, but from one-third to one-half of the House candidates must view the outcome with some uncertainty, although the proportion of districts with extremely close results is ordinarily less. Figure 20.2 shows the distribution of House districts in 1948 and 1952 according to the division of their vote between the parties.

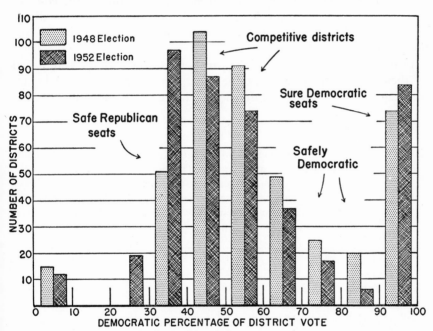

Figure 20.2. Distribution of Congressional Districts According to Democratic Percentage of Major-Party Vote, 1948 and 1952

The fact that a presidential election does not affect the results of campaigns for House seats in the sure districts, Republican or Democratic, does not necessarily mean that an election throws into the House blocs of

[8] For an analysis of some of the oddities of electoral behavior in House districts, see Duncan MacRae, Jr., "Occupations and the Congressional Vote, 1940–1950," *American Sociological Review*, 20 (1955), pp. 332–340.

Representatives unresponsive to the broad verdict of the election. Certainly, Democratic Representatives from sure metropolitan districts in recent Democratic administrations have been loyal supporters of the party program. Even the southerners defected principally on issues of peculiar regional concern. At least on domestic issues Republicans from sure rural districts have tended to be quite as consistent followers of the party line as have those from closer districts. Yet the fact that a district is sure usually means that its people have a deep concern over an issue or set of issues which will produce dissidence in their Representatives if the national leadership runs counter to that concern. Moreover, Representatives from the sure districts acquire seniority in the House and gain the advantage that comes with legislative experience. Hence, the special concerns of the steadfast party areas find especially strong representation in the councils of the party. The disproportionate contribution of sure districts to the contingent of experienced House members is indicated, for a sample election, by the data of Table 20.7.

While the House strength of the parties fluctuates with the vote polled by their presidential candidates, the gross relationship, shown in Figure 20.1 can lead to erroneous inferences. The return of House majorities

Table 20.7

Close Districts and First-Termers: Proportion of Representatives First-Termers, 1952, According to Size of Margin in District Congressional Vote, Nonsouthern Districts

District Per Cent Republican	Total Seats	First-Termers	Others	Per Cent First-Termers
40–44	13	1	12	7.6
45–47.4	15	2 [a]	13	13.3
47.5–49.9	17	8 [b]	9	47.0
50–52.4	11	6 [c]	5	54.5
52.5–54.9	14	8 [d]	6	57.1
55–59	34	5	29	14.7
60–64	48	4	44	8.3

[a] Both of these first-term Democrats succeeded Democrats.

[b] Of these eight first-term Democrats, four came from new districts, two succeeded other Democrats, and two (Pfost of Idaho and Miller of Kansas) succeeded Republicans.

[c] Of these first-term Republicans, three replaced Democrats, one succeeded another Republican, and two came from new districts.

[d] Of these eight first-term Republicans, four succeeded Democrats, three succeeded Republicans, and one came from a new district.

along with presidential pluralities may suggest that the electorate grants a clear mandate of preference for the majority party of the moment. In fact, the voters speak far more equivocally. Despite the apparent correlation between congressional and presidential voting, one popular majority may elect the President and another, the House. The President may owe his election to one constituency and his party's House majority, or at least a goodly number of its members, to another.

Something of the nature of the electoral decision can be discerned if one pushes behind the aggregate relationships shown by Figure 20.1 and compares, district by district, the congressional and presidential vote, as has been done for two presidential elections in Table 20.8. The greater the strength of a party's presidential candidate, as one moves from district to district, the greater are the chances that his party's congressional candidate will carry the district. Yet in some districts, the Democratic presidential candidate will have a plurality as Republicans win the House seats, while in others the Republican presidential candidate will carry the day as his fellow Republicans go down to defeat in the House races.

The reasons for these divergent results within congressional districts

Table 20.8

Relation Between Presidential Vote in Congressional Districts and Results of House Elections, 1952 and 1956

District Republican Presidential Percentage	Results of Congressional Races					
	1952			1956		
	Total Districts	Number R	Per Cent R	Total Districts	Number R	Per Cent R
15–19	4	0	0.0	5	0	0.0
20–24	4	0	0.0	8	0	0.0
25–29	11	0	0.0	8	0	0.0
30–34	14	0	0.0	14	0	0.0
35–39	36	1 [a]	2.8	20	0	0.0
40–44	33	0	0.0	25	0	0.0
45–49	37	2	5.4	30	1	3.3
50–54	56	17	30.4	63	13	20.6
55–59	87	60	69.0	86	33	38.4
60–64	82	71	86.6	86	70	81.4
65–69	49	47	95.9	58	52	89.7
70–74	21	21	100.0	24	24	100.0
75–79	1	1	100.0	8	8	100.0
Total	435	220		435	201	

[a] Jacob Javits won New York's 21st district.

throw light on both the nature of our party system and the character of the electoral verdict. The chances are that two broad sets of factors account for most of the instances of deviation from party regularity. First, the elements of strength and weakness in the congressional candidates and in the district party organizations help to shelter local candidates from national trends. Second, the peculiar policy and personal appeals of the presidential candidates contribute also to their special weakness or strength in particular types of districts. The interaction of these two broad variables produces coincidence and divergence in district voting for President and Representative.

The data of Table 20.8 suggest that within congressional districts the electorate is more strongly attached to local party and perhaps to individual Representatives than to a party's presidential candidates. The party that has become dominant within the congressional politics of a district has a capacity, often remarkable, to withstand the ebb and flow of sentiment in the competition for the Presidency. This ability to hold a district often depends in part on the drawing power of a sitting Representative whose name has become known and who has by favors and services to his constituents, perhaps over a long period, cemented to himself a faithful personal following. Yet often more than personal popularity is involved. The party organization may have a strength quite independent of that of the sitting Congressman, or the voters of the district may lean fairly persistently toward candidates of his party for most offices but now and then split their ticket for the Presidency.

The data suggest that partisan shifts in congressional voting lag behind shifts in presidential voting; or that partisan loyalties are somewhat less volatile in local races than in presidential contests. From this capacity to resist the general trend it would be expected that a number of districts, Republican and Democratic, would stand steadfast in their customary congressional allegiance in the face of conquest of the district by the opposition presidential candidate. Yet quite apart from this phenomenon, which may be common to a great many close districts, occasionally individual congressional candidates dramatize an issue peculiar to the district, or themselves, so skillfully that they can win even though the opposition polls a huge presidential plurality in the district. For example, in 1952, a Democrat, Howard S. Miller, won election from Kansas' 1st district as Eisenhower drew almost 70 per cent of the vote. Mr. Miller, said to have been the first Democrat elected to Congress from this area, accomplished this feat by opposing the construction of Tuttle Creek Dam, a flood control project that had outraged those whose lands would have been inundated. In the same year, Gracie Pfost, of Idaho, defeated an incumbent Republican for Congress in a district that went over 60 per cent for

Eisenhower, and thereby established herself as a formidable lady politician. In New York, beginning in 1946, Republican Jacob Javits won a normally Democratic district by a combination of good luck, strife among the Democrats, and conspicuous espousal of non-Republican policies.

Other elements of the relationship between presidential and congressional voting may be identified if we transfer our attention to the second factor productive of incongruency in presidential and congressional voting—the peculiarities of the presidential contest. Each presidential candidate tends to have a set of appeals, and to attract a following, that does not match precisely the popular congressional support of the party. The peculiarities of his strength may extend the area of his pluralities into congressional districts that his party is unable to carry. On this broad point, the data of Table 20.8 are instructive. Consider the 1952 congressional results in relation to the strength of General Eisenhower, district by district. The popular appeal of the General won for him many congressional districts carried by Democratic congressional candidates. Some of these districts were, to be sure, southern districts in which no Republican ran for the House or in which the Republican candidate was extremely weak. On the other hand, few Republicans won House seats in districts carried by Adlai Stevenson.

Inspection of instances of split results in congressional districts in several elections suggests that the electorate often acts consistently on matters of policy even though it may have to split tickets to do so. It may choose a pro-Eisenhower Democrat in preference to an anti-Eisenhower Republican as it votes for Eisenhower. Or it may vote for a Roosevelt but return to the House a Republican who will be pro-Roosevelt on matters of critical concern to the district. Other, less recondite, reasons also explain much of the deviation between presidential and congressional voting. A presidential candidate may have a strong appeal in a district in which his party, long moribund locally, is simply unable to muster a House candidate who commands much respect.

This discussion of the divergence between patterns of congressional and presidential electoral support, which differs both in degree and in form from election to election, should not obscure the broader fact that the same people who support a winning President also support in relatively high degree the congressional candidates of his party. Broadly the electorate rallies to the support of a presidential candidate and his fellow partisans, although many exceptions occur that contribute to the special character of the American party system.[9] Not a great deal is known about

[9] See the analysis of ticket-splitting in 1956 by Angus Campbell and Warren E. Miller, "The Motivational Basis of Straight and Split Ticket Voting," *American Political Science Review*, 51 (1957), pp. 293–312. They found splitting between national and

the extent of straight-ticket voting, but even General Eisenhower, a presidential candidate with an unusually marked personal rather than partisan following, drew great numbers of voters to the Republican congressional cause. Of the 33,900,000 who voted for the General in 1952, approximately 8,100,000, or so it may be estimated, had voted for Mr. Truman in 1948. Of these switchers, on the order of 5,200,000 also supported the Republican congressional ticket in 1952. The remaining 2,900,000 split their ticket to support Democratic congressional candidates, a phenomenon especially marked in the South.[10]

Party at midterm: the minority. The congressional campaigns in presidential years are overshadowed, even swallowed up, by the effort to win the Presidency. The centripetal influence of the fight for the Presidency tends to pull together all factions of the party. Powerful forces operate to bring all good men to the aid of their party to elect a President and a Congress as well. The cohesive drives of the presidential battle are absent in midterm elections. The parties may become fractionalized, for they lack the mechanism, and often the will, to rally their cohorts to disciplined battle.

The problem of presenting a solid front to the electorate may be especially difficult for the minority party. When a deep-seated conflict exists for control of the minority, its latent inner contradictions may materialize in the most glaring form at the midterm campaign. The campaign may be in reality a battle of every man for himself, and there may be no party front presented against the Administration. The extreme situation manifested itself in a declaration by the late Senator Robert A. Taft in 1941: "No Republican National Convention can be held before next year's

state and local candidates to be more common than between presidential and congressional candidates. In the North 76 per cent of the Eisenhower voters voted straight Republican at the national level in 1956 in contrast with 89 per cent in 1952. In the South the movement was in the opposite direction, 46 per cent against 21 per cent in 1952. In 1956 one out of 10 Stevenson voters split for a Republican Representative or Senator. Rural areas had the lowest proportions of straight-party voting, a fact consistent with the greater awareness of rural people of the identity and role of legislators. A Gallup poll in April, 1942 found that 50 per cent of the respondents were unable to name their Representative; far more farmers knew the name of their Representative than did citizens of cities over 500,000. The National Opinion Research Center found in 1944 that only 31 per cent of the sample questioned could name both Senators correctly. Such lack of knowledge is conducive to straight-ticket voting as is the form of the ballot. In those House districts in which Eisenhower gained from 1952 to 1956 Republicans replaced Democrats more frequently in the states with party-column ballots than in those with office-bloc ballots.

[10] These estimates rest on the finding by Campbell, *The Voter Decides*, p. 17, that 24 per cent of the Eisenhower vote consisted of 1948 Truman supporters and on the division of the sample of these voters between straight-ticket voter and splitters as reported at p. 25.

elections and the party National Committee clearly has no authority to make such declarations. I see no reasons why each Senator should not run on his own foreign policy." [11]

The special difficulties under which the minority may labor are illustrated by the Republican attempt to form a line of battle for the 1950 congressional elections. Soon after the 1948 campaign a struggle developed between the Dewey and Taft wings of the party. Hugh Scott, Jr., chairman of the national committee and a Dewey appointee, proposed to hold a national conference to draft a "fighting and forward-looking" program of "moderation" on which to wage the 1950 campaign. Republican leaders of House and Senate, more disposed toward the Taft wing, had no enthusiasm for "moderation," and Mr. Scott was soon replaced as national chairman by Guy Gabrielson. The new chairman obtained authority from the national committee to create a committee consisting of representatives of the national committee and of the Republican groups in the House and Senate to draft a program for 1950. When the committee eventually came into being its Senate members were named by Senator Taft and its House members by Representative Martin, the Republican House leader.

After negotiation between the groups named by the congressional leaders and the group appointed by the chairman of the national committee, a policy statement was unveiled "supplementing the Republican platform of 1948." Although it dealt with several questions, it declared that the "major domestic issue today is liberty against socialism." On this slogan it was hoped that the party could unite, but protests swelled up from the ranks. The statement gratified only the Old Guard. The Republican state chairman of New York, a Dewey man, observed that the statement "did not offer enough in specific appeal to all the voters of the nation to make it a lasting, persuasive or overly binding document." A group of dissident Republican leaders met in Philadelphia and adopted a declaration of principles of their own, "a positive" program. They argued for "affirmative and constructive solutions of the tremendously intricate and difficult problems facing the nation."

The Republican party thus went forth disunited into the fray. At midterm the minority lacks the machinery to produce a decision on party policy that will be accepted as binding by all the important segments of the party. Though the pronouncements of the national convention are not necessarily embraced by all elements of the party, in presidential campaigns policy differences may be submerged or their solution may be postponed. At midterm the intraparty discussion must focus on issues and is-

[11] *Quoted in Toward a More Responsible Two-Party System,* A Report of the Committee on Political Parties, American Political Science Association (1950), p. 52.

sues alone. Perhaps there is no better way to activate latent differences than to bring issues up for discussion.

Yet the minority is not invariably bedeviled by problems of the same magnitude as confronted the Republicans in 1950. In the 1954 campaign, the Democrats, with the Stevenson bloc in fairly secure command of the party apparatus, avoided extensive fighting among themselves and saved their ammunition for Republicans. Stevenson, who stumped the country in support of the congressional ticket, set a general tone for the Democratic campaign to which most congressional and senatorial candidates could attune their special local appeals. Thus, a conference of 40 Democratic House and Senate candidates foregathered at Sioux Falls, South Dakota, and issued a manifesto describing "the things the Republican Administration has done to break faith with the American farmer and to injure our farm economy," and provided a regional emphasis for one of the general lines of attack adopted by the national leadership.

Party at midterm: The majority. The occasional serious tribulations of the minority party in arriving at a midterm program are not to be explained simply by the obstreperousness, or cussedness, of human nature. Fundamentally a different type of leadership tends to develop in the House and Senate wings of the party than among those who focus on winning presidential campaigns. Both parties are plagued by the divergence between the two types of leaders, but it may be especially marked in the minority when its congressional representation has been reduced to the hard core of standpatters from sure districts. The image of the minority in the eyes of the country may be formed by the pronouncements and behavior of its congressional leaders of an extreme wing. The sober citizen may well shudder when he wonders whether the minority will elect a President of the same hue as the more vocal elder statesmen of the congressional minority.

The vicissitudes of the Administration at midterm are far less forbidding than are those of the minority. The Presidency provides an organizing center for the party whose congressional and presidential elements ordinarily close ranks for the conduct of the campaign. In truth, the President and his program create the central issue of the campaign, and the midterm election becomes in a sense a referendum on the conduct of the government by him and his party. Yet the exact role that the President himself should play in the midterm campaign has not been neatly crystallized. Under some circumstances at least, the country does not accept it as entirely proper for the President to ask the country to uphold his policies by electing a Congress of his party.

Woodrow Wilson's 1918 appeal for a Democratic Congress is a notable illustration of the problem of the proper stance for a President to assume in the midterm campaign. In his manifesto Wilson declared that the elections of 1918

occur in the most critical period our country has ever faced, or is likely to face in our time. If you have approved of my leadership, and wish me to continue to be your unembarrassed spokesman at home and abroad, I earnestly beg that you will express yourselves unmistakably to that effect by returning a Democratic majority to both the Senate and the House of Representatives. . . . The leaders of the minority in the present Congress have unquestionably been pro-war, but they have been anti-administration. At almost every turn since we entered the war they have sought to take the choice of policy and the conduct of the war out of my hands and put it under the control of instrumentalities of their own choosing. This is no time either for divided council or for divided leadership.

Veteran Democratic politicians regarded the issuance of this statement as a major blunder, however much they may have agreed with its premises. And to it they attributed the disasters Democrats suffered in the elections of 1918, although doubt may be entertained about the correctness of that interpretation. The late Arthur Mullen, Nebraska Democratic leader, characterized the statement as the "most suicidal document ever sent out from the White House." He argued that had Wilson's appeal been for the election of men who had supported his policies, not those of his party, it might have had contrary effects.[12]

When the midterm rolls around, the pundits resurrect the events of 1918 and consider what the incumbent President should do. In 1942, another delicate time politically, Roosevelt met the problem differently than Wilson had. Ed Flynn, the Democratic national chairman, in February, 1942 delivered himself of a rip-roaring partisan speech in which he pointed to the "vast confusion" that would result from the election of a Republican Congress. Only a major military defeat, he thought, could be a greater misfortune. What would the President's comment be? To the reporters he said, "When the country is at war, we want Congressmen, regardless of party, who will back up the Government of the United States and who have a record of backing up the country in an emergency, regardless of party." The President may have believed that few Republicans met the tests he set up, but, if so, he thought it impolitic to say so.

An active role by the President in the midterm campaign is perhaps becoming a more accepted practice of our politics. At any rate under circumstances different from those of 1918 and 1942 Presidents have exerted themselves to win the election of a Congress of their party at the midterm. In 1950 the Democratic party made a vigorous campaign. Presi-

[12] A. F. Mullen, *Western Democrat* (New York: Funk, 1940), p. 182.

dent Truman made a straightforward plea for approval of the policies of the Administration by the return of greater majorities in House and Senate. Beset by dissent in his own party, he sought the election of a larger contingent of northern liberal Democrats, lest his program be completely blocked by a combination of the conservative Democratic splinter with the Republican minority.

In the preliminaries to the 1954 elections Eisenhower took a lofty and detached view; he believed that his own participation should be limited to a defense of the Administration's record on a high plane and that the Presidency should not be involved in particular partisan struggles in states and districts. In due course intelligence from the grass roots indicated that the Republican congressional majority was in peril and the President joined in the fray. He dispatched most of the cabinet to the stump to preach the gospel of Republicanism and he himself made flying trips to states with closely fought senatorial contests. In a broadcast he argued that "you can't have one car with two drivers at the steering wheel and expect to end up any place but in the ditch—especially when the drivers are set on going in different directions. You cannot have efficient Federal government when the Congress wants to follow one philosophy of government and the Executive branch another." He called for the "election of a Republican-led Congress." Even those Republicans who had steadfastly opposed the President's program in Congress echoed these sentiments and strove mightily to get aboard the presidential coattails.

Similarly, as the congressional elections of 1958 approached, the Republican national committee and the President bestirred themselves to rouse the faithful to do battle. The national committee in 1957 conducted a series of regional sessions of Republican national committeemen and other leaders to lay plans for the campaign, to estimate the possibilities of success, and to make propaganda. The President addressed most of them by telephone from Washington.

Whatever role the President chooses to take in the campaign, the majority, by its possession of control of the government, has the means to bring its forces into more or less orderly line for the conduct of the campaign. This accomplishment requires co-ordination of the endeavors of the party's national senatorial and congressional committees, a task apt to be considerably simpler for the Administration than for the minority. For the majority also the task of adopting a general policy for the campaign presents no overwhelming difficulty. The performance of the Administration must be the platform, a circumstance that tends to put the majority on the defensive at the midterm. Yet the record on occasion is supplemented by a more or less formal policy statement. In 1950, for example, the Democratic national committee laid out a statement of party principles which adhered largely to the Fair Deal program as enunciated in 1948. In 1954 the Republican national committee convened at Cincinnati and issued a platform with the theme of "Peace, Progress, and Prosperity." [13]

The nature of the midterm contest encourages a strategy of concentration, since the Administration is most seriously threatened in the close districts—which number from 50 to 100. Campaign resources may be amassed in districts where they will presumably yield the greatest return. Thus, in 1954 the Republicans sent into the 4th district of Missouri, in an effort to hold the seat, the Vice-President, the Secretary of Agriculture, the Secretary of Commerce, and the Speaker of the House. All these endeavors, it may be noted, were to no avail. Similarly, the Administration may subject to intensive fire the seats won earlier by the minority by a narrow margin, a tactic which rarely yields results but does compel the minority to exert itself to hold these seats.

Nature of the midterm verdict. Since the electorate cannot change administrations at midterm elections, it can only express its approval or disapproval by returning or withdrawing legislative majorities. At least such would be the rational hypothesis about what the electorate might do. In fact, no such logical explanation can completely describe what it does at midterm elections. The Founding Fathers, by the provision for midterm elections, built into the constitutional system a procedure whose strange consequences lack explanation in any theory that personifies the electorate as a rational god of vengeance and of reward.

The President's party, whether it basks in public favor or is declining in public esteem, ordinarily loses House strength at midterm—a pattern that, save for one exception, has prevailed since the Civil War. The exception occurred in 1934 when the popularity of the Roosevelt policies was on the ascent.[14] Given the regularity of this pattern, the loss of House strength by the Administration at midterm does not necessarily result from withdrawal of popular favor. An exceptionally heavy loss, however, may reflect the development of a hostile public sentiment and may even portend a defeat in the following presidential election.

Explanation of the Administration's loss at midterm must be sought not so much by examining the midterm election itself as by looking at the pre-

[13] In 1953 the Democratic national committee considered a proposal to hold a midterm national convention to set policy for the 1954 congressional campaign. Democratic congressional leaders killed the proposal. Such a convention would, they argued, center on areas of disagreement and accentuate intraparty strife.

[14] The details of the pattern are set out by Key, "If the Election Follows the Pattern," *New York Times Magazine*, October 20, 1946. See also O. C. Press, "The Prediction of Midterm Elections," *Western Political Quarterly*, 9 (1956), pp. 691–698.

ceding presidential election. The presidential campaign mobilizes party strength behind the winning presidential candidate and apparently has the secondary effect of capturing some marginal congressional seats, and of holding a few other such seats, for candidates of the President's party. At the midterm the absence of the supportive power of the presidential campaign allows some districts, usually held by the narrowest margin, to sag over the line to the opposition.[15] The opposition can at the midterm make the most both of the blunders of the Administration and of its own strength, for it does not have to overcome the momentum given to the Administration candidates by the tide that ran two years earlier. While the absence of the President's coattails evidently contributes in large measure to the midterm drop, detailed inspection of campaigns in individual districts will identify from time to time issues and circumstances quite peculiar to a district that may be determinative.

Despite the impartiality with which the electorate votes out members of the President's party, be it Republican or Democratic, at the midterms, the results of the individual contests add up to a broad decision in terms of party. Consider the manner in which the electorate acts at midterm. The aggregate result of the election is not the product of a random shifting of districts, some from the President's party to the minority, some from the minority to the Administration. Such movements in both directions would be expected if district results were the chance product of local issues, candidate popularity, and other such matters unconnected with party. The movement is, however, mainly in one direction. The President's fellow partisans lose seats to the outs and only under exceptional circumstances do they capture districts from the outs; the outs retain the seats they have and gain others from the Administration.

Illustrative of the pattern of the midterm shift is Table 20.9, which analyzes the House elections of 1950 in relation to the results by district in 1948. The Democrats had virtually no hope of gaining seats they had lost in 1948. They picked up only one such district, one in which a state Republican organization disciplined the Representative by defeating him in the general election. On the other hand, Republicans won 30 seats from Democrats, and of these 25 had been Democratic in 1948 by less than five percentage points. Usually the Administration at the midterm loses a rather large proportion of the seats it won by narrow margins at the preceding presidential election.

Lest it be thought that the 1950 results represent a unique event rather than a recurring pattern, the findings of a comparison between the out-

[15] Louis Bean estimates that the coattail effect, on the average, pulls about 20 Representatives into office with the President. See his *The Mid-Term Battle* (Washington: Cantillon Books, 1950), ch. 5.

Table 20.9

Results of 1950 Congressional Elections Related to 1948 Division of
Major-Party Vote by Districts

1948		1950					
Per Cent Democratic	Number of Districts	Districts Unchanged		Shifted to Republican		Shifted to Democratic	
		Number	Per Cent	Number	Per Cent	Number	Per Cent
0–30.0	15	15	100.0				
30.1–35.0	19	18	94.7			1 [a]	5.3
35.1–49.9	133	133	100.0				
50.1–52.5	27	13	48.1	14	51.9		
52.6–55.0	26	15	57.7	11	42.3		
55.1–57.5	18	14	77.8	4	22.2		
57.6–60.0	20	19	95.0	1	5.0		
60.1–100.0	170	170	100.0				
Total	428 [b]	397	92.8	30	7.0	1	0.2

[a] First district of New York. Kingsland Macy was defeated by a Democrat.
[b] Florida districts reapportioned in 1949, excluded. Also excluded was California's 5th district, where a Democrat had replaced Republican Richard Welch in a 1949 special election.

come of the House elections in 1952 and 1954 are presented in Table 20.10. The 1954 election fitted the pattern of the 1950 election but in reverse. Republicans captured extremely few 1952 Democratic seats and quite peculiar cicumstances prevailed in these districts. On the other hand, the Democrats made enough gains, chiefly among seats Republican in 1952 by slender pluralities, to win control of the House. The transfer of control, unusual at the first midterm election after a President takes office, came not from exceptionally heavy Republican midterm losses but from the fact that the 1952 Republican House majority was so slight that a normal midterm sag sufficed to reduce it to a minority.

Reflection about the relationships shown in Tables 20.9 and 20.10 ought to bring some revision of the common assertion that congressional elections are determined by local considerations, by the personality of candidates, all more or less independent of the national party battle. The data of these tables suggest that the balloting represents an episode in the ebb and flow of the fortunes of the parties nationally; the Representatives in the normally close districts are the casualties of battle. Personality and local considerations play a part, but it would require a truly remarkable distribution of attractive personalities to explain why in 1950 only sitting Democrats needed to worry about their fate while in 1954 only sitting

Table 20.10

Results of 1954 House Elections Related to Republican Percentage of 1952 Popular Vote for Representatives by District

1952 Republican Per Cent of Vote	Number of Districts	1954 Districts Unchanged		Shifted to Democratic		Shifted to Republican	
		Number	Per Cent	Number	Per Cent	Number	Per Cent
0–9	85	84	98.8			1 [a]	1.2
10–29	21	21	100.0				
30–39	39	38	97.4			1 [b]	2.6
40–44	23	23	100.0				
45–49	45	42	93.3			3 [c]	6.7
50–54	41	23	56.1	18	43.9		
55–59	53	51	96.2	2	3.8		
60–69	98	94	95.9	4 [d]	4.1		
70 and over	30	30	100.0				

[a] This was the Dallas, Texas, district.

[b] The 15th district of Ohio had been held by a Democrat whose personal following enabled him to carry a heavily Republican district. An appointment to a federal commission removed him from the 1954 competition.

[c] These Republican gains were: the 1st district of Kansas, normally Republican, but won by a Democrat in 1952 on a local issue; the 6th of California, where Democrat Robert L. Condon was defeated; the 1st of Florida (St. Petersburg).

[d] Two of these districts had first been picked up by the Democrats in special elections: the 6th of New Jersey and the 9th of Wisconsin. Another of the four was the normally Democratic district that had been held by Jacob Javits of New York.

Republicans were under a like necessity. The misfortunes of the "ins" may be attributable to a variety of considerations—power policy in one district, farm policy in another, labor policy in another—but the common denominator of the midterm electoral decision as a whole is a pro-Democratic or a pro-Republican turn.

Constitution, Electoral Practices, and Party System

While the details of the patterns of behavior involved in the interrelationships of constitutional system and party system are intricate, their combined broad effect may be simply stated. They both reflect and contribute to the peculiar nature of the American political system. The basic arrangement that puts teeth into the system of separated powers is the independent election of President, of Senate, and of House of Representatives. The formal electoral autonomy of each of the major organs of government introduces divisive factors into the party system and, in turn, the unifying forces of party react upon the constitutional system and modify the formal separation of the organs of government.

Through the electoral system each major party seeks to extend its control over President, House, and Senate, and to a degree succeeds. Yet, paradoxically, the interworkings of party and electoral system contribute also to the uniqueness and independence of President, House, and Senate. Neither party seems able to mobilize its forces with equal success—or perhaps to mobilize the same forces—in the fight for the Presidency and for Congress. The winning presidential candidate draws support not available to his congressional associates. In part this divergence in sources of support flows from the peculiar appeals of each successful presidential candidate. To some extent it flows from imperfections in the manning and operation of the party apparatus on the congressional level. It results, too, from features of the constitutional system—the staggered terms of the Senate and the off-year elections of the House—which stimulate attempts by legislators to establish themselves within their constituencies independently of party.

One broad consequence of the ensemble of arrangements, formal and informal, is to limit the range of decision made by the electorate in the national polling. Great oscillations of public sentiment and feeling are to some extent blocked or at least damped. Shifts of public attitude seem to be most sensitively and completely reflected in presidential voting; they are obstructed in the congressional voting. The incapacity of the winning party to field a congressional ticket equal in popular strength to its presidential candidate trims the scope of the triumph of the party victorious in the presidential voting. Whether such limitations on popular decision are to the public good presents another question. Doubtless at times they protect the Republic from its foolish whim of the moment; at others, they may form defenses for special interests against public wrath.

In another way the general scheme contributes significantly to the character of the political order by creating points of power and authority that cannot be brought readily under central domination. That is, they assure a dispersion or decentralization of power within the party structures. In the dominant party of the moment the standpat districts provide foundations for party factions not beholden to the national leadership and immune to the depredations of the opposition. The resultant cleavages within the majority are duly recorded on the front pages every day. Less commonly recognized are the consequences of the electoral system for the party of the opposition. The system operates, as we have shown by a variety of analyses, to strengthen the minority within the Congress and thereby to assure the maintenance of points of power with a vested interest in resisting the accumulation of power about the President who leads the current majority. The minority almost invariably places in the Congress, even in years of presidential elections, members who would under a more tightly articulated party system be defeated. The effects of the off-year elections further re-enforce this capacity of the minority to survive.

The total effect of all these arrangements in decentralizing and restraining power and in maintaining obstructions to the majority of the moment is congenial to the popular American political philosophy, through which runs a strain of deep distrust of authority. Yet these constitutional virtues may also be defects, in particular the division of authority between the parties, possible because of the midterm elections. In grave circumstances divided partisan control could be disastrous. Even in normal times such elections may place legislative leadership in the hands of those not under the moderating influence of the knowledge that their party is responsible for the administration in all its day-to-day aspects. Governmental departments may be harassed by an opposition congressional majority whose sole motive is to embarrass the Administration. When asked how he would run the House if the Republicans should win in 1946, Joe Martin is said to have replied: "Why, that'll be simple. I'll open each session with a prayer and I'll end it with a vote for a new probe."

The fact that our parties are American parties—and not European parties—makes the division of control of the government between the parties less serious than it might be. If the parties were tightly disciplined and doctrinally disparate, midterm elections could result in an intolerable stalemate. As it is, the parties have adapted themselves to the system and sufficient cross-party collaboration prevails to keep the basic business of government in motion. But there should be no blinking the fact that the midterm elections have their effects. Democratic capture of the House in 1930 made it impossible to cope with the depression in accord with the program of Herbert Hoover. Republican victory in 1946 probably accentuated inflationary tendencies through the rejection of Truman's policies on taxes and economic controls. Democratic control of Congress after the 1954 elections retarded, if it did not block, the pro-business policies of the Republicans.[16]

The division of governmental control flowing from the midterm elections has led to proposals for constitutional reform.[17] After the Democratic defeat in the election of 1946, Senator J. W. Fulbright, of Arkansas,

[16] At an earlier time the loss of the House by the President's party usually preceded a loss of the Presidency at the next election. The midterm verdict was but a step toward a shift in party control of the government. More recently the loss of Congress has not been uniformly an omen of the coming loss of the Presidency.

[17] See W. G. Carleton, "Our Congressional Elections: In Defense of the Traditional System," *Political Science Quarterly*, 70 (1955), pp. 341-357.

proposed that President Truman resign, having first appointed as Secretary of State, who was then in line for succession to the Presidency, a person acceptable to the Republican congressional leadership. He argued that it was desirable to have "at all times, but especially in a time of tense international relations and confusion at home, a government capable of functioning in a definite positive manner." As things stood, he foresaw only stalemate for two years. Acceptance of the proposal would have amounted to a step toward parliamentary government.[18] Others have suggested that the House be elected for terms of four years to run concurrently with that of the President. If both House and Senate were elected concurrently with the President, forces would be loosed which might in the long run alter drastically the relations of President and Congress as well as the character of the party system.[19]

[18] Mr. Truman is said to have remarked, in irreverent allusion to Senator Fulbright's tenure as a Rhodes scholar, that what this country needs is more land-grant colleges.

[19] Congressional elections have been subjected to very little analysis. The chief books are C. A. M. Ewing, *Congressional Elections, 1896–1944* (Norman: University of Oklahoma Press, 1947); Malcolm Moos, *Politics, Presidents and Coattails* (Baltimore: Johns Hopkins Press, 1952); Louis Bean, *The Mid-Term Battle* (Washington: Cantillon Books, 1950). An acute analysis of factors in the midterm House elections has been made by Ruth C. Silva, "A Look Into a Crystal Election Ball," *New York Times Magazine*, October 10, 1954.

21 | Electoral Participation

THE EARNEST campaigns of the Junior Chamber of Commerce to get out the vote sometimes provoke an amused cynicism or even hostile criticism. Persons with an antidemocratic bent may regard such efforts as a stupid endeavor to induce people ignorant of both the candidates and the issues to cast a blind vote. The sophisticates may smile at the work of the JayCees as the harmless antics of humorless activists not likely to affect the political system markedly either for good or for ill. In fact solemn admonitions to the citizenry to go to the polls influence the turnout only slightly, if at all. Yet, for the student of politics, the broad question of electoral participation is by no means trivial. Examination of popular participation in the political process may suggest crucial insights into the nature of the political order. Even variations in the character of the act of voting may serve as indices of fundamental characteristics of the state. An extremely small voter turnout may reflect disillusionment and lack of faith in the democratic process among those who stay at home. It may also result from a widespread belief that affairs are proceeding so well that people need not be deeply concerned.

Political participation by the citizen may involve far more than the simple act of voting. Discussion of public issues, contributions to party causes, work in the chores of campaigns and of election days, the acquisition of information about candidates and issues, and the travail of reflection about public problems are other forms of participation. The varying extent of these types of participation within electorates may be associated with profound differences in the nature of political systems. A state in which large numbers of citizens spring to campaign duties as the political conflict warms up may differ radically from one in which the citizenry regards politics as a matter for a small official or professionalized political class. A political order in which the citizen believes that about all he can do is vote yes or no by no means resembles one in which large numbers of citizens believe that they can bestir themselves, convert their fellows, and affect the course of events by their own efforts.

Obviously the full significance of political participation becomes apparent only when nations sharply differing in the character of citizen involvement in the political process are contrasted. While the data for such contrasts are not available, a good deal is known about the character and extent of participation in the United States. A summary of that information will provide a basis for reflection about some of the broad questions associated with participation.

Trends in Presidential Voting

Commonly in the United States popular interest in voting attains its highest level in presidential elections. The intensity of campaign effort reaches a peak in races for the Presidency, and the media of communication bring presidential politics most compellingly to public attention. Yet even in presidential elections participation does not match the levels of interest shown in the national elections of most other western democracies.

A broad picture of presidential voting since 1896 appears in the graphs in Figure 21.1. Since 1920, a substantially smaller proportion of the potential electorate has voted in presidential elections than voted in the 1890's. In 1896 almost 80 per cent of the enfranchised population came to the polls; in the period 1920–1956, between 49 and 63 per cent. Such a change in the level of interest may seem, when it appears as a tiny dip in a line on a chart, a small shift. The magnitude of the alteration in voting habits may be better grasped if an estimate is made of the numbers who would have voted in a recent election had the 1896 turnout rate prevailed. The 1952 vote reached a high level, but if the same proportion of eligibles had voted as in 1896, about 16,500,000 more persons would have gone to the polls. With a potential electorate of around 100,000,000 a change in turnout rate of one percentage point means that a million fewer, or more, persons vote.

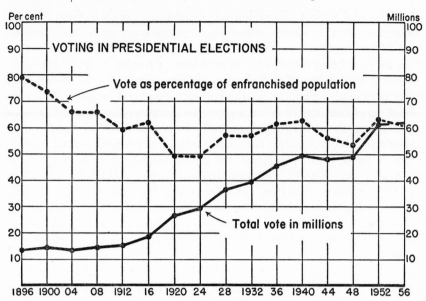

Figure 21.1. Total Presidential Vote and Vote as a Percentage of the Potential
Electorate, 1896–1956

Problems in measuring turnout. Although the graphs in Figure 21.1 indicate correctly the long-run trend in participation in presidential voting,
they do not provide an absolute measure of popular interest comparable
with the figures usually cited for other countries. Editors often seize upon
a figure of around 60 per cent turnout, as in the elections of 1936, 1940, and
1952, compare it with much higher participation figures for Great Britain,
Holland, or Norway, and bemoan the lack of appreciation of the blessings
of liberty among our citizenry.

One would obtain a measure of interest in presidential voting more
comparable with the figures for other countries, if he drew into Figure
21.1 a graph 6 or 7 percentage points higher than the one that appears
there. The percentages shown rest on the proportions of the potential
electorate actually voting—that is, in recent decades, of the proportion of
citizens 21 and over.[1] Not all such persons possess the technical qualifications for voting. A goodly number cannot meet the requirements for residence. Others may have lost the privilege through criminal conviction.
Others may be confined in institutions. Still others may be disqualified
because of their inability to meet other suffrage requirements. The partici-

[1] In the estimation of the potential electorate for computation of the percentages
underlying Figure 21.1 allowance was made for the varying practices among the
states before 1920 regarding woman suffrage, as well as for the differing rules on the
requirement of citizenship for voting.

pation figures for other countries commonly do not include such disqualified categories in the base from which participation rates are computed. Even after allowance for the shortcomings of our measure of participation,[2] the fact remains that the levels of interest in American national elections are lower than those of other major democracies. Whether that differential indicates that the body politic is in an unhealthy state is another matter.

Explanations for variations in turnout. A major question posed by the trend of voting is why the decline in electoral interest since the 1890's. The blunt truth is that nobody knows the answer. A frequent explanation has been that the enfranchisement of women in 1920 brought into the electorate large numbers of persons not in the habit of voting. Yet popular interest began to shrink before the adoption of the woman suffrage amendment. A fairly steady decline occurred from 1896 to 1916. Woman suffrage undoubtedly accounted, at least in substantial part, for the drop in turnout rates in 1920 and in 1924. It took some time for women to become initiated into the mysteries of voting and even now larger proportions of women than of men do not vote.

Woman suffrage accounts only for a part of the difference in popular interest at mid-century and in the 1890's. David Riesman has suggested that profound changes in the American character may underlie an increasing apathy towards matters political.[3] Others have surmised that faith in the efficacy of political action has weakened since the fiery political battles of the 1890's. Although the trend may indicate some change in the American polity, its full explanation remains in the realm of speculation.

Some of the lesser fluctuations in turnout revealed by Figure 21.1 find relatively simple but plausible explanation. The climb in turnout from 1924 to 1936 may be attributed in part to the gradual habituation of women to voting. The hotly fought campaign of 1928 probably deserves credit for bringing more voters to the polls, and the campaigns of 1936 and 1940, both of which centered on deeply felt issues, stimulated voter interest to an even higher pitch. The dip in turnout in 1944 resulted from the numbers of persons in the armed services as well as from the inability

---

[2] Incidentally not even the number of persons who cast a ballot in a presidential election is known precisely. Some voters either do not mark the ballot for a presidential candidate or they spoil their ballot and it is not counted. The vote for minor candidates is almost certainly incompletely reported. In Rhode Island in 1954, 3.18 per cent of the persons who went through the voting machines, as shown by the mechanical counters, did not record a choice for governor. This proportion had ranged from 8 to 10 per cent when paper ballots were used. If a 3 per cent slippage is assumed to prevail in presidential voting—which may be high—the total turnout in 1952 was on the order of 2,000,000 in excess of the presidential vote of 61,550,000.

[3] See *The Lonely Crowd* (New Haven: Yale University Press, 1950).

of many migrants to war-manufacturing centers to fulfill residence requirements for voting. Whether the upsurge in electoral interest in 1952 and 1956 moved the participation level to a new plateau remains to be seen. In any event, attempts to explain that sharp increase in voting make it evident that considerable mystery remains about the causes for the great fluctuations in popular participation.

Variations with Type of Election

Not so many Americans may vote, but those who do work harder at it than do the electors of most other countries. The American voter is marched to the polls far more frequently than are his counterparts elsewhere. In a single year there may be, at different times, municipal primaries, municipal elections, presidential primaries, primaries to nominate candidates for state offices, the presidential election, and perhaps a special election or so. When the voter makes his way to the polling booth, he is confronted, too, by a number of choices unapproached in other countries. A single primary ballot may contain the names of literally dozens of aspirants for nomination for various offices. The general election ballot itself may require the expression of choices for a dozen or more offices. Moreover, the ballot may include a series of propositions or issues; the elector must act on proposed constitutional amendments, initiated measures, referred questions, charter amendments, bond issues, and other such matters. The American voter, in short, has a formidable task.

Participation in state and local elections. Not unexpectedly electoral participation differs considerably among types of elections, and these variations in interest point to some of the factors affecting turnout. Sharp contrasts exist in campaigns. The salience of the personalities and issues of national politics ordinarily command the attention of far more people than do the less dramatic questions of state politics. These differences appear markedly by comparisons of the vote in the years of presidential elections and in the off year. Illustrative is Figure 21.2, which indicates the proportion of the potential electorate of Ohio voting for governor during the period 1920–1954. The saw-toothed graph points to the effect of the presidential campaign in drawing voters to the polls. As they vote for President, they incidentally mark their ballot for governor. In the gubernatorial elections held in the off years without benefit of the drum beating of the rivals for the Presidency, the turnout drops sharply. The Ohio pattern occurs uniformly in other states. Thus the total vote in New York's 1954 gubernatorial election dropped about two million from the 1952 presidential turnout.

When elections of officials of cities, counties, and other local govern-

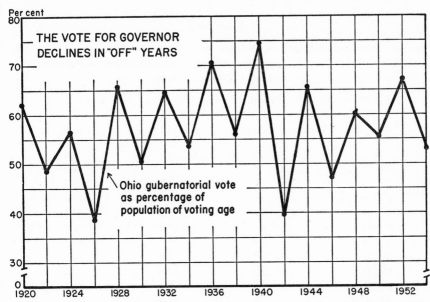

Figure 21.2. Percentage of Citizens 21 Years of Age and Over Voting in Ohio Gubernatorial Elections, 1920–1954

ments occur at a time different from that of the presidential election, turnout tends to be low. Since about 1900, in an attempt to insulate municipal affairs from the influences of national politics, more and more local elections have been scheduled in off years or at times other than the November political season. This timing of local elections has resulted in a reduction in turnout. The information available does not permit an estimate of the modal rate of turnout in local elections over the entire country. Wide variations occur from place to place and doubtless from time to time within the same community. The range of variation is suggested by Table 21.1, which classifies 324 Massachusetts local elections of February and March, 1940, according to the relation of the turnout to the vote in the presidential election held later in the year. In a few localities the local vote amounted to less than 10 per cent of, and in a few it exceeded, the presidential vote. About half the local elections attracted a vote of less than 70 per cent of the presidential vote.[4]

[4] In 1940 the Massachusetts presidential vote amounted to 78.7 per cent of the citizens 21 and over. In a town with a presidential vote at the state rate, a local vote equal to 25 per cent of the presidential vote would have been about 20 per cent of the citizen population 21 and over. A local vote equal to 75 per cent of the presidential vote would have been 59 per cent of the potential electorate. In almost half of the town elections in the table the vote in the local election probably amounted to less than 50 per cent of the potential electorate.

Table 21.1

Local Government Elections Attract Fewer Voters Than the Presidential Sweepstakes: Vote in 324 Massachusetts Local Elections as Percentage of 1940 Presidential Vote [a]

Local Vote as Percentage of Presidential Vote	Number of Local Elections	Per Cent Distribution of Elections	Cumulative Distribution of Elections
0–9	5	1.5	1.5
10–19	8	2.5	4.0
20–29	9	2.8	6.8
30–39	18	5.6	12.4
40–49	19	5.9	18.3
50–59	45	13.9	32.2
60–69	60	18.5	50.7
70–79	68	21.0	71.7
80–89	58	17.9	89.6
90–99	27	8.3	97.9
100–109	6	1.3	99.7
110–114	1	0.3	100.0
Total	324	100.0	

[a] The 324 elections included 311 town elections and 13 city elections held in 1940, principally in February and March.

Popular interest in primaries. The use of direct primaries for the nomination of party candidates gives American voters the opportunity to vote in a type of election virtually restricted to this country. Outside the South popular interest in party primaries is far lower than that in general elections. Comparatively few voters determine who are to be the candidates in the general election campaign. In about three-fourths of the primaries held in a sample of states, analyzed in Table 21.2, less than 35 per cent of the potential electorate voted on the nomination of gubernatorial candidates. On the other hand, in three-fourths of the general elections in the same states more than 50 per cent of the potential electorate went to the polls. In the primary of the weaker party of a state or district the vote tends to be low in relation to the vote for that party's candidate in the general election. By the same measure, popular interest in the primary of the dominant party usually is considerably higher.

Voting on issues. Another type of electoral chore peculiarly American is voting on issues. Some types of questions under American practice are commonly settled by popular vote rather than by the actions of officials. Amendments to state constitutions and to city charters are submitted to

Table 21.2

Popular Interest in Primaries: Distribution of 176 Gubernatorial Primaries and Associated General Elections According to Percentage of Potential Electorate Voting [a]

Participation Rate	Number of Primaries [b]	Percentage Distribution	Number of Elections	Percentage Distribution
Under 20	31	17.6	0	0.0
20–24	23	13.1	0	0.0
25–29	37	21.0	2	1.1
30–34	39	22.2	5	2.8
35–39	15	8.5	10	5.7
40–44	5	2.8	8	4.5
45–49	10	5.7	17	9.7
50 and over	16	9.1	134	76.2
Total	176	100.0	176	100.0

[a] The primaries and elections included in this tabulation were those held in the period 1926–1952 in the following states: Vermont, North Dakota, Maine, Wisconsin, Michigan, New Hampshire, Pennsylvania, Kansas, Massachusetts, Illinois, Wyoming, Ohio, Colorado, West Virginia, and Missouri.

[b] In this column one primary equals a pair of simultaneous primaries, Republican and Democratic. Thus in 31 primaries, so defined, less than 20 per cent of the potential electorate voted for Republican or Democratic aspirants for the gubernatorial nomination.

the voters for approval. In some jurisdictions bond issues fall under the same rule. In some states voters may, by petition under the initiative procedure, place a proposal for a law or constitutional amendment on the ballot. In a similar fashion, in some states acts of the legislature may be suspended and subjected to popular approval or rejection.

On all these types of issues wide variations in voter interest prevail. Proposed amendments to state constitutions excite the interest of relatively few voters. Often they deal with technical questions or with matters that concern few people. In truth, they often must be voted on, not because they deserve popular attention, but because the constitution contains matters which should be handled by statute. On the other hand, when a measure on the ballot deals with a hot issue or with one that affects significantly the interests of important groups in society, a much higher level of voting interest will exist. These differences are illustrated by the data of Table 21.3, which contrasts the proportions of voters who go to the polls that express a choice on different sorts of measures in California, a state whose electors vote on many issues. The proportions voting on constitutional amendments tend to be considerably lower than the proportions voting on initiated and referred measures. The difference flows, not from the form of the issue, but from the substantive differences that usually exist between the two categories of questions. Initiated measures deal with matters in which some organized group has an intense interest and other groups usually are in opposition with equal intensity. The spirited campaign efforts by the groups concerned lead far larger proportions of the voters to express a preference on such measures than on questions dealing with technical or relatively unimportant constitutional amendments.

Factors influencing turnout rates. Several types of elections have been described whose varying character affects the level of popular participation. Other differentiations among elections also bear on participation but they are less readily identified than are those that have been indicated. For example, the closeness of the contest, or the anticipated closeness, seems to be associated with variations in electoral turnout. When the outcome seems to be a foregone conclusion, electoral interest is apt to be low and efforts to get out the vote are likely to be comparatively weak. Perhaps the most striking demonstration of this factor may be found in the variations in participation among the states in the voting for President. Historically, the outcome of the contest for presidential electors in the southern states has not been in much doubt. For that and other reasons, the turnout in the presidential voting in these states has been far lower than in states in which a spirited battle for the electoral vote usually occurs. The differences among the states in presidential voting appear in the map in Figure 21.3, which shows the rates of turnout by states in the 1956 elec-

Table 21.3

Voter Interest in Issues: Measures on California Ballot, 1948–1954, According to Percentage of Voters Expressing a Preference [a]

Per Cent of Voters Who Cast Ballots for Presidential or Gubernatorial Candidates	Number of Measures Submitted by Legislature	Number of Initiated and Referred Measures	Total
90–94	0	7	7
85–89	3	4	7
80–84	13	5	18
75–79	21	0	21
70–74	15	0	15
65–69	5	0	5

[a] In presidential years, the presidential vote was used as the total number of voters; in the off years, the gubernatorial vote was the base for computation of percentages.

PER CENT VOTING

Under 50

50-64

65-69

70 and over

Figure 21.3. Geographical Differentials in Electoral Participation: Percentages of Estimated Potential Electorate Voting in Presidential Election of 1956, by States tion. When it is said that the anticipated closeness of the contest and the associated intensity of campaign effort bear upon the size of the turnout, it should also be noted that the rate of turnout does not necessarily respond immediately when the electoral division changes from, say, 60–40 to 55–45. Rather, when elections are matters of form, as in presidential voting in southern states over a long period, states develop habits of political participation that are not quickly altered. Such persistent levels of participation may rest also on factors other than the intensity of the contest. States tend to have fairly stable levels of participation in comparison with other states over long periods of time; a state with a high rate of voting at one election also ranks high at the next election.

For most of the mentioned differentials in voting interest, commonsense explanations suggest themselves. A campaign that evokes enormous efforts by the party organizations to get out the vote, that presents the electorate with dramatic issues, that commands the attention of the media of communication will stir far more interest than a campaign whose outcome seems to the voter to be of slight immediate importance. The clashes of candidates whose personalities engage the emotions of masses of people will pull more voters to the polls than will contests between nonentities. Similarly, when the voter is confronted by issues or questions about which he has no information or which he cannot readily understand, he is apt to pass over those items on the ballot. Or, if the outcome of an election seems assured, fewer people will vote than if it looks like a horse race.

These variations in participation among elections have practical consequences that politicians take into account in the scheduling of elections. When the tide of national politics is running in favor of a party, state and local elections may be timed to occur simultaneously with the presidential voting. The greater turnout as well as the pull of the presidential candidate may give advantage to the state and local candidates on his ticket. State and local elections may be scheduled at times other than the presidential election also on the assumption that the lower turnout at such times will affect the results.

It is a nice question whether the higher turnout in presidential voting tends to make the national government more responsive than state governments to the great surges of sentiment that sweep the country. Or, to put the question in another way, whether a different constituency, a different shade of opinion, may not tend to be dominant in state affairs from that which moves the national government. If this should be true, variations in levels of voting may be among the factors conducive to federal centralization on the assumption that a smaller and generally more conservative voting constituency tends to form around state governments.

Group Differentials in Political Participation

The general political situation in which an elector finds himself—the type of election, the nature of the campaign—determines to some extent whether he actually votes. Regardless of the general situation, persons with certain social characteristics are more likely to vote than are persons without those characteristics. Marked variations exist in the extent to which various types of people vote. These differentials persist from election to election and occur consistently in all western democracies.

Demographic correlates of voting and nonvoting. The facts about differentials in voting and nonvoting among various population categories may be stated quite simply. Higher proportions of men than of women vote, although the gap between them in political interest has narrowed since 1920. The grant of the franchise did not immediately bring women to the polls; they gradually acquired voting habits. The percentage of income groups going to the polls increases from step to step up the economic ladder. Electoral interest increases with education. On the educational scale, voting participation occurs least frequently among those with a grade school education, most frequently among those with college training. The young and the old manifest less electoral enthusiasm than do those in the middle years. Metropolitan dwellers turn out in larger proportions in presidential elections than do residents of rural areas. Usually political interest declines from level to level as one goes down the scale of occupational status. Negroes, even in the North, vote in lesser degree than do whites. Persons with strong party loyalties turn out to the polls in relatively larger numbers than do those weakly identified with party or those with independent inclinations. Most of these differences, which have been demonstrated to exist by a large number of inquiries, are shown in detail for a pair of presidential elections in Table 21.4.

Apparently education and income are the demographic characteristics most closely associated with electoral participation. Sharp differences prevail in the participation rates of the highest and lowest income groups, and about the same contrasts exist between the voting interest of those with college and grade school education. Income and education are fairly closely correlated, yet they are independent in their bearing on variations in electoral interest. Thus, among grade schoolers voting participation increases with income. High-income persons with little formal education vote in about as high degree as do college persons of equivalent income. Similarly, low-income, college-trained persons show lower rates of electoral participation than do persons of similar education who have managed

Table 21.4

Demographic Characteristics in Relation to Voting and Nonvoting in Presidential Elections of 1948 and 1952 [a]

Characteristics	1948		1952	
	Voted	Did Not Vote	Voted	Did Not Vote
Sex				
Male	69%	31%	79%	21%
Female	59	41	69	31
Age				
21–34	56	44	68	32
35–44	66	34	76	24
45–54	75	25	79	21
55 and over	63	37	77	23
Education				
Grade school	55	45	62	38
High school	67	33	80	20
College	79	21	90	10
Income				
Under $2000	46	54	53	47
$2,000–2,999	61	39	68	32
$3,000–3,999	74	26	76	24
$4,000–4,999	75	25	83	17
$5,000 and over	82	18	88	12
Occupation				
Professional and managerial	75	25	88	12
White-collar	81	19	81	19
Skilled and semiskilled	71	29	74	26
Unskilled	50	50	60	40
Farmers	42	58	67	33

[a] Based on interviews with national samples of voters by Survey Research Center reported by Angus Campbell and others, *The Voter Decides* (Evanston: Row, Peterson, 1954), pp. 70-73.

to make their way into the higher-income groups. Within income categories, voting interest tends to vary with levels of education.

From such data the inference is often drawn that persons with a stake in public affairs and with wider ranges of knowledge and information tend, as one might expect, to show the highest levels of interest in voting. That is perhaps true, but it should be remembered that these facts are drawn from observations of presidential voting and doubtless do not reveal what variations, if any, may exist in behavior in other types of elections. For example, in a municipal primary, city employees, without regard to level of income or education, may vote in extremely high degree and wield a controlling influence.

Motivational factors in voting and nonvoting. While electoral participation is clearly associated with demographic characteristics such as education and income, the explanation of voting and nonvoting in these terms represents a low order of analysis. Upper-income people do vote in high degree but the fact confronts us that a great many poor people also vote. Obviously income is not the sole determinant of voting interest. Some common factor must bring into the active electorate rich and poor, the college-trained and the grade schoolers.

Recent researchers have sought to go beyond demographic analysis and to identify the motivations that bring people to participate in the political process. From these studies, the most notable of which have been made by Angus Campbell, it becomes evident that factors other than income, education, and other such characteristics bear on political participation. Concern about issues, for example, bears significantly on voting and on other forms of political participation. Persons who are both keenly sensitive to the disagreements between the parties on issues and hold strongly felt attitudes of their own about those issues tend to vote in high degree. Those unaware of party stands and with no strong feelings of their own stay away from the polls in droves. Campbell developed a rough measure of these factors, which he called a measure of the extent of issue orientation, and checked the relationship between it and voting in the 1952 presidential election. Only 11 per cent of those persons with the highest extent of issue orientation failed to vote, whereas 58 per cent of those with the lowest score on issue orientation did not vote.

Campbell also attempted to measure the sense of political efficacy, that is, to determine the extent to which the citizen felt that it made any difference whether he voted or participated otherwise in politics. Of those persons with a high sense of political efficacy, only 13 per cent did not vote. Of those with a low score on this measure, 47 per cent did not vote. In another exploratory study, Campbell sought to measure the sense of citizen duty, which represents the degree to which a person feels that he ought to vote as a matter of civic obligation, although he may well believe that his actions will not affect the course of human events. Again, the degree of participation varied along the scale measuring the sense of citizen duty. Of those groups with the highest sense of citizen duty, only 15 per cent failed to vote in 1952 while at the low point of the scale, 73 per cent did not vote.

These patterns of motivation associated with high degrees of political participation are positively associated with demographic correlates of participation, but the psychological motives operate independently. That is, issue orientation, the sense of political efficacy, the sense of citizen duty, and other such attitudes become more marked as income increases and as one goes up the educational scale. Yet within each income level, for example, participation varies with the extent of issue orientation or the sense of political efficacy. Extremely sharp contrasts in voting participation prevail, for example, between persons with a grade-school education who have a sense of political efficacy in high and low degree. Similarly, low-income persons with a low sense of citizen duty are far less likely to vote than are low-income persons with a high sense of citizen duty.[5] The inquiries that produced these findings establish the proposition that certain types of attitudes lead to voting; other attitudes are likely to be associated with nonparticipation. Another sort of problem is raised by the question of how some individuals come to be equipped with one set of attitudes, others with another. The chances are that these varying attitude patterns are precipitated by the complex of developmental experiences that make a man what he is, such as family influences, formal education, and group associations.

Students of electoral behavior have identified many other factors associated with voting and nonvoting. Persons with strong party attachments are more likely to vote than are independents. Degree of exposure to political discussion and communication affects voter turnout. Of special importance is group affiliation. Persons not affiliated with voluntary groups, such as churches, labor unions, and the like, are less likely to vote than are individuals with several group connections. Perhaps the way to put the matter is that persons less completely integrated into the life of the community are less disposed to participate in its politics. Persons who sense an awareness of the relevance to them of government policies are more disposed to vote than are those without such awareness.[6]

When the analysis of participation shifts from simple demographic correlation to motivational factors, the underlying significance of electoral participation becomes more nearly discernible. If the affairs of the state were so conducted that an extremely large proportion of the population felt that voting was a pointless exercise because things were fixed anyway, the political health of the Republic would not be good. What dire conse-

[5] All these and other related matters are reported in detail by Angus Campbell, Gerald Gurin, and Warren E. Miller, *The Voter Decides* (Evanston: Row, Peterson, 1954).

[6] For an analysis of studies of participation, see S. M. Lipset and others, "The Psychology of Voting: An Analysis of Political Behavior," *Handbook of Social Psychology*, Gardner Lindzey, ed., (Boston: Addison Wesley Press, 1954), II, pp. 1124–1175. For the most extended treatment of voter participation, see the forthcoming volume by Robert E. Lane.

quences might follow under such circumstances is problematic, but conceivably the populace would be open to the blandishments of men advocating cures by nondemocratic methods. Or a generally depressed civic morale might be an indicator that democratic procedures had already been converted into a farce. The operation of a democratic order may require the existence of a widespread belief among the voters in the reality of their role in the system.

Participation differentials and the fortunes of parties. The identification of differentials in electoral participation among groups within the population suggests the mundane question whether they affect the fortunes of parties on the American scene. Those elements of the population with lowest voting rates consist in larger measure of persons with Democratic rather than Republican predispositions. Democratic strength has been drawn disproportionately from among the lower-income groups, the less well educated, and skilled and unskilled workers.

Democratic candidates would have been strengthened, at least in recent decades, by compulsory voting or by some other means of bringing out substantially the entire electorate. Analysis after analysis has shown a higher preference for the Democratic cause among those who stayed away from the polls than among those who voted. In November, 1940 those who told *Fortune* interviewers that they did not expect to vote were better than four to one for Roosevelt. In 1952 the Survey Research Center found that 54 per cent of the nonvoters in its national sample preferred Stevenson as against the 44.5 per cent of those who voted. The inability of the Democrats to bring their full potential strength to the polls does not result solely from their dependence on groups with generally low voting rates. Democratic businessmen or Democratic college-trained people are less apt to vote than are their opposite numbers among the Republicans.[7]

The fact that Democrats are less inclined to take themselves to the polls than Republicans does not mean that an increase in the total turnout will be accompanied invariably by an increase in the Democratic proportion of the total vote. If at one election the turnout is 55 per cent of the potential vote and at the next 60 per cent, the effect of the increase on the partisan division will depend in part upon the sectors of the population from which the increment in vote comes. If the additional vote arises largely from groups with a Democratic predisposition, the Democratic proportion of the total vote will increase. Between 1944 and 1948 in some areas the vote in the prosperous wards declined as that in the poorer wards increased. These shifts in participation contributed to the Democratic vic-

[7] See Angus Campbell, "The Case of the Missing Democrats," *New Republic*, July 2, 1956.

tory in 1948. The obvious fact should also be noted that matters other than turnout rate affect the division of the vote. About the same proportion of the potential electorate voted in 1932 as in 1928, but the division of the vote between the two parties shifted markedly. A great many Hoover voters of 1928 had become skeptical of the blessings of the New Era.

Upsurges in turnout and shifts in party strength. The relation of differentials in group participation and in percentages of the eligibles voting to party fortunes obviously raises complex problems of analysis. Another kind of change in participation, however, seems to be clearly related to sharp changes in the attractiveness of the parties to the voters. An unusually rapid rate of growth in the total number of voters from one election to the next is accompanied by an exceptionally high rate of increase in the number of supporters of one of the parties but not of the other. At least this relationship has prevailed since 1890. It is as if a huge number of potential voters were waiting in reserve to be brought into the active electorate and mainly to the ranks of one of the parties by some new set of circumstances.

From 1892 to 1896 the total turnout increased by 14.7 per cent as the Republican vote grew by 35.5 per cent and the Democratic vote declined by 1.1 per cent from the combined Democratic-Populist vote of 1892. The 1916 presidential turnout exceeded that of 1912 by 23.2 per cent, an unusually high quadrennial rate of increase. Wilson's 1916 vote grew by 45 per cent from 1912 while that of Hughes was only 12 per cent over the combined Taft-Roosevelt vote of 1912. Similarly, the period 1948–1952 marked an unusually sharp increase in the total number of voters, accompanied by a Republican rate of growth about four times that of the Democrats. When the national political struggle warms up enough to bring a substantial increase in electoral interest, factors are probably at work to shift voters from party to party as well as to nudge more of them to the polls.

Varieties of Participation and the Political System

Most studies of electoral participation have been microscopic: they focus on the individual and attempt to identify the characteristics or the motives that lead him to vote or not to vote. Such analyses, illuminating though they are, throw little light on the larger question of the relation between the extent and nature of citizen participation and the character of the political system in the large. The significance of variations in the nature and extent of participation probably can be grasped only by extensive cross-national analyses, although some tentative speculations may be ventured. They should be read with the probability in mind that the nature of the political order may affect patterns of participation as well as the reverse.

A useful distinction to make is that between electoral participation limited to the simple act of voting and more active types of political participation. The act of voting may have different motivations and different meanings and it may occur in different degrees among national political systems. Of somewhat greater interest, perhaps because less is known about them, are those types of political participation that go beyond voting. Each man has one vote, but nothing is plainer than that men differ widely in their political influence. Some persons talk up their beliefs, criticize or praise the government, and push their ideas through their membership in this group and that. They may discuss the campaign with their friends and acquaintances and endeavor to persuade them of the error of their ways or to re-enforce them in their sensible agreement with themselves. They may attend rallies, coffee hours, and party dinners. They write their Congressmen. They serve the party's cause by working at the polls, ringing doorbells, addressing envelopes, or doing other such chores. They may even become party functionaries, minor or great, and they may contribute to the campaign chest and solicit others to aid the worthy cause. Such activists may not limit their efforts to campaigns alone; they join the Chamber of Commerce, a trade union, a reform league, and thereby have other avenues for the dissemination of their views. In a sense they may vote many times.[8]

Variations in voting. Variations in voting participation alone may be either quantitative or qualitative. Such differences may appear by comparisons of the behavior of the same electorate at different times; they may also appear by comparison of the electorates of different nations at the same time.

The question of the significance of quantitative variations in voting has stimulated speculation. The graph of varying proportions of the electorate going to the polls has been likened to a fever chart of the body politic. Social tensions, or so the argument goes, increase with the rate of participation. It seems clear that participation rates provide no unidimensional measure of the temperature of political conflict either within a single nation or between nations. The turnout rates are affected by many factors, some of which have been touched on in this chapter. Turnout rates do provide a rough measure of the extent of political involvement within the population and perhaps of extent of the sense of citizen efficacy. An electorate, defined by universal suffrage, that habitually turns out to the extent

[8] See W. Buchanan, "An Inquiry into Purposive Voting," *Journal of Politics,* 18 (1956), pp. 281–296.

of 10 per cent is probably associated with a radically different structure of power than one that has a habitual participation rate of 85 per cent. Virginia, where an extremely small proportion of the potential electorate votes in the decisive Democratic primaries, has a radically different sort of political order than New York with its far higher participation rate. Variations in participation do not alone account for differences in the structure of power; the nature of political leadership may affect participation and vice versa.

Qualitative differences in the act of voting are doubtless of far greater significance than quantitative variations; nor are qualitative differences necessarily measured by the differences or fluctuations in participation. Not a great deal is known of the meaning of voting and nonvoting to the electorate, although the act of voting varies in significance to the individual. The casting of the ballot may be associated with an intensity and anxiety of concern that marks this action as but a step toward the manning of the barricades. Nonvoting may be the product of disillusionment and lack of faith in the democratic process. Voting may be a gesture of alliance with a fellow religionist or unionist or Pole, an act almost without political consequences, often fortuitous. It may be an act performed after careful deliberation about the general weal. It may be an action associated with a belief that it affects the course of events; it may be pure ritual. Obviously the extent of the distribution of varying sorts of attitudes within the electorate about voting itself is associated with important characteristics of the political order, but knowledge of these matters is limited.

Variations in other types of political participation. Popular participation in government involves a great deal more than the simple act of voting. Those who wish to influence the course of events must bestir themselves to do far more than vote. The people who pick up the ball and carry it have been labeled as activists, as politists,[9] as opinion leaders. They constitute a small proportion of the entire electorate, but the chances are that differences in the size, composition, and behavior of this group are associated with significant variations in the nature of political orders.

The activists may constitute varying proportions of the entire electorate. If the realm of the activists is occupied by a small and exclusive class, perhaps consisting largely of professional politicians, a different sort of system exists than when large numbers of citizens convert themselves into energetic, though amateur, politicians when campaign time rolls around. Self-government is a term mainly for oratorical rather than scientific dis-

[9] Alfred de Grazia applies the term politists to the activists. See his *Elements of Political Science* (New York: Knopf, 1952), ch. 3.

course, yet the reality of self-government may be approached as participation becomes more general within the electorate.

Ease of access to the ranks of the activists may be an important index of the nature of the political order. The odds are that in the United States movement into the ranks of the activists encounters a relatively low level of obstruction. That movement may be observed with special clarity in those endeavors that may have nothing to do with elections but are calculated to influence public policy. A small group of citizens may become exercised about a public problem; it stirs up a noise and pressures the city council into action; it then relapses into inactivity. Another crowd agitates for congressional legislation and a remarkably few people can at times put a bill through Congress.

This movement into and out of the ranks of the activists also evidently exists in presidential politics and it may be a significant characteristic of the American system. The development of a general concern about the character of the government, the appearance of a popular leader, or the unfolding of a great cause—to be either supported or opposed—may activate the latent amateur politician in millions of citizens. They spring to action and the campaign eventuates in a verdict by the electorate, decisive at least for the moment. At other times, the political activists may be far less numerous within the electorate. When things seem to be moving along satisfactorily, people may attend to their plowing. When concern arises, however, the ranks of the attentive and active public are swelled, some sort of solution is fought through, and the amateur politicians go back to their callings. At least, a look backward at presidential elections suggests that something on this order must occur.

No trustworthy information exists on variations in the size of the politically-active sector of the population through time, but a few exploratory analyses have been made of the incidence within the American electorate of types of political participation other than voting. In a study of the 1952 presidential campaign the Survey Research Center asked the respondents in its national sample whether they had given money or bought tickets to help the campaign for one of the parties, whether they had attended meetings or rallies, whether they had worked for one or the other parties or candidates, and whether they had talked to anybody to try to show them how they should vote.

Of the entire sample, only 4 per cent reported that they had given money, bought tickets, or otherwise contributed to the campaign. Seven per cent had attended political meetings or rallies while 3 per cent had done work for one or the other of the candidates. Of the total sample, 11 per cent had engaged in at least one of these formal activities. If the percentage is projected to the entire electorate, it might be estimated that in the neighborhood of 10,000,000 persons participated in at least one of these ways in the campaign. A much larger number, 27 per cent of the sample, reported that they had talked with other people to show them why they should vote for one of the parties or candidates.[10]

While the data indicate that a small proportion of the electorate engages in the more formal types of political participation, the distribution of the high participators within the electorate suggests some inferences about the significance of the American pattern of participation. Generally political activity and participation become more common within the population as one goes up the income scale, up the educational ladder, and up the hierarchy of occupations. The data on variations in extent of political participation by income level appear in Table 21.5. Only 15 per cent of those with incomes under $2,000, and 41 per cent of those with incomes of $5,000 or over ranked as high participators.

From the data of Table 21.5 one might leap to the conclusion that persons in the above-average income brackets constitute most of those who engage in more than average political activity. That inference can be checked, however, by another arrangement of the data which is shown in Table 21.6. The income levels of $5,000 and over account for a share of the high participators somewhat larger than their proportion of the entire electorate. Nevertheless persons with more than average political activity to their credit are dispersed widely in the population among all in-

Table 21.5

Division of Income Classes According to Variations in Level of Political Participation in 1952 Presidential Elections [a]

| Income Bracket | Political Participation Level | | | Number |
	Low Did Not Vote	Medium Voted Only	High Voted and Other [b]	
Under $2,000	47%	38%	15%	315
$2,000–$2,999	31	51	17	255
$3,000–$3,999	24	50	26	364
$4,000–$4,999	17	49	34	233
$5,000 and over	13	46	41	415

[a] Based on a special tabulation of national sample interviewed in 1952 study by Survey Research Center, by courtesy of Angus Campbell, Director of the Center.

[b] Respondents classified as high participators had given money, bought tickets, attended rallies, worked for a party or a candidate, talked to other people to try to influence their vote, or engaged in more than one of these activities.

[10] Campbell, *The Voter Decides*, p. 30.

come and educational levels. No doubt finer measures of political activity would indicate somewhat sharper differentiations among population classes in particular types of political activity, such as in making political contributions. The chores and debates of politics, however, are by no means the exclusive preserve of any small political caste or class.[11]

Table 21.6

Distribution of Persons with High Levels of Political Participation in 1952 Presidential Election Among Income Classes [a]

Income Bracket	High Participators [b]		Total Sample	
	Number	Per Cent	Number	Per Cent
Under $2,000	49	11.2	315	19.9
$2,000–$2,999	44	10.1	255	16.1
$3,000–$3,999	93	21.3	364	23.0
$4,000–$4,999	80	18.4	233	14.7
$5,000 and over	170	39.0	415	26.3
Total	436	100.0	1,582	100.0

[a] Based on a special tabulation of a sample interviewed in 1952 study by Survey Research Center, by courtesy of Angus Campbell, Director of the Center.
[b] The activities requisite for classification as a high participator are indicated in the note to Table 21.5.

Although the data on the distribution and character of political participation that goes beyond the simple act of voting are most fragmentary, the importance of the pattern of mass political activity in determining the character of the political order seems self-evident. A low level of all forms of political participation may at times simply reflect a well-founded general satisfaction with the conduct of public affairs. Yet if an electorate loses the capacity to bestir itself to high levels of activity when the occasion warrants, the chances are that a basic alteration in the location and responsiveness of authority within the society has occurred.[12]

[11] These findings are paralleled by another survey reported by J. L. Woodward and Elmo Roper, "Political Activity of American Citizens," *American Political Science Review*, 44 (1950), pp. 872–885. Tables from the Woodward and Roper article are reproduced in the third edition of this text at pp. 578–579.
[12] Only a few major studies of electoral participation have been cited in this chapter. The footnotes to Chapter 19 in each of the first three editions of this text, cumulatively, provide a fairly complete guide to the American literature on the topic.

22 | The Electorate

NOT ALL nations that have universal suffrage are democratic, but all democratic nations have universal suffrage. Even dictatorial regimes are moved to bolster their position by mock election ceremonies and thereby to pay tribute to the potency of the conceptions underlying popular government. Universal suffrage, now regarded as commonplace, did not come about in a day. Popular governments at first allowed only a small part of the populace to vote. In western democratic societies the suffrage has been gradually extended to new groups; each extension has been in response to the demands of a group emerging from political subordination and demanding a voice in the management of public affairs. Whether by the acquisition of suffrage these new groups always gained power and influence or merely won a symbol of emancipation may be questioned. Nevertheless, the step-by-step extension of the suffrage has brought with it far-reaching changes in the methods and strategy of politics. In monarchical and aristocratic regimes the gaining of power might be a matter of personal intrigue among a small group of people. Success depended on the possession of qualities and the employment of techniques quite different from those necessary to gain the favor of the electorate under a system of universal suffrage.

A broad popular suffrage is, then, a constant that conditions both the method and the substance of American politics. Its development in the United States is principally of historical interest; the story is none the less important for an understanding of American politics. The first great suffrage battle broke down property-owning and taxpaying qualifications for manhood suffrage. The outcome of this struggle marked the decline of the colonial and early American aristocracies and the rise in power and influence of the common man. The question of Negro suffrage was debated and, in the main, settled against the Negro prior to the Civil War. The Fifteenth Amendment was designed to extend the suffrage to the Negro, but its effectiveness was long delayed. The third great dispute over the suffrage turned on the question of its extension to women. While the elimination of property-owning and taxpaying qualifications was accomplished by state action, questions of the vote for Negroes and for women became issues of national politics and raised problems of the expediency of national control of suffrage in the federal system.[1]

Property and the Vote

Early property qualifications. Until the triumph of Jacksonian Democracy, property-holding and taxpaying qualifications for the exercise of the suffrage were common. The American Revolution had brought no

[1] The Federal Constitution adopted state definitions of suffrage for the election of Senators and Representatives. Members of the House were to be chosen by "the people of the several states, and the electors in each state shall have the qualifications requisite for electors of the most numerous branch of the state legislature."—Art. I, sec. 2. The same qualifications for voters for Senators were embodied in the Seventeenth Amendment, which made Senators popularly elective. Subject to the federal constitutional prohibitions of denial of the vote on account of race, color, or sex, the states fix the qualifications of voters, but the elector's right to vote for presidential electors, Senators, and Representatives is derived from the Federal Constitution and Congress may take steps to protect this right. The constitutional arrangement results in considerable diversity in the details of suffrage legislation. Dudley O. McGovney summarizes the state laws and argues for uniformity through federal action in *The American Suffrage Medley* (Chicago: University of Chicago Press, 1949). Residents of the District of Columbia do not have the vote. They persistently seek amendment of the Constitution to permit them to vote in presidential elections. Congress could itself grant to the residents of the District the franchise to elect their local officials, but the District commissioners are appointed by the President, and Congress, in effect, acts as a city council for Washington. In 1955 Congress provided a system of registration and elections in the District for national committeemen and committeewomen of the parties, for delegates to the national convention, and for certain members of local party committees. See R. M. Scammon, "Washington Votes Again," *National Municipal Review*, 45 (1956), pp. 328-333.

abrupt change in the fundamental nature of suffrage requirements. Changes were made but they were towards lowering, not eliminating, the property qualification.

The nature of the suffrage qualifications of the colonial period is illustrated by a Virginia act of 1736 which limited the vote for members of the legislature to persons with a freehold of 100 acres, "if no settlement be made upon it" or 25 acres "with a house and plantation." A town or city resident might vote as a freeholder "in any house or lot." Georgia, North Carolina, and New Jersey also defined suffrage requirements in terms of acreage of real estate. In New Hampshire, New York, and Rhode Island, the qualifications were in terms of value of real estate; the pre-Revolutionary requirement in New York, for example, was ownership of real estate worth 40 pounds. In other colonies the requirement was ownership either of real estate or of personal property. In Pennsylvania a person owning 50 acres or other property worth 50 pounds might become an elector. In Massachusetts ownership of real estate yielding 40 shillings annual income or of other property worth 40 pounds gave the right to vote. In South Carolina the suffrage came with ownership of fixed amounts of property or the payment of ten shillings in taxes. During the Revolution eight of the 13 states altered their suffrage requirements, "and the modifications were not such as to indicate that statesmen had abandoned the principle that only property holders should vote. The only tendency manifest was to reduce the amount." [2]

The effect of colonial restrictions on the vote is somewhat problematic. Figures on voting at that time, and even on population, are unreliable. McKinley attempted to estimate the numbers entitled to vote and the numbers actually voting in colonial days, but the data justified only the conclusion that the potential electorate varied "from one-sixth to one-fiftieth" of the population and the proportions of actual voters varied over the same range.[3] The effects of so restricted a suffrage may be better visualized if they are considered in relation to the present electorate. Like limitations today would exclude tens of millions from the vote.

Elimination of property requirements. After the American Revolution the general pattern was, first, to eliminate the property-owning qualification and to substitute a taxpaying requirement, which was, in turn, removed. South Carolina substituted a taxpaying requirement for the property re-

[2] K. H. Porter, *A History of Suffrage in the United States* (Chicago: University of Chicago Press, 1918), p. 10. On aspects of the evolution of the suffrage, see H. F. Gosnell, *Democracy, The Threshold of Freedom* (New York: Ronald, 1948), chs. 2–7.

[3] A. E. McKinley, *The Suffrage Franchise in the Thirteen English Colonies in America* (Philadelphia: University of Pennsylvania, 1905), pp. 38–39.

quirement in 1778; Georgia, in 1789; Delaware, in 1792; Maryland, in 1810; Connecticut, in 1818; Massachusetts, in 1821; New York, in 1821; Rhode Island, in 1842. A few states did not go through the step of substituting taxpaying for property holding. Virginia persisted in the property qualification until 1850 when it was removed; at that time the taxpaying requirement was generally passing out of use.

The struggle over the property qualification in Virginia illustrates the kind of cleavage that occurred in the older states. The demand for the extension of the suffrage came primarily from the more recently settled western section of the state; it was resisted by the tidewater section. In the constitutional convention of 1829–1830, the westerners cited Thomas Jefferson in support of a broadened franchise; easterners, such as John Randolph of Roanoke, opposed the change, successfully for the time being. He refused to be struck down by the authority of Jefferson, a man of "theory and reveries." Randolph said: "Such is the wisdom of our existing form of government that no proposition can be brought forward with a view to making an inroad that can demand a respectable majority. The lust of innovation has been the death of all republics. All men of sense ought to guard and warn their neighbors against it."

In the states of the West the conflict between frontier and tidewater, between an aristocratic group enjoying the suffrage and a democratic group clamoring for its extension, did not occur as in Virginia. The newer states came into the Union with no property or taxpaying requirements, or only nominal ones. In these states no aristocracy existed to assert a position of special status. Nor were their landed classes threatened in their hegemony by a growing urban population. The spectre of ultimate control of the state by the city of New York haunted Chancellor Kent in his famed speech in the New York constitutional convention of 1821 in opposition to a proposal to abolish property qualifications for voters for the state senate:

. . . The apprehended danger from the experiment of universal suffrage, applied to the whole legislative department, is no dream of the imagination. It is too mighty an excitement for the moral condition of men to endure. The tendency of universal suffrage is to jeopardize the rights of property and the principles of liberty. There is a constant tendency in human society—and the history of every age proves it—there is a constant tendency in the poor to covet and to share the plunder of the rich; in the debtor to relax or to avoid the obligations of contract; in the indolent and profligate to cast the whole burthen of society upon the industrious and virtuous; and there is a tendency in ambitious and wicked men to inflame those combustible materials. It requires a vigilant government, and a firm administration of justice, to counteract that tendency. Thou shalt not covet; thou shalt not steal; are divine injunctions induced by this miserable depravity of our nature.

A similar anxiety was expressed by a member of the Pennsylvania constitutional convention of 1837:

But, Sir, what does the delegate propose? To place the vicious vagrant, the wandering Arabs, the Tartar hordes of our large cities on the level with the virtuous and good man? . . . These Arabs steeped in crime and in vice, to be placed on a level with industrious population is insulting and degrading to the community. . . . I hold up my hands against a proceeding which confers on the idle, vicious, degraded vagabond a right at the expense of the poor and industrious portion of this commonwealth.[4]

If such opposition to the broadening of the suffrage is read through modern eyes, it may be too readily dismissed as only an attempt by the rich and well-born to maintain their special prerogatives. That was certainly a part of the picture, but sincere anxieties existed about the viability of governments grounded on mass suffrage. In part, that fear rested on the actuality of subordination of many men without property to the will of others. In a day with no secret ballot (and no trade unions) employers could often command the vote of their employees, and agricultural landlords could often control their tenants.[5] Apart from such relationships that created predictable difficulties, the successive extensions of the suffrage marked steps in the creation of new governmental practices on the face of the earth; and moves into the unknown are always fraught with risk. Yet in due course property and taxpaying qualifications were swept away, although in some jurisdictions a remnant persists in the limitation of voting on bond issues to persons paying property taxes.

The Negro and the Vote

The question of the vote for the Negro has generated the most troublesome problem in the definition of American suffrage. Proposals to extend the suffrage have invariably generated anxieties among those whose positions might be endangered thereby. That rule has applied with special force to the question of Negro suffrage. The geographical concentration of the Negro population in the South made the grant of the vote to the Negro a threat to the regional political and social system. Not only would the suffrage be extended to the propertyless and the uneducated, but it would be given to blacks not long out of slavery who would, it was feared, gain dominance over their erstwhile masters. Moreover, since the pressure for Negro suffrage came originally almost entirely from outside the

[4] Quoted by Porter, *op. cit.*, p. 92.
[5] See Chilton Williamson, "American Suffrage and Sir William Blackstone," *Political Science Quarterly*, 68 (1953), pp. 552–557.

South, the debate over the question was a forensic continuation of the Civil War, a factor conducive to the solidification of southern resistance.

Grant of Negro suffrage. The initial grant of Negro suffrage was a phase of the power politics of the post-Civil War period. Negro suffrage had no part in the reconstruction schemes of Presidents Lincoln and Johnson, but the so-called radical group in Congress favored suffrage. Their leaders calculated that the grant of suffrage would enable Negroes, in combination with white union men, to control the southern states. In some northern states, the move would also bring support to the Union party, as the Republicans of the day called themselves.

While the northern states, somewhat reluctantly, granted the vote to the Negro, its extension to the South required coercive measures. The Reconstruction Act of 1867 imposed Negro suffrage upon the former Confederate states. It declared the governments of those states to be provisional until, among other things, new constitutions were formulated by "delegates elected by the male citizens of said states, twenty-one years old and upward, of whatever race, color or previous condition." Another step toward Negro enfranchisement was the Fourteenth Amendment, which became effective in July, 1868. It provided for a reduction of congressional representation of those states that abridged the right of suffrage, a penalty which has never been exacted. The Fifteenth Amendment, adopted in 1870, went more directly to the question of Negro suffrage by forbidding the states to deny or abridge the right to vote "on account of race, color, or previous condition of servitude."

With the enfranchisement of the Negro, rule of the southern states by a combination of Negroes and carpetbaggers ensued for about eight years, a rule that rested ultimately on military force. Southerners are perhaps prone to exaggerate the horrors of reconstruction, but the results were not considered good by even the most sympathetic observers. Extravagance, corruption, and administrative incompetence prevailed.[6]

White control re-established. Federal reconstruction policy united southern whites, formerly divided between the Whig and Democratic parties. They determined to use whatever tactics were necessary to regain control. The activities of the Ku Klux Klan were the most striking example of the method of intimidation used to discourage Negro political activity. The return of white supremacy in the South was finally sanctioned by the negotiations connected with the Hayes-Tilden contest over the Presi-

[6] See Paul Lewinson, *Race, Class, and Party* (New York: Oxford University Press, 1932).

dency. The bald and oversimplified version of the deal is that the Presidency went to the Republican, Hayes, and a policy of federal nonintervention in racial matters went to the South. The withdrawal of federal troops from the South by Hayes in 1877 removed the props from the remaining reconstruction governments.[7]

Despite the new disposition to leave the Negro question to the South, the constitutional injunction against state abridgment of the right to vote on account of color remained. Probably private intimidation was the chief means of disfranchisement, but a variety of legal means was also used. Gerrymandering legislative districts against the Negro was a favorite device, as were "elaborate and confusing registration schemes, and devious complications of the balloting process."[8] Some states made conviction for petty larceny a disqualification for voting, on the theory that this infraction of the law occurred more frequently among the blacks. Control of the electoral machinery, regained by the whites, facilitated election fraud to reduce the effective Negro strength.

In the 1890's more refined techniques were developed to deal with Negro suffrage. By this time new political disputes had arisen among southern whites. The new combination of business, railroad, financial, and planting classes came to be challenged by the radical agrarians. Each side was tempted to enlist the Negro in its support, a costly sort of campaigning under the political customs of the day. The strongest compulsions existed for the conflicting factions of southern whites to unite on the question of Negro suffrage. Only by effective disfranchisement could political dispute among the whites follow its natural course.

In this situation the problem facing the southern constitution-makers was how to circumvent the Fifteenth Amendment in a manner to disfranchise Negroes legally and at the same time leave the way open for all whites to vote. The Mississippi constitutional convention of 1890 was fertile in the invention of contrivances to serve these purposes, and during the following 10 or 15 years its handiwork found imitation in other states. To vote, the elector was required by the new constitution to pay a two-dollar poll tax and, if requested, to present his tax receipt at the polls. The assumption was that Negroes were neither inclined to pay the tax nor habituated to the preservation of records. A two-year residence requirement was imposed, on the theory that Negroes were more migratory than whites. Legislative districts were gerrymandered to discriminate against the sections of the state most heavily populated by Negroes. Conviction for bribery, burglary, theft, arson, obtaining money under false pre-

---

[7] See C. Vann Woodward, *Reunion and Reaction, The Compromise of 1877 and the End of Reconstruction* (Boston: Little, Brown, 1951).

[8] Lewinson, *op. cit.*, p. 65.

tenses, perjury, forgery, embezzlement, murder, or bigamy was made a disqualification. If the Negro passed all these bars, there remained the literacy test, to become effective in 1892. With it was coupled an "understanding" clause, the crowning achievement of the Mississippi convention. The clause read that after 1892 qualified voters must be able "to read any section of the state constitution; or to be able to understand the same when read to him, or give a reasonable interpretation thereof." [9] Illiteracy was common among both Negroes and whites, but in the administration of the alternative test—the "understanding" clause—discrimination against Negroes was definitely contemplated.

Constitutional politics of Negro suffrage. By the turn of the century southern states had generally disfranchised the Negro. Their constitutional forms did not explicitly exclude the Negro from the vote, but their practices ran in direct contradiction to the express prohibitions of the Federal Constitution. The political branches of the national government, persuaded that only large-scale applications of force could put meaning into the formal right of Negro suffrage in the South, were disposed to let matters rest. Their inertness threw the whole question into the hands of the Supreme Court, which was thus left with the task of its solution.

Litigants were not lacking to bring the question to the attention of the Supreme Court, which in decisions strung out over nearly half a century dealt first with this and then that aspect of the matter. At times it avoided decision by a convenient disinclination to peer beyond legal form. At other times it struck down obviously unconstitutional practices only for them to be replaced by others. Whether such mundane thoughts entered the minds of the Justices, it was as if the Court were engaged in a delaying action with the hope that time would bring a moment propitious for reconciliation of practice with the Constitution.

Eventually, after many years and after many bouts in the rarefied atmosphere of the chambers of appellate courts, the time came when the possibilities for legal circumvention of the Constitution had been exhausted. The series of cases by which that point was reached provide much fare for the connoisseurs of constitutional interpretation, but here only the high points need be recounted. In Williams v. Mississippi,[10] decided in 1898, the Supreme Court had to examine the suffrage question as it reviewed the indictment of Williams for murder. Mississippi law required that jurors be elected. Negroes could not be electors: the effect of the state's constitutional provision was to "abridge the suffrage of the colored

---

[9] W. A. Mabry, "Disfranchisement of the Negro in Mississippi," *Journal of Southern History*, 4 (1938), pp. 318–333.
[10] 170 U.S. 213 (1898).

electors in the State of Mississippi on account of previous condition of servitude." If colored persons could not be electors, they could not, under the state law, become jurors. This coupling of suffrage abridgment with the qualifications for jury duty, it was contended, constituted a deprivation of the equal protection of law by the state, a matter prohibited by the Fourteenth Amendment. The Court found that the constitution and statutes of Mississippi did "not on their face discriminate between the races" and that it had "not been shown that their actual administration was evil, only that evil was possible under them."

In 1903, in Giles *v.* Harris,[11] the Supreme Court had before it the suffrage provisions of the Alabama constitution that permitted permanent registration as a voter before 1903 of all persons "of good character . . . who understand the duties and obligations of citizenship under a republican form of government," as well as all persons who served in the Revolutionary and certain other wars, together with their descendants. Giles, a Negro, alleged, what everybody knew, that the constitutional provisions were part of a conspiracy to disfranchise Negroes because of their race and, therefore, were void under the Federal Constitution. The Court, in an opinion by Mr. Justice Holmes, refused to order the election officers of Alabama to place the name of Giles and other Negroes on the voting lists. In the opinion he expressed doubt about what the Court could do to enforce such an order if it were issued and concluded that relief against political discrimination would have to come either from the people of the state or from the political departments of the United States government.

In 1915 the Supreme Court held void one technique for discriminating against Negroes in favor of illiterate whites. It invalidated the "grandfather clause" of the Oklahoma constitution.[12] The "grandfather clause" was usually a temporary means for permanently registering as voters all those persons who could vote, or whose ancestors could vote, prior to the adoption of the Fifteenth Amendment. Those whose ancestors could not vote at that time had to cross some other hurdle, such as a literacy test, to establish their right to vote. In conjunction, these two requirements meant that whites who could show that they or their ancestors could vote prior to the adoption of the Fifteenth Amendment could gain registration regardless of their literacy and that Negroes, who were legally barred from the vote prior to the Fifteenth Amendment, were in large measure barred by the literacy test. The Court looked behind the form to the intent and held the clause void.

White primary litigation. The white primary provided the constitutional questions for most of the litigation on the question of Negro suffrage.

[11] 189 U.S. 475 (1903).
[12] Guinn *v.* United States, 238 U.S. 347 (1915).

Circumstances made the white primary an especially effective method for political neutralization of the Negro. Long before the rise of the direct-primary method of nomination in the South, Negroes had been excluded from participation in the affairs of the Democratic party. Most Negroes were Republicans, and the gradual movement of most white southerners into the Democratic party, coupled with the adoption of the direct-primary nominating procedure, created a situation ideally suited for a solution of the Negro question in a manner satisfactory to the whites. The limitation of participation in the direct primaries to whites, which was in due course formalized in party rules, permitted whites to settle their political disputes in the primary. The state then went through the formality of ratifying the nominees of the Democratic primary at the general election; a few Negroes might vote on that occasion but their vote would be to no avail because the election results had already been settled in the white primary.

The litigation over the white primary involved a simple constitutional principle, but it took two decades to settle the matter. The question was whether action by a political party in excluding Negroes from its primaries could in some way be used to get around the federal constitutional clauses that prohibited discrimination by the state. The Fifteenth Amendment forbids denial of the vote "by the United States or by any state" on account of race or color; the Fourteenth Amendment prohibits denial by "any state" of the equal protection of the laws. Could a political party accomplish by its own rule what the state was forbidden to do by law?

The judicial merry-go-round was put in motion by an ill-advised action of the Texas legislature. Despite the white primary rule, Negroes commonly voted in the San Antonio primaries. A disgruntled candidate, having lost the Negro vote and the nomination, induced the state legislature to pass a law which declared Negroes ineligible "to participate in a Democratic primary election held in the State of Texas." An action so obviously made by the state could hardly pass muster with the courts. The Supreme Court in 1927 held the law to be an "obvious infringement" of the equal-protection clause of the Fourteenth Amendment.[18] The legislature immediately repealed the legislation and substituted an act authorizing every political party "to prescribe the qualifications of its own members" through its state executive committee. The Democratic state executive committee then adopted a white primary rule, which was quickly challenged. The Court dodged the question whether a political party, as a private organization, might limit its membership to whites. It based its decision on the view that the party's state executive committee had acted under legislation which made it, in effect, an agent of the state. The

[18] Nixon *v.* Herndon, 273 U.S. 536 (1927).

exclusion of Negroes by a party committee acting under state authority constituted a denial of equal protection by the state.[14]

The rebuff by the Supreme Court stimulated the juridical imagination of Texas Democrats, and in 1932 another rule limiting participation in the direct primary to whites was adopted, not by the legislature, not by the state executive committee of the party, but by the party's state convention. Was the convention's action that of a private voluntary association, or was it the action of an instrumentality of a state and as such an infringement of the equal-protection clause? The Court examined the legal nature of parties in Texas and found them to be "voluntary associations for political action" and not "creatures of the state." As a private association the party might exclude Negroes without infringing the equal-protection clause, which applied only to action by a state.[15]

The ingenuity of the constitutional lawyers had not been exhausted and they eventually raised new questions. Enemies of the white primary took courage from the Supreme Court's 1941 decision in the Classic case.[16] In that decision the Court upset the general belief, based on the Newberry case, that the federal government had no power to regulate primaries held under state authority. The contention in the Classic case was that the constitutional provision directing that the House of Representatives be "chosen . . . by the people in the several States" (Art. I, sec. 2) created a right of the voter under the Federal Constitution that might be protected by federal action. The Court accepted this reasoning and upheld indictments of New Orleans election officials charged with fraud in a primary to nominate a United States Representative and, hence, with violation of a provision of the criminal code making it an offense to deprive a citizen of any right or privilege under the Constitution. The Court observed: "Where the state has made the primary an integral part of the procedure of choice, or where in fact the primary effectively controls the choice, the right of the elector to have his ballot counted at the primary is . . . included in the right protected by" Article I, section 2, of the Constitution, just as in an election.

The Classic opinion intimated that the Court might be in a mood to change its mind, and a Texas Negro, who had been excluded from a Democratic primary, brought another suit. In 1944 the Supreme Court, in Smith v. Allwright,[17] overruled its earlier decision approving the white

[14] Nixon v. Condon, 286 U.S. 73 (1932).

[15] Grovey v. Townsend, 295 U.S. 45 (1935).

[16] United States v. Classic, 61 S. Ct. 1031 (1941).

[17] 321 U.S. 649 (1944). For a review of the chain of cases, see O. Douglas Weeks, "The White Primary: 1944–1948," American Political Science Review, 42 (1948), pp. 500–510.

primary. The reasoning was that the primary in Texas was an "integral part" of the machinery for choosing officials. Although the state convention had acted on its own authority in excluding Negroes, in other aspects the primary was regulated by state law, and the state provided procedure by which the party certified its nominees for inclusion on the general election ballot. By such action the state endorsed and enforced the discrimination against Negroes. Under these circumstances, discrimination by the party had to be treated as discrimination by the state. The Court held the action to be prohibited by the Fifteenth Amendment.

Reactions to the Allwright decision. Smith *v.* Allwright overturned the legal doctrines on which southern states had based white primaries. In one sense the most remarkable consequence of the decision was the degree of its acceptance and the extent to which Negroes came to vote in primaries. In a few states, principally states of the Deep South, reaction to the decision was bitter and their legal lights began to look for loopholes in the decision. The Classic case had laid down two tests for determination whether a primary came under federal control: (1) when it is an "integral part" of the election machinery by law; (2) when it in fact "effectively controls the choice." Smith *v.* Allwright turned on the "integral part" test. The test of "control of choice" in the Classic case was dictum and perhaps not good law, the lawyers argued. Possibly a way to preserve the "white primary" would be to repeal all state laws concerning the conduct of primaries and leave the matter entirely to party rule. Exclusion of Negroes from such a private primary by party authorities could not be regarded as a denial or abridgment of the right to vote on account of race or color *by a state* in violation of the Fifteenth Amendment.

To determine whether the "control of choice" test of the Classic case was mere dictum or law, the South Carolina legislature in 1944 repealed all laws relating to the conduct of primaries and left nominations subject solely to management by party authorities. A Negro, denied the right to vote in the 1946 primaries, sued for damages. In the suit it was stipulated that since 1900 every governor, member of the General Assembly, United States Representative, and United States Senator for the state had been a nominee of the Democratic party. If 47 years was enough, the Democratic primary indubitably controlled the choice. The only question was whether that control brought a privately conducted primary within the constitutional prohibition against racial discrimination.

United States District Judge J. Waties Waring, a Charlestonian of impeccable South Carolina connections, found that the South Carolina plan fell before the Constitution. The primary controlled choice. He dismissed the contention that the Democratic party should be regarded as a private club: ". . . private clubs and business organizations do not vote and elect a President of the United States, and the Senators and members of the House of Representatives of our national congress; and under the law of our land, all citizens are entitled to a voice in such selections." The federal circuit court upheld the district court and the Supreme Court declined to review the decision.[18] South Carolina Democratic party authorities did not comply with the decision with alacrity. The party, in essence, limited membership to whites but permitted Negroes to vote in the primaries, provided that they met various requirements including an oath to support the principles of the Democratic party. It required another suit to compel admission of Negroes to party membership.[19] In 1950 South Carolina, more or less reconciled to the proscription of the white primary, sought to keep Negro voting to a minimum by the requirement that voters, black or white, be able to read and write or, alternatively, own property assessed at $300 or more.

Alabama rejected South Carolina's stratagem of attempting to get around Smith *v.* Allwright by repealing the primary laws. Without state regulation of the primaries, Gessner T. McCorvey, chairman of the state Democratic executive committee, said that he did not "know how such elections could be properly policed." There would be no punishment for fraud. "My own idea," he said, "is that the way to handle the situation with which we are confronted is to see that only properly qualified persons are permitted to register." To limit registration to "properly qualified persons," Alabama in 1946, by a narrow popular margin, amended its constitution to require as a condition for registration ability to read and write, to "understand and explain" any article of the United States Constitution, "good character," and an understanding of "the duties and obligations of good citizenship under a republican form of government." The effectiveness of the Alabama scheme necessarily depended on systematic discrimination against Negroes in its administration by the county boards of registrars. In January, 1949 a federal district court saw what everyone knew: ". . . that this amendment was intended to be, and is being used for the purpose of discriminating against applicants for the franchise on the basis of race or color." It was, therefore, "both in its object and the manner of its administration," unconstitutional. The Supreme Court declined to overrule the lower court decision.[20]

---

[18] Elmore *v.* Rice, 72 F. Supp. 516 (1947), 165 F. 2nd 387 (1947), 68 S. Ct. 905 (1948).

[19] Brown *v.* Baskin, 78 F. Supp. 933 (1948).

[20] Davis *v.* Schnell, 81 F. Supp. 872 (1949), 69 S. Ct. 749 (1949). In 1951 Alabama, again by a narrow margin, adopted another constitutional amendment calculated to give boards of registrars leeway to reject Negro applicants for registration.

A special session of the Mississippi legislature in 1947 considered ways and means of avoiding the consequences of the Allwright case. Leaders of a move to follow the South Carolina precedent and leave nominations to the unregulated actions of party authorities were blocked by sober citizens sensitive to criticism from outside the state. Nonparticipation by Negroes flowed largely from social inhibitions other than statute anyway. The legislature limited itself to the adoption of a scheme declaring ineligible to participate in party primaries persons not in "accord with the statement of the principles of the party holding such primary." The "principles" adopted by the Democratic party under this authority included propositions thought to be unacceptable to Negroes, such as opposition to fair employment practices legislation. In 1954, after the agitation of the segregation question had stirred up concern, Mississippi tightened its voting requirements.

Arkansas had earlier developed the scheme of prescribing a requirement of adherence to party principles repugnant to Negroes as a means of discouraging Negro participation in primaries. The Democratic party convention of 1944 limited party membership to whites but permitted nonmembers to vote in the primary provided they met tests of allegiance to party principles. Among the principles was the "preservation of existing laws relating to the segregation of races in schools, public conveyances and other lawfully designated places." The exclusion of blacks from party membership made them ineligible for party posts and ineligible to run as candidates in the primary, clearly unconstitutional limitations. In 1950 the restriction of party membership to whites was removed.[21]

It might be supposed that every conceivable mode to circumvent the decision in Smith *v.* Allwright had been tried and found wanting, but in 1953 the Supreme Court considered another means of evasion in the Jaybird case. The Jaybird Democratic Association of Fort Bend County, Texas, had since 1889 conducted a primary of its own before the official nominating primary. The winner of the Jaybird primary entered the regular Democratic primary and ordinarily won the official party nomination without opposition. No legal bar existed to voting by Negroes in the official primary although the nominations had, in effect, been settled earlier in the Jaybird primary. This set of circumstances gave the Supreme Court some difficulty. How could it be contended that the action of the Jaybird Association was action by the state in abridgment of the Negro's right to vote. Justice Black's opinion characterized the practice: "For a

---

[21] Oklahoma sought to deal with Negro candidates by prescribing that they should be identified as such on the primary or election ballot. In 1955 the statute was held to deny equal protection. See McDonald *v.* Key, 224 F. 2d 608 (1955).

state to permit such a duplication of its election processes is to permit a flagrant abuse of those processes to defeat the purposes of the Fifteenth Amendment." [22]

Technique in defuzing political explosives. While the United States was not completely out of the woods on the question of Negro suffrage after Smith *v.* Allwright, that decision both marked and stimulated substantial progress toward bringing practice into accord with formal constitutional doctrine. The long and tortuous path the Supreme Court followed to reach that decision suggests some reflections on the art of handling difficult political issues. In truth, in 1900 the constitutional provisions on Negro suffrage could have been given reality in the South only by powerful measures of coercion. The Supreme Court had not the instruments of power and the political arms of government had no disposition to intervene.

Instead of making decisions that would have been only empty exhortations the Court followed a delaying tactic for decades. Never for long, however, did it completely foreclose opportunity for litigants to raise the constitutional question in another form. Negroes faced, not an absolute blockage of hope, but rather a long, a painfully long, series of provisional barriers. Meanwhile, in spite of delay in the legal sphere, social changes were taking place to give the question a different political reality. Urbanization in the South created circumstances radically different from the rural plantation society—circumstances under which many whites feared far less the probable consequences of Negro suffrage. As the generations went by, the educational and economic status of Negroes improved. Within the South itself, many whites began to agitate for civic rights for Negroes. At times their concern was that of a political leadership which hoped to enlist Negroes on its side, but more generally it was a concern over the conflict of principle and practice or a response to external criticism.

Alteration in the objective circumstances paved the way for constitutional decisions that might have some reality. In fact, even before Smith *v.* Allwright, the white primary was dying. More and more Negroes were voting in Democratic primaries. A rapid increase in Negro voting followed the decision. Generally, the freest exercise of Negro suffrage occurred in the cities and in the states around the rim of the South with relatively few Negroes in their population. The most marked informal resistance and the most marked increase in the rigor of the application of literacy tests and other such limitations took place in the states and areas with the highest proportions of Negro population. In such areas resistance

[22] Terry *v.* Adams, 345 U.S. 506 (1953).

hardened further in the mid-fifties as the debate on school desegregation developed. Yet the constitutional doctrines with respect to Negro suffrage had far greater reality than they had had even twenty years earlier.[23]

In those localities where the Negro was denied the right to vote, his only recourse was to sue the election or registration officials, a costly and unsatisfactory remedy. In 1957 Congress tried to put more meaning into the constitutional right to vote. It authorized the Attorney General to bring civil actions in the federal courts to restrain interference, actual or threatened, with the right to vote. The government thereby assumed the cost of litigation theretofore borne principally by private organizations such as the NAACP and lent its authority and dignity to efforts to make effective the constitutional prohibition against denial of the vote on account of color. The congressional debate turned largely on the issue of the mode of enforcement of court orders. The diehard southern opponents sought the guarantee of a jury trial, on the assumption that few southern juries would send a man to jail for frightening a Negro away from the polls. The diehard advocates defended the customary right of judges in equity proceedings to clap into jail without a jury trial violators of their orders. The compromise adopted assured jury trials in cases of "criminal" contempt but continued the power of courts "to secure compliance with or to prevent obstruction of" their orders by civil contempt proceedings without a jury. The exact meaning of this differentiation remained to be worked out by experience. Even before the passage of the legislation the Attorney General could have acted, without much indirection, under laws penalizing conspiracies to deprive persons of their constitutional rights. Yet the congressional action had great significance, for it made it clear that the Attorney General should enforce the right to vote. It remained equally clear that the problem of Negro suffrage in the South could not be solved solely by a spate of lawsuits brought by the Attorney General.

[23] The question of the vote for Indians raised constitutional issues similar to those of Negro suffrage. Not until the Nationality Act of 1924 did all Indians possess United States citizenship. Before that time about two-thirds of the Indians had acquired citizenship by treaties and by legislation applicable to particular tribes. The laws of various western states, however, continued to deny the vote to Indians until invalidated in the late 1940's by decisions of state courts and inferior federal tribunals. The extent to which Indians exercise the suffrage varies greatly from place to place. On the legal background, see Felix S. Cohen, *Handbook of Indian Law* (Washington: Government Printing Office, 1942); N. D. Houghton, "The Legal Status of Indian Suffrage in the United States," *California Law Review*, 19 (1931), p. 507; Luella Gettys, *The Law of Citizenship* (Chicago: University of Chicago Press, 1934).

Woman Suffrage

The crusade for woman suffrage in its beginning was closely related to the abolition movement. Woman, because of her extensive legal disabilities under the common law, was compared with the slave. And, in truth, the legal rights of the married woman were closer to those of the slave than to those of free white men. The movement for the removal of legal disabilities of women and for the right of suffrage gained headway prior to the Civil War and kept under way until the adoption of the Nineteenth Amendment to the Constitution in 1920. This long campaign produced an immense quantity of literature from both advocates and opponents of suffrage. Eventually the case for suffrage came to rest on variations of the doctrine of equality and freedom. An early formulation by an advocate of woman suffrage before the Massachusetts constitutional convention of 1853 was as follows: [24]

I maintain first that the people have a certain natural right, which under special conditions of society manifests itself in the form of a right to vote. I maintain secondly that the women of Massachusetts are people existing under those special conditions of society. I maintain finally, and by necessary consequence, that the women of Massachusetts have a natural right to vote.

Rationalizations of opponents of woman suffrage. The rationalizations of the opponents of woman suffrage were of a low order, and at this late date it is difficult to see how they could have been uttered with such sobriety and piety. A few extracts from a statement by Senator Joseph E. Brown of Georgia in 1884 will illustrate the tone of the argument. He argued that "the Creator intended that the sphere of the males and females of our race should be different." Man, he contended, was "qualified for the discharge of those duties that require strength and ability to combat with the sterner realities and difficulties of life." Among these duties were military service, road construction, labor in the fields, and government. The management of government he thought, was "a laborious task, for which the male sex is infinitely better fitted than the female sex." "On the other hand," the argument continued, "the Creator has assigned to woman very laborious and responsible duties, *by no means less important* than those imposed upon the male sex, though entirely different in their character. In the family she is a *queen*. She alone is fitted for the discharge of the sacred trust of wife and the endearing relation of mother." And, the good Senator said, "when the husband returns home weary and worn in the discharge of the difficult and laborious tasks assigned him, he finds in the good wife solace and consolation which is nowhere else afforded." How

[24] Quoted by Porter, *op. cit.*, p. 141.

could the wife, he asked, with all the "heavy duties of citizen, politician and officeholder resting upon her shoulders, . . . attend to the more sacred, delicate, refining trust . . . for which she is peculiarly fitted by nature? Who is to care for and train the children while she is absent in the discharge of these masculine duties?" The Senator could not bear to visualize the burden of public duties thrust upon women.[25]

The Senator's argument embodied the stock objections to woman suffrage, and it amounted to little more than saying, "Woman's place is in the home." But women were everywhere coming out of the home. Women were beginning to enter the professions; they were working in factories, shops, and stores; in the West they were laboring in the fields; they were making their way into colleges and universities; and some of them came to control great wealth. And as these changes progressed, the demand for woman suffrage became louder and more insistent.

What of the opposition to woman suffrage? Although much of it was simply inertia and resistance to change, a part was based on a belief that substantial interests would be endangered by the extension of the franchise to women. One of the official historians of the suffrage movement states that following 1896 the

. . . Republican party was in complete control of the Government at Washington and was largely dominated by the great financial interests of the country, and this was also practically the situation in the majority of the States. The campaign fund controlled the elections and the largest contributors to this fund were the corporations, which had secured immense power, and the liquor interests, which had become a dominant force in State and national politics, without regard to party. Both of these supreme influences were implacably opposed to suffrage for women; the corporations because it would vastly increase the votes of the working classes, the liquor interests because they were fully aware of the hostility of women to their business and everything connected with it.[26]

The liquor interests foresaw correctly the attitudes of women voters; they have tended to favor restrictions on the liquor traffic in higher degree than do men. Corporate employers, however, had less reason to become exercised: nonvoting has been especially marked among women of working-class families.[27]

[25] The argument is quoted in full by Susan B. Anthony and Ida Husted Harper, *The History of Woman Suffrage* (New York: the Authors, 1902), Vol. IV, pp. 93–100.
[26] Ida Husted Harper, *The History of Woman Suffrage* (New York: National American Woman Suffrage Association, 1922), Vol. V, p. xviii.
[27] In 1952 there was among women a slightly higher preference for General Eisenhower than prevailed among male voters. See Louis Harris, *Is There a Republican Majority?* (New York: Harper, 1954), ch. 7.

Woman suffrage in state and local elections. The earlier victories for woman suffrage were in connection with school elections. Kentucky in 1838 granted school suffrage to widows and unmarried women with property subject to taxation for school purposes; Kansas in 1861 was the first state to give the vote on school questions to all women. Michigan, Utah, Minnesota, Colorado, New Hampshire, and Massachusetts followed by 1880; by 1890 school suffrage had been gained by women in 14 states and territories. Wyoming was the first state to grant women the privilege of voting in all elections. It did so as a territory in 1869, and when it was admitted to the Union in 1890 its constitution put men and women on the same plane regarding the suffrage. Three other western states soon followed Wyoming: Colorado in 1893, and Utah and Idaho in 1896. After 1896 the suffrage movement began to encounter stiffer opposition, and no state was brought into the suffrage fold until the Progressive movement was fully under way. Here again western states were more receptive to the idea of woman suffrage. Equal suffrage was granted by Washington in 1910; California in 1911; Arizona, Kansas, and Oregon in 1912; and Montana and Nevada in 1914.

Militant movement for nation-wide suffrage for women. The progress toward nation-wide suffrage through action by individual states had been slow, and during the period from 1913 to 1919 more militant tactics were adopted by one set of suffrage advocates. Influential in the change of method was Mrs. O. H. P. Belmont, who had observed the activities of the English suffragettes. Mrs. Belmont, a sympathetic commentator writes, "was practically the only leader formerly associated with the conservative forces who had the courage to extricate herself from the old routine propaganda and adventure into new paths. She always approached the struggle for liberty in a wholesome revolutionary mood." [28] The leader of the fight in the field, however, was Alice Paul, an able and resourceful woman. The activities of these and other women in leadership of the militant campaign for the adoption of nation-wide woman suffrage constitute one of the most instructive chapters in agitation in American politics.

The militant suffragettes began with rather mild tactics in the 1914 congressional elections. By that time women had been enfranchised in several western states, and their campaign was concentrated in those states. The Democratic party, as the majority party, was to be held responsible for the failure to propose a constitutional amendment granting woman suffrage. All Democratic candidates for Congress in the woman suffrage states were opposed regardless of their individual stand on the suffrage question. Only 20 of 43 Democratic candidates in the nine suffrage states won.

[28] Doris Stevens, *Jailed for Freedom* (New York: Boni & Liveright, 1920), p. 32.

"It was generally conceded," Miss Stevens says in her excellent primer on agitation, "that we had contributed to these defeats." [29] Congressmen and other politicians began to accord a more respectful ear to the suffrage advocates; and in their platforms of 1916 both parties advocated the grant of woman suffrage by state action. This was not satisfactory to the militant suffrage leaders, who organized in the election of 1916 a protest vote against the Democratic party. Undoubtedly the Democratic opposition to national suffrage cost it many votes in the suffrage states.

When Congress and President Wilson temporized, new tactics were adopted. Early in 1917 the women began to picket the White House and won acres of newspaper space over the country. Day after day, in both good weather and bad, the women carried their banners before the White House. The routine was varied by the occasional march of a delegation to present a petition to the President; sometimes the delegations were received, sometimes not. The militant tactics of the Woman's party aroused criticism, and the government played into the hands of the suffragettes by adopting a policy of suppression. After six months of picketing, the demonstrators were arrested for "obstructing traffic." Others took their place; they were arrested; still others took their position on the picket line.

At their trials the women either stood mute or made speeches for liberty and woman suffrage; they refused to pay their fines on the ground that to do so would be an admission of guilt; they insisted on serving their terms in jail: "As long as the government and the representatives of the government prefer to send women to jail on petty and technical charges, we will go to jail. Persecution has always advanced the cause of justice." [30] Thus spoke one of the defendants. To the workhouse went the suffragettes. Martyrdom had the desired effect; a stream of telegrams in protest began to reach the President and Congressmen. Other women went on the picket line and thence to jail. This tactic generated publicity for the cause and created a housing problem for the District of Columbia penal authorities. And the primitive facilities of the penal institutions were given nation-wide publicity.

A dramatic touch was added to the campaign by the prisoners' claim to treatment customarily accorded political prisoners. In all civilized nations, the contention was, persons imprisoned for political offenses were accorded different treatment from that given the ordinary criminal. To re-enforce their claim for this status, the prisoners went on a hunger strike. This tactic, Miss Stevens says, brought "the Administration face to face with a more acute embarrassment. They had to choose between more

[29] *Ibid.*, p. 36.
[30] *Ibid.*, p. 102.

stubborn resistance and capitulation." The Administration unwisely resorted to forced feeding of the prisoners, not pleasant for the prisoners and productive of horrendous newspaper stories. But women continued to come to Washington from all over the nation and added to the prison population. The trials furnished glorious opportunities for propaganda for the cause. An elderly woman was given a light sentence and the judge urged her to pay the fine rather than go to jail: "Your Honor, I have a nephew fighting for democracy in France. He is offering his life for his country. I should be ashamed if I did not join these brave women in their fight for democracy in America. I should be proud of the honor to die in prison for the liberty of American women."

In January, 1918 the House passed the proposed suffrage amendment, but the necessary two-thirds majority was lacking in the Senate. A great demonstration was arranged by the women before the White House. Additional arrests occurred; as each speaker rose to talk, she was dragged away to the waiting patrol wagons. Another hunger strike ensued and, finally, the prisoners were released. But additional demonstrations occurred; more women were sent to prison; and those released went aboard a "Prison Special" to tour the country and enlist support.

The President was finally won over to the cause of nation-wide woman suffrage. In 1919 the newly elected Republican House passed the proposed amendment, and Wilson turned enough pressure on the Democratic Senators to win a two-thirds majority. By August, 1920 the necessary three-fourths of the state legislatures had ratified the amendment, which provided that "the right of citizens of the United States to vote shall not be denied or abridged by the United States or by any State on account of sex."

Militant tactics won the battle, but it need not be concluded that any sort of political agitation may be carried on solely by picketing the White House, going to jail, and indulging in hunger strikes. The women leading the movement had the backing of local associations and societies over the entire country, and the ordinary strategy of propaganda and pressure went on while the more spectacular acts were being committed in Washington. Moreover, many of the leaders of the movement were persons of high social and economic standing. One of the imprisoned women, for example, had a short time earlier been a guest at the White House. They were women who could not be thrown in jail without regard to the political consequences. Also, the ground had been prepared for the militant climax to the campaign by long years of agitation and education.

The movement also illustrates the problem of government in handling a determined agitation. Mrs. Belmont quoted Wilson who had written: "Governments have been very successful in parrying agitation, diverting it, in seeming to yield to it and then cheating it, tiring it out or evading it. But the end, whether it comes soon or late, is quite certain to be the same." Mrs. Belmont drew a parallel: "While the government has endeavored to parry, tire, divert, and cheat us of our goal, the country has risen in protest against this evasive policy of suppression until today the indomitable pickets with their historic legends stand triumphant before the nation." [31]

The Regulation of the Suffrage

The states establish specific requirements to vote subject to federal constitutional limitations contained chiefly in the Fourteenth, Fifteenth, and Nineteenth Amendments. The equal-protection clause of the Fourteenth Amendment has been construed to prohibit discrimination by a state along lines of color in the definition of the electorate. The Fifteenth Amendment explicitly forbids denial of the right to vote "by the United States or any state on account of race, color, or previous condition of servitude." The Nineteenth Amendment prohibits denial "on account of sex." While a catalog of suffrage rules state by state would serve no useful purpose, an indication of the principal types of qualifications fixed by state constitution and law is in order.[32]

Poll taxes. The poll tax, a head tax as a prerequisite for voting, by 1957 remained in use in only five southern states: Alabama, Arkansas, Mississippi, Texas, and Virginia. Under this type of suffrage requirement an annual tax of from one to two dollars must be paid before one becomes eligible to vote. In Alabama, Mississippi, and Virginia liability for the poll tax is cumulative; that is, a person may not pay the poll tax for the election year only and gain the suffrage; he must either pay the tax annually for several years before the election or in the election year pay the delinquent taxes for the period of cumulation prior to the election. Until 1953 in Alabama the tax liability could cumulate to $36, but a constitutional amendment of that year reduced the period of cumulation to two years at $1.50 per year.

An important motive in adoption of the poll tax in the southern states was the disfranchisement of the Negro, the supposition being that whites

[31] Quoted in *ibid.*, p. 246. The suffragettes may not have had a steam roller but the steady din of their agitation must have been about as soothing as the rattle of a pneumatic hammer. Senator Boies Penrose, Pennsylvania boss and foe of woman suffrage, the story goes, was taunted by a suffragette and told that he might as well be for woman suffrage because it was coming anyway. The Senator's retort was: "So is death, but I don't have to go out and meet it halfway."

[32] A table showing voting requirements in all the states appears in *Book of the States, 1956–1957* (Chicago: Council of State Governments, 1956), pp. 84–85.

would pay the tax and that Negroes would not. In operation, however, the poll tax together with some of its incidental features, such as the requirement of payment long in advance of the election, disfranchises a substantial number of whites as well as blacks. It is charged, although the case is not well established, that the adoption of the poll tax in southern states was connected with a desire to disfranchise the poorer whites as well as the blacks. The timing of the adoption gives a plausibility to this view, for the tax, save in Georgia, went into effect after other methods had made the blacks timid about approaching the polling places. The tax came at about the time the Populists, the Farmers Alliance, and other political dissenters were threatening the ruling oligarchies.

Dissatisfaction with the "tax on voting" has led to movements for its repeal both by state action and by federal action. North Carolina abandoned it in 1920, Louisiana in 1934, Florida in 1937, Georgia in 1945, and South Carolina in 1950. Tennessee's legislature, estopped from repeal by a decision of the state's supreme court, in 1949 and 1951 granted exemptions from the tax so broad as to amount to repeal; in 1953 by constitutional amendment the tax was eliminated. Repeal has been agitated in other states, and unsuccessful attacks have been made on the constitutionality of the tax as applied to voting in federal elections.[33]

Poll-tax opponents have not been content with seeking state action. They have advocated federal legislation to make the poll tax illegal as a requisite for voting in presidential and congressional elections. The leadership in the agitation, which has been more or less continuous since 1940, has rested mainly in the hands of liberal groups outside the South. They have worked on the theory that the poll tax restricted the southern electorate so drastically that conservative southerners had great advantage in campaigns for congressional seats. The way to cope with southern Bourbons is to go to the roots of their power and to eliminate the poll tax, which, so the argument runs, disfranchises the lesser economic classes, both colored and white. Anti-poll-tax legislation has passed the House of Representatives, but southern Senators invoked the right of filibuster to block Senate action. Advocates of federal legislative action have been handicapped by doubts about its constitutionality, and proposals for a federal constitutional amendment to outlaw state poll taxes have been put forward as an alternative approach.

The importance of the poll tax in accounting for the character of southern congressional representation has been exaggerated. Reactionary and progressive southern Senators come from states with poll taxes and from states without such taxes. The tax contributes to low popular participation

---

[33] Breedlove *v.* Suttles, 302 U.S. 277 (1937); Pirtle *v.* Brown, 118 F. 2d 218 (1941).

in southern primaries and elections, but it has been only one of many factors in the peculiar political order of the South and probably a relatively unimportant one. Its limited significance may help account for the fact that 10 southern Senators in 1953 sponsored a resolution to propose a constitutional amendment to eliminate the tax as a suffrage requirement, although their move may well have been a tactical step to strengthen their position on other questions of civil rights.[34]

Literacy tests. Literacy tests have been used to exclude from the suffrage classes of persons thought not to possess the qualities necessary for responsible citizenship and, incidentally, to protect the position of those established in the seats of power. Recent immigrants and Negroes have been the principal targets of the literacy tests. Connecticut in 1855 and Massachusetts in 1857 were the first states to adopt a literacy test. In both states the older groups were challenged in their hegemony by the waves of new immigrants. In Connecticut the Know-Nothing representatives in the legislature brought about the submission of the literacy amendment to the state constitution. In Massachusetts the Irish had aligned themselves with the Democrats, and the native American and Whig members of the legislature combined to propose the literacy amendment to the constitution. In 1890 Mississippi adopted a literacy test as one of a battery of expedients to exclude the Negro from the franchise; other southern states soon followed the Mississippi precedent.

About one-third of the states retain the literacy test in one form or another. Usually its administration is by registration officials in whose hands the requirements often become meaningless save when the test is arbitrarily applied to exclude Negroes from the vote. In New York the educational authorities administer the test, and a substantial number of those tested fail.[35]

In several southern states in which the literacy test was designed chiefly to exclude Negroes, alternative means were developed to permit illiterate whites to vote. Mississippi in 1890 contrived the arrangement by which a person unable to read a section of the state constitution might be registered if he could "understand" any section when read to him and give a "reasonable interpretation" thereof. The assumption was that registrars would find that illiterate whites had the capacity to "understand" and "interpret" the constitution. Several states adopted the Mississippi plan,

---

[34] For a detailed analysis of the poll tax, see Key, *Southern Politics*, chs. 27–28.

[35] In the early 1920's about one-fifth of those tested in New York failed. That proportion in recent years has declined to less than 10 per cent, a trend that probably reflects both the declining number of immigrants in the population and generally increasing literacy.

and others also established property ownership as an alternative to literacy. In recent decades the tendency has been to eliminate the "understanding" and property-holding alternatives to literacy.

In a few instances the "understanding" alternative has been converted into a requirement in addition to literacy. In Louisiana the constitution requires, *inter alia*, that a person be able to read any clause in the state or national constitution *and* to "give a reasonable interpretation" of any such clause. Discriminatory administration of such requirements along racial lines has been held unconstitutional in a case arising in Alabama. Nevertheless, with the object of coping with a growing Negro vote, Mississippi in 1954 amended its constitution to require, as a supplement to the literacy test, that an applicant for registration be able to interpret any section of the state constitution "to the satisfaction" of the county registrar. Literacy tests and related franchise requirements took on more importance in the South after the judicial invalidation of the white primary.[36]

Citizenship. All states now require United States citizenship as a prerequisite to the exercise of the suffrage. "For the first time in over a hundred years, a national election was held in 1928 in which no alien in any state had the right to cast a vote for a candidate for any office—national, state or local." [37] During the nineteenth century at least 22 states and territories gave aliens the right to vote, provided, of course, that they met other requirements, such as that of residence. Often it was required that aliens should have taken the first steps in the naturalization procedure. About 1875 the elimination of alien suffrage began. By 1900 only 11 states continued the right; by 1925 the privilege remained only in Arkansas. In that state a 1926 judicial decision declared effective a constitutional amendment voted in 1920 but theretofore held inoperative, and thereby wiped out the last voting privilege of aliens.

Age. In 1956 all states, except Georgia and Kentucky, required that a person be 21 years of age to vote. Agitation to lower the voting age to 18 developed during World War II. In 1943 Georgia lowered the voting age to 18 years. The campaign slogan was "Fight at 18, vote at 18." Legislative consideration in many other states at about the same time led to no action. In 1946 the Democratic party in South Carolina adopted the 18-year rule

[36] On southern literacy tests, their alternatives, and supplements, see Key, *op. cit.*, ch. 26.

[37] L. E. Aylsworth, "The Passing of Alien Suffrage," *American Political Science Review*, 25 (1931), pp. 114–116. Until 1928 Rhode Island required naturalized citizens to own real estate to vote in city council elections, a rule that handicapped Democratic candidates. See M. S. Stedman, Jr., and S. W. Stedman, "The Rise of the Democratic Party of Rhode Island," *New England Quarterly*, 24 (1951), pp. 329–341.

for participation in its primaries, but this liberalization was later abandoned. In 1954 President Eisenhower supported a proposal to amend the Federal Constitution to fix the age qualification at 18, but the Senate defeated the plan. In 1952 South Dakota voters, by a 700-vote margin, rejected a constitutional amendment to set the age qualification at 18 years, and in 1955 Kentucky voters adopted such an amendment to their constitution.[38]

Residence. Every state requires a minimum period of residence in the state, most commonly one year, as a voting qualification. Most states also have a supplemental requirement of a minimum residence in the county and voting district. In Alabama, for example, a person must have resided two years in the state, one year in the county, and three months in the voting district. Michigan, Oregon, Idaho, Indiana, and certain other states require only six months' residence in the state. Mississippi requires two years' residence in the state and one year in the voting district, but reduces the latter period to six months for ministers of the gospel, a recognition of the itinerant character of their calling.

The geographical mobility of the American population gives the residence requirement a greater significance than might be supposed. In the early 1950's annual census surveys showed that between 3 and 4 per cent of the people lived in a different state than they had one year earlier; roughly the same proportion lived in a different county of the same state than it had one year earlier. Residence requirements thus probably exclude over 5 per cent of the potential electorate from the ballot. In 1954 Wisconsin adopted a law to permit voting for presidential electors, but not for state and local officers, by persons who had been residents of the state for less than a year but who would have been qualified to vote in the state from which they came had they remained there.[39]

Disqualifications. The constitution and laws of each state exclude certain categories of persons from the suffrage. The disqualifying factors vary from state to state. Most states exclude the insane, idiots, and incompetents from the suffrage. In a few states "immoral" persons are not entitled to vote; in some states inmates of prisons are explicitly excluded from the vote. A similar end is achieved in other states that deny the suffrage to

[38] For a review of discussion of the matter, see H. J. Abraham, "Reduce the Voting Age to 18?" *National Municipal Review*, 43 (1954), pp. 11–15.

[39] By a concurrent resolution adopted in 1956 Congress recommended to the states the "consideration" of legislation on the order of that adopted by Wisconsin in 1954. Ralph M. Goldman estimates that 5,000,000 persons were prevented from voting in 1954 by residence requirements.—"Move—Lose Your Vote," *National Municipal Review*, 45 (1956), pp. 6–9.

persons convicted of certain crimes. The crimes that disqualify in most states are felonies and election bribery. In some states disqualification follows conviction for treason, bigamy, defalcation, perjury, larceny, forgery, arson, embezzlement, and other specified acts. In South Carolina, for example, an imposing list of felonies and misdemeanors operates to wipe out the right to vote. It includes burglary, obtaining money or goods under false pretenses, robbery, adultery, wife beating, house breaking, receiving stolen goods, breach of trust with fraudulent intent, fornication, sodomy, incest, assault with intent to ravish, miscegenation, and crimes against the election laws.

Suffrage and Political Power

The broadening of the suffrage over the centuries has been associated with a radical change in the nature and distribution of political power. The discussion and decision of matters of state formerly rested with a comparatively small proportion of the population, an aristocracy, oligarchy, or ruling class. Leadership—and, perhaps it might be said, the power of decision—continue to be vested in a comparatively small proportion of the population. Yet the conditions of exercise of power have radically changed. The wishes and probable actions of a vast number of people at the polls must be taken into consideration in the exercise of public power. Suffrage is the basis for the welfare state.

There is an odd feature about the expansion of the suffrage that needs some reflection by those seeking to comprehend the nature of political power. Disfranchised groups have gained the right to vote without being able to exert the power of the suffrage. If political power rested on the vote alone, groups enjoying that right could merely have refused to share it with others. But the disfranchised have had power enough to demand and to obtain the vote. On the other hand, a group such as the Negroes, who received the legal right to vote through the gift of others, has not been powerful enough to make the legal right universally effective in the southern states.

Obviously it is difficult to conclude that the suffrage is the sole cause either of legislation enacted for the benefit of formerly disfranchised classes or of the power enjoyed by these groups. Movements for the broadening of the suffrage have ordinarily gone hand in hand with movements for substantive legislation. Before 1850 agitators for legislation for the benefit of the working man often also fought for the repeal of property and taxpaying qualifications on voting. The woman suffragists were not interested in the suffrage alone; they were also concerned with the removal of the legal disabilities of women and with such matters as the regulation of the liquor traffic and the promotion of general civic decency.

Once a group has gained the suffrage it is in a more powerful position to promote and to protect its cause, but it first must gain, without the ballot, enough power to win the vote. Perhaps the doctrine and practice of popular government contain an inner logic that leads inevitably to the expansion of the suffrage. Once voting is initiated, it is a most troublesome problem to justify in principle the suffrage for one class and not for another. Moreover, if competition for power prevails, invariably some of those within the privileged circle will hope for allies by the admission of their friends from without.

23 | Registration, Elections, Ballots

Once it is determined that persons possessing specified qualifications shall be entitled to vote, it is necessary to establish machinery and procedures to effectuate that general policy. Although the machinery of elections may be a matter of administrative detail, it is a singularly important one. The implementation of the principle of popular elections should require only simple procedures to permit the qualified electors, and no others, to express their choice and to assure an honest and expeditious count of the ballots. Yet the laws governing elections are most intricate and many election procedures are bitterly disputed because different parties or factions believe their fortunes will be affected thereby. The conclusion of a student of the history of voting legislation in New Jersey could be applied more widely. He reviewed scores of legislative acts all but a few of which "were intended for no other purpose than to insure the supremacy of the temporarily dominant party." [1] The leading authority on American elections observed in 1929 that "little progress has been

[1] R. P. McCormick, *The History of Voting in New Jersey* (New Brunswick: Rutgers University Press, 1953), p. 163.

made in the technique of elections in this country. Probably no other phase of public administration is so badly managed. Our elections have been marked by irregularities, slipshod work, antiquated procedure, obsolete records, inaccuracies, and many varieties of downright fraud." [2] Despite improvements in many jurisdictions, the conclusion would not have to be changed materially today.

The conduct of elections, even for presidential electors, Senators, and Representatives, is a responsibility of the states, which usually regard their duty as discharged when they have enacted bulky volumes of election laws to guide the work of the officials in the voting precincts. The mastery of the minutiae of these laws is an essential for the grass-roots political worker; this discussion, however, can touch only the broadest problems in the management of elections which turn principally around the process of registration and the actual conduct of the election.[3]

Registration Systems

The function of a registration system is the preparation of a list of names of persons who meet the suffrage requirements of the jurisdiction. On election day the officials in charge of voting permit those persons to vote whose right to do so has been established through the registration procedure. Party affiliation may also be indicated at the time of registration and the registration records thus become the means for limiting primary participation to party members in states with closed primaries.

The development of registration systems furnishes an illuminating illustration of the factors underlying administrative procedures and what is often called red tape. Originally in small rural communities individuals presenting themselves at the polls were usually known to the election officials, to the watchers at the polls, and to their neighbors. The officials at the polls knew of their own knowledge whether the person requesting a ballot met the suffrage requirements. The formality of establishing this fact could be cared for on election day, if, indeed, any attention was given to the matter at all. With the development of urban society, more formal procedures became necessary to identify those entitled to vote.

The impersonality of urban relationships greatly facilitates certain types of election-day frauds, such as the colonization of voters, personation, and the use of repeaters. It is not to be inferred that voting frauds have been, or are, limited to urban communities; conditions there merely facil-

---

[2] J. P. Harris, *Registration of Voters in the United States* (Washington: Brookings, 1929), p. 3.

[3] In courses that emphasize practical politics students should dig into the details of the election laws of their state. In most states the Secretary of State (or other election official) issues a compilation of the election laws.

itate types of frauds that involve voting by legally unqualified persons. Consequently, with the growth of cities legislatures began to adopt registration laws, particularly in the post-Civil War period. Formalized procedures came into use under which individuals might establish in advance of the election those facts, such as residence, age, citizenship, and other matters, necessary to qualify them to vote. The inclusion of a name on the resulting list of registrants constitutes evidence on election day that the person named is entitled to vote. Thus administrative formalities arise to replace the common knowledge of the smaller community. The influence of urbanization is evident in many registration laws that apply only to large communities or fix more rigorous requirements for larger cities.[4] In the southern states registration systems were not a product of urbanization but were established to enforce the literacy tests and other voting qualifications peculiar to the region.[5]

Registration systems of a variety of types are used in the states to prepare the voting lists. Registration may be permanent or periodic: that is, an elector may be enrolled on the lists permanently, or there may be a complete reregistration at intervals. Registration may be personal or nonpersonal: that is, for registration, personal application by the elector may be required, or the authorities may prepare a voting list from their own knowledge or from information at their disposal. Registration may be compulsory or noncompulsory: that is, either a person's name must be on the list to qualify him to vote, or he may be permitted on election day to establish by appropriate evidence that he possesses the voting qualifications if his name is not on the list.

[4] Urban political leaders at times attribute the greater stringency of laws applying to cities to a rural desire to reduce the urban vote. If city voters are required to go to the polls once to register and again to vote and rural people do not have to make a special trip to the polls to register, the contention is that popular participation in voting in the cities is reduced.

[5] Registration authorities in the southern states apply the suffrage requirements in a manner to meet whatever the local situation demands, subject to suit instigated by the NAACP, a hazard which has made it difficult in some localities to fill the post of registrar. For an account of discriminatory practices against both whites and blacks which would set off a civil commotion almost anywhere else in the United States, see Donald S. Strong, *Registration of Voters in Alabama* (University, Ala.: Bureau of Public Administration, 1956). See also O. H. Shadgett, *Voter Registration in Georgia* (Athens: University of Georgia, 1955). Estimates of Negro registration in 1956 by the Southern Regional Council indicate that perhaps not over 5 per cent of Mississippi Negroes 21 and over were registered in that year and probably not over 10 per cent of Alabama Negroes. In other southern states the proportions ranged from about 20 per cent in Virginia to 40 per cent in Florida. Within individual states proportions of Negroes registered varied widely from county to county. Discrimination by registration officials accounts only partly for low registration among Negroes.

Periodic and permanent registration. In recent years the chief controversy over registration in the United States has turned on the issue of periodic versus permanent registration. The older form of periodic registration is being gradually displaced by permanent registration. About three-fourths of the states use some form of permanent registration either on a state-wide basis or in designated cities or counties. Under periodic registration completely new lists of voters are prepared annually, biennially, or quad-rennially. The customary procedure provides for the decentralized prep-aration of the lists by registration boards sitting usually at the polling place in each precinct. During specified days the boards sit and receive the re-quests of individuals for the inclusion of their names on the lists. Such is the more general practice under systems of periodic registration, though not all such systems fit this pattern. Louisiana, for example, requires a quadrennial registration of all voters in most of its parishes, but the voter may register at any time at a central place in each parish rather than only on certain days at the polling places.[6]

Its defenders contend that periodic registration produces clean lists. When all would-be voters must come to the registration places shortly before the election to get their names on the list, presumably those who have died since the last registration, those who have moved from the pre-cinct, and those disqualified in other ways will not be included on the new lists. This plausible *a priori* assumption appears to be unsupported by ex-perience. Certain cities notorious for registration and election frauds have employed periodic registration; the decentralized and more or less irre-sponsible conduct of registration in the polling places throughout a city facilitates the padding of the lists. Understandings between registration officials of different parties (who supposedly police each other) may result in the falsification of the lists; the name of a nonexistent person on the regis-tration lists permits that name to be voted in the party primaries. Even if the registration officials are honest, the conditions of urban society are such that many precinct registration officials have no personal knowledge of the residence or identity of those applying for registration.

Permanent registration involves a single appearance by the applicant

[6] The scheduling of times at which registration may occur can have untoward con-sequences. If, for example, registration is limited to specified days, persons who hap-pen to be ill at the time are unable to register. One local analysis revealed that about one-quarter of the nonregistrants had been either ill or absent from the locality on registration day. See P. Bradley and A. H. Cope, "A Community Registration Survey," *American Political Science Review*, 45 (1951), pp. 775–778. Labor leaders occasionally complain that registration offices are open only at times when workers have to lose a half day's pay to register. Such an administrative practice affects, at times deliberately, the balance of partisan strength.

for registration before the registration officials. His name remains on the register until he dies, until he changes his residence, or until he becomes otherwise disqualified. This convenience to the voter is the strong justification for permanent registration. The absence of periodic reregistration, however, requires the substitution of other means to purge the rolls of disqualified persons. In the newer permanent systems a continuous revision of the lists occurs. Changes may be made on application of the voter, who has, let us say, moved from one precinct to another. Or the registration officials may act on the basis of information available to them. The central registration staff may examine death certificates and strike names from the voting lists. From court records may be obtained the names of persons adjudged insane or convicted of crimes that disqualify them from voting. In some instances corrections are made on the basis of information on removals provided by utility companies.

In areas where transiency is high or fraudulent registration is suspected, a house-to-house canvass may be conducted to check the lists. Commonly registrations are cancelled because of failure to vote in a specified number of elections. To keep the permanent lists current is no mean task, for in some years of the 1950's about 20 per cent of the population moved into a different residence. The central staff in charge of the revision of the registration records is usually also vested with the responsibility of accepting the applications of new electors for registration. Except for a short interval prior to elections the acceptance of new registrations is continuous rather than restricted to a few days during the year as under the periodic system.

On the issue of fraudulent registration (and hence potential fraudulent voting) neither system is foolproof. The evidence certainly indicates that the system of permanent registration creates an administrative situation in which it is possible to bring about less fraud in registration if there is a will to do so. The decentralized preparation of the rolls by temporary employees (generally recruited because of their loyalty to the party organization) characteristic of periodic registration results in administrative machinery impossible of supervision by the city or county registration authorities. Precinct registration officials are usually not disinterested individuals; their ward organization may even be eager to have fictitious names on the lists. With a small permanent staff in charge of the continuous revision of the permanent lists it is more nearly possible to avoid these influences through supervision. Furthermore, it is possible in a central office to have access to more trustworthy evidence pertaining to residence, removal, or loss of voting privilege than is usually available to the precinct officials. It does not follow, to be sure, that the list under permanent registration will be freer of names of persons unqualified to vote. Yet if the political and administrative will is present, it is more feasible to maintain clean lists under permanent registration than under the periodic system. If that will is absent, fraud and error may be as prevalent under permanent registration as under other systems.

From the standpoint of cost, permanent registration appears, on the basis of available evidence, to be preferable to periodic registration. Once a system of permanent registration has been installed, the principal items of cost are for the support of a small central staff to accept new registrations and to revise the records and for special canvasses. In periodic registration, on the other hand, personnel to accept registrations in every precinct from the entire electorate is necessary, and an entirely new set of records must be purchased at each registration, a characteristic that endears the periodic system to printers who cater to election officials. Jurisdictions with permanent registration also tend to use more modern record-keeping and filing systems than is customary under periodic registration.[7]

Personal and nonpersonal registration. Registration may be personal or nonpersonal. The systems that have been described, under which the elector must make personal application to have his name placed on the registration list, are personal systems. Under a nonpersonal system the lists are prepared by official agencies from information at their disposal. In the United States the nonpersonal scheme generally involves an annual revision by the precinct registration board, which meets to revise the list of the prior year and to add names of new electors in the precinct. The list is usually then posted for the information of the electors of the precinct, and a second meeting of the board is held to permit the appearance of those persons whose names have been omitted and to hear challenges against names incorrectly included in the list. Party workers often keep a close watch over the work of the registration board to assure that their members are registered. In the United States this form of registration is limited in the main to rural or semirural areas, since in only the smaller communities do the precinct registration officials possess the necessary knowledge to maintain the lists.[8] In European countries greater reliance

---

[7] See Joseph P. Harris, *Model Voter Registration System* (New York: National Municipal League, rev. ed., 1957). For a study of registration in major population centers, see R. F. Ray, *Report to Governor Thomas E. Dewey on Permanent Personal Registration of Electors* (Albany, 1952).

[8] See Harris, *Registration of Voters in the United States*, pp. 101–102. Nonpersonal registration is used in over half the election districts in upstate New York. In 1950 registration in ten of the 57 upstate counties of New York exceeded the numbers of citizens 21 and over as reported by the census. In another 11 counties registrants numbered between 90 and 100 per cent of the citizenry of voting age. In New York City, with personal registration, only 53.5 per cent of the citizens 21 and over were regis-

on nonpersonal registration prevails. On the Continent elaborate continual censuses of the population make it possible to keep the registration records up to date without personal application for registration by the electors.

Compulsory and noncompulsory registration. The classification of registration systems as compulsory or noncompulsory is determined by whether it is mandatory that a person's name be on the list before he is permitted to vote. Under the noncompulsory system it is possible for a voter to be "sworn in" at the polls; that is, he makes an affadavit that he meets the suffrage requirements and is supported in this statement by witnesses. The noncompulsory system exists primarily as a concession to those groups that originally opposed registration in any form. The possibility of "swearing in" voters leaves a loophole for fraud.[9]

There is no formal system of registration in two states. In Texas and Arkansas lists of those entitled to vote are prepared from the records of those who have paid poll taxes or established their eligibility to vote under provisions of law exempting them from the tax. These arrangements constitute, in effect, periodic systems of registration.

In the debates of recent decades over the form of registration systems, the National Municipal League and the League of Women Voters have advocated permanent registration, while most party organizations have favored periodic registration. The party position has been in the main dictated by the petty patronage connected with the employment of precinct registration officials rather than by any refined estimate of the effects of different registration systems on the outcome of the party battle. Those effects, if any, are difficult to appraise. Certainly any administrative hurdle in the path to the polling booth reduces the total turnout, and periodic registration is more of an obstacle than is permanent registration. Cities are probably handicapped in state politics when their voters must register periodically while the outstate operates under permanent registration. The chances are also that administrative obstacles to voting have more severe effects in the lower reaches of the educational and economic scale, a factor which may tip the scales one way or another when cleavages along such lines prevail in the voting. Since party organizations must devote

---

tered; in the state outside the city the percentage was 79.8. Upstate Republicans in New York have usually expressed great anxiety about the dangers of padded voting lists in New York City, but it is evident that most of the deadwood is on the upstate rolls.

[9] It is recorded, how correctly one cannot say, that in Chicago's ninth ward on April 3, 1883 among those "sworn in" were George Washington, Thomas Jefferson, John Hancock, James Madison, and Abraham Lincoln. Each of these distinguished men, the story goes, voted the straight Democratic ticket. See Bruce Grant, *Fight for a City* (Chicago: Rand McNally & Co., 1955), p. 67.

great quantities of energy to registration campaigns, they should themselves benefit from registration systems that make it simple for the voter to register and stay registered.

Elections

In the United States, state and local governments conduct elections, even for federal elective officials. And within the states, elections, although governed by state legislation, are generally administered by local governments, with little or no supervision by state agencies.[10] In the consideration of election administration, therefore, attention must be concentrated on counties, cities, or whatever unit of local government is responsible for the conduct of the balloting.[11] Commonly those officials charged with the conduct of the general election are also responsible for the direct primaries, although in several southern states party organizations manage the primaries.[12]

Election organization. The task of conducting an election involves preparation of ballots; designation of polling places; making of arrangements for quarters for the polls; selection, instruction, and supervision of precinct officials to conduct the voting; preparation and distribution to the polling places of booths, ballots, voting machines, and supplies needed on election day; identification of voters as they come to the polls; presentation of ballots to the voters; general management of the polling place on election day; and counting of the ballots after the voting. Conduct of elections is, then, a large and tedious but relatively simple administrative task. It is, moreover, a highly seasonal operation. The dates of elections are fixed by statute. The peak load on the election machinery falls quadrennially on the first Tuesday after the first Monday in November, the date set by Congress for the choice of presidential electors at which time—save in Maine—Senators and Representatives are also chosen. The midterm elections of Senators and Representatives also occur with similar uniformity, thanks to an act of Congress. State constitutions and statutes generally set elections for state officials on the same date as the presidential and

[10] The only comprehensive treatment of election management is by J. P. Harris, *Election Administration in the United States* (Washington: Brookings, 1934). For a guide through the legal maze in one state, see Judith N. Jamison, *Local Election Administration in California* (Los Angeles: Bureau of Governmental Research, University of California, 1952). For a study illustrative of the role of state election authorities, see G. A. Schubert, Jr., *The Michigan State Director of Elections* (ICP Case Series, No. 23, University of Alabama Press, 1954).

[11] Federal power is exerted in elections through the Corrupt Practices Act and the Hatch Act. Occasionally fraud in elections of federal officials is reached obliquely through prosecution under a section of the Federal Criminal Code punishing conspiracy to deprive persons of rights guaranteed by the Constitution.

[12] On southern practice, see Key, *Southern Politics*, pp. 444-450.

congressional polling, although this practice is not universal. Furthermore, the widest variation prevails among the states in the scheduling of direct primaries and state and local elections.

In the more populous cities and counties a board of election commissioners is usually responsible for the conduct of elections. In other places the county board may be the chief local election authority; or the city clerk or the county clerk may be the responsible official. It is the duty of the central county or city authority to select precinct officials, to procure and distribute election equipment and supplies to the precinct polling places, to make arrangements for polling places, and to supervise (generally ineffectively) the work of the precinct election officials who manage the polling places on election day. The control of the city or county election machinery is a prize eagerly sought by the party organizations. Its control gives the organization the patronage of the election machinery and also, at times, can be used to obstruct embarrassing inquiries into the conduct of elections.

The city or county is divided into precincts of various sizes, each of which usually includes a few hundred voters. The polling place in each precinct is manned on election day by a group of precinct officials. Their titles, which vary from jurisdiction to jurisdiction, may be "judge of elections," "election inspector," or "clerk." They determine whether persons presenting themselves at the polling place are entitled to vote; give such persons ballots or access to the voting machine; count the ballots and report the results to the central election authority.

In form, precinct officials are appointed by the central election commission or agency of the city or county, but in most jurisdictions they are, in fact, named by the party organizations. The law usually prescribes that precinct officials shall be divided between the two major parties; in practice, the precinct captain or committeeman of each party has the privilege of naming the election officials to which his party is entitled in his precinct. These election-day jobs are a part of the patronage at the disposal of the precinct captain and are used by him to reward his followers in the precinct. It hardly needs to be observed that the method of appointing precinct officials has never resulted in election machinery notable for clerical accuracy or efficiency, but the procedure has gotten a thankless job done. In the piping days of full employment the attractiveness of a one-day job with long hours and small pay declined, and manning the polls became a problem of positive recruitment, not one of fending off eager applicants for picayune political plums.[13]

---

[13] Reluctance to undertake the tiresome chore of manning the polls appeared from coast to coast. In Oakland, California, in 1954 the elderly and infirm persons who could be recruited to man the precincts could cope with the paper work only with

In the conduct of the polling, the first step is to determine whether the register of voters contains the name of the person who applies for a ballot. If the name is on the list the person is usually given a ballot without further ado. At this stage, however, the right of a person to vote may be challenged. Challenges are infrequent, but, if a challenge is made, various types of evidence may be offered to establish the right of the person in question to vote. Comparison of the voter's signature with that in his application for registration furnishes a means of identification in those jurisdictions using this registration practice. Some registration systems include in the records a description of the voter: height, color of eyes, color of hair, and the like. Such descriptions are practically worthless as a means of identification.

As votes are cast, a list is prepared of those who have voted. The party watchers also check off on their lists the names of those who have voted; as the day wears on, they dispatch runners to bring in the laggards. An incidental but important feature of the voting in machine-controlled precincts is the provision for assistance to the voter in marking his ballot. Persons incapable of marking the ballot may usually request assistance in this task; the reasons justifying a request for assistance vary from state to state, but they include illiteracy (in those states without a literacy test), blindness, and other physical infirmities. Under this provision the secrecy of the ballot may be destroyed, and bargains between party workers and voters may be carried out.

Counting the ballots. At the proper time (in some jurisdictions before the closing of the polls) the counting of the ballots begins. The procedure for counting is often prescribed in minute detail by statute. The statute may require one election official to read from each ballot the choices expressed, while two other election officials (one from each party) watch. The choices are supposed to be tallied independently by two clerks, and both counts are supposed to check at the conclusion of the process. In practice these statutory provisions tend to be ignored, for the simple reason that to follow them slavishly would make the count almost interminable. The laws, for example, often prescribe that the vote on each ballot on all offices shall be recorded at one time. In practice, often the count is made on a single office at a time. The law usually requires that the tally sheet shall actually be made as the count proceeds, but in practice the

difficulty; one hardy 80-year-old woman remained on duty as her three associates fell ill. In Bristol, Rhode Island, party leaders were dismayed to discover that they could not find enough people in their organizations to meet the needs of the election authorities. And in some localities officials had to invoke long-unused laws that permitted them to compel persons to serve.

count is often made and then the official tally sheets are filled in. Otherwise the clerks run into difficulty in making their tallies match. Apart from outright fraud, error is likely to creep into the count. The long ballot, the weariness of election officials, and often their indifferent clerical capacities lay the basis for considerable honest error in counting.[14]

After the completion of the count, the precinct election officials prepare a certificate indicating the number of votes received by each candidate and the number of votes cast for and against each proposition on the ballot. This certificate, together with the ballot box, is sent to the central election authority—election commissioners, city council, county clerk, or whatever agency is vested with authority—and the results are "canvassed"; that is, the returns from all the precincts are added and the outcome of the election is pronounced. In some jurisdictions the canvassing authority "canvasses" the voting machines—that is, checks the readings of the counters on the machines against the reports by the precinct officials. For state offices the county and city results are certified to some state authority—usually the secretary of state—who canvasses or totals the results from all the counties of the state. The process of canvassing is a simple exercise in arithmetic; and the results have been known, usually long before the official canvass, through tabulations made unofficially by newspapers, party officers, and others.

Election contests. Provision is generally made to permit a contest of the result of an election as declared by the official canvassing authorities. The contest is sometimes heard by the election officials, sometimes by the courts, and, if legislators are involved, usually by the legislative body, which is generally the sole judge of the qualifications of its members. The ease with which a recount may be brought about varies from jurisdiction to jurisdiction. In some instances a recount may be had as a matter of right; in others, proof must first be made of misconduct or errors by election officials. In some states recounts are discouraged by the requirement that the petitioner for a recount finance the work—a rule that may nip in the bud frivolous requests for recounts but which also ignores the public interest in both competent and honest election administration. When a recount is not improbable, precinct election officials might be expected to strive for accuracy in their work.[15]

[14] The hours during which the polls are open tend to be quite long in order to accommodate persons who wish to vote before or after work. About half the states have laws requiring employers to give time off for voting, in some instances without deductions from wages. On the anti-docking clauses, see Day-Brite *v.* Missouri, 342 U.S. 421 (1952), and Illinois Central R.R. Co. *v.* Commonwealth, 305 Ky. 632 (1947). For a summary of legislation, see *Labor Law Journal,* 3 (1952), pp. 719–721.

[15] Two recent gubernatorial elections in Michigan have been followed by recounts. In 1950 the initial tabulation gave G. Mennen Williams a plurality of 1,301 in a total

Civilian absentee voting. An aspect of election administration of some importance is provision for voting by those persons who are unable to appear at the polling place on election day. Absentee-voting laws originated during the Civil War to permit voting by military personnel, but the extension of the absentee-voting privilege to civilians occurred principally after 1900. By 1955 all states except New Mexico and South Carolina had adopted some form of absentee-voting legislation for the benefit of civilians. Even by 1936, according to an estimate by Paul G. Steinbicker, about 2 per cent of the votes cast in the presidential election were absentee votes.[16]

State laws on the subject of absent voting by civilians are characterized by almost infinite variation. One point of difference pertains to the geographical limits on absent voting. In a few instances the voter must be outside the territorial limits of the state before he may exercise the absentee-voting privilege. In others, he qualifies to vote absentee if he is home ill or bedridden. Some states specify rather narrow ranges of causes of absence to qualify, as, "in the usual course of business"; others merely specify absence. Another point of difference concerns the elections to which absentee-voting provisions apply. New Hampshire, for example, permits absentee voting only in general elections; Tennessee, in "any election for any purpose whatsoever."

To cast an absentee ballot an elector must apply to the appropriate election officials within a prescribed period preceding the election. When he mails his ballot to the election officials, it must be accompanied by an affidavit showing compliance with the requirements of the legislation. These requirements vary but include such matters as a certificate by a notary public or other officer that the person entitled to the ballot actually marked it—a precaution against abuse of the absentee-voting privilege.

Absentee-voting procedures, it is often said, are particularly susceptible of fraudulent manipulation. The bases for such charges are suggested by North Carolina's experience. In that state absent voting is permitted in the general election but not in the primary. The local gossip is to the effect that the Democratic legislature made this arrangement to give a little leeway to Democrats, who control the election machinery, in the state's western counties in which the outcome of the battle between Republicans and Democrats is close. In the election of governor in 1944 the

of over 1,800,000 votes. His lead grew to 4,157 after a partial recount. In 1952 Williams' initial plurality of 8,618 (in a total vote of over 2,800,000) increased to 9,978 after a partial recount. For an exhaustive study of these recounts, see S. J. Eldersveld and A. A. Applegate, *Michigan's Recounts for Governor, 1950 and 1952: A Systematic Analysis of Election Error* (Ann Arbor: University of Michigan Press, 1954).

[16] "Absentee Voting in the United States," *American Political Science Review*, 32 (1938), pp. 898–907. For a tabular analysis of state legislation, see *Book of the States, 1954–1955,* p. 91.

absent vote (military and civilian) constituted 6.7 per cent of the state total and in 25 of the 100 counties the absent vote exceeded the plurality of the winning candidate. The absent vote was highest in the western counties; it exceeded 15 per cent of the total vote in seven counties. In one county 25.7 per cent of the total ballots were absentee. Generally the percentage of absentee ballots increased with the closeness of the contest from county to county. One hypothess would be that fraud had occurred; another, that when the contest is close greater efforts are made to get out the vote.[17]

Soldier voting. A considerable body of legislation has developed to facilitate absentee voting by military personnel. The problem of voting procedures for the military became of special importance in World War II. Large numbers of men and women were in uniform and their dispersion over the globe created difficult problems in the administration of absent voting. In the evolution of federal legislation on soldier voting the issue has arisen over the extent to which Congress should, or could constitutionally, go in protecting the right of soldiers to vote in view of state control of registration and voting. Under the legislation in force prior to the 1956 election, Congress limited itself to recommendations to the states to enact legislation to facilitate absentee voting by servicemen, members of the merchant marine, civilian employees of the United States, members of welfare or religious organizations attached to the armed services, and their spouses and dependents. The Department of Defense maintains a staff with the duty of collecting information about state laws on the topic, of stimulating state legislation to simplify soldier voting, of making available to troops information on voting procedures, and of expediting the transmission of ballots. Most states have enacted legislation to permit soldier voting but some of the laws are severely limited in their workability. Some states, for example, permit absentee voting but persist in requiring registration in person; others make ballots available too late to permit them to be received by soldiers in remote places in time to return them to the polling officials before election day.

The spread of large numbers of American military personnel over the world makes the problem of absentee voting one of an entirely different magnitude than when the principal concern was to make it possible for the occasional traveling salesman or locomotive engineer away from home

---

[17] When the kinds of people most disposed to trouble themselves to cast absentee ballots are disproportionately concentrated in one party, that party gains advantage. In 1956 the Rhode Island courts held the state's absent voting-statute unconstitutional, a decision which threw out the absentee votes and gave the governorship to a Democrat instead of a Republican.

to vote. In 1944 the 2,691,000 effective military ballots (about 30 per cent of the potential) accounted for over 5 per cent of the vote cast in the presidential election. Even in 1956 persons in or attached to the armed services made up a potential absentee vote of about 3,000,000.[18]

Fraud. The American election system has gained an unenviable reputation for fraud, although electoral fraud occurs far less frequently than is commonly supposed. Often a day or so before the voting, candidates charge that the wicked opposition is conspiring to steal the election and on the day after the election the losers may claim that they have been robbed. Sometimes indictments for electoral fraud amount to nothing more than political persecution. Charges and rumors of election irregularities are displayed prominently in the press. The truth about the incidence of electoral fraud cannot readily be discovered. If it could be, the findings probably would be that fraud has declined over the long term. Yet fraud has occurred on a large scale and votes are still stolen from time to time. The publicized records of shady practices in the big cities are matched by relatively unpublicized stolen elections in the country. In corruptly ruled localities the psychological effect of fraud may contribute more than do the stolen votes to the power of the machine. Opposition is likely to falter if the belief prevails that elections are fixed whatever the actual vote may be. A hair-raising volume could be put together descriptive of electoral frauds; space permits here only the indication of the nature of a few broad types of irregularities.

Fraud and error in registration lay the basis for electoral fraud. When the lists of voters contain false names or the names of persons who have moved away, the party organization may readily find persons to vote those names, provided that the precinct election officials are willing to connive in such an arrangement. How do such names get on the registration lists? The lists may be padded with imaginary names by the registration officials in keeping with a plan to vote the names later. Superfluous names may be on the list merely because of failure to purge the lists of names of persons who have died, moved from the precinct, or otherwise lost their eligibility to vote. When the names of persons who die are left on the lists, the basis is laid, as the argot runs, for "voting the cemetery."

Lists with superfluous names are a condition precedent to a simple and

[18] See B. A. Martin, "The Service Vote in the Elections of 1944," *American Political Science Review*, 39 (1945), pp. 720–732; "Findings and Recommendations of the Special Committee on Service Voting," *American Political Science Review*, 46 (1952), pp. 512–523; *Hearings*, Subcommittee on Elections of the Committee on House Administration, House of Representatives, 82d Cong., 2d sess. on H.R. 7571 and S. 3061 (1952).

easy type of fraud. On election day fictitious names on the registration lists may be voted in various ways. Sometimes the machine employs repeaters or floaters to go from precinct to precinct to vote under false names already on the listing in each precinct. To organize and manage a squad of repeaters is expensive, and the task of voting the names on the registers may be left to the precinct election officials, aided by the precinct party workers. A Philadelphia precinct official testified, for example:

> We didn't record a man as voting unless he actually voted, or unless we knew he could be depended on. For example, I was sure my mother wouldn't come to the polls, so it was quite safe to cast her ballot for her. The people who live next door to us are the right sort, but they're lazy and like to stay at home. So I told them I would cast their votes for them. But we played the game fair.[19]

When a person votes under the name of some other person, the act is called personation. When there is no attempt at deception but a wholesale voting of names on the registers (or not on the registers) by the election officials, the practice is known as "ballot-box stuffing." This practice is cheaper and easier than the organization of repeaters and personators. Cruder practitioners of fraud make no effort to give an appearance of legality to their work and duly record as having voted persons whose names do not appear on the registration lists.[20]

Another point at which fraud may occur is during the counting of the ballots. Occasionally the count is a farce: the vote is determined arbitrarily or by agreement among the election officials and the attendant party workers. This type of fraud is most likely to occur at primaries, when the only persons with an interest may be the machine workers for each party organization, and at general elections in precincts where the minority party is either powerless or a subsidiary of the majority. During the count ballots may be altered or removed and substitutions made. Alterations may have several objects. A long ballot may be marked for only a few offices. The counting official may take up the burden where the elector stopped and finish the laborious exercise of the suffrage. The purpose of alteration may be to change the vote completely. For example, in Chicago investigators for the Citizens' Association reported that "after the polls closed many 'straight' Republican ballots were converted into 'straight' Democratic ballots by the simple expedient of erasing the cross in the Republican party circle and putting a cross in the Democratic party

[19] A. F. Macdonald, "Philadelphia's Political Machine in Action," *National Municipal Review*, 15 (1926), pp. 28–35.

[20] The charges against the defendants in a Chicago case were that "in 31 instances they allowed persons using the same names to vote twice; that they permitted 26 persons to vote who were not registered, and they let 24 persons whose names had been stricken from the poll books cast ballots."—*Chicago Daily News*, August 10, 1934.

circle." [21] Alteration of the ballot may have as its object the spoiling of a ballot so that it will be thrown out. A cross may be altered, for example, to make it appear to be an identifying mark, invalidating the ballot.[22]

Sometimes fraud or trickery occurs in the certification of the results. The ballots may be accurately counted and recorded on the tally sheets but the certificate reporting the results of the precinct doctored. An old trick is the transposition of figures. The candidate receives, for example 49 votes; in certifying this item it may be written 94. Or perhaps the report is prepared without even this sort of attempt to camouflage fraud as error.

The cruder practitioners of electoral fraud leave a trail as plain as that of a bleeding black bear trodding freshly fallen snow. If one precinct reports no votes for a candidate while the surrounding precincts give him a substantial vote, an odor of fraud or error is in evidence. Or if a precinct board reports more votes than the precinct has voters, a fair presumption may be raised that the election code has been transgressed. The annals are replete with such instances of patent irregularity. Yet to pin the guilt on crooked election officials in a court of law is not always easy. In truth, the well-managed political machine sees that the election records, are, on their face, in meticulous accord with the niceties of electoral jurisprudence. The young assistant district attorney trying to make a reputation by the prosecution of an election fraud case against such an organization should steel himself against disappointment.

Ballots

Certain additional features of election management are connected with the ballot and the voting machine. These may be regarded as fairly humdrum matters of administrative detail, but some questions of ballot form are still the subject of spirited disputes. These matters of form, like others connected with the voting process, may have effects that give advantage to one party or the other in particular situations.

Secrecy of the vote. Although secrecy of the ballot has become commonplace, the general use of secret methods of voting is a relatively recent development in American politics. In the colonial period and in the early history of the United States the more prevalent form of voting was the oral, or viva-voce, method. Under this arrangement each voter would appear before the election officials and announce orally the candidate whom

[21] Quoted by Harris, *Election Administration in the United States*, p. 352.
[22] There is a recondite jurisprudence defining precisely what constitutes a valid cross mark. See Spencer Albright, "Legislation on Marking Ballots," *Southwestern Social Science Quarterly*, 21 (1940), pp. 221–226.

he desired to support. Oral voting gradually gave way to a system of voting by ballots, which by no means assured secrecy of voting. At first, ballots were printed privately rather than by public authority. The parties or candidates furnished separate ballots to the voters. The Democratic ballot might be of pink paper; the Republican, white. These and other such characteristics of privately printed ballots enabled observers at the polls to know which ballot an elector dropped into the box.[23]

Serious concern over the absence of secrecy in voting arose soon after the Civil War when intimidation and bribery of voters became rife. It will be recalled that the groups benefiting from the earlier restricted suffrage clung desperately to their privileged status and, as they were compelled to yield to the demands for a broader suffrage, predicted dire results for those of property and substance from the enfranchisement of the masses. After the Civil War the full effects of the broadened suffrage began to be felt, and concerted attempts were made to neutralize these effects by bribery and intimidation. The lack of secrecy of voting facilitated bribery, since a person was not inclined to purchase a commodity of whose delivery he was not assured. Similarly, the lack of secrecy of the vote enabled those in a position to intimidate to apply their sanctions. Without secrecy of the ballot, employers might control the votes of their workmen; landlords, the votes of their tenants; creditors, the votes of their debtors.

Many states, to ensure secrecy, enacted regulatory legislation to govern the private printing of ballots; but these measures were uniformly ineffective, and those desiring a truly secret vote turned toward the Australian ballot. This ballot, so named because of the place of its origin, was printed by public authority. It contained the names of the candidates of all parties and was coupled with methods of election administration designed to ensure secrecy of voting. The agitation for the new type of ballot originated in large measure from labor and other minority groups that believed their political strength to be diminished by the intimidation and bribery prevailing under the existing system of balloting. They were joined in their advocacy in some states by urban reform groups and on occasion by the minority political party. Thus, the early agitation for the Australian ballot was led by people outside the governing cliques; eventually the reform gained broader support.[24]

In the United States the first Australian-ballot law was enacted by the

---

[23] E. C. Evans, *A History of the Australian Ballot System in the United States* (Chicago: University of Chicago Press, 1917), pp. 6–7.

[24] See John H. Wigmore, *The Australian Ballot System* (Boston: Boston Book Company, 2d ed., 1889). For a defense of nonsecret voting, see John Stuart Mill, *Representative Government*, ch. 10.

Kentucky legislature in 1880. This measure applied only to municipal elections in Louisville; the state constitution explicitly required viva-voce voting at elections of state officers. By 1900 a large proportion of the states had adopted the Australian ballot. By 1942 forty-five states used this type of ballot; action by South Carolina in 1950 brought the Australian ballot to all the states, although in some states procedures continued to prevail under which the secrecy of the ballot might be violated.[25]

Intimidation and bribery remain but not to the degree that existed before the introduction of the Australian ballot. The secrecy of the ballot may be destroyed, as we have seen, by statutory provisions to permit "assistance" to illiterate, blind, or otherwise incapacitated voters.[26] Another device sometimes used to destroy the secrecy of the vote and to facilitate purchase is the "endless chain" or "Tasmanian dodge." Under this scheme it is necessary to obtain an official ballot; the purchaser of the vote marks the ballot as he desires it to be voted, delivers it to the bought elector who enters the polling place and procures a ballot. In the booth the voter substitutes the marked ballot for the fresh one, inserts the marked ballot in the ballot box, and delivers the fresh ballot to the party worker. This ballot is marked, given to another voter who repeats the process; the chain goes on unbroken. To check this practice over half of the states employ a system of numbered ballots. When a voter receives a ballot, the number is recorded opposite his name; before he is permitted to deposit the ballot he must show the numbered stub (the ballot is folded so as to show only the number) to the election officials who tear it off. In some instances a venal voter may mark his ballot so as to identify it to the election officials and those watching the count; in this way the purchaser may assure himself that he has received delivery. Identification of an individual ballot in this way is illegal; ballots signed plainly fall within the proscription, but other types of symbols designed to identify are more difficult to deal with.

Consequences of public provision of ballots. It should be observed that Australian-ballot laws constituted an entering wedge for the detailed regulation of party activity. When it was decided that public authorities should print ballots containing the names of the candidates of all parties,

[25] In several southern states a number is written on the ballot as it is cast which corresponds to a number alongside the name of the voter on the polling list. The practice has been defended on the ground that it permits, when an election is contested, the ballot boxes to be opened and the ballots cast by disqualified persons to be thrown out.

[26] One aspect of ballot secrecy for which no solution is apparent is suggested by the warning of ecclesiastical authorities to their parishioners as they instructed them how to vote in a recent election: "The Australian ballot is not secret to God."

it became necessary to define by law "party" and to fix the procedure that the party should follow in certifying its nominations for inclusion on the ballot. Otherwise the agency in charge of ballot preparation might be faced with the problem of deciding which of several party lists should be printed, without having any legal standard for its decision. It was also necessary to require that nominations be made far enough in advance of an election to give time to print the ballot.

Their power to decide, at least in the first instance, whether particular names shall be placed on the ballot is another factor that makes the control of election authorities of value to party organizations. This power is of special significance with respect to the primary ballot. Where party organizations actively support a slate in the primary, the elections board often enforces a meticulous observance of the election laws on anti-organization candidates for nomination who present petitions to gain a place on the ballot. When such a petition can be thrown out on a technicality, the anti-organization candidate rarely receives the benefit of the doubt.

Minor parties often face legal obstacles in getting their candidates on the general election ballot. A party is sometimes defined in terms of the number of votes cast for its candidates at the preceding election. In Ohio, for example, "when any political party fails to cast 10 per cent of the total vote cast at an election for the office of governor it shall cease to be a political party within the meaning of this act." By raising the percentage required to keep party candidates on the official ballot, legislatures sometimes discriminate against minor parties. Usually, however, provision is made to permit a new party to place its candidates on the ballot by petition. In Oklahoma, for example, any "political party presenting a petition of 5,000 names of voters . . . shall have the names of its candidates for state and local offices placed on a ballot."

The fixing of the number of signatures at a high figure frustrates the desire of minor parties to have the names of their candidates on the ballot. In Illinois to put the candidates of a new party on the ballot a petition with 25,000 signatures is required. Moreover, the petition must contain the signature of 200 registered voters in each of at least 50 counties. In 1948 Illinois Republicans sought unsuccessfully to have this act declared void in order that Henry Wallace's Progressives might get on the ballot and divert support from the Democrats. Often the time of petitioning for a place on the ballot is fixed to discourage splinter candidacies. If minor-party petitions must be filed before the primaries or conventions, those disgruntled by major-party actions on nominations cannot put an independent or third-party candidate on the ballot. Such a rule in Oklahoma kept both the Wallace Progressives and the Thurmond Dixiecrats off the 1948 ballot of that state.

Ballot forms. Once it is decided that the ballot shall be provided by public authority, it must be determined how the names of candidates shall be arranged on the ballot. Two principal types of ballot forms have developed, although variations on these forms also exist. They are the office-block ballot, in which all candidates for each office are grouped together, and the party-column ballot, in which all the candidates of each party for all offices are grouped together in parallel vertical columns.

The party-column ballot, used in about 30 states, is sometimes called the Indiana-type ballot because the Indiana law of 1889 has served as a model for other states.[27] In most states using the party-column ballot it is possible to vote for all the candidates of a single party for all offices by making a single cross in the circle at the head of the column containing the party's candidates. In some states the party emblem is carried at the top of its column, a feature which, in less literate days, was of some utility in guiding the voter to the right column on the ballot. To vote a split ticket on a party-column ballot usually requires the recording of a choice for each office, a path the voter will presumably hesitate to follow when he has the alternative of simply making a single cross mark. Professional party workers generally favor the use of the party-column ballot because it encourages straight-ticket voting. A sample party-column ballot is reproduced in Figure 23.1.

In contrast with the party-column ballot is the office-block, or, as it is sometimes called by virtue of its origin, the Massachusetts ballot. Names of all candidates, by whatever party nominated, for each office are grouped together on the office-block ballot, usually with an indication alongside each name of the party affiliation. The supposition is that the voter will be compelled to consider separately the candidates for each office, in contrast with the encouragement given to straight-ticket voting by the party-column ballot. Pennsylvania uses a variation on the office-block ballot: the candidates are grouped according to office but provision is made for straight-ticket voting by a single mark.[28]

[27] For a tabular analysis prepared by Spencer Albright of the ballot laws of all the states, see *Book of the States, 1954–1955*, p. 82.

[28] Another classification of ballots is partisan and nonpartisan. The partisan ballot includes either party symbols or other identification of the party affiliation of the candidates. The nonpartisan ballot, which lacks such identification, is used in the attempt to take certain kinds of elections "out of party politics," chiefly judicial and municipal elections. Still another ballot classification is the consolidated and nonconsolidated ballot. A consolidated ballot includes all offices and questions being voted

Figure 23.1. Specimen Party-Column Ballot [a]

[a] This 1956 ballot differs from the pure Indiana form in that the presidential and vice-presidential candidates appeared on a separate ballot.

The Commonwealth of Massachusetts

List of Candidates nominated, to be voted for in Lawrence, Ward 6, Precinct 8, November 6, 1956

SPECIMEN BALLOT

Edward J. Cronin
SECRETARY OF THE COMMONWEALTH
of Massachusetts

Penalty for wilfully defacing, tearing down, removing or destroying a list of candidates or specimen ballot, fine not exceeding one hundred dollars

Figure 23.2. Specimen Office-Block Ballot

693

Expectations of short-term partisan advantage often underlie changes in ballot forms. In Ohio, in 1949, for example, friends of Republican Robert A. Taft spent over $85,000 in successful advocacy of an initiated proposal to substitute the office-block ballot for the party-column form. They believed that such a change would aid Taft in the 1950 senatorial election. Frank Lausche, a popular Democratic candidate would, it was thought, lend strength to the entire Democratic ticket through the party-column ballot. After his 1950 victory Taft guessed that the new ballot was responsible "for something between 100,000 and 200,000" of his total majority of 430,000.[29]

While these short-term maneuvers for partisan advantage interest the knave in all of us, the issue of ballot form has implicit within it larger considerations about the roles of both the electorate and the party system. The party-column ballot would seem to be the appropriate accompaniment of a party system under which the respective party leaderships could nominate candidates more or less in accord with the party program. With the party as an active and integrating element in the electoral and governing process, the voter can sensibly vote a straight ticket. The rise of the office-block ballot, however, represents in a sense a change in the role of the party system, or at least a lowering of expectations of its capacity to screen aspirants for nominations. The nominating processes often result in the award of places on the party ticket to the most varied assortment of individuals. To vote consistently at the general election the voter may need to split his ticket. By the same token, the emphasis on the individual associated with the office-block ballot tends perhaps further to weaken

on at an election on a single ballot. In some jurisdictions, candidates for federal office may be listed on one ballot, candidates for state office on another, and constitutional amendments and propositions on still another. In some instances the consolidated ballot has been divided to deprive a party's state and local candidates of the strength from a popular presidential candidate or vice versa. For a collection of facsimiles of ballots, see C. O. Smith, *A Book of Ballots* (Detroit: Bureau of Governmental Research, 1938).

[29] The position of a candidate's name on the ballot or voting machine may give advantage or disadvantage. The election of a long list of individuals to fill relatively inconspicuous offices, as councilmen or judges, tends to be associated with position advantage. Similarly in primaries ballot position gives advantage. A careful analysis of these matters has been reported by D. S. Hecock and H. M. Bain, Jr., *The Arrangement of Names on the Ballot and Its Effect on the Voter's Choice* (Detroit: Wayne University Press, 1956). See also Howard White, "Voters Plump for First on List," *National Municipal Review*, 39 (1950), pp. 110–111. Some jurisdictions rotate the order of names on the ballot from precinct to precinct; some leave the assignment of order on the ballot to a lottery by the election authorities. In the drawing of names from hats some remarkable departures from the laws of chance have occurred; in Jersey City the Democratic slate won top place in nine consecutive city elections.

party as each candidate attempts to attract attention to himself, and only incidentally to his party, in the campaign.[30]

Long versus short ballot. Whether the ballot is in form a party-column or an office-block ballot, it is usually a long ballot containing a large number of names and perhaps constitutional amendments and other propositions on which the voters are asked to express an opinion. In 1932 the "average party-column ballot consisted of 565 square inches of paper, on which were printed over 102 names and three propositions." In the office-block states the ballot averaged 349 square inches and contained the names of 77 candidates and four propositions. In the off year of 1934 the average ballot had an area of 398 square inches, and the average voter was asked to express 22 choices.[31] The number of expressions of opinion demanded of the American voter constitutes a greater burden than is borne by any other voter in the world. The ballot is so long, in fact, that the voter wearies and often refrains from voting on offices or measures towards the bottom. Not uncommonly as many as 25 to 30 per cent of those voting fail to mark a choice on obscure constitutional amendments, and the less conspicuous offices almost invariably attract a far lower vote than do the offices at the head of the ticket. In the larger states these partial nonvoters may number in the hundreds of thousands or even exceed a million.

The long ballot is a problem not in election administration but in the design of governmental structure. The ballot merely adapts itself to the requirements of the governmental system. It is relevant to note that the short ballot has been a major plank in the platform of the governmental reformers. To reduce the number of popularly elective state and local offices is, the argument goes, to tailor the task of the electorate to a manageable size. The voter, confronted by only a few choices, could presumably make more informed decisions than when he must find his way through long lists of candidates of whom he never heard who are running for offices about which he knows nothing.

An incidental aspect of the movement to reduce the acreage of ballot

---

[30] A study of voting in the 1956 presidential election throws light on the effects of ballot form. About the same proportions of persons strongly identified with parties voted straight tickets in multiple choice states and in single choice states. The office-block form was associated with a higher degree of ticket splitting among weak identifiers and independents. See Angus Campbell and W. E. Miller, "The Motivational Basis of Straight and Split Ticket Voting," *American Political Science Review*, 60 (1957), pp. 293–312.

[31] Albright, "General Election Ballots in 1934," *Southwestern Social Science Quarterly*, 16 (1936), pp. 85–95.

paper has concerned the election of the President. The custom has been to place on the ballot the names of all the presidential electors pledged to each presidential candidate. Of course, for over a century the presidential electors have had no function save that of a rubber stamp, yet their names have been on the ballot in conformity with the legal theory that people vote, not for the presidential and vice-presidential candidates, but for electors. Shortening the ballot presented the legal problem of determining how to remove the electors' names from it and at the same time provide for the popular selection of electors.[32] Iowa solved the legal problem in 1919 when it enacted legislation to remove the electors' names from the ballot and at the same time adopted the legal fiction that a ballot marked, let us say, for the Democratic presidential candidate was really a vote for the Democratic electors from the state.[33] The Iowa technique of meeting the legal problem is the method generally used. Spencer Albright points out that the presidential short ballot really received its impetus from the use of the voting machine, which, because of its limitations, required a vote for all the presidential electors of a party at one stroke of the lever. In the 1956 election over half of the states used the presidential short ballot. Since most states permit a vote for all electors by marking a single cross, the presidential short ballot does not reduce the burden of the electorate materially, but it does reduce the sheer size of the ballot.

Voting machines. Since 1892 when the city of Lockport, New York, made the first use of voting machines, the voting machine has been gradually taking the place of the paper ballot.[34] In 1898 Rochester, New York, adopted the machine as the sole method of voting, and several other New York cities followed during the next year. Laws in over three-fourths of the states permit the use of machines in all or some localities of the state. Most of these laws, however, merely authorize the local governments, which usually administer elections, to install voting machines. Hence the degree of their use varies greatly among the states with permissive legislation. The Automatic Voting Machine Corporation estimates that in the 1952 presidential election about 40 per cent of the votes were cast by machine.

In essence the voting machine is a mechanical device for recording and

[32] The Constitution, Art. II, sec. 2, provides: "Each state shall appoint, in such manner as the Legislature thereof may direct, a number of electors equal to the whole number of Senators and Representatives to which the State may be entitled."

[33] L. E. Aylsworth, "The Presidential Short Ballot," *American Political Science Review*, 24 (1930), pp. 966–970. Ruth C. Silva, "State Law on the Nomination, Election, and Instruction of Presidential Electors," *American Political Science Review*, 42 (1948), pp. 523–529.

[34] On voting machines, see J. P. Harris, *Election Administration in the United States*, ch. 7; Albright, *The American Ballot*, ch. 4.

Figure 23.3. Face of Voting Machine. Photograph courtesy of Automatic Voting Machine Corporation.

counting automatically the choices registered by the voter. It is provided with a face equipped with levers corresponding to each candidate or proposition to be voted upon. On its face, adjacent to each lever, is a printed paper indicating the candidate for whom a vote will be recorded if that lever is pulled down. In operating the machine, the voter pulls a lever to close the curtains to conceal himself. This movement clears the machine for operation, for unless the curtain is closed the machine cannot be operated. The voter then pulls the lever to indicate his choices. Machines are manufactured with a single lever to pull to vote a straight ticket, corresponding to the party-column ballot. If the law of the state concerned prescribes the office-block ballot, the machine is designed to require the movement of a lever for each office. After lowering the levers to indicate his choices, the voter pulls the lever to open the curtain, which movement also actuates the counters to record his choices. At the close of the polls a panel on the back of the machine covering the counting devices is removed, and the election officials read off, record, and report the total vote indicated for each candidate.

The advocates (and manufacturers) of the voting machine are voluble in its praise. It prevents certain types of fraud and error in the conduct of elections. The "Tasmanian dodge," for example, cannot be worked on a voting machine. It prevents, too, the fraudulent spoiling of ballots by election officials during the count. Fraud and error in the count are impossible. The danger of fraud in reporting the precinct results is minimized, since it is a simple matter to compare the machine with the report of the vote by the precinct election officials. The machine makes the results available quickly after the closing of the polls, for it is not necessary to count ballots. The machine speeds up the voting process itself.

The manufacturers strongly contend that the substitution of the machine for the paper ballot reduces election costs. The Automatic Voting Machine Corporation concludes that it is generally possible to amortize the cost of the machines over a period of from 10 to 12 years through savings over paper ballots. The use of the machine permits a reduction in the number of precincts, with a consequent reduction in the number of election officials. Nor are so many election officials necessary. The machine, however, carries with it new costs, such as the expense of storage and of being set up for use. It is plain enough that election authorities, if they have the will, can bring about savings to offset some, if not all, costs of the machines. Even if machines increased election costs, the assurance of a quick and accurate count and other desirable features of the machines might be worth the cost.[35]

[35] Further technological innovation may occur in mechanical voting. Richland, Washington, an unincorporated community which elects an advisory city council without the necessity of conforming with the minutiae of election legislation, has experimented with accounting-card ballots marked with a special pencil to permit counting by a mark sensing machine. See P. Marrill, "Accounting Cards for Ballots," *American City*, May, 1955, p. 123. For a suggestion of an electronic voting system under which votes would be recorded at a central point and totals would be available "literally within seconds after the closing of the polls," see G. D. Braden, "The Voice of the People," *National Municipal Review*, 41 (1952), pp. 136–141.

Part Five

PARTY AND THE
GOVERNMENT

THE ORATORICAL theory of democracy has it that like-minded people, Republicans or Democrats, manage to form a majority in support of a set of candidates committed to a program of action who, when elected, proceed as officials to carry out that program. Such a view vastly oversimplifies the linkage between popular will and governmental action.

The party that runs the government is, in a sense, a party different from the one that won the election. To win elections requires machinery for the designation of candidates and for drumming up voter support—the electioneering apparatus. To manage governments requires another type of party, a grouping of parliamentarians and administrators more or less bound together in common cause under common leadership. The "party-in-the-government" must have an independence of the electioneering machinery outside; otherwise, it would be unable to fulfill its constitutional responsibilities. The party's national committee would be, in fact, the government. Nor can it be irrevocably bound by promises or commitments made by national conventions; otherwise, it would not be free to cope with problems as they developed. Indicative of these necessities is the existence of governmental party organs separate from the electioneering machinery. These are most visible in the party machinery in House and Senate, but the President and the partisans clustered about him in the executive branch of the government could be regarded as a party group comparable to a House or Senate party caucus.

Though a distinction may be made between electioneering apparatus and party groups within the government, both have common foundations and common problems. The questions that plague parties as they seek unity in national conventions and in campaigns project themselves into the party groups in the government. The elements of homogeneity and diversity in each party following are reflected in the workings of the party in the government, which also responds to the dominant policy orientations of that following. Yet all these influences are modified as they accompany the victorious candidates into office. The success of a slate of candidates transforms a group of partisans into a government. A President in the White House must act differently from a presidential candidate on the stump.

24 | Party Leadership in Legislation

ELECTIONS are dramatic episodes in the struggle for power. The high visibility of party activity in campaigns screens the fact that there are two radically different kinds of politics: the politics of getting into office and the politics of governing. The machinations of the outs as they struggle to gain control stem historically from virtual conspiracies to overthrow the government; a successful challenge at the polls against a party in power amounts to a legitimized coup d'etat. When a party gains power it is transformed; once challenger and critic, it becomes the government—and it hopes to remain the government.

The art of winning office differs from that of governing but the politics of governing is a continuation of the politics of winning office. In campaigns a high premium goes to skills in swaying the multitude. Harvesting the fruits of victory requires deftness in the politics of governance, and these skills in maneuver, in compromise, in persuasion are not those of mass electioneering. The preservation of the winning combination demands a nicely balanced recognition of the claims of factions and interests associated in the victorious party, a sense of decent restraint lest rapacity hasten the day of defeat, an adequate magnanimity toward the vanquished, a capacity to transmute partisan triumph into an advance of the general interest, as well as prowess in the rough in-fighting that occurs as the opposition seeks to discredit those in power.

A distinction can be made between the functions of parties in campaigns and in the conduct of government. In a sense, the two functions are performed by two different parties. The party has its organization outside the government to nominate candidates and to campaign for their election. On the other hand, the party members occupying legislative and executive posts have responsibility for conduct of the government. The party group within the representative body has its own organization and its own identity quite independent of the party outside the government. In nations with parliamentary governments a clear line is drawn between the parliamentary party and the party outside the government. In fact, on occasion the vote-gathering organization even has a name different from that of the parliamentary group. In the United States the notion of a dual personality of party is not so commonly recognized. Nevertheless, the distinction serves to give emphasis to the importance of adequate attention to the two separate functions of party.

Governmental Structure and Party Government

Party performance in the conduct of government is conditioned by the nature of governmental institutions, a proposition of peculiar importance in the comprehension of the role of party in American government. It has been the fashion to assert that the structure of government is a matter of indifference: whatever its character may be, the dominant social forces will express themselves through it. Such reasoning may be valid if one is concerned with broad social movements sweeping through long periods of history. But in the day-to-day conduct of government the nature of the governmental mechanisms is of great significance. Structure and procedure not only influence what can be accomplished and the way it is accomplished, but they sometimes determine the outcome of issues. The interaction between party forces and governmental mechanisms operates in both directions. In the long run party forces also influence the form and nature of institutions, but these influences usually produce gradual change. More clearly perceptible is the fact that, in the everyday business of governing, the institutional tools that party leaders work with modify, divert, and distort as well as reflect the political forces of the moment.

Party and government in Britain. The problems of the formulation and execution of a party program under the presidential form of government are thrown into bold relief by a comparison of that system with the British system of responsible cabinet government. Under the latter scheme undisputed and undivided party leadership is vested in the cabinet, a body formed of the leaders of the majority party in the House of Commons. Cabinet members steer the course of legislation in the House of Commons, and individually they head the administrative departments of government. Thus there is unified in the hands of the cabinet both legislative leadership and executive power. The cabinet governs and is, appropriately, referred to as the Government.

The cabinet governs, but it governs subject to the approval of the House of Commons and ultimately of the nation. Approval by the House of Commons, however, means the support of the majority within the House, from which cabinet members are generally recruited. Although the cabinet, in its power to dissolve Parliament and call an election, has a weapon with which to discipline its followers, the maintenance of party unity depends fundamentally on the enunciation by the cabinet of a party program that will satisfy the party in the House. The members of the Commons tend to reflect, in turn, the attitudes and opinions of their constituents. If the party majority in the Commons cannot be satisfied, at least according to the literary theory of the British constitution, the cabinet may lose its majority and thereby lose office, an event that would precipitate a general election. In practice, by the mysterious usages of the British constitution, elections come about by other means.

In constitutional theory the cabinet may be overthrown; practically, it could be overthrown only by a split in the majority party. Such action would bring in its train a general election; members of the majority do not take lightly the responsibility of causing an election and of imposing upon themselves the expense of a campaign. Yet the threat of dissolution is not a major instrument in the maintenance of the unity of the majority. Cabinet measures that arouse intense criticism may be modified to quell discontent in the party ranks and in the country. The cabinet may even withdraw a measure that threatens party unity. In some situations a minister may be "thrown to the wolves" to satisfy the party or the public. In extreme instances the majority party may change party leadership and, hence, the cabinet, to retain the confidence of the House and of the country.

The machinery of cabinet government thus facilitates the formation and execution of party policy. Party leadership and governmental leadership are in the same hands. The cabinet itself is recruited from among the legislators, and its members are those who have proved themselves in the Commons and have gained the support of their fellows. Consequently it is probable that most shades of opinion within the party will be represented in the government and will, in turn, be reflected in the measures the government proposes. The convention of collective accountability of the cabinet—all members share blame for a sour policy or for the ineptness of a colleague—doubtless brings differing views to bear in decisions on individual policy proposals.

Party discipline in the House of Commons flows in part from the nature of party operations in nominations. A high degree of centralization prevails within the party on candidacies. A local Conservative or Labour association nominates persons approved by the national leadership and at times persons suggested by the party's central office. The mandate of the member of Commons is in a sense not to represent his constituency but to collaborate with and to support the leadership of his party in the conduct of the government. The institutional context of the election of Commoners thus imposes upon them a different type of obligation than is supposed to rest upon the American legislator.

Separation of powers and the splintering of party leadership. By contrast the major features of the cabinet system enable us to obtain a better understanding of the effects of the structure of American government on the formation and execution of party policy. The unity of party in government is too often regarded as the result of the disciplinary effect of individual penalties and sanctions. More fundamentally, party unity rests on consensus on programs and policy. The structure of American government impedes the formation of a party policy that would reconcile the differences within the party in control of the government. In the absence of such a policy, party unity is apt to be disrupted. Although the most prolonged consultation and negotiation would not produce party programs on which all Republicans or all Democrats would unite on all questions, the governmental structure makes difficult the unification of party within the limits of what is feasible.

The obvious structural feature that handicaps party government is the separation of powers, which splinters party leadership. The President, as the head of his party, occupies the premier position in the definition of party policy. But there is no assurance that his program will meet with the approval of all factions of his party in the House and Senate. The machinery of government does not routinely assure consultation with all factions of the party in the formulation of the presidential program. The independence of executive and legislature creates institutional jealousies and misunderstandings.

In short, British government is party government. The prime minister is the party boss and the members of the cabinet are his lieutenants. The American system, on the other hand, creates three independent centers of party and governmental power: the House, the Senate, and the Presidency. Even if the same "party" controls all three, the majority "parties" of the House, the Senate, and the Presidency are separate entities with no acknowledged obligation to work together and no satisfactory routine procedure for doing so. "At Westminster," says Holcombe, "party government is the essence of constitutional government, but at Washington there is both party government and constitutional government." [1] Yet, for government to function, the obstructions of the constitutional mechanism must be overcome, and it is the party that casts a web, at times weak, at times strong, over the dispersed organs of government and gives them a semblance of unity.

Presidential Leadership

"A President," as Merriman Smith has said, "is many men." [2] He is the symbolic head of the nation, the President of all the people, the constitutional monarch of the Republic. He must also be a workaday executive who directs the administration and exercises leadership in the solution of contentious issues. But first of all he must be a politician, a politician who has bested all other politicians to climb to the top of the heap within his own party and to triumph over the opposition at the polls. In the fulfillment of his role as leader in the legislative process, he may act on one occasion as President; at another moment, he may operate as leader of his party; or, he may play both roles simultaneously as he seeks to obtain enactment of his legislative program. Whether he is acting in one capacity or in the other is not always obvious, but that he tends to be the chief legislator there can be no doubt. Nor is there much doubt that his effectiveness as chief legislator depends on his success in building and managing party support. "There have been," observes Holcombe, "Presidents who have tried to govern without benefit of any organized partisan support, but they have never succeeded well enough to make their methods a model for imitation." [3]

Executive initiative in legislation. The position of the President, as Chief Executive and as leader of his party, makes of his office the only point about which leadership of the party in the conduct of the government may be established. Most of the great legislative issues are posed by the President. He advocates action and sets the terms of the debate on great

[1] "The Changing Outlook for A Realignment of Parties," *Public Opinion Quarterly,* 10 (1946–1947), pp. 455–469.
[2] *A President Is Many Men* (New York: Harper, 1948).
[3] A. N. Holcombe, "Presidential Leadership and the Party System," *Yale Review,* 43 (1954), pp. 321–335.

questions. He must also concern himself with the mass of minor legislation necessary to keep the wheels of government turning: appropriations, amendments to existing legislation, developments and modifications of government operations. In this range of matters, legislative initiative falls peculiarly within the province of the President and his administrative associates. These legislative proposals emerge mostly from the experience of the administrative departments from which detailed innovations in public policy must mainly come, albeit not without nudging and needling by Congressmen.

By and large the Presidency, not Congress, is the center of legislative initiative. It is the President who determines the major issues on which Congress acts; and it is the President who attempts, with or without success, to bring his party colleagues in the House and the Senate to the support of his policy. As Professor Ford pointed out:

It is the rule of our politics that no vexed question is settled except by executive policy. Whatever may be the feeling of Congress toward the President, it cannot avoid an issue which he insists upon making. And this holds good of presidents who lose their party leadership as with those who retain it. Tyler, Johnson, and Cleveland, although repudiated by the parties which elected them, furnished the issues upon which party action turned.[4]

At one stage the President's role may be characterized by powerful advocacy of a new substantive program; at another his role may appear to be more one of leadership in strategy, timing, and the fixing of priorities on fairly routine matters. In either role, the President does not "think up" all the laws. Most major new policies have behind them a long and persistent agitation, which may have had its leadership among members of Congress; and a significant statute may rest on the accumulated findings of a generation of congressional committees.[5] Yet it remains for the President to pull the proposal out of the ruck of mere discussion, to elevate it to the stature of a party issue, and to support its passage with the strength of his Administration.

Partisan foundations for collaboration and conflict. Both collaboration and conflict characterize the relations of the President with Congress. Those ingredients occur in different proportions from time to time, but invariably they have a foundation in the enduring nature of the party system. Republican (or Democratic) Senators and Representatives, like the people who vote them into office, are not a homogeneous lot in their

[4] H. J. Ford, *The Rise and Growth of American Politics* (New York: Macmillan, 1898), pp. 283–284.
[5] See L. H. Chamberlain, *The President, Congress, and Legislation* (New York: Columbia University Press, 1946).

philosophies of government. Democratic (and Republican) Senators and Representatives tend to divide into factions; the nature of the President's problem of party leadership depends partially upon the division of strength among the different factions of his party.

Commonly when a President goes into office a substantial number of the legislators of his party stand committed to the broad policy orientation of the President. Such legislators, although they may quibble on matters of detail, respond generally to presidential leadership. On the other hand, his party commonly has also another group of legislators who, on a wide range of issues, depart from the general spirit of the presidential outlook. Their political fate may be bound up with that of the President, but they speak for the antipresidential wing of the party. If they are to follow the President, they have to be wheedled or bought. Eisenhower came into office, for example, along with a number of Republicans who professed to be attached to the new Republicanism and also with others, perhaps more numerous, who adhered to the old-style Republicanism. Roosevelt and Truman could rally northern, metropolitan Democratic legislators to the support of their legislative programs; the conservatives of the southern wing often broke party lines on economic questions, while southerners of all political hues resisted presidential leadership on race questions.

These broad differences within the majority party fundamentally condition the task of presidential leadership and fix limits on party action. They rest, of course, not so much on the personal beliefs of legislators as on the fact that the legislators reflect shadings of view within the mass of the party. The contingent of midwestern isolationists with which Eisenhower had to cope, for example, spoke for an ancient stream of attitude within the party. Nor are these ideological cleavages within parties new.

Apart from these ideological cleavages which may control on a cluster of issues, a President holds or loses the support of his fellow partisans on individual issues for other reasons. The legislator remains extremely sensitive to the peculiar needs and desires of his constituency, a factor that may move him from the party ranks when constituency interest conflicts with the party program. At times the conflict may not be so much between a constituency interest and the party program as between a pressure group and presidential leadership. A legislator may have to decide whether to follow the lobbyists of the American Legion or the American Farm Bureau Federation or his party leadership, and not infrequently the lobbyists win.

Varying conceptions of presidential role in legislation. The presidential role of legislative leadership varies among Presidents with their conceptions of the proper role of the office. In this century Democratic Presidents have subscribed to the doctrine that the Chief Executive should provide forceful presidential leadership, while Republican Presidents have, with the exception of Theodore Roosevelt, leaned toward a more restricted view of their role. Woodrow Wilson pictured himself as something of a prime minister with an obligation to lead his party in the fulfillment of its program and he proceeded accordingly to act vigorously and effectively.[6] Franklin D. Roosevelt exerted a leadership in legislation hardly matched by any other President, while Harry Truman, if not invariably successful in his dealings with Congress, never left the solons in doubt about the legislative objectives of the White House.

Warren Gamaliel Harding, a man not given to theorization, evidently believed that the business of legislation should be left to Congress. A handful of Senators had been active in bringing about his nomination in part because they hoped to take the initiative in legislation from the White House. Nor did Coolidge provide firm legislative leadership. Hoover says that on coming to the Presidency he "felt deeply that the independence of the legislative arm" should be "respected and strengthened." He had, he says, "little taste" for forcing action by Congress.[7] Eisenhower also brought to office a restricted notion of the duties of the President with respect to legislation.

These partisan differences in executive roles have been neither a matter of chance nor the result solely of the personal qualities of the Chief Executives. They emerge, rather, from the differing characteristics of Republican and Democratic parties. The Democratic party has been the party of reform and innovation; reform and innovation must inevitably be driven through Congress by aggressive executive leadership. The Republican party, on the other hand, has been far less a party of innovation; its policy commitments in the main could be fulfilled either by legislative inaction or by comparatively modest modifications of existing law.

Even when Congress is not confronted by the divisive issues of reform and innovation, the manner in which it conducts the normal flow of legislative business may be mightily affected by the manner in which the President operates. When the President is unable to lead, the party in power tends toward a policy of drift. When the President abdicates his legislative leadership, there is no place for the mantle to fall.[8]

[6] "The President," said Wilson, "is expected by the nation to be the leader of the party as well as the chief executive officer of the Government, and the country will take no excuses from him. He must play the part and play it successfully, or lose the country's confidence. He must be Prime Minister, as much concerned with the guidance of legislation as with the just and orderly execution of law; and he is the spokesman of the nation."

[7] *Memoirs, 1920–1933* (New York: Macmillan, 1952), p. 217.

[8] See Norman J. Small, *Some Presidential Interpretations of the Presidency* (Baltimore: Johns Hopkins Press, 1932), ch. 5.

Institutional rivalries and jealousies. No matter what party is in power or what President is in office, a deep antipresidential sentiment permeates Congress, and exists even among members of the President's own party. Representatives and Senators develop a loyalty to Congress as an institution and a regard for its place in the constitutional system. Legislators rather encourage the notion that the assertion of presidential leadership somehow violates our constitutional commandments and is a governmental sin to be committed, if at all, surreptitiously. The dignity of Congress is redressed by an occasional setback to the President. He may be reversed and rebuked for apparently no reason save an assertion of congressional power. But congressional enunciation of the rights and privileges of the legislative branch may be a mere cloak for allegiance to substantive policies in conflict with those of the President. "It is traditional that those who, yielding to other pressures, fail to ratify presidential proposals should disguise their opposition as an endeavor to maintain the integrity and independence of the legislative branch of the government." [9]

Executive leadership and popular rule. People with a yearning for orderliness would like to see develop a state of affairs under which a President could rally his party in Congress to his support with a minimum of pyrotechnics. Yet a President may not be doing his job unless he gets into a fight with Congress now and then. Congress, by the nature of its composition, becomes the stronghold of particular interests—and the special interests certainly ought to be represented. As the bulwark of particularism, Congress is a center of resistance to actions in the general interest and an initiator of actions to benefit partial interests. The President may attempt to block special group pressures or to divide and placate by proposing more moderate measures. His proposals may clash with the narrower and more parochial interests that bring their influence to bear upon the individual Senator and Representative. Ford commented many years ago:

> The situation is such that the extension of executive authority is still the only practical method of advancing popular rule. This disposition of American politics to exalt executive authority causes some critics of our institutions to infer that democracy tends towards personal rule. Appearances seem to corroborate this theory; but all that it really amounts to is that at the present stage of our political development American democracy, confronted by the old embarrassments of feudalism, compounded from new ingredients, instinctively resorts to the historic agency for the extrication of public authority from the control of particular interests—the plenitude of executive power.[10]

[9] O. R. Altman, "First Session of the Seventy-fifth Congress, January 5, 1937, to August 21, 1937," *American Political Science Review*, 31 (1937), p. 1083.
[10] *Op. cit.*, pp. 356–357.

Those comments, written over half a century ago, retain their fundamental validity. The country perhaps could not tolerate an unending warfare between the President and Congress. On the other hand, long-continued peaceful relations between Chief Executive and Congress would probably indicate that all was not well with the Republic.

Presidential program and party unity. Each President must deal with a party representation in Congress that includes shadings of attitudes and factions of greater or lesser cohesiveness. The extent to which the President can carry along with him his fellow partisans of the Congress depends in part on the measures that he chooses to promote. By avoidance of divisive issues, he may maintain the fullest support of his party for those matters on which substantial agreement prevails. It might be possible for a President, through consultation, to submit legislative programs that would command virtually unanimous agreement within the party. Such a program would, however, have been formed to exclude contentious matters and many of the measures included would have had their sharp corners rounded off.

The most careful formulation of presidential legislative recommendations undoubtedly facilitates lawmaking, but it may be fortunate that Presidents can urge projects that may even not be well matured and that are certain of defeat. Campaign promises and presidential recommendations at times represent objectives that are unattainable in the short run. The enactment of great public measures is not a matter of a moment. Agitation, discussion, and consideration may occur over long periods before great aims are achieved. If parties and Presidents were limited in their programs to those objectives capable of immediate enactment, the energetic advocacy of great causes would be handicapped. It may be a happy feature of the constitutional system that the President can urge, without risk of overthrow of the government by parliamentary vote, the adoption of proposals certain to be defeated in the short run. Presidents, to achieve greatness, must perhaps have in them a strain of evangelism and utopianism as well as the knack of keeping the governmental routines in operation.

Sanctions for party discipline. The President's greatest resource in rallying legislative support is the fact that he and a substantial block of the Congressmen of his party stand for broadly the same program. Concurrence of view, not command, underlies their agreement. Genuine Eisenhower Republicans or Truman Democrats generally work together on legislation. The unity of policy consensus, however, can be re-enforced by weapons at the President's disposal, which may also be used to bring to his support other individuals, either generally or on particular measures.

The major formal means for putting the presidential program before Congress are the message on the state of the union, the budget, and the economic report. The message on the state of the union carries out the President's constitutional duty to "give to the Congress information of the state of the Union," and to "recommend to their consideration such measures as he shall judge necessary and expedient." The budget embodies the President's financial program. The economic report, made under the terms of the Employment Act of 1946, reviews the state of the economy and may contain recommendations for legislation. In addition, the President makes specific recommendations in special messages to Congress and may indicate his views in communications to individual members of Congress.

These communications put the President's legislative program on the record, but unless the President follows through with unceasing negotiation and persuasion his recommendations may die with the echo of the voice of the reading clerk. In some instances the President may appeal over the heads of Congress to the public for support of his measures.[11] By this means a President who advocates popular measures may direct varying degrees of pressure upon Congress. That pressure may induce legislators to seek to be known as supporters of a popular President. Obviously the supposed advantage to a legislator of such an identification varies enormously from time to time as does the skill of Presidents in mobilizing popular support. At the first congressional session after his inauguration, Herring comments that Franklin Roosevelt

displayed remarkable skill in manipulating the attention of Congress and of the public. His messages to Congress were strategically timed and positive and specific in character. Disagreement with his proposals was interpreted by the general public as obstructionism. . . . His radio talks to the nation served the double purpose of reassuring the people and breaking down resistance in Congress. Legislators were made only too well aware of the temper of their constituents.[12]

Another weapon is that of the patronage. The President by the control of appointments may reward or punish, but the bargaining power does not rest exclusively on his side. Legislators, too, have votes with which to bargain. Nevertheless, a judicious deference to legislative patronage recommendations may build party solidarity in Congress. Woodrow Wilson,

[11] Of course, every time the President makes a public statement about legislation he is appealing for public support although he may not explicitly ask the voters to "write their Congressman."

[12] "First Session of the Seventy-third Congress, March 9, 1933, to June 16, 1933," *American Political Science Review,* 28 (1934), p. 67.

thus, had his troubles with the conservative and progressive elements of his party, but from a realistic utilization of patronage there resulted, says Link, "the establishment of the President's nearly absolute personal mastery over the Democratic party and the Democratic members of Congress." [13] Patronage has its limits. A Democratic President scarcely expects to obtain southern senatorial support for civil rights legislation by allocating a few jobs. Nor would a Republican President expect to manage his reactionary wing so cheaply. Yet a systematic correlation of patronage allocation and legislative performance has its utilities in maintaining the loyalties of the faithful.

A patronage of policy also has its uses in specific situations. Senators and Representatives, of necessity, must concern themselves with questions of local and individual concern. White House support may clear the way for a special measure of interest to a Senator; a word from the same source may initiate a project in a Representative's district. The administrative departments have their own axes to grind with Congress and they make their own deals, but in a significant legislative battle sufficient centralization of policy patronage may develop at the White House to sway the votes necessary to carry the day. [14]

Consultation between the President and his party leaders in Congress may aid in the development of programs and strategies apt to attract the maximum party support. Legislative leaders can advise the President on the temper of Congress; they can warn of obstacles. The President may enlist the leaders in his cause or he may be enlisted in their cause. [15] Con-

[13] A. S. Link, "Woodrow Wilson and the Democratic Party," *Review of Politics*, 18 (1956), p. 156. The Postmaster General had a list of Senators who were the "real friends" of the Administration and "entitled to priority" in patronage; a group of less zealous supporters could claim only "secondary consideration."—J. M. Blum, *Joe Tumulty and the Wilson Era* (Boston: Houghton Mifflin, 1951), p. 157.

[14] The Eisenhower Administration in 1954 obtained Senate approval of the St. Lawrence Waterway, a project that had been hanging fire for years. Shortly before the Senate vote, Secretary of the Interior Douglas McKay had put the wheels in motion for a start on the Upper Colorado River Reclamation Project. Only two of the ten Senators from the states to be affected voted no on the Waterway. Just before the Senate vote, the Senate Committee on Foreign Relations expedited a recommendation to spend $3,000,000 for a survey of the power potentialities of Passamaquoddy Bay; the Maine Senators, longstanding opponents of the Waterway, saw their way clear to vote for it. The chairman of the Joint Chiefs of Staff turned up opportunely in support of the Seaway as a defense measure. Patronage alone was not enough. Since the Waterway had been first rejected by the Senate in 1934, the steel industry had had to go to Canada for iron ore, a circumstance that dissolved influential opposition to what had earlier been opposed as a "socialist ditch."

[15] Jack Garner reported that Roosevelt "talked the legislative leaders into a lot of things and we seldom talked him out of anything permanently."—Bascom Timmons, *Garner of Texas* (New York: Harper, 1948), p. 228.

sultation between congressional leaders and the President can do no harm and may on occasion expedite the march of legislative business.[16]

From time to time President Truman caused the Democratic national chairman to ask national committeemen and state chairmen to attempt to bring Democratic Senators and Representatives to the support of Administration recommendations. It cannot be said that these attempts had much effect. In truth, national party authorities seem to be unable either to help or to harm congressional candidacies. Without some demonstration that support of the party leadership has a bearing on his own political fortunes, the individual Senator or Representative is not likely to be deeply moved by the requests of party functionaries.[17] On the other hand, when the state chairman, national committeeman, or other such party official has a powerful position in his own bailiwick, he can, if he is so disposed, see that his Congressmen regularly support the Administration.[18]

All these instruments employed in the relationships between President and Congress are, of course, expedients rather than a formalized battery of means for bridging the gap between the executive and legislative departments. They are brought into play as circumstances and presidential preferences dictate rather than in any regular or predictable way. Their existence reflects the fact that the American constitutional system is not designed to be a party government but that its operation requires at times that it approximate party government.[19]

[16] Such conferences may be the occasion for agreement between the President and his congressional leaders on a legislative schedule. For example, in February, 1953 Senate Majority Leader Robert A. Taft and House Majority Leader Joseph W. Martin, Jr., met with the President and agreed upon an eleven-point legislative program: a reorganization bill, appropriation bills, Hawaiian statehood, Taft-Hartley Act amendments, extension of power to allocate materials for defense, tidelands legislation, extension of reciprocal trade, customs simplification bill, extension of old-age and survivors insurance, extension of act for aid to schools in critical areas, and the addition of two members to the board of commissioners of the District of Columbia.

[17] An extreme instance of independence of partisan ties is indicated by these remarks of Senator Langer, of North Dakota: "I want to make it plain that the people of North Dakota do not care whether I am here as a Democrat or Republican. . . . I may say that after I received the Republican nomination for United States Senator the first time, the Republican National Committee donated money to my opponent in the primary.

"Mr. President, I owe the Republican Party in North Dakota absolutely nothing. Not only that, the Republican nominee for President refused to travel on the same train with me. He had my opponent in the primary on the train with him and introduced him to the people of North Dakota."—*Congressional Record* (daily ed.), January 11, 1950, p. 331.

[18] Blocks of Representatives from boss-ridden cities sometimes provide sure votes for the leadership but not much other contribution to the legislative process.

[19] On the Presidency, see E. S. Corwin, *The President* (New York: New York Uni-

Mechanisms of Party Government in Congress

The majority party must fulfill its responsibility for the management of legislation through a complex institutional apparatus. Its chief spokesman, the President, participates in the work of Congress only from the other end of Pennsylvania Avenue. Unlike its British counterpart, the American majority must manage two legislative houses, each of which regards itself as more than the equal of the other. Within each chamber, the majority must bring an intricate organizational apparatus under its control. Since the American Congress is a creative legislative body and not an organ for the registration of approval or disapproval of measures originating elsewhere, its management requires a high order of leadership, a mastery of the arts of diplomacy, and patience in intrigue.

The fundamental characteristics of the American parties—their diversity of composition, their dominant policy orientations, their inner contradictions—manifest themselves in bold relief in the membership of the party groups in the House and Senate. Moreover, as the majority grasps control of the machinery of the House and Senate, all its shadings of interest and ideology also find lodgment at points of power in the legislative organization. The organization of legislative direction becomes a mixture of centralization and decentralization, with factions of the majority, often minorities of the majority, in control of critical points in the legislative machinery. This circumstance starkly exposes to public view the problems of maintaining sufficient majority cohesion to control the significant legislative decisions.

The basic instruments of party control of the legislative machinery are the House Democratic caucus, the House Republican caucus, and the comparable groups within the Senate. It is through these groups, which are unknown to the formal rules of Congress and which meet in private, that the majorities in House and in Senate agree upon persons to staff the formal and informal organization of the respective houses. The party caucus produces party solidarity on the question of who is to manage the legislative machinery, but only infrequently does the caucus even attempt to solidify the majority on questions of what shall be put through the machinery.

Legal and extralegal mechanisms for party control of House. For the guidance of the deliberations of each House of Congress, the majority

versity Press, 1940); Pendleton Herring, *Presidential Leadership* (New York: Farrar and Rinehart, 1940); Harold Laski, *The American Presidency* (New York: Harper, 1940); W. E. Binkley, *President and Congress* (New York: Knopf, 1947); Sidney Hyman, *The American President* (New York: Harper, 1954); Clinton Rossiter, *The American Presidency* (New York: Harcourt, Brace, 1956).

party establishes extralegal machinery and uses in an extralegal way the formal machinery of Congress. The broad features of the machinery in both houses are similar, and in both the party mechanism has arisen to meet the need for leadership and direction common to all large decision-making bodies. As James Madison said in *The Federalist*, "in all legislative assemblies, the greater the number composing them may be, the fewer will be the men who will in fact direct their proceedings." And the control of the party organization in the House, with its 435 members, is much tighter than it is in the Senate with its mere 96 members.

The House majority is led and directed by a set of party leaders who, though they are agreed upon by the party caucus, gain leadership by proving in the day-to-day work of Congress that they possess the qualities to command the deference of their colleagues. The major posts of formal authority brought under party dominion are the Speakership, the Rules Committee, and the standing committees of the House. Next in importance to the Speaker is the majority leader, an official not of the House but of the party group; the majority whip serves as a lieutenant of the majority leader. The minority also has its floor leader and its whip. Both the majority and minority parties in the House have a "steering committee," but these are "an informal and little-used device." They "seldom meet and never steer." [20] Each party caucus also has a committee on commitees which nominates the majority and minority members of each of the standing committees of the House.

If the holders of all these posts constituted a cohesive inner clique of the majority, the leadership could readily determine the course of legislative action. The practices of the House, however, result in a representation of most of the factions of the majority in the roster of officials and leaders of the House. On those routine questions on which the leadership is not divided—and there are many of them—the House acts expeditiously and with a minimum of friction and fuss; on those questions that divide the leadership of the majority, party management breaks down.

Speaker of the House. First among the leaders of the House majority is the Speaker. He achieves his position by working his way to the top of the heap during years of service in the House and ordinarily moves to the Speakership from the floor leadership of his party group. He occupies a place of power in the party as well as among his colleagues in the House. The eminence and influence of the Speaker are made clear by mention

[20] Joint Committee on the Organization of Congress, Report (Senate Report 1011, 79th Cong., 2d sess., 1946), p. 12. Of late the House Republicans have called their steering committee the policy committee.

of such men as Sam Rayburn, Joseph W. Martin, Jr., John Nance Garner, and Nicholas Longworth.

Before a drastic revision of House rules in 1910–1911, the Speaker, as an agent of the majority, dominated the House. In addition to his power as presiding officer to grant recognition and to decide points of order, he appointed committees and sat as a member of the powerful Rules Committee. Speaker Cannon, a standpat Republican, did not exercise his power in a manner to hold the confidence of all factions of his party. The progressive wing joined with Democrats to divide and disperse the Speaker's authority.[21] Stripped of the prerogative of appointment and of membership on the Rules Committee, the Speaker remains with his diminished powers a leader and agent of the majority. Designated in form by the House, he is in fact chosen by the majority caucus. The Speaker acts as a party agent in guiding the conduct of House business, but as Hasbrouck has observed, the rules of the House "have so developed as a vehicle for the program of the majority that the Speaker need only apply them, to serve, on the whole, the ends of his own party. There is seldom need for him to discriminate as a moderator in order to promote his aims as a political leader." [22] Yet when he has discretion he does not hesitate to use it to the advantage of the majority, and he collaborates with his juniors in the inner circle in planning majority strategy.

Majority leader. The majority floor leader plays a role in the direction of the work of the House second in importance only to that of the Speaker. The floor leader is elected by the party caucus, and his duties are so onerous that he serves on no legislative committee.[23] He functions as a sort of field commander who leads and guides the majority in the legislative battle. He keeps in close touch with the chairmen of legislative committees and, in consultation with other important party figures, guides the course of party action in the House. Subject to his responsibility to

[21] See Blair Bolles, *Tyrant from Illinois* (New York: Norton, 1951).

[22] P. D. Hasbrouck, *Party Government in the House of Representatives* (New York, 1923), p. 85. Quoted by permission of The Macmillan Company, publishers.

[23] The selection of the floor leader by the caucus may become a test of strength between factions of the majority. In 1946, for example, when the Republicans won control of the House, their floor leader, Joseph Martin, was scheduled to move into the Speakership, and a majority floor leader had to be chosen. With considerable muttering the conservative aspirants for the post withdrew and yielded the leadership to Charles A. Halleck who was regarded as affiliated with the Dewey, or anti-Taft, wing of the party. In such situations decisions are often made without a formal vote to avoid exacerbation of intraparty differences. Relative strengths can be appraised without the drawing of swords.

his party followers, he arranges the work schedule of the House; and in this task he consults frequently with the minority leader to assure, in so far as practicable, a mutually acceptable schedule of debate.[24]

The majority leader and the Speaker usually serve as links between the President and the House, at least when the Administration has a House majority. In varying degrees the majority leader is an organ of the Administration as well as of the party in the House. He may have obtained his post with Administration support and commonly he leads the legislative battles of the Administration on the House floor and helps to defend the work of the administrative departments against their critics.[25]

Party whip. Another agent of the party leadership is the party whip, a functionary appointed for each party by its floor leader. He serves as a sort of top sergeant for the leadership. One of his duties is to keep in close touch with the members: to communicate the wishes of the party leaders to the rank and file, and to attempt to keep them in line with the party program. He informs them of the schedule of the House and scours Washington to bring absent members to the floor when their attendance is imperative. He canvasses the members to determine their attitude on questions that endanger party unity. In all this work each party's whip is aided by assistants of his appointment who deal with members from specific regions.

Rules Committee. The formal instrumentality for control of the procedure of the House is the Rules Committee. The majority party, but not necessarily its majority faction, holds a majority of the seats on this com-

---

[24] Illustrative are these extracts from a statement of the legislative program for the following week by Majority Leader McCormack on July 21, 1956: "Mr. Speaker, on Monday three District bills will be called up for consideration: . . . Also on Monday there will be a call of the bills on the Consent Calendar. The following bills will be called up under suspension of the rules: . . . There will be eight contempt proceedings called up on Wednesday. For the balance of the week the program is as follows: . . . It does not necessarily follow that these bills will be called up in the order I have stated them. Then, of course, there is the usual reservation about conference reports, and any further program will be announced later."—*Congressional Record* (daily ed.), July 21, 1956, p. 12637.

[25] Suggestive of the function of executive-congressional linkage of the party leadership is the following statement by Republican minority leader Joseph W. Martin in a debate on the Upper Colorado project: "To my Republican friends I want to particularly ask that you support the President of the United States. He has given a program to the American people. This is part of his program, and we should give him a fair chance to fulfill his desire. Let us give these Mountain States a chance to live, and let us uphold the proposal of the President of the United States."—*Congressional Record* (daily ed.), March 1, 1956, p. 3303.

mittee which exercises powers crucial to the management of the House. Consideration of major measures is governed by special rules that it recommends to the House. It may kill a bill by refusal to recommend a rule; it may expedite legislation by recommending appropriate rules; it may limit debate drastically; it may limit the amendments to be offered to bills; it may, in effect, determine the form of the question to be voted on by the House.[26] The committee may even control the substance of the measures submitted to the House by declining to grant a rule until the legislative committee modifies the bill to meet its wishes.[27]

On those measures on which substantial agreement exists within the majority, the Rules Committee facilitates the work of the House leadership. The committee's actions that excite comment, however, bear on contentious bills that divide the majority. Almost inevitably on the committee are members at odds with the Administration on at least some of its program. Thus, in 1954 Speaker Martin had to enlist the AFL to reenforce Administration pressure on the committee to obtain a rule to permit the House to vote on an Eisenhower public housing proposal; most of the Republicans on the committee opposed public housing. On the other hand, in the same year the committee expedited action on a bill to cut excise taxes which the President opposed. During the Roosevelt and Truman Administrations the committee was often at odds with the House leadership and with the President. Right-wing Democrats on the committee joined with Republicans to obstruct the Administration program.

While power on the order of that of the Rules Committee needs to be exercised to guide the flow of House business, whether it should be in the

[26] Illustrative is the rule for the consideration of the Housing Act of 1956: *"Resolved, That upon the adoption of this resolution it shall be in order to move that the House resolve itself into the Committee of the Whole House on the State of the Union for the consideration of the bill (H.R. 11742) to extend and amend laws relating to the provision and improvement of housing. . . . After general debate, which shall be confined to the bill, and shall continue not to exceed 2 hours . . . , the bill shall be considered as having been read for amendment. No amendments shall be in order to the said bill except that it shall be in order for any member of the Committee on Banking and Currency to move to strike out all after the enacting clause of the bill H.R. 11742 and insert as a substitute the text of the bill H.R. 12328, and such substitute shall be in order, . . . but shall not be subject to amendment."—Congressional Record* (daily ed.), July 25, 1956, p. 13131.

[27] Thus, the comment of Representative Eberharter: The Rules Committee "developed a habit of studying legislation that had been studied for maybe weeks or months by the legislative committees. The committee began to dissect that legislation and make up their own minds as to whether or not it was good legislation. Many a chairman of a legislative committee which had considered legislation for months and months was ordered by the Committee on Rules to change the provisions of legislation before a rule would be granted."—*Congressional Record* (daily ed.), January 3, 1951, p. 11.

hands of an irresponsible body raises another question. After their 1948 victory Democrats cast about for ways and means to circumvent the committee in order that they might enact, or at least attempt to enact, their campaign promises into legislation. The solution, adopted in 1949 over opposition of the right wing of the southern wing of the party, was the 21-day rule which empowered the Speaker to recognize chairmen of legislative committees to bring directly to the floor of the House bills which the Rules Committee had sat on 21 days. In 1950 the Administration forces beat off a proposal, supported by a bloc of southern Democrats and Republicans, to repeal the rule. In the Eighty-first Congress the Speaker permitted eight Administration measures to come to a vote under the rule, each of which the House passed. After the elections of 1950, newly elected Republicans in 1951 joined with dissident Democrats to repeal the 21-day rule.

There are defenders of the power of the Rules Committee to make decisions perhaps contrary to the ostensible will of the majority of the House. Faced by an insistent and irresistible clamor, the House, by the inaction of the committee, may be saved the embarrassment of a vote. Or the members, hell-bent for election, may be denied an opportunity to pass an unwise but apparently popular measure. Others argue that the legislative machinery should, as a matter of principle, contain within itself means by which minorities may block action on irreconcilable questions. Whatever the rationalizations, in practice the Rules Committee hampers as well as facilitates party control of the House.[28]

Standing committees. The majority claims for its members the chairmanship and a majority of the members of each of the House committees, but the manner of assignment to committee posts often obstructs the work of the majority leadership. The majority (through its committee on committees selected by the caucus) controls assignments of members to committees, but once on a committee a member moves upward by seniority until he becomes chairman (or ranking minority member). Committee chairmen are thus designated by the fortuitous coincidence of political and biological longevity. They may or may not be in harmony with the dominant faction of the party in the House; they may or may not belong to the President's faction of the party. The seniority rule has the great virtue of avoiding the squabbles that would arise under other methods of choice; it also often weakens majority control. The rule propels into committee chairmanships members from those districts most firmly at-

[28] While the seniority rule seems to be about as durable as the Constitution, it would be an interesting experiment to except the Rules Committee from it.

tached to the majority, and sure Democratic districts or standpat Republican districts often diverge from the presidential policy orientation.

Committees exercise great powers over legislation through their capacity to report or not to report bills and through their prerogatives in the amendment and rewriting of measures. The committees "form miniature legislatures with a high degree of autonomy," and their chairmen can ordinarily prevent committee action even though they may not be able invariably to control the committee affirmatively.[29] When committee chairmen work in harmony with the House leadership, they may exercise their powers to accomplish the party program. When the chairman does not see eye to eye with the Administration or the House leadership, he can cause trouble by his power to bottle up in committee measures whose passage is desired by the leadership.[30]

The powers enjoyed by committees and by committee chairmen point to a basic problem in legislative management. The accomplishment of the work of the House demands a division of labor and a delegation of functions to committees. Yet the fulfillment of the responsibility of the House as a whole requires that it not be a rubber stamp for its committees. House committees enjoy prerogatives that few great legislative assemblies permit their committees to arrogate unto themselves. The tendency of committees to become special pleaders for particular interests, quite apart from

[29] Revolts of committee members against dominance by the chairman are so infrequent that they attract attention. In 1953 the House Government Operations Committee voted to deprive its chairman, Clare E. Hoffman, Republican of Michigan, of his power to appoint special investigating subcommittees. The House later, with the encouragement of the Republican majority leader, gave to the chairmen of the subcommittees of Hoffman's committee control of funds for subcommittee staff. Presumably in the absence of the rule of seniority the occasion would not arise for such drastic action toward a committee chairman.

[30] A spectacular illustration of the problem is provided in the 1953 battle by the Eisenhower Administration to obtain a brief extension of the excess profits tax. Representative Daniel A. Reed, chairman of the Ways and Means Committee, the senior Republican of the House, and one of the finest surviving specimens of genuine, Old-Guard Republicanism, declined to bring the bill to a vote in his committee. To pry the bill from his committee, the Republican leadership pushed through the Rules Committee a resolution to call up the measure despite the lack of committee action. With this threat over his head, Reed called a meeting of his committee which voted down his ruling that consideration of the bill was not in order and reported the bill for passage. So well established is the power of a chairman to obstruct, that to steamroll Mr. Reed required great exertions by Republican leaders both in Congress and the Administration. Mr. Reed seemed to believe that the customary prerogatives of committee chairmen were elements of the Constitution: "I do not propose to betray the people of this country who are entitled to the constitutional procedures of this government."

the political idiosyncracies of committee chairmen, militates against the leadership in the execution of a general program of legislation. A first essential in the execution of a program in the general weal is the power to batter down the more outrageous demands of narrow interests. The strategic advantages enjoyed by committee chairmen handicap efforts in that direction.

Mechanisms of party control: Senate. Superficially, the formal apparatus of party control in the Senate resembles, in the main, that of the House. The majority group designates majorities on each legislative committee; it has its floor leader, its whip, and its caucus. The Senate also adheres to the rule of seniority in the designation of committee chairmen. Unlike the Speaker of the House, the Vice-President, as presiding officer of the Senate, has been, over the long run, more likely to be tolerated than looked to as a legislative leader, although both John N. Garner and Richard Nixon played active roles in the politics of the Senate. The House and Senate, despite their mechanical similarities, are not alike. Given the greater looseness of party ties in the Senate and its higher visibility, the intraparty factional battles for control of the party apparatus usually reveal more starkly the fissures within the party groups than does the struggle for control of the House.

In the maneuvers for control of leadership of the Republican Senate group a recurring pattern is a struggle between Old Guard and so-called new-style Republicans, usually won handily by the Old Guard. In the organization of the Senate after the 1952 election, the announcement by Senator Robert A. Taft that he would be available as majority leader stilled talk of other candidacies for the post. The Administration had to deal with a Senate leadership which included no Eisenhower enthusiasts in posts of great importance and consisted mainly of men distinctly cool toward the General's foreign policies.[31] After the death of Senator Taft, William F. Knowland was moved up to the majority leadership, an action regarded as an Eisenhower victory at the time since the possible alternatives were men irrevocably opposed to the Administration's foreign policy. Senator Knowland opposed only parts of it.[32] As majority leader,

[31] In addition to Senator Taft, the top leadership included Eugene D. Millikan, of Colorado, as chairman of the party conference; William F. Knowland, chairman of the policy committee; Leverett Saltonstall, an early Eisenhower man who was re-elected to his post as majority whip; and Styles Bridges, of New Hampshire, president pro tempore of the Senate, a position which usually goes to the senior member of the majority.

[32] In 1949 a group of "modern" Republicans failed to grasp control from the Old Guard. Kenneth Wherry of Nebraska won out for floor leader over William F. Knowland. Senator Taft was returned to his post as chairman of the policy com-

the Senator was given to public expression of disagreement with the Administration program as well as to public expression of his views of the direction in which it should go.[33]

The Democratic Senate group, since it is less homogeneous than the Republican group, must seek leaders who can bridge the gaps within the party rather than leaders who typify the dominance of one wing of the party. Thus, in 1951 the Senate Democrats chose a new majority leader in a contest between Senator E. W. McFarland of Arizona and Joseph C. O'Mahoney of Wyoming. O'Mahoney represented the Fair Deal wing of the party. McFarland, on the other hand, had not gone along with the Truman program on civil rights, although on other legislation he had been regarded as an Administration follower. The southerners and the moderates united on McFarland, who, at least to some degree, straddled both factions. Similarly, in 1953 the Democrats chose Lyndon Johnson, of Texas, as floor leader. A tumult would have been stirred by an attempt to install a deep-dyed southerner, such as Russell of Georgia; nor would the South have taken kindly to a man of the views of Lehman of New York. The post fell to a man so located on the political spectrum that he could seek to maximize party unity, relatively unembarrassed by demands of his own constituency save on petroleum questions.

The filibuster and party government. A special feature of Senate procedure is the absence of an effective closure rule. Debate may be shut off only by concurrence of two-thirds of the Senate membership. On motions to amend the closure rule, even two-thirds of the members cannot force an end to discussion. The effect of unlimited debate is that a determined minority can talk a bill to death by holding up the business of the Senate until the majority yields. The major beneficiaries of the practice have been southerners who invoke the right of filibuster, or threaten to do so, to kill bills proposing federal action on the rights of the Negro, although on occasion other minorities also indulge in dilatory debate.

When proposals to permit easier closure have arisen, the majority of the Senate has agreed to perpetuate the right of minorities to obstruct action. The right of filibuster is defended on the ground that legislation with drastic consequences should not be enacted over the determined opposi-

mittee over Senator Lodge of Massachusetts. The Old Guard, in a conciliatory gesture, designated Senator Saltonstall of Massachusetts as party whip.

[33] Knowland opined that the majority leader has a dual responsibility. "One is to represent the views of his party in the Senate, and in a kind of broad sense of the Senate itself, to the White House. Secondly, he is to interpret the views of the Administration to his party, and where he finds that there are differences between the two, try to work out areas of agreement with regard to those differences."

tion of a numerous minority in the country. To that prudent principle great deference is accorded even in the absence of its formalization in such practices as the filibuster. The right of minority veto of Senate action means that some types of legislation could be enacted, no matter how numerous a party's majority might be, only under the spur of a more determined and more intense popular sentiment than has yet been aligned in their support.[34]

Party policy and party unity. The majorities of both House and Senate maintain a high degree of cohesiveness on questions of the organization of their respective chambers. They take control of the instruments to guide the legislative process yet they do not maintain sufficient unity to determine the outcome of all substantive issues. To a degree party groups split because of inadequate machinery and insufficient use of existing machinery to develop party programs and to hold in line the party members, but party disunity rests more fundamentally on the divergence of the elements within each party.

The classic means by which a majority may predetermine the results of a representative assembly is a caucus, a private session of a majority whose members commit their votes in advance of action in the assembly. Democratic and Republican caucuses of the House and Senate convene to agree upon slates of officials, and in the chambers the party groups cohere in opposition to each other on these organizational matters. Only most infrequently are caucuses convened to decide the party position on legislative questions; nor does the caucus attempt to fix the vote of its members on such matters as do the caucuses in some state legislatures.[35]

Whatever party discipline prevails in the Congress comes from the exertions of the Administration and the House and Senate leadership rather than from imposition by the party caucus of its will. The caucus has, to be sure, certain disciplinary powers, but they are exercised only rarely and then against recalcitrant members for actions outside the Congress. Professor Berdahl's careful survey of the record suggests that the sin most likely to bring caucus displeasure is bolting the party in a presidential campaign.[36] Western insurgent Republicans supported La Follette for the Presidency in 1924. The Republican Senate conference adopted a

[34] Recent attempts to modify the Senate closure rule have been sponsored chiefly by northern Democrats although they have also had the support of a few Republican senators.

[35] See C. O. Smith and G. L. Field, "The Responsibility of Parties in Congress: Myth and Reality," *Southwestern Social Science Quarterly*, 34 (1953), pp. 23–39.

[36] C. A. Berdahl, "Some Notes on Party Membership in Congress," *American Political Science Review*, 43 (1949), pp. 309–321, 494–508. See also his *Our Two-Party System* (Bureau of Public Administration, University of Mississippi, 1951).

resolution to exclude the "disloyal" Senators (La Follette, Ladd, Brook-hart, and Frazier) from the conference and not to name them to "fill any Republican vacancies on Senate Committees." Within two years, however, the conference relented.[37]

The caucus does not, and perhaps cannot, serve as a means of hammer-ing out a party program on which its members can unite to push through the House or Senate. The reason is simply that to bring together partisans with irreconcilable disagreements is more likely to exacerbate than to compose their differences. Moreover, to attempt to control by caucus action the vote of the deviant members would run counter to the political mores which place a high value on independence. The late Senator Wil-liam E. Borah for decades was a thorn in the side of the Republican leadership. A constituent chided him for opposing the Republican Ad-ministration: "What would you have a Senator do?" he replied. "Sincerely represent his views, however inadequate they may be, or act as an intellectual prostitute for some party organization?" It is one of the glories of the American system of legislation that it has enough play in it to allow room for courageous and righteous men to rise above their party. One of the drawbacks is that by the same token the machinery gives considerable license to the scoundrel.

The belief persists, correctly enough, that the roots of party disunity rest in the lack of agreement on party program. The cure is said to be the contrivance of means for the development or negotiation of agree-ment on party programs to which most party members can subscribe or be induced to support. The Joint Committee on the Organization of Con-gress in its 1946 report proposed the creation of "policy committees" by both parties in both houses. These committees would formulate legislative policy programs to be made public. The Joint Committee proposed no means of party discipline; each member would be "free to vote as he saw fit, but the record of his action would be available to the public as a means of holding both the party and the individual accountable." [38] These committees would have funds "for the maintenance of a high-grade sec-retariat to assist in study, analysis, and research on problems involved in policy determination."

The House struck from the congressional reorganization bill the pro-vision for policy committees. It was reported that the Speaker and other Democratic leaders feared that such a committee would encroach upon their traditional sphere of authority. The Senate, however, adopted the

[37] In 1955 the Republican Senate conference rejected a motion by Senator Clifford P. Case to remove Senator Joseph R. McCarthy from the Committee on Govern-ment Operations.
[38] Joint Committee on the Organization of Congress, *op. cit.*, pp. 12–14.

policy committee proposal. It provided funds "for the maintenance of a staff for a majority policy committee and a minority policy committee in the Senate, consisting of seven members each, for the formulation of overall legislative policy of the respective parties, the members of such staffs to assist in study, analysis, and research on problems involved in policy determinations." The practical result of this provision was the transformation of the party steering committees of each party in the Senate into "policy committees."

Two impressions emerge from the records of the Senate policy committees. One impression is that the minority policy committee, other things being equal, can more easily be developed into an instrument of policy formation and leadership than can the policy committee of the majority, at least when Senate majority and Administration are in the hands of the same party. Under the leadership of Senator Taft the Senate Republican committee before 1952 became a fairly effective instrument for the expression of majority policy and for leadership. The Democratic Senate policy committee evidently became more significant after the Democrats lost the Administration. The main reason for this difference is that the President remains the chief spokesman for the majority; a Senate policy committee will be overshadowed by him unless it wishes to engage in open warfare with its President, a rather unprofitable endeavor.

Another equally plain proposition is that mere creation of a party policy committee is not in itself apt to have consequences of much import one way or another. For the committee to be effective it must be the instrument of a leader or a handful of leaders who have risen to positions of command. By his qualities as leader rather than by his formal post as chairman of the policy committee (and later leader), Senator Taft managed the Republican Senate group. After his death, the Senate policy committee declined sharply in influence.[39]

Party cohesion and the governmental system. The fact that the American Congress has to be managed by an extraordinary amount of pulling and

[39] The bibliography on Congress is voluminous and but a few titles can be cited: F. M. Riddick, *The United States Congress* (Washington: National Capitol Publishers, 1949); Ernest Griffith, *Congress, Its Contemporary Role* (New York: New York University Press, 1951); G. H. Haynes, *The Senate of the United States* (Boston: Houghton Mifflin, 1938); G. B. Galloway, *The Legislative Process in Congress* (New York: Crowell, 1953); J. M. Burns, *Congress on Trial* (New York: Harper, 1949); Bertram Gross, *The Legislative Struggle* (New York: McGraw-Hill, 1953); W. S. White, *Citadel* (New York: Harper, 1957); Roland Young, *Congressional Politics in the Second World War* (New York: Columbia University Press, 1956); Hugh A. Bone, "An Introduction to the Senate Policy Committees," *American Political Science Review*, 50 (1956), pp. 339-359.

hauling, maneuvering and compromising, rather than by the quiet and orderly registration of party majorities gives rise to criticism, to proposals for party reform, and to no little bewilderment among our allies around the world.[40]

The painful fact probably is that the characteristics of the party groups in Congress reflect fundamental features of our party system, not readily susceptible to alteration. The accidents of history and the necessities of forming a following large enough to elect a President bring discordant elements under each party umbrella. No institutional contrivance within the party groups in Congress can close their deeper cleavages. Beyond this, monolithic party groupings within Congress could very well alter in a fundamental way the character of the constitutional system. Disciplined majority groups in House and Senate could be antipresidential as well as pro-Administration. The balance moves between "presidential" and "congressional" government. The solidification of party groups in the Congress might well turn the balance against the President. It is not certain that tightly disciplined legislative partisanship would be compatible with a strong Presidency, at least without the most radical alteration of the party system.

The Place of Party in Legislation

The members of the majority unite to control the machinery of Congress, but on substantive matters they often break ranks. So imperfect is the mobilization of party strength that some commentators dismiss party as irrelevant to the business of legislation. In fact, the appraisal of the place of partisanship in Congress presents perplexing questions to which there are no pat answers. The role of party in Congress differs from decade to decade, from session to session, from issue to issue, and even from legislator to legislator. The most plausible path toward a comprehension of the place of party is to identify some of these variations in the behavior of the party membership in Congress.

Party unity and disunity. In most parliaments a high degree of unity prevails in the party groups. In Congress party solidarity on roll calls is exceptional, yet party appears to be the strongest and most persistent factor associated with the actions of Senators and Representatives. Party considerations, however, exert a far more powerful influence on some types of questions than on others, while on some matters partisanship is virtually nonexistent.

One large segment of the business of Congress remains largely outside the field of party warfare. Much of its work consists of private bills or

[40] The classic critique is Woodrow Wilson's *Congressional Government* which is available in a paper bound edition (New York: Meridian Books, 1956).

measures of local or particular application and they are commonly passed by unanimous consent or without objection. In the 1955 session of the Senate, for example, most of the debate concentrated on only 23 of the 1,325 bills and resolutions passed by the Senate. In the House the legislative debate was directed to 106 measures as the House passed 1,597 bills and resolutions.[41]

The majority fulfills its duty when it sees that these measures not of general import receive thorough and rational consideration. That duty is met through committee management and through some monitoring of measures by the leadership. In each house the party leaders designate "official objectors" who are obliged to post themselves on measures on the private and consent calendars and to raise objection when they deem it advisable.[42] The mode of handling these measures indicates the live-and-let-live character of the American party system. If the majority asserted full control of these matters, the party system would be something other than what it is. If only majority members could sponsor local or special bills with any hope of passage, a partisan capture of the Congress would be much more of a "total" victory than it is.

On those questions settled by a roll-call vote in House or Senate,[43] party affiliations of legislators have a bearing on their vote although the degree to which the division of the vote parallels the party division varies greatly from roll call to roll call. In the 1940's, according to Turner's findings, about 15 per cent of the House roll calls were party votes— that is, at least 90 per cent of the Democrats opposed at least 90 per cent of the Republicans. In contrast, in the era of McKinley about half the roll calls were party votes.[44]

While roll calls with the parties almost solidly opposed to each other are fairly infrequent—about one out of six in the 1940's—there are significant differences in the voting behavior of Republicans and Democrats on a high proportion of roll calls. That is, the bulk of the Democrats, although less than 90 per cent, will oppose the bulk of the Republicans. Or party differences may be marked even though majorities of both parties vote on the same side of the issue. Of the Republicans, for example, 80 per cent might vote aye along with 55 per cent of the Democrats.

[41] F. M. Riddick, "The Eighty-Fourth Congress: First Session," *Western Political Quarterly*, 8 (1955), pp. 612–629.

[42] Riddick, "The Eighty-Third Congress: First Session," *Western Political Quarterly*, 6 (1953), p. 777.

[43] In the 1956 session the Senate passed 1,555 bills and resolutions and had 136 yea-and-nay votes; the House passed 1,236 bills and resolutions and had 74 yea-and-nay votes.

[44] Julius Turner, *Party and Constituency: Pressures on Congress* (Baltimore: Johns Hopkins Press, 1951), p. 28.

Given these characteristics of group behavior, the ascertainment of the relationship between party affiliation and voting becomes a matter of the measurement of degrees of party unity and loyalty. Once a technique of measurement is contrived, the problem remains of estimating the significance of party as party in the legislative process. On these matters great effort and considerable ingenuity have been expended, but it must be said that the number of uncontroverted general propositions that can be made on the subject is not numerous.

Obviously, the extent to which majority legislators support the Administration program is a critical determinant of the role of the party group. A rough measure of this dimension of party loyalty is the percentage of the roll calls on which the legislator votes for the President's recommendations. A Republican might have voted, for example, 10, 50, or 90 per cent of the time to effectuate Eisenhower's recommendations. An impression of the behavior of the party groups in the House based on such a measure appears in Figure 24.1. That chart rests on scores assigned to each Representative, that is, the percentage of his votes in support of the presidential position on 36 critical roll calls in the House in 1953 and 1954.

The chart makes it plain that a substantial difference existed between Democrats and Republicans on this set of issues. Republicans had, far more frequently than Democrats, records of high consistency in concurrence with Eisenhower. Yet, within each party group the voting scores were spread over a wide range. Most frequently Republicans supported the General on from 80 to 90 per cent of the roll calls. A goodly number had even higher support scores and a handful followed the party position less than half the time. The chart also shows clearly the existence of substantial ranges of agreement between the parties even on these warmly contested questions. Few Democratic Representatives had records of high consistency in opposition; the modal Democratic Representative concurred with the Eisenhower position between 40 and 50 per cent of the time.[45]

Commonly the party groups cohere more tightly on some types of questions than on others, and their identification throws some light on

---

[45] Although scores constructed on the same principle as those underlying the chart are widely used, the student should be warned of their limitations. The essence of the trouble is that two men with different voting records may have identical scores. One man could be pro-Administration on one-half of the roll calls and another pro-Administration on the other half and each would have a score of 50. The scores used in Figure 24.1 are not *Congressional Quarterly* scores but an index built on a smaller number of votes that more sharply separates the parties. For further analysis based on the index, see Key, "The Eisenhower Program and the Congressional Elections," *Christian Science Monitor*, October 5 and 7, 1954.

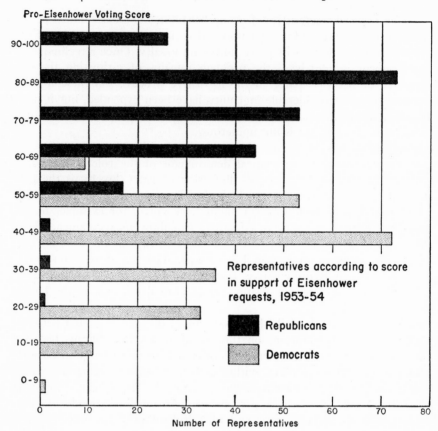

Figure 24.1. Partisan Differences in Voting in the House of Representatives: Distribution of Republican and Democratic Representatives According to Their Score in Support of Eisenhower Legislative Requests, 1953–54

the role of the party group in the conduct of legislative business. Of 145 House roll calls in 1953 and 1954 reported by the *Congressional Quarterly*, a majority of the Republicans opposed a majority of the Democrats on 64. On the remaining 81 roll calls, majorities of Democrats agreed with majorities of Republicans.

In these sessions—which may be presumed to be typical—party lines tended to be most tightly drawn in the earlier stages of the consideration of bills. Votes on rules for the consideration of measures, on amendments, and on moves to recommit saw party lines on the average most clearly drawn. On the other hand, majorities of Republicans and Democrats were far more frequently in agreement on votes on final passage of bills and on conference reports.[46] In terms of subject matter, party solidarity seemed on the average to be greatest on what might be called administrative matters: appropriations, the organization of the government. Roll calls on program matters divided the parties less consistently.[47]

These differences suggest the special importance of the party group in supporting the leadership in the guidance of the course of business of the House and in the enactment of appropriations and other such measures necessary to keep the wheels of government turning. They also point to the narrowness of the differences between parties on many substantive issues. Fairly sharp differences turn up on proposed amendments to program measures, but once the amendments have been adopted—and the measure often watered down—party differences decline.[48]

A House or Senate leadership without a substantial bloc of regular partisan supporters would be mightily handicapped, but the fact remains that the party regulars are infrequently numerous enough to form a stable majority. The leadership must always solidify its own forces as well as it can and often pick up votes from across the aisle to carry the day. With its extremely narrow margins in House and Senate in 1953 and 1954, for example, the Republican leadership often depended on Democrats to provide the votes necessary to enact the President's requests. On 61 issues carried by the President's forces in the House, the outcome depended on Democratic support in 34 instances, according to *Congressional Quarterly* analyses. In the Senate on 103 such issues, the successful outcome required Democratic votes in 87 instances.

Roots of party unity and disunity. Party groups at times cohere; at other times they fly apart. These variations result not from the whim or caprice of the legislator. On some matters powerful forces operate to unite each party group in opposition to the other. On others, equally impelling forces operate to pull splinters or factions away from the position of the party

[46] The average index of likeness of Republican and Democratic groups on 73 roll calls at the earlier legislative stages was 51; on 72 roll calls at the final stages, 81. The index is the complement of the difference between the percentages of the two party groups voting in the same direction. With 80 per cent of the Democratic group voting yea and with 10 per cent of the Republicans voting yea the difference would be 70 and the index 30, indicative of a low level of likeness.

[47] The average index of likeness on 30 roll calls on administrative matters in the early legislative stages was 42; on 22 program roll calls at the same stage, the average index of likeness was 51.

[48] In the 1953 and 1954 sessions the average index of likeness on final passage of 20 program measures was 77; at the earlier stages of the procedure the average index was 51.

group. These behaviors of legislators have roots in their constituencies. The determinism of the representative relationship both contributes to the ˌtendencies toward party unity and to the desertions of the leadership.

The diverse elements comprehended within each party make almost every congressional roll call unique in the way it divides the legislative chamber and the party groups. Yet durable factional elements within each party can be relied upon to bolt the party on certain categories of issues. Perhaps the best advertised factional group within a party is the Democratic southern wing. The members of that faction may be the most regular of the regular on the routine run of legislation, but they uniformly bolt on proposals for federal action with respect to the Negro.

Southern solidarity is restricted to the racial question. On other matters southern Democrats vary. Like their constituents, southern Democratic legislators range from the reactionary to the liberal. The outlook of a state's Senator depends on what faction of the state's Democratic party

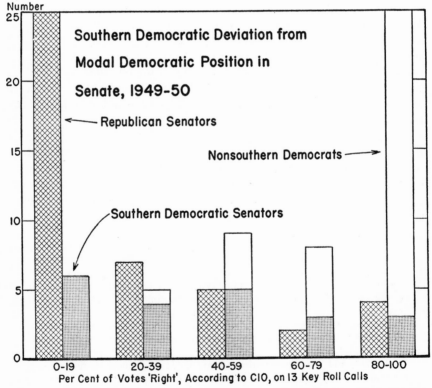

Figure 24.2. Republican and Democratic Senators According to Their Degree of Support of Measures Favored by CIO in 1949 and 1950

he represents. These remarks are supported by the data in Figure 24.2, which shows the distribution of Senators, Republican and Democratic, according to their stands on 13 issues of concern to the CIO in the 1949 and 1950 sessions of Congress.[49] Most Democrats outside the South voted "right," while most Republicans voted "wrong" on most of these issues. Southern Democrats, however, are scattered, as may be seen from the chart, all along the measuring rod. Some consistently supported the position of the Administration; others opposed with equal regularity. Still others fell between these extremes.[50] Republicans, too, as the chart shows, had members scattered all across the political spectrum.[51]

A cleavage on foreign policy has plagued the Republican congressional groups, a split which, like the internal divisions of the Democrats, apparently rests on differences among the party voters. The impact of events from 1916 to 1952 and the positions of the parties during this period attracted one type of voter into the Republican ranks, another to the Democratic. Those resentful of American participation in "Democratic wars," those isolationist by belief, and those dubious of international cooperation found the Republican position more congenial. Faithful Democrats found themselves committed to a more internationalist position, and the party drew to its ranks many who gave a high priority to internationalism. This process of polarization of attitudes continuing over the decades profoundly affected the policy orientation of the two parties, although it did not neatly divide all voters into two camps. Partisan differences must be described in terms of modalities, not dichotomies.

These differences among the voters are mirrored in the behavior of the party groups in Congress, with the consequence that the Eisenhower Administration found it difficult to muster sufficient congressional support to govern. Republican members of the House, for example, gave fairly consistent support to orthodox Republican domestic policies; on the other hand, the largest group of consistent supporters of the Administration on foreign policy issues were among the Democrats. A goodly proportion of

[49] The chart is based on data in *The CIO News*, August 14, 1950. The 13 roll calls included two on the Taft-Hartley Act, one each on minimum wages, organization of the NLRB, and unemployment compensation administration. The others dealt with foreign aid, public power, crop loans, natural gas, rent control, housing, and civil rights.

[50] Nonsouthern Democrats most disposed to deviate from the Administration position came from the border and mountain states: Oklahoma, Maryland, Kentucky, Nevada, New Mexico, Colorado.

[51] Those who departed most often from the bulk of their colleagues were Langer (North Dakota), Morse (Oregon), Lodge (Massachusetts), Aiken (Vermont), Ives (New York), Tobey (New Hampshire). Vermont, New Hampshire, and Maine resemble the South in reverse; a Senator's Republican label is less controlling than his factional affiliation at home.

the Republican members could be relied upon to oppose the Administration, although the Republican group included men of all shadings of view on foreign policy. At times the Republican Senate group acted as if it were in opposition to the Administration; in 1956 the major challenges to Eisenhower's foreign policy measures were led by Senator Styles Bridges, the chairman of the Republican policy committee.

To indicate the problem of the Eisenhower Administration in building Republican support for both its foreign and domestic measures, Figure 24.3 compares Democratic and Republican House members according to

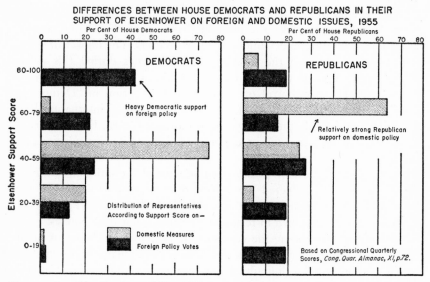

Figure 24.3. Distribution of Republican and Democratic Representatives According to Their Scores in Support of Eisenhower Requests on Domestic and Foreign Policy Matters, 1955

their scores in support of the General's 1955 requests in the foreign and domestic categories. Almost 40 per cent of Republican House members opposed the Administration foreign policy position at least 40 per cent of the times they voted; a bit more than 40 per cent of the Democrats supported the Administration on at least 80 per cent of their votes. The hard core of the isolationist Republican wing is usually said to be midwestern. Most of the consistently isolationist Republican Senators are from the interior of the country, but the data on Republican Representatives suggest that Republican isolationism may not be so much a product of sectionalism as it is a reflection of ruralism. Republicans from rural districts in all sections of the country are on the average more isolationist than their colleagues from the urban districts. Many of the rural districts happen to be in the Midwest.[52]

One Republican splinter has liberal leanings which cut down party solidarity on some types of House roll calls. Again, this deviation from the party norm appears to have a foundation in the grass roots. In Figure 24.4 appears a distribution of Republican (and Democratic) Representa-

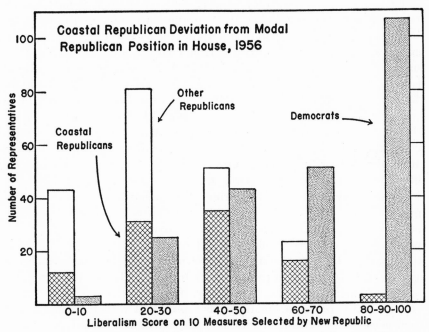

Figure 24.4. Distribution of Republican and Democratic Representatives According to Their Score in Support of Liberal Position on 10 Roll Calls, 1955–56

tives according to their scores on 10 roll calls in 1956. Their votes on these roll calls, selected by the *New Republic*, divided the "liberals" from the "conservatives" by the standards of that journal. While the liberal-conservative issue did not divide the party groups as sharply as it had in

[52] In 1955 Republicans from the most rural districts had an average score of 40 in support of Eisenhower foreign policy requests while their colleagues from the most urban districts averaged 63. Variation in support existed among regions, but within each region the rural-metropolitan difference held. Within the Democratic group, the average for the Democrats from the most rural districts was 59; for those from the most urbanized, 75. These averages are of *Congressional Quarterly* scores, the data underlying Figure 24.3.

earlier years, the modal Democratic position was high on the liberalism scale; the modal Republican position, low. Nevertheless, Republicans are scattered all across the chart in departure from the modal Republican position. A preponderance of these deviant Republicans hailed from states of the Pacific and Atlantic coasts. Many of the coastal Republicans held seats in metropolitan districts and they operated under constituency influence that pushed them up the liberalism scale.[53]

These analyses, though they identify the constituency foundations of recurring cleavages within the party groups in Congress, greatly oversimplify the reality. For analytical purposes the legislator may be regarded as under "pressures" from party and from constituency. When these pressures coincide, each re-enforces the other. When they diverge, the legislator is "cross-pressured" and may be pulled from the party position. Now, the particular legislators who are under conflicting pressures differ from vote to vote with the form and potential impact of the issue upon the constituencies. On one vote this group of legislators may be under conflicting pressures; on the next vote a different group will be similarly affected.[54] A year later, with a different state of public opinion, votes on like questions may break the party groups differently.

Constituency interests may disrupt party solidarity; the same forces may unify the party group. Given the issues of recent decades, it might be expected that Democratic Representatives from northern, urban working-class districts would vote alike in high degree. Such, indeed, turns out to be true. Julius Turner demonstrated in great detail the association between constituency characteristics and the voting records of Representatives. The essence of his analysis was that variations in the voting records of Representatives were associated with partisanship and such constituency characteristics as metropolitanism or ruralism, native-born or foreign-born population, and the sectional location of the district.

[53] The chart is based on data in the *New Republic*, October 15, 1956.

[54] Illustrative is the 1956 Senate vote on a measure to end federal control of natural gas prices. Democratic Senators from gas-producing states were pulled from the party position by constituency considerations; northern liberals were re-enforced in their party loyalty by the interests of their constituencies. Republican Senators who happened to be from gas-consuming states were drawn from their party position to the support of governmental regulation of private enterprise. In a 1954 House vote on flexible farm prices, Democrats from metropolitan districts veered from the general party position of support for rigid prices. Republicans from midwestern farm districts were similarly drawn away from the Eisenhower line of flexible prices. For a study of like conflicts between party and constituency on tariffs, see R. A. Watson, "The Tariff Revolution: A Study of Shifting Party Attitudes," *Journal of Politics*, 18 (1956), pp. 678–701. See also J. Roland Pennock, "Party and Constituency in Postwar Agricultural Price-Support Legislation," *Journal of Politics*, 18 (1956), pp. 167–210.

For the period he analyzed, Democratic representatives from northern, metropolitan, foreign-born districts had, on the average, the highest loyalty to the Democratic House group in voting on roll calls; that is, they voted with the majority of the party group most consistently. Among the Republicans those from rural, native-born districts in the interior of the country had on the average the highest records of loyalty to their party group. Other combinations of constituency characteristics were associated, on the average, with lower records of party loyalty.[55]

Turner found that if constituency characteristics are held constant—that is, if the records of Representatives from similar districts are compared—a difference persists between Republican and Democratic legislators. Perhaps the moral is that party unity, to the extent that it exists, rests in large measure on similarities of district characteristics and, inferentially, similarities of district attitudes and interests. Were there enough metropolitan working-class districts to elect a majority of the House, that majority could readily be molded into a disciplined and cohesive majority. Or if the rural, native, interior districts were numerous enough to elect a majority, it could be shaped into a united working Republican majority. The obdurate facts of our geography and demography prevent either party from putting together a majority of Representatives from districts with similar characteristics. Although more assiduous work by party leadership could doubtless produce a higher degree of party unity, for the foreseeable future the varying qualities of the constituencies will place limits on party unity in Congress.[56]

Bipartisanship in foreign affairs. In domestic affairs the erraticism introduced into government action by the weakness of party ties may not be disastrous for the Republic. Delay for a year or two or ten may merely mean that things have to go along as they have been. Incapacity to act may have more grave consequences in external affairs. A stability of policy when stability is required, a flexibility of policy when flexibility is in order, a firmness in adherence to commitments, a point of manageable

[55] For comparisons of the records of Representatives from many categories of districts, see Julius Turner, *Party and Constituency: Pressures on Congress* (Baltimore: Johns Hopkins Press, 1951). D. B. Truman finds that some of the variance among Representatives' voting records is accounted for by a tendency of members of state delegations to vote together. See his "The State Delegations and the Structure of Party Voting in the United States House of Representatives," *American Political Science Review*, 50 (1956), pp. 1023–1045.

[56] An essential assumption of these remarks is that political survival requires deference by a Representative to his constituency. Turner presents data to suggest that Representatives who deviate markedly from the norm established by others from similar constituencies tend to be vulnerable in campaigns.

power from which to negotiate—all these and other characteristics are requisite to the conduct of foreign relations.

To organize internal politics in a manner to support our external politics an ostensible departure from partisanship has occurred in the practice of a bipartisan foreign policy. In practice collaboration between the parties has included participation of important minority leaders in negotiations, consultation of minority leaders, understandings between presidential candidates to restrict campaign debate on foreign policy, and a deliberate appeal across party lines in the Congress by the Administration for support on foreign policy questions. Given the two-thirds rule for consent to ratification of treaties as well as the looseness of majority discipline, a substantial and strongly led minority can immobilize the United States in its external politics. A major fruit of bipartisan collaboration in the 1940's was the reversal of the isolationist policies of the 1920's and 1930's and the greater involvement of the United States in world politics. Roosevelt had seen at first hand Wilson's failure as he attempted to execute such a policy on partisan lines, and he strove to avoid that fate by enlisting support from the Republican minority.

Probably what successful bipartisanship amounts to is the capacity of the President to hold most of his own party together and to command, as well, the support of a substantial splinter of the opposition. Thus, Roosevelt and Truman managed to hold the northern and southern Democrats together on foreign policy questions, a unity induced in part by the rewards and penalties available to the Administration. They recruited Republican support mainly in the East, although the great Republican foreign policy leader was Senator Vandenberg, of Michigan. Republicans from the interior could be relied upon to provide the principal opposition to the Administration's foreign policy.[57] With the Eisenhower Administration pursuing a generally similar foreign policy, the same cleavages remained. A Republican President could command some support from Republican legislators that a Democratic President could not, but the General enjoyed the cordial distrust of the isolationist wing of his party and had to recruit Democratic support for his measures. That support, while often decisive, was less complete than would have been accorded to a Democratic President.[58]

---

[57] See H. Bradford Westerfield, *Foreign Policy and Party Politics* (New Haven: Yale University Press, 1955), and George L. Grassmuck, *Sectional Biases in Congress on Foreign Policy* (Baltimore: Johns Hopkins Press, 1951).

[58] The potency of the bipartisan appeal in foreign policy may be indicated by the average index of likeness on various sorts of roll calls at the early legislative stages in the House in 1953 and 1954. On administrative matters the average index of likeness was 42; on program matters, 51; on foreign policy, 79.

Split partisan control. The common objectives of partisan allies in the House, the Senate, and the Presidency provide, or so the theory runs, the basis for collaboration among the organs of the government in the achievement of national purpose. Even when the nominees of the same party control both the Presidency and the Congress, as the foregoing discussion makes clear, partisan co-ordination of the independent organs of government lacks perfection. When one party controls the Presidency and another the House or Senate, the normal rivalry between executive and legislature is aggravated by party differences.

The occasional existence of division in partisan control of the Presidency and Congress points both to some of the characteristics of the party system and to the importance of party in the governing process. If the parties were disciplined groups dedicated to divergent programs, a division of partisan control would hamstring the government. In fact, sufficient comity prevails between the parties so that an opposition Congress, although it may heckle and harass, at least provides appropriations and enacts the necessary legislation to keep the government in operation.

In a negative way the eras of divided control underline the significance of party in the total governing process. Although the specific circumstances differ from time to time, Presidents have rarely been able to carry through notable legislative proposals with Congress in the hands of opposition majorities. On the other hand, opposition congressional majorities are themselves unable to assume the leadership in great affairs against the wishes of the President. They may block the President; they may, if they can muster enough votes to override a veto, repeal or whittle down existing legislation. But they can take the initiative in no great undertaking that requires executive collaboration in its fulfillment. Common partisan control of executive and legislature does not assure energetic government, but division of party control precludes energetic government.

Long-run impact of party on public policy. In these pages the emphasis has been on the solidarity and disunity of party groups in the short-run and on the consequent necessity for ceaseless maneuver to form combinations to govern. Another way to speculate about party and public policy is to look at the course of governance over a far longer period of time. The long-run view may yield an estimate of the role of party far different from that which emerges from the microscopic examination of yesterday's votes in the House or Senate.

At intervals a new majority wins control of the Presidency and Congress and its ascent to power marks a reorientation of legislative action. The program may or may not be solidly opposed by the minority legislators; some of the majority may grudgingly support or even oppose. Yet that the party system in its totality is the vehicle for these shifts in direction and tempo of legislation there can be little doubt. Wilson's New Freedom and Roosevelt's New Deal illustrate surges of party strength associated with new directions in legislation. Harding's "normalcy" had its repercussions in congressional action. Eisenhower's victory brought a new tone in domestic legislation.

The new majority party is the vehicle for the expression of these great shifts in public sentiment that become perceptible as we look backward. It perhaps becomes such, not necessarily through the attractiveness of its program or the adroitness of its campaigners, but because it was, as the minority, an instrument conveniently at hand for use when the need arose. Yet when the workings of party in legislation are examined microscopically rather than through the broad sweep of history, the party group appears as a most cumbersome and imperfect piece of machinery.

Parliamentary Party and Presidential Party

From these excursions into the workings of party in legislation there should emerge a sharper recognition of the contrast between the presidential party and the parliamentary party. As it appears in the struggle for the control of the Presidency, the American party is relatively highly disciplined. The process of presidential nomination brings most of its factions and splinters to the support of the candidate, and its presidential electors, if they win their states, cast their votes in support of the party's nominee.

It could almost be said that we have one party system for the purposes of the Presidency; another, for the Congress. The necessities of presidential politics conceal the reality of a multiplicity of parliamentary parties concealed behind the labels of Republican and Democratic. The lines separating these subparties do not appear in the organization of the party in the country for electoral purposes; they become apparent only in the workings of the party in the House and Senate; even there the lines dividing them are blurred. Southern Democrats unite against their northern brethren only on some issues; the Republicans of the interior at times make common cause with their colleagues from the coastal regions.

The institutional apparatus accommodates itself to the interplay of centripetal and centrifugal forces within each major party, permitting expression to both yet permitting neither to triumph completely. Within each party the drives toward unity, the common denominator of shared interests of all factions, the solidarity contrived of compromise find expression in the presidential candidate or in the President. In the workings of Congress, the forces of particularism, of section, of class, of all types of subgroups within the party enjoy comparatively free play—a luxury made tolerable by the stability introduced into the government by an executive whose tenure is beyond reach of mercurial parliamentary majorities.

25 | Administration as Politics

THE VICTORIOUS political party has responsibility for the formulation of a legislative program and for the leadership and guidance of legislative operations. It has a responsibility, too, for the direction of the work of the administrative departments of the government. It executes its lawmaking duties by organizing the legislative bodies and by leading the majority as best it can. On the administrative side it is enabled to carry out its program by presidential designation of secretaries and assistant secretaries and like officials in charge of the administrative departments and agencies of government. They, in turn, have, within limits, the authority to designate their principal assistants. A relatively small number of persons, politically loyal to the chief executive and to the party in power and presumably attached to its program, has the function of guiding the machinery of government in fulfillment of the party's responsibility to the electorate.

The control of administration is in some respects more difficult than the fulfillment of party responsibility for legislation. Often the party leaders in the legislative body come to their tasks better equipped than do the partisans at the head of departments. They have had experience in the House or Senate on the minority side, whereas cabinet members often approach their tasks innocent of experience in federal administration. Furthermore, the President and department heads do not enjoy undisputed sway in the management of administration. Their fellow partisans in Congress usually like to take a hand in the matter and consider that they have a responsibilty for the conduct of administration. The administration, like the majority in Congress, contains within itself centrifugal forces that strain the capacity of the President, in his role as chief administrator, to prevent special interests from dominating particular administrative agencies, at least on some questions.

Administration consists of more than the management of routines. In some of its aspects it is like the legislative process, between-election politics; it must cope with similar problems and its practice requires similar skills. Great administrative decisions, like legislative acts, may involve a reconciliation of conflicting interests and must be made with an alertness to their general public acceptability. Nor is the task of the President in the leadership of federal administration simply one of the issuance of directions to subordinates: the arts of compromise, of negotiation, of persuasion have as great a relevance in the White House as in the halls of Congress.

Administrative Agencies: Actors in the Political Process

The majority party must control the administrative apparatus if it is to impress upon the government its conception of the public interest. Under the laws they administer most executive agencies have wide discretion, the exercise of which may touch party policy. Moreover, administrative agencies are originators of proposals for legislation and often exert an influence in the making of new policy. These drives toward new policy and alterations in old policy must at least not run counter to the dominant inclinations of the party in power. The President acts both as Chief Executive and as party leader in the direction of the administration.

Administrative agencies not ciphers. The administrative agencies are not as clay in the hands of the President and his partisan associates. They tend to have a tradition, an outlook, and a policy inclination of their own. To budge them from their predetermined paths is not always easy. Vast aggregations of public servants, military and civil, organized into well-knit hierarchies and animated by common aims and spirit have a potency in the political process that is often underestimated or even ignored. Government departments and agencies at times act as spokesmen or representatives before legislative bodies and the public for segments of society that they serve. Through the prosecution of research that reveals public needs and points toward public action, administrative agencies often initiate movements leading to new public policy. In the politics of appropriations almost every administrative bureau or department seeks to maintain or enlarge the scope of its operations; moreover, associations of employees of governmental units attempt to bring about the passage of legislation improving the conditions of their employment.

In one respect administrative agencies are like the associations we have called pressure groups: they operate continually, in Republican and Democratic administrations alike, to advance their interests; indeed, often the closest working relations are maintained between a pressure organization and the governmental agencies in which it is interested. Pressure groups and administrative departments are elements in the pattern of politics that may be jarred and realigned by the results of an election but are rarely completely thrown from power. The administrative organization exerts its strength through transient department heads and Presidents, no matter what party is in power. With close relationships between its headquarters personnel in Washington and Congress it is able to make its wishes known to Congress either through the department head or through unofficial channels. Often with a personnel distributed over the nation, it is sometimes able to stir up, by discreet measures, pressure from home to bear on Congress. With almost a monopoly of information in its sphere of interest, the administrative organization is able to release or withhold data in such a fashion as to influence the course of legislative action.

Representative role of administrative agencies. A factor that conditions the task of the President in the direction of administration is the representative role of administrative agencies. Pressure groups and administrative agencies themselves often contend that the agency has a duty to act in furtherance of the interests of the group it serves. This is a doctrine of bureaucratic representation: that the Department of Labor should speak for and represent the interests of labor in making recommendations for new legislation; that the Department of Agriculture should promote vigorously the interests of the farmer and ignore those of other groups; and so on. A characteristic statement of this notion is one made in 1943 by the National Co-operative Milk Producers' Federation:

> Eleven months from now the people will go to the polls. They will decide many important issues. One of the greatest issues which farmers will help decide will be on the question of who controls the Department of Agriculture. We believe that the organized farmers of America will demand of both political parties that they will provide a reconstituted Department of Agriculture

to serve agriculture. Other Departments of Government serve the groups for which they are named. The Department of Agriculture today is not being permitted to function for the farmers. We call for definite pledges on this great fundamental issue.[1]

With agency after agency attached to the interests of particular groups and under pressure to promote partial interests, the President as the leader of the administration has no little difficulty in bringing about the operation of the government in accord with a party program dedicated to the general welfare. The prevailing practice is that the administrative agencies represent the interests they serve.[2] Many of them owe their existence to the groups they serve. As new groups or classes rise to power and influence they are recognized through the establishment of governmental departments. The creation of the Department of Agriculture was the first recognition of an economic class in the administrative structure; later the departments of Commerce and Labor were established.

The degree to which an administrative agency becomes an attorney for its constituency varies with circumstances. The Veterans' Administration is rarely in a position to oppose the interests of the veterans. On the other hand, when an agency is subjected to pressure from conflicting interests, it may enjoy a greater freedom in formulating and advocating its recommendations. The Department of Agriculture cannot satisfy completely the beet-sugar growers, the beet-sugar refiners, the Louisana cane-sugar growers, and the seaboard cane-sugar refiners. When different interests play on an administrative agency, the agency may seek to work out a program of legislative recommendations appeasing divergent interests in so far as practicable, or it may work its own program completely.

Administrative agency and its congressional allies. By their close communion with interests in society administrative agencies may gain a certain independence of presidential direction. By the same token they become beholden to those groups upon whose support they depend. These group relations often extend over into alliances involving the administrative agency, the pressure group, and Congress. Long-lived administrative agencies develop friends in Congress whose policy interests parallel those of the agency. At times a bureau or agency may become virtually independent of the President so powerful is its support in Congress. These relationships make it difficult to bring the work of such agencies into line with the President's program and in so far as it is a party program they tend to vitiate party responsibility. To the extent

[1] National Cooperative Milk Producers' Federation, *A Dairy Policy for 1944*, p. 7.
[2] See Charles Wiltse, "The Representative Function of Bureaucracy," *American Political Science Review*, 35 (1941), pp. 510–516.

that a President fails as a legislative leader he is also apt to fail as chief administrator; when Congress has the whiphand in legislation, it also tends to undercut the President as Chief Executive.

A politics of self-preservation. In the objectives they seek administrative agencies are almost as varied as they are numerous. Yet most agencies seek to maintain, if not to expand, their activities and to assure the retention of administrative arrangements they regard as satisfactory. Every bureau is eager to obtain appropriations to carry out its program on an adequate scale, and few bureau chiefs believe that last year's appropriation was enough. An organization's prestige is measured in part by the size of its appropriations and the number of its employees, and aside from such considerations in seeking appropriations the personnel of an agency is animated by a faith in the worth of the work that is being done and by a belief that the public interest will be advanced by the appropriation of the amount requested. Persons employed by the government, like those employed elsewhere, are apt to have enthusiasm about what they are doing.

The administrative agency usually exerts its strength to defend itself and its program from attack in legislative bodies. Administrators tend to have a vested interest in the law they enforce; and, when its enemies attack, the agency is quick to line up its legislative friends in defense. A special type of legislative proposal that arouses intense interest of administrators is a reorganization bill. Comprehensive schemes to reorganize the administration through legislation have invariably been defeated in Congress in large measure through the pressure exerted by the bureaucracy. Only with the greatest of difficulty did Franklin D. Roosevelt obtain the passage of a reorganization measure delegating to the President the power to shift administrative units from one department to another; yet certain agencies succeeded in bringing about the adoption of amendments excepting them from the operation of the act. The Army Corps of Engineers, for example, which has been one of the most persistent opponents of administrative reorganization, has succeeded in maintaining the *status quo* for itself.[3] Fights on questions of administrative organization are sometimes battles between two federal agencies for jurisdiction over a particular matter, such as the dispute between the Department of

---

[3] See Arthur Maass, *Muddy Waters* (Cambridge: Harvard University Press, 1951). The capacity of administrative agencies, often in association with their pressure-group allies and congressional friends, to resist reorganization suggests the limitations of presidential control over administration. See Avery Leiserson, "Political Limitations on Executive Reorganization," *American Political Science Review*, 41 (1947), pp. 68–84.

Agriculture and the Department of the Interior over the Forest Service. The Forest Service, with its far-flung field service closely knit into the life of the communities served, has gained strong public support and has successfully resisted efforts to transfer it to the Department of the Interior.

Institutional inertia and policy direction. From the public prints it might be supposed that administrative agencies ceaselessly seek to enlarge their functions and to advance their cause. Such drives for power exist but quite as prevalent is an institutional inertia almost gyroscopic in its effect. The responsibilities of political direction may require that an agency be jolted from its ancient ruts. Some political heads of agencies impress their views on the organization they direct, but at times the department as an institution has a momentum and a pattern of action that escape direction. "The department" over a long period builds up a tradition, a policy, and, one could almost say, a "personality" of its own. A point of view comes to permeate the organization; and, if new recruits do not have the departmental attitude, they acquire it in time. These departmental traditions are difficult to bring to life on paper, but they are of enormous importance in the determination of the direction in which the department will exert its influence in the legislative process. Moreover, departmental policy tends to harden into a tradition that resists alteration. The institutional pattern of ideas comes to be set in a certain fashion, and it tends to stay that way.[4] In consequence, chief executives and legislative bodies often have to seek advice on public policy from outside the existing administrative services to offset the force of tradition. Under extreme conditions about the only way to get a job done may be to establish a new agency.

Exploitation of administrative resources. Partisan control of administration may be regarded as a simple exercise of command. If it is that and nothing more it is apt to be both sterile and futile. Few political heads of departments know enough to tell their staffs what to do; their task is to use in the public interest the resources of their departments. From the permanent staffs of government agencies emerge ideas for action and plans

[4] Public lands, including forested lands, were at one time in the custody of the General Land Office of the Department of the Interior. After considerable political pyrotechnics forests were assigned to the Department of Agriculture for protection and management. "The national forest idea ran counter to the whole tradition of the Interior Department," said Gifford Pinchot, who was chief of the Bureau of Forestry of the Department of Agriculture in Theodore Roosevelt's Administration. "Bred into its marrow, bone and fiber, was the idea of disposing of the public lands to private owners."—"How the National Forests Were Won," *American Forests and Forest Life*, October, 1930.

for improving the efficiency of administration. From the same source may come judgments, informed by experience, on the wisdom or probable repercussions of contemplated courses of action. The thinking and planning of the civil servant may approach the intelligent and informed exercise of a trusteeship of the public welfare. The effective political head of an agency finds ways to blend the resources of his department with his own skills in political maneuver and to accommodate the mandates of his party and the creative capacities of the permanent service.

Politicians cannot think up all the laws; a skillful administrative politician may be the midwife who brings to fruition the ideas of his staff. In some spheres administrative officials possess what amounts to a sovereignty of competence. Since a large proportion of legislation consists of modifications of old policy, those in charge of the administration are in possession of information and experience basic to the formulation of changes. For example, in the application of tax laws the Bureau of Internal Revenue discovers loopholes facilitating evasion and suggests remedies to Congress. A crusading Food and Drug Administration urges changes in the law in order to broaden its coverage to protect the public and to make effective enforcement more feasible. Scientists of the Department of Agriculture discover means to control a pest and recommend suitable measures. The Children's Bureau calls attention to high rates of infant mortality and agitates for a program to bring about a reduction. In every sphere of governmental activity the influence of the expert knowledge and of the long experience of the administrative official makes itself felt in new legislation.

Broad problems of political direction. These remarks pose in general terms the problem of political direction of administration. Scores of administrative entities, if we observe the reality that some departments are units only in name, constitute a vast and cumbersome apparatus which the victorious party must bring under its control. Each of the major agencies enjoys the support, and perhaps opposition, of organized interests. Each has its friends in Congress. Each may be of particular concern to some faction or group within the party. Party can meet the requirements of accountability only if it can bring under control those actions of the administrative apparatus most likely to touch party policy or to produce party embarrassment. The nature of that problem of control may be illuminated by an examination of the modes of action of administrative agencies and the techniques of direction by the President.

Administration and Public Policy: Methods

Embedded in the administrative agencies are powerful particularistic drives that seem at times to threaten to fragment the government. The

President presides over the unruly assemblage of administrative institutions and attempts to maintain within it a semblance of order and a harmony with party policy on at least the major questions. Hierarchical etiquette makes the President the boss of the administrative apparatus, but by custom, and on occasion a bit of insubordination, administrative agencies enjoy considerable freedom in the promotion of their objectives.

Public-relations activities of administrative agencies. The techniques of administrative agencies in presenting their case to the public and to the lawmakers are fundamentally similar to those employed by private lobbying groups. Almost every governmental agency conducts some sort of public-relations program, but only a small proportion of the publicity issued by administrative agencies is concerned with the promotion of proposed courses of public policy. The objectives of the bulk of governmental publicity are the performance of a function, such as the dissemination of information on improved farming methods by the Department of Agriculture, or the furnishing of information to the public on the course of public affairs, such as the news releases issued by the Department of State.[5]

Administrative agencies are concerned with the creation of a reservoir of good will among the general public that can be drawn on when specific legislative proposals are under consideration by the legislative body. A "good" press and a "good" name are of great value in convincing Congress of the necessity for an increased appropriation or for other legislation requested by the agency. On the other hand, a "bad" press can make the agency's relations with Congress difficult. Sometimes the public-relations strategy is to dramatize the agency through publicizing its chief. The Federal Bureau of Investigation furnishes an excellent example of this technique. Other agencies do not build up a single personality but seek to create a public opinion favorable to the service as an institution. Still other agencies seek to propagate an idea.

None of the types of public-relations activities cited involves an appeal for public support for any particular policy advocated by the agency; rather, they are calculated to establish a favorable general attitude toward the personalities, services, and ideas concerned. If this type of generalized publicity is effective, an underlying sentiment is formed that is likely to help when specific legislation is under consideration by Congress.

---

[5] Of 286 government press releases, containing a total of over 200,000 words, issued during the week of December 3–9, 1947, four were designed to influence legislation; 23 apparently represented an effort to influence policy; the remainder were mainly factual reports on programs, progress, policy, and other matters of public interest. See Dick Fitzpatrick, "Measuring Government Publicity: Volume of Press Releases," *Journalism Quarterly*, 26 (1949), pp. 45–50.

A different type of publicity—a sort of administrative guerilla warfare —flows from the informal and often surreptitious relations of administrators with journalists. Information is fed to these persons who report it "on high authority" or as from "informed sources." By this means Congress may be needled, the President nudged, a fire lighted under a superior, or officials in another department may be stirred to action or to anger. The most spectacular examples of this practice occur when the Navy, the Air Force, and the Army engage in psychological warfare through the press. Bitter debates among the bureaucrats tend to spill over into the press.

While there are critics of the public-relations activities of administrative agencies, in truth, an agency, if it is to function effectively, must develop support in Congress, from its clientele and from the public generally. An act of Congress is not enough to establish it firmly, particularly if its operations affect some powerful group adversely. As an agency recruits sufficient support to assure a degree of stability, however, it thereby gains a degree of autonomy which may limit presidential direction. Agencies may, in rare instances, completely escape presidential control.[6]

Administrative agencies and the legislative process. Since a large proportion of the legislative output either originates in administrative experience or affects administrative operations, administrative agencies play an extremely important role in the process of lawmaking as a whole. They originate legislative proposals; they attempt, at times, to defeat proposals originating from other sources; and, at other times, they seek to bring about alterations in proposals pending in the legislative bodies. To carry out these activities the agency must have facilities for drafting and for responsible consideration of proposals.[7] It must also watch the course of legislation to keep informed on proposals that might affect its work; otherwise, legislation might be enacted that would be either difficult to administer or would tie the agency in knots.[8]

Most legislation is routine and arouses no controversy. It seeks to ac-

[6] See Robert de Roos and Arthur A. Maass, "The Lobby That Can't Be Licked, Congress and the Army Engineers," *Harper's Magazine*, August, 1949.

[7] See E. E. Witte, "Administrative Agencies and Statute Lawmaking," *Public Administration Review*, 2 (1942), pp. 116–125.

[8] To be differentiated from legislative proposals by administrative agencies are bills initiated by organizations of public employees. Such groups are prolific sources of bills on retirement, leave, compensation, and related matters. For an analysis of their activities in one congressional session, see R. L. Frischknect, "Federal Employee Unions and the First Session, Eightieth Congress," *Western Political Quarterly*, 1 (1948), pp. 183–185.

complish objectives that, by common consent, are wise and necessary for the conduct of public business. Congress routinely requests the advice of administrative agencies on legislation. Representatives of the administrative agencies appear before the committees of Congress and present information indicative of the need for action or the advisability of inaction. The relation of the agency to Congress is often not so much one of advocacy as of consultation with committeemen who have a responsible concern about the administrative operation in question.

Administration bills that propose a major change in public policy are likely to arouse opposition and to call for a vigorous presentation of the department's case. Under these circumstances the department may call on its allies among the pressure groups for assistance in dealing with Congress. When the objectives of the Department of Agriculture, for example, are coincidental with those of the American Farm Bureau Federation, the lobbyists of the Federation will appear, present testimony, buttonhole members of Congress, and perhaps focus upon Congressmen pressure from their constituencies. Or if the Farmers' Union is with the Department and the Federation against it, the Department may plan its legislative strategy in consultation with Union officials. Connections exist between nearly every administrative unit and private associations, which are of great importance in the promotion of legislation. There is a deep-seated congressional jealousy of "bureaucrats," and the bureaucracy is restricted in the methods that it may use in dealing with Congress. If it seeks to stir up popular pressure on Congress in support of specific legislation, it is likely to arouse criticism and resentment in Congress; but its allied private pressure groups may turn the pressure on Congress more freely.

It is chiefly in political disputes involving questions of high policy that the Administration attempts to focus a supporting public sentiment on Congress. And the important figures in these affairs are not petty bureaucrats but the principal leaders of the Administration. On these great questions the President or cabinet members may appeal to the country for support in coping with Congress.

Administration, party, and Presidency. The fulfillment of party responsibility and the achievement of party purpose require that the administrative agencies be brought under party control. In this endeavor the role of the President is crucial. Two broad methods are at his disposal to impress upon the machinery of government his party's policies: the power of appointment and removal; the authority to review and superintend operations of administrative agencies.

The relevance of the power of appointment for party policy becomes most evident when control of the Presidency shifts from one party to another. Republican cabinet officers ordinarily have a different policy orientation from that of Democratic department heads. Appointments and removals of officials of subcabinet rank will also be tinged by policy considerations as well as by greed for patronage. The affiliations of appointees often parallel the obligations and commitments of the incoming party and foreshadow the course of its actions.[9] Undoubtedly an incoming party tends to replace a higher proportion of the upper levels of the bureaucracy than is necessary to gain effective control of the administrative apparatus. After the election of 1952 this result came about in part from the demands for patronage from a party long out of power and in part from the unfamiliarity with governmental practice of many of the top-level Republican appointees. Victims of their own propaganda, they believed themselves to be surrounded by New Deal bureaucrats engaged in a conspiracy to sabotage the Eisenhower crusade, a point of view that became less marked as the businessmen learned their way around Washington.

While the power to appoint the heads of agencies is essential, it does not solve the problem of direction of the administrative apparatus. The President has a continuing task of guiding and co-ordinating the work of the administrative agencies which, left to their own devices, go off in all directions. In this task he has the assistance of the White House staff, headed under Eisenhower by Sherman Adams. The Bureau of the Budget serves as a staff aid to the President in the review of budget requests; it is bad form for an agency head to seek from appropriations committees a greater sum than is recommended in the President's budget. Agency legislative proposals are required to be cleared through the Bureau of the

[9] The early Eisenhower appointments included officials who had been strongly on record as opposed to the programs they were to administer: "The new head of the Rural Electrification Administration is regarded in his home state of Minnesota as an opponent of REA projects; the new head of the Housing and Home Finance Administration fought hard and consistently in Congress against the program he is now to administer; an arch protectionist who voted against the Reciprocal Trade Program when he was in the House has been appointed to the Tariff Commission; an Assistant Secretary of Interior appears to oppose conservation and has testified that the public lands should ultimately be turned over to private citizens; the new general counsel of the Department of Health, Education and Welfare is a former congressman who voted to restrict social security coverage; the new chairman of the Federal Trade Commission previously made his living representing interests who did battle with the Commission; and the President's original appointee to head the Bureau of Mines was so articulate in his opposition to the Mine Safety Law he was to administer that the congressional committee forced the White House to withdraw his name."—H. M. Somers, "The Federal Bureaucracy and the Change of Administration," *American Political Science Review*, 48 (1954), pp. 138–39.

Budget for advice on their conformity with the President's program.[10] The Council of Economic Advisers aids in the co-ordination of economic policies of the government departments, while the President has at his disposal the National Security Council to simplify the task of riding herd on those responsible for diplomatic and military policies.[11]

As the President seeks to maintain control over the unwieldy administrative system he acts only partly as a party chieftain. Were there no parties or elections, the chief executive would have to be equipped with machinery to aid in co-ordinating and directing the administrative system. Yet in his role as principal administrator the President must look to the achievement of the aims of his party, and he himself makes a substantial proportion of the record upon which his party must stand at the next election.

Limitations on Administrators

By various means Congress has sought to limit the activities of administrative agencies designed to influence public opinion and legislative action. In these endeavors it has been motivated in part by congressional jealousy of the growing power and influence of the bureaucracy, in part by adherence to the theory that administrative agencies should have no place in the initiation of legislation, and in part by congressional resentment of the actions of particular administrative agencies in specific situations.

Prohibition of employment of "publicity experts." The first statutory limitation on public-relations activities applicable to all administrative agencies was enacted in 1913. It grew out of the announcement of a civil service examination to select a "publicity expert" for the Office of Public Roads. The duties of this position were to "consist of the preparation of news matter relating to the work of the Office of Public Roads and securing the publication of such items in various periodicals and newspapers, particularly in country newspapers." The desire was to obtain the services of a man "whose affiliations with newspaper publishers and writers is extensive enough to insure the publication of items prepared by him."

[10] See R. E. Neustadt, "Presidency and Legislation: The Growth of Central Clearance," *American Political Science Review*, 48 (1954), pp. 641–671; Arthur Maass, "In Accord with the Program of the President?" *Public Policy*, IV (1953), pp. 77–93.

[11] These remarks give only the faintest notion of the enormity of the President's task in directing administrative agencies, each with its own traditions, its own connections with the pressure groups, its peculiar alliances in Congress, its habits and conceptions of the public interest. For a case study revealing the concrete problems in one area, see R. J. Morgan, "Pressure Politics and Resources Administration," *Journal of Politics*, 18 (1956), pp. 39–60.

The phraseology of the announcement could not have been better calculated to arouse animosity in Congress. Congressman Gillett observed: "The different departments of the administration certainly are not very modest in finding men and means to put before the country in the press the duties and purposes of their administration." And Congressman Fitzgerald agreed "that there was no place in the Government Service for an employee whose sole duty was to extol and to advertise the activities of any particular service of the Government." The outcome was the following enactment: "No money appropriated by this or any other act shall be used for the compensation of any publicity expert unless specifically appropriated for that purpose." [12]

Congress has made no specific appropriation for the employment of publicity experts. Consequently there has resulted, says McCamy, the "evasive hiring of publicity experts under such titles as 'Director of Information,' 'Chief Division of Information and Education,' 'Chief Informational Officer,' 'Editor-in-Chief,' 'Assistant to the Director' or 'Assistant to the Administrator,' 'Supervisor of Information Research,' 'Assistant to the Chairman,' or 'Director of Publication.' " [13] The fact is, however, that many laws authorize administrative agencies to carry on educational work or to inform the public, and the expenditure of funds for publicity work can be legally justified under these authorizations. The principal effect of the legislation of 1913 has been to outlaw the title "publicity expert."

Prohibition of expenditures to influence Congress. In 1919 Congress enacted the following legislation:

> No part of the money appropriated by any act shall, in the absence of express authorization by Congress, be used directly or indirectly to pay for any personal service, advertisement, telegram, telephone, letter, printed or written matter, or other device, intended or designed to influence in any manner a member of Congress, to favor or oppose, by vote or otherwise, any legislation or appropriation by Congress.[14]

Indicative of the practices toward which the legislation was directed is the statement in congressional debate that this clause would "prohibit a practice that has been indulged in so often, without regard to what administration is in power—the practice of a bureau chief or the head of a department writing letters throughout the country, for this organization, for this man, for that company to write his Congressman, to wire his

[12] 38 Stat. L. 212.

[13] J. L. McCamy, *Government Publicity* (Chicago: University of Chicago Press, 1939), p. 7.

[14] 41 Stat. L. 68.

Congressman, in behalf of this or that legislation." The law does permit executive employees to communicate with members of Congress at the request of Congressmen or through "the proper official channels" on legislation or appropriations.

Further statutory limitations on publicity by governmental agencies were imposed by Congress in 1939. By an act effective July 1 of that year, Congress prohibited administrative agencies from sending through the mail free of postage, books, documents, pamphlets, and like materials unless a request had been received. This limitation was adopted as the result of the objections of some Congressmen to the practice of New Deal agencies of transmitting large volumes of publicity matter through the mails.

Enforcement of prohibitions by criticism. In practice the principal sanction for the enforcement of these limitations on administrative agencies is the possibility of adverse criticism in Congress, to which the executive officers of the government are extremely sensitive. The absence of a body of case law interpreting the statutes as applied to different kinds of situations makes it difficult to say precisely what is prohibited. The law does not prevent recommendations of new legislation through proper channels—the President and the heads of departments. The chief effect of the regulatory legislation seems to be to discourage administrative agencies in openly organizing support throughout the country for or against specific bills.

The kinds and tenor of congressional criticism of administrative activity in relation to public policy may be illustrated by a few examples. In 1940 Congressman Smith of Ohio assailed Nathan Straus, administrator of the United States Housing Authority, and members of his staff for "gumshoeing about the Capitol and offices of Congressmen lobbying for the passage of the housing bill." He described the activities of Mr. Straus and his staff as "perfidious action" and announced that "every bureaucrat should be put in jail for lobbying to put his schemes through Congress." In 1953 members of the House Committee on Ways and Means talked ominously of referring the matter to the Department of Justice when the Secretary of the Treasury sought to persuade the NAM and the Chamber of Commerce not to oppose a short-term extension of the excess-profits tax.

Similarly, in 1945 Senator Robert A. Taft made an extended criticism of the Treasury Department for its "information" activities in support of the Bretton Woods agreements. The Senator showed that the department had circulated hundreds of thousands of pamphlets and that its staff had spoken at many meetings and to many organizations in support of the agreements. He contended that such action violated the statute of 1919 and that it also subverted the normal constitutional processes by enabling the administration to organize and direct public pressure upon Congress. Such practices raise genuinely important constitutional issues, but congressional attitudes seem to be grounded more on the particular issue than on the principle involved. A legislator seems more likely to become critical if he opposes a particular measure that is being aided by the administrative propaganda than if he favors it. Thus, in 1946 when President Truman instructed the admirals to refrain from lobbying against the establishment of a Department of National Defense the congressional opponents of service consolidation objected vociferously that the experts were being muzzled and other high crimes and misdemeanors committed.

Administrative agencies are also subjected to criticism from private sources for their efforts, alleged or real, to influence congressional action. In the battle in 1933 over the revision of the Pure Food and Drug Act, for example, Daniel A. Lundy, an advertising man connected with the Home Drug Company of Minneapolis, manufacturers of "Prescription No. 69," a self-administered cure for gallstones, directed a letter to each member of Congress denouncing Walter Campbell, chief of the Food and Drug Administration. He demanded that Campbell be "dismissed and prosecuted for his alleged gross violations and abuse of authority, in spending government money without permission of the Congress . . . to influence passage of the unconstitutional Tugwell-Copeland-Sirovich Food and Drug bills." [15] In 1948, evidently at the behest of opponents of conscription, the Secretary of the Army was put on the carpet by a House committee to respond to charges that the Army was improperly spending public funds to propagandize for universal military training.

Outbursts such as those cited have a common origin. They come from critics, inside and outside Congress, of the policies fostered by the administrative agency concerned. Attacks on administrative action are usually part of a campaign against a specific piece of legislation. Phrased in extravagant language, they are designed to discredit the administrative agency by branding it as a lawbreaker. These attacks may keep administrative agencies within legal bounds, but, within the sphere of legality, there is large scope for administrative lobbying. The President and other policy-forming officials have a responsibility to recommend to Congress courses of action; Congressmen, in turn, rely on administrative officials and employees for advice and assistance. The administration remains one of the most important influences on the course of legislative action.

---

[15] Ruth deForest Lamb, *American Chamber of Horrors* (New York: Farrar & Rinehart, 1936), p. 297.

Legal limitations of the sort discussed are likely to be ineffective in stemming the tide of administrative publicity calculated to influence public opinion and the course of legislative action. In some respects, as Harold Stoke has pointed out,[16] the growth of administrative publicity reflects a profound change in the nature of our governmental arrangements. To executive agencies has shifted in considerable measure the initiation of legislative policy. A corollary of this change is the development of administrative propaganda and education to aid in the crystallization of public sentiment concerning new policies. In another respect administrative agencies have themselves become lawmakers through congressional delegation of authority. To make administrative rules and regulations publicly acceptable, propaganda or education has to be carried on as a substitute for the discussion and debate that earlier served in a more exclusive degree to manufacture public consent to governmental action. Yet there remains a serious problem in the definition of the sphere of permissible official propaganda that is in keeping with the theory of representative government.[17]

Independent Commissions and the Party Program

The party in power has the responsibility and the means for controlling the ordinary government departments and agencies. Its appointees head these agencies, and departmental policy is expected to be in accord with the Administration program. The independent commissions, however, have broad policy-making power and are beyond the ready and effective control of the government of the day. Their independence is justified on the ground that in their quasi-judicial activities the commissions must impartially determine private rights in relation to law. By that independence, however, the commissions come to determine political or policy questions with only a tenuous political responsibility. An Administration may come into power pledged to adopt altered policies in important

[16] "Executive Leadership and the Growth of Propaganda," *American Political Science Review*, 35 (1941), pp. 490–500.

[17] There is no denying, says Arthur Macmahon, "that the public-relations activities of governmental agencies may be dangerous for democratic society. Especially when large resources are involved, an agency should not be more interested in perpetrating itself than in enlightening public opinion. The eagerness to win public support may pass beyond the boundary of cultivating consent into demanding obedience. The formula of public relations for modern administration is elusive. The kind of advocacy that prejudices responsible government must be avoided. Yet administrators must be left adequately equipped to fulfill their responsibilities. Careful and continuous scrutiny by legislatures and citizens is the best guarantee that the limits of desirable administrative informational activity will be observed."—*The Administration of Federal Work Relief* (Chicago: Public Administration Service, 1941), p. 292.

spheres, but it may find itself blocked by the fact that the regulatory commissions are controlled by men appointed by prior Presidents of a different persuasion on policy.

The situation may be illustrated by a report by David F. Houston, then Secretary of Agriculture, covering a cabinet meeting early in Woodrow Wilson's first Administration:

The matter of railway rates was considered at some length. It was agreed that the situation ought to be met squarely and promptly. One of the members (Lane) said that some of the rates on certain goods were too low. They had been made in the interest of owners of industries along the line: Those he said should certainly be raised, but those on all competing roads would have to be raised also. . . .

It was agreed that the matter was one for the Interstate Commerce Commission and that it should either raise or reclassify rates or insist on greater efficiency in management. It was agreed that no pressure of any sort could be brought to bear on the Commission. The impropriety of approaching it or its members was recognized.[18]

Here the President and the cabinet, with political responsibility for the conduct of government, agreed that the situation "ought to be met squarely and promptly." But it was also agreed that the matter was one for the Interstate Commerce Commission, and that it was improper to suggest action by the commission.

When President Coolidge in 1925 appointed William E. Humphrey to the Federal Trade Commission, that body came to be dominated by a Republican majority, and its policy in the enforcement of the prohibition of "unfair methods of competition" in interstate commerce was drastically softened. Yet for the previous five years the commission had not been in accord with the policy of the Republican Administration. The shift in the commission's attitude with the appointment of Humphrey is indicated by a speech that he made:

Under the old policy of litigation it [the Commission] became an instrument of oppression and disturbance and injury instead of a help to business. It harassed and annoyed business instead of assisting it. Business soon regarded the commission with distrust and fear and supicion—as an enemy. These was no cooperation between the commission and business. Business wanted the commission abolished and the commission regarded business as generally dishonest.[19]

[18] From *Eight Years with Wilson's Cabinet* (copyright, 1926, Doubleday, Doran and Company, Inc.), Vol. I, pp. 86–87.

[19] Quoted by Herring, *Public Administration and the Public Interest* (New York: McGraw-Hill, 1936), p. 125.

It is difficult to see how a commission that attempted to prevent "unfair methods of competition" could be "a help to business," except to those businesses injured by unfair competition. When Franklin D. Roosevelt came into office, his conception of the role of the Federal Trade Commission was more nearly in accord with the ideas of the Wilsonian period and he requested the resignation of Humphrey in the following terms: "I do not feel that your mind and my mind go along together on either the policies or the administering of the Federal Trade Commission, and, frankly, I think it best for the people of this country that I should have a full confidence." Humphrey resisted the removal order, and the Supreme Court decided that Congress could limit the power of the President to remove members of commissions exercising quasi-judicial powers. The decision made more difficult the harmonization of the policies of the independent regulatory commissions with the objectives of the party in power.

Harding and Coolidge had their troubles with the Tariff Commission, a body with only power to advise on tariff rates. In 1923 Harding wrote to Culbertson of the Tariff Commission:

I only venture to say at this time that I think it is altogether desirable to hold up a declaration of broad policy until I can sit down and go over the entire situation with the commission. As I understand it, the commission is the agency of the President in dealing with the tariff problem, and my intimate association and final responsibility in all matters lead me to believe that it is highly essential for a thorough understanding before embarking on any definitely defined course.

When the question of reappointment of one member of the commission arose, Coolidge offered the appointment on condition that an undated letter of resignation be signed by the appointee. Refusal to accede to the condition resulted in failure to receive reappointment. Although the Tariff Commission occupies a position different from that of the ordinary regulatory commission, these incidents illustrate the difficulties of bringing about a congruity of political power and responsibility in the areas carved out for the independent commissions.

The limitations on the President's power of removal often mean only that a new Administration is delayed in gaining a majority of the members of an independent commission. That delay may be brief or it may be extended. Only eight months elapsed, for example, before the Eisenhower Administration obtained control of the National Labor Relations Board and introduced a narrower conception of the board's functions. On the other hand, over four years passed before it had a majority of the TVA board. Yet even when an Administration names the personnel of an independent agency, the mode of operation of such agencies places them to a degree beyond Administration direction. That end was sought by the architects of the independent agencies, but it has its vexing consequences for Presidents.

What has happened in the creation of the independent commissions is that Congress, unable itself to deal with specific problems, has handed over to the independent commissions power to arbitrate differences between divergent social and economic interest. The standards to guide the commissions have been extremely vague guideposts, such as "fair," "just," "reasonable," "the public interest," and "the public convenience and necessity." In settling these differences the commissions have adopted a procedure of impartiality, with many features and appearances of the judicial process; but in reality they are declaring policy as Congress does when it decides like issues. Then, too, mixed with these lawmaking functions is the duty of deciding the rights of individuals, which may be more or less purely judicial in nature.

The commissions' assumption of an independent and impartial attitude and their tendency to isolate themselves from the Administration's planning and contriving to meet new situations limit their usefulness in an important way. Impartiality and the judicial viewpoint—no matter how essential they are in settling individual cases under established law—are likely to be incompatible with the exercise of leadership in the formation of new policies, in the anticipation of problems, and in the preparation of policies to meet problems as they arise. The Interstate Commerce Commission apparently had something of this sort in mind when it reported:

There is need for readjustments between and within the different branches of the transportation industry, for the consideration of present tendencies and their probable results, for the avoidance of uneconomic and wasteful practices, and in general for the determination, creation, and protection of the conditions most favorable to the development of a transportation system which will best serve the public interest. There is a field here both for continuing study and research and for active, aggressive, and consistent leadership on the part of Government wihch has never been occupied. The real problem is to fill that void in the best possible way.[20]

With one important governmental agency dealing with certain aspects of the transportation problem, however, it is virtually impossible for another, such as is suggested by the remarks of the commission, to undertake with success the function of research and aggressive leadership.[21]

[20] Interstate Commerce Commission, *52d Annual Report* (1938), pp. 24–25.
[21] Thus, in 1955 the Eisenhower Administration proposed, on the basis of the report of a cabinet committee, a revised transportation policy. The Interstate Com-

The problem of working out the proper relationship of the independent regulatory commissions to the government as a whole remains unsolved. It seems obvious that a more suitable *modus operandi* will have to be devised, but how it will be done is unclear. Herring states the dilemma:

The President has certainly no right to intervene on behalf of any private party who may come before a commission, but this does not mean that he has no concern with its general interpretation of the law. Can some way be found for admitting his influence upon policy without causing interference with the commission's judicial activities? How can the chief executive, for example, be given a means of exerting his influence in national transportation problems without disrupting the work of the Interstate Commerce Commission? [22]

Friction will exist until the question is worked out.[23] The urgency of the need for a satisfactory solution increases as the breadth of governmental regulation grows. Since the various aspects of the economic system dealt with by different independent commissions and ordinary government departments are interrelated, a co-ordinated government policy becomes more and more essential. It is the responsibility of the party in control to devise and execute such a program, but an Administration is limited in that responsibility by the independence of the regulatory commissions.

The Place of Bureaucracy in a Democracy

The administrative services are not inert mechanisms that translate the will of the legislature into action. These services themselves are a significant force in the state and play an important role in the determination of what is to be done in the name of the state. Yet their importance is not so great as might be inferred from the more extravagant diatribes against the bureaucracy.

The trend of events, however, suggests inquiries into the shape of things to come for administrative services and parliamentary institutions. The growing volume and complexity of public functions have reduced to a

---

merce Commission unanimously took exception to the Administration recommendations in a statement to the congressional committees considering them.

[22] *Op. cit.*, p. 224. See Marver Bernstein, *Regulating Business by Independent Commission* (Princeton: Princeton University Press, 1955), and S. P. Huntington, "The Marasmus of the ICC: The Commission, the Railroads, and the Public Interest," *Yale Law Journal*, 61 (1952), pp. 467–509.

[23] One proposal is the assignment of quasi-judicial functions to the commission and the placement of policy responsibility and responsibility for staff management and the initiation of action upon an officer subject to removal by the President. Such an arrangement of the work of the National Labor Relations Board produced results not entirely happy; yet when policy differences arose the President could, and did, request the resignation of Robert N. Denham, the Board's general counsel, in 1950.

fiction the theory of separation of powers and the parallel doctrine of the separability of politics and administration. Representative bodies, the institutional embodiment of democratic ideology, have by the compelling force of events lost both power and prestige. Their role in the initiation of public policy has been diminished by losses to pressure groups and administrative agencies; their authority to decide many issues has, of necessity, been delegated to the administrative services. They have been driven toward a role of futile and uninformed criticism, at its worst motivated either by partisan or picayune considerations.

The administrative services have, in terms of the distribution of both formal governmental power and informal political influence, been the chief heirs of the declining representative bodies. In a culture whose traditional theory has been that political issues should be decided by popularly elected representatives, what are the dangers and problems of the growing importance of the administrative service? Charles E. Merriam pointed out that as we emerge from the era of corruption, incompetence, and ignorance in administration

. . . the new possibilities are those of arrogance and indifference to the public, lack of sympathy approaching harshness and cruelty, devotion to inflexibility and routine, grumbling at theory and change; procrastination, quibbling and delay; or the opposite of too great and rash speed without adequate preparation of the public for the change.

Above all there is the ever impending danger of the desire for personal self-perpetuation and expansion of power, bureaucratic parochialism of the pettiest type; the sabotage of the ends of office by placing the machinery or the person above the function he is there to serve; or the effort of the administrator to take over the role of the policy maker, by various devices, direct or otherwise.[24]

Although tendencies in these directions are discernible, there are offsetting factors. In the initiation and formation of public policy the power of group and class drives, as has been shown, is fundamental. Yet private groups find it difficult, even when the best of intentions are granted, to exert their strength for the general welfare. The legislative programs of administrative agencies, however, tend to incorporate the objectives of private groups and to temper and to modify them in the public interest. Indeed, in many situations of policy parturition it seems that the bureaucracy is the only participant animated by a devotion to the common welfare. In this connection Gaus and Wolcott inquire:

At what point in the evolution of policies in the life of the community shall the process take place of transforming a specialist point of view and program,

[24] "Public Administration and Political Theory," *Journal of Social Philosophy*, 5 (1940), pp. 305–306.

through compromise and adjustment, into a more balanced public program? Much of this process must take place in the administrative agencies through the selection of personnel, their continued in-service training, the content and discipline of their professions, researches, and responsibilities, the attrition of interbureau and interdepartmental contact and association, and the scrutiny of their work, by the over-all administrative staff and auxiliary agencies and by Congress. If there is the proper attention to these matters, the viewpoint of the civil service will differ from the surrogacy that one expects from the officials of a pressure group.[25]

A possible line of development, then, would be the direction and harnessing of the power, knowledge, and skills of the administrative services so that they might constitute a force in the initiation of public policies calculated to promote the common weal. The development of an administrative corps of this character depends in large measure on the further development of techniques of organization and supervision whereby the political heads of administrative services may better overcome the parochialism of the permanent staffs and liberate their talents. This problem of the overhead organization of governmental departments and of the government as a whole is of prime importance in the determination of the direction in which the powers of the bureaucracy will be exerted. Politically responsible officials in collaboration with Congress have the task of orienting public policy, but in the absence of effective techniques for organizing and directing the administration their efforts are likely to be either obstructed or ineffectively carried out by the administrative services. Recent years have seen much attention given to the organization of administration for policy planning.

The danger of the rise of a bureaucracy aggressively grasping for unwarranted power is probably much less than the danger of drifting into a condition in which the bureaucracy is a purely negative force. A seasoned bureaucracy, without heroic measures to the contrary, tends to become attached to the time-honored ways of doing things, hostile toward innovation, lacking in initiative, and timid. These qualities are admirable at the right time and place, but the next few decades in the United States will hardly be the time and place for pleasant habituation to the customary.

This is not to argue for a bureaucracy that will usurp the functions of Congress and the President; the contention is, rather, that present conditions demand a bureaucracy that will minimize the magnitude of the tasks of Congress and the President. How may that be done? The pressure on Congress may be reduced by the development of procedures

[25] *Public Administration and the U.S. Department of Agriculture* (Chicago: Public Administration Service, 1940), p. 283.

within the administration for the satisfactory settlement of matters un-worthy of the attention of Congress; by the eradication of parochialism within administrative agencies and the consequent submission of legisla-tive recommendations that are more likely to meet the desires of Con-gress; and by the development of internal controls that would reduce the task of congressional surveillance of the administration. The task of presidential direction of the administration increases in difficulty with the growth of the number of administrative agencies; the impression of the President's policy on particularistic administrative agencies becomes an almost impossible job (yet that is the President's responsibility and duty). To make the functions of Congress and the President actual as well as nominal, it is essential to have a bureaucracy dedicated to seeking out the general welfare, yet mindful of the final authority of Congress and the President in defining how the general welfare shall be promoted.[26]

The problem of bureaucracy is in part not a problem of bureaucracy at all. It is rather a question of attracting into party service an adequate supply of men competent to manage and control the bureaucracy from their posts as the transient but responsible heads of departments and agencies. Publicists have been greatly exercised about making the civil service attractive enough to draw able men to it as a career. Of no less importance is the attraction of even abler men to the service of parties to direct and carry responsibility for the direction of the career staffs. It is through such persons who owe their posts to the victorious party that popular control over government is maintained.

[26] See the reflective comment by Norton E. Long, "Bureaucracy and Constitution-alism," *American Political Science Review*, 46 (1952), pp. 808–118.

Index